Lecture Notes in Artificial Intelligence   10607

Subseries of Lecture Notes in Computer Science

LNAI Series Editors

Randy Goebel
  University of Alberta, Edmonton, Canada
Yuzuru Tanaka
  Hokkaido University, Sapporo, Japan
Wolfgang Wahlster
  DFKI and Saarland University, Saarbrücken, Germany

LNAI Founding Series Editor

Joerg Siekmann
  DFKI and Saarland University, Saarbrücken, Germany

More information about this series at http://www.springer.com/series/1244

Somnuk Phon-Amnuaisuk · Swee-Peng Ang
Soo-Young Lee (Eds.)

Multi-disciplinary Trends in Artificial Intelligence

11th International Workshop, MIWAI 2017
Gadong, Brunei, November 20–22, 2017
Proceedings

Springer

Editors
Somnuk Phon-Amnuaisuk (ID)
Universiti Teknologi Brunei
Gadong
Brunei Darussalam

Swee-Peng Ang
Universiti Teknologi Brunei
Gadong
Brunei Darussalam

Soo-Young Lee
Korea Advanced Institute of Science
and Technology
Daejeon
Korea (Republic of)

ISSN 0302-9743   ISSN 1611-3349 (electronic)
Lecture Notes in Artificial Intelligence
ISBN 978-3-319-69455-9   ISBN 978-3-319-69456-6 (eBook)
https://doi.org/10.1007/978-3-319-69456-6

Library of Congress Control Number: 2017956768

LNCS Sublibrary: SL7 – Artificial Intelligence

Printed on acid-free paper

This Springer imprint is published by Springer Nature
The registered company is Springer International Publishing AG
The registered company address is: Gewerbestrasse 11, 6330 Cham, Switzerland

Preface

On behalf of the organizing committee, it is an honor and a great pleasure to welcome you to the 11th Multi-disciplinary International Workshop on Artificial Intelligence (MIWAI 2017) held from November 20–22, 2017, in Brunei.

MIWAI is an annual event, initiated back in 2007 in Thailand under the title "Mahasarakham International Workshop on Artificial Intelligence." The event has evolved to be an international workshop with participation from around the world starting from 2011 where MIWAI was held in Hyderabad (India). Subsequently, the event was held in Ho Chi Minh City (Vietnam), Krabi (Thailand), Bangalore (India), Fuzhou (China), Chiang Mai (Thailand), and this year in Brunei.

MIWAI solicits papers from all areas of artificial intelligence. It aims to bring together researchers from around the world in the field of artificial intelligence, to exchange ideas, present recent results, and discuss possible collaborations. This year, the international Program Committee consisted of over 120 researchers from 30 countries. A total of 82 submissions from 30 countries were submitted to the event for double-blind peer-review. Of these, 40 submissions were deemed suitable for presentation and to be included in this book. The acceptance rate is around 49%. Besides the papers published in the proceedings, the technical program included two keynote speeches by Ah-Hwee Tan and Guang-Bin Huang, and three public lectures by Laszlo T. Koczy, Peter Haddawy, and Junmo Kim.

The host organization for MIWAI 2017 was the Centre for Innovative Engineering (CIE), one of the research units of Universiti Teknologi Brunei (UTB). The Organizing Committee wishes to express gratitude and appreciation to the following organizations: Springer, IEEE-Computational Intelligence Society, World Federation Soft Computing, and Brain Science Research Center (KAIST) for their technical support; the members of the MIWAI 2017 Program Committee for their time and invaluable effort in the double-blind peer-review process; the keynote speakers and public lecturers who generated an academically stimulating atmosphere; the MIWAI Steering Committee members and MIWAI conveners for their support and suggestions; the UTB advisory board and all members of the local Organizing Committee for their professional team work; and Universiti Teknologi Brunei for its institutional and various supports.

On behalf of the Organizing Committee, we would also like to express our gratitude to Hjh Zohrah binti Haji Sulaiman, our Vice Chancellor, for her guidance and support, which were essential to the success of this event. Finally, we would like to thank all the participants for taking an interest in MIWAI 2017.

September 2017

Somnuk Phon-Amnuaisuk
Swee-Peng Ang
Soo-Young Lee

Organization

Organizer

Centre for Innovative Engineering, Universiti Teknologi Brunei, Brunei Darussalam

Honorary Advisors

Hjh Zohrah Binti Haji Sulaiman	Universiti Teknologi Brunei, Brunei Darussalam
Sujin Butdisuwan	Mahasarakham University, Thailand

MIWAI Steering Committee

Arun Agarwal	University of Hyderabad, India
C. Raghavendra Rao	University of Hyderabad, India
James F. Peters	University of Manitoba, Canada
Jérôme Lang	University Paris-Dauphine, France
Leon Van Der Torre	University of Luxembourg, Luxembourg
Patrick Doherty	University of Linkoping, Sweden
Rajkumar Buyya	University of Melbourne, Australia
Rina Dechter	University of California, Irive, USA
Srinivasan Ramani	IIIT Bangalore, India

Conveners

Richard Booth	Cardiff University, UK
Chattrakul Sombattheera	Mahasarakham University, Thailand

UTB Advisory Board

Noor Maya Binti Hj Md Salleh	Universiti Teknologi Brunei, Brunei Darussalam
Zuruzi bin Abu Samah	Universiti Teknologi Brunei, Brunei Darussalam
Ady Syarmin bin Hj Md Taib	Universiti Teknologi Brunei, Brunei Darussalam
Jennifer Hiew Lim	Universiti Teknologi Brunei, Brunei Darussalam
Hamdani Bin Hj Ibrahim	Universiti Teknologi Brunei, Brunei Darussalam

Conference Committee

General Chairs

Somnuk Phon-Amnuaisuk	UTB, Brunei
Soo-Young Lee	KAIST, Korea
Peter Haddawy	Mahidol University, Thailand

Program Chairs

Swee-Peng Ang	UTB, Brunei
Jonathan H. Chan	KMUTT, Thailand

Publicity Chairs

Siti Asmahlati Bolkini binti A. Haji Ahmad	UTB, Brunei
Derong Liu	Chinese Academy of Sciences, China
Laszlo T. Koczy	BME, Hungary
Seiichi Ozawa	Kobe University, Japan
Weng-Kin Lai	TARUC, Malaysia

Invited Session Chairs

Fushuan Wen	UTB, Brunei
Shing-Chiang Tan	MMU, Malaysia

International Program Committee

Azizi Ab Aziz	Universiti Utara Malaysia
Arun Agarwal	University of Hyderabad, India
Grigoris Antoniou	University of Huddersfield, UK
Nureize Arbaiy	UTHM, Malaysia
S.M.N. Arosha Senanayake	Universiti Brunei Darussalam, Brunei
Adham Atyabi	Yale University, USA
Thien-Wan Au	Universiti Teknologi Brunei, Thailand
Joscha Bach	MIT Media Lab, USA
Costin Badica	University of Craiova, Romania
Sotiris Batsakis	University of Huddersfield, UK
Tarek Richard Besold	University of Bremen, Germany
Raj Bhatnagar	University of Cincinnati, USA
Antonis Bikakis	University College London, UK
Laor Boongasame	King Mongkut University of Technology Thonburi, Thailand
Tossapon Boongoen	Royal Thai Air Force Academy, Thailand
Veera Boonjing	King Mongkut's Institute of Technology Ladkrabang, Thailand
Richard Booth	Cardiff University, UK
Darko Brodic	University of Belgrade, Serbia
David Camacho	Universidad Autonoma de Madrid, Spain
Thanarat Chalidabhongse	Chulalongkorn University, Thailand
Rapeeporn Chamchong	Murdoch University, Australia
Dehua Chen	Donghua University, China
Zhicong Chen	Fuzhou University, China
Sung-Bae Cho	Yonsei University, Korea
Sook-Ling Chua	Multimedia University, Malaysia

Thien Pham Cong	Ho Chi Minh City - Nong Lam University, Vietnam
Broderick Crawford	Pontificia Universidad Catolica de Valparaiso, Chile
Minh-Son Dao	Universiti Teknologi Brunei, Brunei
Abdollah Dehzangi	University of Iowa, USA
Patrick Doherty	Linkoping University, Sweden
Abdelrahman Elfaki	University of Tabuk, Saudi Arabia
Worrawat Engchuan	Centre for Applied Genomics, Canada
Vladimir Estivill-Castro	Griffith University, Australia
Ibrahim Faye	Universit Teknologi PETRONAS, Malaysia
Lk Foo	Multimedia University, Malaysia
Ulrich Furbach	University of Koblenz, Germany
Hock-Guan Goh	Universiti Tunku Abdul Rahman, Malaysia
Hui-Ngo Goh	Multimedia University, Malaysia
Bok-Min Goi	Universiti Tunku Abdul Rahman, Malaysia
Jinguang Gu	Wuhan University of Science and Technology, China
Jingzhi Guo	University of Macau, SAR China
Peter Haddawy	Mahidol University, Thailand
Wai-Lan Hoo	TARUC, Malaysia
Zhisheng Huang	Vrije University Amsterdam, The Netherlands
Jason Jung	Chung-Ang University, South Korea
Manasawee Kaenampornpan	Mahasarakham University, Thailand
Mohan Kankanhalli	National University of Singapore, Singapore
Kok-Chin Khor	Multimedia University, Malaysia
Ven-Jyn Kok	Universiti Kebangsaan Malaysia, Malaysia
Jérôme Lang	CNRS, LAMSADE, Université Paris-Dauphine, France
Idris Abdul Latiff	Universiti Kaula Lumpur, Malaysia
Phooi Yee Lau	Universiti Tunku Abdul Rahman, Malaysia
Kittichai Lavangnananda	King Mongkut's University of Technology, Thonburi, Thailand
Dianne Mei-Chong Lee	UiTM Negeri Sembilan, Malaysia
Yun-Li Lee	Sunway University, Malaysia
Chee-Kau Lim	University of Malaya, Malaysia
Chern-Hong Lim	TARC, Malaysia
Tiang-Hoo Lim	Universiti Teknologi Brunei, Brunei
Emiliano Lorini	IRIT, France
Martin Lukac	Nazarbayev University, Kazakhstan
Penousal Machado	CISUC, University of Coimbra, Portugal
Michael Maher	University of New South Wales, Australia
Sebastian Moreno	Universidad Adolfo Ibañez, Chile
Debajyoti Mukhopadhyay	Maharashtra Institute of Technology, Thailand
Raja Kumar Murugesan	Taylors University, Malaysia
Kavi Narayana Murthy	University of Hyderabad, India
Sven Naumann	University of Trier, Germany
Keng Hoong Ng	Multimedia University, Malaysia

M.C. Nicoletti	FACCAMP and UFSCar, Brazil
Shahrul Azman Noah	Universiti Kebangsaan Malaysia, Malaysia
Supakit Nootyaskool	King Mongkut's Institute of Technology Ladkrabang, Thailand
Worapat Paireekreng	Dhurakij Pundit University, Thailand
Kitsuchart Pasupa	King Mongkut's Institute of Technology Ladkrabang, Thailand
Laurent Perrussel	IRIT, Universite de Toulouse, France
Duc-Nghia Pham	MIMOS Berhad, Malaysia
Sheung-Hung Poon	Universiti Teknologi Brunei, Brunei
Mvnk Prasad	IDRBT, India
Wiboon Prompanich	King Mongkut's Institute of Technology Ladkrabang, Thailand
Tho Quan	Ho Chi Minh City University of Technology, Vietnam
Imran Rahman	Universiti Sains Malaysia, Malaysia
Vadlamani Ravi	Institute for Development and Research in Banking Technology, India
Andre Rossi	Université de Bretagne-Sud, France
Jose H. Saito	Universidade Federal de São Carlos, Brazil
Aknine Samir	LIRIS Laboratory, Lyon 1 University, France
Riyanarto Samo	Institut Teknologi Sepuluh Nopember, Indonesia
Myint Myint Sein	University of Computer Studies, Yangon, Myanmar
Ali Selamat	Univertsiti Teknologi Malaysia
S.H. Shah Newaz	Universiti Teknologi Brunei, Brunei
Peter D. Shannon	Universiti Teknologi Brunei
Jun Shen	University of Wollongong, Australia
Alok Singh	University of Hyderabad, India
Dominik. Slezak	University of Warsaw and Infobright, Poland
Virach Sornlertlamvanich	SIIT, Thammasat University, Thailand
Frieder Stolzenburg	Harz University of Applied Sciences, Germany
Olarik Surinta	Mahasarakham University, Thailand
Ilias Tachmazidis	University of Huddersfield, UK
Soon-Jian Tan	Universiti Teknologi Brunei, Brunei
Jaree Thongkam	Mahasarakham University, Thailand
Supot Tiarawut	Chulalongkorn University, Thailand
Chuan-Kang Ting	National Chung Cheng University, Taiwan
Chau Vo	Ho Chi Minh City University of Technology, Vietnam
Chalee Vorakulpipat	NECTEC, Thailand
Junzo Watada	Waseda University, Japan
Ukrit Watchareeruetai	King Mongkut's Institute of Technology Ladkrabang, Thailand
Paul Weng	SYSU-CMU JIE, France
Kevin Wong	Murdoch University, Australia

Kuntpong Woraratpanya   King Mongkut's Institute of Technology
Ladkrabang, Thailand
Chai Wutiwiwatchai   Human Language Technology Laboratory,
NECTEC, Thailand
Li Xu   Fujian Normal University, China
Jingtao Yao   University of Regina, Canada
Wai Yeap   Auckland University of Technology, New Zealand
Vivian Suet-Peng Yong   Universiti Teknologi PETRONAS, Malaysia
Morteza Zaker   Amirkabir University of Technology, Iran

Local Organizing Committee

Secretariat

Dk Norhafizah Binti Pg Hj Muhammad

Finance

Hjh Nur'azmina Hj Lingas

Registration

Ak Muhammad Rahimi bin Pg Hj Zahari

Event Organizer

Muhd Robin Yong Bin Abdullah

Publication

Uditha Ratnayake
Noor Deenina binti Mohd Salleh

Media and PR

Siti Noorfatimah Hj Awg Safar

Accommodation/Transportation

Hj Ismit bin Hj Mohamad

Health, Safety, and Environment

Zuliana binti Hj Nayan

Parking and Traffic

Muslim bin Hj Lakim

General Services

Mariatul Kiptiah Binti Ariffin
Muhammad Khairul Fadhli Bin Sani
Nur Amalina Binti Haji AbdManaf
Shiqah Natasya Binti Muhammad Hadi

Webhosting Contact

Panich Sudkhot   MSU, Thailand

Contents

Deep Learning and Its Applications

Document Analysis

Intelligent Information Systems

Swarm Intelligence

Knowledge Representation and Reasoning

Inference and Learning in Probabilistic Argumentation

Nguyen Duy Hung[(⊠)]

Sirindhorn International Institute of Technology, Pathum Thani, Thailand
hung.nd.siit@gmail.com

Abstract. Inference for Probabilistic Argumentation has been focusing on computing the probability that a given argument or proposition is acceptable. In this paper, we formalize such tasks as computing marginal acceptability probabilities given some evidence and learning probabilistic parameters from a dataset. We then show that algorithms for them can be composed by finely joining a basic PA inference algorithm and existing algorithms for the corresponding tasks in Probabilistic Logic Programming or even Bayesian networks.

Keywords: Probabilistic Argumentation · Probabilistic Logic Programming · Probabilistic graphical models · Machine learning

1 Introduction

Probabilistic Argumentation (PA) is a recent line of research in AI to combine the strengths of argumentation theory and probability theory. Various models of PA have been proposed, notably [8,10,12,13,19]. However this line of work focuses only on the semantics and appropriate structures for PA frameworks. Inference tasks for PA has been limited to computing the probability that a given argument is acceptable, as done in [18], or computing the probability that there exists an acceptable argument supporting a given proposition, as done in [11]. In this paper, we first formalize such tasks as computing marginal acceptability probabilities given some evidence and learning probabilistic parameters from a dataset. We then show that algorithms for them can be composed by finely joining a basic PA inference algorithm (computing the acceptability probability of a single proposition) and existing algorithms for the corresponding tasks in Probabilistic Logic Programming (PLP) or even Bayesian networks (BNs). While doing so, we focus on Probabilistic Assumption-based Argumentation - a PA model using Assumption-based Argumentation (ABA [2]) to structure arguments. However our approach is applicable to other PA models as well.

It is worth noting that in comparsion with PA, PLP has a much longer history where one of the early known works is attributed to Poole [14]. Shortly after, in his seminal work [16] Sato shows that definite logic programs augmented with probabilistic elements subsume probabilistic graphical models such as BNs. So he defined a probabilistic logic program as consisting of a set of ground

© Springer International Publishing AG 2017
S. Phon-Amnuaisuk et al. (Eds.): MIWAI 2017, LNAI 10607, pp. 3–17, 2017.
https://doi.org/10.1007/978-3-319-69456-6_1

probabilistic facts F and a definite program Π whose heads do not occur in F. The probability measure on the interpretations of F is then extended to produce a probability measure of LHMs (Least Herbrand Models) of definite programs $\{\Pi \cup F' \mid F' \subseteq F\}$. However, when Π is extended with negations, LHM may not exist and hence some generalization of LHM has to be used. In particular, the state-of-the-art PLP languages (e.g. ProbLog [9], PROBXHAIL [3], PRISM [17], ICL [15], LPAD [20]) generalize Sato's distribution semantics to normal logic programs using either the well-founded semantics or the answer set semantics. Since the well-founded and answer set semantics of normal (and even much more generalized) logic programs correspond to the grounded semantics and the stable semantics of argumentation [7], PABA can be used to emulate PLP languages. However, one might hypothesize that the reverse is not possible since PABA is equipped with many argumentation semantics (details in Sect. 2) that do not have correspondences in PLP. Hence, one may abandon the idea that PABA tasks can be solved by first translating the given PABA framework into a PLP program then harness existing PLP algorithms to address the tasks. Indeed what we are doing in this paper can be seen as refining this idea to make it work. Intuitively, we need to use a basic inference procedure for PABA (e.g. the ones in [11]) to solve the logical, argumentative part of the given problem. The remaining part, which should be purely probabilistic, can be dealt with by PLP and even Bayesian network (BN) algorithms.

The rest of this paper is structured as follows: Sect. 2 presents the background; Sect. 3 formalizes PA inference and learning tasks; Sects. 4 and 5 develop PABA inference and learning algorithms; Sect. 6 demonstrates our prototype implementation in Prolog; Sect. 7 presents related work and concludes. Because of the lack of space, we omit the proofs of technical results.

2   Background

2.1   Abstract Argumentation

An AA framework [4] $\mathcal{F}$ is a pair (AR, Att) where AR is a set of arguments, $Att \subseteq AR \times AR$ and $(A, B) \in Att$ means that A attacks B. $S \subseteq AR$ attacks $A \in AR$ iff $(B, A) \in Att$ for some $B \in S$. $A \in AR$ is acceptable wrt to S iff S attacks every argument attacking A. S is conflict-free iff S does not attack itself; admissible iff S is conflict-free and each argument in S is acceptable wrt S; complete iff S is admissible and contains every arguments acceptable wrt S; a preferred (aka credulous) extension iff S is a maximal (wrt set inclusion) complete set; the grounded extension iff S is the least complete set; a stable extension iff it is a preferred extension and attacks each argument that does not belong to it. An argument A is accepted under semantics $sem \in \{cr, gr, st\}$[1], denoted $\mathcal{F} \vdash_{sem} A$, iff A is in a sem extension. A is skeptically preferred accepted, denoted $\mathcal{F} \vdash_{sk} A$, if A is in each preferred extension. It is well-known that gr is the most skeptical semantics while cr is the least skeptical: $\mathcal{F} \vdash_{gr} A \implies \mathcal{F} \vdash_{sem} A \implies \mathcal{F} \vdash_{cr} A$.

---

[1] credulous/grounded/stable semantics. There are many other semantics. For a review, readers are referred to, e.g. [1].

2.2 Assumption-Based Argumentation

As AA ignores the internal structure of argument, an instance of AA called Assumption-Based Argumentation (ABA [5,6]) defines arguments by deductive proofs based on assumptions and inference rules. Assuming a language $\mathcal{L}$ consisting of countably many sentences, an ABA framework is a triple $\mathcal{F} = (\mathcal{R}, \mathcal{A}, \overline{})$ where $\mathcal{R}$ is a set of inference rules of the form $r : l_0 \leftarrow l_1, \ldots, l_n$ $(n \geq 0, l_i \in \mathcal{L})^2$, $\mathcal{A} \subseteq \mathcal{L}$ is a set of assumptions, and $\overline{}$ is a (total) one-to-one mapping from $\mathcal{A}$ into $\mathcal{L}$, where $\overline{x}$ is referred to as the *contrary* of x. Assumptions do not appear in the heads of inference rules.

A *(backward) deduction* of a conclusion q supported by a set of premises Q is a sequence of sets $S_1, S_2, \ldots, S_n$ where $S_i \subseteq \mathcal{L}$, $S_1 = \{q\}$, $S_n = Q$, and for every i, where σ is the selected proposition in S_i: $\sigma \notin Q$ and $S_{i+1} = S_i \setminus \{\sigma\} \cup body(r)$ for some inference rule $r \in \mathcal{R}$ with $head(r) = \sigma$.

An argument for $q \in \mathcal{L}$ supported by a set of assumptions Q is a deduction from q to Q and denoted by (Q, q). An argument (Q, q) attacks an argument (Q', q') if q is the contrary of some assumption in Q'.

A proposition q is said to be credulously/groundedly/stably accepted in ABA $\mathcal{F}$, denoted $\mathcal{F} \vdash_{cr} q$ (resp. $\mathcal{F} \vdash_{gr} q$, $\mathcal{F} \vdash_{st} q$) if in the AA framework consisting of above defined arguments and attacks, there is an argument for q accepted under the credulous (resp. grounded/stable) semantics.

2.3 Probabilistic Assumption-Based Argumentation

A PABA framework [8] represents a probability distribution of ABA frameworks. The focus of this paper is a subclass of PABA called Bayesian PABA [11] where the probabilistic information is represented by a Bayesian network.

Definition 1. *A (Bayesian) PABA framework $\mathcal{P}$ is a tuple $(\mathcal{A}_p, \mathcal{N}, \mathcal{F})$ where*

- *$\mathcal{F} = (\mathcal{R}, \mathcal{A}, \overline{})$ is an ABA framework,*
- *$\mathcal{A}_p = \{x_1, \ldots, x_m\}$ is a set of positive probabilistic assumptions[3] such that no probabilistic assumption occurs in $\mathcal{A}$ or in the head of a rule in $\mathcal{R}$, and*
- *$\mathcal{N} = (G, \Theta)$ is a Bayesian network of Boolean variables such that for each assumption $x_i \in \mathcal{A}_p$, $\mathcal{N}$ has a corresponding Boolean node X_i (with possible values $\{x_i, \neg x_i\}$)[4].*
  The probability distribution induced by $\mathcal{N}$ is denoted by $Pr_{\mathcal{N}}(.)$.

The semantics of PABA is defined as follows.

Definition 2. *– A **possible world** is a maximal (wrt set inclusion) consistent subset of $\mathcal{A}_p \cup \neg \mathcal{A}_p$.*
$\mathcal{W}$ denotes the set of all possible worlds, and for each $\omega \in \mathcal{W}$, $\mathcal{F}_\omega$ denotes the ABA framework $(\mathcal{R}_\omega, \mathcal{A}, \overline{})$ with $\mathcal{R}_\omega \triangleq \mathcal{R} \cup \{p \leftarrow | p \in \omega\}$.

---

[2] For convenience, define $head(r) = l_0$ and $body(r) = \{l_1, \ldots l_n\}$.

[3] Elements of $\neg \mathcal{A}_p = \{\neg x \mid x \in \mathcal{A}_p\}$ are called negative probabilistic assumptions.

[4] G is a directed acyclic graph over $\mathcal{X} = \{X_1, \ldots, X_m\}$ and Θ is a set of conditional probability tables (CPTs), one CPT $\Theta_{X|par(X)}$ for each $X \in \mathcal{X}$.

- *The **acceptability probability of a proposition** q **under semantics** sem, denoted $Pr_{sem}(q)$, is the probability that there is an acceptable argument for q under sem, i.e.* $Pr_{sem}(q) \triangleq \sum\limits_{\substack{\mathcal{F}_\omega \vdash_{sem} q}}^{\omega \in \mathcal{W}} Pr_{\mathcal{N}}(\omega).$

Example 1. Let's consider a PABA framework $\mathcal{P} = (\mathcal{A}_p, \mathcal{N}, \mathcal{F})$ where

- $\mathcal{F} = (\mathcal{R}, \mathcal{A}, \overline{})$ where $\mathcal{A} = \{\sim howl, \sim bark\}$ with $\overline{\sim x} = x$ and $\mathcal{R}$ describes how an alarm and a dog responds to earthquakes and burglaries by:

  $alarm \leftarrow burglary, earthquake, p\_alarm1$
  $alarm \leftarrow burglary, \neg earthquake, p\_alarm2$
  $alarm \leftarrow \neg burglary, earthquake, p\_alarm3$
  $bark \leftarrow burglary, \sim howl$ $howl \leftarrow earthquake, \sim bark$
- $\mathcal{A}_p = \{burglary, earthquake, p\_alarm1, p\_alarm2, p\_alarm3\}$ and $\mathcal{N}$ is depicted in Fig. 1[5].

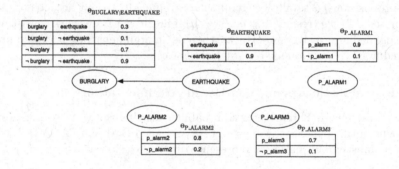

Fig. 1. Bayesian network $\mathcal{N}$

It is easy to see that for a possible world $\omega \in \mathcal{W}$ ($|\mathcal{W}| = 2^5$): $\mathcal{F}_\omega \vdash_{cr} bark$ iff $\omega \supseteq s_0 = \{burglary\}$, thus $Pr_{cr}(bark) = \sum\limits_{\omega \supseteq s_0}^{\omega \in \mathcal{W}} Pr_{\mathcal{N}}(\omega)$; $\mathcal{F}_\omega \vdash_{gr} bark$ iff $\omega \supseteq s_1 = \{burglary, \neg earthquake\}$, thus $Pr_{gr}(bark) = \sum\limits_{\omega \supseteq s_1}^{\omega \in \mathcal{W}} Pr_{\mathcal{N}}(\omega)$.

2.4 Probabilistic Logic Programming

Assuming a finite Herbrand base[6], a (normal) logic program (LP) Π is a finite set of ground clauses of the form $l_0 \leftarrow l_1, ..., l_n$, where l_0 is an atom and l_i is

---

[5] Probabilistic parameters are made up for the sake of illustrations and so is the dependency of burglaries on earthquakes.

[6] We shall make use of usual notations in FOL such as atoms, literals, Herbrand base, interpretations, etc. without precise definitions.

a literal (an atom or an atom preceeded by $\sim$, which denotes Negation as Failure). If Π is free of negations (aka a definite program) then the semantics of Π is defined by the well-known Least Herbrand Model (LHM) which coincides with the least of all models when Π is interpreted as a FOL theory. In [16] Sato points out that definite logic programs augmented with probabilistic elements subsume probabilistic graphical models such as Bayesian networks. Concretely, Sato's distribution semantics defines a probabilistic (definite) program as consisting of a set of ground probabilistic facts F and a definite program Π whose heads do not occur in F. The probability measure on the interpretations of F is then extended to produce a probability measure of LHMs of definite programs $\{\Pi \cup F' \mid F' \subseteq F\}$. However, when Π contains negations, LHM may not exist and hence some generalization of LHM has to be used. In particular, the state-of-the-art Probabilistic Logic Programming (PLP) languages (e.g. ProbLog [9], PROBXHAIL [3], PRISM [17], ICL [15], LPAD [20]) generalize Sato's distribution semantics to normal logic programs using either the well-founded semantics or the answer set semantics. Concretely, a PLP program is often defined as a tuple $R = (\Pi, \Theta :: F)$ consisting of a normal logic program Π and a finite set of probabilistic facts $\Theta :: F = \{p_1 :: f_1, p_2 :: f_2, \ldots, p_n :: f_n\}$ where each $p_i :: f_i \in \Theta :: F$ represents that a fact $f_i \leftarrow$ occurs in the deterministic program with probability p_i. Probabilistic facts are assumed to be independent, and hence each normal logic program $\Pi \cup F'$ is associated with a probability $Pr(F') \triangleq \prod\limits_{f_i \in F'} p_i \cdot \prod\limits_{f_i \in F \setminus F'} (1 - p_i)$. The probability of a literal q is then defined by

$$Pr(q) \triangleq \sum_{\substack{F' \subseteq F \\ (\Pi \cup F') \models_{sem} q}} Pr(F'),$$ with sem being the supported semantics (e.g. the

well-founded semantics in the case of ProbLog [9] and the answer set semantics in the case of PROBXHAIL [3]).

3 PABA Task Definitions

Inference for Probabilistic Argumentation has been focusing on computing the probability that a given argument or proposition is acceptable[7]. If what is given is a set of propositions $\mathbf{e} = \{q_1, \ldots, q_n\}$ rather than a single proposition q, one is interested in computing the following probabilities.

Definition 3. *Given a set of propositions $\mathbf{e}, \mathbf{q}$ and a semantics sem.*

- $Pr_{sem}(\mathbf{e}) \triangleq \sum\limits_{\substack{\omega \in \mathcal{W} \\ \forall q \in \mathbf{e}: \mathcal{F}_\omega \vdash_{sem} q}} Pr_{\mathcal{N}}(\omega)$, *the probability that for each $q \in \mathbf{e}$, there is an acceptable argument for q under semantics sem (or just the acceptability probability of evidence $\mathbf{e}$, for short).*

- $Pr_{sem}(\mathbf{q} \mid \mathbf{e}) \triangleq \dfrac{Pr_{sem}(\mathbf{q} \cup \mathbf{e})}{Pr_{sem}(\mathbf{e})}$, *the marginal acceptability probability of $\mathbf{q}$ given evidence $\mathbf{e}$.*

---

[7] When discussing a PABA inference task, we always refer to an arbitrary but fixed PABA framework $\mathcal{P} = (\mathcal{A}_p, \mathcal{N}, \mathcal{F})$ if not explicitly stated otherwise.

Hence we have several new inference tasks.

Definition 4. *Given a set of propositions e, q and a semantics sem.*

- *$EVID(e, sem)$ task: compute $Pr_{sem}(e)$*
- *$MARG(q, e, sem)$ task: compute $Pr_{sem}(q \mid e)$*
- *$MAP(Q, e, sem)$ task: compute $argmax_{q \in Q} \, Pr_{sem}(q \mid e)$ (given some set Q containing possible values for q).*

A PABA learning task is then defined as follows.

Definition 5. *Let $(\mathcal{A}_p, \mathcal{N}, \mathcal{F})$ be a PABA framework where $\mathcal{N} = (G, \_)$ is a Bayesian network with unknown CPTs, and $D = \{e_1, \ldots, e_M\}$ be a dataset (i.e. each $e_m \in D$ is a set of propositions). Construct PABA framework $\mathcal{P}_{\hat{\Theta}} = (\mathcal{A}_p, (G, \hat{\Theta}), \mathcal{F})$ where*

$$\hat{\Theta} = argmax_{\Theta} \prod_{m=1}^{M} Pr_{sem}^{\Theta}(e_m)$$

where $Pr_{sem}^{\Theta}(.)$ refers to the function $Pr_{sem}(.)$ of the parameterized PABA framework $(\mathcal{A}_p, (G, \Theta), \mathcal{F})$.

For convenience, we will use a notation $\langle (\mathcal{A}_p, (G, \_), \mathcal{F}), D \rangle$ to refer to a PABA learning task. ProbLog and BN learning tasks will be referred to by analogous notations.

4 Algorithms for PA Inference Tasks

A basic PA inference algorithm, which just computes $Pr_{sem}(q)$, can be viewed as translating (implicitly or explicitly) a given proposition q to a compact representation of all possible worlds in which q is acceptable under semantics *sem*. In this section, we first formalize this translation, borrowing some concepts and results from [11] (Definitions 6–8 and Theorem 1). We then lift this translation to the level of evidences and datasets (Definitions 9 and 10) to provide a basis for developing algorithms for the other inference tasks stated in Definition 4.

Definition 6. *– A partial world s is a subset (not necessarily proper) of a possible world and has probability $Pr_{\mathcal{N}}(s) = \sum\limits_{\substack{\omega \in W \\ \omega \supseteq s}} Pr_{\mathcal{N}}(\omega)$.*

– A frame $\mathcal{S}$ is a set of partial worlds and has probability $Pr_{\mathcal{N}}(\mathcal{S}) = \sum\limits_{s \in \mathcal{S}} Pr_{\mathcal{N}}(s)$[8].

---

[8] That is, a partial world is interpreted as a conjunction of probabilistic assumptions, while a frame is interpreted as a disjunction of partial worlds (In other words, a DNF over probabilistic assumptions).

Definition 7. *A partial world s is said to be **sufficient** for a proposition q under semantics sem (for short, **sem-sufficient** for q) if $\mathcal{F}_{s'} \vdash_{sem} q$ for any partial world $s' \supseteq s$.[9]*

Definition 8. *(Translating a proposition)*

- *A frame $\mathcal{S}$ said to be a frame **for a proposition** q **under a semantics** sem (for short, a **sem-frame** for q) if each partial world in $\mathcal{S}$ is sem-sufficient for q.*
- *A sem-frame $\mathcal{S}$ for a proposition q is **complete**, written $q \xLongrightarrow{sem} \mathcal{S}$, if for each possible world $\omega \in \mathcal{W}$ where $\mathcal{F}_\omega \vdash_{sem} q$, $\omega \supseteq s$ for some partial world $s \in \mathcal{S}$.*

Theorem 1. *1. For any proposition q and semantics sem, there exists a frame $\mathcal{S}$ such that $q \xLongrightarrow{sem} \mathcal{S}$.*
2. If $q \xLongrightarrow{sem} \mathcal{S}$ then $Pr_{sem}(q) = Pr_{\mathcal{N}}(\mathcal{S})$.

Example 2 (Continue Example 1). It is easy to verify that:

$$bark \xLongrightarrow{cr} \{\{burglary\}\}; \; howl \xLongrightarrow{cr} \{\{earthquake\}\}$$
$$alarm \xLongrightarrow{cr} \{\{burglary, earthquake, p\_alarm1\},$$
$$\{burglary, \neg earthquake, p\_alarm2\}, \{\neg burglary, earthquake, p\_alarm3\}\}$$

Definition 9 *(Translating evidence). We say that evidence $e = \{q_1, \ldots, q_n\}$ is **sem-translatable** to a frame $\mathcal{S}$, written $e \xLongrightarrow{sem} \mathcal{S}$, if there exists frames $\mathcal{S}_1, \ldots, \mathcal{S}_n$ such that*

1. $q_i \xLongrightarrow{sem} \mathcal{S}_i$ for each $q_i \in e$, and
2. $\mathcal{S}$ consists of the partial worlds in $\{s_1 \cup \cdots \cup s_n \mid s_1 \in \mathcal{S}_1, \ldots, s_n \in \mathcal{S}_n\}$.[10]

Example 3 (Continue Example 1). Consider $\mathbf{e}_1 = \{bark, alarm\}$ and $\mathbf{e}_2 = \{bark, howl\}$, we have

- $\mathbf{e}_1 \xLongrightarrow{cr} \mathcal{S}_{\mathbf{e}_1} = \{\{burglary, earthquake, p\_alarm1\}, \{burglary, \neg earthquake, p\_alarm2\}\}$
- $\mathbf{e}_2 \xLongrightarrow{cr} \mathcal{S}_{\mathbf{e}_2} = \{\{burglary, earthquake\}\}$

From Theorem 1, it is not difficult to prove the followings.

Theorem 2. *1. For any evidence e, there exists a frame $\mathcal{S}$ such that $e \xLongrightarrow{sem} \mathcal{S}$.*
2. If $e \xLongrightarrow{sem} \mathcal{S}$ then $Pr_{sem}(e) = Pr_{\mathcal{N}}(\mathcal{S})$.

The above theorem provides a basis for solving PABA inference problems. For example an $EVID(\mathbf{e}, sem)$ task can be solved by first translating $\mathbf{e} \xLongrightarrow{sem} \mathcal{S}$ (using some basic PABA inference algorithms such as the ones in [11]), then computing $Pr_{\mathcal{N}}(\mathcal{S})$. In the second step, computing $Pr_{\mathcal{N}}(\mathcal{S})$ can be done by Bayesian network algorithms on network $\mathcal{N}$, or by PLP inference algorithms on a PLP program representing $\mathcal{N}$ and $\mathcal{S}$. Concretely,

---

[9] Note that $\mathcal{F}_{s'}$ is the ABA framework obtained from $\mathcal{F}$ by adding a set of facts $\{p \leftarrow \mid p \in s'\}$.
[10] Note that if $s = s_1 \cup \cdots \cup s_n$ is inconsistent, then s is not a partial world and hence $s \notin \mathcal{S}$.

Lemma 1. *Suppose that $\mathcal{S}$ is a frame in a PABA framework $\mathcal{P} = (\mathcal{A}_p, \mathcal{N}, \mathcal{F})$ and R is the ProbLog program obtained from a ProbLog program representing $\mathcal{N}$ by adding a set of rules $\{q \leftarrow s \mid s \in \mathcal{S}\}$ where q is a new proposition not occurring in $\mathcal{P}$. Then $Pr_{\mathcal{N}}(\mathcal{S})$ coincides with the probability of q wrt R.*

Example 4 (Continue Example 3). $EVID(\mathbf{e}_1, cr)$ task can be solved by first translating $\mathbf{e}_1 \overset{cr}{\Rightarrow} \mathcal{S}_{\mathbf{e}_1}$, then computing $Pr_{\mathcal{N}}(\mathcal{S}_{\mathbf{e}_1})$ which can be done by querying the probability of proposition q in the following ProbLog program[11].

Listing 1.1. A ProbLog program for solving EVID task

```
% rules representing the original Bayesian network (Fig. 1)
0.1::earthquake.
0.9::p_alarm1.
0.8::p_alarm2.
0.7::p_alarm3.
0.3:: p_burglary_when_earthquake.
0.1:: p_burglary_when_noearthquake.
burglary :- earthquake,p_burglary_when_earthquake.
burglary :- not earthquake,p_burglary_when_noearthquake.
% rules for solving the given EVID task
q :- burglary, earthquake,p_alarm1.
q :- burglary, not earthquake, p_alarm2.
```

5   Algorithms for PA Learning Tasks

Now we switch our attention to PA learning tasks.

Definition 10 *(Translating dataset). We say that a dataset $D = \{\mathbf{e}_1, \ldots, \mathbf{e}_M\}$ is **sem-translatable** to a set of frames $\{\mathcal{S}_{\mathbf{e}_1}, \ldots, \mathcal{S}_{\mathbf{e}_M}\}$, written $D \overset{sem}{\Longrightarrow} \{\mathcal{S}_{\mathbf{e}_1}, \ldots, \mathcal{S}_{\mathbf{e}_M}\}$, if $\mathbf{e}_m \overset{sem}{\Longrightarrow} \mathcal{S}_{\mathbf{e}_m}$ for each $\mathbf{e}_m \in D$.*

Continue Example 3, we have $\{\mathbf{e}_1, \mathbf{e}_2\} \overset{cr}{\Rightarrow} \{\mathcal{S}_{\mathbf{e}_1}, \mathcal{S}_{\mathbf{e}_2}\}$.

Theorem 3. *1. For any dataset $D = \{\mathbf{e}_1, \ldots, \mathbf{e}_M\}$, there exists a set of frames $\{\mathcal{S}_{\mathbf{e}_1}, \ldots, \mathcal{S}_{\mathbf{e}_M}\}$ such that $D \overset{sem}{\Longrightarrow} \{\mathcal{S}_{\mathbf{e}_1}, \ldots, \mathcal{S}_{\mathbf{e}_M}\}$.*

2. If $D \overset{sem}{\Longrightarrow} \{\mathcal{S}_{\mathbf{e}_1}, \ldots, \mathcal{S}_{\mathbf{e}_M}\}$ then $Pr_{sem}(D) \triangleq \prod_{m=1}^{M} Pr_{sem}(\mathbf{e}_m) = \prod_{m=1}^{M} Pr_{\mathcal{N}}(\mathcal{S}_{\mathbf{e}_m})$.

The following definition describes how to translate a PABA learning task into a BN learning task.

---

[11] Readers are referred to http://problog.readthedocs.io/en/latest/cli.html for details about ProbLog concrete syntax.

Definition 11. *We say that a PABA learning task $\langle(\mathcal{A}_p, (G, \_), \mathcal{F}), D\rangle$ with $D = \{e_1, \ldots, e_M\}$ is sem-translatable to a BN learning task $\langle(G', \_), D'\rangle$, written*

$$\langle(\mathcal{A}_p, (G, \_), \mathcal{F}), D\rangle \overset{sem}{\Longrightarrow} \langle(G', \_), D'\rangle$$

if the following conditions hold.

1. *There exists frames $\mathcal{S}_{e_1} = \{s_{11}, \ldots, s_{1|\mathcal{S}_{e_1}|}\}, \ldots, \mathcal{S}_{e_M} = \{s_{M1}, \ldots, s_{M|\mathcal{S}_{e_M}|}\}$ such that $D \overset{sem}{\Longrightarrow} \{\mathcal{S}_{e_1}, \ldots, \mathcal{S}_{e_M}\}$.*
2. *G' is obtained from G by adding,*
   - *for each $s_{mi} \in \mathcal{S}_{e_m}$ ($m \in \{1, \ldots M\}$), an AND gate representing the conjunction $\bigwedge s_{mi}$, and*
   - *for each $\mathcal{S}_{e_m}$, an OR gate representing the disjunction $\bigvee \mathcal{S}_{e_m}$.*
3. *$D' = \{\{obj(e_1)\}, \ldots, \{obj(e_M)\}\}$[12]*

Example 5 (Continue Example 3). Consider a PABA learning task $\langle(\mathcal{A}_p, (G, \_), \mathcal{F}), D\rangle$ with $D = \{e_1, e_2\}$. We have $\langle(\mathcal{A}_p, (G, \_), \mathcal{F}), D\rangle \overset{cr}{\Longrightarrow} \langle\mathcal{N}', D'\rangle$ where

- $\mathcal{N}' = (G', \_)$ is shown in Fig. 2. Note that there are three AND gates and one OR gate added by condition 2 of Definition 11 where
  - AND1, AND2, AND3 represents conjunctions *burglary $\wedge$ earthquake*, *burglary$\wedge$earthquake$\wedge$p_alarm1* and *burglary$\wedge\neg$earthquake$\wedge$p_alarm2* respectively,
  - OR represents disjunction $\bigvee \mathcal{S}_{e_1}$
- $D' = \{\{obj(e_1)\}, \{obj(e_2)\}\}$

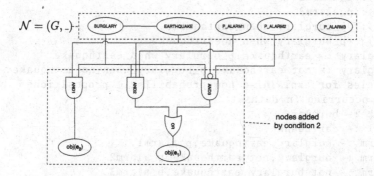

Fig. 2. Bayesian network $\mathcal{N}'$

The correctness of translation $\langle(\mathcal{A}_p, (G, \_), \mathcal{F}), D\rangle \overset{sem}{\Longrightarrow} \langle(G', \_), D'\rangle$ is ensured by the following theorem.

---

[12] *obj(.)* maps evidences to sentences of the underlying language.

Theorem 4. *1. Given any PABA learning task $\langle(\mathcal{A}_p, (G,\_)\mathcal{F}), D\rangle$, there always exists a BN learning task $\langle(G',\_), D'\rangle\rangle$ such that $\langle(\mathcal{A}_p, (G,\_), \mathcal{F}), D\rangle \stackrel{sem}{\Longrightarrow} \langle(G',\_), D'\rangle$*

2. If $\langle(\mathcal{A}_p, (G,\_), \mathcal{F}), D\rangle \stackrel{sem}{\Longrightarrow} \langle(G',\_), D'\rangle$ and $\hat{\Theta}$ is a solution of the BN learning task, then $\hat{\Theta}$ is also a solution of the PABA learning task.

The following definition describes how to translate a PABA learning task into a ProbLog learning task.

Definition 12. *We say that a PABA learning task $\langle(\mathcal{A}_p, (G,\_), \mathcal{F}), D\rangle$ sem-translatable to a ProbLog learning task $\langle(\Pi, \_::F), D\rangle$, written*

$$\langle(\mathcal{A}_p, (G,\_), \mathcal{F}), D\rangle \stackrel{sem}{\Longrightarrow} \langle(\Pi, \_::F), D\rangle$$

if $(\Pi, \_::F)$ is the ProbLog program obtained from a ProbLog program representing $\mathcal{N}$ by adding, for each non-probabilistic proposition q occurring in D (i.e. $q \in \bigcup D \setminus (\mathcal{A}_p \cup \neg\mathcal{A}_p))$, a set of rules $\{q \leftarrow s \mid s \in \mathcal{S}_q\}$, where $q \stackrel{sem}{\Longrightarrow} \mathcal{S}_q$.

Example 6 (Continue Example 5). The PABA learning task $\langle(\mathcal{A}_p, (G,\_), \mathcal{F}), D\rangle$ is cr-translatable to a ProbLog learning task $\langle(\Pi, \_::F), D\rangle$ which, in the concrete ProbLog syntax, is given as follows.

Listing 1.2. A ProbLog learning task

```
% rules representing the Bayesian network (Fig. 1) where
    unknown parameters are tagged with t(_)
t(_)::earthquake.
t(_)::p_alarm1.
t(_)::p_alarm2.
t(_)::p_alarm3.
t(_):: p_burglary_when_earthquake.
t(_):: p_burglary_when_noearthquake.
burglary :- earthquake,p_burglary_when_earthquake.
burglary :- not earthquake,p_burglary_when_noearthquake.
% rules for explaining non-probabilistic propositions
    occurring in dataset
bark :- burglary.
howl :- earthquake.
alarm :- burglary,earthquake,p_alarm1.
alarm :- burglary,not earthquake,p_alarm2.
alarm :- not burglary,earthquake,p_alarm3.
% Dataset D = {e1,e2}
% e1 = {bark, alarm}
evidence(bark,true).
evidence(alarm,true).
--------------------------
% e2 = {bark, howl}
evidence(bark,true).
evidence(howl,true).
```

Theorem 5. *1. Given any PABA learning task $\langle(\mathcal{A}_p, (G, \_), \mathcal{F}), D\rangle$, there exists a ProbLog learning task $\langle(\Pi, \_::F), D\rangle$ such that $\langle(\mathcal{A}_p, (G, \_), \mathcal{F}), D\rangle \stackrel{sem}{\Longrightarrow} \langle\Pi, \_:F, D\rangle$.*

2. Suppose $\langle(\mathcal{A}_p, (G, \_), \mathcal{F}), D\rangle \stackrel{sem}{\Longrightarrow} \langle\Pi, \_::F, D\rangle$. If $\hat{\Theta}$ is a solution of the ProbLog learning task, then $\hat{\Theta}$ is also a solution of the PABA learning task.

6 Prototype Implementation

In this section, we demonstrate a prototype implementation of our PABA learning method using our running example[13]. As described by Fig. 3, a learning process with input $\langle(\mathcal{A}_p, (G, \_), \mathcal{F})\rangle$ proceeds in three steps:

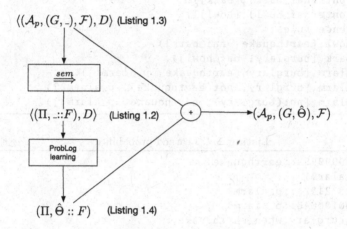

$\langle(\mathcal{A}_p, (G, \_), \mathcal{F}), D\rangle$ (Listing 1.3)

$sem \Longrightarrow$

$\langle(\Pi, \_::F), D\rangle$ (Listing 1.2)

ProbLog learning

$(\Pi, \hat{\Theta} :: F)$ (Listing 1.4)

$+$

$(\mathcal{A}_p, (G, \hat{\Theta}), \mathcal{F})$

Fig. 3. PABA learning

1. Translate $\langle(\mathcal{A}_p, (G, \_), \mathcal{F}), D\rangle \stackrel{sem}{\Longrightarrow} \langle(\Pi, \_::F), D\rangle$ using Definition 12. Here we use the basic PABA inference algorithms of [11] to translate $q \stackrel{sem}{\Longrightarrow} \mathcal{S}_q$ for each proposition q occurring in D. As code Listing 1.3 illustrates, an input PABA learning task $\langle(\mathcal{A}_p, (G, \_), \mathcal{F}), D\rangle$ is specified with the following predicates: iObservables([...]), iObservable(.) declare propositions that might occur in dataset D; iNas([...]) declares the set of assumptions in $\mathcal{F}$; contr(...) refers to the contrary of an assumption; iRule(..., [...]) declares an inference rule of $\mathcal{F}$; iPas([...]) declares the set of probabilistic assumptions in $\mathcal{A}_p$. The output ProbLog learning task $\langle(\Pi, \_::F), D\rangle$ of this sample PABA learning task has been shown in code Listing 1.2.

2. ProbLog learning: This step simply calls ProbLog to learn unknown probabilities tagged by t(_). Code Listing 1.4 shows the resulted ProbLog program where unknown probabilities are filled.

---

[13] Download link of this implementation: http://ict.siit.tu.ac.th/~hung/Prengine/2.0.

3. Export the learning solution: This step simply extracts the probabilities learned by ProbLog and populate them in $(\mathcal{A}_p, (G, \_), \mathcal{F})$ to have a complete PABA framework $(\mathcal{A}_p, (G, \hat{\Theta}), \mathcal{F})$.

Listing 1.3. The specification of the PABA learning task in Example 5

```
% Declare non-probabilistic propositions occurring in dataset
iObservables([bark,howl]).
iObservable(alarm).
% Declare pro. assumptions
iPas([burglary, earthquake, p_alarm1, p_alarm2, p_alarm3]).
% Declare logical assumptions
iNas([naf_bark, naf_howl]).
iRule(contr(naf_bark),[bark]).
iRule(contr(naf_howl),[howl]).
% Inference rules
iRule(howl,[earthquake, naf_bark]).
iRule(bark,[burglary, naf_howl]).
iRule(alarm,[burglary, earthquake, p_alarm1]).
iRule(alarm,[burglary, not(earthquake), p_alarm2]).
iRule(alarm,[not(burglary), earthquake, p_alarm3]).
```

Listing 1.4. Learned probabilities

```
0.999999999989::earthquake.
1.0::p_alarm1.
0.968928721025::p_alarm2.
0.380860100846::p_alarm3.
1.0::p_burglary_when_earthquake.
0.629569982574::p_burglary_when_noearthquake.
burglary :- earthquake, p_burglary_when_earthquake.
burglary :- not earthquake, p_burglary_when_noearthquake.
bark :- burglary.
howl :- earthquake.
alarm :- burglary, earthquake, p_alarm1.
alarm :- burglary, not earthquake, p_alarm2.
alarm :- not burglary, earthquake, p_alarm3.
```

7   Conclusions and Related Work

Various models of Probabilistic Argumentation have been proposed [8,10,12,13, 19] in the literature, however inference tasks for PA has been limited to the basic problem of computing the acceptability probability for a single argument, as done in [18], or computing the probability that there exists an acceptable argument supporting a given proposition, as done in [11]. In this paper, using PABA [8], we formalize such tasks as computing marginal acceptability probabilities given some evidence and learning probabilistic parameters from a dataset.

We show that algorithms for them can be composed by finely joining a basic PABA inference algorithms and existing algorithms for the corresponding tasks in PLP or and even BN. Intuitively, such a basic PABA inference procedure is used to solve the logical, argumentative part of a given task. The remaining part, which should be purely probabilistic, can be dealt with by either PLP or BN algorithms. In this paper, we also provide a prototype implementation of PA learning using this approach. To the best of our knowledge, learning has been unexplored so far in the PABA literature.

One might question the benefits of machine learning in probabilistic argumentation when compared with machine learning in traditional formalisms. As discussed widely (e.g. in [3]), learning in Artificial Neural Networks (AN) aims to build a network of computational units, aka neutrons, each of which outputs a single value weighting the inputs from connected neutrons. However, these weights do not afford an easy interpretation, other than that they are chosen to minimize the difference between the network output and the expected result of a unknown real-valued function under discovery. Machine learning using Bayesian statistics aim to find parameters for a probabilistic model (e.g. a Bayesian network) that maximizes the likelihood of the data. Probabilistic models are typically easier to interpret than ANs, partly because dependencies between random variables often represent causal relationships, though understandings of the learned model still demand the interpretations of probabilistic parameters. Combining logic-based learning and Bayesian statistics, as done in PLP, results in symbolic models that subsume any probabilistic models [16] and afford easier interpretations. As mentioned, the state-of-the-art PLP languages use either the well-founded semantics (e.g. ProbLog [9], PRISM [17], ICL [15], LPAD [20]) or the answer set semantics (e.g. PROBXHAIL [3]) of normal logic programs, which are often implemented using respectively the well-known Prolog top-down SLDNF resolution or Answer-set bottom-up solvers (e.g. clingo). Since the well-founded and answer set semantics of normal (and even much more generalized) logic programs correspond to the grounded semantics and the stable semantics of assumption-based argumentation [7], PABA can be used to emulate PLP languages. Moreover, PABA allows users to comprehend not only the significance of individual inference rules, but also the interactions of arguments for and against a certain conclusion. However, we believe that a major benefit of PABA learning comes from the range of argumentation semantics which could not be found in PLP. In general the more credulous a semantics is, the better it can handle conflicting datasets. For illustration, let's revisit the dataset $D = \{e_1, e_2\}$ in our Example 5. We can say that evidence $e_2 = \{bark, howl\}$ is somehow conflicting (recall the rules $bark \leftarrow burglary, \sim howl$ and $howl \leftarrow earthquake, \sim bark$). Under the grounded semantics, we have $Pr_{gr}(e_2) = 0$ and hence any learning algorithm following $\hat{\Theta} = argmax_\Theta \, Pr_{gr}^\Theta(e_1) \times Pr_{gr}^\Theta(e_2) = argmax_\Theta \, 0$ would have to return an arbitrary result or even fail[14]. However, under the credulous

---

[14] Prolog-based PLP languages using SLDNF resolution such as ProbLog fail to learn this dataset because SLDNF resolution does not terminate if queried ?-bark, howl.

semantics, $Pr_{cr}(\mathbf{e}_2) = Pr_{\mathcal{N}}(\{earthquake, burglary\})$, and as demonstrated in the paper body, the learning process can still produce a sensible result.

References

1. Baroni, P., Giacomin, M.: Semantics of abstract argument systems. In: Simari, G., Rahwan, I. (eds.) Argumentation in Artificial Intelligence, pp. 25–44. Springer, Boston (2009). doi:10.1007/978-0-387-98197-0_2
2. Bondarenko, A., Dung, P.M., Kowalski, R.A., Toni, F.: An abstract, argumentation-theoretic approach to default reasoning. Artif. Intell. **93**(1), 63–101 (1997)
3. Broda, K., Law, M.: PROBXHAIL: An Abductive-Inductive Algorithm for Probabilistic Inductive Logic Programming (2016)
4. Dung, P.M.: On the acceptability of arguments and its fundamental role in non-monotonic reasoning, logic programming and n-person games. Artif. Intell. **77**(2), 321–357 (1995)
5. Dung, P.M., Kowalski, R.A., Toni, F.: Dialectic proof procedures for assumption-based, admissible argumentation. Artif. Intell. **170**(2), 114–159 (2006)
6. Dung, P.M., Mancarella, P., Toni, F.: Computing ideal skeptical argumentation. Artif. Intell. **171**(10–15), 642–674 (2007)
7. Dung, P.M., Son, T.C., Thang, P.M.: Argumentation-based semantics for logic programs with first-order formulae. In: Baldoni, M., Chopra, A.K., Son, T.C., Hirayama, K., Torroni, P. (eds.) PRIMA 2016. LNCS (LNAI), vol. 9862, pp. 43–60. Springer, Cham (2016). doi:10.1007/978-3-319-44832-9_3
8. Dung, P.M., Thang, P.M.: Towards (probabilistic) argumentation for jury-based dispute resolution. In: COMMA 2010, pp. 171–182 (2010)
9. Fierens, D., Van Den Broeck, G., Renkens, J., Shterionov, D., Gutmann, B., Thon, I., Janssens, G., De Raedt, L.: Inference and learning in probabilistic logic programs using weighted boolean formulas. Theory Pract. Logic Program. **15**(3), 358–401 (2015)
10. Gabbay, D.M., Rodrigues, O.: Probabilistic Argumentation: An Equational Approach, CoRR (2015)
11. Hung, N.D.: Inference procedures and engine for probabilistic argumentation. Int. J. Approx. Reason. **90**, 163–191 (2017)
12. Hunter, A.: A probabilistic approach to modelling uncertain logical arguments. Int. J. Approx. Reason. **54**(1), 47–81 (2013)
13. Li, H., Oren, N., Norman, T.J.: Probabilistic argumentation frameworks. In: Modgil, S., Oren, N., Toni, F. (eds.) TAFA 2011. LNCS (LNAI), vol. 7132, pp. 1–16. Springer, Heidelberg (2012). doi:10.1007/978-3-642-29184-5_1
14. Poole, D.: Logic programming, abduction and probability. New Gen. Comput. **11**(3), 377 (1993)
15. Poole, D.: The independent choice logic and beyond. In: De Raedt, L., Frasconi, P., Kersting, K., Muggleton, S. (eds.) Probabilistic Inductive Logic Programming. LNCS, vol. 4911, pp. 222–243. Springer, Heidelberg (2008). doi:10.1007/978-3-540-78652-8_8
16. Sato, T.: A statistical learning method for logic programs with distribution semantics. In: Logic Programming, Proceedings of the Twelfth International Conference on Logic Programming, Tokyo, Japan, 13–16 June 1995, pp. 715–729 (1995)

17. Sato, T., Kameya, Y.: New advances in logic-based probabilistic modeling by PRISM. In: De Raedt, L., Frasconi, P., Kersting, K., Muggleton, S. (eds.) Probabilistic Inductive Logic Programming. LNCS, vol. 4911, pp. 118–155. Springer, Heidelberg (2008). doi:10.1007/978-3-540-78652-8_5

18. Thang, P.M.: Dialectical proof procedures for probabilistic abstract argumentation. In: Baldoni, M., Chopra, A.K., Son, T.C., Hirayama, K., Torroni, P. (eds.) PRIMA 2016. LNCS (LNAI), vol. 9862, pp. 397–406. Springer, Cham (2016). doi:10.1007/978-3-319-44832-9_27

19. Thimm, M.: A probabilistic semantics for abstract argumentation. In: ECAI, vol. 242, pp. 750–755. ISO Press (2012)

20. Vennekens, J., Denecker, M., Bruynooghe, M.: Cp-logic: a language of causal probabilistic events and its relation to logic programming. Theory Pract. Logic Program. **9**(3), 245–308 (2009)

Spatial Problem Solving in Spatial Structures

Christian Freksa$^{(\boxtimes)}$ ⓘ, Ana-Maria Olteţeanu ⓘ,
Thomas Barkowsky ⓘ, Jasper van de Ven ⓘ,
and Holger Schultheis ⓘ

Bremen Spatial Cognition Center, University of Bremen, Bremen, Germany
freksa@uni-bremen.de

Abstract. The ability to solve spatial tasks is crucial for everyday life and therefore of great importance for cognitive agents. In artificial intelligence (AI) we model this ability by representing spatial configurations and spatial tasks in the form of knowledge *about* space and time. Augmented by appropriate algorithms, such representations enable the generation of knowledge-based solutions to spatial problems. In comparison, natural embodied and situated cognitive agents often solve spatial tasks without detailed knowledge about underlying geometric and mechanical laws and relationships. They directly relate actions and their effects through physical affordances inherent in their bodies and their environments. Examples are found in everyday reasoning and also in descriptive geometry. In an ongoing research effort we investigate how spatial and temporal structures *in the body and the environment* can support or even replace reasoning effort in computational processes. We call the direct use of spatial structure *Strong Spatial Cognition*. Our contribution describes cognitive principles of an extended paradigm of cognitive processing. The work aims (i) to *understand* the effectiveness and efficiency of natural problem solving approaches; (ii) to *overcome* the need for detailed representations required in the knowledge-based approach; and (iii) to *build* computational cognitive systems that make use of these principles.

Keywords: Cognitive systems · Spatial cognition · Spatial problem solving · Strong spatial cognition

1   Introduction: AI and Cognitive Systems

Cognitive agents – be they humans, animals, or autonomous robots – comprise brains or computers connected to sensors and actuators. These components are arranged in the agents' bodies in ways that allow them to interact with one another and with their spatial environments. In this paper, we consider the entire aggregate (cognitive agent including its body and the environment) as a *full cognitive system* (Fig. 1). We investigate how spatial processes performed by an agent in the environment can support computational processes.

Consider the *distribution*, *coordination*, and *execution* of spatial tasks among the system components of spatially situated cognitive agents. In a pure information processing/AI approach, the elements of the spatial problem outside the brain or computer would be considered "outside the system." Inside the system they are

© Springer International Publishing AG 2017
S. Phon-Amnuaisuk et al. (Eds.): MIWAI 2017, LNAI 10607, pp. 18–29, 2017.
https://doi.org/10.1007/978-3-319-69456-6_2

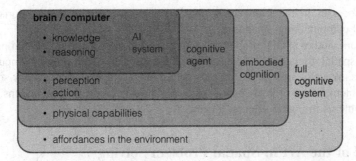

Fig. 1. Structure of a full cognitive system. (Adapted from Freksa 2015b, p. 11)

described in terms of some knowledge representation language or pattern. This allows the computer to perform formal reasoning (or other computational processing) on the knowledge representation. To obtain this knowledge representation, physical, topological, and geometric relations in the problem configuration must be transformed into abstract *information*. The tasks then can be performed entirely on the information processing level, where physical, topological, and geometric relations and physical affordances no longer persist.

However, the classical information-processing oriented division between (a) brain or computer and (b) perception, action, body, and environment, is only one way of distributing the activities involved in cognitive processing. As in natural problem solving approaches, we can include the spatial problem domain as part of the system and (1) maintain some of the spatial relations in their original form; (2) simulate spatial relations and interactions through motion models; or (3) use *mild abstraction* (Freksa et al. 2018) for their representation.

One of the pillars of knowledge representation research is that processing structures of problem solving processes differ within and across types of representation (cf. Marr 1982). Most importantly, certain processing structures facilitate certain forms of processing (Sloman 1985; Larkin and Simon 1987). In particular, certain *spatial* structures facilitate certain forms of *spatial* problem solving (Barkowsky et al. 1994; Freksa 2013, 2015a, b; Freksa and Schultheis 2014; Freksa et al. 2016; Furbach et al. 2016). *Spatial* problem solving is a particularly interesting and important class of problems that mobile cognitive agents, such as most animals and autonomous robots, must deal with all the time. Accordingly, we investigate structures that specifically facilitate solutions to spatial problems. However, it has been argued that spatial cognition can provide mechanisms for non-spatial problem solving, as well (e.g. Lakoff and Johnson 1980); thus, if successful for spatial problem solving, the importance of this research may extend into other domains of cognition.

From depictive (constructive) geometry we know that certain computation can be replaced by geometric construction (and vice versa). Often, constructive procedures appear simpler than the corresponding computations and they also lead more frequently to insights into the nature of the problem and the solution. Our approach aims at relating *spatial constructions* and the corresponding *computations* in their respective underlying structures (substrates) in order to assess and compare the spatial problem solving processes in the framework of a full cognitive system that comprises both spatial and computational operations.

Our work studies spatial problems, identifies principles of solving spatial problems inside the spatial domain, and compares spatial approaches with purely computational approaches. We also investigate how to determine a suitable approach for solving a spatial problem from a problem specification and how to control spatial actions to solve spatial problems in a goal-oriented manner.

2   State of the Art in Spatial Problem Solving

Spatial problem solving has been a fundamental research topic in AI from the very beginning. Initially, spatial relations were treated like other features: task-relevant aspects of the domain were formalized and represented in some kind of data structure; general computation and reasoning methods were applied; and the result of the computation was interpreted in terms of the target domain. Taking into account the ubiquity of space and time in real environments, approaches have been developed that give spatial and temporal relations a special status and that are specifically tailored towards specific aspects of space (such as topology, orientation, and distance). In the following overview we consider five perspectives that have been taken for solving spatial problems. Most approaches take into account several of these perspectives.

2.1   Knowledge-Based Perspectives (K)

Knowledge-based approaches have dominated AI for most of the past 60 years. In such approaches, facts and relations about space in general and about specific problem domains are encoded as knowledge that describes the domain. Problem solving is then performed by computation that operates on the description level. Ontologies have become a much-used approach to formally describe properties of domains (e.g., Bateman et al. 2010 for the spatial domain). Commonsense reasoning, being one of the oldest research areas of AI, makes extensive use of formalized spatial knowledge. Yet, as Davis and Marcus (2015) point out, progress in the field has been slow. Qualitative spatial reasoning (Egenhofer and Franzosa 1991; Freksa 1991b; Cohn and Renz 2008; Dylla et al. 2017) has been an active research area since the late 1980s; specific knowledge about spatial relations and spatial operations defines spatial structures and makes up spatial calculi for reasoning on the basis of human-understandable spatial concepts. Some cognitive robotics approaches include qualitative spatial calculi (Mansouri and Pecora 2013; Wolter and Wallgrün 2012) to provide knowledge-based support for object identification, spatial orientation, and robot actions in space.

2.2   Computational Adaptation and Learning (L)

As manual encoding of extensive knowledge is cumbersome, learning algorithms have been developed that generate spatial information from sensor data (e.g. SLAM - Thrun et al. 2005; Frese et al. 2005) or generate new knowledge about spatial actions from rudimentary knowledge (Wörgötter et al. 2015). Deep Learning (Goodfellow et al.

2016) and 'cognitive computing' (Modha et al. 2011; Kelly 2015) approaches combine a multitude of methods in order to derive new knowledge from vast amounts of data. Whereas SLAM specifically exploits spatial structure in the sensor data, the latter two approaches do not necessarily require perceptual or other spatial input; they are mainly used for processing knowledge in an abstract form. Adaptation and learning approaches typically make use of large amounts of behavioral correlations rather than relying on the internal domain structure.

2.3   Analogical Representation and Analogical Reasoning (A)

Analogical reasoning pays particular attention to the structure of the represented domain and to the processes operating on them. Sloman (1971, 1975) analyzed structural characteristics in comparison to descriptive ('Fregean') representations as well as effects of representational structures on the processing characteristics. In the spirit of analogical representation and reasoning and in recognition of the power of two-dimensional visualization and perception, the field of *Diagrammatic Reasoning* evolved (Glasgow et al. 1995; Goel et al. 2010). This research area was motivated by (i) papers by mathematicians and other theoreticians who confessed that they obtain their insights and understanding of problems not by looking at formulas but by drawing and studying diagrams; and by (ii) influences of cognitive psychology that acknowledge essential differences between processing 2D layouts and processing their linearized descriptions. In his famous book *How to solve it,* Polya (1956) analyzed cognitive processes that lead from problem statements to their solutions. Diagrams visualize spatial and spatialize non-spatial situations to make them accessible to visual perception and spatial analysis. In AI, Funt (1980) and Chandrasekaran (2006) have proposed retina-like and more general perceptual representational structures that make certain aspects of spatial configurations – such as spatial neighborhood, shape, or size – directly accessible to computational processes.

2.4   Biology-Inspired Approaches (B)

Alternative autonomous systems inspired by biological role models have been proposed in biocybernetics and AI research. Such systems perceive their environment and act in a goal-oriented manner. For example, Braitenberg's (1984) vehicles demonstrate smart spatial behavior without requiring explicit symbolic representation of spatial information; these vehicles directly replicate specific aspects of neural sensory-motor connectivity that implicitly responds to spatial arrangements and inherent spatial structures. From an engineering perspective, Brooks (1991) proposed the *subsumption architecture* to implement intelligent reactive systems without representing knowledge about the domain. Like Braitenberg, Brooks emphasizes physical interaction with the environment as a primary source of constraints on the design of intelligent systems. He argues for focusing on the interface to the real world, in order to avoid the need for reliance on a representation. In their elaborate book, Pfeifer and Scheier (1999) describe this class of approaches as a new way of understanding intelligence *(Nouvelle AI).* Goel et al. (2012) use biological role models for conceiving design systems that manifest cognitive, collaborative, conceptual, and creative characteristics.

2.5   Cognition-Based Approaches (C)

In *The design of everyday things*, Norman (2013) distinguishes 'knowledge in the world' from 'knowledge in the head'. Maintaining features and relations in their original form and context corresponds to what Norman calls *knowledge in the world*. Use of knowledge in the world involves the use of perception in order to solve problems. He explains why people need both types of knowledge to manage everyday tasks. Gibson (1979) introduced the notion of *affordance* to characterize conditions that permit actions in physical environments. As Gibson developed his theory in the context of visual perception, the notion was understood by various authors (including initially by Norman) to refer exclusively to conditions that can be perceptually identified; different uses of the notion *affordance* have caused considerable confusion in the cognitive science community that seems to have scared some researchers away from what is a highly beneficial notion, if used in a well-defined manner.

Qualitative spatial relations have provided a conceptual framework to comprehend space-specific structures and processes underlying topological and geometric affordances (Freksa 1991a; Gooday and Cohn 1994; Egenhofer and Mark 1995). Wintermute and Laird (2008) proposed to augment qualitative representation and reasoning in cognitive architectures by quantitative simulations of spatial relations and interactions, in order to make physical affordances accessible to computational approaches. A Dagstuhl Seminar (Rome et al. 2008) approached the topic of affordance-based robot control as a perspective on directly coupling perception, action, and reasoning in real-time. Raubal and Moratz (2008) present an extended theory of affordances that differentiates between different kinds of affordances in order to characterize functional models of affordance-based agents. Kirsh (2013) discusses human imagination and the role of (i) physical interaction; (ii) thinking with brain and body; (iii) physically performing vs. watching; and (iv) thinking with things for effective cognition and for finding answers to sometimes long-standing questions. In our work we address these issues with a constructive approach and theoretical analysis.

3   Spatial Solutions to Spatial Problems

The Strong Spatial Cognition team at the Bremen Spatial Cognition Center[1] has studied example problems from the literature such as the shortest route problem (Dreyfus and Haugeland 1974), Archimedes' volume comparison problem (Vitruvius 2007), and classical geometric construction problems. We demonstrated or outlined spatial procedures to solving these problems (Freksa 2013, 2015a, b; Freksa and Schultheis 2014; Freksa et al. 2016, 2018). In collaboration with other universities we started to investigate approaches to compare formal and spatial solutions to solving spatial problems (Furbach et al. 2016).

Previously, in the framework of the CRC/TR 8 Spatial Cognition, the team had investigated spatial relations in geographic maps and varieties of formal representations. *Mild abstraction* (Freksa et al. 2018) was identified as a form of analogical

---

[1] http://bscc.spatial-cognition.de.

representation employed in geographic paper maps to facilitate physical operations such as perception, route-following with a finger, and manipulation in similar ways as in the represented real-world domain. Mild abstraction may abstract only from few aspects, while preserving structural spatial properties Perception is required to use mildly abstracted representations – but the perception task typically is easier than the same task under real-world conditions, for example due to the modified scale.

4 The Strong Spatial Cognition Paradigm

Our work largely builds on the perspectives **A**, **B**, and **C** outlined in the state-of-the-art section. Also, **K** is important for the meta-level of planning and organizing sub-tasks of spatial problem solving. **L** only peripherally plays a role, as we prescribe spatial structure that learning approaches would derive. In our approach, we specifically target the direct use of spatial structure. For example, we study the concept of a 'string' as a deformable 1D spatial entity whose length is invariant under shape transformations (Freksa et al. 2016). A certain class of spatial problems requires length comparison, while absolute length is irrelevant (e.g., the shortest path problem). Arbitrarily shaped strings are difficult to compare with regards to their length. Simple spatial *pull* and *align* operations, however, can transform arbitrarily shaped strings into straight and aligned strings that are easily compared through perceptual operations. Similar operations can be found for other aspects of space, such as angles.

With our work, we take an important step beyond the state of the art and introduce a paradigm shift: we aim at preserving spatial structure and directly exploit features of simultaneous spatial transformations. Initially we represent spatial objects and configurations using the objects and configurations themselves or their *physical* models, rather than via abstract representations. The core advantages of this approach are: information loss due to early representational commitments is avoided; and no decision needs to be made beforehand about which aspects of the world to represent in a certain way, which aspects to abstract away, and which spatial reference frame to use. This can be decided partly during the problem solving process. Then, additional contextual information may become available that can guide the choice of the specific abstraction to be used.

Even more important: objects and configurations frequently are aggregated in a natural and meaningful way; for example, a chair may consist of a seat, several legs, and a back; if I move or deform one component of a chair, I automatically (and simultaneously!) move or deform other components and the entire chair, and vice versa (cf. the frame problem, McCarthy and Hayes 1969). This property is not intrinsically given in abstract representations of physical objects; but it is an extremely important property from a cognitive point of view, as no computational processing cycles are required for simulating the physical effects or for reasoning about them. Thus, manipulability of physical structures may become an important feature of cognitive processing, and not merely a property of physical objects.

Our approach is to *isolate* and *simplify* the specific spatial problem to be solved, e.g. by removing task-irrelevant entities and features from the spatial configuration or by *reconstructing the essence* of the spatial configuration through mild abstraction. In general, it will be difficult to prescribe the precise preprocessing steps for solving a problem; but for the special case of spatial problems it is feasible to provide useful heuristics. These can serve as meta-knowledge which can be used to control actions on the physical level. After successful preprocessing, it will be possible in certain cases to 'read' an answer to the problem through perception directly off the resulting configuration; in other cases, the resulting spatial configuration may be a more suitable starting point for a knowledge-based approach to solving the problem.

A main hypothesis of our approach is that the 'intelligence' of cognitive systems is located not only in specific abstract problem-solving approaches, but also – and perhaps more importantly – in the capability of recognizing characteristic problem structures and of selecting particularly suitable problem-solving approaches for given tasks. Formal representations may not facilitate the recognition of such structures, due to a bias inherent in the abstraction. This is where *mild abstraction* can help.

The insight that spatial relations and physical operations are strongly connected to cognitive processing may lead to a different division of labor between the perceptual, the representational, the computational, and the locomotive parts of cognitive interaction than the one we currently pursue in AI systems: rather than putting all the 'intelligence' of the system into computing, our approach aims at putting more intelligence into the interactions between components and structures of the full cognitive system. More specifically, we aim at exploiting intrinsic structures of space and time in order to simplify the tasks to be solved.

We hypothesize that the flexible assignment of physical and computational resources for cognitive problem solving may be closer to the workings of natural cognitive systems than an almost exclusively computational approach. For example, when we as cognitive agents search for a certain object in our environment, we have at least two strategies at our disposal: we can represent the object in our mind and try to imagine and mentally reconstruct where it could or should be – the classical AI approach; or we can visually search for the object in our physical environment. Which is better (or more promising) depends on a variety of factors including memory, physical effort, the size of the physical environment, etc.; frequently a clever combination of both approaches will be best.

Strong Spatial Cognition research is primarily carried out as basic cognitive systems research: we identify and relate a set of cognitive principles and ways of combining them to obtain cognitive performance in spatio-temporal domains. We bring together three areas of expertise: (1) **cognitive systems research** – to investigate cognitive architectures and trade-offs between explicit and implicit representations; (2) **theory** – to characterize and analyze the resulting structures and operations; and (3) **implementation** – to construct and explore various cognitive system configurations.. The Strong Spatial Cognition approach aims at developing and exploring a novel paradigm for cognitive processing based on the integration of results obtained in various disciplines of cognitive science.

5 Example of Strong Spatial Cognition Problem Solving[2]

Suppose an agent's task is to identify the shortest route that connects a location A with a location B given several possible paths in a route network that can be chosen. A classical knowledge-based approach would (i) represent the lengths of the route sections, (ii) compute various alternatives of configuring these sections to connect A and B and (iii) determine the option with the smallest overall length. Note that the lengths of the route sections need to be known to use this approach although the absolute length of the resulting route is not of interest. Also note that several alternatives have to be computed and compared before the one route of interest can be identified.

Dreyfus and Haugeland (1974) describe a spatial approach to this task. Here we present a mildly abstracted version of a route network: a map in which all regions that do not correspond to routes are missing; the routes are represented here by colored

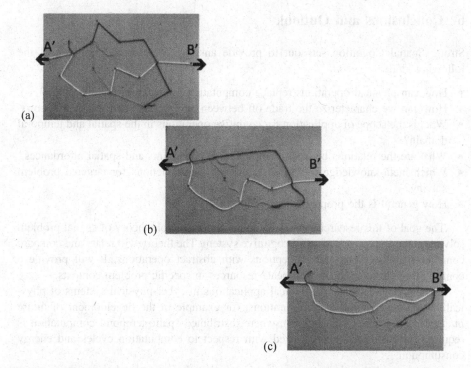

Fig. 2. Determining the shortest route from point A to point B by physical manipulation of a mildly abstracted representation of a route network. (a) The (non-elastic) strings corresponding to route segments preserve the relative distance relations of the original route segments. The distance relations are invariant with respect to physical manipulations (pulling apart strings at A' and B') which distort angles and shapes of the route network (b) and (c). The shortest route is identified as the route corresponding to the straight connection between A' and B' in (c).

---

[2] This example is adapted from Freksa (2015b) pp. 81–82.

strings. We obtain a deformable map consisting only of route representations that preserve the relative lengths of the original route sections (Fig. 2a).

The map permits certain spatial reconfigurations of the network through deformation, while preserving topology and important geometric constraints. In particular, an agent can (carefully) pull apart the positions A' and B' on the string map (Fig. 2b) that correspond to locations A and B until a string of route sections forms a straight line between these positions (Fig. 2c); due to the *geometric properties of the representation*, the route sections corresponding to the sections on the straight line represent the shortest route between A and B.

This approach avoids computation by reducing the problem to the relevant single dimension of length on which a basic geometric principle *straight line is shortest connection* can be directly applied. In this example, computational problem solving operations have been replaced by spatial operations.

6   Conclusions and Outlook

Strong Spatial Cognition sets out to provide answers to research questions of the following kind:

- How can physical operations replace computation in spatial problem solving?
- How can we characterize the trade-off between computation and physical action?
- What is the scope of application for cognitive operations in the spatial and temporal domain?
- What are the relations between computational constraints and spatial affordances?
- Which meta-knowledge is needed to control spatial actions for targeted problem solving?
- How general is the proposed paradigm?

The goal of this research is to develop an implementable theory of spatial problem solving in the framework of a full cognitive system. The theory will relate and compare concrete spatial actions and perceptions with abstract operations. It will provide a control structure to adequately allocate resources in specific problem contexts.

Ultimately, we envision technical applications in cyber-physical systems of physically supported cognitive configurations, for example in the development of future *intelligent materials* ('smart skin'), where distributed spatio-temporal computation is required but needs to be minimized with respect to computation cycles and energy consumption.

Our approach builds on research on spatial and temporal relations, their representation in memory, and qualitative spatial and temporal reasoning. We pursue broadly applicable cognitive principles, which can be configured to help design tomorrow's intelligent assistants. Our philosophy is to understand and exploit pertinent features of space and time as modality-specific properties of cognitive systems. Such features will enable powerful specialized approaches in the domain of space and time, as space and time are most basic for perception and action and are ubiquitous in cognitive processing. Furthermore, there are strong arguments that space and time-based approaches will not be limited to the spatial and temporal domains, as most of human cognition is rooted in the interaction in space and time (e.g. Lakoff and Johnson 1980). The understanding and use of spatial and temporal structures will be beneficial for both cognitive science and cognitively inspired systems and AI approaches.

References

Barkowsky, T., Berendt, B., Egner, S., Freksa, C., Krink, T., Röhrig, R., Wulf, A.: The Realator: how to construct reality. In: Rodríguez, R.V. (ed.) ECAI 1994 Workshop W12 Spatial and Temporal Reasoning, Amsterdam (1994)

Bateman, J.A., Hois, J., Ross, R., Tenbrink, T.: A linguistic ontology of space for natural language processing. Artif. Intell. **174**, 1027–1071 (2010)

Braitenberg, V.: Vehicles: Experiments in Synthetic Psychology. MIT Press, Cambridge (1984)

Brooks, R.A.: Intelligence without representation. Artif. Intell. **47**, 139–159 (1991)

Chandrasekaran, B.: Multimodal cognitive architecture: making perception more central to intelligent behavior. In: Proceedings of AAAI, pp. 1508–1512 (2006)

Cohn, A.G., Renz, J.: Qualitative spatial representation and reasoning. In: van Harmelen, F., Lifschitz, V., Porter, B. (eds.) Handbook of Knowledge Representation, pp. 551–596. Elsevier, Amsterdam (2008)

Davis, E., Marcus, G.: Commonsense reasoning and commonsense knowledge in artificial intelligence. CACM **58**(9), 92–103 (2015)

Modha, D.S., Ananthanarayanan, R., Esser, S.K., Ndirango, A., Sherbondy, A.J., Singh, R.: Cognitive computing. Commun. ACM **54**(8), 62–71 (2011)

Dreyfus, H., Haugeland, J.: The computer as a mistaken model of the mind. In: Brown, S.C. (ed.) Philosophy of Psychology, pp. 247–258. Palgrave Macmillan, London (1974)

Dylla, F., Lee, J.H., Mossakowski, T., Schneider, T., van Delden, A., van de Ven, J., Wolter, D.: A survey of qualitative spatial and temporal calculi: algebraic and computational properties. ACM Comput. Surv. (CSUR) **50**(1), 7:1–7:39 (2017)

Egenhofer, M.J., Franzosa, R.D.: Point-set topological spatial relations. Int. J. Geogr. Inf. Syst. **5**(2), 161–174 (1991)

Egenhofer, M.J., Mark, D.M.: Modeling conceptual neighborhoods of topological line-region relations. Int. J. Geogr. Inf. Syst. **9**(5), 555–565 (1995)

Freksa, C.: Conceptual neighborhood and its role in temporal and spatial reasoning. In: Singh, M., Travé-Massuyès, L. (eds.) Decision Support Systems and Qualitative Reasoning, pp. 181–187. North-Holland, Amsterdam (1991a)

Freksa, C.: Qualitative spatial reasoning. In: Mark, D.M., Frank, A.U. (eds.) Cognitive and Linguistic Aspects of Geographic Space, pp. 361–372. Kluwer, Dordrecht (1991b)

Freksa, C.: Spatial computing – how spatial structures replace computational effort. In: Raubal, M., Mark, D., Frank, A. (eds.) Cognitive and Linguistic Aspects of Geographic Space, pp. 23–42. Springer, Heidelberg (2013). doi:10.1007/978-3-642-34359-9_2

Freksa, C.: Computational problem solving in spatial substrates – a cognitive systems engineering approach. Int. J. Softw. Inf. **9**(2), 279–288 (2015a)

Freksa, C.: Strong spatial cognition. In: Fabrikant, S.I., Raubal, M., Bertolotto, M., Davies, C., Freundschuh, S., Bell, S. (eds.) COSIT 2015. LNCS, vol. 9368, pp. 65–86. Springer, Cham (2015b). doi:10.1007/978-3-319-23374-1_4

Freksa, C., Barkowsky, T., Dylla, F., Falomir, Z., Olteteanu, A.-M., van de Ven, J.: Spatial problem solving and cognition. In: Zacks, J., Taylor, H. (eds.) Representations in Mind and World. Routledge, New York (2018)

Freksa, C., Olteteanu, A.-M., Ali, A.L., Barkowsky, T., van de Ven, J., Dylla, F., Falomir, Z.: Towards spatial reasoning with strings and pins. In: Advances in Cognitive Systems 4, Poster Collection #22, pp. 1–15 (2016). http://www.cogsys.org/papers/ACS2016/Posters/Freksa_et.al-ACS-2016.pdf

Freksa, C., Schultheis, H.: Three ways of using space. In: Montello, D.R., Grossner, K.E., Janelle, D.G. (eds.) Space in Mind: Concepts for Spatial Education, pp. 31–48. MIT Press, Cambridge (2014)

Frese, U., Larsson, P., Duckett, T.: A multigrid relaxation algorithm for simultaneous localization and mapping. IEEE Trans. Robot. 21(2), 196–207 (2005)

Funt, B.: Problem-solving with diagrammatic representations. Artif. Intell. 13(3), 201–230 (1980)

Furbach, U., Furbach, F., Freksa, C.: Relating strong spatial cognition to symbolic problem solving – an example. In: Proceedings of 2nd Workshop on Bridging the Gap Between Human and Automated Reasoning, IJCAI, New York (2016). arXiv:1606.04397v1 [cs.AI]

Gibson, J.J.: The Ecological Approach to Visual Perception. Lawrence Erlbaum, New Jersey (1979)

Glasgow, J., Narayanan, N.H., Chandrasekaran, B. (eds.): Diagrammatic Reasoning: Cognitive and Computational Perspectives. AAAI Press, Menlo Park (1995)

Goel, A.K., Jamnik, M., Narayanan, N.H.: Diagrammatic Representation and Inference. Springer, Berlin (2010). doi:10.1007/978-3-642-14600-8

Goel, A.K., Vattam, S., Wiltgen, B., Helms, M.: Cognitive, collaborative, conceptual and creative – four characteristices of the next generation of knowledge-based CAD systems: a study in biologically inspired design. Comput. Aided Des. 44(10), 879–900 (2012)

Gooday, J.M., Cohn, A.G.: Conceptual neighbourhood in temporal and spatial reasoning. In: ECAI 1994, Amsterdam (1994)

Goodfellow, I., Bengio, Y., Courville, A.: Deep Learning. MIT Press, Cambridge (2016)

Kelly III, J.: Computing, cognition and the future of knowing. IBM Research: Cognitive Computing. IBM Corporation (2015)

Kirsh, D.: Embodied cognition and the magical future of interaction design. ACM Trans. Comput.-Hum. Interact. 20(1), 3:1–3:30 (2013)

Lakoff, G., Johnson, M.: Metaphors we Live by. University of Chicago Press, Chicago (1980)

Larkin, J.H., Simon, H.A.: Why a diagram is (sometimes) worth ten thousand words. Cogn. Sci. 11, 65–99 (1987)

Mansouri, M., Pecora, F.: A representation for spatial reasoning in robotic planning. In: International Conference on Intelligent Robots and Systems (IROS) - Workshop on AI-Based Robotics (2013)

Marr, D.: Vision. MIT Press, Cambridge (1982)

McCarthy, J., Hayes, P.J.: Some philosophical problems from the standpoint of artificial intelligence. Mach. Intell. 4, 463–502 (1969)

Norman, D.A.: The Design of Everyday Things. Basic Books, New York (2013)

Pfeifer, R., Scheier, C.: Understanding Intelligence. MIT Press, Cambridge (1999)

Polya, G.: How to Solve it. Princeton University Press, Princeton (1956)

Raubal, M., Moratz, R.: A functional model for affordance-based agents. In: Rome, E., Hertzberg, J., Dorffner, G. (eds.) Towards Affordance-Based Robot Control. LNCS, vol. 4760, pp. 91–105. Springer, Heidelberg (2008). doi:10.1007/978-3-540-77915-5_7

Rome, E., Hertzberg, J., Dorffner, G. (eds.): Towards Affordance-Based Robot Control. LNAI, vol. 4760. Springer, Berlin (2008). doi:10.1007/978-3-540-77915-5

Sloman, A.: Interactions between philosophy and artificial intelligence: the role of intuition and non-logical reasoning in intelligence. Artif. Intell. 2, 209–225 (1971)

Sloman, A.: Afterthoughts on analogical representation. In: Schank, R., Nash-Webber, B. (eds.) Theoretical Issues in Natural Language Processing (TINLAP-1), pp. 431–439 (1975)

Sloman, A.: Why we need many knowledge representation formalisms. In: Bramer, M. (ed.) Research and Development in Expert Systems, pp. 163–183. Cambridge University Press, New York (1985)

Thrun, S., Burgard, W., Fox, D.: Probabilistic Robotics. MIT Press, Cambridge (2005)

Vitruvius, M.V.: De Architectura. Book IX, pp. 9–12, text in English, University of Chicago (2017). Accessed 21 Mar 2007

Wintermute, S., Laird, J.E.: Bimodal spatial reasoning with continuous motion. In: Proceedings of AAAI, pp. 1331–1337 (2008)

Wörgötter, F., Geib, C., Tamosiunaite, M., Aksoy, E.E., Piater, J., Xiong, H., Ude, A., Nemec, B., Kraft, D., Krüger, N., Wächter, M., Asfour, T.: Structural bootstrapping – a novel, generative mechanism for faster and more efficient acquisition of action-knowledge. IEEE Trans. Auton. Mental Dev. 7(2), 140–154 (2015)

Wolter, D., Wallgrün, J.O.: Qualitative spatial reasoning for applications: new challenges and the SparQ toolbox. In: Hazarika, S.M. (ed.) Qualitative Spatio-Temporal Representation and Reasoning, pp. 336–362. IGI Global (2012)

Transfer Learning-Based Case Base Preparation for a Case-Based Reasoning-Based Decision Making Support Model in the Educational Domain

Pham Thanh Tri, Vo Thi Ngoc Chau[(⊠)], and Nguyen Hua Phung

Ho Chi Minh City University of Technology,
Vietnam National University – HCMC, Ho Chi Minh City, Vietnam
{1570234, chauvtn, nhphung}@hcmut.edu.vn

Abstract. Decision making support in the educational domain is very important for the success of the students, especially for that of the in-trouble students who are asked to stop their study. As a further work of early prediction of the in-trouble students, our current work is thus dedicated to a decision making support model in the educational domain for the problem of study extension of those in-trouble students. Different from the existing educational decision support systems and their models, our model is developed with a combination of case-based reasoning and transfer learning. This combination stems from a more practical context where there are little target data and corresponding target cases available for decision making support. Therefore, our model utilizes case-based reasoning for its problem solving process while making use of transfer learning for case base preparation with not only the limited number of target data but also the larger number of source data. In addition, with the instance-based transfer learning-based method, the case base of our model can be constructed and maintained over the time so that new target cases can be supported with enough similar cases for forming their proper solutions. An empirical study on real data sets has shown that our initial work is promising to have a rich case base for the proposed educational decision making support model.

Keywords: Decision making support model · Case-based reasoning · Instance-based transfer learning · TrAdaBoost · Educational data mining

1 Introduction

In the educational domain, success of each student in study at university is a main concern of any educational organization in the world. Many existing works on educational data mining have been proposed for educational data analysis in general and early prediction of student success/failure in particular. Some examples are given in [2, 10–12, 15, 16]. Although the educational data mining area has had a remarkable achievement of different kinds of mining models and patterns, few works have taken such discovered knowledge into account for particular decision making support.

© Springer International Publishing AG 2017
S. Phon-Amnuaisuk et al. (Eds.): MIWAI 2017, LNAI 10607, pp. 30–43, 2017.
https://doi.org/10.1007/978-3-319-69456-6_3

In addition to the works on educational data mining, a large number of the existing works on decision support systems in the educational domain have been introduced with many various purposes. Using different technologies and architectures, some typical educational decision support systems are presented in [4, 13, 20, 22]. These systems can provide the decision makers with valuable information and knowledge for their decision making process on several predefined problems. Nevertheless, none of them has examined decision making support in the context where there are little data available in the target domain of the problems to be supported.

Generally speaking, bringing the mining models and patterns discovered from educational data to decision making support is a need in the educational domain. Meanwhile, the target data are not always rich and thus, sometimes insufficient for decision making support. In such situations, data shortage might lead to a challenge for a decision making support model based on case-based reasoning where a lot of data are required for case base construction. That fact needs to be considered especially for the educational domain where study status of each student is just updated after each semester or each year. The update speed in the educational domain is low for enriching the case base of the case-based reasoning-based model with the new target cases whose solutions must be confirmed in the real world.

In recent times, combining transfer learning and case-based reasoning has been of interest for decision making support. Examining the approach of case-based reasoning as a transfer learning method discussed in [9], our paper presents an initial work on a combination of transfer learning and case-based reasoning in the educational domain and shows how promising such a combination is, in order to cope with the afore-mentioned practical context of the limited number of target data. In particular, we define an educational decision making support model based on case-based reasoning and transfer learning. The educational problem supported with our model is considering study extension for the in-trouble students. Case-based reasoning provides a problem solving process for our model while transfer learning enables us to exploit the data and their corresponding cases in multiple source domains for the case base of our model. Indeed, the model has the case base prepared with both target and source data. It has no distinction between the resulting target and source cases in its decision making support. In addition, the case base of our model can be enriched over the time with a transfer learning-based method. This ability makes our model updated as much as possible for sustainability with the new target cases that need appropriate solutions.

The rest of our paper is structured as follows. In Sect. 2, we propose a decision making support model in the educational domain based on case-based reasoning and transfer learning along with three main subprocesses related to the case base of the model. In Sect. 3, we show how our transfer learning-based case base preparation can be made. A short empirical study on real data sets is also given in this section. For a comparison between our work and the existing related works, Sect. 4 presents a lit-erature review. We intend to leave our literature review till Sect. 4 after the presen-tation of our proposed work because to the best of our knowledge, our decision making support model based on case-based reasoning and transfer learning is the first one for the educational domain and as a result, the readers can have our model in mind while reading the literature review on the other existing related works in comparison with ours. Finally, we conclude our current work and state some future works in Sect. 5.

2   Towards a Decision Making Support Model in the Educational Domain Based on Case-Based Reasoning and Transfer Learning

2.1   Model Definition

Based on case-based reasoning and transfer learning, a decision making support model in the educational domain is defined in this section. As discussed in [9], case-based reasoning and transfer learning have an interrelationship in knowledge discovery. In particular, [9] summarized three main combination approaches such as: case-based reasoning as a transfer learning method, case-based reasoning for problem learning, and case-based reasoning to transfer knowledge. In our work, the proposed model is somewhat following the first approach. It treats the target cases and source cases equally in solving problems in the target domain. In addition, it has a case base enriched by the transfer learning method with those from the source domain. By doing that, our model is significant for the educational domain where little data have been collected. Therefore, the context of our decision making support model is associated with little target data and more source data. Within such a context, in Fig. 1, we sketch our proposed decision making support model for education problems based on case-based reasoning and transfer learning. This figure provides us with a general view on our model in the educational domain.

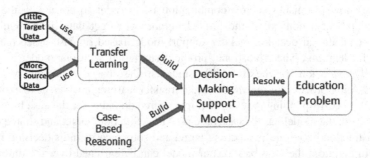

Fig. 1. The proposed decision making support model based on case-based reasoning and transfer learning for an education problem

Displayed in Fig. 2, our architecture of the proposed model introduces the role of each method in the model. Transfer learning is responsible for case base construction while case-based reasoning for solving an education problem with a solution of a similar previous problem associated with a case prepared in the case base. It is realized that the effectiveness of the model depends on the richness of the case base. If the number of cases is limited or the cases in the case base are inappropriate for the given problem, the capability of decision making support of the model is lowered. This is because the case base provides the intelligence for the decision making support process of the model. Therefore, it is regarded as the heart of our model.

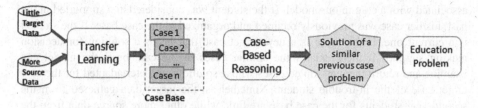

Fig. 2. The architecture of the proposed decision making support model

In Fig. 3, we detail the aforesaid architecture of the model around the case base. In this case base-centered architecture, the model is viewed with three marked regions corresponding to three subprocesses related to the case base. They are: (1) Construction, (2) Use, and (3) Maintenance. In region (1) Construction, transfer learning is utilized. In region (2) Use, case-based reasoning is conducted. In region (3) Maintenance, an examination on the case base is performed to ensure its effectiveness over the time. These three regions are described below along with their subprocesses.

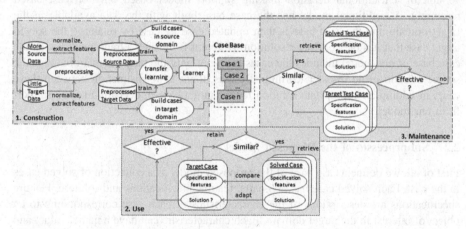

Fig. 3. The detailed case base-centered architecture of our decision making support model

In short, our decision making support model based on case-based reasoning and transfer learning is delineated in the educational domain. Given a program A which is considered as a main program in our decision making support, data were collected for each student studying with this program A along their study path starting from the second year till the end of the study period of time. In particular, we have the second-year data, the third-year data, and the fourth-year data from the corresponding second-year students, third-year students, and fourth-year students. The model is developed to support the study extension problem for the second-year students being asked to stop their studies with the program A. This is because we have higher priority to early detection of in-trouble students so that support can be given to them sooner and they can have more chance to succeed in their study for a degree ultimately. Each in-trouble student is associated with a case in our model. If the student was considered and supported in the past, his/her case was previously retained and organized in the case base. If the student is a current one, his/her case is a new target case that needs a solution for decision making support. If there exist some similar cases in the case base, the model can examine and return them as solved cases whose solutions are later adapted for the new target case of the in-trouble student. Nonetheless, the target data gathered from the second-year students for the case base are little while other more source data from the third-year and fourth-year data are available. Enriching the case base with the source cases is done for our proposed model so that more cases can be examined to supply the solutions appropriate for the new target case. Thus, the decision making support model can be more effective in use.

As compared to the existing works that have been proposed for educational decision making support such as [4, 13, 20, 22], our decision making support model based on case-based reasoning and transfer learning is novel. It is also interpretable to decision makers as their decision making process is naturally expressed with the problem solving process of case-based reasoning. Besides, it is practical as the context set up in our work stems from real situations. Above all, it provides an advanced version of a traditional decision making support model based only on case-based reasoning. A traditional model has the case base built with the data available in the target domain and the case base is then updated case by case by retaining the solved target case that has the confirmed solution. Different from such a traditional model, the case base of our model includes the cases from not only the target domain but also the source domain using transfer learning. Besides, there is no distinction between these cases in finding an appropriate solution for the target case in decision making support from our model.

2.2   Subprocesses of the Proposed Model

First of all, we define a case base of the proposed model as a collection of solved cases in the past. Each solved case has two parts: feature specifications and solution. Feature specifications are descriptions of the characteristics of each case corresponding to an object of interest in the target domain. Each characteristic can have a name, value, and constraints if any recorded when the object is observed in the real world. Solution is a specific solution along with its effectiveness for the object in the real world with respect to the problem supported by the model. Particularly for the study extension problem of the in-trouble students in the educational domain, each solved case is associated with one in-trouble student. Feature specifications are the attributes and their values describing each student. They are name, age, gender, hometown, family status, economic status, work status, study status of each semester, grades of the courses taken so far, reason for study stop, etc. Solution is the extension status ("allowed", "not allowed") along with other supporting information such as reason for extension status, extension period of time, next study plan, financial support, etc. and with its real effectiveness such as final study status ("graduate", "study", "study stop"). For each solution, we expect a positive effectiveness to be "graduate" or "study" so that permission for extension can be regarded as an effective decision. Otherwise, our cost and effort have been wasted.

Similar to each solved case in the case base, a new target case is defined for each in-trouble student who is now under consideration for an extension. This target case is different from a solved case only in solution. For each target case, solution is questionable so that the model must process to find an appropriate one from some similar solved cases for it.

In addition to solved cases and new target cases, our model has been built with solved test cases and target test cases. These test cases are defined in the same way as any solved case with feature specifications and solution. They are just different from solve cases in their role. Indeed, they are used internally for model examination so that the case base can be maintained over the time.

Secondly, three subprocesses manipulating the aforementioned various cases with the regions marked in the case base-centered architecture in Fig. 3 are detailed. These subprocesses also complete the design of our model.

(1) Case Base Construction Subprocess with Transfer Learning

In the early stage of model development, the case base construction subprocess has a very important impact on the success of our model. The content of the case base determines how much support the model can give to its decision maker for each new target case. The richer content, the more support. Therefore, little target data might be insufficient for case base construction. Aware of this fact, we consider our model in the situation where transfer learning is needed for processing both little target data and more source data.

As shown in region (1). Construction, this subprocess starts with preprocessing on both target and source data with normalization and feature extractions so that all the data can be represented in the same feature space and ready for the transfer learning process. The transfer learning process is then applied to obtain a learner. This resulting learner helps us to get the appropriate positive instances from which the cases in both source and target domains can be prepared accordingly. Those cases are used to update the case base.

This mechanism is also invoked once our model is maintained. As of that moment, the case base is too over the time.

(2) Problem Solving Subprocess with Case-Based Reasoning

Once the case base of the model is ready, the problem solving subprocess can be put in use. This subprocess is mainly based on case-based reasoning. In particular, for each target case whose solution is not available, a collection of the solved cases which are the most similar to the target case is retrieved from the case base. The k-nearest neighbor method can be applied in this step. After that, these solved cases are further examined in such a way that their specification features are compared with those of the target case. The most similar solved case is considered for solution adaptation. As a result, a solution to the problem of the target case is prepared from the solution of the most similar solved case and returned as supporting information for the decision maker. In the future, the effectiveness of the solution of the target case will be observed and recorded. If its solution can be confirmed effectively, the target case along with its solution is then included in the case base. Retaining a target case and its solution in the educational domain takes time. This is because after one semester, one year, or till the end of the study path of the in-trouble student corresponding to the target case, we will have the resulting effectiveness of his/her study extension. Therefore, the richness of the case base increases slowly with the retention of a target case in our real world.

(3) Case Base Maintenance Subprocess

Although not a required one, the case base maintenance subprocess plays an important role in the sustainability of the proposed model over the time. This subprocess is an additional one with which our model is equipped as compared to the existing case-based reasoning-based models. Indeed, it checks the effectiveness of the model on the tested target cases via checking the effectiveness of the solved cases present in the case base. Such a check ensures the availability of the solved cases to support coming real target cases. If yes, no change is made on the case base. Otherwise, the case base needs to be updated with new solved cases from the target domain, source domain, or both. In detail, the check in maintenance is similar to what has been done in the problem solving subprocess based on case-based reasoning while the update in maintenance is similar to what has been done in the case base construction subprocess based on transfer learning. Therefore, there is an iterative process underlying the proposed model to keep the model as effective as possible when time goes by.

3 Transfer Learning-Based Case Base Preparation

In order to deal with the limited number of target cases in the target domain, more cases in other source domains are considered. However, it is non-trivial for us to align source cases with target cases for proper support of new target cases in the target domain. Thanks to transfer learning, case base preparation for our model is facilitated.

3.1 A Transfer Learning-Based Method for Case Base Construction

As previously mentioned, transfer learning is utilized for case base construction in the development of our proposed model. Due to the instance-based nature of case-based reasoning, instance-based transfer learning methods are chosen in our transfer learning-based method. As an initial work on this topic as of this moment, our work takes into account TrAdaboost and its more recent variant MultiSourceTrAdaboost [21]. Among the existing instance-based transfer learning methods, TrAdaboost [5] is popular as an instance-based transfer learning version of the well-known boosting algorithm Adaboost [7]. Nevertheless, other instance-based transfer learning algorithms like TransferBoost [6] can be examined in this method alternatively.

The following is our transfer learning-based method for case base construction. It includes four main steps. It can be conducted with any existing instance-based transfer learning algorithm.

```
Input:
    Dₜ : a target data set
    Dₛ : one or many source data sets
    D'ₜ : a target data set that contains the positive in-
    stances for selection
    D'ₛ : a source data set that contains the positive in-
    stances for selection
    ITL : an instance-based transfer learning method
Output:
    CB : the case base enhanced with both target cases and
    source cases
Precondition: the number of instances in Dₜ is much
smaller than that in Dₛ: |Dₜ|<|Dₛ|.
Process:
    Step 1: Build a learner Lₜ in the target domain using
    ITL on Dₜ and Dₛ
    Step 2: Apply Lₜ on positive instances in D'ₜ and D'ₛ to
    get a set R of correctly predicted positive instances
    Step 3: Prepare the target cases Cₜ and the source cases
    Cₛ with feature specifications and solutions correspond-
    ing to the target and source instances in R
    Step 4: Enhance the case base CB with not only the tar-
    get cases Cₜ but also the source cases Cₛ
```

Different from the use of a transfer learning method in a traditional way, the use of an instance-based transfer learning method in our work is also applied on source instances for case selection. The rationale behind the selection of those source cases stems from the stability of their associated positive instances in the source data with respect to the positive instances in the target data. This is because the resulting learner that has been constructed for the target instances can correctly recognize those source instances, leading to no distinction between source instances and target instances. As a result, their cases can be treated equally and thus, those source cases can be added into the case base in the target domain. By doing that, the case base of our proposed model is enriched with more data in the source domains. In addition, this method is used to support the maintenance of the model, i.e. the case base, over the time.

3.2 An Empirical Study on Case Base Construction

Using the transfer learning-based method discussed above, an empirical study on case base construction in the educational domain is conducted. In our experiments, real data are used. They are collected from 1334 second-year, third-year, and fourth-year students studying in the Computer Science program in 2005–2008 [1] at Faculty of Computer Science and Engineering, Ho Chi Minh City University of Technology, Vietnam National University - Ho Chi Minh City. Our target data set is the one with the second-year students and our source data sets with the third-year students and with the fourth-year students. In addition, we use course grades as feature specifications and study extension as solution of each in-trouble student. Each in-trouble student is a student who got a study-stop request. Besides, we use two labels such as study-stop and non-study-stop for case base construction.

In this empirical study, we would like to check if a transfer learning method is suitable for case base construction as compared to a corresponding non-transfer learning method on the target data. If yes, we would like to check how better a transfer learning method is for case selection from the source data.

Experimental results are shown in Tables 1 and 2, respectively. Analysis of these experimental results is given for each issue as follows.

Table 1. Accuracy with different percentages of tested positive instances in the target data

Percentage of tested positive instances	Adaboost	TrAdaboost	MultiSourceTrAdaboost	TaskTrAdaboost
11.21%	70.40%	72.65%	**79.82%**	52.91%
36.77%	72.65%	**75.78%**	74.44%	62.33%
51.96%	57.84%	60.78%	57.35%	**62.25%**
55.60%	54.71%	**61.44%**	44.39%	56.05%
72.98%	38.51%	42.53%	54.60%	**78.16%**
91.60%	33.57%	35.66%	51.05%	**91.61%**

Table 2. Incorrect instances from the source data selected with different number of instances in the target data

Number of instances in the target domain	Adaboost	TrAdaboost	MultiSourceTrAdaboost
50	164	**75**	96
100	113	**61**	70
150	96	**49**	73
200	100	**43**	50

For the first issue, in Table 1, we recorded the accuracies of Adaboost [7], TrAdaboost [5], MultiSourceTrAdaboost [21], and TaskTrAdaboost [21] with different percentages of the tested positive instances (i.e. instances corresponding to the in-trouble students labeled "study-stop") in the target data. For this experiment group, we used only 22 instances in the target data set for training and the rest for source data sets to simulate the context where there is the limited number of target data. Among the results, the results from the transfer learning-based methods are often better. Another interesting point is that TrAdaboost and MultiSourceTrAdaboost following an instance-based transfer learning approach outperform the others with smaller percentages of the tested positive instances, while TaskTrAdaboost following a parameter-based transfer learning approach with higher percentages of the tested positive instances.

Therefore, we can draw two concluding remarks such as: (i). the transfer learning-based methods are suitable for case base construction and (ii). the instance-based transfer learning algorithms can be considered more for the model when the number of the positive instances is limited, corresponding to the lower percentages of the tested positive instances which are less than 50%.

From the previous experimental results in Table 1, we further examined the instance-based transfer learning methods with TrAdaboost and MultiSourceTrAdaboost as compared to the non-transfer learning method with Adaboost for the second issue. In Table 2, we used different number of the instances in the target data along with the source data to select the instances from the source data for enriching the case base. We recorded the number of the incorrect instances from the source data selected after the training process of each algorithm. The experimental results show that TrAdaboost and MultiSourceTrAdaboost can select more instances correctly than Adaboost. Compared to each other, TrAdaboost seems to be more suitable than MultiSourceAdaboost when examined on our educational data sets. However, it is hard for us to have a firmed statement about their performances at this moment. This is because the effectiveness of our model needs to be further checked with not only the case base construction sub-process but also the problem solving and maintenance subprocesses.

Through the experimental results and the concluding remarks that we have obtained in analysis above, the use of instance-based transfer learning is promising for case base construction. As soon as a case base is prepared properly, our proposed decision making support model based on case-based reasoning and transfer learning is accomplished for academic affairs. With this advanced model, we hope our in-trouble students can have more support in time and moreover, another chance to succeed in their study.

4 Related Works

In this section, an overall review of several existing related works is presented. With the related works in [2, 10–12, 15, 16], we show a need of supporting the in-trouble students in our model. With those in [4, 13, 20, 22], we distinguish our decision making support model from other kinds in the existing decision support systems. With those in [3, 9, 14], a combination of transfer learning and case-based reasoning is discussed in comparison with ours.

First, it has been realized that predicting the success of the students in studying in particular as well as analyzing the educational data in general is significant and popular in the educational data mining area. Many existing works such as [2, 10–12, 15, 16] have been proposed. In [2], the authors predicted the success of the students based on their study records and social behavior data using the existing supervised learning methods and social network analysis. Also performing a student classification task, [10] exploited multiple data sources to enrich the characteristics of each student in the task. In contrast, our work has made use of multiple data sources for case base construction. In [11], the prediction of the student dropouts in distance higher education was carried out with the existing semi-supervised learning methods. Not for the students at university but for high-school students, [12] predicted the failure of students based on their general survey, specific survey, and current grades with an evolutionary algorithm.

Also supporting the secondary-school students, [15] proposed modeling the problem of grouping the students into different classes based on their profiles as a resource allocation problem. This problem is then resolved with two different solutions: the first one based on a solution to a constraint satisfaction optimization problem and the second one based on the Ant Colony Optimization (ACO) algorithm. The ACO-based solution appeared to be suitable for this class allocation problem to obtain many different sets of student profiles at school. As for the work in [16], several different communities of the students were generated from their behavior information in various experiments. The k-means algorithm and so-called Normalized Compression Distance were used in their solution. As a further work after educational data analysis and early drop-out prediction, our work pays more attention to the support of the in-trouble students who are predicted to drop out. Therefore, our work has a significant contribution to facilitate the ultimate success of those in-trouble students in the real world.

Second, we are aware of several decision support systems in [4, 13, 20, 22]. These systems were developed with many different purposes in their various contexts. In [4], the authors aimed at the architecture of a decision support system for their university's educational mission, training, and academic services. Different from our work, [13] focused on a decision support system for strategic planning about educational resources, distribution and usage of those resources at universities. This system was developed as a Web application using a multilayered client-server architecture. Not for administrative support, [22] concentrated on support of discovering who students were, how students worked, and how students used virtual courses based on data warehousing technology and data mining techniques. Different from the previous ones, [20] was investigated for educational decision making support of the predefined academic problems related to undergraduate students. A three-tiered Web-based modular architecture along with data mining techniques was considered for this system. As compared to these decision support systems, our work is dedicated to a decision making support model for educational problems. This model is an important ingredient of an educational decision support system. As for technical issues, our model is based on case-based reasoning and transfer learning while the existing systems have not yet taken into account such a combination in their development.

Third, case-based reasoning is a famous problem solving framework. It has many applications in a diversity of domains. Some of them are listed in [8, 17–19] for concurrent product engineering, mechanical design, and medical fields. On the other hand, transfer learning is a learning paradigm that enables knowledge and experiences gained from learning on several source tasks to be utilized in learning on other target tasks. There are three well-known approaches to transfer learning: instance-based transfer learning, feature-based transfer learning, and parameter-based transfer learning. As both target and source data in our work are in the same feature space, only instance-based transfer learning and parameter-based transfer learning algorithms based on Adaboost [7] were considered. Typical examples of instance-based transfer learning algorithms are TrAdaboost [5], MultiSourceTrAdaboost [21], and TransferBoost [6]. A typical example of parameter-based transfer learning algorithms is TaskTrAdaboost [21]. In this paper, we have brought case-based reasoning and transfer learning to a decision making support model in the educational domain. In the development of our model, their combination helps us deal with a more practical situation of a traditional case-based reasoning-based decision making support model. This approach has not yet been investigated thoroughly in the existing works. Indeed, as previously mentioned, [9] has summarized three interrelationship approaches to a combination of case-based reasoning and transfer learning: case-based reasoning as a transfer learning method, case-based reasoning for problem learning, and case-based reasoning to transfer knowledge. Our work has followed the first approach with the case base construction subprocess based on transfer learning and the problem solving subprocess based on case-based reasoning. As a result, our decision making support model can overcome the limited number of target cases in the target domain by exploiting source cases in many other source domains with no distinction between them. Moreover, the maintenance subprocess linked to transfer learning is introduced for the sustainability of the model over the time. Different from ours, [3] presented the use of case-based reasoning in transfer learning. In particular, their case base was used as heuristics to improve the efficiency of the learning process in the target domain. The resulting meta algorithm was confirmed to outperform the non-transfer learning versions and other transfer learning algorithms for reinforcement learning. Quite similar to ours, [14] showed the use of transfer learning in process-oriented case-based reasoning. The workflow cases were transferred from a source domain to a target domain based on generalization and abstraction of workflows and structural analogies between the vocabularies of the source and target domains. In detail, their proposed transfer process included two phases: build time and transfer time. The first phase was responsible for transfer knowledge creation with ontologies and analogical mapping while the second phase for applying transfer knowledge on the workflows from the source domain. The underlying routine of their transfer process is an exhausted search for transformation paths from source workflows to target workflows. By contrast, the transfer process in our model is based on instance-based transfer learning algorithms, dealing with the data and their corresponding cases in both target and source domains at the instance level, not at the structure level. Last but not least, the application domain of our model is the educational domain while that in [3, 14] is not.

Aware of the aforementioned existing works, we believe that our proposed decision making support model based on case-based reasoning and transfer learning is a promising model for an educational decision support system. With this model along with early detection of in-trouble students, it is expected that the detected students can have proper and in-time support toward an ultimate success in study at university.

5 · Conclusions

In this paper, we have defined an educational decision making support model based on case-based reasoning and transfer learning. Developed in the first phase, a case base is our current focus. Therefore, we have introduced a case base-centered architecture of the proposed model where three subprocesses are addressed: case base construction, problem solving, and maintenance. In the case base construction subprocess, transfer learning has been examined with the promising experimental results from the instance-based transfer learning algorithms on real data sets. In the problem solving subprocess, case-based reasoning is used to find a solution from the most similar previous cases for the new target case. In the maintenance subprocess, the effectiveness of the case base and therefore, the effectiveness of the model can be maintained over the time.

In comparison with the traditional decision making support models based on only case-based reasoning and the current one from the existing decision support systems in the educational domain, our proposed model has its own merits in a more practical context where there exist little target data for building a case base of the model. Besides, its sustainability is also considered when the case base is updated not only with the confirmed target cases but also with the source cases. These two features of our model can be achieved with instance-based transfer learning on both target and source data.

As an original model, our proposed model is still in its infancy. At this moment, we are completing the proposed decision making support model with a comprehensive case-based reasoning process for academic affairs. In addition, more investigation in transfer learning for case base construction will be made with an examination on how effective an enhanced case base can be in the proposed model. We also plan to integrate the resulting model into a knowledge-driven educational decision support system in an academic credit system. Last but not least, we will collect more data from other programs and examine the model in the inter-program context.

Acknowledgments. This research is funded by Vietnam National University Ho Chi Minh City, Vietnam, under grant number C2016-20-16.

References

1. Academic Affairs Office, Ho Chi Minh City University of Technology, Vietnam. http://www. aao.hcmut.edu.vn. Accessed 29 June 2017
2. Bayer, J., Bydzovska, H., Geryk, J., Obsivac, T., Popelinsky, L.: Predicting drop-out from social behaviour of students. In: Proceedings of the 5th International Conference on Educational Data Mining, pp. 103–109 (2012)
3. Bianchi, R.A.C., Celiberto Jr., L.A., Santos, P.E., Matsuura, J.P., de Mantaras, R.L.: Transferring knowledge as heuristics in reinforcement learning: a case-based approach. Artif. Intell. **226**, 102–121 (2015)
4. Bresfelean, V.P., Ghisoiu, N., Lacurezeanu, R., Sitar-Taut, D.-A.: Towards the development of decision support in academic environments. In: Proceedings of the ITI 2009 31st International Conference on Information Technology Interfaces, pp. 343–348. IEEE (2009)
5. Dai, W., Yang, Q., Xue, G.-R., Yu, Y.: Boosting for transfer learning. In: Proceedings of the 24th International Conference on Machine Learning, pp. 193–200 (2007)
6. Eaton, E., desJardins, M.: Selective transfer between learning tasks using task-based boosting. In: Proceedings of the 25th AAAI Conference on Artificial Intelligence, pp. 337–342 (2011)
7. Freund, Y., Schapire, R.E.: A decision-theoretic generalization of on-line learning and an application to boosting. J. Comput. Syst. Sci. **55**(1), 119–139 (1997)
8. Haque, B.U., Belecheanu, R.A., Barson, R.J., Pawar, K.S.: Towards the application of case-based reasoning to decision-making in concurrent product development (concurrent engineering). Knowl.-Based Syst. **13**, 101–112 (2000)

9. Klenk, M., Aha, D.W., Molineaux, M.: The case for case-based transfer learning. AI Mag. **32**, 54–69 (2011)
10. Koprinska, I., Stretton, J., Yacef, K.: Predicting student performance from multiple data sources. Artif. Intell. Educ. **9112**, 678–681 (2015)
11. Kostopoulos, G., Kotsiantis, S., Pintelas, P.: Estimating student dropout in distance higher education using semi-supervised techniques. In: Proceedings of the 19th Panhellenic Conference on Informatics, pp. 38–43 (2015)
12. Márquez-Vera, C., Cano, A., Romero, C., Ventura, S.: Predicting student failure at school using genetic programming and different data mining approaches with high dimensional and imbalanced data. Appl. Intell. **38**, 315–330 (2013)
13. Mansmann, S., Scholl, M.H.: Decision support system for managing educational capacity utilization. IEEE Trans. Educ. **50**(2), 143–150 (2007)
14. Minor, M., Bergmann, R., Müller, J.-M., Spät, A.: On the transferability of process-oriented cases. In: Proceedings of the International Conference on Case-Based Reasoning: Case-Based Reasoning Research and Development, pp. 281–294 (2016)
15. Nogareda, A.M., Camacho, D.: A constraint-based approach for classes setting-up problems in secondary schools. Int. J. Simul. Model. **16**(2), 253–262 (2017)
16. Gonzalez-Pardo, A., Rosa, A., Camacho, D.: Behaviour-based identification of student communities in virtual worlds. Comput. Sci. Inf. Syst. **11**(1), 195–213 (2014)
17. Qi, J., Hu, J., Peng, Y.: Hybrid weighted mean for CBR adaptation in mechanical design by exploring effective, correlative and adaptative values. Comput. Ind. **75**, 58–66 (2016)
18. Schmidt, R., Gierl, L.: Case-based reasoning for medical knowledge-based systems. In: Studies in Health Technology and Informatics, pp. 1–34 (2000)
19. Tabatabaee, H., Fadaeiyan, H., Alipour, A., Baghaeipour, M.R.: Using case-based reasoning for diagnosis in medical field. Bull. Env. Pharmacol. Life Sci. **4**(11), 102–114 (2015)
20. Vo, T.N.C., Nguyen, H.P.: A knowledge-driven educational decision support system. In: Proceedings of the 2012 IEEE RIVF International Conference on Computing and Communication Technologies, pp. 1–6 (2012)
21. Yao, Y., Doretto, G.: Boosting for transfer learning with multiple sources. In: Proceedings of the IEEE Conference on Computer Vision and Pattern Recognition, pp. 1855–1862 (2010)
22. Zorrilla, M., Garcia, D., Alvarez, E.: A decision support system to improve e-learning environments. In: Proceedings of EDBT, pp. 1–8. ACM (2010)

Multi-level Search of a Knowledgebase for Semantic Parsing

Anupiya Nugaliyadde$^{(\boxtimes)}$, Kok Wai Wong, Ferdous Sohel,
and Hong Xie

Murdoch University, Perth, WA, Australia
{a.nugaliyadde, k.wong, f.sohel, h.xie}@murdoch.edu.au

Abstract. In this paper, we present a semantic parser using a knowledgebase. Instead of relying on filtering the concepts extracted from the knowledgebase, we use all the concepts to create the parser. A simple search is conducted on ConceptNet for the words in the input sentence. In this paper, two proposed techniques are used to extract concepts from the ConceptNet 5. The reason for proposing two techniques in this paper is to address the issue of removing the supervision and training process. The first approach extracts all concepts from ConceptNet 5 for each input word. The extracted concepts are used to search again in ConceptNet 5, which creates multiple levels of search results. This deep concept structure creates a multi-level search to create the semantic parse result. The second approach follows the same first step of extracting concepts using the input text. However, the extracted concepts are passed through a relationship check and then used for the second level search. Concepts are drawn from 2 levels of searching in ConceptNet. The extracted concepts are used to create the parser. Furthermore, we use the initial concepts extracted to search again in ConceptNet. The parser we created is tested on Free917, Stanford Sentiment dataset and the WebQ. We achieve recall of 93.82%, 94.91% for Stanford Sentiment dataset, accuracy of 77.1%, 79.2% for Free917 and 26.5%, 38.2% for WebQ respectively for the two approaches. This shows state-of-the-art results compared to other methods for each datasets.

1 Introduction

Computational language understanding requires the conversion of text to computationally understandable structures [1]. Semantic parsing converts a natural language utterance into a logical form, which can be used to produce denotations [2]. These denotations are used for many natural language understanding tasks such as semantic role labeling, Word Sense Disambiguation (WSD), query processing, Information Extraction (IE) and Question Answering (QA) [3]. Most recent research on semantic parsing focus on machine learning [4, 5] which requires supervision and training. Various techniques have been introduced to improve semantic parsing by reducing supervision [2]. In order to achieve this we use a knowledge base, ConceptNet [6], to fully remove supervision.

Semantic parsing requires a combination of natural language with logic in order to construct the best results [5]. In order to construct a set of proper logical predicate, a

© Springer International Publishing AG 2017
S. Phon-Amnuaisuk et al. (Eds.): MIWAI 2017, LNAI 10607, pp. 44–53, 2017.
https://doi.org/10.1007/978-3-319-69456-6_4

knowledgebase is required. Berant and Liang [5] use a knowledgebase to paraphrase and semantically parse a sentence. Knowledgebases have a potential to achieve complex sematic parsing. Poria et al. [7] use the ConceptNet 3 to manually extract concepts for semantic parsing of sentences. Even though conceptNet contains an imperative set of concepts for semantic parsing and use these concepts to removes supervision. We introduce two novel approaches. Two approaches are explored as one method focus on more concepts and the other does a basic filter depending on the relationships. The proposed techniques use ConceptNet 5 [6] as it is the updated version from ConceptNet 3. Furthermore, concepts are extracted from ConceptNet using two levels: (i) the concepts are first extracted for the input sentence words (level 1) and (ii) the extracted concepts are passed to ConceptNet 5 and extract concepts for the second time (level 2). These two levels of search create a multi-level search. The extracted concepts are matched with each other to generate semantic parsed output. The two approaches are different as approach 2 filters concepts at the level 1 based on relationships and do the concept extraction at level 2. However, for approach 1, the concepts are extracted and finalised in one level. We aim to use the concepts to create a logical format. As an example: "when was the United Nations founded?" our approach focuses on producing;

$$(!fb:organization.date\_founded \ fb : en.united\_nations) \qquad (1)$$

Our novelty is based on using a multi-level search on ConceptNet with automatic extractions of concepts from the Conceptnet 5. The proposed approaches hold an information rich semantic parsing results.

2 Background

There are many semantic parsing approaches introduced in the recent years. Most research have focused on machine learning approaches. Machine learning approaches such as deep neural networks [2] and SVM [8] have been used. Learning approaches for semantic parsing requires learning a pattern to extract information in order to create the semantic parser. Even though learning method are capable of learning complex patterns and extract information for a semantic parser, they are not capable of generating unavailable information in the text. Therefore, there should be a method of extracting unavailable information. A knowledgebase has the capability of providing the unavailable information through the input text.

Wordnet [9] is a knowledgebase which holds lexical information. The lexical information held in Wordnet has the capability of providing the unavailable information [10]. Therefore, an information rich results are generated through the use of a knowledgebase. ConceptNet 5 [6] is a complex knowledgebase which holds a number of concepts for each word. ConceptNet 5 holds pre-existing lexical and semantic features for words and phrases. This also provides unseen information that cannot be extracted from the context. These concepts from Conceptnet holds more information which could be used for semantic parsing [7], and use dependency parsing to get the semantic relationships between words. Conceptual information is gathered using the

ConceptNet ontology. The concepts from the text are sent to the ConceptNet and the semantics are then retrieved. This focuses on identifying concepts from the inputs and passing the concept to the Conceptnet to find the relationships. ConceptNet is used in order to give the machine a better understanding of the sentence.

Through paraphrasing [5], ConceptNet allows parser to identify more complex concepts to support sematic parsing. Through the use of paraphrasing, the machine learning approaches require less training and supervision in semantic parsing as it provides an insight by utilising more information to support the semantic parser [2]. Therefore, our approach aims to achieve a semantic parser which uses ConceptNet to remove supervision and training.

3 Methodology

Our research focuses on creating a semantic parser with the use of ConceptNet 5 using a multi-level of search. Basic steps of our method is shown in Fig. 1. The left panel shows the steps and the right panel shows how an example is parsed. The first step is Part Of Speech (POS) tagging the input. Using the tagged sentences, phrases will be identified. The phrases and words are then searched in ConceptNet 5. The extracted concepts are validated and used to for semantic parsing.

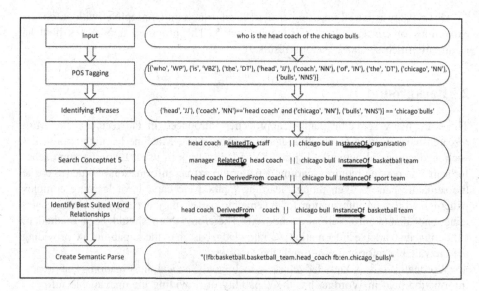

Fig. 1. The main steps in the proposed methods

ConceptNet 5 is used to map words with the knowledge to support semantic parsing. Using pre-existing knowledge of ConceptNet 5 for each word and word phrase, we generate a knowledge structure as shown in Fig. 2. Furthermore, as shown in Fig. 2, initially the words and word phrases are searched from ConceptNet 5 which created the level 1 search results. Level 1 results are then searched in ConceptNet 5 in order to generate level 2 results. The results in level 2 are used for the parser.

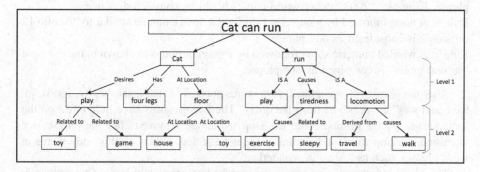

Fig. 2. Level structure generated, shows a sample set of data extracted from Conceptnet 5

Our methodology can be divided into two phases; generating the lexical representation and semantic representation generation. We use POS tagging to identify and processed the information to create the lexical representation. The lexical representation is used to create the semantic representation through the ConceptNet 5. The two approaches presented in the paper differ at the final phase of generating semantic representation.

3.1 Lexical Phase

The main task in the lexical phase is POS, which is shown in Fig. 1. This step is important as the tags for the words are used to identify the phrases from words. A given query is tagged using NLTK POS tagger Yih et al. (2014) since this method is a simpler tagging method without using any learning method. The tagged query is used in order to create phrases. The initial step is used in order to combine words which should be search together in ConceptNet 5 as the example "what causes prostate cancer?" if prostate and cancer were searched separately in ConceptNet 5, it would generate irrelevant results for the given query. When tagged using the NLTK POS tagger it will generate:

[('what','WP'), ('causes','VBZ'),('prostate','NN'),('cancer','NN')]

The tags are used to create the phrase. We use the following seven rules which are a subset of the rules used in Poria et al. [7] for creating the multi-word expressions/ phrases that will be searched from the ConceptNet 5.

Rule 1: Names which fall together such as "Barack Obama" are combined together to create a phrase.
Rule 2: Nouns which fall together are also combined together such as "farmer's market" to create a phrase.
Rule 3: Nouns which follow the pattern of a noun followed by a plural of another noun ['NN', 'NNS'] such as "city officials" are also combined together to create a phrase.

Rule 4: Names such as "Alice in wonder-land", which follow the pattern of ['NNP', 'IN', 'NNP'] are combined together to create a phrase.

Rule 5: Numeric value before a noun or set of nouns is combined together to create a phrase. Example: "2003 cricket world cup"; should be considered as one.

Rule 6: A noun followed by a numeric value and a noun example similar to "Apollo 12 mission"; is considered as one phrase.

Rule 7: A worded numeric value followed by a noun or nouns as shown in the example "second grade" is combined as one phrase.

After the phrases are generated, stop words such as "a, an, is, at, be, by, for, is, in, were and was" are removed from the query. These stop words have little effect on the semantically parsed results. Since the stop words are removed after the phrases are identified, the stop words in the phrases are not affected. This is used on stop words in word phrases such as "Alice in wonderland".

The generated phrases and words are searched automatically in the ConceptNet 5. In order to search the ConceptNet 5 the words and phrases are passed to the ConceptNet 5 API. This generates related words and their relationship (concepts) to the searched word/phrase.

The ConceptNet 5 was searched in two levels. The levels described are shown in Fig. 2 for the example of: "cat can run". The two levels created in our methods are based on the two stages of information extraction. The initial concept extraction for the information creates the level 1 and the next concept extraction creates the level 2. These approaches do not use any hand written rules in extracting the concepts as well as semantically parsing the query.We have taken two approaches to improve semantic parsing.

The step "search in ConceptNet 5" (shown in Fig. 1) is achieved by using these two approaches. They are described as follows.

3.2   Approach 1

Figure 3 shows the steps in Approach 1. The search mentioned in Fig. 3 is based on extracting concepts from ConceptNet 5. All the concepts extracted at level 1 are searched again in ConceptNet 5. The concepts drawn from level 2 are used to semantically parse the query. The relationships and the related words are mapped with each other in order to generate the logic format. The logical format is based on lambda format. The lambda expressions predicate is created using these extracted concepts. The lambda expressions variable is extracted from query itself. The related words at the level 2 and their relationships are further used to enhance the semantic logical format to be generated. The relationships are identified by matching words in the concepts

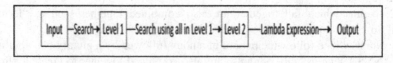

Fig. 3. Approach 1 block diagram

extracted. As shown in Fig. 2 "cat" and "run" both have "play" in common. With that information it can be stated that the words have a semantic similarity.

In this approach, words from the query are not eliminated although they do not show any relationships at the level 1 of ConceptNet 5 search. There are a larger set of concepts in Conceptnet 5 compared to the earlier versions. These extracted concepts can be used to improve on the sematic parsing as well as further elaborating a sentence.

3.3 Approach 2

As shown in Fig. 4 the initial search is similar to Approach 1, where level 1 search results are extracted from ConceptNet 5 for each word or phrase in the query. The results generated from level 1 for each word and phrase is compared. The relationships with each word and phrase are identified and the rest of the words are dropped. The identified related words and phrases are passed to the ConceptNet 5 to further extract the concepts. The generated concepts in the level 2 are used in order to create the semantic par-ser. The extracted concepts are used in developing the parser using the words and their relationships in level 2. The filter applied to the level 1 results in reducing level 2 search in ConceptNet 5. This reduces a substantial amount of search in ConceptNet 5 in level 2, this reduces the computational intensity in generating the final semantic parse logical format.

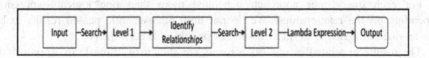

Fig. 4. Approach 2 block diagram

3.4 Semantic Phase

Our approaches use the ConceptNet 5 without any filter similar to Poria et al. [7] therefore it is information rich. The ConceptNet 5 provides words and their relationships to develop the logical format for semantic parsing. The logical format is created using lambda format. We create the predicate of the lambda expression using the concepts extracted from the ConceptNet 5 and pass the variable from the query. This can be explained further through the use of the example query "what is serge made out of", the target lambda expression is:

$$(!fb:fashion.textile.fiber\ fb:en.serge) \tag{2}$$

The predicate "fashion.textile.fiber" is generated using the concepts drawn using ConceptNet 5 and serge is directly extracted from the query. Hence this can be considered to improvise the calculations for semantic parsing. This also provides more information which is not revealed in the given query. Therefore that information is not missed out when parsing the query.

4 Results and Discussions

Our approach was tested on the Stanford Sentiment dataset and Freebase. The dataset comprises of 11 855 and 917 open domain queries respectively. The queries are similar to queries which are passed to a question answering system or search engine. The two approaches were tested using all the data in Stanford Sentiment dataset which includes both the training and testing datasets.

The queries in the datasets were converted into a lambda format. The lambda format supports a direct search from a corpus. The lambda format generates logical format. Given the example, "when was starry night painted" generates the related words and their relationships from the ConceptNet 5. Our approaches will finally generate,

> when RelatedTo time
> paint Related To art
> starry night InstanceOf artwork

based on the above relationships and generated words (2) shows the logical format.

$$(!fb : visual\_art.artwork.date\_completed\, fb : en.starry\, night) \qquad (3)$$

For each query, our approach generated more than one logical expression depending on the relationships. We do not limit our semantic passed results to be one-on-one but generate as many results as possible for each query.

The results generated in our experiments are shown in Table 1. In Approach 1, results generated in level 1 and level 2 are used for semantic parsing separately. This enabled us to identify and observe the improvement in providing more concepts in order to achieve semantic parsing. We use,

True Positive = TP
False Positive = FP
False Negative = FN
Total Number of Queries = TNQ
Precision = TP/(TP + FP)
Recall = TP/(TP + FN)
Accuracy = TP/TNQ

Table 1. Tested results on Stanford Sentiment dataset using the Conceptnet 5

	Approach 1		Approach 2
	Level 1	Level 2	Level 2
Precision	81.77%	82.37%	85.68%
Recall	91.96%	93.29%	94.39%
Accuracy	90.95%	95.48%	97.04%

Overall the results in Approach 2 achieved a high recall rate of 94.39%, due to the high level of concepts available. The concepts are not omitted therefore rich information is used for semantic parsing. Validating the concepts from the first level to the next level reduces the false negative results. An improvement of 1.33% of recall rate is visible from Approach 1 to Approach 2. The reduction of false negative can be stated to be important for tasks similar to question and answering query optimization. Hence reduce the missing important information.

The results generated in Approach 1 show that when moving from level 1 to level 2, the recall improves from 91.96% to 93.29%. This validates our hypothesis that when provided with more concepts the results improve.

Although a high recall is shown, precision is reduced due to the high number of false positive results created in Approach 1. We address this issue by applying a filtration method in Approach 2. As shown in the results the recall as well as the precision improves. Therefore, the use of a filter after the level 1 search seems to generate better results.

Approach 2 can be compared with Approach 1 in the aspect of computational intensity. Approach 2 reduces the searches in the level 2 due to the relationship-filter. Both approaches have a computational complexity of $O(nc)$, where n being the processing complexity and c being the number of iterations. However, it is evident that Approach 2 has a less computational complexity than Approach 1. The value of c in Approach 2 will be lower than in Approach 1 since the number of iterations is less. Since Approach 2 uses filters this reduces the number of false negative results. Approach 2 shows superior performance in both results and computational costs.

Poria et al. [7] use ConceptNet 3 and extracts the concepts manually for selected 300 utterance of Stanford sentiment dataset. We surpass by automating the extraction of the concepts using ConceptNet 5. Furthermore we search two levels in ConceptNet 5 to identify the semantic relationships and create the logical format for 11 855 queries. Bordes et al. [11] present a semantic parsing framework which requires both Concept-net and WorldNet. ConceptNet is used in order to enrich the WordNet's relationships using the method. Our method only relies on the ConceptNet 5. Therefore our approach holds fewer dependencies compared to the above method. Furthermore we extract both the words and the relationships in the ConceptNet 5 for semantic parsing. Therefore using the relation-ships the logical representation can be created with a stronger relationship that the other semantic parsing methods. Our method also shows a potential of improving the logical representation hold additional information.

We compare the results generated in Approach 2 with Poria et al. [7] results for semantic parsing. This is the closest match to our method. We use 917 queries, in contrast they only use 300 manually selected queries. Furthermore, our approach extracts concepts automatically in which they manually extract the concepts from ConceptNet. ConceptNet 3 held separate editions for English and Brazilian Portuguese Havasi et al. [12] with the Global Mind. ConceptNet 5 contains all languages of ConceptNet simultaneously as well as a collection of large collection of knowledge bases Havasi et al. [12].

As for our current knowledge, we have not found semantic parsing technique using ConceptNet 5 with brute search and there are a few techniques is ConceptNet 3. For the sake of comparative analysis we tested our approaches on ConceptNet 3 as well. The results are shown in Table 2. As shown in Table 2, our approaches outperformed the existing method of Poria et al. [7]. Poria et al. [7] method achieved a precision of 92.21%, and our Approach 1 and Approach 2 achieved 94.56%, 95.24% respectively. It should be further noted that we used 3 times more queries than Poria et al. [7]. We had 11 855 queries while Poria et al. [7] used only 300 manually selected queries. Again, as consistent with the results for ConceptNet 5, Approach 2 produced better results than Approach 1.

Table 2. Results using Conceptnet 3

	Poria et al.	Approach 1	Approach 2
Precision	92.21%	93.82%	94.91%
Number of queries tested	300	11 855	11 855

Furthermore it can be confidently stated that unlike the methods which requires training Herzig et al. [13] our methods can be used without training. We further test our method with the ConceptNet 5 on the freebase dataset the WebQ to compare with the Berant et al. [2], the current state of the art method on the freebase and WebQ Question-Answer pairs are generating accuracies of 71.3% and 32.9% respectively. Our approaches showed the accuracies of 77.1% for approach 1 and 79.2% for approach 2 for the free917 dataset, and 36.5% for approach 1 and 38.2% for approach 2 for the WebQ dataset (Table 3).

Table 3. Accuracies for Free917 and webQ datasets

	FREE917	WebQ
Berant et al.	71.3%	32.9%
Approach 1	77.1%	36.5%
Approach 2	79.2%	38.2%

5 Conclusion

Two fully automatic approaches are proposed and presented for semantic parsing using rich information extracted from ConceptNet 5. Approach 1 uses the results generated through level 2 for semantic parsing of the queries. Approach 2 filters the concepts generated from level 1 and passes to level 2. Both approaches produce information rich results since a multi-level concept extraction is done from ConceptNet 5.

Our experiment results for Approach 1 showed that when more concepts are available, the precision, recall and accuracy improves. Results generated from Approach 1 and Approach 2 have recall values of 93.29%, 94.39% and precision of 82.37%, 85.37% respectively for Stanford Sentiment dataset. Furthermore, we test on Free917 and WebQ in which we achieve 77.1%, 79.2% and 36.5%, 38.2% respectively for each approach. The results of Approach 2 indicated that with the use of a filter the results improved.

Our experiments showed that with the use of more concepts, the semantic parsing can be further improved. These show the capability of enhancing semantic parsing through the complex concepts extracted from ConceptNet.

Acknowledgment. We would like to acknowledge Rob Speer, of Common Sense Computing Group, MIT Media Lab for providing the JSON objects that were required to do our experiments on ConceptNet 3.

References

1. Allen, J.: Natural Language Understanding. Pearson, London (1995)
2. Berant, J., Chou, A., Frostig, R., Liang, P.: Semantic parsing on freebase from question-answer pairs, pp. 6–18 (2013)
3. Nugaliyadde, A., Wong, K.W., Sohel, F., Xie, H.: Reinforced memory networks for question answering. In: The 24th International Conference on Neural Information Processing, Guangzhou, China (2017, in press)
4. Pradhan, S.S., Ward, W.H., Hacioglu, K., Martin, J.H., Jurafsky, D.: Shallow semantic parsing using support vector machines. In: HLT-NAACL, pp. 233–240 (2004)
5. Berant, J., Liang, P.: Semantic parsing via paraphrasing. In: ACL, vol. 1, pp. 1415–1425 (2014)
6. Speer, R., Havasi, C.: ConceptNet 5: a large semantic network for relational knowledge. In: Gurevych, I., Kim, J. (eds.) The People's Web Meets NLP, pp. 161–176. Springer, Heidelberg (2013). doi:10.1007/978-3-642-35085-6_6
7. Poria, S., Agarwal, B., Gelbukh, A., Hussain, A., Howard, N.: Dependency-based semantic parsing for concept-level text analysis. In: Gelbukh, A. (ed.) CICLing 2014. LNCS, vol. 8403, pp. 113–127. Springer, Heidelberg (2014). doi:10.1007/978-3-642-54906-9_10
8. Agarwal, B., Poria, S., Mittal, N., Gelbukh, A., Hussain, A.: Concept-level sentiment analysis with dependency-based semantic parsing: a novel approach. Cogn. Comput. **7**(4), 487–499 (2015)
9. Miller, G.A.: WordNet: a lexical database for English. Commun. ACM **38**(11), 39–41 (1995)
10. Shi, L., Mihalcea, R.: Putting pieces together: combining FrameNet, VerbNet and WordNet for robust semantic parsing. In: Gelbukh, A. (ed.) CICLing 2005. LNCS, vol. 3406, pp. 100–111. Springer, Heidelberg (2005). doi:10.1007/978-3-540-30586-6_9
11. Bordes, A., Glorot, X., Weston, J., Bengio, Y.: Joint learning of words and meaning representations for open-text semantic parsing. In: Artificial Intelligence and Statistics, pp. 127–135 (2012)
12. Havasi, C., Speer, R., Alonso, J.: ConceptNet 3: a flexible, multilingual semantic network for common sense knowledge. In: Recent advances in Natural Language Processing, pp. 27–29. John Benjamins, Philadelphia (2007)
13. Su, Y., Yan, X.: Cross-domain Semantic Parsing via Paraphrasing. arXiv preprint arXiv: 1704.05974 (2017)

Design of a Cloud Brokerage Architecture Using Fuzzy Rough Set Technique

Parwat Singh Anjana$^{(\boxtimes)}$, Rajeev Wankar, and C. Raghavendra Rao

School of CIS, University of Hyderabad, Hyderabad 500046, India
anjana.uoh@gmail.com, rajeev.wankar@gmail.com, crrcs@gmail.com

Abstract. Cloud computing offers numerous services to the cloud consumers such as infrastructure, platform, software, etc. Due to the vast diversity in available cloud services from the user point of view, it leads to several challenges to rank and select the potential cloud service. One of the plausible solutions for the problem can be obtained with the use of Rough Set Theory (RST) and available in the literature. Unfortunately, Rough Set Theory cannot deal with numerical values. One of the classical solutions to this problem can be obtained by using Fuzzy Rough Set. To the best of our knowledge, there is no working Fuzzy-Rough Set based brokerage architecture available which is used for minimizing attributes, search space and for ranking the service providers. In this paper, we proposed a Fuzzy Rough Set based Cloud Brokerage (FRSCB) architecture, which is responsible for service selection based on consumers Quality of Service (QoS) request. We propose to use Fuzzy Rough Set Theory (FRST) to minimize the number of attributes and searching space. We also did the QoS attribute categorization to identify functional and non-functional requirements and behavior of the attributes (static/dynamic). Finally, we develop an algorithm that recommends potential cloud services to the cloud consumers.

Keywords: Cloud computing · Quality of Service · Cloud brokerage · Fuzzy Rough Set · Reduct · Cloud Service Provider Ranking

1 Introduction

Cloud computing services are very useful to most business owners, especially for small sized organizations. From the user point of views, we need an additional layer on top of the service provisioning to enable functions such as service discovery and monitoring. This extra layer of computing is known as a Cloud Brokerage system. According to Gartner [1] A cloud broker is an individual or organization that consults, mediates and facilitates the selection of cloud computing solutions on behalf of an organization. It serves as a third party between a Cloud Service Provider (CSP) and organization buying the provider's products and solutions. In [1] cloud broker services are classified into three categories as *(1) Service Intermediation* broker system improve the given service by adding some special capabilities and offers the value added service, *(2) Service Aggregation*

S. Phon-Amnuaisuk et al. (Eds.): MIWAI 2017, LNAI 10607, pp. 54–68, 2017.
https://doi.org/10.1007/978-3-319-69456-6_5

broker system combines the number of services into one new service to provides data integration and security of data movement between cloud consumer and providers, and *(3) Service Arbitrage* broker system which is very much similar to service aggregation; the only difference is that number of services being aggregate are not fixed. Cloud brokers can help consumers by giving access to multiple providers through one contract vehicle. They provided financial reporting and budgeting policy which can remove acquisition barriers and allow timely provisioning of cloud services. The proposed architecture is service arbitrage broker designed using the Fuzzy Rough Set Technique (FRST) that provides user with an opportunity to select the service provider based on the Quality of Service (QoS) parameter set by them based on the Service Level Agreement (SLA).

Major contributions of this work include: (1) The design of a cloud brokerage architecture, which helps a user in ranking and selecting a suitable CSP, based on their QoS requirements. (2) Categorization of QoS attributes in two types to determine their static/dynamic behavior, functional/non-functional characteristics. Also, introduce experience of past users and performance in consideration to improve CSPs ranking and selection procedure further. As well, it restricts the CSPs to provide the best services to contest in the next service assignment actively. (3) The prime focus is on search space reduction and the composition of the dynamic QoS parameters for CSP ranking to benefit cloud users from diversity in the cloud market. (4) Introduced network layer attributes which are not part of the user request to rank CSPs because network QoS attributes also play a critical role in service offerings. (5) To provide one more level of customization in the description of user QoS requirements, we proposed user-assigned weights to QoS attributes so that a user can also prioritize their needs. In case if a user is not interested in assigning weights Golden Section Search Method [2] is employed to assign best weights to the attributes. Finally giving a choice to the user to select the best service provider from the ranked list of CSPs.

The rest of the paper is organized as follows. Section 2 gives an overview of existing cloud services selection techniques and related work. Section 3 presents an overview of the Rough Set, Fuzzy Set, and Reduct. Section 4 covers the proposed Fuzzy Rough Set based Cloud Brokerage (FRSCB) architecture with its key components. Section 5 presents the ranking mechanism with a case study example. Finally, we conclude this paper in Sect. 6 with some suggestion on the future work.

2 Literature Survey

Sun et al. [3] presented a brief study of existing cloud service selection techniques to address service discovery and selection challenges. They studied and classified the service selection techniques based on the five different perspectives. They characterized the existing service selection approaches into four groups based on seven dimensions. According to their work following are the existing cloud service selection approaches:

- Multi-Criteria Decision Making Based Approaches
  - AHP/ANP based Technique
  - MAUT based Technique
  - Outranking based Technique
  - Simple Additive Weighting based Technique
- Multi-Criteria Optimization Based Approaches
  - Dynamic Programming based Technique
  - Greedy Algorithm based Technique
- Logic-Based Approaches

Garg et al. [4] proposed an SMICloud framework based on the "Service Measurement Index (SMI)" attributes defined in the "Cloud Service Measurement Index Consortium (CSMIC) [5]". The SMICloud framework allows users to compare different CSPs based on their QoS requirements along with other dimensions, and finally, select the best CSP to satisfy user QoS requirement. They presented an overview of Service Measurement and Key Performance Index (KPI) attributes, described SMICloud framework and shows how the QoS attribute matrices can be modeled. Also presented ranking mechanism and explained with a case study. Their framework provides a high-level overview of QoS requirements that is required by the cloud users for selecting an appropriate service. There is no globally accepted metrics available for CSP selection which define these KPIs and ranks CSPs.

Ganghishetti and Wankar [6] proposed a Cloud-QoS Management Strategy (C-QoSMS) for IaaS cloud where framework allocates the resources by considering the SLA. They used a soft computing technique to assign the best service to the users with minimum searching time. The performance of their developed system has been analyzed concerning the number of requests. Later on, they extend their framework known as Modified C-QoSMS [7] in which they compared the results of presented framework with cloud brokers using Round Robin and Random algorithms. The C-QoSMS framework did not consider gray valued attributes, not scalable, and designed only for amazon instances. The C-QoSMS framework uses Rough Set. Hence discretization of the numerical value is required for the ranking of CSPs. In proposed FRSCB, we need not obliged to perform the discretization as we are using the FRST. We identified the functional and non-functional requirements, and also include gray valued attributes which help in ranking the CSPs.

3   Background

3.1   Fuzzy Set Theory (FST)

Zadeh [8] proposes an approach known as Fuzzy Set in 1965 to deal with the vagueness of the data. In this technique, elements of a set can belong to the set by mean of a degree k such that $0 <= k <= 1$. In traditional set theory, an element can belong to the set or can not. To understand this let an example where a person can be healthy or unhealthy in traditional set theory, while in

FST, we can say that a person is healthy (or unhealthy) in 70% (to the degree 0.7). A membership function in FST can be given using the following Eq. 1. Where, A is a set of elements and a is an element of A i.e. $a \in A$.

$$\mu_a(A) \in [0, 1] \tag{1}$$

3.2 Rough Set Theory (RST)

Rough Set Theory (RST)has vital importance in the area of artificial intelligence and cognitive sciences, especially in the fields of expert systems, decision-based systems, knowledge discovery system, knowledge acquisition, inductive reasoning, etc. Pawlak proposed a new mathematical approach known as RST [9] to deal with the vagueness of data. "The vagueness of data can be expressed using the concept of the boundary region of the sets. If boundary region is empty, then set is called crisp otherwise called vague or rough, it means that our knowledge about that set is not sufficient to define precisely [9]". Rough Set can also be viewed as a practical implementation of Frege's idea of vagueness where boundary region is used to express the uncertainty, and the rough set can be defined using approximation theory [10].

3.3 Reduct

A Reduct of the system is the minimal subset of attributes that give the same classification power of elements of the universe as the whole set of attributes [11], or we can say that attributes that do not belong to a reduct are irrelevant concerning the classification of elements of the universe. Therefore to simplify the system, we can remove some attribute such that we can still discern objects of the new system as the original one. Let dependency between two attribute sets A, B is $A \implies B$ then it may happen that set B depends on a subset A' of the set A but not on the whole set A. Hence, we are interested in finding this subset, and for this, we need the notion of a Reduct. Let $A', B \subseteq A$. Obviously, if $A' \subseteq A$ is a B-reduct of A, then A' is a minimal subset of A such that

$$\gamma(A, B) = \gamma(A', B) \tag{2}$$

- We can say that attribute $a \in A$ is B dispensable in A, if A-positive region of B: $POS_A(B) = POS_{(A-a)}(B)$; otherwise a is B indispensable in A.
- If all attributes $a \in A$ are A indispensable in A, then A will be called B independent.
- $A' \subseteq A$ is a B reduct of A, iff A' is B independent and $POS_A(B) = POS_{A'}(B)$.

3.4 Need of Fuzzy Rough Set

The limitation of the RST is that it works only with discrete values, where only categorical attributes exist. In fact, numerical, interval valued and fuzzy features also exist in real world data. For example, information as shown in the Table 3 can not be handled by RST. One plausible solution to deal with this problem is discretion the numerical data by using any of discretization techniques so that numerical value can be converted into categorical and then analyze the information using RST. Alternatively, to resolve this problem, FST can also be employed. But some time data is presented in the form of numeric as well in categorical, therefore, to deal with such hybrid information we need a hybrid technique known as Fuzzy Rough Set Technique (FRST). We employed this model to determine all possible reducts of the systems.

4   Proposed Approach

4.1   FRSCB Architecture

In this section, we present proposed "Fuzzy Rough Set based Cloud Brokerage (FRSCB) Architecture" as shown in Fig. 1. The FRSCB architecture can be used as a service broker to rank the cloud service provider and to select the best service provider among them. The term best means, the element of all QoS attributes by the vendor best matches with the requirement of the user.

The Quality of Service (QoS) is a broad term which is used to represent the overall experience a user or application will experience over the web. User QoS requirement may consist of different type of attributes such as numeric, gray valued, static, and dynamic. Dynamic attributes are those attributes which change over time such as virtual machine performance while static attribute such as cost does not. In this work, we characterized the QoS attributes in two different types which help in identifying the functional and non-functional requirements of the user. The $Type1$ category consists of static and dynamic attributes while $Type2$ category consists of numeric and gray valued attributes. As shown in the Table 1.

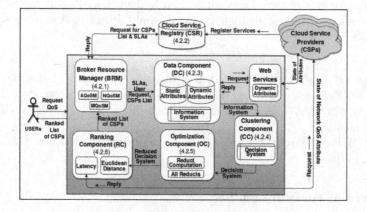

Fig. 1. FRSCB architecture

Table 1. QoS attribute categorization

QoS parameter	Top level attribute	Sub attributes	Attribute type		Unit (Matrices)
			Type1	Type2	
Accountability	Accountability	Levels	Static	Numeric	Levels (1–10)
Performance	CPU	CPU speed	Dynamic	Numeric	GHZ
	Memory	Memory read	Dynamic	Numeric	Mb/s
		Memory write	Dynamic	Numeric	Mb/s
	Storage/Disk	Disk read	Dynamic	Numeric	Mb/s
		Disk write	Dynamic	Numeric	Mb/s
	Network (VM)	In bound	Dynamic	Numeric	bits/s
		Out bound	Dynamic	Numeric	bits/s
	Response time	Range	Dynamic	Numeric	Second
		Avg value	Dynamic	Numeric	Second
Cost	VM	VM cost	Static	Numeric	$/Hr or $/M
	Storage	Storage cost	Static	Numeric	$/Gb
	Data transfer	In bound	Static	Numeric	$/Gb
		Out bound	Static	Numeric	$/Gb
Agility	Capacity	Disk	Dynamic	Numeric	Gb
		CPU	Dynamic	Numeric	GHZ
		Memory	Dynamic	Numeric	Gb
	Elasticity	Time	Dynamic	Numeric	Seconds
Assurance	Serviceability	Free support	Static	Gray value	Boolean (0/1)
		Support type	Static	Gray value	24/7, phone
	Availability	Service	Dynamic	Numeric	%
	Failure	Failure rate	Dynamic	Numeric	%
	Service stability	Upload time	Dynamic	Numeric	Seconds
		CPU	Dynamic	Numeric	GHZ
		Memory	Dynamic	Numeric	Gb/S
Security	Data	Data security	Static	Gray value	Security levels
	Platform	Platform sec.	Static	Gray value	Security levels
	Network	N/w security	Static	Gray value	Security levels
Trustworthiness	Trust level	Trust level	Dynamic	Gray value	Levels
	User feedback	Satisfaction	Dynamic	Gray value	Levels
	Recovery	Mode	Dynamic	Gray value	Modes

The functional QoS requirements such as CPU performance, disk, and main memory can easily be quantified while non-functional such as security, type of supports, and user feedback are not straightforward to quantify. In proposed architecture, we have three sub-components as Application Layer QoS Manager (AQoSM), Network Layer QoS Manager (NQoSM), and Machine Layer QoS Manager (MQoSM) which deals with functional and non-functional requirements. We designed Information System (IS) as shown in Table 3 by using the numbers of QoS attributes such as Accountability, Availability, Cost, etc. There are different network layer parameters such as throughput, latency, bandwidth. We considered latency to determine any delay that may occur during the communication over the network. More specifically, from cloud point of view, latency becomes very critical attribute for latency-sensitive applications. The interactive characteristics of such application require predictable and small latency since people usually prefer quick response [12]. If the latency is high, then it directly degraded user experience which impacts on revenue [13]. The increasing use of cloud services leads to the unpredictability of response time and critical performance barrier for latency-sensitive applications because of shared resources. Since cloud grows in the number of users and scale, to ensure guaranteed QoS, latency becomes essential property [14]. In our approach, different weights are assigned by the user to the latency, and QoS attributes based on their importance to rank the service providers. In the case when a user does not assign the weights system will assign based on relative importance of the latency and other QoS attributes. To decide the optimal weights, Golden Section Search Method [2] was employed and made as a default method for assigning the weights.

4.2 FRSCB Components

FRSCB architecture has been divided into several components such as Broker Resource Manager, Cloud Service Registry, Data Component, etc., these components are responsible for the overall functionality of the system, ranking of Cloud Service Providers (CSPs), and finally selection. The CSPs register their service offering along with QoS parameters in the Cloud Service Registry (CSR); then FRSCB algorithm is invoked whenever a user submits a request.

4.2.1 Broker Resource Manager (BRM)

BRM is one of the central components of FRSCB. It takes users QoS request and returns the ranked list of CSPs, also ensures the QoS requirements of the user and the application when remote services are accessed. After receiving a user request at the very beginning, it fetches the list of available CSPs, their service offering information along with SLAs, and sends all the information to the Data Component (DC). Once ranking process is completed, it is responsible for sending the ranked list to the user and execution of the selected service. BRM consists of three sub-components as AQoSM, NQoSM, and MQoSM to deal with functional and non-functional QoS requirements. These sub-components of BRM play a significant role to coordinate with the service providers cloud manager for service execution and to measure the QoS once service execution started. Elements of the AQoSM includes the availability (service up and down-time), security and privacy (authentication and authorization mechanisms), user feedback, cost, service and user information (service and user Ids). NQoSM includes network related information which is used to maintain the QoS over the network to deliver predictable results. It consists accountability, assurance, and networking (including bandwidth, latency, throughput, and error rate) QoS parameters. NQoSM attributes are independent of the user request, but they are very critical for CSPs ranking and selection. MLQoSM is similar to the type of applications which requires an interaction between the user and the application such as visualization applications. Elements of MQoSM includes the performance (CPU frequency, disk, memory), agility (capacity, elasticity), the number of virtual machines (VMs), and scalability QoS parameters.

4.2.2   Cloud Service Registry (CSR)

It is a global Registry service used to record QoS parameter where all CSPs need to register their services and QoS provisions. Whenever a new CSP starts their services, they need to register their capabilities, QoS offerings, along with SLAs. In our design, we assume that there is a standard global CSR where all CSPs already registered their services. We fetch the information about the service providers and QoS parameters from this CSR to design the Information System (IS). In the absence of this global CSR, the CSPs need to register their services in our local CSR registry.

4.2.3   Data Component (DS)

This component is responsible for designing of the IS based on the information it gets from the brokerage resource manager. Subsequently, it also identifies the type of QoS attribute, selects the IaaS provider from the list of all CSPs. Once the identification of QoS attributes is done and the user requests consists dynamic attributes in the request, this component fetches the current state of that attributes from CSP using web-services.

4.2.4   Clustering Component (CC)

This component performs the $K - means$ [15] clustering over the IS obtained during the Data Component. After performing K-means clustering, the CSP who offers the similar services are grouped under the same cluster. Different clustering labels are attached to each cluster. The number of clustering label depends on the IS. We used *Elbow* method [16] to decide the optimal number of clusters (i.e. k-value). These clustering labels are used as a decision attribute to design the Decision System (DS). In proposed DS, we kept Decision Attribute at the end of the table (last column).

4.2.5   Optimization Component (OC)

Optimization component tries to reduce the searching space with the help of Reduct computation, for this, it determines all reduct of the DS using Fuzzy Rough Set Technique (FRST) and selects the best reduct i.e. selects the reduct which consists the maximum overlapping with user requested attributes. Finally, design the Reduced Decision System (RDS) based on the chosen reduct.

4.2.6   Ranking Component (RC)

This component does the ranking of CSPs. It first calculates the *Euclidean Distance* of each CSP from user QoS request in RDS by considering attribute values of each CSP and user QoS request. Then it determines the *Latency* of CSPs. Further, it calculates the *Total Score* of each CSP by performing addition of *Euclidean Distance* and *Latency*. Finally, send the ranked list to BRM. Here, it is important to note that before addition, weight must be assigned to QoS attributes and Network attributes for ranking. The user can assign different weights to rank the cloud service providers. In case if the user does not assign any weight then the system will assign 66.67% weight to QoS attributes (AQoSM and MQoSM) and 33.33% weight to Network QoS attributes (NQoSM). To decide the optimal weights, Golden Section Search Method [2] was employed. User selected QoS attribute must be given more weight over network attributes (*Latency*).

Algorithm 1. FRSCB Algorithm

Input: User QoS Request and Weights
Output: Ranked List of Cloud Service Providers (CSPs)
    STEP [A]
        (i) User QoS Request to FRSCB, along with QoS attribute
    STEP [B]
        (i) BRM←User Request
        (ii) BRM←fetch list of all CSP from CSR
    STEP [C]
        (i) categories User request
            (a) if(Dynamic Attribute)
                (i) Fetch attributes Favourable values in WSC and send it to DC
            (b) if(Static Attribute)
                (i) no Fetch
        (ii) extract IaaS providers from Data obtained in STEP [B](i)
        (iii) generate IS using STEP [C](i),[C](ii)
    STEP [D]
        (i) Clustering Label←K-Means Clustering(IS)
        (ii) Clustering Label of STEP [D](i)←Decision Attribute
        (iii) generate DS←using IS and Decision Attribute
    STEP [E]
        (i) find all *Reduct(DS)*
        (ii) select BEST reduct from STEP [E](i)
        (iii) generate RDS based on STEP [E](ii)
    STEP [F]
        (i) find Euclidean Distance of CSP selected in STEP [C](ii) using STEP[E](iii), [A](i)
        (ii) get Latency of respective CSP
        (iii) rank SP by assigning weightage to QoS Attributes and Latency
        (iv) return ranked list of service provider to BRM
    STEP [G]
        (i) BRM returns the CSPs List to respective User-Id
        (ii) User select one CSP and send CSP-Id to FRSCB
        (iii) FRSCB interacts with respective CSP using BRM for resource reservation and service execution.
/* BRM: Broker Resource Manager; CSR: Cloud Service Registry; DC: Data Component; WSC: Web Services Component; IS: Information System; DS: Decision System; RDS: Reduced Decision System; NRM: Network Resource Manager; CSP: Cloud Service Provider; ED: Euclidean Distance. */

---

5   CASE STUDY: Ranking Cloud Services Based on User QoS Requirements

Implementation of our work has been done in *R − language* [17] and *RStudio* [18] is used as a development environment. In proposed architecture, a GUI is developed with the help of $fgui$ [19] package to submit the user QoS request to the system. We have used 15 more frequently referred CSPs along with 15 QoS attributes. We considered one Network Layer Parameter ($Latency$) for designing the Information System (IS). To create a synthesized IS we have referred SMI-Cloud framework [4], CloudSim [20], more frequently referred CSPs, their SLA, and other internet resources. Designed IS is shown in Table 3. Here it is important to mention that nowadays CSPs are not providing this information; therefore, we performed our experiment on synthesized data. However, we tried to get as much as real time information of QoS attributes. For the retrieval of real-time values of Performance, Assurance, and Network QoS attributes, including Availability, Data In Bound, Out Bound, Service Up/Down Time, and Latency we used Cloud Harmony API's [21]. There is no single globally acceptable standardization available in the literature for standardizing some of the non-functional QoS attributes such as Accountability, Security, and Support which are not easy to quantify. In proposed architecture, for Accountability, Security, and Supports we introduced different levels which can be extended easily.

Accountability includes the functions which are used to measure various CSP specific characteristics. These characteristics are crucial to build the consumer trust. A cloud user would like to store their critical data and deploy the application on the cloud, where they are provided accountability of security exposures and compliance. Accountability includes functionalities such as auditability, agreement, data ownership, etc. In our proposed work, accountability has ten different levels vary from 1–10 and user can select their desired value.

Security consists the number of important Key Performance Indicators (KPI) including firewall policies, certificates provisioning (SSL), the configuration of virtual machines, access control, log management, encryption or masking of sensitive data. The principal objective of security control is to mitigate threats caused by human errors, improve operational performance and implant safety mechanism into the cloud. An information assurance framework [22] for cloud developed by the European Union Network Information Security Agency (ENISA) consists of 10 first-degree indicators, 69 second-degree indicators, and 130 third-degree indicators. In [23], Cloud Control Matrix (CCM) presented by Cloud Security Alliance (CSA), which gives fundamental principle that the CSPs have to meet and to support users to estimate the security. Based on the risk of threats we presented ten different levels of security (1–10) from simple ($level - 1$) to complex ($level - 10$) can be easily extended. Every level has the combination of one or more security KPIs to ensure the security. For example, at $level - 1$, the provider gets authenticated; at $level - 2$, multi-factor authentication takes place where both client and provider gets authenticated; and at the further levels, various multi-factor authentication, fine granular authorization, firewall policies, privileged accounts (access controls), application identity takes place for security. A user can select the desired value from 1 to 10.

A dynamic support system in the cloud will help in improving customer experience, reduce cost and complexity, and achieve effective SLAs. In our proposed work, Support has ten different levels (1–10). For instance, smaller the level

Table 2. User QoS request

	Availability (%)	Accountability Level (1-10)	Number of VMs	VM Cost ($/h)	CPU Frequency (Hrz)	Memory (GB)	Service Response Time(s)	Security Levels (1-10)	Support Type (1-10)	User Feedback (0-5)
User Request	95.95	2	2	0.76	3.3	12	150	5	10	5

Table 3. Information system

SP ID	Availability (%)	Accountability Level (1-10)	Number of VMs	Cost				Capacity			Service Response Time (sec)	Security Level (1-10)	Support Level (1-10)	User Feedback (0-5)
				VM Cost ($/h)	Inbound $/m	Outbound $/m	Storage Cost $/m	CPU Frequency (Hrz)	Disk (GB)	Memory (GB)				
SP 1	99.95	4	2	0.54	12	12	12	1.8	1512	12	120	1	3	5
SP 2	100	8	4	0.34	11	15	11	2.5	712	16	180	1	2	1
SP 3	99.91	4	2	0.65	9	17	15	2.2	360	12	120	2	3	4
SP 4	99.95	9	1	0.37	10	14	23	3.4	1512	14	100	3	3	3
SP 5	98.99	3	2	0.63	12	14	13	1.8	512	18	90	2	2	2
SP 6	99.95	2	2	0.76	8	13	10	3.3	1712	12	150	2	3	5
SP 7	99	1	3	0.47	10	12	12	2.3	1624	18	195	3	3	2
SP 8	100	8	4	0.74	9	15	9	2.2	1524	14	125	1	2	2
SP 9	95.56	5	2	0.54	11	16	12	2.5	624	16	150	3	3	3
SP 10	99.36	6	6	0.44	8	15	12.6	3.3	512	24	120	1	3	0
SP 11	99	2	3	0.32	12	12	13.8	2.3	524	14	100	3	2	1
SP 12	100	4	2	0.76	9	16	11.2	2.1	712	12	120	3	3	2
SP 13	100	9	5	0.43	11	17	11	3	1254	16	90	3	3	5
SP 14	99.12	6	1	0.4	7	11	9.9	2.2	1812	22	105	1	2	1
SP 15	98	7	2	0.66	12	13	13	2.7	1412	18	160	2	3	1

($level - 1$) represents the poor support where CSPs provides support through email only. In the Average support ($level - 5$), they provide email and phone support for a fixed period, while in the higher extensive support ($level - 10$), they provide $24 * 7$ phone and quick email support with immediate solutions.

We fetch the information about QoS parameters from Cloud Service Registry to design the initial Information System (IS). For dynamic attributes web services are used to fetch the real-time information. A generated IS is shown in Table 3. K-Means clustering is applied on IS to get the clusters; different clustering labels are attached to each cluster. Further clustering labels are used as decision attribute to design the Decision System (DS) as shown in Table 4. The optimal number of clusters will be identified before the clustering iteration using *Elbow Method* [16]. The proposed system will consider values of QoS attribute and weights submitted by the user to rank the CSPs. Let us look at a user QoS request as shown in Table 2.

To get all possible reducts of the Decision Systems (DS), we need to construct the Discernibility Matrix [24, 25] based on Fuzzy Rough Set Theory (FRST) [8]. Once we have the discernibility matrix, we can compute all decision reducts of the DS. We used function *all_reduct_computation*() of package RoughSets [26] to compute all possible reducts. The attributes of the reducts have the potential to make a decision while other attributes do not have that possibility of decision making; hence, they are not part of the Reduct. The number of reducts depends on the 'α' precision value. We did the analysis of the effect of precision value on our system. Figure 2a shows the change in the number of reducts on our DS based on precision value. We set the precision value to 0.05 as default and got following reducts:

Reduct-1 *[Accountability, Availability, CPU Frequency, Data In-bound Cost, Disk, Number of VMs, Security, Service Response Time, Support, VM Cost]*

Table 4. Decision system

SP ID	Availability (%)	Accountability Levels (1-10)	Num. of VMs	Cost VM Cost ($/h)	Cost Data Inbound ($/m)	Cost Data Outbound ($/m)	Storage Cost ($/m)	Capacity CPU Frequency (Hrz)	Capacity Disk (GB)	Capacity Memory (GB)	Service Response Time (sec)	Security Levels (1-10)	Support Levels (1-10)	User Feedback Levels (0-5)	Clustering Label
SP 1	99.95	4	2	0.54	12	12	12	1.8	1512	12	120	1	3	5	3
SP 2	100	8	4	0.34	11	15	11	2.5	712	16	180	1	2	1	1
SP 3	99.91	4	2	0.65	9	17	15	2.2	360	12	120	2	3	4	5
SP 4	99.95	9	1	0.37	10	14	23	3.4	1512	14	100	3	3	3	3
SP 5	98.99	3	2	0.63	12	14	13	1.8	512	18	90	2	2	2	5
SP 6	99.95	2	2	0.76	8	13	10	3.3	1712	12	150	2	3	5	4
SP 7	99	1	3	0.47	10	12	12	2.3	1624	18	195	3	3	2	4
SP 8	100	8	4	0.74	9	15	9	2.2	1524	14	125	1	2	2	3
SP 9	95.56	5	2	0.54	11	16	12	2.5	624	16	150	3	3	3	1
SP 10	99.36	6	6	0.44	8	15	12.6	3.3	512	24	120	1	3	0	5
SP 11	99	2	3	0.32	12	12	13.8	2.3	524	14	100	3	2	1	5
SP 12	100	4	2	0.76	9	16	11.2	2.1	712	12	120	3	3	2	1
SP 13	100	9	5	0.43	11	17	11	3	1254	16	90	3	3	5	2
SP 14	99.12	6	1	0.4	7	11	9.9	2.2	1812	22	105	1	2	1	4
SP 15	98	7	2	0.66	12	13	13	2.7	1412	18	160	2	3	1	3

Table 5. Service provider ranking

SP ID	Availability (%)	Accountability (1-10)	No. of VMs	Cost VM Cost $/h	Cost Data Inbound $/m	Capacity CPU Freq. Hrz	Capacity Disk GB	Service Response Time (sec)	Security (1-10)	Support (1-10)	Euclidean Distance *weightage	Latency (ms) *weightage	Total Score
SP 6	99.95	2	2	0.76	8	3.3	1712	150	2	3	82.89	32.1	114.99
SP 1	99.95	4	2	0.54	12	1.8	1512	120	1	3	86.96	29.1	116.06
SP 15	98	7	2	0.66	12	2.7	1412	160	2	3	83.79	34.9	118.69
SP 9	95.56	5	2	0.54	11	2.5	624	150	3	3	83.2	38	121.20
SP 2	100	8	4	0.34	11	2.5	712	180	1	2	87.16	34.35	121.51
SP 10	99.36	6	6	0.44	8	3.3	512	120	1	3	86.59	35.55	122.14
SP 3	99.91	4	2	0.65	9	2.2	360	120	2	3	86.92	35.25	122.17
SP 8	100	8	4	0.74	9	2.2	1524	125	1	2	85.95	36.9	122.85
SP 7	99	1	3	0.47	10	2.3	1624	195	3	3	91.07	32.25	123.25
SP 11	99	2	3	0.32	12	2.3	524	100	3	2	92.97	33.6	126.57
SP 12	100	4	2	0.76	9	2.1	712	120	3	3	87.05	39.6	126.60
SP 14	99.12	6	1	0.4	7	2.2	1812	105	1	2	91.16	39.3	130.46
SP 4	99.95	9	1	0.37	10	3.4	1512	100	3	3	93.89	37.35	131.24
SP 13	100	9	5	0.43	11	3	1254	90	3	3	98.32	36.3	134.62
SP 5	98.99	3	2	0.63	12	1.8	512	90	2	2	97.37	40.8	138.17

Reduct-2 *[Accountability, Availability, CPU Frequency, Data In-bound Cost, Disk, Security, Service Response Time, Storage Cost, Support, VM Cost]*

From the above reducts, we select the $Reduct - 1$ to design the Reduced Decision System (RDS). $Reduct - 1$ is chosen to generate the RDS because it has a higher number of QoS attribute matching with user request than $Reduct - 2$. For the above *User Request*, $Reduct - 1$ have seven QoS attributes matching, while $Reduct - 2$ only six. The same strategy is followed to select the best reduct when we have two or more reducts. In original IS as shown in Table 3 we are having 14 QoS attributes while after reduction of the information using the concept of reduct we have 10 QoS attributes. The % of data reduction we achieved here is approximately 28.5%. The number of reducts depends on the QoS attributes values and α precision. If we have a huge IS system with a large number of service providers and QoS attributes, Reducts will significantly minimize the searching space and help in getting better ranking of the CSPs.

At present, more than five hundred CSPs are offering their services. The website Cloud Service Market [27] and Cloud Harmony [21] makes an attempt to develop a common platform for CSPs to register their services, where more than 500 CSPs have been registered. Now, with the help of *User QoS Request* and *RDS*, we determine the *Euclidean Distance* of each CSPs. Next, we determine

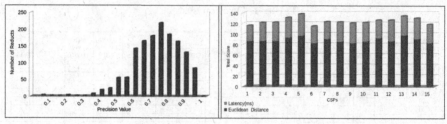

(a) Change in the number of Reducts with
Precision Value ($0 <= \alpha <= 1$).

(b) Service Provider Ranking based on Total Score.

Fig. 2. Results: service provider ranking

the *Total Score* of CSPs by the addition of *Euclidean Distance* with their respective *Latency* by assigning the weights as given by the user. We proposed 66.67% weightage to *Euclidean Distance* and 33.33% weightage to *Latency* in case if the user does not specify any weight. Finally, rank the CSPs in ascending order of their *Total Score* as shown in Table 5 and Fig. 2b. Here, smaller the *Total Score* represent the better Service Provider. *Service Provider* − 6 provide the best service as per-user QoS request.

6   Conclusions and Future Work

With the advancement of Internet technologies, cloud computing has become an important tool to fulfill various on-demand resource needs of the user. Currently, there are more than five hundred CSPs who are providing different services with different QoS and SLAs. From the user's point of view implementation of a cloud computing strategy become a very challenging task as it involves various management and operational aspects. There are several approaches to deal with such challenges, but for comparing different CSPs and their service offering, there is a need for cloud service broker. We proposed an efficient and effective cloud service broker FRSCB to meet the service requirements of the users. In our work, we categorized the QoS attributes in different types, that helps to identify the functional and non-functional QoS requirements of the users. The FRST is used to minimize the searching space. The proposed architecture is more stable and scalable than the previous work carried out in this field (rough set for cloud brokerage). The Euclidean distance is used to move to the model ideal value (zero line) which indicates the enhanced performance of the system. Our architecture can be more useful for the new cloud users who want to select the potential service provider to meet his/her QoS requirements. In future, we are planning to implement the proposed architecture for the on-line system by dynamically fetching information about QoS attributes and networking attributes provided by different CSPs.

References

1. Cloud Service Broker. https://www.techopedia.com/definition/26518/cloud-broker. Accessed June 2016
2. Zhao, B., Tung, Y.-K.: Determination of optimal unit hydrographs by linear programming. Water Resour. Manage. **8**(2), 101–119 (1994)
3. Sun, L., Dong, H., Hussain, F.K., Hussain, O.K., Chang, E.: Cloud service selection: state-of-the-art and future research directions. J. Netw. Comput. Appl. **45**, 134–150 (2014)
4. Garg, S.K., Versteeg, S., Buyya, R.: A framework for ranking of cloud computing services. Future Gener. Comput. Syst. **29**(4), 1012–1023 (2013)
5. Cloud Service Measurement Index Consortium (CSMIC), SMI framework. http://csmic.org. Accessed June 2016
6. Ganghishetti, P., Wankar, R.: Quality of service design in clouds. CSI Commun. **35**(2), 12–15 (2011)
7. Ganghishetti, P., Wankar, R., Almuttairi, R.M., Rao, C.R.: Rough set based quality of service design for service provisioning in clouds. In: Yao, J.T., Ramanna, S., Wang, G., Suraj, Z. (eds.) RSKT 2011. LNCS, vol. 6954, pp. 268–273. Springer, Heidelberg (2011). doi:10.1007/978-3-642-24425-4_36
8. Zadeh, L.A.: Fuzzy sets. Inf. Control **8**(3), 338–353 (1965)
9. Pawlak, Z., Skowron, A.: Rudiments of rough sets. Inf. Sci. **177**(1), 3–27 (2007)
10. Skowron, A., Jankowski, A., Swiniarski, R.W.: Foundations of rough sets. In: Kacprzyk, J., Pedrycz, W. (eds.) Springer Handbook of Computational Intelligence, pp. 331–348. Springer, Heidelberg (2015). doi:10.1007/978-3-662-43505-2_21
11. Jensen, R., Shen, Q.: Rough set-based feature selection. In: Rough Computing: Theories, Technologies, p. 70 (2008)
12. Gray, W.D., Boehm-Davis, D.A.: Milliseconds matter: an introduction to microstrategies and to their use in describing and predicting interactive behavior. J. Exp. Psychol.: Appl. **6**(4), 322 (2000)
13. Schad, J., Dittrich, J., Quiané-Ruiz, J.-A.: Runtime measurements in the cloud: observing, analyzing, and reducing variance. Proc. VLDB Endow. **3**(1–2), 460–471 (2010)
14. Foster, I., Zhao, Y., Raicu, I., Lu, S.: Cloud computing and grid computing 360-degree compared. In: Grid Computing Environments Workshop, GCE 2008, pp. 1–10. IEEE (2008)
15. Jain, A.K.: Data clustering: 50 years beyond k-means. Pattern Recogn. Lett. **31**(8), 651–666 (2010)
16. Tibshirani, R., Walther, G., Hastie, T.: Estimating the number of clusters in a data set via the gap statistic. J. R. Stat. Soc.: Ser. B (Stat. Methodol.) **63**(2), 411–423 (2001)
17. R Core Team: R Language Definition. R Foundation for Statistical Computing, Vienna, Austria (2000)
18. R Development Environment. https://www.rstudio.com/. Accessed June 2016
19. CRAN-package fgui: GUI interface. https://cran.r-project.org/web/packages/fgui/index.html. Accessed June 2016
20. Calheiros, R.N., Ranjan, R., Beloglazov, A., De Rose, C.A., Buyya, R.: CloudSim: a toolkit for modeling and simulation of cloud computing environments and evaluation of resource provisioning algorithms. Softw.: Pract. Exp. **41**(1), 23–50 (2011)
21. Cloud Harmony. http://cloudharmony.com. Accessed June 2016

22. Catteddu, D., Hogben, G., et al.: Cloud computing information assurance framework. In: European Network and Information Security Agency (ENISA) (2009)
23. Cloud Security Alliance (CSA): Cloud Control Matrix (CCM). https:// cloudsecurityalliance.org/group/cloud-controls-matrix/. Accessed June 2016
24. Jensen, R., Shen, Q.: New approaches to fuzzy-rough feature selection. IEEE Trans. Fuzzy Syst. **17**(4), 824–838 (2009)
25. Pawlak, Z.: Rough sets. Int. J. Comput. Inf. Sci. **11**(5), 341–356 (1982)
26. CRAN-package roughsets. https://CRAN.R-project.org/package=RoughSets. Accessed July 2017
27. Cloud service market: a comprehensive overview of cloud computing services. http://www.cloudservicemarket.info. Accessed June 2016

Generating Tutorial Interventions for Teaching Situation Awareness in Dental Surgery – Preliminary Report

Narumol Vannaprathip[1(✉)], Peter Haddawy[1,2], Holger Schultheis[2], and Siriwan Suebnukarn[3]

[1] Faculty of ICT, Mahidol University, Nakhon Pathom, Thailand
narumol.van@student.mahidol.ac.th,
peter.had@mahidol.ac.th
[2] Bremen Spatial Cognition Center, University of Bremen, Bremen, Germany
schulth@informatik.uni-bremen.de
[3] Faculty of Dentistry, Thammasat University,
Pathum Thani, Thailand
ssiriwan@tu.ac.th

Abstract. Situation awareness is known to be a critical skill in surgical decision making. While a few simulators have been developed to teach surgical decision making, none explicitly address teaching situation awareness skills. In this paper we present a knowledge representation framework that captures the key elements in reasoning about situation awareness. The framework makes use of concepts from AI planning and uses PDDL to represent surgical procedures. We describe tutorial feedback strategies identified in a preliminary observational study of endodontic surgery. We then present algorithms that implement these strategies using the knowledge representation framework. We show how the representation supports generating a number of tutorial interventions observed in teaching sessions by expert endodontic surgeons. We finally describe the contributions of our work.

Keywords: Surgical decision making · Situation awareness · Intelligent Tutoring System · Pedagogical intervention · AI planning · Knowledge representation

1 Introduction

Using simulation for teaching surgical skills has become popular due to the limitations and challenges in the traditional Halstedian apprenticeship approach. Existing surgical simulations have focused mainly on technical skills and have not fulfilled their potential in supporting the teaching of decision making skills [1] even though 75% of important events in the operating room are related to decision making [2]. The few simulators that have been developed for teaching surgical decision making [3] focus on correct choices of actions in individual procedures and less on teaching the underlying decision making skills and on developing an understanding of the reasons for appropriate actions.

© Springer International Publishing AG 2017
S. Phon-Amnuaisuk et al. (Eds.): MIWAI 2017, LNAI 10607, pp. 69–74, 2017.
https://doi.org/10.1007/978-3-319-69456-6_6

An essential skill in surgical decision making is situation awareness (SA) [4, 5]. Situation awareness can be characterized as "the perception of the elements in the environment within a volume of time and space, the comprehension of their meaning, and the projection of their status in the near future" [6]. Perception involves gathering the relevant information from the environment at a specific point in time. Comprehension is the ability to interpret and understand the current situation with respect to the goal. Projection involves mentally seeing the future status and understanding the associated consequences.

In earlier work, we addressed the issue of incorporating essential perceptual cues in a simulator for teaching dental surgery as a step toward addressing the teaching of SA [7]. In the present paper, we take a further step by developing a representation and pedagogical module capable of generating tutorial dialog to teach SA skills.

2 Observational Study

After approval from the Institution's Ethics Committee, an oral surgical unit within Thammasat University teaching hospital was used to collect the data. An observational study of five teaching sessions (one trainee per session) of endodontic treatment was conducted. Each trainee carried out root canal treatment on a patient under the supervision of an endodontist. Actions and discussions during and after surgery were recorded via video camera and transcribed. They were analyzed to identify the teaching strategies and their triggers. The content of each teaching intervention was examined based on Endsley's situation awareness framework [6]. We found eight strategies for teaching situation awareness, which are elaborations of eight of the 27 teaching behaviors identified by Hauge et al. [8]. We have implemented six of these strategies and in this paper we present two of them. The first strategy responds to incorrect student actions by pointing out undesired outcomes and their causes (Strategy 1). The second strategy is a retrospective discussion in which the tutor queries the student's understanding of the task after completion (Strategy 2).

3 Representation and Algorithm

We use a subset of the Planning Domain Definition Language (PDDL) [9] to represent surgical procedural knowledge such as sequences of actions, action parameters, dependencies between actions, and action effects that vary depending on the state in which the action is executed; and to represent the elements of Endsley's SA framework [6], including perceivable elements of the domain and the processes of comprehension and projection. Facts relating to the three elements of the SA framework are represented by three types of propositions: perception, comprehension, and projection. The relation between perception and comprehension propositions is represented with domain rules. Actions have conditional effects (projections) and perception and comprehension propositions can appear in the condition formulas. The effects represent both the desired and relevant undesired action outcomes.

We use PDDL4J [10] as a parser for PDDL version 3.1, which is the latest version at the time of implementation. Because the derived_predicates in PDDL4 J do not support negated propositions in the domain axioms, we use the axiom module from PDDL version 1.2 instead. Given a set of actions, domain rules, perception propositions in the current state, and an action chosen by the student with its parameters, the system uses forward chaining and plan projection to generate a directed graph data structure representing the various SA components and their relationships (Fig. 1). Perceptions (P nodes) link to comprehensions (C nodes). P nodes and C nodes can influence the outcomes of actions or projections (Pj nodes) by linking to the conditions (AC nodes) of actions (A nodes). Take, for example, the Try Main Cone step in which the gutta percha main cone is fitted to the root canal. To insert the main cone (action), a student has to be aware that the root canal is irrigated (perception), which means the root canal is clean (comprehension), resulting in an uncontaminated root canal (projection) after the action. In some cases, perceived information needs no interpretation and can be used directly to determine action outcomes. For example, to define main cone size we need only know the master apical file (MAF) size (perception). Figure 1 shows a portion of the graph data structure for the Try Main Cone step.

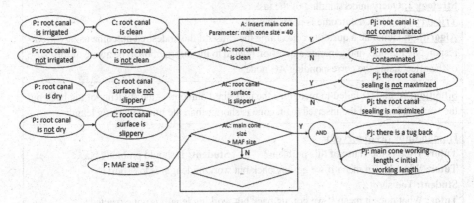

Fig. 1. A partial model of the Try Main Cone step

Following action projection, the status of task completion and the correctness of the action outcomes trigger selection of a teaching strategy. Once the strategy is selected, the corresponding template containing the tutoring message and required SA nodes is loaded. To generate an explanation, starting from the Pj nodes, the pedagogical module traces back to the parent P nodes through intermediate AC and C nodes and inserts the relevant information into the template. The propositions are transformed into English didactic phrases. Figures 2 and 3 show the comparison of the observed human tutor intervention and the content generated by the automated tutor for strategies 1 and 2 of the rubber dam application step and the try main cone step, respectively.

Strategy 1: Explain why the action is incorrect by pointing out the undesired outcome and its causes   **Trigger:** Student's action is incorrect   **Algorithm:** Trace back from the Pj node of the undesired outcome to its parent AC node
Situation: Student applied a rubber dam covering the patient's nose
Human tutor (as observed):   **Tutor:** Open some areas for breathing. Otherwise, the patient gets syncope. Look there is no area for breathing.
Automated tutor: **Tutor:** You insert the rubber dam and clamp *[Action]* such that the position of rubber dam covers the nose of the patient *[AC node]*. The patient is at risk of syncope *[Pj]*.

Fig. 2. Human and automated tutor intervention for strategy 1

Strategy 2: Query understanding of the task   **Trigger:** The desired outcome is not achieved   **Algorithm:** Generate a question concerning the cause of the undesired outcome using the corresponding Pj node, and generate a question related to the information to be aware of the cause of the effect using the corresponding AC node.
Situation: A student failed to recognize the undesired outcome – the student got tug back but the working length of the inserted main cone is shorter than the initial working length.
Human tutor (as observed):   **Tutor:** What is the cause of this problem?　　**Student:** It should probably be….   **Tutor:** What does it mean if we got tug back but working length is too short?   **Student:** Too short…   **Tutor:** What does it mean if we got tug back but working length is not expected?   **Student:** It is too large.　　**Tutor:** Yes,
Automated tutor: **Tutor:** What causes presence of tug back resistance *[Pj]* and the working length of the main cone less than the initial working length *[Pj]*?   　1) the main cone size is greater than the MAF size *[AC node]*   　2) the main cone size is less than the MAF size *[AC node]*   　3) the root canal is clean *[AC node]*   　4) the main cone size equals the MAF size *[AC node]*   **Student:** Answer (number): 3　　**Tutor:** This is not correct.   **Tutor:** What kind of information do you need to decide for the main cone size [AC node]?   　1) the root canal is irrigated *[P node]*　　2) the root canal is dried *[P node]*   　3) the MAF size *[P node]*　　4) the root canal is not irrigated *[P node]*

Fig. 3. Human and automated tutor intervention for strategy 2

4   Discussion and Conclusion

This paper has presented a novel approach to represent surgical procedural knowledge and generate tutorial interventions to teach situated decision making in dental surgery. The PDDL representation is able to capture key elements of the surgical procedure and Endsley's SA framework to support rich tutorial dialog. Our approach combines three features that render it particularly suitable for its target domain: It (a) allows for conditional effects, (b) is modelled on the SA framework, and (c) supports automatic generation of feedback. This combination is not available in previous work on Computer Interpretable Guidelines (CIG) [11], Intelligent Tutoring Systems [12–15], and Plan Critiquing [16–18]. While many representations that have been used for Intelligent Tutoring Systems (See [19] for an overview) possess a subset of these three features, none of the existing systems support all of these features in combination. For example, constraint-based models [12] and qualitative models [13] do not support conditional action effects. Representations used for CIGs also do not support conditional effects since their purpose is to represent recommended actions. The representations employed in Plan Critiquing are not tailored to teaching SA [16, 18].

Our implementation is yet preliminary with a number of ways it can be improved. The teaching strategies are currently limited to explanations concerning outcomes of single steps in a procedure. We cannot yet handle explanations involving interactions among steps. The current implementation also assumes that actions have deterministic outcomes even though some possible effects of an executed action may not actually happen in surgery. Such risks can be represented using non-deterministic effects. We plan to represent the non-deterministic effects using the `oneof` operator from NDDPL [20]. In addition to these extensions, next steps will include integrating the pedagogical module into our existing virtual reality simulator [21] and evaluating the quality of the generated feedback.

Acknowledgements. We thank the Faculty of Dentistry, Thammasat University for the support of the observational study. We gratefully acknowledge funding by the Hanse-Wissenschaftskolleg Institute for Advanced Study, Delmenhorst, Germany (Haddawy, Suebnukarn), the Santander BISIP Scholarship (Vannaprathip), and the Thailand Research Fund (RDG6050029).

References

1. Andersen, D.K.: How can educators use simulation applications to teach and assess surgical judgment? Acad. Med. **87**, 934–941 (2012)
2. Spencer, F.: Teaching and measuring surgical techniques: the technical evaluation of competence. Bull. Am. Coll. Surg. **63**, 9–12 (1978)
3. Lin, D.T., Park, J., Liebert, C.A., Lau, J.N.: Validity evidence for Surgical Improvement of Clinical Knowledge Ops: a novel gaming platform to assess surgical decision making. Am. J. Surg. **209**, 79–85 (2015)
4. Flin, R., Youngson, G., Yule, S.: How do surgeons make intraoperative decisions? Qual. Saf. Health Care. **16**, 235–239 (2007)

5. Schulz, C.M., Krautheim, V., Hackemann, A., Kreuzer, M., Kochs, E.F., Wagner, K.J.: Situation awareness errors in anesthesia and critical care in 200 cases of a critical incident reporting system. BMC Anesthesiol. **16**, 4 (2016)

6. Endsley, M.R.: Toward a theory of situation awareness in dynamic systems. Hum. Factors J. Hum. Factors Ergon. Soc. **37**, 32–64 (1995)

7. Vannaprathip, N., Haddawy, P.: Desitra : a simulator for teaching situated decision making in dental surgery. In: 21st International Conference on Intelligent User Interfaces, IUI 2016, pp. 397–401. ACM (2016)

8. Hauge, L.S., Wanzek, J.A., Godellas, C.: The reliability of an instrument for identifying and quantifying surgeons' teaching in the operating room. Am. J. Surg. **181**, 333–337 (2001)

9. Kovacs, D.L.: BNF definition of PDDL 3.1. Unpublished Manuscript from IPC-2011 website (2011)

10. Pellier, D.: PDDL4J. https://github.com/pellierd/pddl4j. Accessed 28 Nov 2016

11. De Clercq, P.A., Blom, J.A., Korsten, H.H.M., Hasman, A.: Approaches for creating computer-interpretable guidelines that facilitate decision support. Artif. Intell. Med. **31**, 1–27 (2004)

12. Mitrovic, A.: A knowledge-based teaching system for SQL difficulties with learning SQL overview of SQL-Tutor. Proc. ED-MEDIA. **98**, 1027–1032 (1998)

13. Evens, M.W., Chang, R.-C., Lee, Y.H., Shim, L.S., Woo, C.W., Zhang, Y., Michael, J.A., Rovick, A.A.: CIRCSIM-Tutor: an intelligent tutoring system using natural language dialogue. In: Proceedings of the Fifth Conference on Applied Natural Language Processing: Descriptions of System Demonstrations and Videos, pp. 13–14. Association for Computational Linguistics (1997)

14. Gertner, A.S., VanLehn, K.: Andes: a coached problem solving environment for physics. In: Gauthier, G., Frasson, C., VanLehn, K. (eds.) ITS 2000. LNCS, vol. 1839, pp. 133–142. Springer, Heidelberg (2000). doi:10.1007/3-540-45108-0_17

15. Graesser, A.C., Person, N.K., Harter, D., Tutoring Research Group: Teaching tactics and dialog in AutoTutor. Int. J. Artif. Intell. Educ. **12**, 257–279 (2001)

16. Miller, P.L.: ATTENDING: critiquing physician's management plan. IEEE Trans. Pattern Anal. Mach. Intell. **5**, 449–461 (1983)

17. Mengshoel, O.J., Wilkins, D.C.: Recognition and critiquing of erroneous agent actions. In: AAAI-96 Workshop on Agent Modeling, pp. 61–68. AAAI Press, Portland (1996)

18. Rymon, R.: Goal-directed diagnosis—a diagnostic reasoning framework for exploratory-corrective domains. Artif. Intell. **84**, 257–297 (1996)

19. Mendjoge, N., Joshi, A.R., Narvekar, M.: Review of knowledge representation techniques for intelligent tutoring system. In: International Conference on Computing for Sustainable Global Development (INDIACom), pp. 2508–2512 (2016)

20. Bertoli, P., Cimatti, A., Lago, U.D., Pistore, M.: Extending PDDL to nondeterminism, limited sensing and iterative conditional plans. In: ICAPS 2003 Workshop on PDDL (2003)

21. Sararit, N., Haddawy, P., Suebnukarn, S.: A VR simulator for emergency management in endodontic surgery. In: Companion Publication of the 22nd International Conference on Intelligent User Interfaces. ACM (2017)

Data Mining and Machine Learning

Validation of Machine Learning Classifiers Using Metamorphic Testing and Feature Selection Techniques

Sadam Al-Azani and Jameleddine Hassine[⊠]

Department of Information and Computer Science,
King Fahd University of Petroleum and Minerals, Dahran, Saudi Arabia
{g201002580,jhassine}@kfupm.edu.sa

Abstract. Testing involves examining the behavior of a system in order to discover potential faults. Given an input for a system, the challenge of distinguishing the correct behavior from potentially incorrect one, is called the "test oracle problem". Metamorphic testing has shown great potential in overcoming the test oracle problem. In this work, we apply metamorphic testing to validate experimentally machine learning classification algorithms, namely Naïve Bayes (NB) and k-Nearest Neighbor (k-NN) individually and in combination (i.e., ensemble classifications methods), using real-world biomedical datasets. Furthermore, advanced feature selection techniques and synthetic minority over-sampling technique (SMOTE) are used in order to generate our test suite and meet the requirements of the specified metamorphic relations. While, this study reveal that NB and k-NN satisfy the specified metamorphic relations, it also concludes that it is not compulsory that the metamorphic relations that are necessary for NB and k-NN individually, are also necessary for their ensemble classifier.

1 Introduction

Machine learning techniques have been widely accepted for providing support in many application domains, such as pattern recognition, bioinformatics, and computational linguistics. Building highly accurate machine learning models for classification, prediction, or clustering is one of the core objectives for solving real-world problems. Hence, it is essential to test and validate machine learning-based applications to ensure their correctness. However, little effort has been devoted to test such applications [13]. Assuring the correctness of machine learning applications remains one the major challenges for their successful deployment, due to the inherent complexity of the computational logics embedded within the learning algorithms. Furthermore, conventional software testing techniques might not be applicable to such applications, due to the lack of test oracle. A test oracle is a mechanism that is used during testing to determine whether a software behaves correctly or not as a result of the execution of a test case. The inability to distinguish the desired behavior from a potentially incorrect behavior is called the "test oracle problem".

© Springer International Publishing AG 2017
S. Phon-Amnuaisuk et al. (Eds.): MIWAI 2017, LNAI 10607, pp. 77–91, 2017.
https://doi.org/10.1007/978-3-319-69456-6_7

The main motivation of this research is to apply metamorphic testing and feature selection techniques in order to validate experimentally machine learning methods. More particularly, we are interested in applying the metamorphic relations, introduced in [13], to validate Naïve Bayes (NB) and k-Nearest Neighbor (k-NN) classifiers and their combination (ensemble classification method), implemented in the WEKA (Waikato Environment for Knowledge Analysis) workbench [11], using real-world bioinformatics datasets.

The contributions of this paper are as follows:

– We employed metamorphic testing to evaluate machine learning classifiers, namely NB and k-NN classifiers, implemented in WEKA-3.6.13, using two publicly available real-life biomedical datasets. Contrary to synthetic datasets (used in [13]), biomedical datasets are characterized by their high dimensionality, multiple classes, noise and missing values, which are known challenges posed to classification algorithms.
– We applied and evaluated NB and k-NN individually and in combination through employing ensemble classification methods.
– We applied feature selection techniques, e.g., CFS and ChiS and SMOTE [1] to generate different test cases, as discussed in Sect. 3.

The rest of this paper is organized as follows. The background of this research and the related work is presented in Sect. 2. Section 3 describes the conducted experiments and presents the obtained results. The conclusions are drawn in Sect. 4.

2 Background and Related Work

Researchers have proposed some techniques to overcome the "test oracle problem" [2,3]. One such attempt, is the one introduced by Davis and Weyuker [3] (called pseudo-oracle). It consists on using multiple implementations of an algorithm to process the same input and then comparing their results. If the results are different, then it can be concluded that there is a defect in one or several implementations. However, this technique may not be always feasible because of the lack of multiple reasonably different implementations. Another technique is to use "metamorphic testing" [2]. Metamorphic testing method employs properties or rules (called, metamorphic relations) of the target function to generate follow-up test cases and verify the outputs automatically [14].

For machine learning, Murphy et al. [7] identified six metamorphic properties namely additive, multiplicative, permutative, invertive, inclusive, and exclusive, which are available in many machine learning applications. The most closely related work to ours is the one by Xie et al. [12,13] in which the authors defined and applied eleven metamorphic relations to validate machine learning classifiers. They were able to detect faults experimentally using synthetic datasets. For a thorough and complete literature survey on metamorphic testing, interested readers are referred to [9].

k-NN is a non-parametric method used for classification and regression. k-NN computes the distance between each training sample and the test sample by using several distance measurements such as Euclidean Distance, Cityblock Distance, Minkowski Distance, etc. NB classifier is a simple probabilistic classifier that applies theorem of Bayes with strong (naïve) independence assumptions between the attributes. A well-known strategy to get accurate classifiers is *ensemble learning*. The ensemble learning consists on combining various learning algorithms to obtain more accurate classifiers compared to single learning algorithms. Several approaches have been proposed to build ensemble classification methods, including *bagging, boosting, voting* and *stacking*. Boosting and bagging combine homogeneous models, while voting and stacking can combine heterogeneous base classifiers [10]. In homogeneous ensemble classifier, the base models are generated using the same classifier (e.g., decision trees), whereas in heterogeneous ensemble classifier, each base model is generated by a different classifier. Voting method is excluded, in this study, since it is preferred when the number of base classifier is odd. Since NB and k-NN are heterogeneous and not odd, we will focus on combining theses classifiers using stacking method.

Stacking combine different base classifiers $(clf_1, clf_2, clf_3, \ldots, clf_n)$ using the second-level classifier (meta-classifier). In the first level, each base classifier is trained using the training set and the predictions of each base classifier $(p_1, p_2, p_3, \ldots, p_n)$ are used to create a new feature representation to train the meta-classifier to generate the final prediction (P_f) (see Fig. 1). The stacking combination level doesn't only depend on the predictions of base classifiers but also on the second level classifier. Therefore, with this ensemble learning method, it is not necessary for metamorphic relations to be achieved if it is necessary for the base classifiers (naïve bayes and k-NN classifiers).

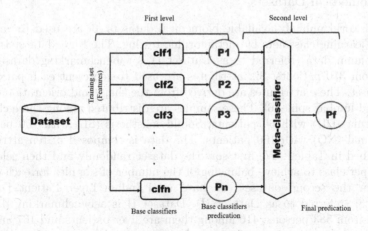

Fig. 1. Stacking-based ensemble learning

It is worth noting that our focus is not to improve the recognition rates but to test and validate the aforementioned algorithms individually and in combination using the metamorphic relations [13].

Feature selection, also called "attribute selection", is an effective technique to get rid of the redundant, noisy, or irrelevant attributes. Feature selection is carried out through searching the space of the attribute subset and evaluating each one by combining a feature evaluator with a search method. In this work, we use Correlation-based Feature Selection (CFS) [4] as feature evaluator along with *Best-first search* method. CFS selects sets of attributes that are highly correlated with the class but uncorrelated to each other [4]. Best-first search method employs greedy hill climbing algorithm with backtracking facility. Furthermore, we use *Chi-Square* (ChiS) to support the outcomes of CFS, as described in Sect. 3. ChiS evaluates attributes with respect to a class through computing the Chi-square statistic [11]. Both CFS and ChiS feature selection techniques are filtering methods. In this work, they are employed to determine the uninformative and informative attributes, which are related to the applied metamorphic relations.

Synthetic Minority Over-sampling Technique (SMOTE) is an over-sampling algorithm that aims to overcome the problem of imbalanced datasets by over-sampling the minority class [1]. This is conducted by generating artificial samples instead of over-sampling with replacement. Generating artificial examples by using SMOTE algorithm relies on the feature space similarities between existing minority examples [5].

3 Empirical Validation

3.1 Biomedical Datasets

Two real-world publicly available biomedical datasets [6] are used to validate machine learning classifiers by metamorphic testing. The First dataset is: Vertebral column data (referred to as Dataset I) is a benchmarking dataset collected from 310 patients. Six attributes are used to represent each patient in the Dataset. These attributes are derived from the shape and orientation of the pelvis and lumbar spine [6]. These samples are distributed among three classes: Disk Hernia (DH) with 60 patients, Spondylolisthesis (SL) with 150 patients and Normal (NO) with 100 patients. The data is composed of ten attributes as described in Table 1. We first sort the dataset randomly and then select 60 samples per class to achieve balancing of the number of samples for each class.

As for the second dataset, we have used Indian Liver Patient Dataset (ILPD) [8] (referred to as Dataset II). Dataset II is a benchmarking dataset collected from 583 persons: 416 among them are liver patients and 167 are not. We also consider only 160 samples for each class to alleviate the problem of imbalanced dataset. The data is composed of ten attributes described in Table 2. Both Datasets are downloaded from University of California at Irvine (UCI) Machine Learning Repository [6].

Table 1. Dataset I attributes

Attribute name	Description	Type of data
PelvicIn	Pelvic incidence	Real
PelvicTilt	Pelvic tilt	Real
LumLAngle	Lumbar lordosis angle	Real
SacralSlope	Sacral slope	Real
PelvicRadius	Pelvic radius	Real
GradeSp	Grade of spondylolisthesis	Real

Table 2. Dataset II attributes

Attribute name	Description	Type of data
Age	Age of the patient	Integer
Gender	Gender of the patient	Categorical
TB	Total Bilirubin	Real
DB	Direct Bilirubin	Real
Alkphos	Alkaline Phosphotase	Integer
Sgpt	Alamine Aminotransferase	Integer
Sgot	Aspartate Aminotransferase	Integer
TP	Total Protiens	Real
ALB	Albumin	Real
AG Ratio	Albumin and globulin ratio	Real

3.2 Experiments and Results

We use NB and k-NN implementations in WEKA-3.6.13 (with its default parameters). Furthermore, two different structures of stacking classifier are used to
concrete the findings and results as follows: (1) NB is used as meta-classifier
(referred to as *Ensemble NB*) and (2) k-NN is used as a meta classifier (referred
to as *Ensemble k-NN*). In what follows, we briefly present the used metamorphic
relations, introduced in [12,13], and describe the adopted procedure.

1. **MR-0: Consistence with affine transformation:** *Applying the same
   arbitrary affine transformation function does not affect the results.*

   In this experiment, the two datasets are used. The source input is designed
   for this metamorphic relation as follows. Seventy percent of each dataset is
   used for training and 30% is used as test data. For the follow-up input, we
   normalized the values to be ranged within the interval [0, 1]. The test data is
   used in both source input and follow-up cases cover all classes. The obtained
   classification accuracy rates are shown in Table 3.

   Analysis: MR-0 is a necessary relation to be achieved using NB and k-NN,
   we found that NB and k-NN meet this metamorphic relation. While MR-0

is necessary for both NB and k-NN and also achieved using both datasets, it is not achieved using the ensemble classifiers, which is not necessary for the ensemble.

Table 3. MR-0 classification accuracy rates (%)

	Dataset I		Dataset II		Dataset I		Dataset II	
	NB	k-NN	NB	k-NN	Ensemble NB	Ensemble k-NN	Ensemble NB	Ensemble k-NN
Source input	72.22	61.11	70.83	59.38	68.52	66.67	70.83	65.63
Follow-up input	72.22	61.11	70.83	59.38	66.67	66.67	70.83	62.5

2. **MR-1.1: Permutation of class labels:** *This rule addresses the effects of swapping the labels of classes. Conducting one-to-one mapping between a class label in the set of labels L to another label in L. If the source case result is l_i, the result of the follow-up case should be $Perm(l_i)$ when applying the permutation function to the set of corresponding class labels C for the follow-up case.*

The same training and testing sets used in MR-0 are used for this relation to generate the source input cases. For the follow-up input, labels of classes are swapped. The results are shown in Table 4.

Analysis: MR-1.1 is necessary for NB only and it is achieved using all classifiers.

Table 4. MR-1.1 classification accuracy rates (%)

	Dataset I		Dataset II		Dataset I		Dataset II	
	NB	k-NN	NB	k-NN	Ensemble NB	Ensemble k-NN	Ensemble NB	Ensemble k-NN
Source input	72.22	61.11	70.83	59.38	68.52	66.67	70.83	65.63
Follow-up input	72.22	61.11	70.83	59.38	68.52	66.67	70.83	65.63

3. **MR-1.2: Permutation of the attribute**: *This relation addresses the effects of reordering the attributes. Permute the set of attributes in both training samples and test cases has no effects in the results.*

The same scenario of MR$_7$0 and MR-1.1 is used to generate the source input tests. For the follow-up input, we permute the attributes for all the samples in the training and the testing data. The results are shown in Table 5.

Analysis: MR-1.2 is necessary for both NB and k-NN and not necessary for the ensemble. The results show that MR-1.2 is achieved using all classifiers.

Table 5. MR-1.2 classification accuracy rates (%)

| | Dataset I | | Dataset II | | Dataset I | Dataset II | Dataset II | |
	NB	k-NN	NB	k-NN	Ensemble NB	Ensemble k-NN	Ensemble NB	Ensemble k-NN
Source input	72.22	61.11	70.83	59.38	68.52	66.67	70.83	65.63
Follow-up input	72.22	61.11	70.83	59.38	68.52	66.67	70.83	65.63

Table 6. MR-2.1 classification accuracy rates (%)

| | Dataset I | | Dataset II | | Dataset I | Dataset II | Dataset II | |
	NB	k-NN	NB	k-NN	Ensemble NB	Ensemble k-NN	Ensemble NB	Ensemble k-NN
Source input	72.22	61.11	70.83	59.38	68.52	66.67	70.83	65.63
Follow-up input (I)	72.22	61.11	70.83	59.38	68.52	66.67	70.83	65.63
Follow-up input (II)	-	-	70.83	59.38	-	-	70.83	58.33

4. **MR-2.1: Addition of uninformative attributes:** *Adding uninformative attributes to both training and testing sets to create the follow-up input has no effect on the test samples that have been classified correctly in the source input.*

Uninformative attributes are irrelevant, redundant or noisy attributes. The same training and testing datasets used for MR-0 and MR-1.1 are used to create the source input tests. For the follow-up input, two different assumptions are investigated:

- Add an attribute, called "AttIrr", with a value of 10 to all samples in the training and testing sets, for both datasets I and II. The results are shown in Table 6.

– Determine the most uninformative attributes in the datasets and repeat them. The least informative attribute is determined by applying the feature selection techniques, i.e., Correlation-based Feature Selection (CFS) [4] and Chi-square (ChiS), which are implemented in WEKA. If the attribute is not selected by CFS and has the lowest rank by Chi-square, we consider it as an uninformative attribute. For Dataset I, CFS selected "SacralSlope", "PelvicRadius", and "Spattributes", while Chi-square ranked the attributes as shown in Table 7. Hence, we don't apply this assumption to Dataset I, because the attributes that are considered as uninformative by CFS have a high rank in Chi-square. For Dataset II, CFS selected "TB", "DB", "Alkphos", "Sgpt", "Sgot", and "TP" attributes as the most significant ones, while it considered "Age", "Gender", and "ALB" as insignificant attributes. By ranking these attributes using Chi-square, "Age" and "Gender" attributes earned the lowest ranks, as shown in Table 8. Hence, we have only considered Dataset II, since it has uninformative attributes. For the follow-up input, we duplicated the "Age" attribute and the results are shown in Table 6.

Table 7. Dataset I ranks using Chi-Square

Rank	Attribute	Rank	Attribute
162.6	GradeSp	97.288	PelvicIn
108.894	SacralSlope	32.308	PelvicTilt
103.28	LumLAngle	25.311	PelvicRadius

Analysis: MR-2.1 is necessary for NB and k-NN. In the first scenario, we found that this relation is achieved for all algorithms. In the second scenario, we found that only NB and k-NN achieve this relation.

Table 8. Dataset II ranks using Chi-Square

Rank	Attribute	Rank	Attribute
63.0823	Sgot	22.6483	ALB
61.4495	TB	21.9955	AGRatio
58.8088	DB	20.0592	TP
57.3952	Sgpt	17.034	Age
54.8701	Alkphos	4.3399	Gender

5. **MR-2.2: Addition of informative attributes**: *Adding informative attributes to both training and testing sets to create the follow-up input has no effects on the test samples that are classified correctly in the source input.*

We used the same training and testing sets used for previous metamorphic relations to create the source input (source input (I)). For the follow-up input, we added an attribute called "AttRel" with values one for class1, two for class2 (for both datasets I and II), and three for class3 (in dataset I) to all samples in the training and testing sets (follow-up input (I)). The results are shown in Table 9.

Analysis: MR-2.2 is necessary only for NB. In the first scenario, we found that if a sample s_1 is classified correctly using the source input test then it is classified correctly in follow-up input test. However, if s_1 is not classified correctly using the source input case then it is most likely classified correctly in follow-up input test. These results are expected and reasonable because the informative attribute is the dominant attribute and it has positive effect to classify those samples that cannot be classified in the first scenario. Hence, the results obtained using this relation improved in the follow-up input cases without impacting those samples that have been classified correctly in the source input case. This relation is achieved using all classifiers. In the second scenario, the samples, classified perfectly in the source input case, are also classified correctly in the follow-up case. Additionally, for Dataset I, two samples that were not classified in the source input case using ensemble based k-NN classifier were classified correctly in the follow-up case. For Dataset II, one sample that was not classified in the source input case using ensemble based k-NN classifier was classified correctly in the follow-up case. These outcomes are expected because, intuitively, adding the informative attributes result in a correct classification of a sample that was not classified correctly in the source input case. As a result, this relation is also achieved using all algorithms.

We have also investigated another scenario, in which the source input (II) is created by excluding the most informative attribute, which is "GradeSp", in the dataset I. Seven samples that belong to class "DH" are used. For the follow-up input (II), we added the informative attribute "GradeSp" along with its corresponding values for training and testing. The results are shown in Table 9. As per Dataset II, the source input (II) was created by excluding the most informative attribute, which is "Sgot". For the follow-up input (II) of Dataset II, we added the informative attribute "Sgot" along with its corresponding values for training and testing. The results are shown in Table 9.

For the remaining metamorphic relations Dataset I is chosen for conducting the experiments because it has more classes than Dataset II.

6. **MR-3.1: Consistence with re-prediction:** *Appending a test sample that has been classified correctly in the source input to the training set will not affect the results in the follow-up input.*

We used 60% of samples (108 samples) for training as source input case (I) and nine samples belonging to "DH" as test cases classified correctly using NB and k-NN. For the follow-up case (I), we appended a sample having a label from the test set to the training set, such that the training set of the follow-up case is increased by one sample. The results of both source case (I) and follow-up case (I) are shown in Table 10.

Table 9. MR-2.2 classification accuracy rates (%)

	Dataset I		Dataset II		Dataset I		Dataset II	
	NB	k-NN	NB	k-NN	Ensemble NB	Ensemble k-NN	Ensemble NB	Ensemble k-NN
Source input I	72.22	61.11	70.83	59.38	68.52	66.67	70.83	65.63
Follow-up input I	96.30	100	80.21	100	100	100	100	100
Source input II	100	100	100	100	100	42.86	100	57.14
Follow-up input II	100	100	100	100	100	71.43	100	85.71

Instead of using all samples which are correctly classified by NB and k-NN, an additional scenario is considered, that consists on replacing one sample with another one that belongs to "DH" and it is not classified correctly by k-NN (Source input II). Then we appended that sample to the training set to generate follow-up input (II). The results of this scenario are illustrated in Table 10.

Analysis: MR-3.1 is necessary for k-NN only. It is achieved using NB and k-NN but is not achieved using the ensemble. The results of k-NN were improved because the added sample has a positive effect on the classification of the samples that were not classified correctly in the input source case, which is a reasonable and expected outcome. However, in case of ensemble based k-NN classifier the results are not expected because this sample has negative impact on classification accuracy.

Table 10. MR-3.1 classification accuracy rates (%)

	Dataset I			
	NB	k-NN	Ensemble NB	Ensemble k-NN
Source input I	100	100	100	66.67
Follow-up input I	100	100	100	77.78
Source input II	100	88.89	100	77.78
Follow-up input II	100	100	100	55.56

7. **MR-3.2: Additional training sample:** *Duplicating all samples in the training set that belong to class l_i to create the follow-up input has no effect on the results for test samples that have been classified correctly as class l_i in the source input.*

Two scenarios are created and then investigated. In the first scenario, we used 60% of samples (108 samples) for training (source input I), we duplicate samples of class "SL" (follow-up input II) and for testing we used 20% (64 samples). The results of this scenarion are shown in Table 11.

Another scenario, consists on taking 25 samples for class1 "DH" and 36 for class2 "NO" and 36 samples for class3 "SL" as training set (source input II). This training set suffers from the imbalanced dataset problem. To achieve balancing, we applied SMOTE technique [1] to add synthetic training samples for the class1 "DH" as follow-up input case II. For testing cases, seven samples belonging to class "DH", classified correctly using NB and k-NN in the source input case II, are used as test samples for both source input II and follow-up input II. The results are illustrated in Table 11.

Analysis: MR-3.2 is necessary for NB and k-NN. This relation is achieved by NB and k-NN, and is not achieved using the ensemble.

Table 11. MR-3.2 classification accuracy rates (%)

	Dataset I			
	NB	k-NN	Ensemble NB	Ensemble k-NN
Source input I	86.11	80.56	86.11	72.22
Follow-up input I	86.11	80.56	86.11	69.44
Source input II	100	100	100	100
Follow-up input II	100	100	100	85.71

8. **MR-4.1: Addition of classes by duplicating samples**: *Duplicating all samples from any number of classes which do not have label l_i should not change the result of the output of the follow-up input.*

   Sixty percent of samples (108 samples) are used for training (source input case). For follow-up input, the samples of classes "NO" and "SL" were duplicated while changing their labels to be "NO*" and "SL*", resulting in the follow-up input having five classes "DH", "NO", "SL", "NO*", "SL*". For the test case, we have selected nine test cases of class "DH" and conducted the experiments. The results are depicted in Table 12.

   Analysis: MR-4.1 is a necessary relation to be achieved using NB only. All classifiers achieve this metamorphic relation.

9. **MR-4.2: Addition of classes by re-labeling samples**: *Given a test case or test sample t_s that is classified as l_i in the source input, removing one entire class of samples (which is not l_i) will not affect the results of t_s in the follow-up input.*

Table 12. MR-4.1 classification accuracy rates (%)

	Dataset I			
	NB	k-NN	Ensemble NB	Ensemble k-NN
Source input	100	100	100	66.67
Follow-up input	100	100	100	100

The same procedure conducted for MR-4.1 is followed here; however, instead of duplicating "NO" and "SL", we relabelled half of each class to "NO*" and "SL*", resulting in having five classes "DH", "NO", "SL", "NO*", "SL*" in the follow-up input. The sizes of training sets of the source input and the follow-up input are equal, while having different number of classes. The results are shown in Table 13.

Analysis: MR-4.2 is a necessary to be achieved using k-NN only. It is achieved using k-NN and NB and is not achieved using the ensemble classifier.

Table 13. MR-4.2 classification accuracy rates (%)

	Dataset I			
	NB	k-NN	Ensemble NB	Ensemble k-NN
Source input	100	100	100	66.67
Follow-up input	100	100	100	55.56

Table 14. MR-5.1 classification accuracy rates (%)

	Dataset I			
	NB	k-NN	Ensemble NB	Ensemble k-NN
Source input with test set (I)	100	100	100	62.5
Follow-up input with test set (I)	100	100	100	50
Source input with test set (II)	100	100	100	75
Follow-up input with test set (II)	100	100	100	100
Source input with test set (III)	100	100	100	68.75
Follow-up input with test set (III)	100	100	100	75

10. **MR-5.1: Removal of classes**: *If the test case or test sample t_s is classified as l_i in the source input, removing samples from other classes rather than l_i will not affect the results of t_s in the follow-up input.*

    The same source input dataset for evaluating MR-4.1 and MR-4.2 is used here. Sixty percent of samples (108 samples) are used for training (source input case). For the follow-up input the class "SL" is removed. That is the follow-up input just contains "DH" and "NO". Three test sets are used to test the source input and the follow-up input: (I) using eight samples belong to "DH" (II) using eight samples belong to "NO" (III) by combining both of the test sets. The results are shown in Table 14.

    Analysis: MR-5.1 is necessary for NB only and it is achieved using NB and k-NN.

11. **MR-5.2: Removal of samples**: *Removing some samples of class l_i to create the follow-up input will not affect the results of those samples that are classified correctly to class l_j in the source input and $l_i \neq l_j$.*

    The same source input dataset of MR-5.1 is used here. For the follow-up input, we removed 50% of samples belonging to classes "NO" and "SL" without any changes for "DH". For the test case, we have selected nine test cases of class "DH" (same as MR-4.1). The results are shown in Table 15.

    Analysis: MR-5.2 is not a necessary relation for all classifiers. However, it is achieved by all classifiers.

Table 15. MR-5.2 classification accuracy rates (%)

	Dataset I			
	NB	k-NN	Ensemble NB	Ensemble k-NN
Source input	100	100	100	66.67
Follow-up input	100	100	100	100

Table 16 describes which of the MRs are necessary for both NB and k-NN (i.e., using "Yes" value), according to [12,13], and for the the combination of them based on our analysis earlier. The experimental results show that NB and k-NN meet all metamorphic relations. As discussed above, we validated and verified that it is not necessary for a metamorphic relation that is necessary for NB and k-NN to be necessary for their combined classifiers.

4 Conclusion

In this work, we have applied metamorphic testing to validate machine learning algorithms NB, k-NN, and their combinations (ensemble classifiers). Several test cases are created and extracted from two biomedical datasets. Different scenarios are investigated to test those classifiers. CFS and ChiS feature selection

Table 16. Results summary

	NB		k-NN		Ensemble	
	Necessary	Achieved	Necessary	Achieved	Necessary	Achieved
MR-0	Yes	Yes	Yes	Yes	No	No
MR-1.1	Yes	Yes	No	Yes	No	Yes
MR-1.2	Yes	Yes	Yes	Yes	No	Yes
MR-2.1	Yes	Yes	Yes	Yes	No	No
MR-2.2	Yes	Yes	No	Yes	No	Yes
MR-3.1	No	Yes	Yes	Yes	No	No
MR-3.2	Yes	Yes	Yes	Yes	No	No
MR-4.1	Yes	Yes	No	Yes	No	Yes
MR-4.2	No	Yes	Yes	Yes	No	No
MR-5.1	Yes	Yes	No	Yes	No	No
MR-5.2	No	Yes	No	Yes	No	Yes

techniques are used to test and validate some related metamorphic relations. In addition, we have utilized SMOTE to add artificial samples to test the classifiers. The experimental results show that metamorphic relations are achieved using NB and k-NN. Furthermore, it is concluded that it is not necessary for a metamorphic relation that are necessary for NB and k-NN individually to be necessary for their combined classifier using stacking-based ensemble learning method.

As future work, we plan to extend metamorphic relations to include other machine learning algorithms.

References

1. Chawla, N.V., Bowyer, K.W., Hall, L.O., Kegelmeyer, W.P.: Smote: synthetic minority over-sampling technique. J. Artif. Intell. Res. **16**(1), 321–357 (2002)
2. Chen, T.Y., Cheung, S.C., Yiu, S.: Metamorphic testing: a new approach for generating next test cases. Technical Report HKUST-CS98-01, Department of Computer Science, Hong Kong University of Science and Technology (1998)
3. Davis, M.D., Weyuker, E.J.: Pseudo-oracles for non-testable programs. In: Proceedings of the ACM 1981 Conference, NY, USA, pp. 254–257 (1981). http://doi.acm.org/10.1145/800175.809889
4. Hall, M.A.: Correlation-based feature selection for machine learning. Ph.D. thesis, The University of Waikato (1999)
5. He, H., Garcia, E., et al.: Learning from imbalanced data. IEEE Trans. Knowl. Data Eng. **21**(9), 1263–1284 (2009)
6. Lichman, M.: UCI machine learning repository. http://archive.ics.uci.edu/ml (2013). Accessed May 2017
7. Murphy, C., Kaiser, G.E., Hu, L., Wu, L.: Properties of machine learning applications for use in metamorphic testing. In: Proceedings of the Twentieth International Conference on Software Engineering & Knowledge Engineering (SEKE 2008), San Francisco, CA, USA, 1–3 July 2008, pp. 867–872 (2008)

8. Ramana, B.V., Babu, M.S.P., Venkateswarlu, N.: A critical study of selected classification algorithms for liver disease diagnosis. Int. J. Database Manag. Syst. **3**(2), 101–114 (2011)

9. Segura, S., Fraser, G., Sanchez, A.B., Ruiz-Cortés, A.: A survey on metamorphic testing. IEEE Trans. Softw. Eng. **42**(9), 805–824 (2016)

10. Sesmero, M.P., Ledezma, A.I., Sanchis, A.: Generating ensembles of heterogeneous classifiers using stacked generalization. Wiley Interdiscip. Rev.: Data Min. Knowl. Discov. **5**(1), 21–34 (2015)

11. Witten, I.H., Frank, E.: Data Mining: Practical Machine Learning Tools and Techniques. Morgan Kaufmann, Burlington (2005)

12. Xie, X., Ho, J., Murphy, C., Kaiser, G., Xu, B., Chen, T.Y.: Application of metamorphic testing to supervised classifiers. In: 9th International Conference on Quality Software QSIC 2009, pp. 135–144. IEEE (2009)

13. Xie, X., Ho, J.W., Murphy, C., Kaiser, G., Xu, B., Chen, T.Y.: Testing and validating machine learning classifiers by metamorphic testing. J. Syst. Softw. **84**(4), 544–558 (2011)

14. Zhou, Z.Q., Huang, D., Tse, T., Yang, Z., Huang, H., Chen, T.: Metamorphic testing and its applications. In: Proceedings of the 8th International Symposium on Future Software Technology (ISFST 2004), pp. 346–351 (2004)

Packer Identification Using Hidden Markov Model

Nguyen Minh Hai[✉] and Quan Thanh Tho

Ho Chi Minh City University of Technology, Ho Chi Minh City, Vietnam
hainmmt@cse.hcmut.edu.vn, qttho@hcmut.edu.vn

Abstract. Most of modern malware are packed by packers to evade
the anti-virus software. Basically, packers will apply various obfuscat-
ing techniques to hide their true behaviors from static analysis methods.
Thus, how to deal with packed malware has always been a tough problem
so far. This paper proposes a novel approach for packer detection using
a combination of BE-PUM tool and Hidden Markov Model. First, BE-
PUM tool is applied to detect the sequence of possible obfuscation techniques embedded in the analyzed binary program. Then, Hidden Markov
Model is used to effectively identify the possibility of packer existence
from the generated sequences. As Hidden Markov is very effective for
pattern recognition, our proposed technique can accurately identify the
packers deployed in binaries files. We have performed experiments on
more than 2000 real-world malwares taken from VirusShare. The result
is very promising.

Keywords: Malware · Obfuscation techniques · Packers · Hidden
Markov Model · BE-PUM

1   Introduction

Most of the modern popular malwares are packed by packers. The main goal of
those packers is to evade the signature based techniques of anti-virus softwares.
It also increases the difficulty of reverse engineering work since it often takes a
very long time for unpacking or decrypting a packed file. As a counter solution,
most of anti-virus software tends to detect packer signature for verifying the
malware. However, since malware can easily modify the packer signature, this
solution cannot determine precisely whether a packed target is a malware or not.

According to [1–4], more than 80% of malware is packed by many kinds of
packers for protecting against anti-virus system. Among them, the most popular
packers are ASPACK[1], FSG[2], PECOMPACT[3],TELOCK[4], UPX[5], and YODA's

---

[1] http://www.aspack.com.
[2] http://fsg.soft112.com.
[3] https://bitsum.com/pecompact.
[4] http://www.telock.com-about.com.
[5] http://upx.sourceforge.net.

© Springer International Publishing AG 2017
S. Phon-Amnuaisuk et al. (Eds.): MIWAI 2017, LNAI 10607, pp. 92–105, 2017.
https://doi.org/10.1007/978-3-319-69456-6_8

Crypter[6]. Figure 2 shows some major steps of analyzing malware. Among them, the phase of identifying and unpacking packer takes a very important step.

In general, we assume that each packer P can be represented by a sequence of obfuscation techniques $O = \{o_1, o_2, \ldots, o_n\}$ where o_i is a number representing a certain obfuscation technique. Figure 1 depicts the sequence of obfuscation techniques in some packers. For example, with packer FSG v2.0, the sequence of the obfuscation techniques are $O = (Overwriting, Overwriting, IndirectJump, Overwriting, StolenByte)$. However, when a malware F is packed by packer P, the sequence of obfuscation techniques is not exactly the same with the value of Fig. 1. The reason is that malware can accidentally adopts these obfuscations itself which contaminates the sequence. Hence, to determine whether F is packed by P, the method of using the exact matching of sequence of obfuscation techniques produces low accuracy.

0	overlapping function	1	overlapping block	2	code chunking
3	overwriting	4	packing/unpacking	5	indirect jump
6	SEH	7	2API	8	obfuscated constant
9	checksumming	10	timing check	11	anti-debugging
12	stolen bytes	13	hardware break point		

Packer Name	Sequence of obfuscation techniques
ASPack v2.12	4_7_3_7_3_12_7_3_3_10_7_4_3_10_7_8_8_4_8_8_8_8_4_4_8_8_8 _8_8_8_8_8_8_4_4_4_4_8_4_4_8_4_8_8_3_8_3_3_7_7_3_12_7_3_3_ 3_7
FSG v2.0	3_3_5_3_5_4_3_5_3_5_3_4_3_5_12
nPack v1.0	3_12_3_12_10_8_8_10_7_8_7_7_8_4_7_12
PECompact 2.0x	9_7_7_7_13_3_10_7_7_3_8_8_4_3_4_8_3_3_12_3_10_8_8_3_7_8_8_ 8_8_8_8_8_8_8_4_7_3_3_3_12_3_3_3_4_3_3_7_3
PEtite v2.1	3_7_3_7_3_8_8_3_8_2_4_4_4_4_4_4_8_8_8_8_4_8_8_4_8_4_8_8_ 8_8_8_8_7_9_3_4_8_8_3_9_4_8_8_4_4_4_7_7_7_7_7_1_3_3_12_8_7 _7_8
tElock 0.99	8_3_9_9_4_4_4_2_4_2_8_8_8_3_2_3_3_2_8_9_13_9_9_9_9_9_4_4_4 _8_9_2_8_8_8_8_8_8_8_8_8_8_8_8_8_8_8_8_8_3_8_3_3_3_8_8_9_9 _9_9_2_9_9_4_3_3
UPX v3.94	4_4_4_8_4_5_3_12_5_3
yoda's Crypter 1.3	4_2_7_8_7_4_1_7_7_9_4_13_4_4_7_3_7_3_12_7_7_7_7_7_7_7_7_ 7_3_3_3_3_4_3_3_7_3_3_2_7_8_4_3_7_7_3_4_3_12_2_8_8_8_4_4_7 _8_3_12_3_0_7_9_4_13_4_7_8_4_7_8_9_4_13_12
UPACK v0.37	8_8_8_3_4_4_3_3_4_7_8_3_3_3_3_3_3_3_3_8_3_8_3_3_8_3_3_4_ 7_3_3_12

Fig. 1. List of obfuscation technique sequences for each packer

---

[6] http://www.yodas-crypter.com-about.com.

In this paper, we introduce a new approach of applying Hidden Markov Model to identify packers. Our key contributions are summarized as follows.

– We have extended the tool, BE-PUM [5,6] as a generic model generator with stubs of detecting obfuscation techniques. During the on-the-fly model generation, BE-PUM records the sequence of obfuscation techniques in each packer [13].
– We propose a new approach of identifying packers based on Hidden Markov Model.
– We perform the experiments on more than 2000 real malware for checking the effectiveness of our approach.

The rest of this paper is organized as followed. Section 2 briefly describes the background knowledge of BE-PUM and packer. Section 3 presents the high-level overview of our method. Section 4 shows our experiments on more than 2000 real-world malwares mainly collected from VirusShare[7]. The final Sect. 5 discusses conclusion of our paper and some future works.

Related Work. There are two main targets for packer analysis. The first one is packer detection which focuses on recognizing the occurrence of packer in targeted file. The main technique for this goal is to detect the packer signature often located in original entry point. This approach is used in many softwares, e.g. PEID[8], CFF Explorer[9]. Since malware can obfuscate the packer signature, this technique can be easily evaded. The second goal is to unpack the packed files. Some remarkable tools following this goal include OllyBonE[10], Renovo [8] and CoDisasm [9].

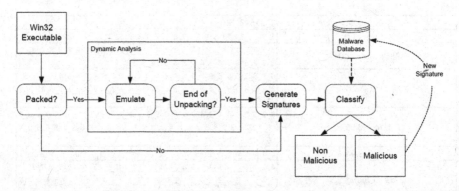

Fig. 2. Major steps of analyzing malware [7]

---

[7] https://virusshare.com/.
[8] https://www.aldeid.com/wiki/PEiD.
[9] http://www.ntcore.com/exsuite.php.
[10] http://www.joestewart.org/ollybone.

OllyBonE, a plugin of OllyDbg[11] aims to unpack code for finding the OEP (Original Entry Point). This tools consists of a Windows kernel driver for implementing the page protection of arbitrary region. The method of finding the OEP in this plugin consists of some steps. It first selects the memory region for protecting with its Windows kernel driver and sets exception break-on-execute for this region. Then it waits for unpacking stub to finish. If control flows transfers to the address inside the protected area, the exception occurs and OEP is found. However, this plugin fails in many cases when packers employs anti-debugging technique e.g. exploiting the special API *IsDebuggerPresent@kernel32.dll*.

Renovo [8] is built on top of an emulated environment, TEM[12] which is a dynamic analysis component of BitBlaze [11]. Renovo stores a shadow copy of memory space of the targeted file for observing and monitoring program execution and memory write at run time. Renovo finds the original entry point by extracting the newly generated code and data.

CoDisasm [9] is a new tool developed by Loria for tackling the problem of self-modifying code and overlapping instruction in disassembly of x86 binaries. CoDisasm presents a new disassembly method, concatic disassembly, which is a combination of CONCrete path execution with stATIC disassembly.

2 Preliminaries

2.1 Packer

Packer [10] is a software which can transform a binary file into another executable. The new binary file preserves the original functionality, but contains a different content on the system for preventing the process of linking between them. Packers are employed on executables for mainly two goals, (i) to reduce the size of binary file, and (ii) to evade detection of anti-virus software. For (i), packer minimizes targeted file by compressing its content and then uncompressing it on-the-fly during the execution. However, existing real-world packers are used mainly for the (ii), i.e. to protect the original file from being observed, analyzed and tampered with. For achieving this goal, packer combines many obfuscation methods which include anti-debugging, anticracking, anti-tracing, anti-reverse engineering, and more for preventing target file from straightforward analysis. These packers are used for protecting the licensed softwares or games from crackers. However, this feature is also applied in malware for protecting them from detection of anti-virus software.

Obfuscation Techniques. Packer supports many obfuscation techniques. We categorize them into 6 groups.

- Entry/code placing obfuscation (Code layout): overlapping functions, overlapping blocks, and code chunking.

---

[11] http://www.ollydbg.de.
[12] http://bitblaze.cs.berkeley.edu/temu.html.

- Self-modification code: Dynamic code which includes overwriting and packing/unpacking.
- Instruction obfuscation: Indirect jump.
- Anti-tracing: SEH (structural exception handling) and Special API (LoadLibrary@kernel32.dll and GetProcAddress@kernel32.dll).
- Arithmetic operation: Obfuscated constants and checksumming.
- Anti-tampering: Checksumming, timing check, anti-debugging, anti rewriting, and hardware breakpoints. Anti-rewriting technique includes stolen bytes and checksumming.

These obfuscation techniques are detected in BE-PUM during the on-the-fly model generation [13].

2.2   BE-PUM

BE-PUM [5] (Binary Emulator for PUshdown Model generation) is a tool that generates a precise control flow graph (CFG) [6], as well as precise disassembly of x86 binary code. It can handle typical obfuscation techniques of malware, e.g., *indirect jump, self-modification, overlapping instructions*, and *structured exception handler (SEH)*, which cover obfuscation techniques introduced by a *packer* [10].

BE-PUM generates a model of binary code in an on-the-fly manner, following to the execution paths. The concolic testing is used at each step for extending a model.

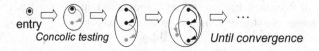

Compared to McVeto [14], which statically detects possible destinations of indirect jumps and confirms their feasibility by symbolic execution, BE-PUM decides the destinations of indirect jumps by concolic testing.

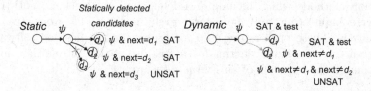

The figure below shows the architecture of BE-PUM, which consists of three components: *symbolic execution, binary emulation*, and *CFG storage*. It applies *JakStab 0.8.3* [15–17] as a preprocessor to compute a single step disassembly, and an SMT solver *Z3 4.4* as a backend engine to generate test instances for concolic testing.

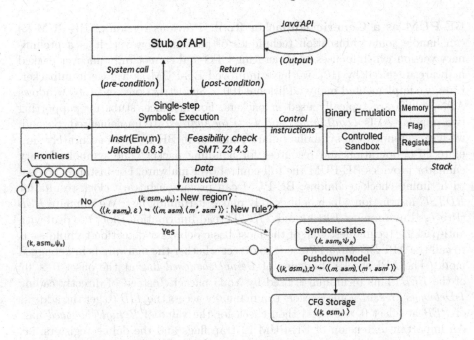

The next Figure shows how BE-PUM executes one-step concolic test. The *binary emulation* either interprets an x86 instruction, or spawns to a Windows API stub. The Windows API stub calls JNA to execute a native shared library in real Windows environment for obtaining the return value and updating the environment.

The *binary emulation* also transfers the *pre-condition P* to the *post-condition P′*. The *path condition* consists of arithmetic constraints on symbolic values only. The *memory model* describes the environment, which sets up the value of registers, memory locations, and flags by arithmetic expressions of symbolic values.

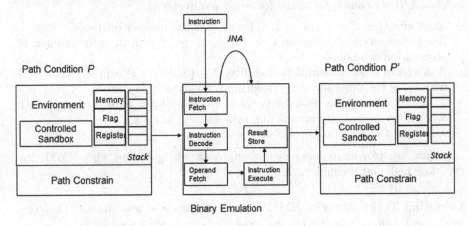

If an exception like the *division by zero* occurs, BE-PUM detects it at the binary emulator, which passes them to the Windows system error handler.

BE-PUM as a Generic Unpacker Tool. Previous version of BE-PUM [5] can handle some obfuscation techniques of packers. However, it is a preliminary version which focuses on generating CFG and cannot fully uncover packed malware. Inspired by [10], we have improved BE-PUM as a generic unpacker. First, we implemented many additional 100×86 instructions and 1500 windows APIs, which are typically used in packers. For instance, stubs for supporting two popular APIs *LoadLibrary* and *GetProcAddress* are implemented. Second, we have extended the symbolic binary emulator in BE-PUM to accurately simulate CPU operation and resources for handling packer. The symbolic binary emulator provides BE-PUM the full control over malware. For instance, to deal with timing check technique, BE-PUM can provide arbitrary clock results for *RDTSC* instruction which deliberately makes it running fast. We simulate *PEB* (Process Environment Block) and *TIB* (Thread Information Block) to deal with anti-packing techniques. One of the most basic debugger detection techniques is to call the API *IsDebuggerPresent* to detect whether the malware is in debugged mode. The API checks the value of *BeingDebbugged* flag at the offset 0×02 of the *PEB*. This technique is used by Yoda packer. Instead of directly calling *IsDebuggerPresent*, some packers can manually access the *TIB* to get the address of *PEB* at offset 0×30 and then check for the value of *BeingDebbugged* flag. An important extension of BE-PUM is, trap flags and the debug registers, i.e. hardware breakpoint and SEH with the trap flag used in Telock packer.

During the on-the-fly model generation, BE-PUM observes and detects the sequences of obfuscation techniques employed in packers [13].

3 Identifying Packer Using Hidden Markov Model

3.1 Hidden Markov Model

Hidden Markov Model (HMM) [18] is a stochastic state transition model which is well-known for pattern recognition [19–21]. In general, a Hidden Markov Model is $\lambda = \{A, B, \pi\}$ consisting of the following parameters:

- A set of states, $S = \{s_1, s_2, \ldots, s_n\}$ with n is the number of states.
- A set of observation symbols, $O = \{o_1, o_2, \ldots, o_m\}$ with m is the number of observation symbols.
- A matrix of state transition probability, $A = \{a_{ij} | a_{ij} = P(q_{t+1} = s_j | q_t = s_i)\}$ with a_{ij} is the probability of transiting from state s_i to state s_j.
- A matrix of emission probability, $B = \{b_j(k) | b_j(k) = P(o_k | q_t = s_j)\}$ with $b_j(k)$ is the probability of emitting symbol o_k at state s_j.
- A vector of initial state probability, $\pi = \{\pi_i | \pi_i = P(q_1 = s_i)\}$.

There are two main tasks in our approach when dealing with HMM, the decoding task and learning task.

Decoding Task. Given an HMM λ and a sequence of observations $O = (o_1, o_2, \ldots, o_T)$, this task computes the most likely sequence of states $s_1, s_2, \ldots, s_T$ which produced λ. This is the pattern recognition task, commonly solved by the Viterbi algorithm [22].

Learning Task. The second task updates the parameters of an HMM based on the training data. The values of A, B and π are determined during this learning process. In our approach, we create one state for each packer. Since each packer is treated equally, the initial state probability is the same for each state $\pi_i = \frac{1}{n}$. Each obfuscation technique is considered as an observation symbol.

For each packer T_{s_i} corresponding to state s_i, we denote $P = \{P_1, P_2, \ldots, P_o\}$ a list of training samples which are packed by T_{s_i}. The probability of emitting symbol o_k at state s_i is the frequency of an obfuscation technique o_k for packer T_{s_i}.

$$b_i(k) = \frac{\sum_{j=1}^{o} f(O_k, P_j)}{\sum_{l=1}^{m} \sum_{j=1}^{o} f(O_l, P_j)} \tag{1}$$

with $f(O_k, P_j)$ is total number of times obfuscation technique O_k occurs in P_j.

Note that, $\sum_{k=1}^{m} b_i(k) = \sum_{k=1}^{m} \left(\frac{\sum_{j=1}^{o} f(O_k, P_j)}{\sum_{l=1}^{m} \sum_{j=1}^{o} f(O_l, P_j)} \right) = 1$.

Then we generate the signature vector V_{s_i} for each state s_i.

$$V_{s_i} = \left\{ \frac{\sum_{j=1}^{o} f(O_1, P_j)}{o}, \frac{\sum_{j=1}^{o} f(O_2, P_j)}{o}, \ldots, \frac{\sum_{j=1}^{o} f(O_m, P_j)}{o} \right\} \tag{2}$$

For two state s_i and s_j, we use the cosine distance [23] to compute the similarity between them.

$$cos(s_i, s_j) = cos(V_{s_i}, V_{s_j}) = \frac{\sum_{k=1}^{m} \frac{\sum_{l=1}^{o} f(O_k, P_l^{s_i})}{o} \frac{\sum_{l=1}^{o} f(O_k, P_l^{s_j})}{o}}{\sqrt{\sum_{k=1}^{m} \left(\frac{\sum_{l=1}^{o} f(O_k, P_l^{s_i})}{o} \right)^2} \sqrt{\sum_{k=1}^{m} \left(\frac{\sum_{l=1}^{o} f(O_k, P_l^{s_j})}{o} \right)^2}} \tag{3}$$

Note that, $cos(s_i, s_i) = cos(V_{s_i}, V_{s_i}) = 1$.

The probability a_{ij} of transiting from state s_i to state s_j is calculated.

$$a_{ij} = \frac{cos(s_i, s_j)}{\sum_{k=1}^{n} cos(s_i, s_k)} \tag{4}$$

Note that $\sum_{j=1}^{n} a_{ij} = \sum_{j=1}^{n} \frac{cos(s_i, s_j)}{\sum_{k=1}^{n} cos(s_i, s_k)} = 1$ with all s_i.

3.2   Running Example

We consider 4 examples in Fig. 3. Among them, 2 files (Demo1, Demo2) are packed by UPX and the others (Demo3 and Demo4) are packed by FSG. The observation sequences of 4 files are described in the Fig. 3(a). This running example contains two states, UPX and FSG which correspond to the two packers. Since UPX and FSG are treated equally, the initial state probability is the same for each state $\pi_{upx} = \pi_{fsg} = \frac{1}{2}$.

We examine the Indirect Jump (IJ) technique, numbered as 5 in packer UPX. Applying formula (1), we calculate the following results.

$$b_{upx}(5) = \frac{\sum_{j=1}^{2} f(5, P_j)}{\sum_{l=1}^{14} \sum_{j=1}^{2} f(O_l, P_j)} = \frac{4}{20} = 0.2$$

Packer Name	Sequence of obfuscation techniques
Demo1	3 4 4 8 4 5 3 12 5 4
Demo2	4 4 4 4 8 3 5 5 12 3
Demo3	3 5 3 5 3 4 3 5 3 5 3 4 3 5 12
Demo4	3 3 5 3 5 4 3 5 3 5 3 4 3 5 12
Target File	3 4 4 8 5

(a) Obfuscation technique sequence

(b) Resulted HMM

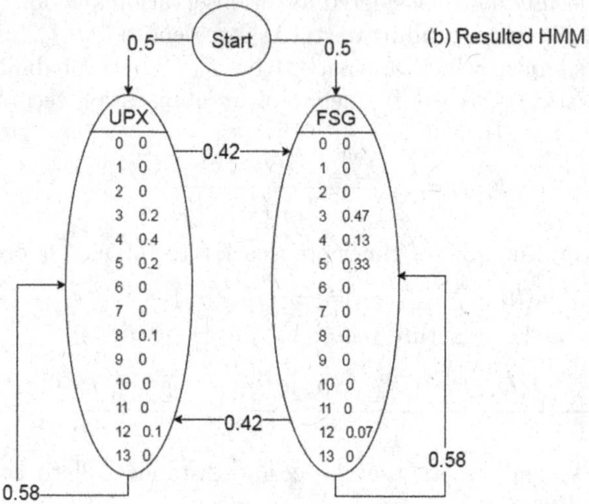

Fig. 3. Running example

Then

$$b_{upx}(4) = \frac{8}{20} = 0.4$$
$$b_{upx}(8) = b_{UPX}(12) = \frac{2}{20} = 0.1$$
$$b_{upx}(3) = \frac{4}{20} = 0.2$$
$$b_{upx}(0) = b_{upx}(1) = b_{upx}(2) = b_{upx}(6) = b_{upx}(7) = 0$$
$$b_{upx}(9) = b_{upx}(10) = b_{upx}(11) = b_{upx}(13) = 0$$

Applying (2), the vector of packer UPX is $V_{upx} = \{0,0,0,2,4,2,0,0,1,0,0,0,1,0\}$. The vector FSG is $V_{fsg} = \{0,0,0,7,2,5,0,0,0,0,0,0,1,0\}$. Then, applying (3) (4)

$$cos(upx, fsg) = \frac{33}{\sqrt{26}\sqrt{79}} = 0.73$$
$$cos(upx, upx) = cos(fsg, fsg) = 1$$
$$a_{upx,fsg} = \frac{0.73}{1.73} = 0.42$$
$$a_{upx,upx} = \frac{1}{1.73} = 0.58$$

The generated HMM is described in Fig. 3(b). We consider a target file F. The obfuscation technique sequence is described in Fig. 3(a). We use the Viterbi algorithm for recognition.

$$p_{upx}(5,5) = 0.00007042762$$
$$p_{fsg}(5,5) = 0.00008414887$$

Since $p_{fsg}(5,5) > p_{upx}(5,5)$, F is packed by packer FSG.

4 Experiments

All experiments are performed on Windows XP built on VMware workstation 10.0. The host OS is Windows 8 Pro with AMD Athlon II X4 635, 2.9 GHz and 8 GB memory.

4.1 Generating HMM with Manually Training Set

We focus on 9 packers, which are ASPACK v2, FSG v2.0, NPACK v1.0, PECOMPACT v2.0, PETITE v2.1, TELOCK v0.99, UPX v3.94, YODA v1.3, and UPACK v0.37-0.39. To generate HMM, we apply 9 packers on 398 Windows executables taken from System32 in Windows XP SP3. The resulted HMM of our approach is presented in Figs. 4 and 5. Since these packers are treated equally, the initial state probability is the same for each state, $\pi_p = \frac{1}{9}$ with all packers p.

Packer Name	AntiDebugging	Checksumming	CodeChunking	IndirectJump	ObfuscatedConst	Overlapping Block	Overlapping Function	Overwriting	Packing/Unpacking	SEH	Stolen Byte	Timing Check	Special API	Hardware BPX
ASPack v2.12	0	0	0	0.21	0.22	0	0	0.16	0.34	0	0.03	0	0.03	0
FSG v2.0	0	0	0	0.44	0.13	0.31	0	0	0	0	0	0	0.13	0
nPack v1.0	0	0	0	0.13	0.06	0	0	0.25	0.25	0	0.13	0	0.19	0
PECompact 2.0x	0	0	0	0.33	0.08	0	0	0.16	0.31	0.02	0.04	0	0.04	0.02
PEtite v2.1	0	0.02	0.02	0.13	0.25	0	0	0.17	0.37	0.03	0	0	0.02	0
tElock 0.99	0	0	0.09	0.15	0.12	0	0	0	0.39	0.23	0	0	0	0.02
UPX v3.94	0	0	0	0.2	0.4	0.2	0	0	0.1	0	0	0	0.1	0
yoda's Crypter 1.3	0.01	0.01	0.04	0.2	0.18	0	0	0.32	0.11	0.04	0	0	0.05	0.04
UPACK v0.37	0	0	0	0.58	0.12	0	0	0.06	0.21	0	0	0	0.03	0

Fig. 4. The matrix of emission probability

Packer Name	ASPack v2.12	FSG v2.0	nPack v1.0	PECompact 2.0x	PEtite v2.1	tElock 0.99	UPX v3.94	yoda's Crypter 1.3	UPACK v0.37
ASPack v2.12	0.6682	0.02	0.03	0.04	0.05	0.02	0.02	0.08	0.06
FSG v2.0	0.01	0.7006	0.02	0.05	0.01	0.07	0.05	0.03	0.07
nPack v1.0	0.001	0.01	0.6015	0.04	0.05	0.08	0.09	0.06	0.07
PECompact 2.0x	0.03	0.01	0.01	0.674	0.001	0.07	0.04	0.09	0.08
PEtite v2.1	0.06	0.003	0.03	0.03	0.6716	0.002	0.07	0.02	0.12
tElock 0.99	0.04	0.02	0.01	0.01	0.03	0.7037	0.07	0.08	0.03
UPX v3.94	0.037	0.01	0.02	0.05	0.03	0.04	0.7543	0.01	0.06
yoda's Crypter 1.3	0.05	0.02	0.03	0.04	0.01	0.03	0.02	0.724	0.07
UPACK v0.37	0.01	0.02	0.01	0.03	0.021	0.04	0.01	0.07	0.8109

Fig. 5. The matrix of state transit probability

4.2 Packer Identification on Real Malware

We have collected 2126 real malware from the VirusShare database. For comparison, each file is scanned by the three popular packer scanners, PEiD, CFF Explorer, and VirusTotal[13]. PEiD is considered as the most popular signature-based detector for packed files. VirusTotal is a free on-line malware scanner,

---

[13] https://virustotal.com/.

which combines the results from many AntiVirus sources, e.g., Kaspersky, Microsoft, and AVG. CFF Explorer is also a popular tool, but its database is quite obsolete.

Figure 6 presents the results of packer identification in BE-PUM, PEiD, CFF Explorer, and VirusTotal. Clearly, our approach produces the better results compared with the method of binary signature using PEiD, CFF Explorer, and VirusTotal.

There are 305 inconsistent examples among results of PEiD, CFF Explorer, VirusTotal, and BE-PUM. We manually investigate all disassembled results by BE-PUM of the 305 examples for checking the accuracy. Table below contains 7 inconsistent samples among 305 examples.

Malware	CFF Explorer	PEiD	VirusTotal	BE-PUM
Backdoor Win32.Rbot.apj	NONE	NONE	UPX	UPX v3.0
Backdoor Win32.VB.yo	NONE	FSG v1.10	NONE	UPX v3.0
Backdoor Win32.Rbot.xf	NONE	FSG v1.10	UPX	UPX v3.0
Trojan-Dropper Win32.Agent.uq	NONE	yoda's Protector v1.02	UPX	UPX v3.0
Trojan-PSW Win32.LdPinch.ei	NONE	Morphine v1.2	UPX	UPX v3.0
Email-Worm Win32.NetSky.ab	PECompact 2.x	PECompact 2.x	PecBundle	PECompact v2.0
Email-Worm Win32.NetSky.ac	PECompact 2.x	PECompact 2.x	NONE	PECompact v2.0

The first file Backdoor.Win32.Rbot.apj is detected as NONE by PEID and CFF Explorer. However, VirusTotal and BE-PUM confirm the file as UPX. This file has the binary signature 68 C4 C2 41 00 67 64 FF 36 00 00 which is disassembled as

```
004922C9:  68 C4 C2 41 00        push 0x41c2c4
004922CE:  67 64 FF 36 00 00      push dword fs:[0x0]
```

whereas the binary signature of UPX v3.0 (in *CFF explorer*) is 60 BE 00 E0 95 00 8D BE 00 30 AA FF 57 which evades PEID and CFF Explorer. For checking the packer label, we compare the assembly code generated by this malware and a manual UPX file. Except for the first 8 instructions, both files produces the similar results as shown in the code below which confirms our result.

Assembly code generated by (a)Backdoor.Win32.Rbot.apj and (b) UPX packed file

(a)   (b)

```
pushl $0x41c2c4
pushl %fs:0
movl %fs:0, %esp
nop
pushl $0x491110
jmp 0x004922f6
nop
ret
```

```
pusha                            pusha
movl %esi, $0x476000             movl %esi, $0x405000
leal %edi, -479232(%esi)         leal %edi, -16384(%esi)
pushl %edi                       pushl %edi
jmp 0x00491132                   jmp 0x004052fa
movl %ebx, (%esi)                movl %ebx, (%esi)
subl %esi, $0xfffffffc           subl %esi, $0xfffffffc
adcl %ebx, %ebx                  adcl %ebx, %ebx
```

The next 3 cases are the same. With Backdoor.Win32.VB.yo, CFF Explorer and VirusTotal produces the same result NONE, PEID detects as FSG v1.0 and BE-PUM identifies this file as UPX v3.0. For confirming the accuracy, we also compare the assembly code generated by this executable and UPX file. As described in the code below, except for first instruction, the generated assembly codes of these two files are equal.

Assembly code generated by (a) Backdoor.Win32.VB.yo and (b) UPX packed file

(a)   (b)

```
jmp 0x0042c791                   pusha

movl %esi, $0x41b000             movl %esi, $0x405000
leal %edi, -106496(%esi)         leal %edi, -16384(%esi)
pushl %edi                       pushl %edi
jmp 0x0042c7b2                   jmp 0x004052fa
movl %ebx, (%esi)                movl %ebx, (%esi)
subl %esi, $0xfffffffc           subl %esi, $0xfffffffc
adcl %ebx, %ebx                  adcl %ebx, %ebx
jb 0x0042c7a8                    jb 0x004052f0
movb %al, (%esi)                 movb %al, (%esi)
incl %esi                        incl %esi
movb (%edi), %al                 movb (%edi), %al
incl %edi                        incl %edi
addl %ebx, %ebx                  addl %ebx, %ebx
```

Packer Name	CFF Explorer	Peid	VirusTotal	Our Approach
ASPack v2.12	183	183	183	219
FSG v2.0	384	384	384	410
nPack v1.0	77	77	77	115
PECompact 2.0x	92	92	92	112
PEtite v2.1	115	115	115	177
tElock 0.99	150	150	150	168
UPX v3.94	360	360	360	430
yoda's Crypter 1.3	150	150	150	150
UPACK v0.37	310	310	310	345

Fig. 6. Experimental results

5   Conclusion

This paper proposed the new approach of packers identification using Hidden Markov Model. A binary model generator BE-PUM was extended to detect sequence of obfuscation techniques. The HMM was then employed to decide the likelihood of the obfuscation technique sequence. For checking the accuracy of our approach, we have performed the experiments on more than 2000 real malware with 9 packers. The accuracy of the our work outperforms the state-of-the-art tools, like *PEiD*, *CFF Explorer*, and *Virus Total*. The drawback is that BE-PUM is quite heavy. For the future work, we also tried a multi-threaded implementation [24], which requires further investigation.

Acknowledgments. This research is funded by Vietnam National Foundation for Science and Technology Development (NAFOSTED) under grant number 102.01-2015.16.

References

1. McAfee: The good, the bad, and the unknown. http://www.techdata.com/mcafee/files/MCAFEE_wp_appcontrol-good-bad-unknown.pdf. Accessed 21 May 2017
2. Santos, I., Ugarte-Pedrero, X., Sanz, B., Laorden, C., Bringas, P.G.: Collective classification for packed executable identification. In: Proceedings of the 8th Annual Collaboration, Electronic Messaging, Anti-Abuse and Spam Conference, Australia, pp. 23–30 (2011)
3. Al-Anezi, M.M.K.: Generic packing detection using several complexity analysis for accurate malware detection int. J. Adv. Comput. Sci. **3**, 32–39 (2016)
4. Osaghae, E.O.: Classifying packed programs as malicious software detected. Int. J. Inf. Technol. Electr. Eng. **5**, 22–25 (2016)
5. Nguyen, M.H., Nguyen, T.B., Quan, T.T., Ogawa, M.: A hybrid approach for control flow graph construction from binary code. In: IEEE APSEC, pp. 159–164 (2013)
6. Hai, N.M., Ogawa, M., Tho, Q.T.: Obfuscation code localization based on CFG generation of malware. In: Garcia-Alfaro, J., Kranakis, E., Bonfante, G. (eds.) FPS 2015. LNCS, vol. 9482, pp. 229–247. Springer, Cham (2016). doi:10.1007/978-3-319-30303-1_14
7. Morgenstern, M., Marx, A.: Runtime packer testing experiences. In: CARO. LNCS, vol. 6174, pp. 288–305 (2008)

8. Kang, M.G., Poosankam, P., Yin, H.: Renovo: a hidden code extractor for packed executables. In: ACM WORM, pp. 46–53 (2007)

9. Bonfante, G., Fernez, J., Marion, J.-Y., Rouxel, B., Sabatier, F., Thierry, A.: CoDisasm: medium scale concatic disassembly of self-modifying binaries with overlapping instructions. In: ACM SIGSAC CCS, pp. 46–53 (2015)

10. Roundy, K.A., Miller, B.P.: Binary-code obfuscations in prevalent packer tools. ACM Comput. Surv. **46**, 1–32 (2013)

11. Song, D., et al.: BitBlaze: a new approach to computer security via binary analysis. In: Sekar, R., Pujari, A.K. (eds.) ICISS 2008. LNCS, vol. 5352, pp. 1–25. Springer, Heidelberg (2008). doi:10.1007/978-3-540-89862-7_1

12. Anti-virus technology whitepaper. Technical report, BitDefender (2007)

13. Nguyen, M.H., Tho, Q.T.: An experimental study on identifying obfuscation techniques in packer. In: 5th World Conference on Applied Sciences, Engineering and Technology (WCSET), 02–04 June 2016, HCMUT, Vietnam (2016). ISBN 978-81-930222-2-1

14. Thakur, A., Lim, J., Lal, A., Burton, A., Driscoll, E., Elder, M., Andersen, T., Reps, T.: Directed proof generation for machine code. In: Touili, T., Cook, B., Jackson, P. (eds.) CAV 2010. LNCS, vol. 6174, pp. 288–305. Springer, Heidelberg (2010). doi:10.1007/978-3-642-14295-6_27

15. Kinder, J.: Static analysis of x86 executables. Ph.D. thesis, Technische Universitat Darmstadt (2010)

16. Kinder, J., Kravchenko, D.: Alternating control flow reconstruction. In: Kuncak, V., Rybalchenko, A. (eds.) VMCAI 2012. LNCS, vol. 7148, pp. 267–282. Springer, Heidelberg (2012). doi:10.1007/978-3-642-27940-9_18

17. Kinder, J., Zuleger, F., Veith, H.: An abstract interpretation-based framework for control flow reconstruction from binaries. In: Jones, N.D., Müller-Olm, M. (eds.) VMCAI 2009. LNCS, vol. 5403, pp. 214–228. Springer, Heidelberg (2008). doi:10.1007/978-3-540-93900-9_19

18. Rabiner, L.R., Juang, H.: Hidden Markov models for speech recognition - strengths and limitations. In: Laface, P., De Mori, R. (eds.) Speech Recognition and Understanding. NATO ASI Series, vol. 75, pp. 3–29. Springer, Heidelberg (1992). doi:10.1007/978-3-642-76626-8_1

19. Kunda, A., He, Y., Bahl, P.: Handwritten word recognition: a hidden Markov model based approach. In: pattern recognition, pp. 283–297, May 1989

20. Rimey, R.D., Brown, C.M.: Selective attention as sequential behavior: modeling eye movements with an augmented hidden Markov model. In: Proceedings of the DARPA Image Understanding Workshop, pp. 840–649 (1990)

21. Bakis, R.: Continuous speech word recognition via centisecond acoustic states. In: Proceedings of ASA Meeting, Washington, D.C., April 1976

22. Forney, G.D.: The Viterbi algorithm. Proc. IEEE **61**, 268–278 (1973)

23. Singhal, A.: Modern information retrieval a brief overview. Bull. IEEE Comput. Soc. Techn. Comm. Data Eng. **24**, 35–43 (2001)

24. Hai, N.M., Tho, Q.T., Anh, L.D.: Multi-threaded on-the-fly model generation of malware with hash compaction. In: Ogata, K., Lawford, M., Liu, S. (eds.) ICFEM 2016. LNCS, vol. 10009, pp. 159–174. Springer, Cham (2016). doi:10.1007/978-3-319-47846-3_11

AIC-Driven Spatial Hierarchical Clustering: Case Study for Malaria Prediction in Northern Thailand

Peter Haddawy[1,2($\boxtimes$)], Myat Su Yin[1], Tanawan Wisanrakkit[1],
Rootrada Limsupavanich[1], Promporn Promrat[1],
and Saranath Lawpoolsri[3]

[1] Faculty of ICT, Mahidol University, Nakhon Pathom, Thailand
`peter.had@mahidol.ac.th`, {`myat.su`, `tanawan.wis`,
`rootrada.lim`, `promporn.prm`}`@student.mahidol.ac.th`
[2] Bremen Spatial Cognition Center, University of Bremen, Bremen, Germany
[3] Faculty of Tropical Medicine, Mahidol University, Bangkok, Thailand
`saranath.law@mahidol.ac.th`

Abstract. Targeted intervention and resource allocation are essential in effective control of infectious diseases, particularly those like malaria that tend to occur in remote areas. Disease prediction models can help support targeted intervention, particularly if they have fine spatial resolution. But there is typically a tradeoff between spatial resolution and predictability of the time series of infection. In this paper we present a systematic method to quantify the relationship between spatial resolution and predictability of disease and to help provide guidance in selection of appropriate spatial resolution. We introduce a complexity-based approach to spatial hierarchical clustering. We show that use of reduction in Akaike Information Criterion (AIC) as a clustering criterion leads to significantly more rapid improvement in predictability than spatial clustering alone. We evaluate our approach with two years of malaria case data from northern Thailand.

Keywords: Malaria prediction · Spatial clustering · Akaike Information Criterion

1 Introduction

Targeted intervention and resource allocation are essential elements of effective control strategies for infectious disease. This is particularly the case for diseases like malaria that are prevalent in less developed and more remote areas in which public health resources are often scarce. A valuable supporting technology is the ability to predict disease with sufficient spatial resolution to effectively target the disease. With case data on infectious disease as well as on related environmental variables now increasingly available in high spatial resolution [1], the data to build high resolution models is not a limiting factor. But in modeling of disease there is typically a tradeoff between the spatial resolution of the model and the accuracy of its predictions. Predictions that are too coarse are not helpful but neither are those that are inaccurate.

© Springer International Publishing AG 2017
S. Phon-Amnuaisuk et al. (Eds.): MIWAI 2017, LNAI 10607, pp. 106–111, 2017.
https://doi.org/10.1007/978-3-319-69456-6_9

While the issue of choice of resolution for modeling has been recognized and discussed in the epidemiological literature [2], previous work has typically chosen spatial resolution for modeling based on existing government administrative boundaries or on boundaries of responsibility of medical clinics. There is as yet no work that has sought to systematically investigate the relationship between resolution and prediction accuracy nor to provide a principled means for generating and selecting among resolutions.

In this paper we introduce a new approach to spatial clustering for disease prediction we call *AIC-driven spatial hierarchical clustering*. The approach uses the concept of reduction in time series complexity, measured in terms of Akaike Information Criterion, as a primary criterion for spatial clustering. We evaluate the approach using two years of weekly village level malaria case data from a region in northern Thailand. We show that we can greatly increase the predictability of malaria cases with only a small amount of clustering and that AIC-driven clustering performs significantly better than clustering based on physical distance alone. Our algorithm produced hierarchical clusters which allow a user to easily explore the resolution/accuracy tradeoff.

2 Related Work

Work on malaria prediction has used numerous techniques including various types of regression, ARIMA models, SIR based models, and neural networks [3]. Models are most commonly built with weekly or monthly temporal resolution. Spatial resolutions include village, district, province, and catchment, with district being the most common.

Most work on clustering in epidemiology has focused on use of spatial scan statistics to identify spatial and temporal clusters of disease [4, 5] with a limited amount of work exploring the direct impact of clustering on disease prediction. Giardina et al. [6] assess the effect of the spatial resolution of remotely sensed land cover and elevation on malaria risk estimation. They investigate three resolutions: 1 km, 500 m and 100 m and find that finer resolution models tend to overestimate the number of infections. Teklehaimanot et al. [7] use data on weekly confirmed malaria cases in ten districts of Ethiopia as well as temperature and rainfall to produce weekly predictions. Districts with similar climactic characteristics are grouped to reduce random error and produce more reliable and precise estimates of weather effects.

Montero and Vilar [10] present a number of model-based, complexity-based and prediction-based time series clustering techniques implemented in R. Their model-based approach fits time series with ARIMA models and measures the similarity between the fitted models. The complexity-based approach determines similarity between complexity measures of time series. Their approach is fundamentally different from our work in that they treat the individual time series separately in fitting the ARIMA models or computing complexity and follow a standard clustering approach. In our work similarity is determined in terms of an ARIMA model fitted to a merger of the time series being considered for clustering. In addition, they do not consider reduction in complexity as a clustering criterion.

3 Algorithm

To be useful for targeted intervention, clusters should be physically compact and they should yield good predictability. To facilitate examining the tradeoff between spatial resolution and prediction accuracy, they should also be hierarchically organized so that the membership does not change dramatically as we move between clustering levels. To achieve this, we use agglomerative hierarchical clustering with physical distance as one attribute. The other attribute, which must be computed on the fly, is the difference between the AIC of each candidate cluster and the average AIC of the two clusters being merged: $AIC (C_1 \cup C_2) - (AIC (C_1) + AIC (C_2))/2$. Each cluster is represented by a single time series and when two clusters are merged, their time series are combined so

```
Intialize Cluster_current_level to incidence time series of vil-
lages 1..n
Intialize Cluster_output to Cluster_current_level
Repeat
  For each pair of candidates Ci and Cj in Cluster_currentlevel
    //AIC Distance
    Set CombinedTS to the combined time series of Ci and Cj
    Set AIC_CombinedTS to GetAIC (CombinedTS)
    Set AIC_Ci to GetAIC (CI)
    Set AIC_Cj to GetAIC (Cj)
    Set AIC_distance to AIC_CombinedTS - (AIC_Ci + AIC_Cj)/2

    //Physical Distance
    Set Lat_Ci to GetAverageLatitude (Ci)
    Set Lat_Cj to GetAverageLatitude (Cj)
    Set Lat_diff to the difference between Lat_Ci and Lat_Cj
    Set Long_Ci to GetAverageLongitude (Ci)
    Set Long_Cj to GetAverageLongitude (Cj)
    Set Long_diff to the difference between Long_Ci and
      Long_Cj

    Compute distance as a combination of Lat_diff,
    Long_diff and AIC_distance using specified distance
    function

    Set Cnew to the new cluster formed by combining the Ci
    and Cj which have the minimum distance
    Set Cluster_current_level to Cluster_current_level - Ci - Cj ∪ Cnew
    Append Cluster_current_level to Cluster_output
Until Cluster_current_level contains only one cluster
Output Cluster_output
```

Fig. 1. Pseudo code of the clustering algorithm using physical distance and AIC

that the new time series represents the number of cases in the cluster region. The underlying idea is to cluster regions when it results in a decrease in AIC. The pseudo code of the clustering algorithm using physical distance and AIC is shown in Fig. 1. It is straightforward to adjust the algorithm to use with the distance measures separately.

4 Data

We demonstrate our approach with the problem of weekly malaria prediction in Tha Song Yang district of Tak province in Thailand. Tha Song Yang comprises 66 villages in which malaria is endemic. The case data for our experiments consists of weekly microscopically confirmed malaria cases obtained from Thailand's national E-Malaria Information System [1] covering each of the villages for the years 2012 and 2013 (99 weeks), providing a total of 6,579 records with 12,800 total cases (*Plasmodium falciparum, Plasmodium vivax*). The numbers of cases per village per week ranges from 0 to 82 with a mean of 2.1.

5 Experimental Setup

The impact of clustering on prediction accuracy was evaluated using 10-fold cross validation. A cluster hierarchy was generated using the training data for each fold and a predictive model was generated for each cluster in the hierarchy. The same hierarchy was then applied to the test data and the predictive models were tested on the clusters there. For malaria prediction we selected three of the most commonly used techniques: linear regression, ARIMA, and ARIMAX. Land surface temperature lagged 5 by weeks was incorporated in the ARIMA and ARIMAX models since previous work [9] showed it to have a considerable influence on malaria incidence in this region. For each predictive model we evaluated the effect of clustering on short-term (1-week) and long-term (4-week) prediction accuracy. Since the incidence values generally increase with cluster size, to compare prediction accuracy of clusters of varying size we need an evaluation metric that is independent of magnitude. We thus use the Symmetric Mean Absolute Percentage Error (SMAPE) [8] which has a range of 0 to 100.

6 Results and Discussion

Table 1 compares results of 4-week ARIMA prediction for clusters created using three different similarity measures: physical distance only, AIC only, and physical distance plus AIC with weight 5. Euclidean distance is used for all three. The table shows the average decrease in AIC value as cluster size increases as well as the average reduction in SMAPE. Averaged over all cluster sizes, the highest average decrease is for AIC only (−32.38), follow by physical distance plus weighted AIC (−26.79), and last physical distance only (−22.50). Results for 1-week prediction and for prediction with ARIMAX and linear regression are similar.

Figure 2 shows the average reduction in SMAPE for the three clustering criteria, for 1-week and 4-week ARIMA predictions. All curves show a sharp early reduction in

Table 1. Average decrease in AIC and in SMAPE for 4-week ARIMA predictions using the clusters resulting from three different clustering criteria.

| Cluster size (#villages) | Physical distance only | | Physical distance with AIC (weight = 5) | | AIC only | |
| | Avg. decrease | | Avg. decrease | | Avg. decrease | |
	AIC	SMAPE	AIC	SMAPE	AIC	SMAPE
2	0.03	−9.92	0.01	−10.19	0.00	−14.63
3	−0.03	−18.33	0.01	−19.92	0.00	−25.49
4	−0.06	−22.47	0.00	−26.65	−0.01	−32.32
5	−0.17	−25.50	−0.04	−29.87	−0.02	−36.98
6	0.19	−23.21	−0.04	−36.16	−0.02	−44.15
...	...	...	...	...	...	...
66	−0.46	−55.11	−0.46	−55.11	−0.46	−55.11
Average	−0.07	−22.50	−0.04	−26.79	−0.04	−32.38

prediction error as cluster size increases. For example, clustering based on physical distance with weighted AIC achieves a reduction of 30 for 4-week prediction with a cluster size of only 5, which is 55% of the maximum reduction of 55 when putting all 66 villages into a single cluster. Note that the portions of the graphs for larger cluster sizes are noisy because some points in the graphs represent only one or a few clusters. The AIC alone and physical distance with weighted AIC clustering criteria perform significantly better than physical distance alone.

We report t statistics for cluster sizes 2–6 since 6 is an inflection point in the graph and beyond cluster size 6 the number of clusters is not sufficient to compute reliable average SMAPE values. For AIC alone vs Physical Distance alone all differences in SMAPE are significant ($p < 0.05$) for both 1 and 4 week predictions. For Physical Distance with AIC vs Physical Distance alone, SMAPE differences are significant for cluster sizes 4–6 for 1 week prediction and cluster sizes 3–6 for 4 week prediction ($p < 0.05$). The overall results for linear regression and ARIMAX are similar to those for ARIMA.

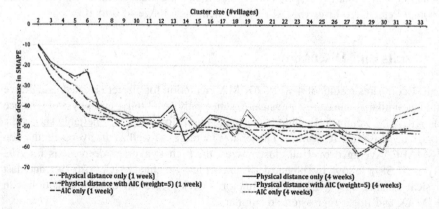

Fig. 2. Average decrease in SMAPE for 1- and 4-week predictions for ARIMA using the cluster results from three different similarity measures.

7 Conclusion

This paper has introduced an approach to spatial hierarchical clustering that enables exploration of the tradeoff between spatial resolution and prediction accuracy. Using malaria data from Northern Thailand we have shown that use of the technique can yield rapid returns, greatly improving prediction accuracy with only a small amount of clustering. Furthermore, use of AIC reduction as a clustering criterion provides significantly better results than use of physical distance alone. We plan to apply the technique to malaria prediction in other regions to further verify our results as well as to apply the technique to prediction of other diseases such as dengue.

The predictive models in this study are relatively simple, using only previous incidence and temperature to predict future incidence. In practice, predictive models often also make use of a wide variety of environmental variables [9]. A next step in this work is to investigate the effect of clustering on more complex prediction models.

Acknowledgements. This paper is based upon work supported by the U.S. Army ITC-PAC under Contract No. FA5209-15-P-0183. This work was also partially supported through a fellowship from the Hanse-Wissenschaftskolleg Institute for Advanced Study, Delmenhorst, Germany to Haddawy and a Santander BISIP scholarship to Su Yin.

References

1. Khamsiriwatchara, A., et al.: Artemisinin resistance containment project in Thailand. (I): implementation of electronic-based malaria information system for early case detection and individual case management in provinces along the Thai-Cambodian border. Malar. J. **11**(1), 1 (2012)
2. Graham, A.J., Atkinson, P.M., Danson, F.M.: Spatial analysis for epidemiology. Acta Trop. **91**(3), 219–225 (2004)
3. Zinszer, K., et al.: A scoping review of malaria forecasting: past work and future directions. BMJ Open **2**, e001992 (2012)
4. Glaz, J., Naus, J., Wallenstein, S.: Scan Statistics. Springer, New York (2001)
5. Alemu, K., Worku, A., Berhane, Y., Kumie, A.: Spatiotemporal clusters of malaria cases at village level, northwest Ethiopia. Malar. J. **13**(1), 223 (2014)
6. Giardina, F., Franke, J., Vounatsou, P.: Geostatistical modelling of the malaria risk in Mozambique: effect of the spatial resolution when using remotely-sensed imagery. Geospatial Health **10**, 232–238 (2015)
7. Teklehaimanot, H.D., Lipsitch, M., Teklehaimanot, A., Schwartz, J.: Weather-based prediction of Plasmodium falciparum malaria in epidemic-prone regions of Ethiopia I. Patterns of lagged weather effects reflect biological mechanisms. Malar. J. **3**, 41 (2004)
8. Makridakis, S.: Accuracy measures: theoretical and practical concerns. Int. J. Forecast. **9**, 527–529 (1993)
9. Haddawy, P., et al.: Spatiotemporal Bayesian networks for malaria prediction: case study of Northern Thailand. In: Studies in Health Technology and Informatics, pp. 773–777 (2016)
10. Montero, P., Vilar, J.A.: TSclust: an R package for time series clustering. J. Stat. Softw. **62**(1), 1–43 (2014)

Multivariate Time Series Clustering Analysis for Human Balance Data

Owais Ahmed Malik$^{(\boxtimes)}$ and Daphne Teck Ching Lai

Faculty of Science, Universiti Brunei Darussalam,
Gadong BE1410, Brunei Darussalam
{owais.malik,daphne.lai}@ubd.edu.bn

Abstract. The evaluation of human balance control patterns is an important tool for identifying the underlying disorders in the postural control system of individuals and taking appropriate actions if required. This study presents the use of the multivariate time-series clustering techniques for analyzing the human balance patterns based on the force platform data. Different multivariate time-series clustering techniques including partitioning clustering with Dynamic Time Warping (DTW) measure, Permutation Distribution Clustering (PDC) and k-means for longitudinal data (KmL3D) were investigated. The cluster solutions were generated using anterior-posterior and medial-lateral center of pressure (COP) displacement data for four balance evaluation conditions namely eyes open on stable surface (EOS), eyes open on unstable surface (EOU), eyes closed on stable surface (ECS) and eyes closed on unstable surface (ECU). The resulted clusters were evaluated based on various cluster validity indexes. Further, suitable association measures were computed between clustering solutions and demographic (age and body mass index) and qualitative balance test (BEST-T) parameters. The clusters generated by Partition Around Medoid (PAM) DTW technique for EOS, EOU and ECS balance conditions demonstrated statistically significant association with all parameters while for ECU balance testing condition, significant associations were observed only for the age parameter of the participants.

1 Introduction

Balance control and postural stability are essential for human beings in order to perform the normal daily life activities such as standing, walking, running etc. A person is able to maintain his/her balance by adjusting the center of mass of the body during static or dynamic activities. This ability is the result of a complex process which depends on the integration of three major components including the visual, vestibular, and somatosensory systems [1]. A change in one or more of these systems, due to age factor or any pathology/injury, may cause impaired balance and increase the risk of fall [2–4]. An early identification of abnormal balancing patterns can help in taking preventive measures and avoiding the risk of fall and other related injuries. In past, efforts have been made to characterize the balance of the body and understand its association with various factors

© Springer International Publishing AG 2017
S. Phon-Amnuaisuk et al. (Eds.): MIWAI 2017, LNAI 10607, pp. 112–125, 2017.
https://doi.org/10.1007/978-3-319-69456-6_10

including age, gender, weight, pathology etc., in order to improve the health care and well being of the individuals [1,2,5,6].

A common technique to quantify the condition of balancing is to measure the displacement of the center of pressure (COP) of the body using stabilography method. In this method, a force platform is used to measure the resultant forces as a time-series data in anterior-posterior (AP) and medial-lateral (ML) directions while a person is standing over it. These forces along with the momentum data are used to compute the COP displacement in respective directions (AP and ML). In a typical balance testing setup, the effect of different surfaces (stable/unstable platforms) and visual conditions (eyes open/eyes closed) on COP displacement is generally evaluated. Mostly, various parameters (e.g. mean AP-ML displacement, mean AP-ML velocity, minimum/maximum AP-ML displacement, RMS values of AP-ML displacements, area and total displacement of sway etc.) are extracted from COP data and used to compare the different balance conditions between two or more groups based on health status, age or gender [7,8]. Recently, the time-frequency domain features have also been found useful for differentiating the balancing patterns of young and old population [9]. However, in literature, there is no agreement on a single best method or set of features to analyze the COP data for understanding and assessing the balance condition of a subject [10].

In this study, we propose the use of multivariate time-series clustering technique for analyzing the COP data for discovering human balance patterns and finding the association between COP displacements (AP and ML) and different demographic and health characteristics of the subjects. Extracting such patterns and associations can help in identifying the abnormal postural control of the individuals with different health conditions. In contrast to the existing studies where clustering was performed based one or more features from the COP data, the whole time-series data for AP and ML displacements have been used for finding the clusters [7–9]. The multivariate time-series clustering of human balance data has not been much explored previously in the literature. Various time-series clustering methods were investigated for this study [11–14] and two techniques, namely Permutation Distribution Clustering (PDC) [11] and partitioning clustering with Dynamic Time Warping (DTW) measure [12,13], were selected due to their support for high dimensional multivariate time-series data analysis. The results of these techniques were compared for different number of clusters for each balance condition (3 trials) performed by the subjects. The cluster solutions were initially evaluated using cluster validity indexes. Furthermore, suitable association measures and significance tests were applied between clustering solutions and four parameters including age (continuous variable), age group (young/old), body mass index (BMI) and Mini-BESTest score (BEST-T) and the results of all 3 trials for each balance condition were compared. Thus, the motivation of the exploratory analysis performed in this study is to identify the time-series structures in the unlabeled balance data set (AP and ML COP data) by organizing the data into similar clusters. These clusters (as labeled classes) will then be used for developing an automated postural control classification system for balance testing activities based on the force platform data.

2   Methodology

Figure 1 shows the steps performed to generate and evaluate the clustering solutions using the time-series clustering techniques. The details about each of these steps are described below.

2.1   Data Set

This study used data from the public human balance evaluation database from Physionet [10,15]. The data set contains both qualitative and quantitative data of balance evaluations for 163 subjects. The important characteristics of the data set are shown in Table 1. The stabilography data were recorded using the force platform at a sampling frequency of 100 Hz while the subjects were standing still for 60 seconds during four different conditions: eyes open on stable surface (EOS), eyes open on unstable surface (EOU), eyes closed on stable surface (ECS) and eyes closed on unstable surface (ECU). For each condition, data were recorded for three trials, resulting in a total of 1930 trials (excluding the 26 trials for 5 subjects who were not able to complete the one or more eyes closed trials). More details about the set up of experiments can be found in [10]. The software for force platform provided 3-D force (F_x, F_y, F_z) and moment of force (M_x, M_y, M_z) data which were filtered using 4th order zero lag 10 Hz low pass filter and the centers of pressure in anterior-posterior (COP_x) and medial-lateral (COP_y) directions were computed [10]. An example of COP time-series data for a subject for four different balance conditions is shown in Fig. 2. Moreover, the data set also contains the results of mini balance evaluation system test for each subject.

Table 1. Characteristics of human balance evaluation data set.

Parameter	Value
No. of subjects	163 (116 females and 47 males)
Age (mean - SD)	46.63 (23.04) years
Age group	Young (<60 years), Old ($\geq$60 years)
BMI (mean - SD)	23.65 (3.36) Kg/m^2

2.2   Data Pre-processing

The anterior-posterior and medial-lateral COP data were extracted for all three trials from the given data set for each subject for four different conditions (EOS, EOU, ECS and ECU). The data for the disabled subjects (as reported in the data set) were removed and COP data (COP_x and COP_y) from 146 subjects were selected as input for clustering techniques. Thus, the data set for a single trial consisted of two variables (COP_x and COP_y), each consisting of 6000 data points (60 sec $\times$ 100 Hz), for a total of 146 subjects ($2 \times 146 \times 6000$).

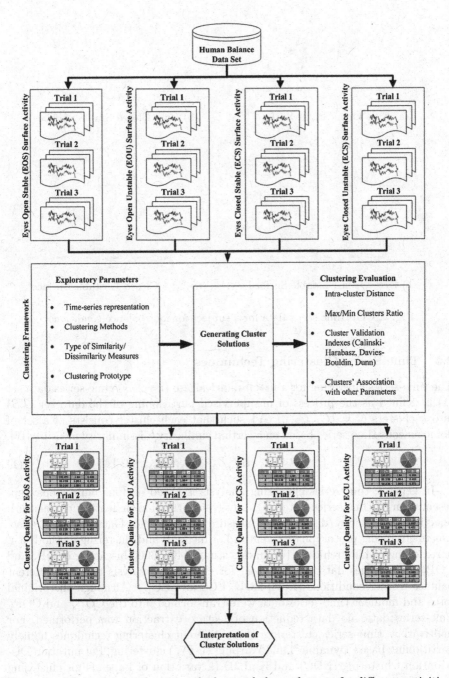

Fig. 1. Overall process for clustering the human balance data set for different activities

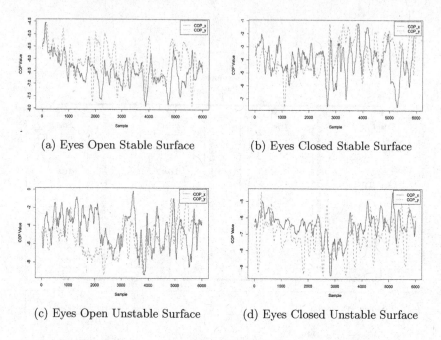

(a) Eyes Open Stable Surface   (b) Eyes Closed Stable Surface

(c) Eyes Open Unstable Surface   (d) Eyes Closed Unstable Surface

Fig. 2. COP time-series data for a subject for four balance conditions

2.3   Time Series Clustering Techniques

The time-series clustering for a $m \times n$ multivariate ($i = 1..v$) time-series data set
(1) is defined as the process of unsupervised partitioning of the data set (TS)
into k clusters $C = \{C_1, C_2, ..., C_k\}$ such that each cluster consists of a set of
homogeneous time-series based on a certain similarity/dissimilarity measure [16].

$$TS = \{ts_{11}^n, ts_{12}^n, ..., ts_{1m}^n, ..., ts_{v1}^n, ts_{v2}^n, ..., ts_{vm}^n\} \tag{1}$$

In general, time-series clustering analysis is based on four main steps: representation of time-series data (e.g. any transformation or feature extraction),
selection of similarity/dissimilarity measure (e.g. shape or feature based), selection of clustering prototype (e.g. centroid or medoid) and clustering method (e.g.
partitioning or hierarchical) [16]. In this study, 146×6000 bi-variate (COP_x and
COP_y) time-series data set was used for clustering analysis for four different
balance testing conditions (EOS, EOU, ECS and ECU). Although the original
force and moment time-series data were transformed into the COP_x and COP_y
time-series data, no data reduction or feature extraction was performed. For
multivariate time-series clustering, three different clustering techniques namely
partitioning based Dynamic Time Warping (DTW) clustering, Permutation Distribution Clustering (PDC) and KmL3D (a variation of k-means for clustering
joint-trajectories) were applied using *tsclust* (dtwclust R package), *pdclust* (pdc
R package) and *kml3d* (KmL3D R package) functions respectively and the results
were compared. The selection of similarity/dissimilarity measure and clustering

prototype was based on the type of clustering algorithm (i.e. DTW or PDC or KmL3D). However, KmL3D was not able to accommodate the entire 60-second balance data. Instead, 600 time points (average of every 1 sec data) were extracted from COP_x and COP_y and experimented but the clusters did not show significant association with other parameters. Thus, no deeper investigation with KmL3D was done. Furthermore, KmL3D is more suitable for longitudinal data, rather than time-series [14]. Similarly, while PDC's time performance was high, taking a few minutes to compute, it tends to produce highly imbalanced clusters. For this reason, no thorough investigations on PDC clusters were continued. The working and relevant details about the DTW method are described below.

DTW is a dynamic programming algorithm that tries to find the optimum warping path between two series. *tclust* function from dtwclust-package in R was used to cluster the given data set with 'partitional' clustering method and 'dtw' distance metric [12]. Partitional clustering creates a hard partition of the time-series data into 'k' clusters (specified by the user), where each cluster has a centroid (a time-series). Two different cetnroid computation methods were used in this study: Partition Around Medoid (PAM) and DTW Barycenter Averaging (DBA). Initially, the cluster centroids were randomly initialized by choosing any one of the series in the data. In the next step, distance between each series and each centroid was calculated using 'dtw' metric, and the series were assigned to the cluster with minimum distance from centroid. The centroids were then recomputed by using either PAM or DBA method and the procedure was repeated until the stopping criterion is met (either no further change in time-series assignment to clusters or maximum number of iterations were reached).

2.4   Selection and Evaluation of Clustering Solutions

Since the selected clustering techniques do not determine the optimal number of clusters automatically, different measures were used to determine and evaluate the cluster solutions. In partitional clustering techniques, the cluster centroids are randomly initialized in the beginning, so the generated clustering solution depends on the initial choice of the centroids. In order to avoid this bias and selecting an optimal clustering solution, the algorithm was repeated at least 10 times for each trial of all activities. Then, a clustering solution was selected for each value of k (the number of clusters to be generated) such that it has (1) minimum score of the product of average and standard deviation of intra-cluster distances, and (2) reasonable distribution of data in each cluster (i.e. the largest to the smallest cluster size is 3 or less). Further, different clustering validity indexes were used to evaluate the cluster solutions found based on the above two measures. In this study, we used three clustering indexes for validation namely Calinski-Harabasz (CH) index [17], Davies-Bouldin (DB) index [18] and Dunn (D) index [19].

Calinski-Harabasz (CH) Index. The Calinski-Harabasz index is defined as

$$CH = \frac{(N-K)}{(K-1)} \frac{BGSS}{WGSS} \tag{2}$$

where K denotes the number of clusters, N is the size of data set, and BGSS and WGSS represent the between (separation) and within (cohesion) cluster sums of squares of the partition, respectively. An optimal cluster solution maximizes this measure.

Davies-Bouldin (DB) Index. Davies-Bouldin index is defined as

$$DB = \frac{1}{K} \sum_{i=1, i \neq j}^{K} max\left(\frac{(\delta_i + \delta_j)}{d(c_i, c_j)}\right) \tag{3}$$

where K is the number of clusters, δ_i is the average distance of all patterns in cluster i to their cluster center c_i, δ_j is the average distance of all patterns in cluster j to their cluster center c_j, and $d(c_i, c_j)$ is the distance of cluster centers c_i and c_j. The number of clusters that minimizes DB is assumed to be the optimal cluster solution.

Dunn (D) Index. The Dunn index is defined as the ratio between the minimal intra-cluster distance (d_{min}) and the largest within-cluster distance (d_{max}).

$$D = \frac{d_{min}}{d_{max}} \tag{4}$$

The intra-cluster distance between two clusters c_i and c_j can be computed by using (5):

$$d_{ij} = min\|M_k^i - M_l^j\| \tag{5}$$

where M represents an observation (record) in the data set.

Similarly, the inter-cluster distance between points of a cluster c_i can be computed by using 6

$$D_i = max\|M_k^i - M_l^i\| \tag{6}$$

Then, d_{min} and d_{max} are computed as the minimum and maximum of d_{ij} and D_i distances for all clusters, respectively.

Finally, the association between different number of clusters and four parameters including age (continuous variable), age group (young/old), BMI and BEST-T for all activities were also investigated to examine the quality of the clusters.

3   Results and Discussion

Clustering solutions tested on all balance testing conditions, EOS, EOU, ECS and ECU, obtained from DTW-DBA and DTW-PAM were evaluated based on cluster quality and cluster meaningfulness.

3.1 Cluster Quality

The solutions presented are chosen based on a combination of (1) minimum score of the product of average and standard deviation of intra-cluster distances of a cluster solution, (2) largest to smallest cluster ratio (3) cluster validity indexes (CVI) values and (4) association measures with the four parameters. As a first step, the cluster solutions for each trial of all activities with the minimum intra-cluster distance and balanced distribution of data among clusters were chosen for further analysis. It was found that DTW-PAM produced less number of clusters consistently that were meaningful than DTW-DBA, so only detailed solutions of DTW-PAM are presented while results from DTW-DBA are not presented. Both DTW-DBA and DTW-PAM took hours to run, however the *dtwclust* package allows the reuse of DTW distance matrix for PAM centroids in contrast with DBA centroids which made DTW-PAM a better choice for clustering the given data set. In the next step, three different clustering indexes were computed for each cluster solution (for each trial of an activity). Tables 3, 4, 5 and 6 show the cluster quality in terms of CH, DB and D. The results based on CVI values were highly inconsistent where solutions that were deemed promising, they did not always produce clusters with significant association with the four parameters.

3.2 Cluster Meaningfulness

To evaluate the meaningfulness of clustering solutions, suitable association measures and significance tests between clustering solutions with parameters BEST-T, age, age group and BMI on the four activities were investigated. Following the motivation of original study where this dataset was collected [10,15], association between the balance data with age and age group are of interest. BEST-T is a parameter of interest because it contains the total score of a qualitative balance test, Mini Balance Evaluation Systems Tests, which we expect to have cluster association. Association of age or BMI with balance have been found in many studies [20–22]. Gender association was not conducted as the number of females is more than twice of males, creating female-biased clusters. The association measures and tests chosen were based on the distribution and data type of the parameters and cluster solution, as shown in Table 2. The results obtained from these evaluations on DTW-PAM clustering are presented in Tables 3, 4, 5 and 6 for EOU, EOS, ECS and ECU tests respectively. Where significant association was found, the p-values in brackets are presented in bold and where significant association was found in all parameters, the number of cluster is underlined.

3.3 Test Conditions

Clusters found in EOU tests tend to have significant association with the parameters, for 3 to 5 clusters for all three trials. In both trials 1 and 2, EOU produced 4 clusters which have significant associations with all four parameters. Clusters found in ECS and EOS tests showed significant association with some of the

Table 2. Association measures and significance test used.

Parameter	Distribution	Data type	Association measure	Significance test
BEST-T	Non-normal	Continuous	Kruskall-Wallis	Chi-sq
Age	Non-normal	Continuous	Kruskall-Wallis	Chi-sq
Age group	Non-normal	Discrete	Cramer's V	Chi-sq
BMI	Normal	Continuous	-	ANOVA

Table 3. Cluster validity, association and significance measures for EOU trials.

k	Cluster validity			Cluster association			
	CH	DB	D	χ^2 BEST-T	χ^2 age	V age group	F-stats BMI
EOU Trial 1							
2	135.071	1.840	0.333	0.177(0.674)	1.722(0.189)	0.046(0.579)	1.573(0.212)
3	83.228	1.894	0.452	13.239(**0.001**)	15.600(*)	0.290(**0.002**)	3.958(**0.021**)
4	50.336	1.996	0.371	10.044(**0.018**)	15.006(**0.002**)	0.255(**0.019**)	2.673(**0.050**)
5	39.970	1.798	0.314	12.398(**0.015**)	13.792(**0.008**)	0.245(0.061)	0.551(0.699)
EOU Trial 2							
2	46.696	1.860	0.377	6.431(0.011)	4.331(**0.037**)	0.055(0.504)	0.897(0.345)
3	75.517	2.013	0.353	16.067(*)	12.287(**0.002**)	0.293(**0.002**)	1.160(0.316)
4	50.681	1.799	0.441	9.816(**0.020**)	13.707(**0.003**)	0.302(**0.003**)	2.953(**0.035**)
5	39.116	1.802	0.487	10.258(**0.036**)	13.261(**0.010**)	0.286(**0.015**)	3.357(**0.012**)
EOU Trial 3							
2	150.916	1.766	0.393	0.875(0.350)	0.324(0.569)	0.075(0.366)	2.114(0.148)
3	72.985	1.804	0.398	4.414(0.110)	8.589(**0.014**)	0.223(**0.025**)	3.134(**0.047**)
4	48.681	1.825	0.514	7.682(0.053)	9.089(**0.028**)	0.237(**0.036**)	5.858(**0.001**)
5	39.079	1.799	0.476	13.311(**0.010**)	16.874(**0.002**)	0.296(**0.009**)	0.778(0.541)

*$p < 0.001$.

parameters. This may suggest the effectiveness of the test conditions for determining stability levels of the young and old, with EOU most effective followed by EOS and ECS. The least effective for elucidating the balance profiles of young and old appears to be the ECU condition, where only in trial 2, significant age and age group association was found with 3 clusters.

Thus, the age and age group significant associations across 3 and 4 clusters for EOU (all three trials), EOS and ECS (in Trial 2) support the original study's hypothesis [10] that the age has influence in the stability of individuals.

3.4   Trials

Clusters found in Trial 3 were observed to have little or no association with BEST-T, age, age group and BMI across all four number of clusters (3 to 5), with the exception of EOU tests. This may suggest that the data from Trial 1 and 2 are more useful than from Trial 3.

Table 4. Cluster validity, association and significance measures for EOS trials.

k	Cluster validity			Cluster association			
	CH	DB	D	χ^2 BEST-T	χ^2 age	V age group	F-stats BMI
EOS Trial 1							
2	157.007	1.693	0.539	3.775(0.052)	1.387(0.239)	0.071(0.387)	0.129(0.720)
3	80.071	1.825	0.440	6.770(**0.034**)	4.029(0.133)	0.164(0.136)	0.093(0.911)
4	54.252	1.662	0.498	4.123(0.249)	0.368(0.947)	0.087(0.772)	0.250(0.861)
5	40.725	1.846	0.491	5.710(0.222)	2.660(0.616)	0.132(0.627)	1.188(0.319)
EOS Trial 2							
2	72.084	1.533	0.310	1.912(0.167)	5.586(**0.018**)	0.187(**0.023**)	1.241(0.267)
<u>3</u>	82.071	1.756	0.374	7.642(**0.022**)	6.703(**0.035**)	0.219(**0.029**)	4.553(**0.012**)
4	55.407	1.852	0.373	10.177(**0.017**)	16.755(**0.001**)	0.303(**0.003**)	2.622(0.053)
<u>5</u>	37.260	1.843	0.292	12.374(**0.015**)	20.236(*)	0.324(**0.003**)	2.804(**0.028**)
EOS Trial 3							
2	151.960	1.828	0.359	0.120(0.729)	0.612(0.434)	0.091(0.268)	0.132(0.717
3	72.132	1.728	0.434	2.439(0.295)	2.946(0.229)	0.119(0.356)	0.575(0.564)
4	51.044	1.817	0.446	0.494(0.920)	1.877(0.598)	0.101(0.680)	0.579(0.630)
5	36.050	1.810	0.434	10.739(**0.030**)	14.722(**0.005**)	0.286(**0.016**)	1.112(0.353)

*$p < 0.001$.

Table 5. Cluster validity, association and significance measures for ECS trials.

k	Cluster validity			Cluster association			
	CH	DB	D	χ^2 BEST-T	χ^2 age	V age group	F-stats BMI
ECS Trial 1							
2	109.411	1.881	0.341	1.133(0.889)	9.317(0.054)	0.216(0.139)	1.419(0.231)
3	70.685	1.743	0.341	1.696(0.428)	6.551(**0.038**)	0.173(0.110)	3.203(**0.044**)
4	47.298	1.685	0.401	6.550(0.088)	8.816(**0.032**)	0.274(**0.010**)	4.219(**0.007**)
5	34.037	1.879	0.402	1.987(0.738)	4.072(0.396)	0.189(0.256)	1.642(0.167)
ECS Trial 2							
2	153.537	1.581	0.387	1.092(0.296)	0.087(0.768)	0.087(0.293)	0.143(0.706)
<u>3</u>	74.329	1.886	0.508	8.230(**0.016**)	9.607(**0.008**)	0.276(**0.004**)	3.549(**0.031**)
4	47.785	1.846	0.539	11.309(**0.010**)	11.982(**0.007**)	0.273(**0.008**)	2.098(0.103)
5	36.471	1.903	0.446	6.503(0.165)	7.025(0.135)	0.178(0.320)	1.201(0.313)
ECS Trial 3							
2	154.693	1.606	0.486	0.248(0.618)	0.014(0.907)	0.014(0.862)	2.358(0.127)
3	54.786	1.855	0.423	1.509(0.470)	0.948(0.622)	0.019(0.975)	0.920(0.401)
4	52.816	1.811	0.441	1.251(0.741)	2.538(0.468)	0.066(0.888)	2.286(0.081)
5	39.220	1.841	0.410	2.860(0.582)	0.621(0.961)	0.143(0.546)	0.724(0.577)

Table 6. Cluster validity, association and significance measures for ECU trials.

k	Cluster validity			Cluster association			
	CH	DB	D	χ^2 BEST-T	χ^2 age	V age group	F-stats BMI
ECU Trial 1							
2	147.592	1.610	0.354	0.428(0.513)	0.303(0.582)	0.073(0.378)	0.008(0.927)
3	54.241	1.728	0.435	1.387(0.500)	5.174(0.075)	0.199(0.053)	0.400(0.671)
4	51.965	1.862	0.370	3.536(0.316)	6.285(0.099)	0.172(0.227)	0.139(0.937)
5	39.809	1.839	0.459	2.393(0.664)	4.370(0.358)	0.169(0.370)	0.489(0.744)
ECU Trial 2							
2	136.982	1.837	0.362	0.204(0.651)	0.384(0.536)	0.070(0.397)	2.226(0.138)
3	72.804	1.925	0.271	5.072(0.079)	8.433(**0.015**)	0.223(**0.027**)	1.416(0.246)
4	51.396	1.910	0.341	3.168(0.366)	5.390(0.145)	0.185(0.170)	0.924(0.431)
5	38.473	1.868	0.321	2.415(0.660)	3.007(0.557)	0.155(0.474)	0.430(0.787)
ECU Trial 3							
2	150.519	1.683	0.332	0.924(0.337)	0.286(0.593)	0.061(0.460)	1.471(0.227)
3	75.213	1.929	0.332	0.717(0.699)	0.815(0.665)	0.076(0.658)	1.161(0.316)
4	50.764	1.827	0.344	1.206(0.752)	0.578(0.902)	0.102(0.680)	0.311(0.818)
5	40.605	1.884	0.397	2.684(0.612)	10.579(**0.032**)	0.218(0.131)	1.883(0.117)

For clustering solutions that consistently demonstrate significant association across few runs, post-hoc tests were conducted to determine which clusters were significantly different based on BEST-T, age and BMI. The results are presented in Table 7, where only clusters in terms with significant difference are reported with their p-values in brackets. With 3 clusters, it can be observed there is significant differences among clusters 1 and 3, and 2 and 3 for BEST-T and Age. For BMI, there is significant differences in cluster 2 and 3. For post-hoc test on 4 clusters, all clusters were found to have significant differences with at least another cluster in terms of BEST-T and Age but not BMI. Clusters 1 and 3 do not appear to vary significantly different in BEST-T, age and BMI, evident via Table 7 and Fig. 3(d) to (f). It platform at a sampling with 3 clusters be a better choice having significant differences between any cluster pair for 3 parameters.

Table 7. Post-hoc test results for EOU Trial 1 for 3 and 4 clusters.

k	Activity	BEST-T	Age	BMI
3	EOU	1&3 (0.004), 2&3 (0.006)	1&3 (0.013), 2&3 (*)	2&3 (0.016)
4	EOU	2&3 (0.004), 3&4 (0.034)	1&2 (0.047), 2&3 (0.002)	2&3 (0.054)

$^*p < 0.001$.

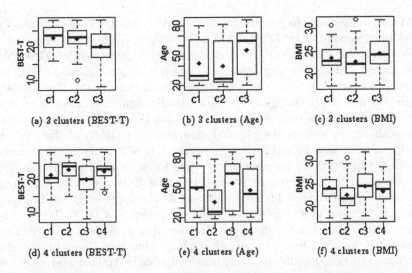

(a) 3 clusters (BEST-T)   (b) 3 clusters (Age)   (c) 3 clusters (BMI)

(d) 4 clusters (BEST-T)   (e) 4 clusters (Age)   (f) 4 clusters (BMI)

Fig. 3. Boxplots showing BEST-T, age and BMI distribution for EOU Trial

Figure 3 shows the boxplots of BEST-T, age and BMI distribution for cluster solutions from EOU Trial 1 for 3 and 4 clusters. We observed that clusters 1 and 2 belonging to the younger group, with lower age median (thick line in the box) and mean (dot in the box) values as opposed to cluster 3. Interestingly, clusters 1 and 2 have higher BEST-T and lower BMI values in terms of median and mean. For the 4-cluster solution, we observe that cluster 2 belonging to the young group, cluster 3 the older group and cluster 1 and 4 a mixture with median and mean near age 50. In these two clusters, those in cluster 4 with slightly lower median age than cluster 1 perform better in terms of BEST-T evaluation despite non-observable differences in terms of median BMI. As the group with lowest age median and mean, cluster 2 has highest BEST-T and lowest BMI median and mean while cluster 3 with highest age median has lowest BEST-T and highest BMI mean and median. This appears to suggest those younger individuals tend to have better balance control. In the 3-cluster solution, clusters 2 and 3 appear to suggest age and BMI influence the balance. Due to the less distinctive nature of cluster 1 and 4 in the 4-cluster solution, the 3-cluster solution appears to be the best, with more distinct clusters that have significant association with the four parameters.

4   Conclusions and Future Work

Three multivariate time-series clustering techniques, DTW (PAM and DBA), PDC and KmL3D, were explored in this study for finding the patterns in human balance data collected over three trials. PDC and KmL3D techniques were not found suitable for this data set. PDC generated highly imbalanced cluster solutions and KmL3D was unable to handle the all 6000 time points of the data set. While comparing the results for DTW-PAM and DTW-DAB, the cluster solutions generated by DTW-PAM were quite consistent as compared to DTW-DBA technique. On EOU data, cluster solutions generated by DTW-PAM demonstrated statistically significant association with age, BEST-T, BMI and age group, particularly with 3 and 4 clusters for all three trials. This indicates the clusters may be meaningful, with statistically significant association with scores obtained qualitatively from using the Mini Balance Evaluation Systems Tests, with age as well as the physical characteristics (BMI) of the subjects. Some meaningful associations with these parameters were found in clusters from EOS, ECS while little or no associations were found in ECU conditions. Trial 3 was observed to have little or no association in EOS, ECS and ECU tests which may suggest the third trial is least useful. The future study will focus on finding cluster associations with individual components of BEST-T and other balance tests reported in the data set. Moreover, the findings of this study will be compared with the feature based clustering techniques. Based on the clusters' characteristics, intelligent algorithms will also be trained and tested for differentiating the young and old groups of adults.

References

1. Winter, D.: Human balance and posture control during standing and walking. Gait Posture **3**(4), 193–214 (1995)
2. Abrahamova, D., Hlavacka, F.: Age-related changes of human balance during quiet stance. Physiol. Res. **57**(6), 957–964 (2008)
3. Shkuratova, N., Morris, M.E., Huxham, F.: Effects of age on balance control during walking. Arch. Phys. Med. Rehabil. **85**(4), 582–588 (2004)
4. Ku, P.X., Osman, N.A.A., Abas, W.A.B.W.: Balance control in lower extremity amputees during quiet standing: a systematic review. Gait Posture **39**(2), 672–682 (2014)
5. Greve, J., Alonso, A., Bordini, A.C., Camanho, G.L.: Correlation between body mass index and postural balance. Clinics (Sao Paulo) **62**(6), 717–720 (2007)
6. Menegoni, F., Galli, M., Tacchini, E., Vismara, L., Cavigioli, M., Capodaglio, P.: Gender-specific effect of obesity on balance. Obesity (Silver Spring) **17**(10), 1951–1956 (2009)
7. Ruhe, A., Fejer, R., Walker, B.: Center of pressure excursion as a measure of balance performance in patients with non-specific low back pain compared to healthy controls: a systematic review of the literature. Eur. Spine J. **20**(3), 358–368 (2011)
8. Palmieri, R.M., Ingersoll, C.D., Stone, M.B., Krause, B.A.: Center-of-pressure parameters used in the assessment of postural control. J. Sport Rehabil. **11**(1), 51–66 (2002)
9. Javaid, A.Q., Gupta, R., Mihalidis, A., Etemad, S.A.: Balance-based time-frequency features for discrimination of young and elderly subjects using unsupervised methods. In: 2017 IEEE EMBS International Conference on Biomedical Health Informatics (BHI), pp. 453–456, February 2017
10. Santos, D.A., Duarte, M.: A public data set of human balance evaluations. PeerJ **4**, e2648 (2016)
11. Brandmaier, A.M.: pdc: an R package for complexity-based clustering of time series. J. Stat. Softw. **67**(5), 1–23 (2015)

12. Sardá-Espinosa, A.: Comparing time-series clustering algorithms in R using the dtwclust package
13. Montero, P., Vilar, J.A.: TSclust: an R package for time series clustering. J. Stat. Softw. **62**(01) (2014)
14. Genolini, C., Alacoque, X., Sentenac, M., Arnaud, C., et al.: kml and kml3d: R packages to cluster longitudinal data. J. Stat. Softw. **65**(4), 1–34 (2015)
15. Goldberger, A.L., Amaral, L.A., Glass, L., Hausdorff, J.M., Ivanov, P.C., Mark, R.G., Mietus, J.E., Moody, G.B., Peng, C.K., Stanley, H.E.: Physiobank, physiotoolkit, and physionet: components of a new research resource for complex physiological signals. Circulation **101**(23), 220 (2000)
16. Aghabozorgi, S., Shirkhorshidi, A.S., Wah, T.Y.: Time-series clustering-a decade review. Inf. Syst. **53**, 16–38 (2015)
17. Caliski, T., Harabasz, J.: A dendrite method for cluster analysis. Commun. Stat. **3**(1), 1–27 (1974)
18. Davies, D.L., Bouldin, D.W.: A cluster separation measure. IEEE Trans. Pattern Anal. Mach. Intell. PAMI **1**(2), 224–227 (1979)
19. Dunn, J.C.: Well-separated clusters and optimal fuzzy partitions. J. Cybern. **4**(1), 95–104 (1974)
20. Vereeck, L., Wuyts, F., Truijen, S., de Heyning, P.V.: Clinical assessment of balance: normative data, and gender and age effects. Int. J. Audiol. **47**(2), 67–75 (2008)
21. Del Porto, H., Pechak, C., Smith, D., Reed-Jones, R.: Biomechanical effects of obesity on balance. Int. J. Exerc. Sci. **5**(4), 1 (2012)
22. Yoon, S.W., Park, W.S., Lee, J.W.: Effects of body mass index on plantar pressure and balance. J. Phys. Ther. Sci. **28**(11), 3095–3098 (2016)

Analysis of District-Level Monsoon Rainfall Patterns in India: A Pilot Study

Sougata Deb[✉], Cleta Milagros Libre Acebedo, Jun Yu,
Gomathypriya Dhanapal, and Niranchana Periasamy

Institute of Systems Science, National University of Singapore, Singapore, Singapore
{e0015161,e0015122,e0015147,e0015354,e0015361}@u.nus.edu

Abstract. Agricultural activities in India are heavily reliant on the monsoon rainfall during July–September every year. Indian Meteorological Department has been issuing rainfall forecasts since 1886. These predictions at a country or broad region level have limited benefits since different areas may see wide variations even when the overall average for India remains stable. This study explored possibilities of creating a cluster of districts as a more granular yet cohesive unit for rainfall forecast, by using different weather and atmospheric variables for past 12 months. Analytically, Principal Component Analysis (PCA) was used to reduce data dimensionality before creating an optimal cluster solution. Subsequently, a set of cluster-level linear regression models was found to perform better than a single regression model based on the entire sample. While district-level predictions showed limited value, the sequential combination of unsupervised and supervised techniques showed promising results at an overall level. These results will serve as a strong baseline for the planned extension of this pilot study which will use advanced machine learning techniques to improve upon the prediction performance further.

1   Introduction

Indian agriculture relies heavily on proper amount and distribution of rainfall during the monsoon season (July–September) [17]. The Indian Meteorological Department (IMD) has been issuing long-range forecasts[1] for average monsoon rainfall in India since 1886. Statistical modeling by using multiple covariates and correlation analysis was introduced by Gilbert Walker [7] during 1904–24. Over the past century, more advanced models were built progressively to improve on the quality of forecasts.

A 16-parameter power regression model was adopted in 1988 [7] which was subsequently revised to two different power regression models [5]. This was done to enable an early monsoon forecast in April, followed by a revised forecast in June. In 2007, IMD shifted to an ensemble forecast combining predictions from two component models [13], multiple linear regression (MLR) and projection pursuit regression. Some independent research [17] on the same data has

---

[1] Defined as at least 10 days ahead as per UK Meteorological Office definition.

© Springer International Publishing AG 2017
S. Phon-Amnuaisuk et al. (Eds.): MIWAI 2017, LNAI 10607, pp. 126–136, 2017.
https://doi.org/10.1007/978-3-319-69456-6_11

recently showed superior performance by using more advanced techniques like Neural Networks. Rainfall studies on other countries demonstrated usage of other regression techniques such as weighted regression [21] to tackle heteroscedasticity of errors, generalized estimating equations [14] to account for panel data relationships and support vector regression [11,16] for its ability to model a large class of non-linear relationships.

In all IMD models, the forecasts were made either at a country level or by 3 broad regions [7], *viz.* north-west, north-east and peninsular regions of India. Similar studies on other countries [3,14,18,21] have also been conducted at a broad region or country level. IMD acknowledged that while successive normal monsoons were observed at country level, drought-hit situations were found in many parts of the country. Hence a more granular rainfall prediction can be immensely helpful to strategize local activities. However, they also stressed that attempts to forecast monsoon over smaller areas like districts become unsuccessful as correlations fall drastically [13]. IMD left this as an area of future research which has been explored as part of this pilot study.

2   Scope, Objective and Methodology

The scope of this pilot was to assess suitability of such an area-level rainfall prediction approach and to create a baseline performance before moving to a full scale research on this topic. Specifically, results of this pilot will help establish the worth of pursuing and developing this approach further. Analytically, the objective was to come up with a cohesive clustering of districts, more granular than the 3 broad geographic regions without impacting the prediction accuracies adversely. This essentially translated to two learning components. First was an unsupervised learning to understand the natural grouping of the districts, followed by a supervised prediction of monsoon rainfall.

Unsupervised learning is a broad domain with numerous approaches and techniques [9], each offering certain benefits over others for specific data characteristics and objectives [4]. In absence of a globally optimal method, the choice primarily depends on the researcher, subject to the specific problem being solved [9]. A focused review of the clustering techniques suited for spatial data suggested frequent usage of techniques ranging from traditional k-means clustering [10,12,19], DBSCAN [4] to more recent evolutionary approaches such as genetic graph-based clustering [22], medoid-based clustering using ant colony optimization [23] and hybrid approaches such as adaptive k-means for overlapped graph clustering [15].

The evolutionary approaches often generated superior results empirically due to their flexibility in approximating any arbitrary non-linear regions [22], while k-means offered simplicity and better interpretability over other advanced techniques such as self-organizing maps [10]. As a result, k-means clustering was chosen for unsupervised learning in this pilot study with a view that more advanced techniques could be leveraged in subsequent phases to drive and quantify further improvements. Results from the usage of k-means clustering should thus be considered a baseline performance in future extensions of this study.

On similar lines, MLR was chosen as the supervised technique for final monsoon rainfall prediction. More generalized regression approaches that had already been used on this problem [7,13] to model non-linear relationships and other machine learning approaches such as neural networks [11,17] and support vector machines [11,16] were reserved for the full scale study. Contrasting the predictions from these methods with MLR predictions will help understand the latent non-linear relationships in future studies.

For unsupervised learning, it was further postulated that clustering based on weather and atmospheric characteristics would be more appropriate than a geographic proximity based clustering envisioned by IMD. Hence, 11 different categories of weather and atmospheric parameters (Table 1) were averaged at month-level for 12 preceding months as the independent variables. This resulted in 132 predictor variables. For consistency with IMD's approach, the 12-month period was chosen as April-March. This allowed usage of the derived *factors* in a regression model in April for predicting the upcoming monsoon rainfall, similar to the early forecast done by IMD.

Table 1. Independent variable categories and key descriptive statistics

Variable	Description	Unit	Range	Std. dev.	Outlier
PPT	Monthly average precipitation	mm	0–2360	20–196	0.8–2.3%
MinT	Minimum temperature	°C	(−24)–32	3.1–5.7	0.9–1.7%
AvgT	Average temperature	°C	(−17)–38	3.1–5.4	1.0–1.8%
MaxT	maximum temperature	°C	(−11)–45	3.2–6.0	0.5–1.8%
Cloud	% sky covered in cloud	%	0–99	8.2–16.9	0.0–1.8%
Vapor	Vapour pressure	hPa	0–39	4.1–6.9	0.0–1.5%
WetD	No. of wet days	days	0–31	1.3–5.2	0.1–2.6%
DiurTR	Diurnal temperature range	°C	3–21	1.3–3.1	0.0–0.7%
GFrost	No. of days with ground frost	days	0–31	0.2–4.7	1.0–2.5%
CropET	Reference crop evapo-transpiration	mm/day	0–9	0.5–1.3	0.0–1.4%
PotnET	Potential evapo-transpiration	mm/day	0–10	0.6–1.3	0.0–1.8%

3   Data Preparation

India had a total of 576 districts (as of 2002) spread over 29 states and 7 union territories (UT). For this pilot, 100 years (1902–2001) of information on 327 (60%) districts were extracted from http://www.indiawaterportal.org/. This translated to 32,700 observations and 132 variables. A Kaiser-Mayer-Olkin [20] test showed a high 0.955 value, confirming the sufficiency and suitability of this sample data for subsequent factor analysis using PCA.

3.1   Data Quality Assessment

None of the variables had any missing values. Additionally, the following quality checks were performed to ensure logical coherence in the variables.

- Temperature: minimum ≤ average ≤ maximum
- Minimum temperature $< 0\,°C \implies$ ground frost > 0
- Evapo-transpiration: reference crop ≤ potential
- Wet Days $= 0 \iff$ average precipitation $= 0$, Wet Days $> 0 \iff$ average precipitation > 0

No exception was found for first three checks. 337 anomalous cases showing wet day > 0 but precipitation $= 0$, were corrected by forcing wet days to 0.

3.2 Univariate Analysis

Two variables, *cloud cover* and *diurnal temperature range* had imputed values for first ten years (1902–1911) for some of the districts. However, no action was required as it impacted only ∼6% of observations. *Ground frost* variables were extremely sparse with ∼50% zero values as it generally does not snow in majority of India.

Outlier Analysis. India being a country with a diverse weather range, some mild (outside $\pm1.5\sigma$ limits, where σ was the sample standard deviation of the variable) and extreme (outside $\pm3\sigma$) outliers were present in most of the variables (Table 1). Analytically, outlier treatment was essential since both PCA and MLR are extremely sensitive to outliers and leverage points. However, these values were the realities which were to be lost as a result of any such imputation. To strike a balance, the imputation was done only for the extreme outliers by capping/flooring them to the corresponding $\pm3\sigma$ limits.

Checking Normality. It is generally accepted that minor deviations from normality do not affect PCA/factor analysis significantly, while normally distributed variables aid the generalizability of solution. Normality of each variable was assessed by fitting a normal distribution on the empirical histogram. Three categories of variables, precipitation, wet days and ground frost showed highly right-skewed distributions, closer to Log-Normal form. Figure 1 shows the distribution of March precipitation as an example. Hence a log transformation[2], $LogVar = Ln(Var + 1)$ was used on all these 36 monthly variables.

Variable Standardization. The variables were measured in different scales and had a wide variation in their variances. This necessitated some standardization to avoid biasing the data distribution in favour of few high-variance ones, *e.g.* precipitation. Standard z-score transformation was used for each raw predictor variable.

3.3 Bivariate Analysis

As a final step before running PCA, the correlation matrix (Fig. 2) created from the standardized data was checked to identify and avoid extreme multi-collinearities (>0.95) and singularities [20]. However, no such variable pairs were

---

[2] +1 was used to tackle the 0 values.

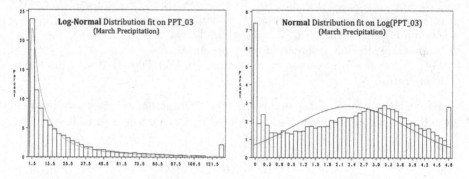

Fig. 1. Example of a variable (March precipitation) requiring transformation

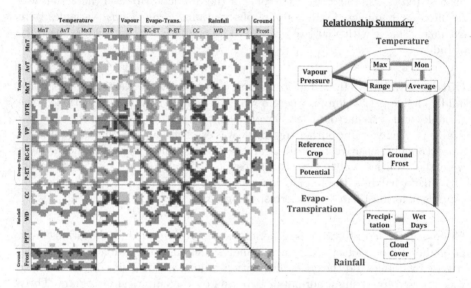

Fig. 2. Bivariate correlation summary for 132 variables

found. This also helped understand the inter-dependencies and validate them against the known meteorological relationships.

E.g. All temperature variables were found to have high positive correlation, both among themselves and across months. This was expected because entire India lies in the northern hemisphere and temperature change affects all districts similarly. Rainfall related variables, precipitation, wet days and cloud cover were correlated among themselves but not within each variable across months. This too, was logical because rainfall in different months (except for monsoon) is sporadic and does not follow the same trend throughout India. These findings indicated that PCA would be able to reduce data dimensionality considerably. The same was supported by Bartlett's sphericity test. High value of the test statistic showed presence of significant correlations in the data [2].

4   Principal Component Analysis

PCA with a VariMax rotation on the 132 standardized variables returned strong results (Fig. 3). Scree plot showed that 50% variability in the data could be explained by the first two *factors* alone. Eventually, first 4 *factors* were selected as the most significant drop in eigen values was observed between factors 4 and 5. A strong 0.7 cutoff was used to interpret factor loadings of the raw variables, as suggested by Comrey and Lee [2]. Profiles of these 4 factors were as below.

- **Factor 1:** *Prevailing winter weather* where most of the temperature, ground frost and evapo-transpiration variables from Oct-Mar loaded heavily
- **Factor 2:** *Pre-monsoon weather volatility* as vapor pressure, diurnal temperature range and evapo-transpiration for Apr-May loaded heavily
- **Factor 3:** *Last year's monsoon temperature* since all temperature variables from Jun–Sep showed high loading
- **Factor 4:** *Last year's monsoon rainfall* since cloud cover, precipitation and wet days variables for Jul-Sep showed high loading

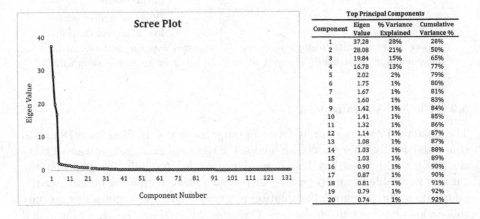

Top Principal Components			
Component	Eigen Value	% Variance Explained	Cumulative Variance %
1	37.28	28%	28%
2	28.08	21%	50%
3	19.84	15%	65%
4	16.78	13%	77%
5	2.02	2%	79%
6	1.75	1%	80%
7	1.67	1%	81%
8	1.60	1%	83%
9	1.42	1%	84%
10	1.41	1%	85%
11	1.32	1%	86%
12	1.14	1%	87%
13	1.08	1%	87%
14	1.03	1%	88%
15	1.03	1%	89%
16	0.90	1%	90%
17	0.87	1%	90%
18	0.81	1%	91%
19	0.79	1%	92%
20	0.74	1%	92%

Fig. 3. Principal component analysis summary

5   Cluster Analysis

K-means clustering based on Euclidean distance was performed using the top 4 factors. Number of clusters was varied between 3–8 to balance between granularity and robustness of the clusters. Analytical validity was measured by Davies-Bouldin Index, which compares the intra and inter-cluster separations and is known to be a robust measure of cluster validity [8]. This resulted in selection of the 5-cluster solution generated by the k-means algorithm.

5.1   Cluster Profiling

Table 2 shows profiling of the 5 clusters by the 4 factors along with brief interpretations based on the factor values. It suggested logical coherence in atmospheric characteristics within each cluster and highlighted the differences among them.

Table 2. Profiling of clusters by factors

Cluster (size)	Factor 1	Factor 2	Factor 3	Factor 4	Interpretation
C1 (30%)	−	+	+	++	Tropical volatile temperature with good monsoon rain
C2 (20%)	−	−	+	=	Extreme weather with low rainfall
C3 (8%)	=	−	=	+	Consistently cold places
C4 (12%)	++	=	−	−	Low monsoon rain; high temp. and rainfall during winter
C5 (30%)	++	++	−	−	Pleasant winter with low monsoon rainfall

++: above average, statistically significant   *+: above average, not significant*
=: below average, statistically significant   *−: below average, not significant*

5.2   Cluster Visualization

The cluster solution essentially formed groups using the districts from 18 Indian states and 4 UTs. This enabled an analysis of the geospatial organization of these clusters for additional insights. It was encouraging to find (Fig. 4A) that the clusters were able to group near-by districts together without using any spatial information. Furthermore, the solution reconciled with the hypothesis that only collocations may not drive the best cluster solution since the algorithm found some districts in west Karnataka and Tamil Nadu to be similar to other districts in Odisa and West Bengal.

To understand this further, two publicly available maps of India (Fig. 4B[3] and 4C[4]) were compared with the district clusters. Map, Fig. 4B depicted the standardized stratigraphic classification and correlation of lithostratigraphic units of India. These were indicative of the different geographic and surface features related to a region which are often found to be correlated with the prevailing weather, including rainfall [1]. Map, Fig. 4C had a more direct interpretation as it grouped regions that observed similar average daily temperatures throughout the year. These demonstrated that the selected factors broadly mapped the different geological and isothermal regions of India while forming the final clusters.

---

[3] http://www.portal.gsi.gov.in/images/GSIimages/static_indgeo.gif.
[4] http://www.mapsofindia.com/maps/india/annualtemperature.htm.

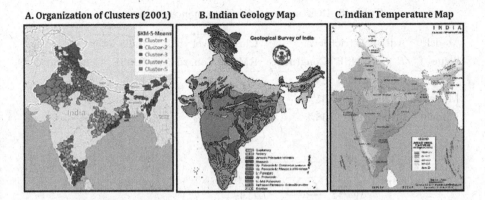

Fig. 4. Geo-spatial visualization of clusters and related phenomena

The cluster map was geospatially more granular than both Fig. 4B and C, with cluster borders often tracking the composite boundaries that would be generated if the isothermal and geological maps were superimposed. This congruence of a weather-driven map with geological and isothermal maps was similar to the findings in [6] though the premise and scope of the referred study was broader than this pilot. These relationships would be beneficial in creating more objective definitions of the 5 clusters, *e.g.* C3 as the high-altitude Himalayan region.

6   Regression Analysis

$Ln(1 + PPT)$ was modeled since all rainfall related predictors were already log-transformed. However, final performance comparison was done using the original values.

As a first baseline, Model-A was built with the same 4 factors used in the clustering analysis. Subsequently, Model-B was built using stepwise selection from all 132 factors and by retaining only the factors which accounted for a partial R^2 of at least 0.01. This resulted in selection of 5 factors for Model-B, with only one coming from the top 4 factors.

Finally, to leverage the cluster solution to its full potential, 5 different linear regression models, one for each cluster was built following the same stepwise selection of factors. This combined suite of predictions was referred to as Model-C. Analysis of regression errors indicated presence of some heteroscedasticity for high rainfall values in all the three models. This was left for future extensions such as applying weighted regression or generalized linear models.

Goodness-of-fit was measured using adjusted R^2 (Table 3). Model accuracy was measured using the same LPA[5] based root mean square error (RMSE) metric adopted by IMD.

---

[5] Long Period Average (LPA) is defined as the average actual monsoon rainfall for 1951–2000.

Table 3. Regression model performance summary

Model	Adj	District level		Cluster level		India level	
Type	R^2	RMSE	Congruence	RMSE	Congruence	RMSE	Congruence
Model-A	0.557	43%	35%	21%	36%	13%	58%
Model-B	0.636	36%	35%	22%	37%	14%	50%
Model-C	0.706	31%	38%	20%	49%	**12%**	**56%**

$$RMSE = \sqrt{\frac{1}{n^*Y} \sum_{i=1}^{Y} \sum_{j=1}^{n} (\frac{\hat{R}_{ij} - R_{ij}}{LPA_j})^2} \qquad n = 327, Y = 100$$

Additionally, the qualitative accuracy metric used by IMD was also checked. This metric categorized the rainfall values as % of LPA into 3 bins (<90%, 90–110% and >110%) and the congruence between actual and predicted categories was measured. Both accuracy metrics were calculated at district, cluster and overall India levels to understand the usability of these predictions. Cluster and country level roll-ups for rainfall were done by the area-weighted averages as suggested by IMD.

7   Conclusions and Future Research

In this study, MLR based predictive models were built for forecasting monsoon rainfall in India with a 3 months' lead time. Application of PCA helped reduce dimensionality significantly, from 132 to 4. All 4 factors were intuitively explainable and logical in their components. This coherence resulted in identification of 5 closely-knit clusters showing significant differences in characteristics from each other. Geo-spatial visualization showed alignment of these clusters both geographically and geologically. Contrasting cluster memberships against the geological and isothermal regions was able to bring out important insights about the cluster characteristics.

The best monsoon rainfall prediction came from a combination of 5 different cluster-level linear regression models with an overall RMSE of 12% and Congruence of 56%. Latest models used by IMD had a 6% RMSE and 68% congruence, based on 1981–2008 data. It should be noted that the empirical results in this study were based on a much longer 1902–2001 period. Same metrics for 1981–2001 showed an RMSE of 10% with a 67% congruence, close to the performance of the live models. While the absolute congruence at cluster level was a low 38%, it suggested that the combination of unsupervised and supervised methods may lead to a better prediction at an overall level when more advanced techniques are applied. It could thus be concluded that a further exploration on this problem will be worth undertaking in future.

Finally, the independent variables used in this pilot study were all surface-level measures that offer only limited predictive power [3]. Other features such as upper air [18,21] and oceanic [7,13] parameters have been proven to lend good predictive power in rainfall prediction. Moreover, the full scale study is expected to use terrain features such as altitude, % farm land, forest cover, distance from the nearest sea etc. as additional variables in both modeling and cluster creation steps.

Acknowledgement. This work was undertaken as part of the Master of Technology in Enterprise Business Analytics program in Institute of Systems Science, National University of Singapore, under the guidance of Dr. Rita Chakravarti. Authors would like to thank Dr. Chakravarti for her guidance and the two anonymous reviewers for their valuable suggestions on this paper.

References

1. Dunne, T.: Stochastic aspects of the relations between climate, hydrology and landform evolution. Trans. Jpn Geomorphol. Union **12**(1), 1–24 (1991)
2. Comrey, A.L., Lee, H.B.: A First Course in Factor Analysis. Lawrence Eribaum Associates Inc., Hillsdale (1992)
3. Omotosho, J.B., Balogun, A.A., Ogunjobi, K.: Predicting monthly and seasonal rainfall, onset and cessation of the rainy season in West Africa using only surface data. Int. J. Climatol. **20**(8), 865–880 (2000)
4. Zaïane, O.R., Foss, A., Lee, C.-H., Wang, W.: On data clustering analysis: scalability, constraints, and validation. In: Chen, M.-S., Yu, P.S., Liu, B. (eds.) PAKDD 2002. LNCS, vol. 2336, pp. 28–39. Springer, Heidelberg (2002). doi:10.1007/3-540-47887-6_4
5. Sen, N.: New forecast models for Indian south-west monsoon season rainfall. Curr. Sci. **84**(10), 1290–1291 (2003)
6. Stenseth, N.C., Ottersen, G., Hurrell, J.W., Mysterud, A., Lima, M., Chan, K.S., et al.: Studying climate effects on ecology through the use of climate indices: the North Atlantic Oscillation, El Nino Southern Oscillation and beyond. Proc. R. Soc. Lond. B Biol. Sci. **270**(1529), 2087–2096 (2003)
7. Rajeevan, M., Pai, D.S., Dikshit, S.K., Kelkar, R.R.: IMD's new operational models for long-range forecast of southwest monsoon rainfall over India and their verification for 2003. Curr. Sci. **86**(3), 422–431 (2004)
8. Kim, M., Ramakrishna, R.S.: New indices for cluster validity assessment. Pattern Recogn. Lett. **26**(15), 2353–2363 (2005)
9. Rokach, L., Maimon, O.: Clustering methods. In: Maimon, O., Rokach, L. (eds.) Data Mining and Knowledge Discovery Handbook, pp. 321–352. Springer, Boston (2005). doi:10.1007/0-387-25465-X_15
10. Aksoy, E.: Clustering with GIS: an attempt to classify turkish district data. In: XXIII FIG Congress, pp. 8–13, November 2006
11. Tripathi, S., Srinivas, V.V., Nanjundiah, R.S.: Downscaling of precipitation for climate change scenarios: a support vector machine approach. J. Hydrol. **330**(3), 621–640 (2006)
12. Bottman, N., Essig, W., Whittle, S.: Why weight? A cluster-theoretic approach to political districting. In: MCM 2007, Department of Mathematics, University of Washington (2007)

13. Rajeevan, M., Pai, D.S., Kumar, R.A., Lal, B.: New statistical models for long-range forecasting of southwest monsoon rainfall over India. Clim. Dyn. **28**(7–8), 813–828 (2007)
14. Ingsrisawang, L., Ingsriswang, S., Luenam, P., Trisaranuwatana, P., Klinpratoom, S., Aungsuratana, P., Khantiyanan, W.: Applications of statistical methods for rainfall prediction over the Eastern Thailand. In: Proceedings of the International MultiConference of Engineers and Computer Scientists, vol. 3 (2010)
15. Bello-Orgaz, G., Menéndez, H.D., Camacho, D.: Adaptive k-means algorithm for overlapped graph clustering. Int. J. Neural Syst. **22**(05), 1250018 (2012)
16. Kisi, O., Cimen, M.: Precipitation forecasting by using wavelet-support vector machine conjunction model. Eng. Appl. Artif. Intell. **25**(4), 783–792 (2012)
17. Kumar, A., Pai, D.S., Singh, J.V., Singh, R., Sikka, D.R.: Statistical models for long-range forecasting of southwest monsoon rainfall over India using step wise regression and neural network. Atmos. Clim. Sci. **2**(03), 322 (2012)
18. Ansari, H.: Forecasting seasonal and annual rainfall based on nonlinear modeling with Gamma test in North of Iran. Int. J. Eng. Pract. Res. **2**(1), 16–29 (2013)
19. Rao, M.V.V., Kumar, S., Brahmam, G.N.V.: A study of the geographical clustering of districts in Uttar Pradesh using nutritional anthropometric data of preschool children. Indian J. Med. Res. **137**(1), 73 (2013)
20. Yong, A.G., Pearce, S.: A beginner's guide to factor analysis: focusing on exploratory factor analysis. Tutor. Quant. Methods Psychol. **9**(2), 79–94 (2013)
21. Chifurira, R., Chikobvu, D.: A weighted multiple regression model to predict rainfall patterns: principal component analysis approach. Mediter. J. Soc. Sci. **5**(7), 34 (2014)
22. Menéndez, H.D., Barrero, D.F., Camacho, D.: A genetic graph-based approach for partitional clustering. Int. J. Neural Syst. **24**(03), 1430008 (2014)
23. Menéndez, H.D., Otero, F.E., Camacho, D.: Medoid-based clustering using ant colony optimization. Swarm Intell. **10**(2), 123–145 (2016)

Deep Learning and Its Applications

Facial Expression Recognition Using a Hybrid CNN–SIFT Aggregator

Tee Connie[✉][iD], Mundher Al-Shabi[iD], Wooi Ping Cheah[iD],
and Michael Goh[iD]

Faculty of Information Science and Technology,
Multimedia University, Melaka, Malaysia
tee.connie@mmu.edu.my

Abstract. Deriving an effective facial expression recognition component is important for a successful human-computer interaction system. Nonetheless, recognizing facial expression remains a challenging task. This paper describes a novel approach towards facial expression recognition task. The proposed method is motivated by the success of Convolutional Neural Networks (CNN) on the face recognition problem. Unlike other works, we focus on achieving good accuracy while requiring only a small sample data for training. Scale Invariant Feature Transform (SIFT) features are used to increase the performance on small data as SIFT does not require extensive training data to generate useful features. In this paper, both Dense SIFT and regular SIFT are studied and compared when merged with CNN features. Moreover, an aggregator of the models is developed. The proposed approach is tested on the FER-2013 and CK+ datasets. Results demonstrate the superiority of CNN with Dense SIFT over conventional CNN and CNN with SIFT. The accuracy even increased when all the models are aggregated which generates state-of-art results on FER-2013 and CK+ datasets, where it achieved 73.4% on FER-2013 and 99.1% on CK+.

Keywords: Facial expression recognition · Dense SIFT · CNN · SIFT

1 Introduction

Automatic facial expression recognition is an interesting and challenging problem which has important applications in many areas like human-computer interaction. It helps to build more intelligent robots which has the ability to understand human emotions. Many other real-world applications such as call center and interactive game development also benefit from such intelligence.

Ekman in early 1970s showed that there are six universal emotional expressions across all cultures, namely disgust, anger, happiness, sadness, surprise and fear [3]. These expressions could be identified by observing the face signals. For example, a smile gesture by raising the mouth corners and tightening the eyelids is a signal of happiness.

T. Connie and M. Al-Shabi—These authors contributed equally to this work.

© Springer International Publishing AG 2017
S. Phon-Amnuaisuk et al. (Eds.): MIWAI 2017, LNAI 10607, pp. 139–149, 2017.
https://doi.org/10.1007/978-3-319-69456-6_12

Due to the importance of facial expression recognition in designing human–computer interaction systems, various feature extraction and machine learning algorithms have been developed. Most of these methods deployed hand-crafted features followed by a classifier such as local binary pattern with SVM classification [20], Haar [24], SIFT [1], and Gabor filters with fisher linear discriminant [12], and also Local phase quantization (LPQ) [23].

The recent success of convolutional neural networks (CNNs) in tasks like image classification [5] has been extended to the problem of facial expression recognition [9]. Unlike traditional machine learning and computer vision approaches where features are defined by hand, CNN learns to extract the features directly from the training database using iterative algorithms like gradient descent. CNN is usually combined with feed-forward neural network classifier which makes the model end-to-end trainable on the dataset.

Like ordinary neural network, CNN learns its weights using back-propagation algorithm. It has two main components namely local receptive fields and shared weights. In local receptive fields, each neuron is connected to a local group of the input space. The size of this group of the input space is equal to the filter size where the input space can be either pixels from the input image or features from the previews layer. In CNN the same weights and bias are used over all local receptive fields. These two components, although make CNN runs faster, but are prone to over-fitting as the same weights are applied to the entire image.

In most cases, CNN requires a lot of training data to generalize well. The availability of large datasets and cheap computational power offered by GPU increase the popularity of CNN. However, this is not the case in facial expression recognition where the datasets are limited. While Scale Invariant Feature Transform (SIFT) [15] and other hand-crafted methods provide less accurate results than CNN [2, 11, 13], they do not require extensive datasets to generalize. Nonetheless, the modeling capacity of the hand-crafted methods are limited by the fixed transformations (filters) that remain the same for different sources of data. In this paper, we propose a hybrid approach by combining SIFT and CNN to get the best of both worlds. Both regular SIFT and Dense SIFT are investigated and combined with CNN model. Figure 1 shows an overview of the proposed approach. The raw image passes through the CNN layers before combined with either SIFT or Dense SIFT features. Both SIFT or Dense SIFT models are trained and evaluated separately. The SIFT and Dense SIFT features are merged with the CNN features at the final stage. Unlike other works, the CNN and SIFT/Dense SIFT features are combined during the training and testing phases. Moreover, the CNN features and fully-connected layers for the SIFT features are trained at same time which makes this work unique. The existence of the SIFT features during the CNN training help the CNN to learn different features representation from SIFT and make CNN and SIFT compliment each other. The contributions of this paper are two-fold: (1) we investigate the impact of combining SIFT and Dense SIFT with CNN feature to increase the performance of facial expression recognition, and (2) designing a novel classifier for facial expression recognition by aggregating various CNN and SIFT models that achieves a state of art results on both FER-2013 and CK+ datasets.

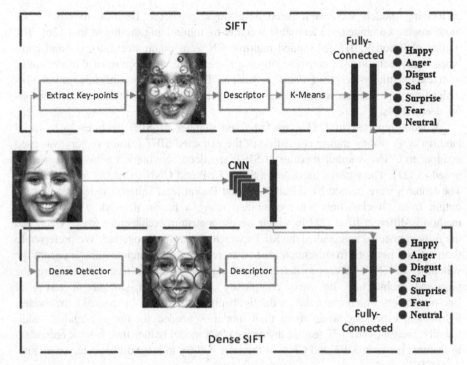

Fig. 1. Overview of the proposed methods

2 Related Work

Automatic facial expressions recognition (FER) has been an active research in the computer vision field. Facial expression and emotion recognition with hand-crafted feature extractors were reported in [2–5]. Many works have also applied convolution neural network in facial expression recognition. In [8] the authors analyzed the features learnt by neural network and showed that neural network could learn patterns from the face images that correspond to Facial Action Units (FAUs). He proposed to ignore the biases of the convolutional layers which gave him an accuracy of 98.3% on the CK+ dataset. The winner of FER-2013 challenge [22] used a CNN layer followed by a linear one-vs-all SVM. Instead of minimization of cross-entropy loss like vanilla CNN, he minimized a margin-based loss with standard hinge loss. The method achieved 71.2% accuracy on a private test. Another study applied deeper neural network by constructing four inception layers after two ordinary convolution layers [18]. Models based on transfer features from pre-trained deep CNN have also been proposed [19, 25]. The importance of pre-processing on increasing the accuracy of the FER model was heavily studied by [14]. Different methods were used to increase the number of examples through rotation correction and intensity normalization.

More recently, ensemble methods such as Bagging or Boosting are applied in facial expressions recognition. Several popular approaches such as [7] used CNN to analyze the videos and deployed deep belief net to capture audio information. The top performing models were then fused as a single predictor. Besides, multiple CNN models were combined via learnable weights by minimizing the hinge loss [26]. The winner of EmotiW2015 [8] trained multiple CNNs as committee members and combined their decisions via construction of a hierarchical architecture of the committee with exponentially-weighted decision fusion. The network architecture, input normalization, and random weight initialization were changed to obtain varied decisions for deep CNNs.

A work reported in [27] extracted fixed number of SIFT features from facial landmarks. A feature matrix consisting of the extracted SIFT feature vectors was used as input to CNN. Another mixture of SIFT and deep convolution networks was proposed in [21]. The authors used dense SIFT, LBP and CNN extracted from AlexNet. The features were trained by linear SVM and Partial least squares regression and the output from all classifiers were combined using a fusion network. Our proposed method is different from [21] in which we use a custom architecture where CNN and the fully-connected layers after the SIFT extractor are trained together. We preferred to design CNN network from scratch other than re-using other architecture to ensure the suitability of CNN features to detecting the expression on the face. Furthermore, the proposed architecture has less complexity and is much smaller in terms of free-parameters which make the model lightweight. It is favorable to make the models lightweight especially when more than model is needed for the aggregator. Additionally, merging the SIFT feature inside the CNN model reduce the possible redundant in features between SIFT and CNN as the later will try to learn different representation from SIFT.

3 Pre-processing

We standardize the size of all images to 48 × 48 pixels. To make the model more robust to noise and slight transformations, data augmentation is employed. Each image is amplified ten times using different linear transformations. The transformations include horizontal flip, rotation with a random angle between (−30, 30), skewing the center area, and zooming at four corners of the image. Some results of applying the transformations are depicted in Fig. 2. Finally, all images are normalized to have zero mean and unit variance.

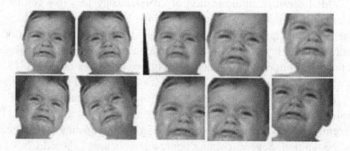

Fig. 2. The ten type of image transformations

4 Deep CNN Architecture

We built a custom CNN network architecture that is designed from scratch. The network consists of six convolution layers, three Max-Pooling layers, followed by two dense fully connected layers. Each time Max-Pooling is added, the number of the next convolution filters doubles. The number of convolution filters are 64, 128, and 256, respectively. The window size of the filters is 3 × 3. Max pooling layers with a stride of size 2 × 2 is placed after every two convolutional layers. Max-Pooling is used to summarize the filter area which is considered as a type of non-linear down-sampling. Max-Pooling is helpful in providing a form of translation invariance and it reduces the computation for the deeper layers.

To retain the spatial size of the output volumes, zero-padding is added around the borders. The output of the convolution layers is flatted and fed to the dense layer. The dense layer consists of 2048 neurons linked as a fully connected layer.

Each of the Max-Pooling and dense layers is followed by a dropout layer to reduce the risk of network over-fitting by preventing co-adaptation of the feature extractor. Finally, a softmax layer with seven outputs is placed at the last stage of the network. To introduce non-linearity for CNN, we used Leaky Rectifier Linear Unit (Leaky ReLU) [17] as follows:

$$f(x) = \max(x, \frac{x}{20}) \tag{1}$$

where the threshold value 20 is selected using the FER-2013 validation set. Leaky ReLU is chosen over ordinary ReLU to solve the dying ReLU problem. Instead of giving zero when x < 0, leaky ReLU will provide a small negative slope. Besides, its derivatives is not zero which make the network learns faster than ReLU. A categorical cross-entropy method is used as the cost function and is optimized using Adam [10] which is an adaptive gradient-based optimization method. All the hyper-parameters of the network such as the size of each layer are validated and fine-tuned against the FER-2013 validation set.

5 Sift and Bag of Key-Points

SIFT [9] is used to extract the key-points from the facial images. After locating the key-points, direction and magnitude of the image gradient are calculated using key-point neighboring pixels. To identify the dominant directions, the gradient histogram is established as shown in Fig. 3. Finally, the SIFT descriptor is determined by partitioning the image into 4 × 4 squares. For each of the 16 squares, we have a vector length of 8. By merging all the vectors, we obtain a vector of size 128 for every key-point.

In order to use the key-point descriptors in classification, a vector of fixed-size is needed. For this purpose, K-means is used to group the descriptors into a set of clusters. After that, a bag of key-points is formed by calculating the number of descriptors that

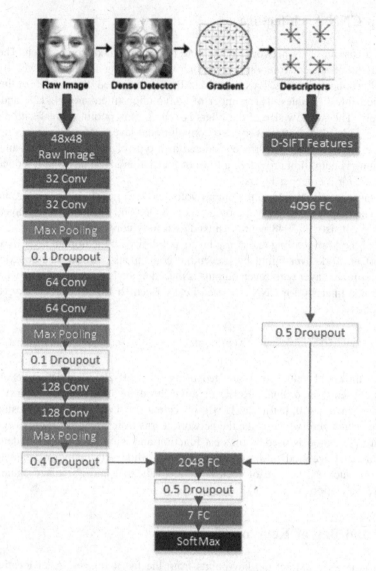

Fig. 3. CNN with dense SIFT

have been included in each cluster. The resulting feature vector has a size of K. After several trials, an optimal size of K = 2048 is found.

The K-vectors found are passed to a fully-connected layer of size 4096 followed by a dropout. The weights of the fully-connected layer is regularized by l2 norm with value 0.01. Finally the output is merged with the CNN model.

In contrast, dense SIFT does not require extraction of key-points from the facial image. Dense SIFT divides the image into equal region of pixels. Each region has a size of 12 × 12 pixels which yields 16 regions for an image. The SIFT descriptor is ran over all the 16 regions and each region is described by 128 features. This yields a total of 2048 features for the whole image.

To increase the accuracy of the model, the outputs from CNN only, CNN with SIFT, and CNN with Dense SIFT are aggregated using average sum. The probability of an input image x containing an expression e is:

$$P(e \mid x) = \frac{A(e \mid x) + B(e \mid x) + C(e \mid x)}{3} \qquad (2)$$

where A, B and C denote the CNN only model, CNN with SIFT model, and CNN with dense SIFT model, respectively. As each model has a SoftMax layer as the last layer, the output is confined in the range from 0 to 1. The best match expression is the one which yields the highest probability,

$$Y(x) = \underset{e \in Expressions}{\arg \max} \ P(e|x) \qquad (3)$$

6 Experimental Results

We tested our models on the FER 2013 and Extended Cohn-Kanade (CK+) datasets. The first is FER-2013 which has very wild facial expression images. The second is the standard CK+ which has a tiny number of samples. The FER-2013 dataset was presented in the ICML 2013 Challenges in Representation Learning [4]. The dataset was retrieved using Google image search API. OpenCV face recognition components were used to obtain bounding boxes around each face. The incorrectly labeled images were rejected by human.

On the other hand, the CK+ [16] is a lab controlled dataset which consists of 327 images from 123 subjects. Each of the image is assigned one of seven expressions: anger, contempt, disgust, fear, happy, sad, and surprise. To make our experiments compatible with other works like [14, 15, 23] and also the FER-2013 dataset, the contempt examples are removed. So we trained our models on 309 images from the other six expressions.

The FER 2013 dataset contains 28709 training images: 3589 validation (public) and 3589 test (private) divided into seven types of expression Angry, Disgust, Fear, Happy, Sad, Surprise and Neutral. Due to label noise, the human accuracy of this data is 68%. Table 1 shows the distributions of the expressions along the FER-2013 and CK+ datasets. The FER-2013 has more samples than CK+ in all categories. Happiness is the most frequent expression in the dataset. The rest of emotion labels except Disgust has quite similar distribution. Figure 4 shows examples of CK+ and FER-2013 datasets. The images in the FER-2013 dataset is by far more challenging as every image has a different pose.

Table 1. Distribution of the emotion labels in the datasets

Expressions	FER-2013	CK+
Anger	4953	45
Disgust	547	59
Fear	5121	25
Happiness	8989	69
Sadness	6077	28
Surprised	4002	83
Neutral	6198	0

Fig. 4. Examples of CK+ and FER-2013 datasets

6.1 Experimental Results for FER 2013

All the models are trained on 28709 examples in the FER 2013 dataset. The public set is used as validation set to tune the hyperparameters while the private set is used as test set. We initialized the weights as described in [6]. Each network is trained for 300 epochs with a batch size of 128.

Figure 5a shows the accuracy of the models on the test data. CNN with Dense SIFT outperforms the CNN only and the CNN with SIFT. Surprisingly the SIFT features did

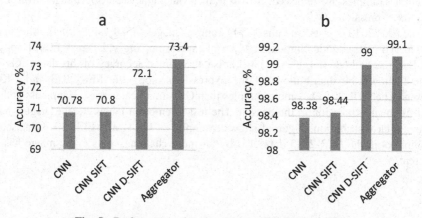

Fig. 5. Performance of the models on FER-2013 and CK

not improve the accuracy over the CNN only model. One possible reason is the SIFT Key-points locator is not suitable for 48×48 small images. In contrast, the Dense SIFT model increased the accuracy of the CNN by about 1%. Dense SIFT has another advantage in which it runs faster than regular SIFT as the key-points locations are already fixed and Bag of Key Points is not needed. The aggregator of the three models improves the result remarkably which surpasses state-of-the-art methods as shown in Table 2. Although the average sum technique is trivial and simple compared to [9], high variations in the model's designs increase the impact of the model's decisions.

Table 2. Classification accuracies of different models on FER

Method	Accuracy %
CNN SIFT	70.8
CNN D-SIFT	72.1
Proposed aggregator	**73.4**
Kim et al. [9]	72.72
Tang [22]	71.2
Mollahosseini et al. [18]	66.4

6.2 Experimental Results for CK+ Dataset

OpenCV Cascade Classifier has been chosen to detect faces landmarks in the images in CK+ and these landmarks are used to crop the faces. The model is pre-trained on FER-2013 training set first and parameter tuning is performed on the CK+ dataset. The advantages of using the pre-trained model are to speed-up the training phase and to increase the overall performance of the model. We use all the 309 images in the dataset for training and testing is performed using 10-fold cross-validation. All the networks are trained only for 20 epochs to prevent overfitting due to the limited size of training set.

The addition of Dense SIFT to CNN has again shown better performance against CNN only and CNN with SIFT models as depicted in Fig. 5b. Both CNN with Dense SIFT model and the aggregator exhibit significant results as shown in Table 3. Moreover, all the models including the CNN only model outperforms state-of-the-art

Table 3. Classification accuracies of different models on CK+

Method	Accuracy %
CNN only	98.38 ± 0.03
CNN SIFT	98.44 ± 0.08
CNN D-SIFT	99 ± 0.07
Proposed aggregator	**99.1 ± 0.07**
Khorrami et al. [13]	98.3
Lopes et al. [18]	96.76
Liu [12]	93.70

techniques. Several factors contribute to this good performance. For example, the eight layers in the deep neural network, extensive pre-processing, D-SIFT fusion with the CNN, and the aggregator of different models increase the discriminative power of the proposed method.

7 Conclusion

In this paper, a hybrid Convolutional Neural Network with Dense Scale Invariant Feature Transform aggregator is proposed for facial expression recognition. We have shown how the Dense SIFT features and convolution neural network could complement each other in improving the accuracy result. The proposed method combines the strengths of hand-craft and deep learning approaches. The Dense SIFT technique is studied and compared with regular SIFT feature extractor in which it shows an advantage over regular SIFT. The performance gain is noticeable when all the models are combined with the aggregator in which it outperforms state-of-the-art methods. Our experiments demonstrate a clear advantage of aggregating Dense SIFT and CNN models by achieving outstanding results on both FER-2013 and CK+ datasets.

References

1. Berretti, S., et al.: A set of selected SIFT features for 3D facial expression recognition. In: 2010 20th International Conference on Pattern Recognition (ICPR), pp. 4125–4128 (2010)
2. Dosovitskiy, A., et al.: Discriminative unsupervised feature learning with exemplar convolutional neural networks. ArXiv:14066909 Cs. (2014)
3. Ekman, P., Friesen, W.V.: Constants across cultures in the face and emotion. J. Pers. Soc. Psychol. **17**(2), 124–129 (1971)
4. Goodfellow, I.J. et al.: Challenges in representation learning: a report on three machine learning contests. ArXiv:13070414 Cs Stat. (2013)
5. He, K., et al.: Deep residual learning for image recognition. ArXiv:151203385 Cs. (2015)
6. He, K., et al.: Delving deep into rectifiers: surpassing human-level performance on ImageNet classification. ArXiv:150201852 Cs. (2015)
7. Kahou, S.E., et al.: Combining modality specific deep neural networks for emotion recognition in video. In: Proceedings of 15th ACM on International Conference on Multimodal Interaction, pp. 543–550. ACM, New York (2013)
8. Khorrami, P., et al.: Do deep neural networks learn facial action units when doing expression recognition? ArXiv:151002969 Cs. (2015)
9. Kim, B.-K., et al.: Hierarchical committee of deep convolutional neural networks for robust facial expression recognition. J. Multimodal User Interfaces **10**(2), 173–189 (2016)
10. Kingma, D., Ba, J.: Adam: a method for stochastic optimization. ArXiv:14126980 Cs. (2014)
11. Li, J., Lam, E.Y.: Facial expression recognition using deep neural networks. In: 2015 IEEE International Conference on Imaging Systems and Techniques (IST), pp. 1–6 (2015)
12. Liu, C., Wechsler, H.: Gabor feature based classification using the enhanced fisher linear discriminant model for face recognition. IEEE Trans. Image Process. **11**(4), 467–476 (2002)
13. Liu, M., et al.: AU-inspired deep networks for facial expression feature learning. Neurocomputing **159**, 126–136 (2015)

14. Lopes, A.T., et al.: Facial expression recognition with convolutional neural networks: coping with few data and the training sample order. Pattern Recogn. **61**, 610–628 (2017)
15. Lowe, D.G.: Object Recognition from local scale-invariant features. In: Proceedings of 7th IEEE International Conference on Computer Vision, vol. 2, pp. 1150–1157 (1999)
16. Lucey, P., et al.: The extended Cohn-Kanade dataset (CK+): a complete dataset for action unit and emotion-specified expression. In: 2010 IEEE Computer Society Conference on Computer Vision and Pattern Recognition – Workshops, pp. 94–101 (2010)
17. Maas, A.L., et al.: Rectifier nonlinearities improve neural network acoustic models. In: ICML Workshop on Deep Learning for Audio, Speech and Language Processing (2013)
18. Mollahosseini, A., et al.: Going deeper in facial expression recognition using deep neural networks. In: 2016 IEEE Winter Conference on Applications of Computer Vision (WACV), pp. 1–10 (2016)
19. Ng, H.-W., et al.: Deep learning for emotion recognition on small datasets using transfer learning. In: Proceedings of 2015 ACM on International Conference on Multimodal Interaction, pp. 443–449. ACM, New York (2015)
20. Shan, C., et al.: Facial expression recognition based on local binary patterns: a comprehensive study. Image Vis. Comput. **27**(6), 803–816 (2009)
21. Sun, B., et al.: Facial expression recognition in the wild based on multimodal texture features. J. Electron. Imaging **25**(6), 061407 (2016)
22. Tang, Y.: Deep learning using linear support vector machines. ArXiv:13060239 Cs Stat. (2013)
23. Wang, Z., Ying, Z.: Facial expression recognition based on local phase quantization and sparse representation. In: 2012 8th International Conference on Natural Computation (ICNC), pp. 222–225 (2012)
24. Whitehill, J., Omlin, C.W.: Haar features for FACS AU recognition. In: 7th International Conference on Automatic Face and Gesture Recognition (FGR 2006), pp. 5–101 (2006)
25. Xu, M., et al.: Facial expression recognition based on transfer learning from deep convolutional networks. In: 2015 11th International Conference on Natural Computation (ICNC), pp. 702–708 (2015)
26. Yu, Z., Zhang, C.: Image based static facial expression recognition with multiple deep network learning. In: Proceedings of 2015 ACM on International Conference on Multimodal Interaction, pp. 435–442. ACM, New York (2015)
27. Zhang, T., et al.: A deep neural network driven feature learning method for multi-view facial expression recognition. IEEE Trans. Multimed. **18**(12), 1 (2016)

Visual-Only Word Boundary Detection

Muhammad Rizki Aulia Rahman Maulana[✉], Retno Larasati[✉],
and Mohamad Ivan Fanany

Faculty of Computer Science, Universitas Indonesia,
Kampus UI Depok, Depok, Jawa Barat 16424, Indonesia
muhammad.rizki33@ui.ac.id, retno.larasati@kcl.ac.uk, ivan@cs.ui.ac.id

Abstract. Word boundary detection is one of the primary components in speech recognition system, which can be learned jointly as part of the speech model or independently as an extra step of preprocessing, reducing the problem into a conditionally independent word prediction. It can also be used to separate Out of Vocabulary (OOV) words in the sentence, thereby avoiding unnecessary computation. By itself, word boundary detection is essential in multimodal corpus collection, in which it allows automated and detailed labeling towards the dataset, be it on sentence or word level. In this research, we proposed a novel approach in word boundary detection, that is, by utilizing only visual information, using 3-Dimensional Convolutional Neural Network (3D-CNN) and Bidirectional-Gated Recurrent Unit (Bi-GRU). This research is important in paving the way for a better lip reading system, as well as multimodal speech recognition, as it allows easier creation of novel dataset and enables conventional word-level visual or multimodal speech recognition system to work on continuous speech. Training was done on GRID video corpus on 118 epochs. The proposed model performed well compared to the baseline method, with considerably lower error rate.

Keywords: Word boundary detection · Word segmentation · 3-Dimensional Convolutional Neural Network · Speech recognition

1 Introduction

One of the critical components in speech recognition system is word boundary detection. Word boundary detection has several functions. Firstly, word boundary detection can be used to separate the Out of Vocabulary (OOV) words [1]. Secondly, word boundary detection can help reduce continuous speech recognition problem into a simpler single word classification problem. Finally, word boundary detection can become part of speech recognition applications that require identification of words or short phrases in speech. Other than the functions mentioned above, word boundary detection systems are significant for data pre-processing. Data pre-processing is needed if the speech recognition system requires further processing of the segments of speech. However, more than half of the recognition errors are caused by word boundary recognizer [2]. For speech

© Springer International Publishing AG 2017
S. Phon-Amnuaisuk et al. (Eds.): MIWAI 2017, LNAI 10607, pp. 150–161, 2017.
https://doi.org/10.1007/978-3-319-69456-6_13

recognition system that requires word boundary detection as a preprocessing step, incorrect detection of word boundary might result in incorrectly recognized speech and also unnecessary increase in computations [3].

For the past two decades, there have been many advances in the research of audio-based word boundary detection. Various methods have been explored to solve audio-based word boundary detection problem using specifically designed audio files [1,3] or noise-induced audio files [4–6]. One of the recent studies using Time Delay Neural Network, showed 66% to 70% precision with around 0.685−0.577 of start time standard deviation and around 0.71−0.684 of end time standard deviation [7].

Notwithstanding the success of studies conducted on audio-based word boundary detection, there are some limitations to the audio files used as input. The primary challenge in audio word boundary detection is to catch the word starting time with a silent first vowel or the end of a word that co-articulates to the next word which becomes more complicated with noise induced audio files.

Regardless of the limitation in its approach, most existing works are based solely on identification of acoustic signal without any consideration about visual information. Studies on visual speech were first conducted to solve the problem on deciphering visual speech. The visual speech recognition system was at first believed to follow the audio-based recognition system success. However, early research did not achieve the desired results, with undesirable performances when dealing with a large vocabulary in a continuous speech recognition task [8].

However, recent studies on lip reading show that visual based speech recognition system's accuracy can be as high as its audio based counterparts [9,10]. Using Deep Learning approach, LipNet [9] outperformed model proposed by Gergen et al. [11] in terms of sentence-level accuracy with GRID corpus dataset. LipNet [9] achieved 9% higher accuracies compared to [11], with up to 95.2% rate of accuracy and 11.6% error rate.

Following this progress on visual speech recognition system, we propose a visual-only word boundary detection using 3-Dimensional Convolutional Neural Network. The dataset that we utilized in this experiment is GRID, a multi-speaker audio-visual sentences corpus. GRID corpus consists of high-quality audio and video recordings of 34 talkers, with each speaking 1,000 sentences [12].

This research was of enormous importance, as it laid out a foundation for other studies in the field of speech recognition. Firstly, visual-only word boundary detection can be fused with audio-only counterparts into multimodal word boundary detection, with which we might solve the problem with word segmentation on noisy audio data. Secondly, visual-only word boundary detection can also be embedded as a preprocessing step for a speech recognition system's architecture which enabled an existing word-level speech classifier to work on sentence-level or even continuous speech. Thirdly, visual-only word boundary detection can help with the creation of a novel multimodal speech dataset with multi-level variations (i.e., word and sentence-level speech).

This paper is organized as follows. A brief overview of the related works on word boundary is described in Sect. 2. Our proposed architecture is explained in Sect. 3. The summarization of our experimental procedures is described in Sect. 4. Then, the results obtained and the report on its evaluation and comparison with the other methods is discussed in Sect. 5. Finally, the main conclusions of our work are summarized in Sect. 6.

2   Related Work

Over the past two decades, research on word boundary detection has been done with the focus on developing various algorithms that can identify word boundaries through acoustic speech. Earlier studies in tackling this problem involve observing energy or pitch frequency pattern across the speech, which is later processed using several kinds of algorithms [1–3].

Earlier studies produced high accuracy prediction using specific audio data. These audio data were pre-prepared and recorded in a controlled silent environment. In reality, speech recognition applications need to identify words in the presence of noise. To get a solid word boundary detection system in a noisy environment, it has been discovered that the use of zero crossing rate or energy is inadequate and unreliable, regardless the complexity of the algorithm [4]. The algorithm trend used in research for audio word boundary detection is then shifted to another parameter. Some studies use the time-frequency energy band to distinguish between speech and noise [4, 13].

The frequency energy in the fixed frequency band $250-3500\,Hz$ is used to improve the information from the time energy data. The way to calculate the time-frequency parameter is by smoothing the sum of time-energy and frequency-energy. Nevertheless, the time-frequency based robust algorithm proposed in [4] uses handcrafted thresholds and rules that are inconclusive as a predictor and are not easy to choose or determined by a non-professional human.

The time-frequency parameter in [4], is then improved to a refined-time-frequency parameter and applied as the base for recurrent self-organizing neural fuzzy inference network [6]. Both time-frequency and refined-time-frequency parameter portray the time and frequency features, with the difference in the frequency band. Instead of a single-band, the frequency band used in refined-time-frequency was multi-band spectrum analysis. Just like the time-frequency parameter, the refined-time-frequency is calculated by smoothing the sum of the time-energy and frequency-energy. As mentioned above, the use of time-frequency parameter requires a handpick threshold value that can be difficult to determine. To solve this problem, Wu and Lin [6] used a recurrent self-organizing neural fuzzy inference network to determine the frequency bands as a threshold adaptively.

With the current technological advancement, speech recognition systems nowadays have become much more accurate and reliable. However, to work in a real−life situation, speech recognition accuracy got lower when faced with disrupted or low−quality noise. As an alternative approach, speech recognition can combine audio and video data to improve the system's performance [11].

The specific word boundary detection system is not as common as word or speech recognition, especially using the deep learning approach. Until now, there has been no research using deep learning method to detect word boundary through visual information. This is surprising because there are a number of research on visual speech recognition that models the problem as a word classification, which inherently needs a robust word boundary detector for it to work on real-world data. Garg *et al.* [14], adopted the use of deep learning technology for word recognition by using Convolutional Neural Network(CNN) and Recurrent Unit with MIRACL-VC1 dataset. CNN here is used to handle the video frames feature, and the Recurrent Unit is used to process the sequence of features. Video frames are stacked together to create a bigger image to be later learned by Long-Short Term Memory(LSTM) Recurrent Unit. This work was later followed by Chung and Zisserman [10]. Chung and Zisserman conducted an empirical study to compare five different deep learning architectures, such as 3D Convolution with Early Fusion (EF-3), 3D Convolution with Multiple Towers (MT-3), Early Fusion (EF), Multiple Towers (MT) [10]. The highest accuracy model was attained by Multiple Towers architecture with 65.4% accuracy on the 333 words dataset. However, without a robust word boundary detection algorithm, those approaches would only be applicable for pre-segmented data which is very far from the real-world settings.

3   Architecture

The architecture of our proposed model (Fig. 1) consists of Fully Connected Neural Network, Bidirectional-Gated Recurrent Units (Bi-GRU) and 3-Dimensional Convolutional Neural Network (3D-CNN) arranged contiguously in layers from top to bottom. The top layer, a Fully Connected Neural Network, works as a binary classifier with Sigmoid activation function. The sigmoid function is frequently used for binary classification since it is bounded between 0 and 1, and is easy to compute. In the middle layer, Bi-GRU works as a global model, and the first (bottom) layer 3D-CNN works as a feature extractor.

3.1   Bidirectional-Gated Recurrent Units

It is not easy to train Recurrent Neural Network (RNN) to capture long-term dependencies because the gradients tend to vanish [15]. One of the solutions for this problem is to use more complex activation function. Gated recurrent units (GRU) are designed to make it easier for RNNs to capture long-term dependencies by having more persistent memory. GRU have been shown to perform well in tasks that require capturing long-term dependencies, including speech recognition [16]. GRU's four fundamental operational stages can be explained with the following equations.

$$z^{(t)} = \sigma(W^{(z)}x^{(t)} + U^{(z)}h^{(t-1)}) \tag{1}$$

$$r^{(t)} = \sigma(W^{(r)}x^{(t)} + U^{(r)}h^{(t-1)}) \tag{2}$$

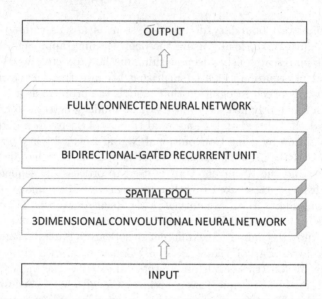

Fig. 1. The proposed architecture. A sequence of input is firstly processed by 3D Convolutional Neural Network and is followed by spatial pooling layer. Bidirectional-Gated Recurrent Unit is then used to process the feature extracted. Finally, Fully Connected Neural Network generates the output

$$\hat{h}^{(t)} = tanh(r^{(t)} \circ Uh^{(t-1)} + Wx^{(t)}) \qquad (3)$$

$$h^{(t)} = (1 - z^{(t)}) \circ \hat{h}^{(t)} + z^{(t)} \circ h^{(t-1)} \qquad (4)$$

The above equations represents the update gate (1), reset gate (2), new memory (3), and hidden state (4) respectively. To update the signal, $z^{(t)}$ is responsible for determining how much of $h^{(t-1)}$ should be carried forward to the next state. Therefore, if $z^{(t)} \approx 1$, most of the $h^{(t-1)}$ is going to be copied out to $h^{(t)}$ and if $z^{(t)} \approx 0$, then most of the $\hat{h}^{(t)}$ is going to be forwarded to the next hidden−state.

On the signal reset gate, $r^{(t)}$ is responsible for determining how important is the $h^{(t-1)}$ to the summarization $\hat{h}^{(t)}$. Irrelevant $h^{(t-1)}$ is interpreted as past hidden state's irrelevancy to the new memory; therefore the past hidden state would be deleted. The new memory generation is created from the combination of a newly observed word $x^{(t)}$, with the past hidden state. The hidden state is generated with the advice of the updated gate.

Other than making a prediction based on the past state, it is possible for RNN to make predictions based on the future state by having the RNN model read through the data backward in time. At each time-step, RNN maintains two hidden layers, one for the left-to-right (forward) propagation and another for the right to left (backward) propagation. The forward and backward parts of the network are independent of each other until the output layer, where the score results produced by both RNN hidden layers are combined to give the final result

[17]. This additional direction in the architecture, from one to two is referred as Bidirectional-RNN [18]. Equations below show the mathematical formulation behind setting up the Bidirectional RNN forward and backward hidden layer, respectively.

$$\overrightarrow{h}_t = f(\overrightarrow{W} x_t + \overrightarrow{V} \overrightarrow{h}_{t-1} + \overrightarrow{b}) \tag{5}$$

$$\overleftarrow{h}_t = f(\overleftarrow{W} x_t + \overleftarrow{V} \overleftarrow{h}_{t-1} + \overleftarrow{b}) \tag{6}$$

$\overrightarrow{W}, \overrightarrow{V}$, and $\overrightarrow{b}$ represent forward weight matrices and bias vector. $\overleftarrow{W}, \overleftarrow{V}$, and $\overleftarrow{b}$ are representing backward weight matrices and bias vector. The equation for final results, with U is the output metric, and c is the output bias, is defined as

$$\hat{y}_t = g(U h_t + c) = g(U[\overrightarrow{h}_t; \overleftarrow{h}_t] + c) \tag{7}$$

3.2   3-Dimensional Convolutional Neural Network

The 3-Dimensional Convolutional Neural Network (3D-CNN) has been success-fully used in video analysis [9,19,20]. One of the advantages of 3D-CNN is the ability to store time as the third dimension. Compared to 2D-CNN that performed the operations spatially, 3D-CNN does the convolution and pooling spatio-temporally. The 3D-CNN formula is defined as

$$y_{xyt} = f(\sum_i \sum_j \sum_k w_{ijk} v_{(x+i)(y+j)(t+k)} + b) \tag{8}$$

where y_{xyt} is a feature map value, f is the activation function, w_{ijk} is a kernel weight and $v_{(x+i)(y+j)(t+k)}$ is an input value.

In our proposed model, the 3D-CNNs are followed by Batch Normalization (BN), an activation unit, 3D dropout and spatial pooling. Batch Normalization is used to reduce the internal covariate shift on the network [21]. The internal covariate shift is decreased by normalizing each example within the batch to avoid the regularization effects. Batch Normalization ensures that normalization operation is appropriately handled by any optimization method. The Batch Normalization can be written as follows.

$$BN_{\gamma,\beta}(x_i) = \gamma(\frac{x_i - \mu_B}{\sqrt{\sigma_B^2 + \epsilon}}) + \beta \tag{9}$$

Rectified Linear Unit (ReLu) is employed as the activation function [22]. The 3D dropout is used to help learn informative features. Lastly, the spatial pooling is the last component before Bi-GRU, to increase the model performance [23]. The spatial pooling helps increase the network performance by alleviating the computational weight and also by detecting spatial feature regardless of small translation that was applied to the input.

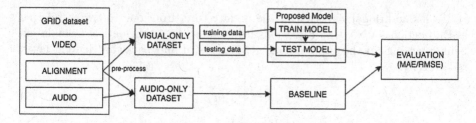

Fig. 2. Flowchart for detecting word boundary.

4   Experiment

4.1   Dataset

In our experiments, we used the audiovisual data in the GRID corpus [12]. GRID corpus consists of high-quality audio and video recordings of 34 talkers, with each speaking 1,000 sentences. The video was recorded at 25 frames per second with two resolution options, 720 × 576 pixels and 360 × 288 pixels which we have used in this paper. Subjects were requested to talk in adequately fast pace to fit each sentence into a 3 s time window, which equals to 75 frames in total.

To pre-process the GRID dataset, we did a facial landmark detection on speaker's mouth, which is followed by computing mouth crop. The facial landmark detection is performed using Histogram of Oriented Gradients feature combined with a linear classifier, image pyramid, and sliding window detection scheme [24]. We used Dlib [25] for our face landmark detection library. With the landmark detector, the mouth area was located, which was later cropped and scaled. Scaling was done to ensure the consistency of mouth size in the video. Lastly, all pixels were remapped into a real value between 0 and 1 for neural network input.

4.2   Training

The training was performed on GRID corpus using our proposed architecture. The model is trained for 118 epochs, with 34000 video data for each epoch. The word boundary is represented as a list of tuple of word start and end frame. We reported the output of our proposed model including the frame number prediction, and compare it with the actual frame number. The words predicted were counted for each video, then the number of words predicted was compared to the word count ground truth, which is six words per video.

As a baseline, a simple prediction model has also been tested for GRID audio data. The prediction model works by detecting words using periods of silence as indicators of where the words boundaries are. The pause between words works as a mark for the sentence and word boundaries. Therefore, the word location was given by inverting the interval between words within the sound signal. The audio-based prediction model is implemented using Python language and inspired by this work [26].

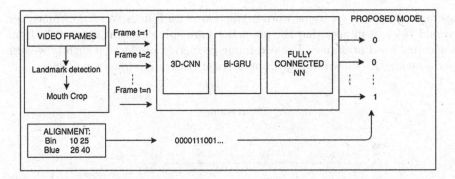

Fig. 3. Procedure for training video and alignment data. Video frames are pre-processed through landmark detection and mouth-cropping. Video alignment are represented as tuple consist of 0 and 1 value. For each video frame, our model predicts either 0 or 1. Prediction result then compared to the video alignment value. 0 represents silent/transition between word, 1 represents word utterance.

5   Results

The evaluation was done using mean absolute error (MAE), and root means squared error (RMSE). Mean absolute error is known to provide a logical framework for evaluating and comparing models [27]. Both MAE and RMSE assesses the quality and measures the accuracy of a predictor. However, RMSE is arguably sensitive to outliers [28]. From the RMSE equation, the errors are squared before they are averaged. Thus, significant errors receive a relatively high weight.

Table 1 compares the performance of our proposed model with the audio based word boundary detection model. Our proposed model performed well with low error results, starting frame difference and ending frame difference. Our proposed model has very low MAE level (0.007) and with RMSE equals 0.136. On the other hand, the audio based word boundary detection model produces larger errors with MAE and RMSE 5.95 and 5.971 respectively.

Table 1. Performance of visual-only word boundary detection model and audio word boundary detection model

Model	MAE	RMSE
3D-CNN + Bi-GRU (visual)	0.007	0.136
Invert interval (audio)	5.95	5.971

Other than the word count, the proposed model also predicted the start and end frame of each word. As mentioned above, the number of frames for each video is 75, consisting of 25 frames for each second. As shown in Fig. 4, the average error for start frame word prediction is 2.5 frames. With 25 frames per second video, it implies that the predictions are only deviating about 0.1 s from the actual word utterance. The end frame prediction produced a slightly weaker performance. As shown in Fig. 5, the average error is 5.2 frames or 0.28 s.

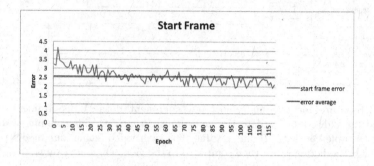

Fig. 4. Start frame difference.

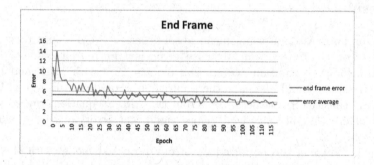

Fig. 5. End frame difference.

We also computed the difference between predicted words count and actual words count by calculating the amount of produced tuple of start and end frame. The average error is 1.4 as shown in Fig. 6 below.

The charts Figs. 2, 3, 4 show the graphic trends where the errors are decreasing throughout the training.

The standard deviation for the start and end time are recorded. The results from the first 5 epochs and last 2 epochs are shown in Table 2. From 118 epochs, the standard deviations for the start time range from 0.272 to 0.588 s. On the other hand, the standard deviations for the end time are generally bigger, ranging from 0.495 to 1.965 s.

Among all the 118 epochs, the third one (epoch 2) has the highest error deviance, both for the start time and end time. As previously mentioned, the fluctuating results show the trend of decreasing error. The decreasing deviations are shown in Table 2 indicates that the prediction is converged towards the actual boundaries of the word.

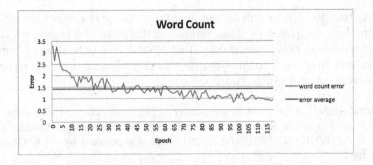

Fig. 6. Word count difference.

Table 2. Standard deviation for start time and end time

Epoch	Start time standard deviation	End time standard deviation
0	0.453 s	1.51 s
1	0.445 s	1.15 s
2	0.588 s	1.96 s
3	0.486 s	1.57 s
4	0.47 s	1.25 s
5	0.465 s	1.14 s
117	0.274 s	0.495 s
118	0.298 s	0.521 s

6   Conclusion

In this paper, we proposed the first visual-only word boundary detection model using deep learning. We show how word boundary can be inferred using only visual information. GRID dataset was used to train the model. Using the same dataset, the visual-only model performed better than the audio based word boundary detection model, with 0.007 mean absolute error, 0.136 roots mean squared error, and 0.28-s maximum error.

7   Future Work

We hope that the results of this paper will encourage future research for more advanced lip reading system and audio-visual based speech recognition. Visual-only word boundary detection can help to create novel datasets, that will open the opportunity to work on continuous speech recognition from conventional word-level visual or audiovisual speech recognition system.

Our proposed model has not been compared with other word boundary models that use deep learning, hence empirical study with other deep learning method is needed. Additionally, we will further investigate the performance of visual-only word boundary compared to other various methods. In the future, we hope to train the model on other visual corpus and build multimodal word boundary detection, and later use it to empower the existing word-level speech recognition model to work on real-world data.

Acknowledgment. This work is supported by Indexed Thesis Publication Grant funded by Directorate of Research and Public Services, Universitas Indonesia under contract No: 411/UN2.R3.1/HKP.05.00/2017 and is supported by GPU Grant from NVIDIA Inc.*

References

1. Rabiner, L.R., Sambur, M.R.: An algorithm for determining the endpoints of isolated utterances. Bell Labs Tech. J. **54**(2), 297–315 (1975)
2. Junqua, J.-C.: Robustness and cooperative multimodal man-machine communication applications. In: Second VENACO Workshop the Structure of Multimodal Dialogue (1991)
3. Ying, G., Mitchell, C., Jamieson, L.: Endpoint detection of isolated utterances based on a modified teager energy measurement. In: 1993 IEEE International Conference on Acoustics, Speech, and Signal Processing ICASSP-1993, vol. 2, pp. 732–735. IEEE (1993)
4. Junqua, J.-C., Mak, B., Reaves, B.: A robust algorithm for word boundary detection in the presence of noise. IEEE Trans. Speech Audio Process. **2**(3), 406–412 (1994)
5. Wu, G.-D., Lin, C.-T.: Word boundary detection with mel-scale frequency bank in noisy environment. IEEE Trans. Speech Audio Process. **8**(5), 541–554 (2000)
6. Wu, G.-D., Lin, C.-T.: A recurrent neural fuzzy network for word boundary detection in variable noise-level environments. IEEE Trans. Syst. Man Cybern. Part B (Cybern.) **31**(1), 84–97 (2001)
7. Tan, C.K.-Y., Kim-Teng, L.: Learning of word boundaries in continuous speech using time delay neural networks (2003). http://bit.ly/2xjbHvq
8. Potamianos, G., Neti, C., Gravier, G., Garg, A., Senior, A.W.: Recent advances in the automatic recognition of audiovisual speech. Proc. IEEE **91**(9), 1306–1326 (2003)
9. Assael, Y.M., Shillingford, B., Whiteson, S., de Freitas, N.: Lipnet: sentence-level lipreading. arXiv preprint arXiv:1611.01599 (2016)
10. Chung, J.S., Zisserman, A.: Lip reading in the wild. In: Lai, S.-H., Lepetit, V., Nishino, K., Sato, Y. (eds.) ACCV 2016. LNCS, vol. 10112, pp. 87–103. Springer, Cham (2017). doi:10.1007/978-3-319-54184-6_6
11. Gergen, S., Zeiler, S., Abdelaziz, A.H., Nickel, R.M., Kolossa, D.: Dynamic stream weighting for turbo-decoding-based audiovisual ASR. In: INTERSPEECH, pp. 2135–2139 (2016)
12. Cooke, M., Barker, J., Cunningham, S., Shao, X.: An audio-visual corpus for speech perception and automatic speech recognition. J. Acoust. Soc. Am. **120**(5), 2421–2424 (2006)
13. Gu, L., Zahorian, S.A.: A new robust algorithm for isolated word endpoint detection. Energy **2**, 1 (2002)

14. Garg, A., Noyola, J., Bagadia, S.: Lip reading using CNN and LSTM. Technical report (2016)
15. Bengio, Y., Simard, P., Frasconi, P.: Learning long-term dependencies with gradient descent is difficult. IEEE Trans. Neural Netw. **5**(2), 157–166 (1994)
16. Graves, A., Mohamed, A.-R., Hinton, G.: Speech recognition with deep recurrent neural networks. In: 2013 IEEE International Conference on Acoustics, Speech and Signal Processing (ICASSP), pp. 6645–6649. IEEE (2013)
17. Irsoy, O., Cardie, C.: Opinion mining with deep recurrent neural networks (2014)
18. Schuster, M., Paliwal, K.K.: Bidirectional recurrent neural networks. IEEE Trans. Signal Process. **45**(11), 2673–2681 (1997)
19. Ji, S., Xu, W., Yang, M., Yu, K.: 3D convolutional neural networks for human action recognition. IEEE Trans. Pattern Anal. Mach. Intell. **35**(1), 221–231 (2013)
20. Tran, D., Bourdev, L., Fergus, R., Torresani, L., Paluri, M.: Learning spatiotemporal features with 3D convolutional networks. In: Proceedings of the IEEE International Conference on Computer Vision, pp. 4489–4497 (2015)
21. Ioffe, S., Szegedy, C.: Batch normalization: accelerating deep network training by reducing internal covariate shift. In: International Conference on Machine Learning, pp. 448–456 (2015)
22. Nair, V., Hinton, G.E.: Rectified linear units improve restricted boltzmann machines. In: Proceedings of the 27th International Conference on Machine Learning (ICML-2010), pp. 807–814 (2010)
23. Boureau, Y.-L., Le Roux, N., Bach, F., Ponce, J., LeCun, Y.: Ask the locals: multiway local pooling for image recognition. In: 2011 IEEE International Conference on Computer Vision (ICCV), pp. 2651–2658. IEEE (2011)
24. Kazemi, V., Sullivan, J.: One millisecond face alignment with an ensemble of regression trees. In: Proceedings of the IEEE Conference on Computer Vision and Pattern Recognition, pp. 1867–1874 (2014)
25. dlib.net/face_landmark_detection.py.html.   http://dlib.net/face_landmark_detection.py.html
26. eddersko/wordboundary. https://github.com/eddersko/WordBoundary
27. Wallach, D., Goffinet, B.: Mean squared error of prediction as a criterion for evaluating and comparing system models. Ecol. Model. **44**(3–4), 299–306 (1989)
28. Pontius, R.G., Thontteh, O., Chen, H.: Components of information for multiple resolution comparison between maps that share a real variable. Environmental and Ecological Statistics **15**(2), 111–142 (2008)

Combination of Domain Knowledge and Deep Learning for Sentiment Analysis

Khuong Vo[1], Dang Pham[1], Mao Nguyen[1], Trung Mai[2(✉)], and Tho Quan[2]

[1] YouNet Corporation, 2nd floor, Lu Gia Plaza, 70 Lu Gia Street, District 11, Ho Chi Minh City, Vietnam
{khuongva, dangpnh, maonx}@younetco.com
[2] Bach Khoa University,
268 Ly Thuong Kiet Street, District 10, Ho Chi Minh City, Vietnam
{mdtrung, qttho}@hcmut.edu.vn

Abstract. The emerging technique of deep learning has been widely applied in many different areas. However, when adopted in a certain specific domain, this technique should be combined with domain knowledge to improve efficiency and accuracy. In particular, when analyzing the applications of deep learning in sentiment analysis, we found that the current approaches are suffering from the following drawbacks: (i) the existing works have not paid much attention to the importance of different types of sentiment terms, which is an important concept in this area; and (ii) the loss function currently employed does not well reflect the degree of error of sentiment misclassification. To overcome such problem, we propose to combine domain knowledge with deep learning. Our proposal includes using sentiment scores, learnt by regression, to augment training data; and introducing *penalty matrix* for enhancing the loss function of cross entropy. When experimented, we achieved a significant improvement in classification results.

Keywords: Sentiment analysis · Sentiment terms · Sentiment scores · Training data augmentation · Deep learning · Penalty matrix · Weighted cross entropy

1 Introduction

Opinion was defined by Oxford Dictionary as the feeling or the thought of someone about something and these thoughts are not necessarily the truth. Therefore, opinion is always an important reference for making decisions of individuals and organizations. Before the Internet, opinions were referenced via friends, family or consumer opinion polls of enterprises. The explosion of information and communication technologies (ICT) leads to a huge amount of information to be read. Some information is quite "big" but not containing much useful information. This causes difficulties for individuals and businesses in consulting, searching, synthesizing information as well as evaluating and tracking customer comments on the products and services of the business. Therefore, *opinion mining/sentiment analysis* has been born and is developed rapidly, strongly and attracting much attention in research communities. According to

S. Phon-Amnuaisuk et al. (Eds.): MIWAI 2017, LNAI 10607, pp. 162–173, 2017.
https://doi.org/10.1007/978-3-319-69456-6_14

Liu [1], opinion has a significant role in daily activities of people due to the fact that important decision is proposed from the consultation of the others.

Research on this topic was conducted at different levels: *term level* [2], *phrase level* [3], *sentence level* [4] and *document level* [5, 6]. In terms of methodologies, approaches related to this problem can be summarized as follows:

- *Lexicon approach*: *sentiments terms* are used a lot in sentiment analysis. There are *positive* terms and *negative* terms. Additionally, there are also opinion phrases or idioms, which can be grouped into *Opinion Lexicon* [7]. Dictionary-based method by *Hu* and *Kim* [8, 9] shows strategies using dictionary for identifying sentiment terms.
- *Corpus-based methods*: *This* method is based on syntax and pattern analysis to find sentiment words in a big dataset [10].

Recently, with the introduction of *TreeBank*, especially *Stanford Sentiment Treebank* [11], sentiment analysis using *deep learning* becomes an emerging trend in the field. Recursive Neural Tensor Network (RNTN) was applied to the treebank and produced high performance [11]. Formerly, the compositionality idea related to neural networks has been discussed by Hinton [12], and the idea of feeding a neural network with inputs through multiple-way interactions, parameterized by a tensor have been proposed for relation classification [13]. Along with the treebank, the famous *Stanford CoreNLP tool* [14] is used widely by the community for sentiment tasks. Besides, convolution-based method continues to be developed for sentiment analysis on sentences [15, 16]. To store occurrence order relationship between features, recurrent neural network systems such as Long Short Term Memory (LSTM) was used in combination with convolution to perform sentiment analysis for short text [17]. Most recently, a combined architecture using deep learning for sentiment analysis has been proposed in [18].

However, when deep learning is used with real datasets from different sentiment domains, we observe that there are some problems arising as follows:

- Each domain has a different set of sentiment terms. For example, for *Smartphone*, positive/negative terms can be *durable, expensive, well-designed, slim*, etc. Meanwhile, in *Airlines*, sentiment terms can be *delay, slow check-in, good service*, etc. Each term carries a different *sentiment score*. To date, these aspects seem not considered much in deep learning approaches.
- Like other neural networks, deep learning uses a *loss function* to evaluate the error of the learning process. Currently, for sentiment analysis approaches, the default loss function assigns the same error rate for different error cases. For example, if a training sample is expected as a *negative* case, the loss function will produce the same error value if this sample is wrongly predicted as positive or neutral cases. Intuitively, misclassification from *negative to positive* should be considered more serious than from *negative to neutral*. We believe that the loss function should assign different values for those cases.

To tackle these problems, we propose the following approaches:

- We use *regression* to learn sentiment scores for sentiment terms. Then, we use these sentiment scores to perform *augmentation* of the dataset to train deep learning models.
- We improve the loss function of the deep learning model by applying a *penalty matrix* so that the system can learn more accurately from errors of different mis-classification cases.

The rest of this paper is organized as follows. In Sect. 2, we recall some background on convolution neural networks (CNN) and sentiment analysis. A general architecture of using CNN for sentiment analysis is presented in Sect. 3. Section 4 shows the contribution of our study about learning sentiment scores using regression and how this score is used for data augmentation. Section 5 discusses the idea of using a *penalty matrix* to improve the loss function. Section 6 presents the results of our experiments. Finally, Sect. 7 concludes the paper.

2 Background

2.1 Convolution Neural Networks (CNN) for Sentiment Analysis

Convolution Neural Network (CNN) is one of the most popular deep learning models. Given in Fig. 1 is the general architecture of such CNN system. The first layer builds the vector from the words in the sentence. Input documents are transformed into a *matrix*, each row of which corresponds a word in a sentence. For example, if we have a sentence with 10 words, each word was represented as a *word-embedding* [19] vector of 100 dimensions, the matrix will have the size of 10×100. This is similar to an image with 10×100 pixels. The next layer will perform *convolution* on these vectors with different filter sets and then *max-pooling* is performed for the set of filtered features to retain the most important features. Then, these features are passed to a fully connected layer with softmax function to produce the final probability output. *Dropout* [20] technique is used to prevent overfitting.

In [16], basic steps of using a CNN in sentiment analysis was detailed in the process by which one feature is extracted from one filter as follows.

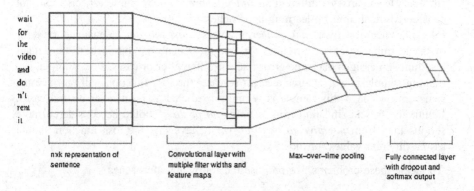

wait
for
the
video
and
do
n't
rent
it

nxk representation of sentence

Convolutional layer with multiple filter widths and feature maps

Max–over–time pooling

Fully connected layer with dropout and softmax output

Fig. 1. Using CNN for text processing [16]

Given a sentence with n words, let $x_i \in R^k$ be e k-dimensional word vector corresponding to the i-th word in the sentence. The sentence can be represented as:

$$x_{i:n} = x_1 + x_2 + \ldots x_n$$

Here, + denotes vector concatenation. Generally, $x_{i:i+j}$ represents the vector from index i to $i + j$. A convolution operator with filter $w \in R^{hxk}$ for h words will produce the feature:

$$c_i = f(W \cdot x_{i:i+h-1} + b),$$

Here, b is the bias and f is a non-linear function. By applying the filter on all windows of the sentence, we will obtain the feature map:

$$c = [c_1, c_2, \ldots, c_{n-h+1}].$$

The max-pooling is applied over the feature map and get the maximum value $\hat{c} = \max\{c\}$ as the feature corresponding to this filter.

2.2 Using Domain Knowledge for Sentiment Analysis

In general, when one performs sentiment analysis for a particular domain, the domain knowledge can be applied as shown in Fig. 2.

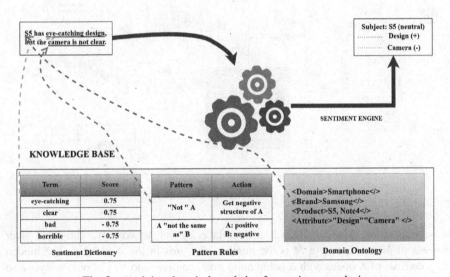

Fig. 2. Applying domain knowledge for sentiment analysis.

Thus, a general system [21] will rely on a *Sentiment Engine* to perform sentiment analysis on a user's comment expressing his opinion. This *Sentiment Engine* will operate based on a *Knowledge Base* consisting of the following components:

– A sentiment dictionary, including the *positive* and *negative* sentiment terms. In particular, those sentiment words will be assigned numerical scores indicating their *sentiment levels*.
– Linguistic patterns used to identify different phrase samples.
– A *Sentiment Ontology* to manage semantic relationships between sentiment terms and domain concepts. For more detail of Sentiment Ontology, please refer to [21].

Obviously, determining the sentiment scores for those sentiment terms is an important task to let such a system operate efficiently. We will present this work in the later part of the paper.

3   The Proposed Deep Architecture

Figure 3 presents an overview of our proposed deep architecture for sentiment analysis. The system includes the following modules:

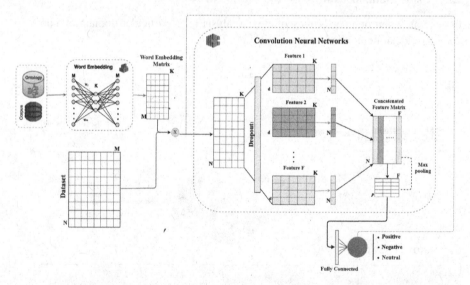

Fig. 3. The overall deep architecture.

Word Embedding Module: This is a three-layer neural network W. The input layer consists of M words where M is the number of words in the dictionary. The hidden layer consists of K nodes with K being quite small compared to N. The output layer also includes M nodes. This network will be trained from an M-word dictionary. Each word w in the dictionary is passed to the input layer of W as a *one-hot vector* corresponding to w. The W network will be trained to recognize the words w' close to w, to be activated by the corresponding nodes in the output layer. w' words can be determined from a predefined domain ontology built by the expert or learned from a co-occurrence between (w, w') in a large corpus in the domain being handled. After W is trained, the w_{ij} weights from the input node i to the intermediate node j will form a word embedding matrix $W_{M \times K}$.

Training Dataset: A set of collected documents. Each of these documents has been labeled {*positive, neutral, negative*} w.r.t to an object that needs to be sentiment-rated. A document with N words will be represented as matrix $D_{N \times M}$, in which the ith row is the one-hot vector corresponding to the ith word in the document. When performing the matrix multiplication $D \times W$, we can obtain an embedded matrix $E_{N \times K}$. Matrix E will be used as the input for next *Convolution Neural Network* module.

Convolution Neural Network: At this stage, the matrix E will be collapsed with a convolutional window, which is a matrix $F_{d \times K}$. The meaning of this matrix F is to extract an *abstract feature* from the *d-gram* analysis of the original text. The system will use f matrices $F_{d \times K}$ as an attempt to learn f abstract features. With the convolution between two matrices E and F being a $N \times 1$ column matrix, we will obtain the last matrix $C_{N \times f}$ by concatenating these column matrices together.

Next, matrix C will be fed into a pooling layer by a window $p \times f$. The meaning of this process is to keep the important *d-gram* sets in consecutive p *d-gram*. Finally, we obtain the matrix $Q_{q \times f}$ with $q = N/p$.

Finally, a fully connected layer will be implemented to aggregate the results and from there conducted back-propagation process.

4 Sentiment Scores Learning

4.1 Problem Definition

In this section, we discuss on learning sentiment score. In a general sentiment system, an adverb is used to modify or qualify a sentiment word. Mathematically, each sentiment word is associated with a sentiment score. If this sentiment word is associated with an adverb, the sentiment score would be scaled by the adverb's score. For example, consider the text *"S5 is very beautiful"*. The final score of the entity S5 (1.125) is calculated by multiplying the score of the sentiment word *"beautiful"* (0.75) with the adverb *"very"* (1.5). Since it is a positive number, one can conclude that this text is a positive mention to the product *S5*.

In general, the final score of a mention is a linear combination of all pair of sentiment word and its associated adverb as follows:

$$f = \sum_{i=1}^{n} a_i s_i = a^T s \tag{1}$$

where (a_i, s_i) is a pair of (adverb-sentiment word) in the text; a_i is set as 1 for every sentiment word s_i that does not have any associated adverb.

4.2   Sentiment Score Learning

4.2.1   Adverb Score Learning

For each mention in a training set of M mentions, let $t^{(m)}$ be the score of the mth mention, $s^{(m)}$ the vector form of the sentiment words, and $b^{(m)}$ the bias (calculated by sum of all sentiment words $s_i^{(m)}$ that do not have any associated adverb). We would like to find the set of adverb's scores w that minimizes the error:

$$\arg_w \min E(w) = \sum_{m=1}^{M} [(w^T s^{(m)} + b^{(m)} - t^{(m)}]^2 \tag{2}$$

The above equation leads to a traditional least square problem. In the context of sentiment analysis, in addition to minimizing the error function E, we also do not want w_i to take a negative value. Furthermore, the norm of w should not to be large (which leads to an overfitting). So, the optimization problem for adverb score learning is formulated as:

$$\arg_w \min \sum_{m=1}^{M} [(w^T s^{(m)} + b^{(m)} - t^{(m)}]^2 + \lambda w^T w \tag{3}$$
$$\text{subject to } w \geq 0$$

where λ is the regularization parameter which stands for the trade-off between error minimization purpose and the overfitting avoidance.

4.2.2   Sentiment Word Score Learning

This process is similar to the adverb score learning problem, but we consider the set of adverb scores w as fixed. We denote $\theta^{(m)}$ as scale parameters which are associated with the sentiment word set s; and set $\theta_i^{(m)} = 1$ if the sentiment word s_i does not pair with any adverb in the mth mention, otherwise $\theta_i^{(m)} = w_i^{(m)}$. Moreover, to model two types of sentiment word (positive and negative), we constrain $s_i > 0$ or $s_i < 0$ depending on whether the ith sentiment word is positive or negative. The optimal set of sentiment words s is the solution of the following optimization problem:

$$\arg_s \min \sum_{m=1}^{M} (\theta^{(m)T} s - t^{(m)})^2 + \lambda s^T s \tag{4}$$
$$\text{subject to } A_s < 0$$

where A is the diagonal matrix such that $A_{i,i} = \pm 1$, indicating whether s_i is positive or negative sentiment word.

4.2.3   Iterative Learning

In this section, we combine the learning process in Sects 4.2.1 and 4.2.2 together to form a dictionary learning algorithm that iteratively trains both the adverbs a and the sentiment word s.

Algorithm 1 Iterative Sentiment Word Learning
1: **procedure** TRAIN
2:    $K \leftarrow$ max iterations
3:    $s \leftarrow$ load sentiment words from database
4:    Initialize $b^{(m)}, t^{(m)}, s^{(m)}$ from *training set*
5:    Initialize λ, A
6:    $k \leftarrow 0$
7: loop for $k < K$:
8:      $w \leftarrow$ solving adverb optimization problem in (3)
9:      Update $\theta^{(m)}$ from w
10:    $s \leftarrow$ solving sentiment word optimization problem in (4)
11:    Update $s^{(m)}$ from s
12:    $k \leftarrow k + 1$

4.2.4   Using Learned Sentiment Scores for Data Augmentation

Data augmentation is a technique commonly used in learning systems to increase the size of training data sets as well as to control generalization error for the learning model by creating different variations from the original data. For example, for image processing, one can re-size an image to generate different variants from this image. In our case, from a dataset of labeled samples, we will generate variants by replacing the sentiment terms in the original data by the other sentiment terms that *have similar absolute scores*.

For example, let us consider an emotional sentence *"Company A is better than Company B. Company B is horrible"*, with the object that needs to be analyzed being *Company B*, the system will first preprocess the sentence as *"Company A is better than **Target**. **Target** is horrible."* Obviously, this sentence will be labeled as negative, w.r.t **Target**.

In this example, we assume that the words such as *horrible, poor, terrible* have similar negative scores after our learning process. In addition, the words *great* and *'amazing* have similar absolute values of opposite sign (i.e. these words have positive scores). Thus, from this sample, we will generate other augmented training samples as follows.

#	Training Data	Label
1	*Company A is better than **Target**. **Target** is poor*	Negative
2	*Company A is better than **Target**. **Target** is terrible*	Negative
3	*Company A is worse than **Target**. **Target** is great*	Positive
4	*Company A is worse than **Target**. **Target** is amazing*	Positive

In our learning system, the generation of augmented positive samples from the original negative samples is important, as this will help the system recognize that the word *Company A* does not play any role in identifying emotions since it appears in both positive and negative samples. Conversely, sentiment orientation will be determined by the sentiment words, including the original words and newly replaced words.

5 Using Penalty Matrix for the Loss Function

In neural network systems, one of the common methods for evaluating the loss functions is *cross entropy* [22]. Generally, a mention sample will be labeled with a 3-dimensional vector y. Each dimension respectively represents a value in [*positive, negative, neutral*]. For example, if a mention is labeled as negative, the corresponding y vector of this mention is (0, 1, 0). After the learning process, a vector of probability distribution over labels of 3-dimensional $\bar{y}$ will be generated, corresponding to the learning outcome of the system. The loss function is then calculated by the cross entropy formula as follows:

$$H(y, \bar{y}) = -\sum y_i \ln(\bar{y}) \tag{5}$$

However, unlike standard classification task, the importance of each label in sentiment analysis (*positive, negative, neutral*) is different. Generally, in this domain, the data is unbalanced. That is, the number of *neutral* mentions are very large, as compared to other labels. Therefore, if a mention is classified as *neutral*, the probability that it is a misclassified case is lower than the case it is classified as *positive/negative*. Moreover, positive and negative are two distinctly opposite cases. Thus, the error punished when a mention, expected as *neutral*, is misclassified as *positive*, should be less than that of the case where a *negative*-expected mention is misclassified as *positive*. The loss function is calculated by the default cross entropy function does not reflect those issues. Thus, we introduce a custom loss function, known as *weighted cross entropy* in which the cross entropy loss is multiplied by a corresponding penalty weight specified in a *penalty matrix*:

According to the penalty matrix in Table 1, one can observe that if a mention is expected to be *negative* but is predicted as *positive* or vice versa, the corresponding penalty weight is 4. Meanwhile, for the case that a mention is expected to be *positive* or *negative* and predicted as *neutral*, the penalty weight is 2. In other words, the former case is considered more serious than the latter. Also, if a mention is expected to be *neutral* and predicted as *positive* or *negative*, the penalty weight is 3. It is obvious that if the prediction and the expectation match to each other, the loss is not weighted as the penalty weight value is 1 (i.e. the loss function will be minimized in this case).

Table 1. The penalty matrix

Predicted/expected	Positive	Negative	Neutral
Positive	1	4	3
Negative	4	1	3
Neutral	2	2	1

Example 1. If y is [0, 1, 0] (*negative*), $\bar{y} = [0.2, 0.3, 0.5]$ (*neutral*), then the default cross entropy will result in 1.204, while the result of weighted cross entropy is 2.408.

Example 2. If y is [1, 0, 0] (*positive*), $\bar{y} = [0.2, 0.7, 0.1]$ (*negative*), the default cross entropy will also result in 1.609, while the result of weighted cross entropy is 6.436.

Examples 1 and 2 show that the weighted cross entropy function gives different loss values to different misclassification cases. Currently, we develop our penalty matrix based on observable intuition. However, in the future, we can rely on the distribution of data to construct this penalty matrix.

6   Experimental Results

We have applied our enhancement on basic deep learning model for sentiment analysis. The data we collected included 1 million social network discussions with labeled sentiment. This dataset is provided by YouNet Media[1], a company that analyzes data on social media channels. The company also provides a set of initial sentiment dictionary that includes positive and negative terms. However, these sentiment terms are manually assigned by sentiment scores of only 4 values in (1, 0.5, −0.5, −1).

Initially, the data were represented as one-hot vectors consisting of 65000 dimensions. After performing the word embedding technique, these vectors were reduced to 320 dimensions. In the Convolution Neural Network, we then used 128 filters. For training, we applied k-fold cross validation strategy with $k = 5$. Since our data is unbalanced between positive, neutral and neutral samples, we use the SMOTE [23] sampling method to balance data.

Besides CNN network model, we also employ the traditional SVM classification method using a *bag-of-word* approach for testing. In our experiment, we enhance the original CNN model with our improvements. In the CNN-*reg* method, we use regression to learn sentiment scores, instead of using default values in the sentiment dictionary. In the CNN-*cross* method, we use weighted cross entropy to calculate the loss function. Finally, the CNN-*total* method combines two enhancement of regression-based data augmentation and weighted cross entropy (Table 2).

Table 2. Experimental results.

	Recall	Precision	F-measure
SVM	81.49%	75.49%	78.38%
CNN	88.32%	85.46%	86.87%
CNN-reg	91.07%	90.18%	90.62%
CNN-cross	87.17%	93.55%	90.25%
CNN-total	90.33%	95.26%	92.73%

---

[1] http://www.younetmedia.com/.

We use the metrics in information retrieval, including recall, precision, and F-measure to evaluate performance. The results showed that CNN-based methods achieved better performance than the traditional SVM method. One can also observe that using regression to calculate sentiment scores for data augmentation has significantly increased recall and precision.

Finally, the use of weighted cross entropy slightly reduces recall, but it makes precision increased significantly, as the system learns better from serious misclassification such as from negative to positive (and vice versa). Finally, the combined CNN-*total* method yields the best results, in terms of F-measure. This demonstrates the advantage of our approach.

7 Conclusion

This paper proposed an approach to improve the accuracy of deep learning for sentiment analysis by incorporating domain knowledge. We introduce two improvements, including using regression to learn the sentiment score for data augmentation and using weighted cross entropy with penalty matrix as an enhanced loss function. When experimented with real datasets, our proposed approach demonstrated significant improvement on the F-measure metric.

Acknowledgments. We are grateful to YouNet Media for supporting real datasets for our experiment.

References

1. Liu, B.: Sentiment analysis and opinion mining. Synth. Lect. Hum. Lang. Technol. **5**(1), 1–167 (2012)
2. Ding, X., Liu, B.: Resolving object and attribute coreference in opinion mining. In: Proceedings of the 23rd International Conference on Computational Linguistics, pp. 268–276. Association for Computational Linguistics (2010)
3. Kim, J., Li, J.J., Lee, J.H.: Discovering the discriminative views: measuring term weights for sentiment analysis. In: Proceedings of the Joint Conference of the 47th Annual Meeting of the ACL and the 4th International Joint Conference on Natural Language Processing of the AFNLP, vol. 1, pp. 253–261. Association for Computational Linguistics (2009)
4. Wilson, T., Wiebe, J., Hwa, R.: Just how mad are you? Finding strong and weak opinion clauses. In: AAAI, vol. 4, pp. 761–769 (2004)
5. Turney, P.D.: Thumbs up or thumbs down?: semantic orientation applied to unsupervised classification of reviews. In: Proceedings of the 40th Annual Meeting on Association for Computational Linguistics, pp. 417–424. Association for Computational Linguistics (2002)
6. Pang, B., Lee, L., Vaithyanathan, S.: Thumbs up?: sentiment classification using machine learning techniques. In Proceedings of the ACL-02 Conference on Empirical Methods in Natural Language Processing, vol. 10, pp. 79–86. Association for Computational Linguistics (2002)
7. Taboada, M., Brooke, J., Tofiloski, M., Voll, K., Stede, M.: Lexicon-based methods for sentiment analysis. Comput. Linguist. **37**(2), 267–307 (2011)

8. Hu, M., Liu, B.: Mining and summarizing customer reviews. In: Proceedings of the tenth ACM SIGKDD International Conference on Knowledge Discovery and Data Mining, pp. 168–177. ACM (2004)

9. Kim, S.M., Hovy, E.: Determining the sentiment of opinions. In: Proceedings of the 20th International Conference on Computational Linguistics, p. 1367. Association for Computational Linguistics (2004)

10. Hatzivassiloglou, V., McKeown, K.R.: Predicting the semantic orientation of adjectives. In: Proceedings of the 8th Conference on European chapter of the Association for Computational Linguistics, pp. 174–181. Association for Computational Linguistics (1997)

11. Socher, R., Perelygin, A., Wu, J., Chuang, J., Manning, C.D., Ng, A., Potts, C.: Recursive deep models for semantic compositionality over a sentiment treebank. In: Proceedings of the 2013 Conference on Empirical Methods in Natural Language Processing, pp. 1631–1642 (2013)

12. Hinton, G.E.: Mapping part-whole hierarchies into connectionist networks. Artif. Intell. **46** (1–2), 47–75 (1990)

13. Jenatton, R., Roux, N.L., Bordes, A., Obozinski, G.R.: A latent factor model for highly multi-relational data. In: Advances in Neural Information Processing Systems, pp. 3167–3175 (2012)

14. Manning, C.D., Surdeanu, M., Bauer, J., Finkel, J.R., Bethard, S., McClosky, D.: The stanford corenlp natural language processing toolkit. In: ACL (System Demonstrations), pp. 55–60 (2014)

15. Zhang, X., LeCun, Y.: Text understanding from scratch (2015). arXiv preprint arXiv:1502. 01710

16. Kim, Y.: Convolutional neural networks for sentence classification. In: Proceedings of the 2014 Conference on Empirical Methods in Natural Language Processing, pp. 1746–1751 (2014)

17. Wang, X., Jiang, W., Luo, Z.: Combination of convolutional and recurrent neural network for sentiment analysis of short texts. In Proceedings of the 26th International Conference on Computational Linguistics, pp. 2428–2437 (2016)

18. Nguyen, D., Vo, K., Pham, D., Nguyen, M., Quan, T.: A deep architecture for sentiment analysis of news articles. In: Le, N.-T., Van Do, T., Nguyen, N.T., Thi, H.A.L. (eds.) ICCSAMA 2017. AISC, vol. 629, pp. 129–140. Springer, Cham (2018). doi:10.1007/978-3-319-61911-8_12

19. Mikolov, T., Sutskever, I., Chen, K., Corrado, G.S., Dean, J.: Distributed representations of words and phrases and their compositionality. In Advances in Neural Information Processing Systems, pp. 3111–3119 (2013)

20. Srivastava, N., Hinton, G.E., Krizhevsky, A., Sutskever, I., Salakhutdinov, R.: Dropout: a simple way to prevent neural networks from overfitting. J. Mach. Learn. Res. **15**(1), 1929–1958 (2014)

21. Nguyen, T., Quan, T., Phan, T.: Sentiment search: an emerging trend on social media monitoring systems. Aslib J. Inf. Manag. **66**(5), 553–580 (2014)

22. Bishop, C.M.: Neural networks for pattern recognition. Oxford University Press, Oxford (1995)

23. He, H., Garcia, E.A.: Learning from imbalanced data. IEEE Trans. Knowl. Data Eng. **21**(9), 1263–1284 (2009)

Hierarchical Attention Network with XGBoost for Recognizing Insufficiently Supported Argument

Derwin Suhartono[1,2]([✉]), Aryo Pradipta Gema[1], Suhendro Winton[1], Theodorus David[1], Mohamad Ivan Fanany[2]([✉]), and Aniati Murni Arymurthy[2]

[1] Computer Science Department, School of Computer Science,
Bina Nusantara University, Jakarta, Indonesia
dsuhartono@binus.edu,
{aryo.gema,suhendro.winton,theodorus.david}@binus.ac.id
[2] Machine Learning and Computer Vision (MLCV) Laboratory,
Universitas Indonesia, Depok, Indonesia
{ivan,aniati}@cs.ui.ac.id

Abstract. In this paper, we propose the empirical analysis of Hierarchical Attention Network (HAN) as a feature extractor that works conjointly with eXtreme Gradient Boosting (XGBoost) as the classifier to recognize insufficiently supported arguments using a publicly available dataset. Besides HAN + XGBoost, we performed experiments with several other deep learning models, such as Long Short-Term Memory (LSTM), Gated Recurrent Unit (GRU), bidirectional LSTM, and bidirectional GRU. All results with the best hyper-parameters are presented. In this paper, we present the following three key findings: (1) Shallow models work significantly better than the deep models when using only a small dataset. (2) Attention mechanism can improve the deep model's result. In average, it improves Area Under the Receiver Operating Characteristic Curve (ROC-AUC) score of Recurrent Neural Network (RNN) with a margin of 18.94%. The hierarchical attention network gave a higher ROC-AUC score by 2.25% in comparison to the non-hierarchical one. (3) The use of XGBoost as the replacement for the last fully connected layer improved the F1 macro score by 5.26%. Overall our best setting achieves 1.88% improvement compared to the state-of-the-art result.

Keywords: Hierarchical Attention Network · XGBoost · Insufficiently supported argument · Shallow learning · Deep learning

1 Introduction

Argumentation has already become a ubiquitous element of our life nowadays. Presenting an array of ideas coherently and logically ordered is the core concept of argumentation itself. A well-organized argument can be a powerful instrument to rationally persuade others of our point of view [22]. Despite the development of literature study focusing on argumentation that has been there for quite a

© Springer International Publishing AG 2017
S. Phon-Amnuaisuk et al. (Eds.): MIWAI 2017, LNAI 10607, pp. 174–188, 2017.
https://doi.org/10.1007/978-3-319-69456-6_15

long time, computational argumentation is still a young research field in natural language processing domain. Computational argumentation studies are focusing on the in-depth analysis for a more comprehensive understanding of the pattern of arguments in natural language texts. Even if, computational argumentation is still a relatively young research domain, there has been diverse interests because of its resemblance with how human create reasonings [34]. For instance, debating technologies [3,29,37], classifying part of texts as argumentative or non-argumentative [31], identifying argument components (claim or premises) for each sentence [32], recognizing 4 classes (major claims, claims, premises, none) of argumentation structures [42].

Besides all of those examples of computational argumentation research, one research that we consider worth exploring, which is to recognize sufficiency of an argument [43]. As what the authors have pointed out, the research that has been done to assess an argument in natural language text is still limited compared to other computational argumentation research subdomain. The existing approaches are to estimate the level of the persuasiveness of an argument [47] to score an entire essay [36] and also to evaluate the acceptability of an argument [7], and no research focuses on the lack of an argument.

In this paper, we also use the same theoretical framework as the state of the art [43] which was proposed in 2006 [26]. Before we can understand how the theoretical framework assess the sufficiency of an argument, we need to understand the structure of an argument. As described in Fig. 1, an argument generally consists of major claim, claim, and premise. Every argument component might have a relation with another argument component. To recognize the sufficiency of an argument, we need to assess premises of the argument, whether they provide enough evidence for supporting or attacking the claim or not. Here is the example to explain the sufficiency theory and their corpus creation standard:

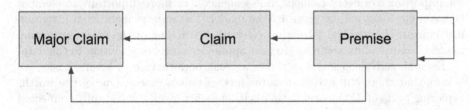

Fig. 1. An argument generally consists of major claim, claim, and premise. The arrows denote the relation between each argument component, whether it is a support relation or attack relation.

Insufficient Argument Example: It is an undeniable fact that tourism harms the natural habitats of the destination countries. As Australia's Great Barrier Reef has shown, the visitors cause immense destruction by breaking corals as souvenirs, throwing boat anchors or dropping fuel and other sorts of pollution.

This argumentation is an insufficient argument mostly due to the lack of support towards the general case. One sample of premise (second sentence) cannot support the entire general idea (first sentence). Therefore, the argument can be deemed as insufficient. Here is the example of a sufficient argument:

Sufficient Argument Example: *Cloning will be beneficial for people who are in need of organ transplants. Cloned organs will match perfectly to the blood group and tissue of patients since they can be raised from cloned stem cells of the patient. In addition, it shortens the healing process.*

This example provides a broader support towards its major claim. Because the premise is to gain benefit, it is safe to say that the two premises: perfectly match organ tissues, shorter healing process, shows benefit. For that reason, this argument is assumed as a sufficient one.

But, despite the contribution given by the state of the art research [43], we certainly believe that there are still a lot of room for improvement for that task, especially to increase the accuracy. The most prominent model is deep learning. The key difference between deep learning algorithm and traditional machine learning techniques is that deep learning does not necessarily need features engineering processes. The entire architecture will generate high level representation of the data which later will be classified. Despite the general assumption that manual features engineering is the key to several task successes, deep learning algorithms are showing good results in natural language tasks [27, 28, 45, 51]. As expected, its development in natural language processing domain is kept giving a promising breakthrough, such as attention mechanism [2]. Attention mechanism is proven to give a state-of-the-art result in translation task [2, 20, 48]. Attention mechanism can be an effective addition to a model by enabling a weighted access to every element of a sequence of data. Thus, it can give the ability to assess the importance of every element in a sequence, the more important an element is, the more focus will be given by the model. The improvement from attention mechanism, Hierarchical Attention Network [51] is one of the most interesting models because of its architecture that applies two level of attention to the data.

Even though deep learning shows a great performance in several tasks, we believe that there still exists areas for further enhancement. One of the worth-exploring parts of deep learning task is its classifier layer, the last fully connected layer. Softmax activation along with its cross-entropy loss function is the most commonly used classifier combination in deep learning [3]. But, we believe that it can be replaced with an empirically proven classifier, XGBoost [9, 10]. XGBoost is an implementation of gradient boosted decision trees designed for speed and performance. Because of its performance, XGBoost is used by a lot of data scientists and accomplish the state-of-the-art results in a bunch of machine learning tasks.

The objective of this research is to empirically analyze the performance of deep learning in recognizing insufficiently supported arguments. Our proposed model for this task is a novel approach using the combination of Hierarchical Attention Network as the feature extractor, and XGBoost as the classifier. This model yields excellent results in this task with 1.88% improvement compared to the state-of-the-art results; 87.05% of accuracy, 84.58% of f1-score and 82.84% of Area Under The ROC Curve score.

2   Related Work

The most related previous work is the sufficiency recognition using SVM (Support Vector Machine) and CNN (Convolutional Neural Network) [43]. Other than this research, the most related work is the general argumentation mining tasks. These include tasks that are focusing on debating elements classification, and argumentation structures classification. In debating elements classification sub-domain, an automatic claim detection on a given contexts [29] and its improvement, which is to detect its negation [5], also the evidence detection on an unstructured text with a given context [37], automatic argumentations summarizer in a political debate [2], and a further improvement from the previous work [29], which is to classify the stance from a given context-dependent claim [3]. Argumentation structure sub-domain includes the identification of arguments in legal texts [31], in news article [18,40], and user-generated web discourse [23].

Different argumentation components to be classified has also been introduced, claims and premises [32], claims and evidences [1], and four classes major claims, claims, premises, and none [42]. However, in an era where deep learning algorithm advancements are actively progressing, it is unfortunate that currently, only a few computational argumentation research that use the algorithms for the proposed model. To the best of our knowledge, research that used deep learning are as follows: predicting convincingness of an argument using Bidirectional LSTM [23], assessing the sufficiency of an argument using CNN [43], and recognizing support relation in arguments pair using a modification of Siamese Network with LSTM and attention mechanism [21]. The rest (majority) of computational argumentation research still rely on handcrafted features, such as context-free grammars [32], structural features, lexical features, and syntactic features [42]. Some research attempted to analyze the use of word vector representations in identifying argument components [44] and its combination with handcrafted features [15].

Other implementations of deep learning models in natural language processing are as follows: CNN for text classification [27,28,51], document-level document classification [45], and Hierarchical Attention Network [49]. Along with Hierarchical Attention Network [49] that has been applied to a lot of traditional natural language tasks, such as topic labeling [46], sentiment analysis [30,33], and spam detection [38]. The result that they get is better than any other model that has been proposed before it.

Not only the sparsity of deep learning presence in the argumentation mining research, but XGBoost is also not well explored in the field of argumentation mining. XGBoost is widely used in from KDD Cup. From 29 challenges winning solutions announced at Kaggle's blog during 2015, 17 solutions used XGBoost [9]. In 2016, KDD cup 2016 winner used XGBoost to rank a research institute contribution based on their number of accepted papers in the future conference [39]. To the best of our knowledge, there is no implementation of XGBoost in argumentation mining yet.

3 Methodologies

Our proposed model is a novel approach using both deep learning and XGBoost as shown in Fig. 2. The flow is described as follows:

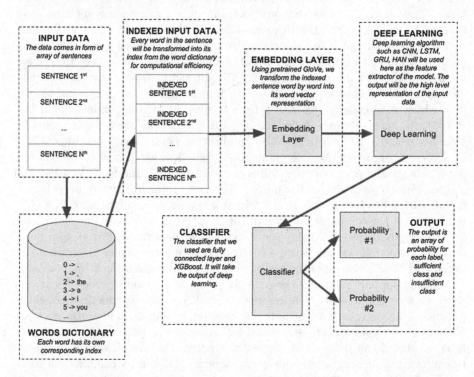

Fig. 2. Our proposed model outline. Starting from the raw input data, and transformed into their word vector representations which will be classified by the classifier after being processed by the deep learning algorithm

For the tokenization, we used Keras tokenizer and text processing tools [12] to create a vocabulary of words. In the beginning of the training process, we fed the entire dataset to the machine to be tokenized word-by-word. For example: the sentence *"i want to play a video game."* will be tokenized into an array of words as such: [*"i"*, *"want"*, *"to"*, *"play"*, *"a"*, *"video"*, *"game"*, *"."*]. The very same treatment will be enforced to every sentence in the dataset. Later, these arrays of words will be kept in a dictionary variable and assigned to its index accordingly. These indices help the computational process become more efficient. But, words alone cannot be mathematically computed. Hence, we need to transform each word into its vector representation. We implemented pretrained 300-dimensions word vectors from Global Vector (GloVe) [35]. We implemented this publicly available pre-trained GloVe as the fixed weight of the embedding layer. Therefore, we did not train the embedding layer along with another layer in the training process.

These arrays of word vector representations will be the input of the deep learning layer. Deep learning layer will act as the feature extractor of each data. Hence, the output of it will be the high-level representations/features of each data. These high-level features will then be the input for the classifier layer. As mentioned in Fig. 2, we implemented two classifiers algorithms, fully connected layer and XGBoost. For the fully connected layer, we implement an end-to-end learning system. Thus, the entire architecture, both deep learning layer and classifier are trained at the same time. For the XGBoost, we implemented transfer learning method. Thus, we firstly trained the deep learning algorithm with fully connected layer. After that, we remove the fully connected layer and replaced it with XGBoost. This XGBoost took the high-level representation computed by the deep learning layer as the input for its training process. Both fully connected layer and XGBoost are trained using softmax function as the objective function. Deep learning algorithms and the classifier algorithms will be further explored in the next subchapter.

Following the original experiment [43], we also treat this task as a binary classification task following their data and annotations. To get comparable results, we also used 20 times 5-fold cross-validation to assess the model. For the training process, we implement early stopping mechanism [4, 8, 50]. In all our model, we apply dropout mechanism [41] to prevent overfitting. It is worth to know that the data distributed by the original paper, the one that we used, is not divided equally for each class. In detail, 33% for the insufficient argument class, 67% for the sufficient argument. Hence, in addition to the model quality metrics, we add Area Under the ROC Curve (ROC-AUC) [14,19] because we believe that ROC-AUC can be the most reliable metrics calculation due to the imbalanced data problem [6].

3.1   Long Short Term Memory (LSTM)

The first model is LSTM [25]. The reason we use LSTM is due to its proven effectivity in handling sequential data and because of its performance that has been proven empirically as one of the best RNN architecture. Not only the one directional LSTM, the Bidirectional LSTM as well [23, 25, 51]. In this paper, we did several experiments using LSTM and Bidirectional LSTM models. The best parameters for LSTM and Bidirectional LSTM in this particular task is using 128 number of units and 0.5 rates for both of dropout and recurrent dropout.

3.2 Gated Recurrent Unit (GRU)

The second model is GRU [11,13]. The reason we use GRU is due to its performance that is on par with LSTM and its computational efficiency. The difference between GRU and LSTM is the number of gates present in both models [13]. GRU has two gates (reset and update) while LSTM has three gates (input, forget, output). Same as the experimental model of LSTM, we also create GRU and Bidirectional GRU [33] as the result comparison. The best parameters for both GRU and Bidirectional GRU in this task are using 128 number of units and 0.5 rates of dropout and recurrent dropout.

3.3 Hierarchical Attention Network (HAN)

Figure 3 shows the architecture of Hierarchical Attention Network [49]. This design used GRU [2], which has been explained in the previous subchapter. As stated in the original paper of Hierarchical Attention Network, this architecture works with two attention mechanism.

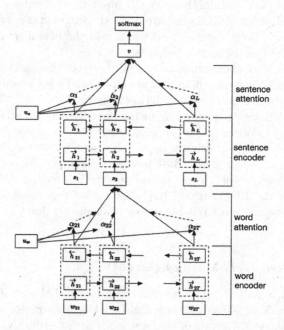

Fig. 3. Hierarchical Attention Network [49]. It contains two level attention that works hierarchically

As shown in Fig. 3, the document will be seen as a four-dimension data ([Batch size, the number of sentences, the number of words in a sentence, vector representation]). In the deepest part of the architecture, they use word-level attention with a Bidirectional GRU [2]. This word-level attention can be seen as a representation of most influential or informative word in that particular sentence. In the outer, they add another attention, the sentence-level attention. Just like the word-level attention, this attention mechanism will also be a representation of the most informative sentence in that document. On top of the architecture, they use softmax layer [24] and use negative log likelihood. Since we use the same model, the whole equation can be seen in the paper. The best settings for Hierarchical Attention Network to recognize sufficient argument are using one layer bidirectional GRU for both word and sentence encoder with 32 number of GRU units. We also applied 0.5 rates of dropout and recurrent dropout. For the optimizer, we implement Nadam [17] with 0.002 learning rate. We use 32 as the batch size.

3.4   Extreme Gradient Boosting (XGBoost)

XGBoost implements gradient boosting algorithm and designed to handle a large-scale data using a fast-parallel tree construction which will cut the training time significantly. As for the classification task, we used softmax probability as the objective function and logistic loss as the loss function. For further enhancement that we made will be discussed in the next sub-chapter.

3.5   HAN + XGBoost

In this model, we did not use an end-to-end architecture. Instead, we used a pre-trained HAN model and popped the last layer, the fully connected layer, and used that as the feature extractor. This method is inspired by the effectiveness of transfer learning [16]. After that process, we used the extracted features as the input for the XGBoost to further be classified into two classes using softmax probability as the objective function. The best hyperparameter setting that we have tried is 1000 epoch, 0.01 learning rate, and ten as the max_depth, and we let another hyperparameter to used the default value provided by the library [10]. Using the best pre-trained model of HAN, which is judged by the cross-validation results, the HAN + XGBoost model can surpass the previous work results. Details of the results are in the next chapter.

4   Experiments

For these experiments, we used keras with tensorflow as its backend. In Table 1, we presented the architecture assessment based on the 20 times 5-fold cross validation, the same setting as the state of the art [43] experiment. The first three results are taken from the state of the art experiment. The LSTM, GRU, BiL-STM and BiGRU which are represented by model number 4–7 are significantly outperformed by the CNN model and also surpassed by SVM. As we can see in the Table 1, those Recurrent Neural Network modifications were surprisingly bad in this task. But, the LSTM and GRU, with an added attention layer, give better results; the ROC-AUC score is $81.97 \pm 2.92\%$ for LSTM+attention and

82.39 ± 3.86% for GRU+attention. BiLSTM+attention and BiGRU+attention give comparable results with the LSTM+attention and GRU+attention. Both get 82.96 ± 3.07% and 82.28 ± 3.50% ROC-AUC score respectively. The model that becomes the focus of our paper, HAN, gives a lower result in comparison to the state of the art [43] CNN. The best HAN model is using 32 GRU units which get 79.32 ± 3.60% F1 score and 84.65 ± 2.92% for ROC-AUC score.

Table 1. Metric scores of models. All of our deep learning models used GloVe. Except HAN, we implemented 64 batch size and 128 units, HAN used 32 batch size and 16, 32, 64, 100, and 128 units. HAN units are denoted by the number inside bracket, ex: HAN (units) (* state of the art [43] published results)

No	Model name	Accuracy (%)	Precision (%)	Recall (%)	F1 macro (%)	ROC-AUC (%)
1	Human upper bound*	91.1 ± 2.2	86.3 ± 5.8	80.8 ± 10.9	88.7 ± 2.6	-
2	SVM*	79.8 ± 2.8	73.1 ± 6.0	64.1 ± 6.1	77 ± 3.2	-
3	CNN*	84.3 ± 2.5	76.2 ± 5.4	78.4 ± 6.8	82.7 ± 2.7	-
4	LSTM	76.20 ± 3.00	79.54 ± 7.76	41.11 ± 12.20	52.75 ± 11.04	67.62 ± 5.02
5	GRU	69.95 ± 3.82	61.58 ± 11.88	28.19 ± 13.44	37.29 ± 13.51	59.74 ± 5.86
6	Bidirectional LSTM	75.10 ± 2.69	76.00 ± 9.38	40.73 ± 11.33	51.62 ± 9.17	66.69 ± 4.27
7	Bidirectional GRU	69.52 ± 2.17	60.93 ± 7.31	29.78 ± 8.90	39.05 ± 8.19	59.81 ± 3.23
8	LSTM + attention	83.79 ± 2.37	76.79 ± 6.55	76.37 ± 8.27	76.01 ± 3.64	81.97 ± 2.92
9	GRU + attention	83.80 ± 2.96	75.69 ± 5.97	78.05 ± 8.74	76.39 ± 4.66	82.39 ± 3.68
10	Bidirectional LSTM + attention	84.39 ± 2.41	76.74 ± 5.65	78.56 ± 8.05	77.19 ± 3.81	82.96 ± 3.07
11	Bidirectional GRU + attention	84.11 ± 2.57	77.22 ± 6.03	76.59 ± 9.01	76.36 ± 4.51	82.28 ± 3.50
12	HAN (16)	85.44 ± 2.78	77.80 ± 5.66	80.74 ± 8.14	78.84 ± 4.44	84.29 ± 3.51
13	HAN (32)	85.66 ± 2.57	78.00 ± 6.03	81.52 ± 7.09	79.32 ± 3.60	84.65 ± 2.92
14	HAN (64)	85.64 ± 2.39	80.54 ± 6.00	77.13 ± 8.41	78.28 ± 4.13	83.56 ± 3.23
15	HAN (100)	85.35 ± 2.49	80.11 ± 5.81	76.61 ± 9.27	77.75 ± 4.62	83.21 ± 3.63
16	HAN (128)	84.57 ± 3.53	79.98 ± 7.27	74.44 ± 10.48	76.30 ± 5.95	82.09 ± 4.42

In Table 2, we used HAN with 32 GRU units as the feature extractor, whose output will be fed to XGBoost. Each model implements 1000 epochs, 0.01 learning rate, and 10 maximum tree depth. The best result is achieved by the 11th model as shown in Table 2. The model achieves 84.58 ± 2.38% F1 score and 82.84 ± 2.49% ROC-AUC score as shown in Fig. 4, which is higher than the state of the art [43] CNN regarding F1 score. Table 3 shows the composition of true negative, true positive, false negative and false positive. As seen in Table 3, it is relatively easy for the model to correctly identify sufficiently supported arguments; with 656:681 ratio of correct identification. On the other hand, identifying insufficiently supported arguments is relatively harder; with 232:348 ratio of correct identification. We conclude that the reason of this problem is derived from the imbalance proportion of insufficiently supported arguments in the dataset. This will be further analysed in the next chapter.

Table 2. Metric scores of HAN 32 units and GloVe embedding with XGBoost. Each model implements 1000 epochs, 0.01 learning rate, and 10 maximum tree depth

No.	XGBoost Params		Accuracy (%)	Precision (%)	Recall (%)	F1 macro (%)	ROC – AUC (%)
	Alpha	Lambda					
1	0.1	1	87.05 ± 1.89	87.92 ± 2.19	82.84 ± 2.49	84.58 ± 2.38	82.84 ± 2.49
2	0.1	1.5	86.94 ± 1.83	87.83 ± 2.08	82.71 ± 2.5	84.44 ± 2.34	82.71 ± 2.5
3	0.1	0.5	87.00 ± 1.77	87.89 ± 2.15	82.78 ± 2.33	84.52 ± 2.23	82.78 ± 2.33
4	0.2	1	87.04 ± 1.85	87.93 ± 2.13	82.83 ± 2.47	84.57 ± 2.34	82.83 ± 2.47
5	0.2	0.9	86.99 ± 1.81	87.90 ± 2.15	82.76 ± 2.42	84.51 ± 2.30	82.76 ± 2.42
6	0.3	1	87.02 ± 1.86	87.93 ± 2.15	82.78 ± 2.48	84.53 ± 2.36	82.78 ± 2.48

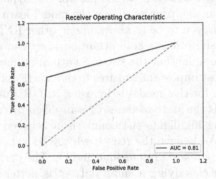

Fig. 4. Area under receiver operating characteristic curve (ROC-AUC) graph. This graph is produced by HAN + XGBoost with its best settings. It achieved 84.58±2.38%

Table 3. Confusion Matrix table yielded by the proposed model with the best hyper-parameter settings

	Sufficient	Insufficient	
Sufficient	656	25	681
Insufficient	116	232	348
	772	257	1029

5 Discussions

We found three important findings in this paper. The first one is the fact that the shallower model can outperform a relatively more complex model. This is proven by the comparison between CNN and SVM with other deep learning algorithms (LSTM, GRU, BiLSTM, and BiGRU). We believe the prevalence of this issue is correlated to the size of the dataset. We postulate that complex models need to train more parameters compared to the shallow one. However, the corpus created [43] is relatively small in comparison to other tasks, such as: sentiment analysis, or spam detector. Analyzing from the experiment results, we drew a conclusion that complex models are not suitable to tasks that did not provide a large dataset.

The second finding is the effectiveness of attention mechanism in a document classification task. As shown in Table 1, LSTM, GRU, BiLSTM, BiGRU with an additional layer of attention can significantly outperform their standard implementations. This finding contradicts our first finding. However, we believe that this occurrence arose because of the attention mechanism behavior. Attention mechanism amplifies the existing features instead of making the model require more features. This can be achieved because attention mechanism gives access to every timestep unit. Identifying which part of the sequence that gives more contribution to the learning process makes the model learn better. Hierarchical attention network is proven to be the best among other RNN models. By taking our second finding assumption, where attention layer can amplify the existing features, it is safe to assume that the two-level attention mechanism enables the model to select the most important features from an array of prominent features. The best modification for this model is by using 32 GRU units.

The third finding is the state-of-the-art result given by combining HAN with XGBoost. This finding highlights the comparison between the fully connected layer and XGBoost. We believe the reason why XGBoost can outperform fully connected layer is fairly related to our first finding. The performance of gradient boosting algorithm in classifying a small dataset is better than deep learning. This task failed to provide a large enough dataset to train an enormous number of parameters that a fully connected layer has. Hence, we experimented with gradient boosting decision tree as the replacement of the fully connected layer. It is proven to increase the entire metrics scores. Consequently we conclude that, XGBoost helps improve a model performance in a classification task, especially when combined with deep learning.

In Fig. 5, we presented the comparison graph between the shallow model, RNN models, RNN models using attention mechanism, hierarchical attention, and hierarchical attention using XGBoost. This graph works as the summary of our findings. "Shallow model" denotes a model with a relatively small amount of the trainable parameters in comparison to the other models, i.e.: CNN. We referred the average of the results of LSTM, GRU, BiGRU, BiLSTM from Table 1 as "RNN models". The "RNN + Attention" refers to the average of four RNN models with attention mechanism results in Table 1. "HAN" refers to the average result of HAN models, and "HAN + XGBoost" refers to the average result of all HAN+XGBoost models from Table 2. We used accuracy, precision, recall, and f1 as the comparative metrics. As seen in the graph, the shallow model outperformed RNN models or the more complex models, attention improved RNN models, HAN further improved it, and lastly XGBoost improved the results of HAN as stated in the findings. Detailed values are presented in Table 4.

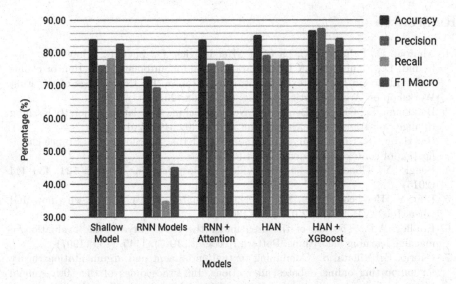

Fig. 5. Model and Accuracy Graph

Table 4. Table for graph on Fig. 5. This table contains the explanation about the results shown in the previous table.

Model	Accuracy (%)	Precision (%)	Recall (%)	F1 Macro (%)	ROC-AUC (%)
Shallow model	84.3 ± 2.5	76.2 ± 5.4	78.4 ± 6.8	82.7 ± 2.7	-
RNN models	72.69 ± 2.92	69.51 ± 6.58	34.95 ± 3.97	45.18 ± 5.48	63.46 ± 4.59
RNN + attention	84.02 ± 2.58	76.61 ± 6.05	77.39 ± 8.52	76.49 ± 4.16	82.40 ± 3.29
HAN	85.33 ± 2.75	79.29 ± 6.15	78.09 ± 6.68	78.10 ± 4.55	83.56 ± 3.54
HAN + XGBoost	86.80 ± 1.81	87.51 ± 2.15	82.66 ± 2.37	84.33 ± 2.27	82.77 ± 2.42

6   Conclusion

In this paper, we proposed a novel model that combine HAN and XGBoost to recognize insufficiently supported arguments. We also presented both shallow and deep learning models for the very same task as comparisons to some previous works. Several findings are also established in this paper, such as: the effectiveness of shallower model for small dataset, the effectivity of attention mechanism, and the state-of-the-art results resulted by our proposed model (HAN + XGBoost). For the future work, we argue that attention, hierarchical attention, and the combination of deep learning and XGBoost have a good prospect in solving other argumentation mining tasks. Even if our model yielded good results, it does not mean that our architecture can already evaluate the logical elaboration of an argument yet. It is definitely an interesting task to be solved in the future.

Acknowledgments. This research was fully funded by "Penelitian Disertasi Doktor" from Ministry of Research, Technology and Higher Education of Indonesia with contract number 039A/VR.RTT/VI/2017.

References

1. Aharoni, E., Polnarov, A., Lavee, T., Hershcovich, D., Levy, R., Rinott, R., Gut-freund, D., Slonim, N.: A benchmark dataset for automatic detection of claims and evidence in the context of controversial topics. In: Proceedings of the First Workshop on Argumentation Mining, pp. 64–68 (2014)
2. Bahdanau, D., Cho, K., Bengio, Y.: Neural machine translation by jointly learning to align and translate. arXiv preprint arXiv:1409.0473 (2014)
3. Bar-Haim, R., Bhattacharya, I., Dinuzzo, F., Saha, A., Slonim, N.: Stance classi-fication of context-dependent claims (2016)
4. Bengio, Y., Goodfellow, I.J., Courville, A.: Deep learning. Nature **521**, 436–444 (2015)
5. Bilu, Y., Hershcovich, D., Slonim, N.: Automatic claim negation: why, how and when. In: NAACL HLT 2015, p. 84 (2015)
6. Bradley, A.P.: The use of the area under the ROC curve in the evaluation of machine learning algorithms. Pattern Recognit. **30**(7), 1145–1159 (1997)
7. Cabrio, E., Villata, S.: Combining textual entailment and argumentation theory for supporting online debates interactions. In: Proceedings of the 50th Annual Meeting of the Association for Computational Linguistics: Short Papers, vol. 2, pp. 208–212. Association for Computational Linguistics (2012)
8. Caruana, R., Lawrence, S., Giles, L.: Overfitting in neural nets: backpropagation, conjugate gradient, and early stopping. In: NIPS, pp. 402–408 (2000)
9. Chen, T., Guestrin, C.: Xgboost: reliable large-scale tree boosting system. In: Pro-ceedings of the 22nd SIGKDD Conference on Knowledge Discovery and Data Min-ing, San Francisco, CA, USA, pp. 13–17 (2016)
10. Chen, T., He, T.: Xgboost: extreme gradient boosting. R package version 0.4-2 (2015)
11. Cho, K., Van Merriënboer, B., Bahdanau, D., Bengio, Y.: On the proper-ties of neural machine translation: encoder-decoder approaches. arXiv preprint arXiv:1409.1259 (2014)
12. Chollet, F.K.: (2015). http://keras.io
13. Chung, J., Gulcehre, C., Cho, K., Bengio, Y.: Empirical evaluation of gated recur-rent neural networks on sequence modeling. arXiv preprint arXiv:1412.3555 (2014)
14. Davis, J., Goadrich, M.: The relationship between precision-recall and ROC curves. In: Proceedings of the 23rd International Conference on Machine Learning, pp. 233–240. ACM (2006)
15. Desilia, Y., Utami, V.T., Arta, C., Suhartono, D.: An attempt to combine features in classifying argument components in persuasive essays. In: 17th Workshop on Computational Models of Natural Argument (CMNA) (2017)
16. Do, C., Ng, A.Y.: Transfer learning for text classification. In: NIPS, pp. 299–306 (2005)
17. Dozat, T.: Incorporating nesterov momentum into adam (2016)
18. Eckle-Kohler, J., Kluge, R., Gurevych, I.: On the role of discourse markers for discriminating claims and premises in argumentative discourse. In: EMNLP, pp. 2236–2242 (2015)
19. Fawcett, T.: An introduction to ROC analysis. Pattern Recognit. Lett. **27**(8), 861–874 (2006)
20. Firat, O., Cho, K., Bengio, Y.: Multi-way, multilingual neural machine translation with a shared attention mechanism. arXiv preprint arXiv:1601.01073 (2016)

21. Gema, A.P., Winton, S., David, T., Suhartono, D., Shodiq, M., Gazali, W.: It takes two to tango: modification of siamese long short termmemory network with attention mechanism in recognizing argumentative relations in persuasive essay. In: 2nd International Conference on Computer Science and Computational Intelligence (2017)
22. Govier, T.: A Practical Study of Argument. Cengage Learning, Boston (2013)
23. Habernal, I., Gurevych, I.: Which argument is more convincing? Analyzing and predicting convincingness of web arguments using bidirectional LSTM. In: Proceedings of the 54th Annual Meeting of the Association for Computational Linguistics (ACL) (2016)
24. Hinton, G.E., Salakhutdinov, R.R.: Replicated softmax: an undirected topic model. In: Advances in Neural Information Processing Systems, pp. 1607–1614 (2009)
25. Hochreiter, S., Schmidhuber, J.: Long short-term memory. Neural Comput. 9(8), 1735–1780 (1997)
26. Johnson, R.H., Blair, J.A.: Logical Self-defense. Idea, New Delhi (2006)
27. Johnson, R., Zhang, T.: Effective use of word order for text categorization with convolutional neural networks. arXiv preprint arXiv:1412.1058 (2014)
28. Kim, Y.: Convolutional neural networks for sentence classification. arXiv preprint arXiv:1408.5882 (2014)
29. Levy, R., Bilu, Y., Hershcovich, D., Aharoni, E., Slonim, N.: Context dependent claim detection (2014)
30. Maas, A.L., Daly, R.E., Pham, P.T., Huang, D., Ng, A.Y., Potts, C.: Learning word vectors for sentiment analysis. In: Proceedings of the 49th Annual Meeting of the Association for Computational Linguistics: Human Language Technologies, vol. 1, pp. 142–150. Association for Computational Linguistics (2011)
31. Moens, M.F., Boiy, E., Palau, R.M., Reed, C.: Automatic detection of arguments in legal texts. In: Proceedings of the 11th International Conference on Artificial Intelligence and Law, pp. 225–230. ACM (2007)
32. Palau, R.M., Moens, M.F.: Argumentation mining: the detection, classification and structuring of arguments in text. In: International Conference on Artificial Intelligence and Law (2009)
33. Pang, B., Lee, L.: Opinion mining and sentiment analysis. Found. Trends Inf. Retr. 2(1–2), 1–135 (2008)
34. Parsons, S., Oren, N., Reed, C.: Computational Models of Argument: Proceedings of COMMA 2014, vol. 266. IOS Press, Amsterdam (2014)
35. Pennington, J., Socher, R., Manning, C.D.: Glove: global vectors for word representation. In: EMNLP, vol. 14, pp. 1532–1543 (2014)
36. Persing, I., Ng, V.: Modeling argument strength in student essays. In: ACL, vol. 1, pp. 543–552 (2015)
37. Rinott, R., Dankin, L., Perez, C.A., Khapra, M.M., Aharoni, E., Slonim, N.: Show me your evidence-an automatic method for context dependent evidence detection. In: EMNLP, pp. 440–450 (2015)
38. Sahami, M., Dumais, S., Heckerman, D., Horvitz, E.: A Bayesian approach to filtering junk e-mail. In: Papers from the 1998 Workshop on Learning for Text Categorization, vol. 62, pp. 98–105 (1998)
39. Sandulescu, V., Chiru, M.: Predicting the future relevance of research institutions-the winning solution of the KDD cup 2016. arXiv preprint arXiv:1609.02728 (2016)
40. Sardianos, C., Katakis, I.M., Petasis, G., Karkaletsis, V.: Argument extraction from news. In: Proceedings of the 2nd Workshop on Argumentation Mining, pp. 56–66 (2015)

41. Srivastava, N., Hinton, G., Krizhevsky, A., Sutskever, I., Salakhutdinov, R.: Dropout: a simple way to prevent neural networks from overfitting. J. Mach. Learn. Res. **15**(1), 1929–1958 (2014)
42. Stab, C., Gurevych, I.: Identifying argumentative discourse structures in persuasive essays. In: EMNLP, pp. 46–56 (2014)
43. Stab, C., Gurevych, I.: Recognizing insufficiently supported arguments in argumentative essays, pp. 980–990 (2017)
44. Suhartono, D., Iskandar, A.A., Fanany, M.I., Manurung, R.: Utilizing word vector representation for classifying argument components in persuasive essays (2016)
45. Tang, D., Qin, B., Liu, T.: Document modeling with gated recurrent neural network for sentiment classification. In: EMNLP, pp. 1422–1432 (2015)
46. Wang, S., Manning, C.D.: Baselines and bigrams: simple, good sentiment and topic classification. In: Proceedings of the 50th Annual Meeting of the Association for Computational Linguistics: Short Papers, vol. 2, pp. 90–94. Association for Computational Linguistics (2012)
47. Wei, Z., Liu, Y., Li, Y.: Is this post persuasive? Ranking argumentative comments in the online forum. In: The 54th Annual Meeting of the Association for Computational Linguistics, p. 195 (2016)
48. Xu, K., Ba, J., Kiros, R., Cho, K., Courville, A., Salakhudinov, R., Zemel, R., Bengio, Y.: Show, attend and tell: neural image caption generation with visual attention. In: International Conference on Machine Learning, pp. 2048–2057 (2015)
49. Yang, Z., Yang, D., Dyer, C., He, X., Smola, A., Hovy, E.: Hierarchical attention networks for document classification. In: Proceedings of NAACL-HLT, pp. 1480–1489 (2016)
50. Yao, Y., Rosasco, L., Caponnetto, A.: On early stopping in gradient descent learning. Constr. Approx. **26**(2), 289–315 (2007)
51. Zhang, X., Zhao, J., LeCun, Y.: Character-level convolutional networks for text classification. In: Advances in Neural Information Processing Systems, pp. 649–657 (2015)

Speed Invariant Bearing Fault Characterization Using Convolutional Neural Networks

Dileep Kumar Appana, Wasim Ahmad, and Jong-Myon Kim[✉]

School of Electrical, Electronics, and Computer Engineering,
University of Ulsan, Ulsan 44610, South Korea
dk.appana@gmail.com, wasimahmad.qc@gmail.com,
jongmyon.kim@gmail.com

Abstract. Unlike traditional machine learning techniques, convolutional neural networks (CNNs), one of deep learning methods, automate the feature extraction process required for an effective classification. In general, CNN based bearing fault diagnosis analyzes raw signals to classify the localized faults. However, bearings are subjected to non-stationary speeds due to various operating conditions, and thus, CNN cannot determine optimal features of the various conditions while analyzing raw signals, reducing classification accuracy. In this paper, we propose a pre-processing step to improve the performance of the CNN based fault diagnosis by extracting envelope spectrums (ES) on the raw signals. As ES demodulates the signals to provide the information inherent in defect frequency of faults and its variations to non-stationary speeds, CNN can learn to extract distinctive features to diagnose bearing defects effectively. The proposed method is evaluated on acoustic emission based low speed bearing data. The trained CNN model is tested on data with different revolutions per minute (RPM), and it achieves the classification accuracy greater than 94.8%.

Keywords: Bearings · Convolutional neural network · Fault diagnosis · Varying rotational speed

1 Introduction

Recent advancements in technology have driven the industries into a new fold of global competitiveness, leading to implementing effective maintenance strategies of its machinery to boost the efficiency and productivity. Rolling element bearings (REBs) being the most fragile machinery component need to be condition monitored as they are prone to approximately 40% of overall machine failures due to varying conditions. To provide a reliable operating plant by avoiding unexpected operational failures of the component and reduce huge economical losses, accurate diagnosis of defects in the bearing is required. Thus, the bearing fault diagnosis is a key issue in this field [1].

To accomplish bearing defect diagnostics, many data-driven approaches have been introduced [2] with signal processing methods being the most popular ones. Utilizing the periodic patterns from the faulty bearing signals, these methods consist on three steps to localize the underlying bearing defects. These are data acquisition, useful

© Springer International Publishing AG 2017
S. Phon-Amnuaisuk et al. (Eds.): MIWAI 2017, LNAI 10607, pp. 189–198, 2017.
https://doi.org/10.1007/978-3-319-69456-6_16

feature extraction and fault localization. In the first stage, data is acquired by probing the sensors to quantify the machine vibration levels. Due to the presence of other machine components, these signals are accompanied by noise [3]. The second stage involves in overcoming the challenges of deterioration due to noise and extracting effective statistical parameters either in time, frequency or time-frequency domains [4] not limited to a single domain. The last stage involves in classification, utilizing predominant classifiers such as k-nearest neighbor (k-NN), support vector machines (SVM), artificial neural networks (ANNs), and so on. Choosing the effective features for determining faults require domain experience. Moreover, the process becomes more expensive if the machinery components are changed as it requires recalibration. Deep learning approaches remove the necessity of retooling and make it adaptable to the operating conditions by providing the architecture that can perform automatic feature extraction and classification.

Convolution neural network (CNN), a deep learning approach, with high performance GPUs is successful in ascertaining as robust pattern recognizing tools. A CNN mainly comprise of three layers: a convolutional layer (CL), pooling layer (PL) and a fully connected layer (FC). The CL identifies the patterns through convolutions for filtering operation using shared weights and biases. Input representations are down sampled using PL in the network to reduce the computational diversity. Stacking single or multiple ConvNet (CL and PL) with a FL at the end enables the network to classify data samples using a Softmax classifier, and forms a deep learning network to identify complex patterns. Though the weights and biases are initialized randomly, a back-propagation algorithm tunes the hyper parameters in the network. The procedure is repeated for a certain number of iterations until the minimum error criterion is met and stopped before it leads to overfitting [5]. Rectified linear unit (ReLU) activates all neurons in the network to ensure an effective filtering process and enhance training by avoiding harmful slowdowns in the network.

The Lenet-5 model is a successful architecture with multiple convolutional and pooling layers connected through a fully connected layer to a classifier that extracts details and classify hand written digits effectively [6]. Extending this to fault diagnosis of temporal vibration signals, Zhang et al. [7] transformed the one dimension (1-D) signal to two dimensional (2-D) image to feed into the network which has the same dimensionalities to classify the faulty patterns. Ince et al. [8] proposed a motor fault detection system that performs 1-D CNN operations inside the deep neural network. With adaptive learning rate computations and temporal vibrational signals reshaped to a 2-D array, Guo et al. [9] performed effective bearing fault diagnosis utilizing the abilities of deep learning method. These CNN-based approaches provide accurate fault diagnosis when raw bearing signal is provided as input to the network. However, it is either required to train different networks for different bearing rotational speeds or perform highly complex computations if the learning rate is kept adaptive to use the same network across different rotational speeds.

Therefore, a real time acoustic emission (AE) analysis based bearing fault diagnosis system using envelope spectrums (ES) and CNN is proposed in study which can classify faults invariant to rpm. AE based analysis has inherent ability to capture the low energy signals, and intrinsic symptoms can be diagnosed at an early stage. Than the raw bearing signals, its ES provide information to CNN to learn about the characteristics of the bearing faults effectively. CNN with self-learning capabilities performs automatic feature extraction from the available information and classify bearing faults that can be in variant to rotational speeds. The efficacy of the proposed method is verified on low-speed bearing dataset with varying rotational speeds of the bearings.

The remaining paper is organized as follows. Section 2 describes the proposed algorithm of fault diagnosis scheme, and Sect. 3 presents performance evaluation of the proposed method. Finally, Sect. 4 concludes this paper.

2 Proposed Methodology

When the roller element strikes, the bearing faults provide implicit information periodically which can facilitate a learning mechanism to diagnose the underlying faults of the bearing efficiently. Therefore, the proposed approach consists of three stage processes: (1) data acquisition of signals with faults in various components of the bearings, (2) preprocessing of acquired data by extracting envelope spectrums on raw signals, and (3) fault classification using a CNN architecture. The overall flow diagram of the proposed method is illustrated in Fig. 1.

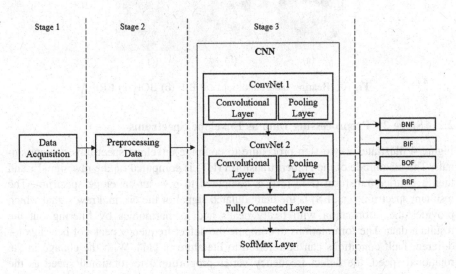

Fig. 1. Proposed methodology for classification using a deep CNN.

2.1 Stage 1 - Data Acquisition

A test bench (see Fig. 2) is employed that acquires data from an induction motor using wide band frequency AE sensors on low-speed bearings, operating at three different bearing rotational speeds of 350, 400, and 450 rpm. Data is sampled at 250 kHz on the drive end of a bearing cylindrical roller bearings when a sensor placed at a distance of 21.48 mm. The bearing elements are equipped with a crack of 12 mm long, 0.35 mm wide, and 0.3 mm deep. With the help of a 2-PCI systems, the sample recordings are

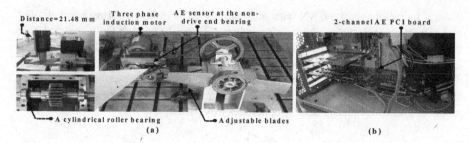

Fig. 2. Test bench (a) bearing fault simulator (b) data acquisition setup

made for one second duration and 90 samples for each bearing condition at each rotational speed. Four bearing conditions (see Fig. 3) are bearing with no fault (BNF), bearing with faults on inner raceway (BIF), bearing with faults on outer raceway (BOF), and bearing with faults on roller elements (BRF).

Fig. 3. Bearing fault conditions (a) BIF (b) BOF (c) BRF

2.2   Stage 2 - Preprocessing Data as Envelope Spectrums

Figure 4 illustrates a two-step procedure to compute envelope spectrums on raw signals. The magnitude of the Hilbert transform (HT) is computed on the raw signal x and then a Fourier transform (FT) [10] is computed to give an envelope spectrum. The resultant spectrum (i.e., ES) is the demodulated signal of the original raw signal which provides the information with faulty peaks and its harmonics by filtering out the resultant data. The formulations to compute the defect frequency peaks of bearings for different fault conditions can be referred to literature in [11]. With the change in the rotational speed, the defect frequency varies proportional to rotational speed as the number of cycles per minute varies. Though the frequency peaks vary the information from ES is enough to enable the signal analysis of the deep network for effective classification that can be invariant to rpm. With defect frequencies as reference spectrums are windowed with a window size of 128. Spectrums of all bearing conditions are normalized before feeding to the network.

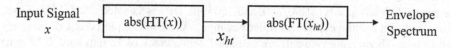

Fig. 4. Preprocessing step - computing envelope spectrum

2.3   Stage 3 - Convolution Neural Network

Lee [12] presented a CNN architecture for effective classification of bearing faults. Referring to this architecture with modifications the description of the network is as follows, and dimensions are tabulated in Table 1.

Table 1. Dimensions of the proposed CNN architecture

Parameters	Dimensions (width x height x depth)	
	Input signal	250000×1
	Preprocessed signal	$128 \times 1 \times 1$
Conv 1	Kernel size	5×1
	Stride	1×1
	Depth	4
	Output	$124 \times 1 \times 4$
Pool 1	Stride	2×1
	Output	$62 \times 1 \times 4$
Conv 2	Kernel size	5×1
	Stride	1×1
	Depth	4
	Output	$58 \times 1 \times 4$
Pool 2	Stride	2×1
	Output	$29 \times 1 \times 4$
Full connected	nodes	64
Softmax	nodes	4

2.3.1   Input to the Network

The standard CNN architecture is fed by reshaped input to the network for analysis. Thus, authors reshaped 1-D temporal signal data to a 2-D array to feed as input to the network. Considering the proposed application to suit real time monitoring systems, 1-D analysis is considered without reshaping the original signal. The inputs are the windowed spectrums computed and are directly fed to the network in the proposed scheme.

2.3.2   Two Layered ConvNet Stack Architecture and Its Parameters

Lee [12] evaluated different structures for effective classification using CNN under varied noisy conditions. For four conditions of bearings, higher accuracy is obtained when four filters are used. Thus, four filters are chosen in this study for available bearing conditions in the ConvNet stack. The kernel size of 5×5 is used in general and considering the time consumption. Thus, a 5×1 size is used in the proposed network as the operations are done in 1-D. The stride in the convolutional layer is kept at 1×1 and in pooling layer at 2×1. 64 hidden nodes are used in the fully connected layer. All the nodes are activated through ReLU activations.

As discussed earlier in Sect. 1, stacking multiple ConvNet is required for a deep learning network. A two layered network along with one fully connected layer which provided a stable classification accuracy [7, 9] is considered. For training the network, a standard mini-batch size of 128 [6] is used.

2.3.3 Optimization

All the hyper parameters are initialized randomly and are optimized using an adaptive moment estimation (Adam) optimizer and a first order gradient based optimization of stochastic objective functions [13] which maintain the exponential moving averages of the gradient and its square. The optimizer is advantageous over other optimizing techniques, having less memory requirements, scaled gradients being invariant to parameter updates, working with the non-stationary setting, step-size hyper parameter with bounded norms, and working with sparse gradients. A little training is enough to accomplish a better convergence. Dropout regularized logistic regression is applied to features for better learning. A constant learning rate decay of 1e-3 is used. The pre-processed signal is fed to CNN instead of raw signal.

2.3.4 Classification

The SoftMax classifier which minimizes the cross-entropy computed on the Softmax function between the probability estimates of the class is used. The Softmax layer provides four outputs, corresponding to four categories of bearing signals.

3   Experimental Results and Discussion

The efficacy of the proposed algorithm is verified on AE bearing data using four types of bearing conditions with varying rpms. Data with same rpm is grouped as one dataset and it comprises four bearing conditions with 90 samples from each condition. In total, three datasets with three different rpms are acquired, and each dataset having 360 samples. In the experiment, the CNN is trained on one rpm data and tested on the remaining rpm data. Extracting envelope spectra demodulates the signals, as illustrated in Fig. 5.

From the Fig. 5, it can be observed that the ES provides the information of bearing condition with frequency peaks. Theoretically, computed defect frequencies are marked for the three faulty conditions. From the figure, it can be noticed that bearing data representing the normal condition does not have any defect frequency peak. They appear only when the faults appear in a bearing, which can be observed in the three bearing fault conditions with peaks at different frequencies. As the defect frequency peaks are visible in ES but not in the frequency spectrum. Therefore, ES provides greater resolutions of fault signatures where the peaks are dependent on the rotational speed. Figure 6 illustrates ES with the variations of defect frequency peaks of different fault conditions when the rotational speeds of the bearings are changed from 350 to 450 rpm.

The time domain characteristics of a raw signal also cannot reveal the variations of faults when rotational speeds are varied. But the extracted spectrums are similar though the peaks are varied with a factor proportional to speed of the bearings. When these spectrums are directly used as input, the CNN learns about the faults with the available information by automating the feature extraction process to discriminate the faults even

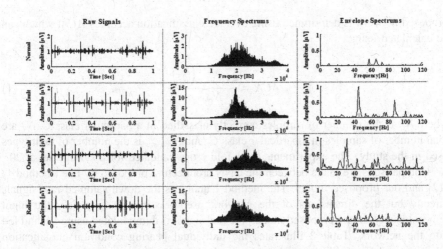

Fig. 5. Representations of bearing conditions (a) Raw signal in time domain, (b) spectrum in frequency domain, (c) envelope spectrum

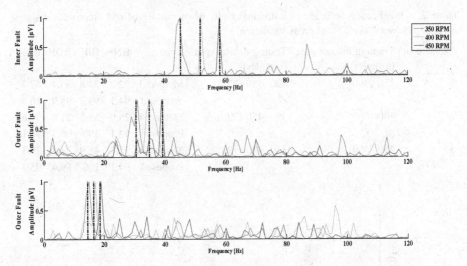

Fig. 6. Variations of envelope spectrum of three faulty conditions with changes in rotational speeds.

if the rpm is changed. A two-layered convolutional and pooling layer architecture utilized by the network learns effectively with dropout rate of 0.5 and constant learning rate that provides stable classification accuracy. The Adam optimizer computes the error with the selected samples from mini batch size and fine tunes the randomly initialized weights and biases of the network by updating the error through a back-propagation technique. The minimum error criterion is met when the number of iterations are set to 70. The number of testing samples are two-folds more than the training samples used. After the completion of the learning process, the precision of the proposed network is determined using average classification accuracy *ACA*, which can be calculated using

$$ACA = \frac{\sum_{N_{classes}} \left(\frac{N_C}{N_T} \right)}{N_{classes}} \tag{1}$$

where N_C is the number of samples correctly classified in a particular class C, N_T are total number of samples in a particular class C, and $N_{classes}$ is the number of fault types used in the study. The experiments are k-fold cross-validated for a k-value set at 20.

Comparisons are made between the CNN architecture proposed by Lee (method 1) [12] and our proposed model. The method 1 analyzes the down sampled raw signals directly but the dimensions of the network used are in 1-D to satisfy the input dimensionality. In the proposed model, the raw signal is demodulated using ES and fed into the network. Table 2 illustrates the individual bearing condition classification accuracy, and Fig. 7 illustrates the average classification accuracies when training and testing of the models are carried out with different rpm datasets, for both methods.

Table 2. Classification accuracy of individual faults when raw signal and preprocessed signal are fed to network via 20-fold cross validation.

Experiment	Training dataset rpm (samples)	Testing dataset rpm (samples)	Type	BNF	BIF	BOF	BRF
1	350 (360)	400, 450 (720)	Method 1	22.2	34.8	36.4	47.4
			Proposed	94.1	99.7	98.9	86.4
2	400 (360)	350, 450 (720)	Method 1	25.9	58.2	21.8	39.6
			Proposed	92.1	100	96.7	96.1
3	450 (360)	350, 400 (720)	Method 1	15.8	48.9	27.3	29.3
			Proposed	94.1	100	89.4	95.7

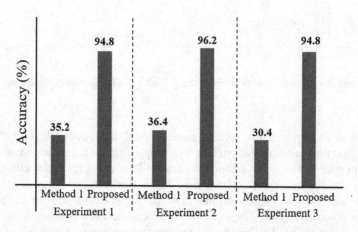

Fig. 7. Comparison of average classification accuracies for method 1 and the proposed method under different shaft speeds.

Figure 8 illustrates the comparison of the training and testing classification accuracies. It can be observed that when the samples are tested from the same rpm dataset, the classification accuracy is above 98%. While the testing is done with samples from different rpm, the classification accuracy is obtained above 94%. Figure 7 demonstrates that the classification accuracy is enhanced as the network learns using ES instead of raw signals. Therefore, ES serves as a useful preprocessing step to make the CNN based bearing fault classification invariant to the rotational speed of the bearings.

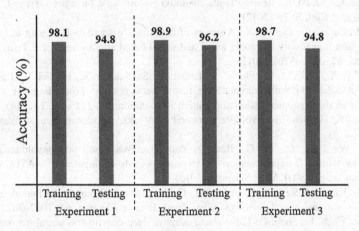

Fig. 8. Comparison of training and testing ACA for the proposed scheme with varied rpms.

4 Conclusions

This paper proposed a new method using envelope spectrum analysis with CNN for characterizing bearing faults on bearing data recorded at low and variable shaft speeds. The proposed method was evaluated by calculating the envelope spectrum of the raw acoustic emission signals and using it as input to the CNN for learning discriminative representations. The CNNs combine the feature learning and classification tasks. The proposed method including the preprocessing step enhances the classification accuracy from 35% to 95%.

Acknowledgements. This work was supported by the Korea Institute of Energy Technology Evaluation and Planning (KETEP) and the Ministry of Trade, Industry & Energy (MOTIE) of the Republic of Korea (Nos. 20162220100050, 20161120100350, 20172510102130). It was also funded in part by The Leading Human Resource Training Program of Regional Neo Industry through the National Research Foundation of Korea (NRF) funded by the Ministry of Science, ICT and Future Planning (NRF-2016H1D5A1910564), and in part by the Basic Science Research Program through the National Research Foundation of Korea (NRF) funded by the Ministry of Education (2016R1D1A3B03931927).

References

1. Appana, D.K., Islam, M.R., Kim, J.-M.: Reliable fault diagnosis of bearings using distance and density similarity on an enhanced k-NN. In: Wagner, M., Li, X., Hendtlass, T. (eds.) ACALCI 2017. LNCS, vol. 10142, pp. 193–203. Springer, Cham (2017). doi:10.1007/978-3-319-51691-2_17
2. Rai, A., Upadhyay, S.: A review on signal processing techniques utilized in the fault diagnosis of rolling element bearings. Tribol. Int. **96**, 289–306 (2016)
3. Harlisca, C., Szabó, L.: Bearing faults condition monitoring-a literature survey. J. Comput. Sci. Control Syst. **5**, 19 (2012)
4. Gao, Z., Cecati, C., Ding, S.X.: A survey of fault diagnosis and fault-tolerant techniques—Part I: fault diagnosis with model-based and signal-based approaches. IEEE Trans. Industr. Electron. **62**, 3757–3767 (2015)
5. Karpathy, A., Toderici, G., Shetty, S., Leung, T., Sukthankar, R., Fei-Fei, L.: Large-scale video classification with convolutional neural networks. In: Proceedings of the IEEE Conference on Computer Vision and Pattern Recognition, pp. 1725–1732 (2014)
6. LeCun, Y.: LeNet-5, convolutional neural networks. http://yann.lecun.com/exdb/lenet (2015)
7. Zhang, W., Peng, G., Li, C.: Bearings fault diagnosis based on convolutional neural networks with 2-D representation of vibration signals as input. In: MATEC Web of Conferences, p. 13001. EDP Sciences (2015)
8. Ince, T., Kiranyaz, S., Eren, L., Askar, M., Gabbouj, M.: Real-time motor fault detection by 1-D convolutional neural networks. IEEE Trans. Industr. Electron. **63**, 7067–7075 (2016)
9. Guo, X., Chen, L., Shen, C.: Hierarchical adaptive deep convolution neural network and its application to bearing fault diagnosis. Measurement **93**, 490–502 (2016)
10. Antoni, J., Randall, R.: On the use of the cyclic power spectrum in rolling element bearings diagnostics. J. Sound Vibr. **281**, 463–468 (2005)
11. Randall, R.B., Antoni, J.: Rolling element bearing diagnostics—a tutorial. Mech. Syst. Sig. Process. **25**, 485–520 (2011)
12. Lee, D., Siu, V., Cruz, R., Yetman, C.: Convolutional neural net and bearing fault analysis. In: Proceedings of the International Conference on Data Mining (DMIN), p. 194. The Steering Committee of The World Congress in Computer Science, Computer Engineering and Applied Computing (WorldComp) (2016)
13. Kingma, D., Ba, J.: Adam: a method for stochastic optimization. arXiv preprint arXiv:1412.6980 (2014)

Neural Network Control Method for Mobile Robot Trajectory Tracking

Pan Yang[ORCID], Sheng Han[✉], and Youfang Lin

Beijing Key Laboratory of Traffic Data Analysis and Mining,
School of Computer and Information Technology, Beijing Jiaotong University,
Beijing 100044, China
shhan@bjtu.edu.cn

Abstract. In this paper, we study movement control problems of nonholonomic mobile robots trajectory tracking and propose an adaptive mixed Pi-Sigma neural network (MPSNN) control method combined effectively with logical reasoning ability of fuzzy control and self-learning ability of neural network control. This method maps Takagi-Sugeno (T-S) fuzzy system to Pi-Sigma neural network (PSNN) structure. It explains the motion state transition process for mobile robot with inference process of T-S fuzzy system and gives neural network certainly physical meaning. The backpropagation iterative algorithm of MPSNN is designed based on the principle of error back propagation and the gradient descent method. The self-learning ability of PSNN is used to adjust T-S fuzzy rules and membership functions on-line to make the trajectory tracking controller of the design have portability and adaptability. In addition, it also designed the quadratic interpolation method to dynamically adjust learning rates in the network and improve the error convergence efficiency. Finally, we design two MPSNN trajectory tracking controllers based on Pi-Sigma neural network and verify the validity and superiority of the proposed method and the designed controller by using MATLAB numerical simulation.

Keywords: Mobile robot · Trajectory tracking control · T-S fuzzy control · Mixed Pi-Sigma neural network · Backpropagation iterative algorithm

1 Introduction

Nowadays, mobile robots are widely used in various fields such as industry, service industry, storage industry, logistics industry, security industry, etc. [1–3]. According to different areas, background of problems and application scenarios are faced with robot have certain differences. But in any application scenarios about the process of motion control of mobile robot, all needs to ensure that mobile robot in the process of movement can quickly and accurately track the given trajectory or goal to achieve trajectory tracking control in real time. Therefore, the research have a long-term practical value.

The object of trajectory tracking control is a set of nonholonomic mobile robot which belongs to a typical nonlinear system [4]. It creates a huge challenge for trajectory tracking control. At present, there are many methods which are mainly divided

© Springer International Publishing AG 2017
S. Phon-Amnuaisuk et al. (Eds.): MIWAI 2017, LNAI 10607, pp. 199–212, 2017.
https://doi.org/10.1007/978-3-319-69456-6_17

into two main categories including traditional [5] and intelligent [6, 7] to solve the problem of trajectory tracking control. And the development direction is the latter. Many of the existing scholars have made some achievements by designing trajectory tracking controller for wheeled mobile robot in trajectory tracking control. Ibrahim [8] introduced and discussed a control strategy for nonholonomic wheeled mobile robots which included a 'steering' controller dealing with the kinematics of the system and another is a velocity controller. Zhao et al. [9] proposed a novel trajectory tracking control approach which combined SMC, PID, neural networks with experts' knowledge to design a kinematic controller and a dynamic controller. Rossomando [10] proposed a sliding mode control method using adaptive neural network to ensure that the neural sliding mode control can achieve a stable closed-loop system for the trajectory-tracking control of a mobile robot with unknown nonlinear dynamics. Liu et al. [11] proposed an improved neural network adaptive sliding mode control method which mostly optimizes network structure parameter by particle swarm optimization algorithm and reduce chattering. Yu and Chen [12] adopted an iterative learning control algorithm to solve the high-precision trajectory tracking issue with time-varying, nonlinear, and strong-coupling dynamics properties and given a rigorous mathematical proof. Wang et al. [13] presented a parameter adaptive controller to improve control performance and solve the speed jump problem existing in conventional back-stepping tracking control. Aissa [14] has taken the integrate performance of neural network and fuzzy inference system to design an ANFIS controller which applied to control the mobile robot safely and reach to target objects. Cuong Nan [15] presented an adaptive trajectory tracking neural network control method using radial basis function (RBF) with robust compensator to achieve the high-precision position tracking and made use of the back-propagation algorithm and the Lyapunov stability theorem. From the above research methods, using traditional control methods need to establish a precise mathematical model about controlled object, so as to achieve more precise control. But the motion model for mobile robot system is usually not accurate and there are many uncertainty factors because of environmental uncertainty. And SMC system [16] can easily bring out the "chattering" phenomenon between different control logic of high speed switching back and forth. Thus, the traditional control method is difficult to fully approach the practical application effect. However, using intelligent control methods can make complex kinematics and dynamics model simpler. Among them, fuzzy control system has flexible logic reasoning which is beneficial to simplifying the derivation process of the state of things and neural network control model has the advantages of self-learning and strong robustness which can fully approximate complex and unknown system during the robot movement.

In view of advantages of the above two intelligent control methods, based on Takagi-Sugeno (T-S) fuzzy control and Pi-Sigma neural network (PSNN) control, this paper proposed a mixed Pi-Sigma neural network (MPSNN) control method. And two MPSNN trajectory tracking controllers are presented. In MPSNN trajectory tracking controller, it designed adaptive T-S fuzzy control rules to explain the derivation process of robot motion state and reflected with PSNN which can be used for studying and optimizing rules and membership functions in T-S fuzzy control system by using back propagation iterative algorithm and gradient descent method. And this paper also designed a quadratic interpolation method to dynamically adjust the network learning rate which can avoid poor performance caused by fixed during back propagation. This research can greatly improve the efficiency of network computing and the accuracy of network output. The controller in the process of numerical simulation in MATLAB, will train data by off-line which have been collected from the SMC simulation to ensure that the method is efficiency and real time.

2 Problem Statement

In this section, we will take a wheeled mobile robot with double drive system as the research object. Assumed that driving wheels of mobile robot move without slipping on a plane, there is only a pure rolling contact between the wheels and the ground. The modeling for mobile robot done in Cartesian coordinates as shown on Fig. 1. In the figure, the XOY represents a global coordinate system and the X_1OY_1 represents a local coordinate system of mobile robot. $(x_c, y_c, \theta_c)^T$ and $(x_r, y_r, \theta_r)^T$ denote the actual position and the desired positon of the current moment during mobile robot movement. θ_e expresses the error of heading angle. v and w indicate the real linear velocity and angular velocity. v_r and w_r indicate the expected linear velocity and angular velocity.

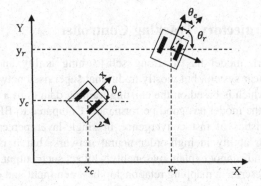

Fig. 1. Robotic position in Cartesian coordinates.

So, representation formula of robot kinematics model is as follows:

$$\begin{cases} \dot{x} = v\cos\theta \\ \dot{y} = v\sin\theta \\ \dot{\theta} = w \end{cases} \tag{1}$$

A mobile robot start with any initial position denoted by $(x, y, \theta)^T$. The motion state in time t is shown in Fig. 1. According to the coordinate transformation formula, we can get mathematical equations for posture error coordinates denoted by $(x_e, y_e, \theta_e)^T$ in mobile robot local coordinates. That is:

$$\begin{bmatrix} x_e \\ y_e \\ \theta_e \end{bmatrix} = \begin{bmatrix} \cos\theta_c & \sin\theta_c & 0 \\ -\sin\theta_c & \cos\theta_c & 0 \\ 0 & 0 & 1 \end{bmatrix} \begin{bmatrix} x_r - x_c \\ y_r - y_c \\ \theta_r - \theta_c \end{bmatrix} \tag{2}$$

Based on the literature [17], the differential equation of position error is as follows:

$$\begin{bmatrix} \dot{x}_e \\ \dot{y}_e \\ \dot{\theta}_e \end{bmatrix} = \begin{bmatrix} y_e w - v + v_r \cos\theta_e \\ -x_e w + v_r \sin\theta_e \\ w_r - w \end{bmatrix} \tag{3}$$

Trajectory tracking for mobile robot as a function about time, the control problem itself is in a given arbitrary initial position and mobile robot trajectory, aim to find a motion control $(v, w)^T$. As time t gets longer and longer, the control volume allows the mobile robot to track the given trajectory movement and arriving to the target point with tending to zero position error. That is:

$$\lim_{t\to\infty} \left\| (x_e, y_e, \theta_e)^T \right\| = 0 \tag{4}$$

3   Design of Trajectory Tracking Controller

The neural network model has a strong self-learning ability and also can fully approximate nonlinear system, but mostly traditional supervised network is to take the form of feed data which is based on the existing training data to fit a series of network parameters so that the model has good performance. Compared to BP network, PSNN has both characteristics of fast convergence in single-layer perceptron and strong non-linear mapping ability in high-order neural network, but it is always lack of physical meaning and cannot explain reasonably why get such output. Considering that fuzzy system can describe a mapping relationship between input and output by a set of fuzzy conditional sentences. Among them, T-S fuzzy system also divides control in a whole nonlinear system into fuzzy approximation in multiple local linear system. It can make up the disadvantages of neural network model while also simplifying the problem. However, the self-learning ability of neural networks can modify fuzzy rules online to solve the problem that traditional T-S fuzzy system is limited to fixed. Therefore, we proposed a control method named MPSNN based on T-S fuzzy control and PSNN control and designed two MPSNN trajectory tracking controllers.

3.1   Takagi-Sugeno Fuzzy System

In T-S fuzzy system [18], systems' rules are defined in the form of "if-then":

$$R^i : If\ x_1\ is A_1^{i_1},\ x_2\ is A_2^{i_2},\ldots,x_n\ is A_n^{i_n}\ then\ y_i = p_0^i + p_1^i x_1 + \ldots + p_n^i x_n \tag{5}$$

Here, x_j represents an input variable; A_j^{ij} represents a fuzzy set; p_r^i represents a truth value parameter; y_i is an output of the system according to rule R^i where $i = 1, 2, \ldots, m; i_j = 1, 2, \ldots, m_j; \prod_{j=1}^{n} m_j = m; j = 1, 2, \ldots, n$ and $r = 0, 1, \ldots, n$. m and n separately denote the total number of fuzzy rules and the total number of input variables. y, an integrated output of this fuzzy system, is equal to the weighted average of each y_i, which is denoted by:

$$y = \frac{\sum_{i=1}^{m} \omega_i y_i}{\sum_{i=1}^{m} \omega_i} \tag{6}$$

Here, the weighted coefficient ω_i includes value from rules R^i applied to the input. That is:

$$\omega_i = \prod_{j=1}^{n} \mu_{A_j^{ij}}(x_j) \tag{7}$$

Here, $\mu_{A_j^{ij}}(x_j)$ expresses a membership value with input x_j which belongs to the fuzzy set A_j^{ij}.

3.2 Pi-Sigma Neural Network

The pi-sigma neural network proposed by Shin and Ghosh [19] which has three layers in network structure, as shown in Fig. 2.

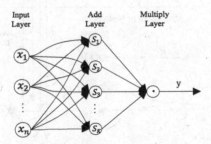

Fig. 2. Pi-Sigma neural network.

Among them, network input x is a vector with n dimensional, and x_i is a component with i in x. Hidden layer of the network contains total of K-neuron, and h_t is an output about the neuron with t in hidden layer, there is:

$$h_t = \sum_{i=1}^{n} (w_{it} x_i + \theta_{it}), t = 1, 2, \cdots, K \tag{8}$$

Here, w_{it} and θ_{it} are respectively on behalf of connection weights and thresholds between an input variable x_i and a hidden neuron with t.

Connection weights between hidden layer and output layer in PSNN are fixed with 1, and the output is:

$$y = \sigma\left(\prod_{t=1}^{k} h_t\right) \tag{9}$$

$\sigma(\cdot)$ means a nonlinear activation function and it is flexible.

3.3   Mixed Pi-Sigma Neural Network Architecture

Based on T-S fuzzy system and neural network structure, we design a MPSNN architecture as shown in Fig. 3, which can be divided into antecedent and subsequent network processing. u, P, W and S respectively represent operations with membership function, multiplication, normalization and add.

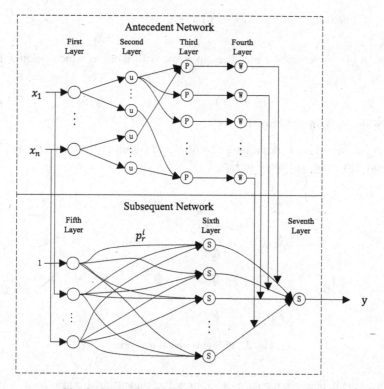

Fig. 3. The mixed Pi-Sigma neural network structure.

Antecedent Network. Antecedent network implements "if" part in T-S fuzzy system. The network output is a weighted coefficient vector $\bar{\omega}$ after normalization.

First Layer: This layer is an input layer and the total number of nodes is denoted by $N_1 = n$. Each neuron node is directly connected with the component x_i in input variables and its output directly enter the second layer.

Second layer: This layer is a fuzzy layer and the total number of nodes is denoted by $N_2 = \sum_{j=1}^{n} m_j$. Activation function in each neuron node use Gauss kernel function. That is:

$$\mu_{A_j^{ij}}(x_j) = exp\left(-(x_j - c_j^{ij})^2 / (b_j^{ij})^2\right) \tag{10}$$

$i_j = 1, 2, \ldots, m_k$, $\prod_{j=1}^{n} m_j = m, j = 1, 2, \ldots, n$. c_j^{ij} and b_j^{ij} denote a central value and a width value for the selected membership function of Gauss. Through this function, the input variable can be converted into a membership degree of the corresponding fuzzy quantity in order to realize the fuzzy operation about input variable.

Third layer: This layer implements an inference by "if" rule and the total number of nodes is denoted by $N_3 = m$. Multiplication reasoning is applied to all the input fuzzy variables within each neuron node to get an adaptive degree for "if" rule in each T-S fuzzy rules. That can be signed by:

$$\omega_i = \prod_{j=1}^{n} \mu_{A_j^{ij}}(x_j) \tag{11}$$

Here, $i_j = 1, 2, \ldots, m_k$; $\prod_{k=1}^{n} m_k = m; j = 1, 2, \ldots, n$.

Fourth layer: This layer is a normalized layer and the total number of nodes is denoted by $N_4 = m$. Each neuron node is normalized to the result of the fuzzy inference layer. That is:

$$\bar{\omega}_i = \frac{\omega_i}{\sum_{j=1}^{m} \omega_j} \tag{12}$$

Here, $i = 1, 2, \ldots, m$. This layer is the last layer of the antecedent network. So, its output results are directly used by the subsequent network.

Subsequent Network. Subsequent network implements "then" part in T-S fuzzy system, combined with the output of antecedent network to produce a combined output y.

Fifth Layer: This layer is an input layer and the total number of nodes is denoted by $N_5 = n + 1$. What is different from the first layer is the addition of a single neuron, $x_0 = 1$.

Sixth Layer: This layer implements an inference by "then" rule and the total number of nodes is denoted by $N_6 = m$. A neuron node corresponds to a subsequent output in T-S fuzzy rule, namely:

$$y_i = p_0^i + p_1^i x_1 + \ldots + p_n^i x_n \tag{13}$$

Here, $i = 1, 2, \ldots, m$.

Seventh Layer: This layer is an output layer and the total number of nodes is denoted by $N_7 = 1$. It is used for matching "if" and "then" rules to realize join operations reasoning for the conclusion of T-S fuzzy rules. That is:

$$y = \sum_{i=1}^{m} \bar{\omega}_i y_i \tag{14}$$

3.4   Backpropagation Iterative Algorithm

According to the MPSNN architecture proposed in the Sect. 3.3, the number of input fuzzy partition within network is usually fixed and equal. Therefore, parameters which need to be adjusted include only c_j^{ij} and b_j^{ij} ($i_j = 1, 2, \ldots, m_j$; $\prod_{j=1}^{n} m_j = m$; $j = 1, 2, \ldots, n$) which come from the membership function in the second layer and $p_r^i (i = 1, 2, \ldots, m; r = 0, 1, \ldots, n)$ which means connection weight coefficient between fifth and sixth layer. Among them, m and n represent the total number of fuzzy rules and the total number of input variables, respectively.

Suppose that the expected output of the network is y_d, and the cost function is defined as:

$$E = \frac{1}{2}(y_d - y)^2 \tag{15}$$

Based on the error back propagation principle and gradient descent method, formulas for calculating the degree of a ladder about the error cost for each layer output value are defined as:

$$\delta^{(7)} = \frac{\partial E}{\partial y} = -(y_d - y) \tag{16}$$

$$\delta^{(6)} = \frac{\partial E}{\partial y_i} = \frac{\partial E}{\partial y} \frac{\partial y}{\partial y_i} = \delta^{(7)} \bar{\omega}_i \tag{17}$$

$$\delta_i^{(4)} = \frac{\partial E}{\partial \bar{\omega}_i} = \frac{\partial E}{\partial y} \frac{\partial y}{\partial \bar{\omega}_i} = \delta^{(7)} y_i \tag{18}$$

$$\delta_i^{(3)} = \frac{\partial E}{\partial \omega_i} = \frac{\partial E}{\partial \bar{\omega}_i} \frac{\partial \bar{\omega}_i}{\partial \omega_i} = \delta_i^{(4)} \frac{\sum_{j=1}^{m} \omega_j - \omega_i}{\left(\sum_{j=1}^{m} \omega_j\right)^2} \tag{19}$$

$$\delta_{ij}^{(2)} = \frac{\partial E}{\partial \mu_{A_j^{ij}}} = \frac{\partial E}{\partial \omega_i} \frac{\partial \omega_i}{\partial \mu_{A_j^{ij}}} = \sum_{\mu_{A_j^{ij}} \in \omega_i} \delta_i^{(3)} \prod_{\substack{t=1 \\ t \neq j}}^{n} \mu_{A_t^{i_t}} \tag{20}$$

Then, formulas for calculating the degree of a ladder about the error cost used to tune parameters are defined as:

$$\frac{\partial E}{\partial p_r^i} = \frac{\partial E}{\partial y_i} \frac{\partial y_i}{\partial p_r^i} = -(y_d - y)\bar{\omega}_i x_r \tag{21}$$

$$\frac{\partial E}{\partial c_j^{ij}} = \frac{\partial E}{\partial \mu_{A_j^{ij}}} \frac{\partial \mu_{A_j^{ij}}}{\partial c_j^{ij}} = -(y_d - y) \sum_{\mu_{A_j^{ij}} \in \omega_i} y_i \frac{\sum_{j=1}^m \omega_j - \omega_i}{\left(\sum_{j=1}^m \omega_j\right)^2} \omega_i \frac{2(x_i - c_j^{ij})}{(b_j^{ij})^2} \tag{22}$$

$$\frac{\partial E}{\partial b_j^{ij}} = \frac{\partial E}{\partial \mu_{A_j^{ij}}} \frac{\partial \mu_{A_j^{ij}}}{\partial b_j^{ij}} = -(y_d - y) \sum_{\mu_{A_j^{ij}} \in \omega_i} y_i \frac{\sum_{j=1}^m \omega_j - \omega_i}{\left(\sum_{j=1}^m \omega_j\right)^2} \omega_i \frac{2(x_j - c_j^{ij})^2}{(b_j^{ij})^3} \tag{23}$$

Therefore, the backpropagation iterative algorithm that was designed to learn and optimize parameters to be tuned is shown below, among them, $\beta_p > 0$, $\beta_c > 0$, $\beta_b > 0$, which are represent as the learning rate parameters of p_r^i, c_j^{ij}, b_j^{ij}, respectively:

$$p_r^i(k+1) = p_r^i(k) - \beta_p \frac{\partial E}{\partial p_r^i} = p_r^i(k) + \beta_p(y_d - y)\bar{\omega}_i x_r \tag{24}$$

$$c_j^{ij}(k+1) = c_j^{ij}(k) - \beta_c \frac{\partial E}{\partial c_j^{ij}}$$
$$= c_j^{ij}(k) + \beta_c(y_d - y) \sum_{\mu_{A_j^{ij}} \in \omega_i} y_i \frac{\sum_{j=1}^m \omega_j - \omega_i}{\left(\sum_{j=1}^m \omega_j\right)^2} \omega_i \frac{2(x_i - c_j^{ij})}{(b_j^{ij})^2} \tag{25}$$

$$b_j^{ij}(k+1) = b_j^{ij}(k) - \beta_b \frac{\partial E}{\partial b_j^{ij}}$$
$$= b_j^{ij}(k) + \beta_b(y_d - y) \sum_{\mu_{A_j^{ij}} \in \omega_i} y_i \frac{\sum_{j=1}^m \omega_j - \omega_i}{\left(\sum_{j=1}^m \omega_j\right)^2} \omega_i \frac{2(x_j - c_j^{ij})^2}{(b_j^{ij})^3} \tag{26}$$

3.5   Design of MPSNN Controller Based on Pi-Sigma Neural Network

This paper uses the above MPSNN architecture to build two MPSNN trajectory tracking controllers which have the same structure and model with double inputs and single output. The first MPSNN controller produces linear velocity (v) with two inputs x_e and $\dot{x}_e$ which represent an error and an error derivative in x axis. The second produces angular velocity (w) with two inputs y_e and θ_e which represent an error in y axis and an error of direction angle. Among them, the total number of membership neurons within each controller is set to $m_k = 5$, and there are $N_1 = n = 2$, $N_2 = \sum_{j=1}^n m_j = 10$, $N_3 = \prod_{j=1}^n m_j = m = 25$, $N_4 = 25$, $N_5 = 3$, $N_6 = 25$, $N_7 = 1$.

4   Simulation Results

This section implements the numerical simulation using the proposed MPSNN trajectory tracking control methodology in MATLAB. In the process of simulation, data used for training network off-line are derived from the data caused by SMC method. To verify the effectiveness of the proposed method and designed controller.

In the simulation experiment, in order to compare the influence of different membership neurons in the controller, we let a target robot track a circular motion, we assume that movement time t = 20 s, expected line velocity $v_r = 10.0\,\text{cm/s}$, expected angular velocity $w_r = 1.0\,\text{rad/s}$. In training phase, training step in each time on-chip is 1000 and training data is derived from a set of pose errors using SMC method to track the circular trajectory under different initial posture errors. In test phase, we expect initial position as $(x_r, y_r, \theta_r)^T = (1, 0, 0)^T$ and actual initial position is set to $(x_c, y_c, \theta_c)^T = (0, 0, 0)^T$. The number of membership neurons is set to $m_k = 3$, $m_k = 5$, $m_k = 7$, $m_k = 9$, and $m_k = 11$. The experimental results are shown below. Among them, Figs. 4, 5 and 6 show the circular trajectory and pose error curves tracked by the MPSNN control method with membership neurons $m_k = 3$, $m_k = 5$ and $m_k = 7$, respectively. In order to more clearly evaluate the effect of different membership neurons on the MPSNN controller, we use mean square error (MSE) and system actual computational time (CT) as the evaluation criteria, as shown in Table 1 below.

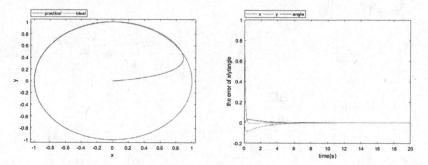

Fig. 4. Left shows the circular trajectory tracking curve and right shows posture error tracking curve with MPSNN control method in case of $m_k = 3$.

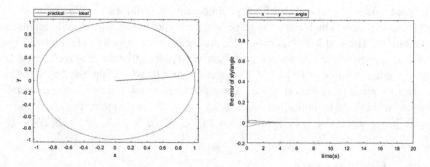

Fig. 5. Left shows the circular trajectory tracking curve and right shows posture error tracking curve with MPSNN control method in case of $m_k = 5$.

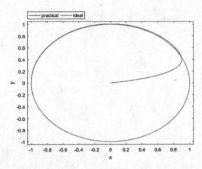 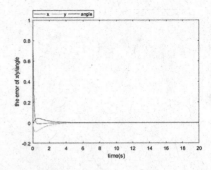

Fig. 6. Left indicates the circular trajectory tracking curve and right indicates posture error tracking curve with MPSNN control method in case of $m_k = 7$.

Table 1. Evaluation criteria in MPSNN control system with different membership neurons.

m_k	MSE	CT(s)
3	0.0037	17.835215
5	0.0011	15.811252
7	0.0032	17.111717
9	0.0021	17.874308
11	0.0045	18.912706

Formula for the MSE is as:

$$MSE = \sum_{i=1}^{CNT} errorPosition(i) * errorPosition(i)'/CNT \qquad (27)$$

Here, CNT represents the total number of path points, and $errorPosition(i)$ represents a $1 * 3$ matrix composed of pose errors.

These experiments show that when membership neuron is set to $m_k = 5$, the robot can quickly adjust the pose error and stably achieve the motion of tracking the circular trajectory. In that case, we got a smallest value in MSE and a shortest CT. So, the MPSNN controller will achieve a best performance.

To compare the influence of different training times in MPSNN controller on experimental results, in the same movement time, training step and movement speed, we make a target robot track a sine curve motion. The expected initial position is defined by $(x_r, y_r, \theta_r)^T = (0, 0, 0)^T$ and the practical initial posture is defined by $(x_c, y_c, \theta_c)^T = (-1.08, -0.07, -pi/6)^T$. After a set of standard data generated by SMC trajectory tracking controller are used to train MPSNN off-line with once time, the experimental result is shown on the left side of Fig. 7. At least four experiments, in turn, we collect trajectory data for mobile robot under the condition of different initial pose error and train MPSNN off-line. At the same time, compared with the controller designed by PSNN model mentioned in Sect. 3.2, more than 20 experiments were conducted and the optimal experimental results were presented on the right side of

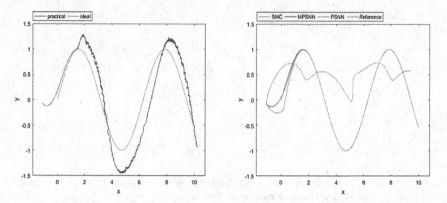

Fig. 7. Left indicates the sine trajectory tracking curve after one training with MPSNN control method and right indicates the comparison of MPSNN control method of training 4 times and SMC method and PSNN method of training at least 20 times (Color figure online)

Fig. 7. Here, the line of red, blue, green and mulberry respectively represent movement trajectory with expected, controlled by MPSNN, controlled by SMC and controlled by PSNN for the target robot. We can see that the training process of the three-layer PSNN model depends entirely on the form of "feeding data". The model can be interpreted poorly, and it is easy to induce the overfitting phenomenon, which cannot control the target object accurately. And Fig. 8 show the posture error tracking curve with MPSNN control method and SMC method. The value of MSE and CT is shown in Table 2 below.

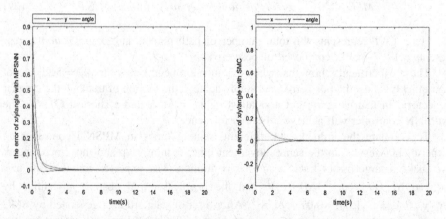

Fig. 8. Left indicates posture error tracking curve with MPSNN control method and right indicates posture error tracking curve with SMC method.

Table 2. Evaluation criteria in the process of tracking sine curve with different control method.

Method	MSE	CT(s)
MPSNN	0.0135	37.622676
SMC	0.0100	37.537927
PSNN	2.4076	23.034386

Although PSNN method has the shortest computational time, MPSNN method is used to design a seven-layer neural network which means that there are more neurons to be calculated and more parameters to be adjusted and more time to be spent. Compared to SMC, MPSNN model has more self-learning ability and flexibility which can adjust and optimize parameters from historical data. These results show that in the case of offline training, the MPSNN trajectory tracking controller can greatly improve the response speed of online processing and avoid overfitting to make the target robot quickly and accurately track the desired trajectory so as to realize trajectory tracking control with tending to zero position error during activity. At the same time, it embodies strong robustness.

5 Conclusion

Combining the advantages of T-S fuzzy control and Pi-Sigma neural network control, this paper designed and implemented a MPSNN controller based on Pi-Sigma neural network. This controller take it as training data with off-line operation in the network which is trajectory tracking control data caused by SMC method. It can avoid the "chattering" phenomenon caused by SMC system between different control logic of high speed switching back and forth. The proposed controller has the following advantages:

(1) The design of this controller does not depend on mathematical model about target object itself, and can fully approximate nonlinear system such as mobile robot, which has highly portability.

(2) The controller embed a design idea about T-S fuzzy system on the Pi-Sigma neural network. The mechanism of T-S fuzzy control is realized by the transfer of neurons. It also uses online learning ability of neural network to adaptively adjust the parameters in membership function within T-S fuzzy control system. It designs a lot of fuzzy rules which does not rely on expert experience and can be adjusted online. Finally, it has highly applicability.

(3) The controller combined with some practical significances in fuzzy control system gives neural network certainly physical meaning and makes network have some abilities about logical reasoning. It has highly interpretability.

(4) After the controller realized off-line training with MPSNN control method, it can greatly improve the online execution speed. In the process of trajectory tracking control, under the condition of unknown error, real-time adjustment of trajectory tracking has be realized. It has strong robustness.

Effectiveness and superiority of above proposed design method about trajectory tracking controller are demonstrated by MATLAB numerical simulations.

References

1. Pinillos, R., et al.: Long-term assessment of a service robot in a hotel environment. Robot. Auton. Syst. **79**, 40–57 (2016)
2. Ni, J., et al.: Bioinspired intelligent algorithm and its applications for mobile robot control: a survey. Comput. Intell. Neurosci. **2016**(1) (2016)
3. Wang, C., Du, D.: Research on logistics autonomous mobile robot system. In: 2016 IEEE International Conference on Mechatronics and Automation (ICMA), pp. 275–280. IEEE, Harbin (2016)
4. Xin, L., et al.: Robust adaptive tracking control of wheeled mobile robot. Robot. Auton. Syst. **78**, 36–48 (2016)
5. Gregor, K., et al.: Wheeled Mobile Robotics: From Fundamentals Towards Autonomous Systems. Butterworth-Heinemann, Oxford (2017)
6. Zi-xing, C.: Advance in research of intelligent control and mobile robots. J. Central South Univ. Technol. (Nat. Sci.) **36**(5), 721–726 (2005)
7. Åström, K.J., Mcavoy, T.J.: Intelligent control. J. Process Control **2**(3), 115–127 (1992)
8. Ibrahim, E.S.B.: Wheeled mobile robot trajectory tracking using sliding mode control. J. Comput. Sci. **12**(1), 48–55 (2016)
9. Zhao, J.B., et al.: Design and implementation of membrane controllers for trajectory tracking of nonholonomic wheeled mobile robots. Integr. Comput.-Aided Eng. **23**(1), 15–30 (2015)
10. Rossomando, F.G., Soria, C., Carelli, R.: Sliding mode control for trajectory tracking of a non-holonomic mobile robot using adaptive neural networks. J. Control Eng. Appl. Inform. **16**(1), 12–21 (2014)
11. Liu, T., Yin, S., Li, H.: Robot trajectory tracking control with an improved neural network adaptive sliding mode control. J. Comput. Inf. Syst. **11**(12), 4401–4411 (2015)
12. Yu, C., Chen, X.: Trajectory tracking of wheeled mobile robot by adopting iterative learning control with predictive, current, and past learning items. Robotica **33**(7), 1393–1414 (2015)
13. Wang, J., et al.: Trajectory tracking control based on adaptive neural dynamics for four-wheel drive omnidirectional mobile robots. Engineering Review: Međunarodni časopis namijenjen publiciranju originalnih istraživanja s aspekta analize konstrukcija, materijala i novih tehnologija u području strojarstva, brodogradnje, temeljnih tehničkih znanosti, elektrotehnike, računarstva i građevinarstva **34**(3), 235–243 (2014)
14. Aissa, B.C., Fatima, C.: Adaptive neuro-fuzzy control for trajectory tracking of a wheeled mobile robot. In: 2015 4th International Conference on Electrical Engineering (ICEE), pp. 1–4. IEEE, Boumerdes (2015)
15. Cuong, P.V., Nan, W.Y.: Adaptive trajectory tracking neural network control with robust compensator for robot manipulators. Neural Comput. Appl. **27**(2), 525–536 (2016)
16. Ngo, Q.H., Hong, K.S.: Adaptive sliding mode control of container cranes. IET Control Theory Appl. **6**(5), 662–668 (2012)
17. Kanayama, Y., et al.: A stable tracking control method for an autonomous mobile robot. In: Proceedings of 1990 IEEE International Conference on Robotics and Automation, pp. 384–389. IEEE, Cincinnati (1990)
18. Li, H., et al.: Model reduction for interval type-2 Takagi-Sugeno fuzzy systems. Automatica **61**, 308–314 (2015)
19. Nie, Y., Deng, W.: A hybrid genetic learning algorithm for Pi-sigma neural network and the analysis of its convergence. In: Fourth International Conference on Natural Computation, ICNC 2008, pp. 19–23. IEEE, Jinan (2008)

What Does a Policy Network Learn After Mastering a Pong Game?

Somnuk Phon-Amnuaisuk[1,2]([✉])

[1] Media Informatics Special Interest Group, Centre for Innovative Engineering,
Universiti Teknologi Brunei, Mukim Gadong, Brunei
somnuk.phonamnuaisuk@utb.edu.bn
[2] School of Computing and Informatics, Universiti Teknologi Brunei,
Mukim Gadong, Brunei

Abstract. Activities in reinforcement learning (RL) revolve around
learning the Markov decision process (MDP) model, in particular, the
following quantities: state values V, state-action values Q, and policy
π. Due to high computational cost, the reinforcement learning problem
is commonly formulated for learning task specific representations with
hand-crafted input features. In this report, we discuss an alternative
end-to-end approach where the RL attempts to learn general task representations, in this context, learning how to play the Pong game from
a sequence of screen snap shots. We apply artificial neural networks to
approximate a policy of a reinforcement learning model. The policy network learns to play the game from a sequence of frames without any
extra semantics apart from the pixel information and the score. Many
games are simulated using different network architectures and different
parameters settings. We examine the activation of hidden nodes and the
weights between the input and the hidden layers, before and after the
RL has successfully learned to play the game. Insights into the internal
learning mechanisms and future research directions are discussed.

Keywords: End-to-end reinforcement learning · Policy optimization ·
Policy gradient learning

1 Introduction

The field of reinforcement learning (RL) has been an active research domain
since the 1990s [1]. RL has been successfully applied to various problem domains
including Game AI [2–4]. It offers a powerful alternative machine learning approach when precise evaluations are not available for describing the interactions
between the system and the environment.

How could RL learn to behave in an environment given that the precise evaluation of actions is not available? RL learns an optimal actions policy by randomly
sampling the state space. Traditionally, a tabular approach is a common choice
of implementation. Various RL learning techniques have been established e.g.,

© Springer International Publishing AG 2017
S. Phon-Amnuaisuk et al. (Eds.): MIWAI 2017, LNAI 10607, pp. 213–222, 2017.
https://doi.org/10.1007/978-3-319-69456-6_18

temporal different learning (TD), *Q-learning*, and *SARSA* [1]. The tabular approach works well when the state space is not too large. However, in many real life
problems, the state space is large and it is likely that RL may only partially learn
a policy. This leads to the instability of the learning algorithms and a fluctuation
in the performance of RL, if the state space is partially experienced during the
learning stage. The way to overcome this is still an open research issue. The
issue can be mitigated if the balance between exploitation and exploration is
maintained during the learning stage. The balance between exploring uncharted
states and exploiting fruitful states ensures that near optimal policy is learned
within a reasonable time.

The domain here is the *Atari Pong game* from the *AI Gym* implementation
(https://gym.openai.com). The Pong game is a simple two-player turn playing
game, where a player (PC, which is the RL in our case) and the non-player
character (NPC which is the AI gym in our case) can take one of the following
three actions: no movement, move the paddle up or move the paddle down. We
are interested in the end-to-end approach where pixel information of the Pong
game are taken as input without manually converting them into other features.
The input to our RL system is just the pixel information and the score after
each served ball. Many implementations have been posted on the OpenAI site
and this implementation is also adapted from those examples[1].

In the RL setup, the PC behaviours are learnt without any direct supervision.
The system learns a policy $\pi(a|s; w)$, i.e., what action a is preferred given a state
s, the w denotes the neural network weight parameters. From the properties
associated with neural network nodes, we hope to gain some insights of what is
learned after the network has successfully learnt to play the Pong game through
examining activation patterns of the hidden layer nodes, patterns of weights in
the policy network, etc.

The rest of the paper is organized into the following sections: Sect. 2 discusses
the background of DRL; Sect. 3 discusses the policy gradient learning; Sect. 4
provides the results and analysis of the weights, as well as activations of hidden
layer; and finally, the conclusion and further research are presented in Sect. 5.

2   Related Works

Recent advances in DL [5], the success story of Deep Q-Network (DQN) [6] and
the introduction of many game test-beds such as AI Gym and Arcade Learning Environment (ALE) [7], have revived interests in AI-game research. One
of the important themes of DL research is the investigation of the *end-to-end*
approach [8,9]. The end-to-end approach expects the system to learn important
discrimination features without manually crafted features or explicit bias from a

---

[1] Our policy network is implemented using a feed forward neural network. It could
successfully learn and win the game with an average score of 5, e.g., 21:16. There are
many other implementations with better scores such as those demonstrated using
asynchronous actor-critic agents (A3C) and long-short term memory (LSTM) learning algorithms.

human programmer. It has been observed that a successfully trained convolution neural network (CNN) in the end-to-end image recognition task could reveal a hierarchical structure of features; simple features at the near input layer such as ridgelet, circular, curvature, grating, etc., to complex features at the output layer such as eyes. There is a clear increment in semantic content [10]. This automated abstraction of conceptual information is, however, not well understood yet.

Traditionally, three popular tactics are employed in tabular reinforcement learning implementations: TD, Q-learning and SARSA [1]. It is so called tabular RL since state values or state-action values are commonly implemented as tables/arrays. In order to curb the computing cost, the table size is manually crafted to the smallest size possible for the problem at hand. For example, in the Pong game, information of the two paddles' positions, the ball's position and the control of the player's paddle could express states. The number of all possible states-actions is the Cartesian product of the possible positions of the two paddles, the ball and actions. When the size of the look-up table is small enough, all entries in the table can be reached through experiential updates and the tabular approach could successfully learn the optimal solution of the task.

We are interested in the end-to-end approach. The size of the state space here is huge since the states are constructed from pixels, in our case, approximately 40 million states. Therefore, a tabular approach will not be practical. Here, we resort to an alternative policy optimization approach to approximate the value function. The action policy is encoded as weights in a policy network $\pi(w)$. The policy network does not represent an approximate value function as a table but as a parameterized functional form using a computational model such as artificial neural networks [11].

There are two main umbrellas of RL policy network learning approaches: a gradient-free approach and a gradient-based approach. The gradient-free approach optimizes the policy π using examples randomly sampled from the state space. The gradient-free learning approach may be guided by mechanisms such as *evolutionary strategy* [12] or other search heuristics. The gradient-free approach can work well when the number of optimized parameters are small since the state space is heuristically explored. For a problem with a large state space, performance may suffer from non-exhaustive experience. Hence the gradient-based approach is preferred [13,14].

3   Policy Gradient Learning in Pong

Policy learning differs from the tabular state values learning or the tabular state-action values learning approach since tabular approach updates its table entry by entry. The tabular approach is inefficient if the state space is large. The large state space often leads to a poor generalization of ability since the whole state space cannot be thoroughly explored. In contrast, policy learning efficiently approximates the policy by back-propagating errors to adjust the weights W of the policy network. It learns all policies at once and converges them to a suboptimal policy.

3.1   Problem Formulation

Let us formulate the Pong game from the end-to-end RL perspective; let s denote an input vector constructed by flattening a 2D array of input pixels, let $\pi(a|s;w)$ denote a policy function which predicts action a, given a state s and the para-metrized weight w. The predicted y from the policy network indicates the best action according to the policy π. The output y is encoded in the *one-hot* encoding fashion. Finally, let W_{ij}^l be a weight matrix of layer l connecting nodes from input set i to output set j, as illustrated in Fig. 1.

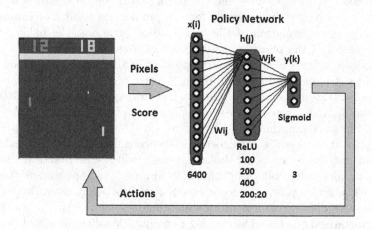

Fig. 1. An end-to-end RL implements a policy gradient network using feed-forward neural network. The network takes a pixel information as input and suggests a player's action output. The network may be constructed with one or more hidden layers.

In the Pong game, an episode is complete when one of the players obtains 21 points. Hence in one episode, a sequence of image frames $s_t \in \mathcal{R}^{high \times width}$, a sequence of actions $a_t \in \{1, 2, 3\}$ that the RL agent has taken and a sequence of reward signals $r_t \in \{-1, 0, 1\}$ constitute a batch of experience for that episode. Since the RL is playing against an NPC, if the NPC wins then the evaluative reward, at that frame t, will be $r_t = -1$, and if RL wins then $r_t = 1$. However while the game is still running the reward $r_t = 0$. Hence, there will be thousands of frames with a lot of evaluative reward $r_t = 0$ and occasionally with $r_t -1$ or 1. The evaluative information at time t must be propagated to earlier actions, $t - 1$ since the merit or the penalty obtained at time t are also contributed by previous actions. This is obtained by propagating the reward along the historical steps of the current game: $r_{t-1} = r_{t-1} + \gamma r_t$, where γ is the discount factor.

After the RL has learnt to play the Pong game with a policy $\pi(w)$, we expect the accumulated return, R to be maximized.

$$R = \sum_{t=0}^{H} \pi(a_t|s_t; w) r_t \tag{1}$$

The above equation maximizes R if the probability of taking an action a_t and the evaluative r_t (after the reward propagation) have high values. In other words, it tells us that R is maximized if the right decision is taken. The decision for these actions are conditioned according to the state and the parameterized neural network weights w.

Without loss of generality to the number of hidden layers, let us consider a neural network with just one hidden layer having the weights, W_{ij}^1 and W_{jk}^2, connecting between the input layer to the hidden layer and the hidden layer to the output layer (see Fig. 1), let the activation functions of layer W^1 and W^2 be the ReLU($\cdot$) and Sigmoid($\cdot$) respectively, and let x_i be a vector constructed by flattening the differences $s_t - s_{t-1}$. The differences between the two frames capture the temporal information. The predicted action y_k can be expressed as:

$$y_k = Sigmoid(\sum_j [\ ReLU(\sum_i [x_i\ W_{ij}^1])\ W_{jk}^2]) \tag{2}$$

The discrepancies between the output y_k and the *biased random label* y_k' forms the loss function:

$$loss = (y_k - y_k')^2 \tag{3}$$

where y_k and y_k' are the one-hot representation of an action a and a corresponding label respectively. It should be noted that the random labels are biased toward the actions recommended by the network. Hence, this can be seen as an *on policy* learning with occasionally random actions.

The loss function above is optimized when the actions taken agree with the labels. However, this does not imply optimal policy. The optimal policy is the policy that maximizes the accumulative return R. Hence the reward r_t also conditions the actions by adjusting the neural network weights. The optimal weights is obtained by updating the weight in the direction of:

$$\Delta w = \alpha[\nabla_w log\pi(a_t|s_t; w)(r_t - b_t)] \tag{4}$$

Table 1. Pseudo Code for policy gradient learning

input: frame pixels and the game score s_0
     a differentiable policy parameterization $\pi(a|s; w)$
output: *policy network weights w*
Initialize *policy network weights w*
for episode $= 1$ to M **do**
    a,r $\leftarrow$ Generate an episode $s_0, a_0, r_0, s_1, a_1, r_1, ..., s_t, a_t, r_t$ following $\pi(\cdot|\cdot; w)$
    a' $\leftarrow$ Generate labels for the episode(labels are biased toward **a**)
    define loss from **a** and **a'**, loss $= (y_k - y_k')^2$
    for each t from t=T to t=0 of each episode:
       $r_{t-1} = r_{t-1} + \gamma r_t$
     $w \leftarrow w + \alpha[\nabla_w log\pi(a_t|s_t; w)(r_t - b_t)]$
endfor

where α is the learning rate and $(r_t - b_t)$ is an advantage of the action a_t over the expected base line b_t. This is one of the variations of the REINFORCE algorithm [11]. In essence, the update increases the probability of an action having more advantage over other actions. Table 1 gives a pseudo code of the policy gradient learning process.

3.2   Simulation

In the end-to-end setting, the inputs to the system are the pixels from the game, the score and the episode complete flag. There are many tuning parameters. Since each experiment takes days to complete (at least 40 h for 20,000 episodes in our computer), variations of selected parameters are reported here. In this simulation, the numbers of hidden nodes, hidden layers and the learning rate are varied. Table 2 below summarizes the settings employed in our simulation.

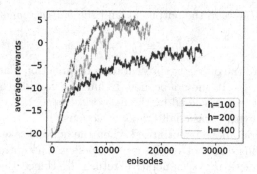

Fig. 2. Summary of average scores observed from the networks with 100, 200, and 400 hidden nodes (single hidden layer), with the learning rate set at 0.001.

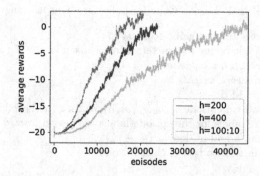

Fig. 3. Summary of average scores observed from the networks with 100:10, 200, and 400 hidden nodes (100:10 denotes two hidden layers), with the learning rate set at 0.0001.

Table 2. Control parameters

Information	Exp 1	Exp 2	Exp 3	Exp 4
Input frame size	80 × 80	80 × 80	80 × 80	80 × 80
Hidden nodes	100	200	400	100:10
Output nodes	3	3	3	3
Learning rate α	0.001	0.001, 0.0001	0.001, 0.0001	0.0001
Discount factor γ	0.9	0.9	0.9	0.9
Network architecture	6400:100:3	6400:200:3	6400:400:3	6400:100:10:3
Activation functions	ReLU Sigmoid	ReLU Sigmoid	ReLU Sigmoid	ReLU ReLU Sigmoid

Figures 2 and 3 show the average scores of different network architectures and different learning rates. It is conclusive that learning does take place in both single hidden layer, or two hidden layer cases, since the average scores of all runs increase with episodes. However, the behaviors of the learning algorithm are dependent on many factors such as weight initialization, learning rate, lost function, etc., it is quite hard to draw any conclusive argument regarding optimal parameters setting from the data that we have.

4 Examining the Network Characteristics

In order to examine the neural network characteristics, after the policy network has successfully trained and can beat the AI Gym, the weights of a trained network are frozen. Then the RL is simulated for 50,000 steps and the activations of the hidden layer nodes and the output actions are recorded. This generates 50,000 pairs of hidden activation pattern and action pairs. An analysis of these pairs reveals the activation patterns for the up, down and still actions. An analysis of the frozen weights associated with each hidden node also reveals weight patterns corresponding to important input patterns. Figure 4 shows plots of hidden layer activations (top-right). The 200 hidden nodes are reshaped into a 20 × 10 image (top-left). It is observed that after the training, all hidden nodes converge into three sets: nodes corresponding to the *still* action, nodes corresponding to the *up* action and nodes corresponding to the *down* action.

Among the *still/up/down* nodes, it would be interesting to see further groupings inside each category. Here, the activation patterns in each *still/up/down* group are further clustered into five clusters using k-means clustering. Their results are shown in three rows; the first row shows five plots of activation strength corresponding to five clusters in the *still* action, the second row for the *up* action and the third row for the *down* action. The bottom pane of the Fig. 4 presents similar information but from a network with 400 nodes in the hidden layer (it is reshaped into a 20 × 20 image).

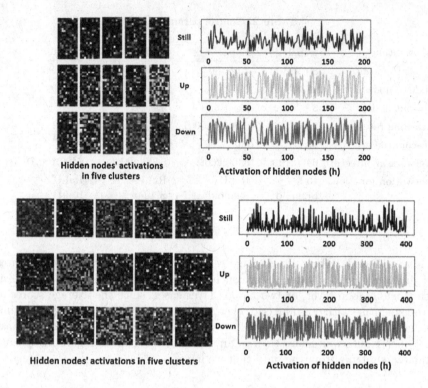

Fig. 4. Activation Patterns from 200 hidden nodes (top) and 400 hidden nodes (bottom). A clear grouping of nodes according to their functions are observed.

Figure 5 shows the plots of weights W_{ij} connecting input x_i to the hidden nodes h_j. There are 6,400 input weights associated to each hidden node. Representing these 6,400 weights as a 80×80 image reveal the game board. The first row of Fig. 5 shows the weights before the learning. No obvious patterns are observed. After the learning, a clear pattern which could be seen as the trajectory of the ball and the paddles emerges, as shown in rows two and three.

This means the node h_j will produce high activation output, i.e., $\text{ReLU}(\sum_i x_i W_{ij})$, if the corresponding pixel x_i is active. The brighter the pixel, the higher the contribution to the hidden node activations. In the case of a single hidden layer, the action y_k are computed from the contributions of hidden nodes $Sigmoid(\sum_j h_j W_{jk})$. The weights W_{jk} linearly combine the contributions from the different hidden nodes. In other words, the W_{ij} learns the representation of the dictionary (can be seen as basis vectors). If the dictionary is complete, every input frame should successfully activate the appropriate hidden nodes, their appropriate combinations and therefore the appropriate actions that optimize the reward.

Fig. 5. Patterns of weights from some random nodes, before the learning (first row) and after the learning (second and third row). Trajectory of the paddlers and the ball can be clearly observed after the learning.

5   Conclusion and Future Direction

Although ANN has been applied as a function approximator for RL before [15], learning function approximation in the end-to-end approach is still an open research area. In this work, we show the results of policy gradient learning and their characteristics under different parameters. The following observations are conclusive from the results: (i) the activation of hidden layers has successfully grouped according to actions: still, up, down; (ii) the weights between the input layer and the hidden layer show a strong correlation between ball trajectories and appropriate actions.

The above two observations share parallel similarities to the dedicated functionality in different brain areas and the concept of Hebbian learning. The policy gradient learning in RL shares many similarities with learning behaviors observed in biological systems, for examples, learning from inexact feedback, and be adaptive on dynamic policy learning. However, there are characteristics that seem to be difficult to realize with the current architecture. For example, does the policy $\pi(w)$ capture a deep gameplay strategy? Is it plausible for complex strategies to be captured by this style of learning mechanisms? Can a seemingly intelligent action performed by $p(a|s; w)$ be claimed as *intuition*? We hope to investigate these sort of questions in our future work.

Acknowledgments. We wish to thank anonymous reviewers for their comments that have helped improve this paper. We would like to thank the GSR office for their financial support given to this research.

References

1. Sutton, R.S., Barto, A.G.: Reinforcement Learning: An Introduction, 2nd edn. MIT Press, Cambridge (2017)
2. Tesauro, G.: TD-Gammon, a self-teaching backgammon program, achieves master-level play. Neural Comput. **6**(2), 215–219 (1994)
3. Phon-Amnuaisuk, S.: Learning chasing behaviours of non-player characters in games using SARSA. In: Chio, C., et al. (eds.) EvoApplications 2011. LNCS, vol. 6624, pp. 133–142. Springer, Heidelberg (2011). doi:10.1007/978-3-642-20525-5_14
4. Silver, D., Huang, A., Maddison, C.J., Guez, A., Sifre, L., van den Driessche, G., Schrittweiser, J., Antonofglou, I., Panneershelvam, V., Lanctot, M., et al.: Mastering the game of Go with deep neural networks and tree search. Nature **529**(7587), 484–489 (2016)
5. LeCun, Y., Bengio, Y., Hinton, G.: Deep learning. Nature **521**, 436–444 (2015)
6. Mnih, V., Kavukcuoglu, K., Silver, D., Rusu, A.A., Veness, J., Bellemare, M.G., Graves, A., Riedmiller, M., Fidjeland, A.K., Ostrovski, G., Petersen, S., Beattie, C., Sadik, A., Antonoglou, I., King, H., Kumaran, D., Wierstra, D., Legg, S., Hassabis, D.: Human-level control through deep reinforcement learning. Nature **518**, 529–533 (2015)
7. Bellemare, M.G., Naddaf, Y., Veness, J., Bowling, M.: The arcade learning environment: an evaluation platform for general agents. J. Artif. Intell. Res. **47**, 253–279 (2013)
8. Krizhevsky, A., Sutskever, I., Hinton, G.E.: Imagenet classification with deep convolutional neural networks. In: Advances in Neural Information Processing Systems, pp. 1097–1105 (2012)
9. Sukhbaatar, S., Szlam, A., Weston, J., Fergus, R.: End-to-end memory networks. In: Advances in Neural Information Processing Systems, pp. 2440–2448 (2015)
10. Zeiler, M.D., Fergus, R.: Visualizing and understanding convolutional networks. In: Fleet, D., Pajdla, T., Schiele, B., Tuytelaars, T. (eds.) ECCV 2014. LNCS, vol. 8689, pp. 818–833. Springer, Cham (2014). doi:10.1007/978-3-319-10590-1_53
11. Williams, R.J.: Simple statistical gradient-following algorithms for connectionist reinforcement learning. Mach. Learn. **8**(3), 229–256 (1992)
12. Phon-Amnuaisuk, S.: Evolving and discovering Tetris gameplay strategies. In: Proceedings of the 19th Annual Conference on Knowledge-Based and Intelligent Information and Engineering Systems (KES 2015), vol. 60, pp. 458–467 (2015). Procedia Comput. Sci
13. Silver, D., Lever, G., Heess, N., Degris, T., Wierstra, D., Riedmiller, M.: Deterministic policy gradient algorithms. In: Proceedings of the International Conference on Machine Learning (ICML), pp. 387–395 (2014)
14. Andrychowicz, M., Denil, M., Colmenarejo, S.G., Hoffman, M.W., Pfau, D., Schaul, T., Shillingford, B., de Freitas, N.: Learning to learn by gradient descent by gradient descent. In: Advances in Neural Information Processing Systems, pp. 3981–3989 (2016)
15. Williams, R.J.: On the use of backpropagation in associative reinforcement learning. In: Proceedings of the IEEE International Conference on Neural Networks, vol. I, pp. 263–270 (1988)

Document Analysis

Minimally-Supervised Sentiment Lexicon Induction Model: A Case Study of Malay Sentiment Analysis

Mohammad Darwich(✉) [iD], Shahrul Azman Mohd Noah [iD],
and Nazlia Omar [iD]

Faculty of Information Science and Technology,
Center for Artificial Intelligence Technology, Universiti Kebangsaan Malaysia,
Bangi, Selangor, Malaysia
modarwish@hotmail.com

Abstract. Vital to the task of mining sentiment from text is a sentiment lexicon, or a dictionary of terms annotated for their a priori information across the semantic dimension of sentiment. Each term has assigned a general, out-of-context sentiment polarity. Unfortunately, online dictionaries and similar lexical resources do not readily include information on the sentiment properties of their entries. Moreover, manually compiling sentiment lexicons is tedious in terms of annotator time and effort. This has resulted in the emergence of a large volume of research concentrated on automated sentiment lexicon generation algorithms. Most of these algorithms were designed for English, attributable to the abundance of readily available lexical resources in this language. This is not the case for low-resource languages such as the Malay language. Although there has been an exponential increase in research on Malay sentiment analysis over the past few years, the subtask of sentiment lexicon induction for this particular language remains under-investigated. We present a minimally-supervised sentiment lexicon induction model specifically designed for the Malay language. It takes as input only two initial paradigm positive and negative terms, and mines WordNet Bahasa's synonym chains and Kamus Dewan's gloss information to extract subjective, sentiment-laden terms. The model automatically bootstraps a reliable, high coverage sentiment lexicon that can be employed in Malay sentiment analysis on full-text. Intrinsic evaluation of the model against a manually annotated test set demonstrates that its ability to assign sentiment properties to terms is on par with human judgement.

Keywords: Sentiment analysis · Opinion mining · Sentiment lexicon · Malay sentiment analysis · Malay sentiment lexicon · WordNet Bahasa

1 Introduction

Sentiment Analysis (SA), or Opinion Mining (OM), is at the crossroads of natural language processing and computational linguistics, and involves the detection and extraction of sentiment, attitude, opinion and emotion from text. A core task is identifying the overall sentiment polarity (or semantic orientation) of a text as having a

S. Phon-Amnuaisuk et al. (Eds.): MIWAI 2017, LNAI 10607, pp. 225–237, 2017.
https://doi.org/10.1007/978-3-319-69456-6_19

positive, negative or neutral connotation. This polarity can be classified as one of a set of predefined discrete classes, or positioned on a continuum between positivity and negativity (e.g. [+1, −1]), where the nearer it is to either end of the scale, the higher its sentiment strength, or intensity. SA has been a rapidly emerging academic field during the past two decades, attributable to applicative interest in industry, warranting significant research effort since its origination. SA is currently exhaustively applied in numerous domains, including commercial products and services, stock market prediction, politics and customer relationship management. Classifying a text in terms of its sentiment properties requires a priori information about the smallest sentiment-carrying units: terms (words and phrases).

However, manually compiling a sentiment lexicon is tedious in terms of annotator time and effort, hence, the emergence of a large volume of research concentrated on automated sentiment lexicon induction. This involves sentiment classification at the 'term' level, the end result of which can aid in the sentiment classification of larger pieces of text. Terms that express a desirable state are considered to possess a positive orientation (e.g. interesting and ecstatic); while those that express an undesirable state are considered to possess a negative orientation (e.g. corrupt and horrid). The task of automated sentiment lexicon generation branches in two directions. It involves utilizing digital dictionaries and lexical resources in a *dictionary-based approach*, or computing co-occurrence statistics derived from text corpora in a *corpus-based approach*.

A re-occurring issue, however, is that most works in the body of literature on sentiment lexicon generation have been conducted for English, attributable to the abundance of readily accessible lexical resources in this language. Conversely, works for low-resource languages such as Malay remain scarce. Malay sentiment analysis has recently started to witness rapid progress both in industry and academia, hence, the need for automated sentiment lexicon induction algorithms specifically constructed for this language.

We proposed a minimally-supervised sentiment lexicon induction model for Malay, which mines a Malay version of WordNet called WordNet Bahasa and a Malay language dictionary named Kamus Dewan. The proposed approach first extracts subjective terms, and then stratifies positive and negative terms based on the direction the terms deviate from objectivity. We utilize WordNet Bahasa for its reliable lexical relations among words, and Kamus Dewan, considering it is among the most widely used publically available Malay dictionaries with human-defined gloss information. The model takes as input only two initial paradigm positive and negative terms, and automatically bootstraps a reliable, high coverage sentiment lexicon that can be applied in Malay sentiment analysis and related tasks.

The remainder of this paper is structured as follows. Section 2 reviews related work for English and low-resource languages. Section 3 presents the proposed sentiment lexicon induction model. Sections 4 and 5 present the evaluation of the model and the results obtained respectively. Section 6 concludes and highlights our plans for future work.

2   Related Work

Several well-regarded manually compiled sentiment lexicons do exist [1]. Due to their high cost in terms of time and effort, however, a large volume of research concentrated on automated sentiment lexicon generation has emerged in the past few years. The dictionary-based approach to generate a sentiment lexicon involves leveraging digital dictionaries and lexical resources (e.g. WordNet) to automatically assign terms with their corresponding semantic orientations [2]. This typically generates a general-purpose, domain-independent lexicon. The corpus-based approach involves exploiting co-occurrence statistics or syntactic patterns in textual corpora using pre-defined seed words [3]. This approach generates a domain-specific lexicon if a corpus from the required domain is used.

In the past few years, the majority of research on sentiment analysis has mostly been for English. Applying readily available off-the-shelf lexicon generation algorithms constructed for English on foreign languages such as Malay is difficult, since resources available in foreign languages are lacking. This is illustrated explicitly by [4], who use bilingual word networks by merging English WordNet with WordNets in foreign languages, and conclude that applying algorithms constructed for English on other languages results in poor accuracy, mainly due to the low amount of resources available in foreign languages.

Moreover, an automated translation of available English sentiment lexicons is also problematic. Mihalcea et al. [5] propose a sentiment lexicon in a foreign language by directly translating an available sentiment lexicon originally in English. An evaluation of this translation approach using manually-labeled annotation demonstrates that only a small amount of words in the target lexicon preserve their original sentiment polarities, post-translation. This is attributable to the fact that polysemous terms may be translated from the source language into different senses than the ones intended in the target language. Wan [6] also attempts a similar technique to derive a Chinese sentiment lexicon from bilingual resources, with relatively poor accuracy. Mohammad et al. [7] investigate this issue in detail and mention that, when text is translated from a source language to a target language, the sentiment of terms is preserved to varying degrees, with great reliance on the machine translation technique involved. Tan et al. [8] compile a Malay sentiment lexicon by manually translating terms in the Affin lexicon to their Malay counterparts, and supplement the lexicon with slang terms commonly used in Malay social media posts. Shamsudin et al. [9] manually compile a sentiment lexicon using WordNet Bahasa to classify Malay social media posts. However, manual annotation defeats the purpose for an automated means of lexicon construction.

Malay sentiment analysis has started to witness rapid progress both in industry (e.g. [10]) and academia (e.g. [11]) during the past few years. In [10], a knowledge base approach combined with supervised classifiers for sentiment classification of Malay text is proposed. In [12], a lexicon for a particular Malaysian dialect, i.e., the Sabah language, is constructed and employed to categorize a social media dataset. In [13], Malay news headlines are classified using a series of supervised classifiers. In [14], Malay newspaper sentences are classified based on the artificial immune concept called the negative selection algorithm, while [15] utilize a series of Malay stemming algorithms, namely, reverse porter algorithm, backward forward algorithm and the immune network algorithm, for sentiment classification of Malay newspaper articles. In [16], noise and its impact on the sentiment classification of Malay movie reviews are investigated. A more recent work by [17] investigate the effects of noise removal and stemming using a series of supervised classifiers.

Although an automatic means of constructing Malay sentiment lexicons would be highly beneficial for sentiment analysis in this language, research concentrated explicitly on automated sentiment lexicon generation in Malay remains scarce. Dar-wich et al. [18] map Malay synsets from WordNet Bahasa onto the English WordNet to generate a multilingual word network. A predefined seed set of positive and negative terms was then expanded by iteratively adding terms connected by the synonym and antonym lexical relations. The underlying intuition here is that the sentiment polarity is preserved as the constructed graph is navigated from seed terms to target terms via these relations. A supervised classifier was used for word-polarity tagging, using textual representations of the expanded seed sets as features. The drawback of this work is that it only considers adjectives. Furthermore, a binary classifier was used, which forces objective terms into the positive or negative class. Another limitation is that it does not utilize gloss information, which may also act as a valuable resource in the sentiment classification of terms.

3 Proposed Sentiment Lexicon Induction Model

We present here a minimally-supervised sentiment lexicon induction model to extract subjective, sentiment-laden terms from digital lexical resources. The model was developed to operate in low resource availability scenarios, and with minimal human involvement. It takes as input only two initial paradigm positive and negative terms, and automatically bootstraps a sentiment lexicon using three main steps:

Step 1. *Generating synonym chains from a word graph using predefined seed terms.* A graph of words (nodes) is first constructed using the synonym relations among them (edges). Initial seed terms are used to form synonym chains by iteratively calling all the synsets corresponding to the member terms within the initial seed synsets. The lexicon is enriched with newly added terms as the synonym chains expand on every iterative call. The intuition here is that the sentiment properties are preserved as the synonym chain is traversed, since synonymous terms are not only related by meaning, but also in terms of their semantic orientation.

Step 2. *Mining the human-defined gloss information of entries in a digital dictionary.* A constituent term contained within the gloss of an entry term is related to the entry term semantically, and so terms within the gloss of the entry are deemed to have a similar semantic orientation to that of the entry itself. For each entry in the digital dictionary investigated, if a subjective term generated from Step (1) matches a constituent term within the gloss of the entry, the entry itself is added to the lexicon.

Step 3.   *Merging the results from Steps (1) and (2).* This allows for maximizing the coverage of the sentiment lexicon by exploiting the two most prominent features of a digital dictionary – its word network as defined by lexical/ semantic relations (e.g. synonymy/hyponymy respectively), and its human-defined gloss information

As previously mentioned, we utilize two widely-used lexical resources for the Malay language, namely, WordNet Bahasa[1] (WNB hereafter; [19]) and Kamus Dewan Third Edition[2] (KD hereafter) by Dewan Bahasa dan Pustaka [20]. The motivation for using a dictionary-based approach here is that a dictionary comprises widespread coverage of the entire span of words defined in a natural language, and is for the most part a 'structured resource', whereby there is high semantic equivalence between an entry term on the left hand, and its corresponding human-defined gloss on the right. Furthermore, it possesses a rich network of lexical/semantic relations such as synonymy/hyponymy respectively. Since WNB does not contain a sufficient volume of gloss information, we supplement it with KD, a publically available Malay dictionary with reliable gloss information.

Although this work involves sentiment classification at the term level, it also subsumes the problem of subjectivity classification, which aims to classify text as either subjective (i.e. opinionated and expresses sentiment) or objective (i.e. factual and does not express sentiment) [21]. The model generates only a set of subjective terms labeled as positive or negative as the final lexicon, while the complement set of objective terms (i.e. terms with a near-neutral or neutral measure of confidence) are filtered out and not retained.

3.1   Generating Synonym Chains from WordNet Bahasa

The Global WordNet Association standardizes independent WordNet versions for many languages. WNB is the prominent standardized Malay version of WordNet, comprising a total of 49,668 synsets, 145,696 senses and 64,431 unique terms. Table 1 illustrates a portion of WNB. The first column shows a sense's offset-pos value, followed by a corresponding POS tag. WNB comprises senses in Malay, Indonesian, as well as general Bahasa (an overlap of both languages) denoted as M, I and B respectively; these can be observed in the 'Language' column. The 'Translation' column contains the translations of English senses to the target language. Note that there may exist one or several translations for an English sense, as can be seen for the offset '15297472', which is associated with three independent translations.

Since a portion of WNB was checked using an automatic technique, a 'goodness' metric is assigned to each sense, which reflects the degree of reliability of the translation to the target language. Y, O, M, L and X represent 'manually checked and good', 'automatically checked and good', 'automatically checked and medium', 'automatically checked and probably bad', and 'manually checked and bad' respectively.

---

[1] http://wn-msa.sourceforge.net/index.eng.html.

[2] http://prpm.dbp.gov.my.

Table 1. Portion of WordNet Bahasa

Offset-pos	Language	Goodness	Translation
15297303-n	B	M	*tempoh percubaan*
15297472-n	B	L	*Percubaan*
15297472-n	B	L	*waktu percubaan*
15297472-n	I	O	*masa percobaan*
15298011-n	B	L	*perbelanjaan*
15298507-n	M	X	*waktu pertanyaan*

The WNB database was cleaned by discarding all senses with 'language = I' and 'goodness = X or L', to discard terms associated with Indonesian only, and terms with poor quality translations.

The only human involvement in the model involves defining two singleton seed sets S^+_{wnb} and S^-_{wnb} by a paradigm positive synset to represent the positive class, and a paradigm negative synset to represent the negative class respectively. The terms *baik* (corresponding to the English synset good.a.01)[3] and *buruk* (corresponding to the synset bad.a.12) were used to define both classes (S^+_{wnb} = [baik] and S^-_{wnb} = [buruk]). Using these predefined seed sets, we generate synonym chains from WNB by iteratively calling all the synsets corresponding to the member terms within the initial synsets. Note that we only add adjectives to the seed sets, since the introduction of nouns and verbs resulted in a high volume of noise (i.e. non-polar terms) in the expanded seed sets. The reason for this is likely because, in linguistics, adjectives have the role of modifier words that express sentiment on other words such as nouns (e.g. *wonderful* day). The seed sets are enriched with newly introduced terms as the synonym chains expand on each iterative call. The intuition here is that the sentiment properties are generally preserved as the synonym chain is navigated, since synonyms are not only related in meaning, but also in terms of their semantic orientation.

Several experiments conducted out using different lengths of chains (1,000, 1,500 and 2,000 synsets for each the positive and negative seed sets). The aim is to determine the optimal coverage-correctness tradeoff, i.e., to retrieve as many polar terms as possible, but without compromising accuracy. The synonym chains were trimmed to the first 1000 synsets, since higher values resulted in the rapid inclusion of non-polar terms. This is because the synonym relations tend to become weaker as the distance from seed terms becomes greater, resulting in the addition of noise to the expanded seed sets. Table 2 shows some statistics for the synsets extracted and their corresponding terms.

Table 2. Statistics for synsets and member terms

Class	Synsets	Unique terms	Tokens
S^+_{wnb}	530	1,053	2,342
S^-_{wnb}	441	888	1,785

---

[3] The convention 'term.pos.sense' is used to define WordNet synsets here. For example, good.a.01 refers to the first sense of the adjective 'good', while bad.a.12 refers to the 12th sense of the adjective 'bad'.

It is critical that the expanded seed sets contain minimal noise, since they are later employed to mine KD for additional subjective terms. Some terms in the synonym chains were picked up several times on multiple independent calls, attributable to the existence of multiple links between two terms in the network. According to the social network theory [22], a node that shares many semantic links with nodes of a particular category, tends to be 'central' to that category. Therefore, according to this theory, this frequency information of term occurrence can be used to compute a confidence measure (cm hereafter) for each term. A cm can be thought of as a measure of centrality, since the more a term occurs in a particular class, the more central it is to that class, and in turn the more likely it belongs. We compute the cm for each term as follows:

$$cm = \frac{posfreq(t) - negfreq(t)}{posfreq(t) + negfreq(t)} \tag{1}$$

where $posfreq(t)$ represents the frequency of occurrence of term t within the positive class, while $negfreq(t)$ represents its frequency of occurrence within the negative class. The denominator is used to constrain the cm to the bounds of $[-1, +1]$. The nearer the cm is to either end, the higher the confidence it belongs to its class. This effectively dampens the confidence of non-polar terms, allowing us to filter them out and retain only terms with a cm above a predefined threshold. In this work, terms with a cm <0.25 were discarded, since they were mostly non-polar. The final expanded sets S_{wnb}^{+} and S_{wnb}^{-} contain 857 positive and 873 negative terms respectively. Table 3 shows some sample terms along with their confidence measures found in the generated synonym chains. The next step involves mining the gloss information of entries in a digital dictionary. Since WNB does not include a sufficient volume of gloss information, we alternatively use KD's gloss information to further increase the coverage of the lexicon.

Table 3. Sample terms and their confidence measures

S_{wnb}^{+}	S_{wnb}^{-}
['bijak', 0.058]	['malang', 1.0]
['cantik', 1.0]	['sedih', 0.974]
['baik', 0.6]	['tidak bersih', 1.0]
['mencintai', 1.0]	['menyinggung', 0.6]
['menarik', 0.196]	['berpenyakit', 1.0]
['pintar', 0.304]	['menyengsarakan', 0.846]
['sehat', 1.0]	['sangat dahsyat', 1.0]

3.2 Mining Kamus Dewan for Subjective Terms

Using the expanded seed sets S_{wnb}^{+} and S_{wnb}^{-} from the previous step, we mine the gloss information of entries in KD to further increase coverage of the lexicon. The *definiendum-definiens* semantic relation (i.e. the relation between an entry itself and a constituent within its gloss) is used with the intuition that a constituent term contained within the gloss of an entry is related to the entry term semantically. In other words, terms within the gloss of the entry are deemed to have a similar semantic orientation to that of the entry. The results after multiple experiments indicate that using only relations between entries and *adjectives* within their glosses tends to yield the best performing results, compared to nouns, verbs and adverbs. Conveniently, the expanded seed sets from the synonym chains generation step contain only adjectives. The 857 positive terms in S^+_{wnb} and the 873 negative terms in S^-_{wnb} are used as the initial seed terms here, while the positive seed set (S^+_{kd}) and negative seed set (S^-_{kd}) involved in this current step of mining KD are initially null sets.

For each of the 55,725 entries in KD, if a term in S^+_{wnb} (S^-_{wnb}) matches an adjective term in the gloss of the entry, the entry itself is added to S^+_{kd} (S^-_{kd}). This matching rule is illustrated in Fig. 1, whereby 'menarik' is matched with a term in the gloss of the entry 'cantik', and so 'cantik' is retrieved to S^+_{kd}. In order to avoid the issue of sentential negation in glosses, if a matched gloss term is preceded by a negation term, the corresponding entry is not retrieved, since negators tend to invert the sentiment of the terms under the scope of negation. Negation in the context of Malay is expressed in the majority of cases using the negators 'tidak', 'bukan', 'jangan' and 'belum' [23, 24]. For example, one of the glosses for the entry term 'buruk' is 'tidak cantik'. The negation rule would avoid the scenario of 'cantik' being matched, and the entry 'buruk' being added to the positive class S^+_{kd} as a result. It is important to note that entry terms of all POSs (i.e. adjectives, adverbs, verbs and nouns) are extracted during this step, but the final lexicon does not include POS information, since entry terms in KD are not all tagged with POS information.

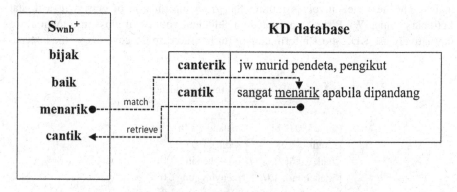

Fig. 1. Matching rule example

An inevitable problem encountered is that objective terms that contain in their glosses subjective terms would be picked up by this algorithm. For example, the term 'sinonim' is defined as 'kata yg sama atau hampir sama maknanya dgn kata lain, mis cantik dgn indah dan cepat dgn pantas, kata seerti', and would be labeled as having a positive connotation because it contains multiple positive terms such as 'cantik' and 'indah'. To dampen the strength of objective terms, a confidence measure (cm) is assigned to the terms in S^+_{kd} and S^-_{kd} using the same method described in the previous section. Terms with a low cm (<0.25) were removed from both sets, which amounted to S^+_{kd} containing 2,134 terms and S^-_{kd} containing 2,586 terms.

3.3 Merging S_{wnb} with S_{kd}

When merging two terms, the average cm assigned to the term in S_{wnb} with S_{kd} is taken. For terms found in both the positive class and the negative classes, the average cm is taken for the term, but the term is only retained in the class assigning it the higher cm, since it is more likely the term belongs to that particular class. The final lexicon is formulated by merging S_{wnb} with S_{kd}. For the positive list, S_{wnb}^+ and S_{kd}^+ contained 857 and 2,134 terms respectively, while their union ($S_{wnb}^+ \cup S_{kd}^+$) amounted to 2,869 terms, after merging the 122 term-intersection. For the negative list, S_{wnb}^- and S_{kd}^- contained 873 and 2,586 respectively, while their union ($S_{wnb}^- \cup S_{kd}^-$) amounted to 3,286 terms, after merging the 173-term intersection. A handful of common stop words (e.g. dan, ada, tetapi, etc.) were removed from the positive and negative lists. Table 4 shows a portion of the resultant sentiment lexicon.

Table 4. Portion of resultant sentiment lexicon

Positive terms	cm	Negative terms	cm
berkilap	1.0	bongkok	0.8
bernas	1.0	gasang	0.75
berfungsi	1.0	sumbing	0.75
unggul	1.0	dukacita	1.0
anggun	0.6	cemburu	0.85
bersemarak	1.0	biasa	1.0
adil	0.8	katik	1.0
biak	1.0	lapuk	1.0

4 Evaluation

We evaluate the model's ability to categorize terms as Positive, Negative or Objective. The induced lexicon only contains terms that were found to be subjective (i.e. positive or negative), while terms found to be objective were not retained, since we are only interested in sentiment-laden terms to be in the final lexicon. However, for evaluation purposes, from the induced lexicon itself, we have randomly selected 1,000 terms from those labeled as Positive, 1,000 terms from those labeled as Negative, and 1,000 terms from those filtered out as Objective. Two human annotators were then trained and requested to manually label of these 3,000 terms as 'POS', 'NEG' or 'OBJ'. The Cohen's kappa value was recorded to be in the 0.81–1 range, indicating 'almost perfect inter-annotator agreement' according to [25]. This gold standard manually annotated test set was then used to compare the *manual* annotation of humans with the *automatic* annotation of the proposed model (i.e. human-machine agreement), in order to arrive at the overall accuracy of the model:

$$Accuracy = \frac{tp + tn}{tp + tn + fp + fn} \qquad (2)$$

where tp, tn, fp and fn represent true positives, true negatives, false positives and false negatives respectively. This evaluation metric is indicative of the model's overall accuracy in the task of ternary sentiment classification of terms.

5 Results and Discussion

Table 5 depicts the accuracy of the model to label positive terms, negative terms, objective terms and the overall accuracy. According to the table, the model achieves comparable accuracy to label subjective terms (63.6% for positive and 61.7% for negative). It performs remarkably higher to label terms as objective (94.6%), attributable to the fact that there exist a significantly larger amount of objective terms in a natural language. The overall accuracy of the model for ternary Positive-Negative-Objective classification of terms is 73.33%.

Table 5. Model accuracy in term sentiment classification

Acc (positive)	Acc (negative)	Acc (objective)	Acc (overall)
63.6	61.7	94.6	73.3

One important observation is that there is a 10.68% drop in accuracy (from 73.33% to 62.65%) when moving from a ternary classification problem to a binary Positive-Negative classification problem. This demonstrates that the former, which involves first classifying terms as subjective or objective, and then classifying subjective terms as positive or negative, is a more challenging problem. This is in line with previous work [26, 27]; the latter work reports a 17% drop in accuracy when moving from a binary to a ternary problem. This is also a more *realistic* problem [27], since in classifying terms as positive or negative while ignoring the objective class, an assumption is made that *the lexical resource or dictionary used only contains subjective terms*, which is not the case in reality. Among the total 55,725 entries in KD, only about 6,155 terms (11%) were labeled as subjective (2,869 positive and 3,286 negative), while the remaining 89% were considered objective. [27] report that nearly a quarter of the terms in the English language contain at least some degree of subjectivity (precisely 24.63%). [26] demonstrate that only a small set of terms are core, prototypical members of their sentiment category, while the remaining become increasingly sentiment-ambiguous when moving towards the fuzzy periphery of the category, and that the majority of terms in a language are unquestionably objective in nature.

Another important observation is that the overall accuracy of the model (73.3%) is only 7.7% lower than the accuracy of humans in labeling terms (i.e. inter-human agreement), which we have taken to be at least 81% (see Sect. 4). Note that the model's accuracy is 4.03% higher than inter-human agreement defined by [28], which is 69.27% (taking the average of 76.19% to label adjectives and 62.35% to label verbs). Possible improvements in accuracy may be possible by dealing with misclassification resulting from noisy gloss information. For example, many objective terms potentially include subjective terms in their glosses, and vice versa.

Liu [29] mentions that a pruning process to manually clean up the resultant sentiment lexicon is a one-time effort. We manually removed any errors and mismatches from the resultant lexicon and made a clean version publically available for future research on Malay sentiment analysis and possibly other natural language processing tasks.[4] The lexicon can be easily read, expanded, modified according to the required task (e.g. domain adaptation), and integrated into any practical sentiment analysis system.

6 Conclusion

This work proposed a minimally-supervised sentiment lexicon induction model specifically for the Malay language. The model mines WordNet Bahasa and Kamus Dewan, first extracting subjective terms, and then stratifying positive and negative terms based on the direction they deviate from objectivity. This involves sentiment classification of terms, but also subsumes the problem of subjectivity classification. We utilize WordNet Bahasa for its reliable lexical relations, and Kamus Dewan, a widely used publically available Malay dictionary. However, this model is dictionary-independent, since any dictionary with lexical relations and gloss information can be employed.

The model takes as input only two initial paradigm positive and negative terms, and automatically bootstraps a reliable, high coverage sentiment lexicon that can be used in Malay sentiment analysis on full-text (and possibly other real-world natural language processing applications). The confidence measures of terms can be used to empirically set an accuracy-coverage trade-off point for the induced lexicon. For example, retaining only terms above a 0.75 confidence measure would yield a smaller, but highly accurate sentiment lexicon; while decreasing this threshold would increase the size of the lexicon, at the expense of accuracy. A clean version of the lexicon is made publically available for future work on Malay sentiment analysis and possibly other natural language processing tasks.

An important limitation in this work is that, although it covers the entire span of the Malay language, it is only able to classify formal terms as defined in the lexical resources utilized. It is not able to detect and classify informal terms such as those commonly used on the Web and social media. Moreover, the resultant lexicon is a general, domain-independent lexicon, and may not perform well on domain-specific text. A corpus-based approach in combination with the proposed approach may be able to solve the aforementioned issues, and is considered future work.

Acknowledgement. This research was partially supported by the Malaysia Ministry of Education Grant FRGS/1/2014/ICT02/UKM/01/1 awarded to the Center for Artificial Intelligence Technology at Universiti Kebangsaan Malaysia.

---

[4] http://lrgs.ftsm.ukm.my/MalaySent.

References

1. Stone, P.J., Dunphy, D.C., Smith, M.S.: The General Inquirer: A Computer Approach to Content Analysis (1966)
2. Baccianella, S., Esuli, A., Sebastiani, F.: SentiWordNet 3.0: an enhanced lexical resource for sentiment analysis and opinion mining. In: LREC, pp. 2200–2204 (2010)
3. Hatzivassiloglou, V., McKeown, K.R.: Predicting the semantic orientation of adjectives. In: Proceedings of the eighth conference on European chapter of the Association for Computational Linguistics, pp, 174–181. Association for Computational Linguistics (1997)
4. Hassan, A., Abu-Jbara, A., Jha, R., Radev, D.: Identifying the semantic orientation of foreign words. In: Proceedings of the 49th Annual Meeting of the Association for Computational Linguistics: Human Language Technologies: short papers. vol. 2, pp. 592–597. Association for Computational Linguistics (2011)
5. Mihalcea, R., Banea, C., Wiebe, J.: Learning multilingual subjective language via cross-lingual projections. In: Annual Meeting-Association for Computational Linguistics. vol. 1, p. 976 (2007)
6. Wan, X.: Co-training for cross-lingual sentiment classification. In: Proceedings of the Joint Conference of the 47th Annual Meeting of the ACL and the 4th International Joint Conference on Natural Language Processing of the AFNLP, vol. 1, pp. 235–243. Association for Computational Linguistics (2009)
7. Mohammad, S.M., Salameh, M., Kiritchenko, S.: How translation alters sentiment. J. Artif. Intell. Res. (JAIR) 55, 95–130 (2016)
8. Tan, Y.-F., Lam, H.-S., Azlan, A., Soo, W.-K.: Sentiment analysis for telco popularity on Twitter big data using a novel Malaysian dictionary. In: ICADIWT, pp. 112–125 (2016)
9. Shamsudin, N.F., Basiron, H., Sa'aya, Z.: Lexical based sentiment analysis-verb, adverb and negation. J. Telecommun. Electron. Comput. Eng. (JTEC) 8(2), 161–166 (2016)
10. Sadanandan, A.A., Osman, N.A., Hussain Saifuddin, M.K., Ahamad, D.N.P., Hoe, H.: Improving accuracy in sentiment analysis for Malay language
11. Nasharuddin, N.A., Abdullah, M.T., Azman, A., Kadir, R.A.: English and Malay cross-lingual sentiment lexicon acquisition and analysis. In: Kim, K., Joukov, N. (eds.) ICISA 2017. LNEE, vol. 424, pp. 467–475. Springer, Singapore (2017). doi:10.1007/978-981-10-4154-9_54
12. Hijazi, M.H.A., Libin, L., Alfred, R., Coenen, F.: Bias aware lexicon-based sentiment analysis of Malay dialect on social media data: a study on the Sabah language. In: 2016 2nd International Conference on Science in Information Technology (ICSITech), pp. 356–361. IEEE (2016)
13. Alfred, R., Yee, W.W., Lim, Y., Obit, J.H.: Factors affecting sentiment prediction of Malay news headlines using machine learning approaches. In: Berry, M.W., Mohamed, A.H., Yap, B.W. (eds.) SCDS 2016. CCIS, vol. 652, pp. 289–299. Springer, Singapore (2016). doi:10.1007/978-981-10-2777-2_26
14. Puteh, M., Isa, N., Puteh, S., Redzuan, N.A.: Sentiment mining of Malay newspaper (SAMNews) using artificial immune system. In: Proceedings of the World Congress on Engineering (2013)
15. Isa, N., Puteh, M., Kamarudin, R.: Sentiment classification of Malay newspaper using immune network (SCIN). In: Proceedings of the World Congress on Engineering (2013)
16. Samsudin, N., Puteh, M., Hamdan, A.R., Nazri, M.Z.A.: Normalization of noisy texts in Malaysian online reviews. J. ICT 12, 147–159 (2013)

17. Arif, S.M., Mustapha, M.: The effect of noise elimination and stemming in sentiment analysis for Malay documents. In: Ahmad, A.-R., Kor, L.K., Ahmad, I., Idrus, Z. (eds.) Proceedings of the International Conference on Computing, Mathematics and Statistics (iCMS 2015), pp. 93–102. Springer, Singapore (2017). doi:10.1007/978-981-10-2772-7_10

18. Darwich, M., Noah, S.A.M., Omar, N.: Automatically generating a sentiment lexicon for the Malay language. Asia-Pacific J. Inf. Technol. Multimed. **5**(1), 49–59 (2016)

19. Bond, F., Lim, L.T., Tang, E.K., Riza, H.: The combined wordnet bahasa. NUSA: Linguist. Stud. Lang. Around Indonesia **57**, 83–100 (2014)

20. Perkamusan, D.: Kamus Dewan. Dewan Bahasa dan Pustaka, Kuala Lumpur (1984)

21. Wilson, T., Hoffmann, P., Somasundaran, S., Kessler, J., Wiebe, J., Choi, Y., Cardie, C., Riloff, E., Patwardhan, S.: Opinionfinder: a system for subjectivity analysis. In: Proceedings of HLT/EMNLP on Interactive Demonstrations, pp. 34–35. Association for Computational Linguistics (2005)

22. Burt, R.S.: Models of network structure. Ann. Rev. Sociol. **6**(1), 79–141 (1980)

23. Idris, A.A.: Modality in Malay (1980)

24. Kroeger, P.: External negation in Malay/Indonesian. Language **90**(1), 137–184 (2014)

25. Landis, J.R., Koch, G.G.: The measurement of observer agreement for categorical data. Biometrics **33**, 159–174 (1977)

26. Andreevskaia, A., Bergler, S.: Mining WordNet for a fuzzy sentiment: sentiment tag extraction from WordNet glosses. In: EACL, pp. 209–216 (2006)

27. Esuli, A., Sebastiani, F.: Determining term subjectivity and term orientation for opinion mining. In: EACL, p. 2006 (2006)

28. Kim, S.-M., Hovy, E.: Determining the sentiment of opinions. In: Proceedings of the 20th international conference on Computational Linguistics, p. 1367. Association for Computational Linguistics (2004)

29. Liu, B.: Sentiment analysis and opinion mining. Synth. Lect. Hum. Lang. Technol. **5**(1), 1–167 (2012)

Analysis of the Reforming Languages by Image-Based Variations of LBP and NBP Operators

Darko Brodić[1(✉)], Alessia Amelio[2],
Radmila Janković[1], and Zoran N. Milivojević[3]

[1] Technical Faculty in Bor, University of Belgrade, V.J. 12, 19210 Bor, Serbia
dbrodic@tfbor.bg.ac.rs
[2] DIMES, University of Calabria, Via Pietro Bucci Cube 44, 87036 Rende, CS, Italy
aamelio@dimes.unical.it
[3] College of Applied Technical Sciences, Aleksandra Medvedeva 20, 18000 Niš, Serbia
zoran.milivojevic@vtsnis.edu.rs

Abstract. This paper proposes an extension of the local binary pattern and neighbor binary pattern as a basis for extracting features needed for recognizing an image which represents a text in specific languages. At the first, the unicode text is, according to its energy status in the text-line area, converted into a gray level image. Then, the extension of the local binary pattern and neighbor binary pattern is proposed. These features are extracted in order to differentiate image-based representations of a text in a given language. At the end, the extracted features are classified by Support Vector Machine and Naive Bayes to establish a difference that can identify different languages. The obtained results prove the accuracy and efficiency of the proposed method when compared with other state-of-the-art methods.

Keywords: Image analysis · Natural language processing · Local binary pattern · Neighbor binary pattern · Adjacent local binary pattern · Classification

1 Introduction

Local Binary Pattern (LBP) [18] and some of its derivations [10,16,17] have been broadly used in image processing and computer vision. Basically, LBP explores local structures of the images. It performs this process by comparing each pixel in the image with its neighboring pixels. The most important characteristics of the LBP are: (i) computational simplicity, and (ii) robustness to image amplitude (illumination) changes. Originally, LBP was proposed for use in texture analysis [19]. Due to its robust characteristics, LBP has been broadly exploited in many applications, such as: (i) image and video retrieval [8], (ii) visual inspection [15], (iii) motion analysis [11], (iv) face image analysis [1], etc.

In this paper, we introduce a wider level of LBP derivations which can be used for the discrimination of evolving languages. In this sense, LBP, Adjacent

© Springer International Publishing AG 2017
S. Phon-Amnuaisuk et al. (Eds.): MIWAI 2017, LNAI 10607, pp. 238–251, 2017.
https://doi.org/10.1007/978-3-319-69456-6_20

LBP (ALBP) as well as Neighbor Binary Pattern (NBP) are used in their various combinations. Furthermore, a new Adjacent Neighbor Binary Pattern (ANBP) is introduced with the analogy to ALBP. The experiment is performed on a database of documents written in Slavonic Serbian language from 18th century (a literary language used by the Serbs in the Habsburg Empire) and Serbian language from 19th and 20th century. Differentiation of these languages is a challenging task. Basically, Slavonic Serbian language is not evolved, but rather reformed into modern Serbian language by introducing: (i) a new Serbian Cyrillic alphabet by following strict phonemic principles and (ii) reforming of the Serbian literary language by modernizing it and distancing it from the Slavonic Serbian language. At the end, the discrimination of these languages is implemented by two different classification tools: (i) Support Vector Machine, and (ii) Naive Bayes. The results obtained by the experiment are very promising.

The paper is organized as follows. Section 2 introduces the proposed algorithm. Section 3 presents the experiment. Section 4 describes the experimental setting. Section 5 gives the results and discusses them. At the end, Sect. 6 draws the conclusions.

1.1   Related Work

We should point out that previously proposed methods for language recognition have typically used a classical statistical approach based on the uni-grams, bi-grams, tri-grams (widely called n-grams) or their combination and variation [9, 20]. However, this process was not universal one for phonetic languages because each new letter in any language was introduced as a new element or variable in this type of analysis.

The application of LBP to the script and language recognition has been completely unexplored. Still, to be analyzed by LBP or its derivations, the language should be transformed into the image space. The first attempt was made in [21]. Basically, the study proposed the conversion of each character into Character Shape Codes (CSC) introducing a general approach to the alphabet of each language along with reducing the number of variables to be analyzed. Similarly, the coding based on the energy profile of each character was proposed in [3]. Furthermore, the study used LBP and ALBP [17] as a basis for the discrimination of different languages. In particular, the new approach was based on the conversion of the written language into codes representing an image and then analyzed it by LBP. Still, this approach was not used for comparison between languages transformed one into another during their reformation through the historical period. A similar approach based on image ALBP was proposed in [5] for discriminating between closely related languages on the example of Serbian and Croatian. A concrete attempt to use the image ALBP for the discrimination of languages evolved over time, i.e. Italian Vulgar and modern Italian, was performed in [6]. Also, the same image features were employed in [4] for distinguishing the South Slavic Medieval labels written in different scripts of the evolving historical period. In the last two cases, the analysis was limited to the Italian language and to the discrimination of the evolving script.

2   The Proposed Algorithm

The proposed algorithm consists of different stages needed for evolving language discrimination:

(i)   establishing the energy profile of each character in the text of each text-line,
(ii) coding each character in the text according to its energy profile,
(iii) establishing a correspondence between coding and equivalent image gray levels,
(iv) exploring local structures of the given image by the application of LBP, NBP and their derivations, and
(v)   discrimination of the extracted features by the classification tools.

Figure 1 shows the overview of the algorithm.

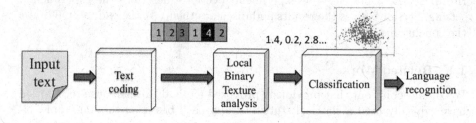

Fig. 1. Overview of the proposed algorithm

2.1   Coding the Text

In the first stage, each character is extracted in the text-line (scanned document) or it is recognized by its unicode value (electronic document). Then, its energy profile is calculated. This characteristic is closely related to the typography. Furthermore, each text-line of the text can be split into four virtual lines, which further define different zones of the same text-line. The virtual lines are:

– top-line,
– upper-line,
– base-line, and
– bottom-line,

establishing the following vertical zones:

– lower,
– middle, and
– upper.

Accordingly, the characters are classified taking into account their position in the vertical zones. Hence, the characters can be classified as:

- base letters (code 1),
- ascender letters (code 2),
- descendent letters (code 3), and
- full letters (code 4) [3],[6].

This classification is illustrated in Fig. 2.

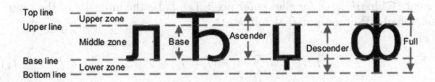

Fig. 2. Coding of the letters

In this sense, each character from the text is converted into the elements from the set G = {1,2,3,4}, which results in an image-like information representing different gray scale levels. Figure 3 illustrates this process on a given text sample.

At the first sight, it seems that the number of alphabet variables is rapidly reduced to 4. However, the new four variables (codes) introduce a new quality of elements, which is general for different alphabets as well as for capital and small letters. It is worth noting that the coding system is based on a character segmentation stage from the Optical Character Recognition (OCR). Hence, it introduces the elements of the document image processing, which is the core of the text writing and the typography.

То поглавље сам већ давно објавио.

21 11111111 111 112 11111 1241111

Fig. 3. Mapping of the initial text to coded text corresponding to image information

2.2 Texture Analysis

The obtained image is subjected to texture analysis for feature extraction. In particular, an extension of LBP and NBP in the form of extended and adjacent LBP and NBP (ELBP, ENBP, ALBP and ANBP) is applied on the image for the creation of the corresponding feature vector.

Local and Neighbor Binary Pattern. LBP is a texture operator that measures the local contrast variations in the image [19]. It is computed by considering a Window of Interest (WOI) whose dimension is 3×3, sliding over the image pixels. Each time, the center pixel in the WOI is compared with the neighboring pixels. Their value is set to 1 if their intensity is higher than the intensity of the center pixel, otherwise it is set to 0. Then, the neighboring intensities are multiplied by different powers of two according to the pixel position, and summed to create a binary label for the center pixel. Let I_c be the intensity of the center pixel. The LBP is computed as follows:

$$LBP_{d,r} = \sum_{i=1}^{d} sign(I_i - I_c) \times 2^{i-1},$$ (1)

where the $sign(x)$ is 1 if $x \geq 0$, and 0 otherwise. I_i is the intensity of the i-th neighbor pixel, d is the number of neighbor pixels, and r is the distance between the neighbor and center pixel. In the case of our image (see Fig. 3), only the left and right neighbors of the center pixel can be considered. Hence, we have $d = 2$, determining a total of $2^2 = 4$ different labels. Also, we set $r = 1$, which is the minimum neighboring distance. At the end, the feature set is a histogram of size 1×4 counting the frequency of each micro pattern over the image.

NBP is just a slight modification of LBP [10]. It proposes a different type of LBP calculation, which does not depend on the center pixel value, but on the value of the previous neighbor pixels in the current set. The NBP is computed as follows:

$$NBP_{d,r} = \sum_{i=1}^{d} sign(I_i - I_{i+1}) \times 2^{i-1}.$$ (2)

In the contrast to LBP, where the comparison of the center pixel and neighbor pixel values is the most important for its calculation, the NBP value only depends on the sequentially mutual neighbor pixel values.

Extended Local and Neighbor Binary Pattern. In the Extended Local Binary Pattern (ELBP), we consider the pixels which are more distant from the center pixel compared to LBP. In this case, the neighbor pixels have distance r set to 2, 3, 4, and 5, i.e. $r > 1$. However, $d = 2$ is again. Hence, it determines a total of $2^2 = 4$ different labels. In this way, we explore the mutual dependence not only of the closest neighbor pixels, but also of the distant ones from the center pixel. Similarly, the NBP is transformed into Extended Neighbor Binary Pattern (ENBP) by introducing a bigger distance into NBP, i.e. setting r equal to 2, 3, 4, and 5, i.e. $r > 1$. In the aforementioned cases, we obtain LBP_r and NBP_r as specific ELBP and ENBP, respectively.

Adjacent Local and Neighbor Binary Pattern. Due to the small feature number, the expansion to ALBP is used for further analysis [17]. It is the combination of two adjacent LBPs in the horizontal direction, i.e. the two horizontal pixels on the left and right of the center pixel. It determines a binary label of 4 elements, for a total of $2^4 = 16$ different labels. At the end, the feature set is a histogram of size 1×16 counting the frequency of each different label over the image.

Making the correspondence between LBP and NBP, we propose ANBP, which is the combination of the NBPs given in the ALBP manner. Accordingly, it is the combination of two adjacent NBPs in the horizontal direction, i.e. the two horizontal pixels on the left and right of the center pixel. Again, it determines a binary label of 4 elements, for a total of $2^4 = 16$ different labels.

Figure 4 illustrates LBP, NBP, ELBP, ENBP, ALBP and ANBP samples and their calculation.

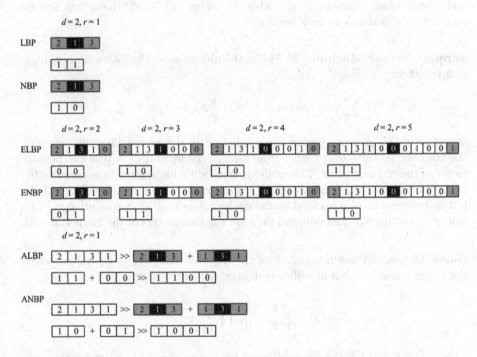

Fig. 4. Illustration of LBP, NBP, ELBP, ENBP, ALBP and ANBP

Finally, the image information is represented by 16 ALBP (with $r = 1$, named as ALBP1), 4 LBP (with $r = 1$, named as LBP1), 4 NBP (with $r = 1$, named as NBP1), 4 ENBP, 4 ELBP (with $r = 2, ..., 5$), 16 ANBP (with $r = 1$, named as ANBP1) features and their combinations. Among all the different types of features and their combinations, we use the combination of ALBP1, ENBP with $r = 2, 3$, ANBP1 and LBP1, which obtained the best performances in this context.

2.3 Classification

The feature vector obtained by the combination of the different patterns is classified by using the Support Vector Machine (SVM) and the Naive Bayes (NB) algorithms. They are well-known machine learning methods, extensively used in the domain of document categorization and image processing, where they obtained better results than the other classifiers [12,13]. Also, we conducted our experiment by employing another classifier, i.e. K-Nearest Neighbors (K-NN) [2]. Classification results demonstrated that SVM and NB perform considerably better than K-NN in this context of evolving language recognition of documents. For this reason, they have been definitively adopted in our case.

Let $T = \{(x_1, y_1), ..., (x_n, y_n)\}$ be a training set of feature vectors $x_1, ..., x_n$ and binary class labels $y_1, ..., y_n$. Also, let $x_j = \{x_j^1, ..., x_j^k\}$ be a test feature vector with k features to be classified.

Support Vector Machine. SVM has the aim to solve the following optimization problem:

$$\min_{w,b,\xi} \ \frac{1}{2} w^T w + C \sum_{i=1}^{n} \xi_i, \quad \text{subjected to} \ \ y_i(w^T \phi(x_i) + b) \geq 1 - \xi_i, \quad i = 1, ..., n \ \ (3)$$

where $x_i \in T$, y_i is its binary class label, ϕ is the kernel function mapping the training vector into a higher dimensional space, and $C > 0$ is the penalty factor of the training error. The model is learned by finding the linear separating hyperplane maximizing the margin [7]. The prediction of the class label of the test feature vector x_j is realized by the decision function: $y_j = sgn(w^T \phi(x_j) + b)$, where sgn is the sign function and w, b are the parameters of the learned model.

Naive Bayes. By assuming that all the features of x_j are independent, given the target value, the NB classifier is defined as [23]:

$$f_{nb}(x_j) = \frac{p(Y = 1)}{p(Y = 0)} \prod_{h=1}^{k} \frac{p(x_j^h | Y = 1)}{p(x_j^h | Y = 0)}, \tag{4}$$

where $p(x_j^h | Y = 1)$ is the probability of observing the value x_j^h given the class label 1 in the training set T, and $p(Y = 1)$ is the probability of observing the class label 1 in the training set T. The same is for the class label 0. The feature vector x_j is predicted to be in class 1 if and only if $f_{nb}(x_j) \geq 1$. Otherwise, it is predicted to be in class 0. For numerical features, the normal distribution function is considered for computing the probability terms:

$$f(w, \mu, \sigma) = \frac{1}{\sqrt{2\pi}\sigma} e^{-\frac{(w-\mu)^2}{\sigma^2}}. \tag{5}$$

Hence, we have $p(x_j^h | Y = 1) = f(x_j^h, \mu_{Y=1}, \sigma_{Y=1})$, where $\mu_{Y=1}$ and $\sigma_{Y=1}$ are respectively the mean and standard deviation of the values of h-th feature corresponding to class label 1. The same is for the class label 0.

3   Experiment

The experiment includes a process of discrimination between documents written in Slavonic Serbian and Serbian languages. Slavonic Serbian was a literary language used by the Serbs in the Habsburg Empire. These two languages represent evolving languages from the mid of 18th till the first decades of the 19th century. It is worth noting that the Serbian language of the 19th century preserved in a similar form till now. The database which is subjected to the experiment is composed of thirty documents. Ten out of the thirty documents are written in Slavonic Serbian language, while the other twenty documents are written in Serbian language. Each document counts from 500 to 1500 characters. Figure 5 shows a sample text written in Slavonic Serbian language.

Честь имамъ всѣмъ Высокопочитаемымъ Читателемъ обявити, да безъ сваке сумнѣ намѣренъ есамъ, ону достохвалну и цѣлому Сербскому Роду преполезну ИСТОРИЮ СЕРБСКУ, от коесамъ цѣло оглавленїе давно сообщїо, печатати.

Fig. 5. Slavonic Serbian language text sample

Figure 6 shows the same text written in Serbian language.

Имам част да најавим свим поштованим читаоцима да сам ја, без икакве сумње, намеран штампати достојну хвале и целом српском народу вредну СРПСКУ ИСТОРИЈУ, од које сам цело поглавље био већ давно објавио.

Fig. 6. Serbian language text sample

Furthermore, a sample of documents used in the experiment database[1] is illustrated in Fig. 7.

Our aim is the evaluation of the extended features in the classification of the evolving languages. In particular, we compare their ability in recognizing the documents of the database as given in Serbian or Slavonic Serbian language with the state-of-the-art ALBP features (with $r = 1$), used in the literature for the discrimination of evolving languages and scripts [4,6].

4   Experimental Setting

The experimentation has been performed in Matlab R2015b on a notebook with Quad-Core CPU at 2.2 GHz, 16 GB RAM and UNIX operating system.

Classification of the feature vectors is performed by SVM and NB algorithms. In the case of NB algorithm, we employ the normal distribution function in Eq. (5) for computing the conditional probabilities, because all values of the feature vectors are numerical ones. In the case of SVM, we run the algorithm

---

[1] Digitalized National Library of Serbia, http://digitalna.nb.rs.

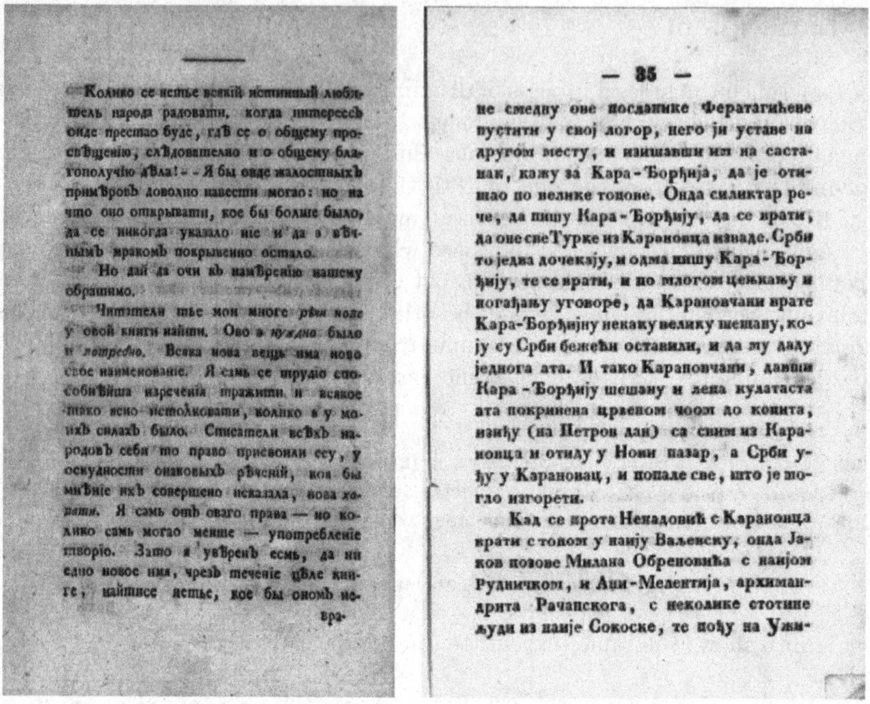

Колико се нетьє всякій истинный любитель народа радовати, когда интерессъ онде престао буде, гдѣ се о общему просвѣщенію, слѣдователно и о общему благополучію дѣла! - - Я бы овде жалостныхъ примѣровъ доволно навести могао: но на что оно отрывати, кое бы болше было, да се никогда указало ніе и да в вѣчнымъ мракомъ покрывенно остало.

Но дай да очи къ намѣренію нашему обратимо.

Читатели тьє мои многе *рѣчи нове* у овой книги найти. Ово в *нуждно* было и *потребно*. Всяка нова вещь има ново свое наименованіе. Я самь се трудіо способнѣйша изреченія тражити и всякое тако ясно истолковати, колико в у моихъ силахъ было. Списатели всѣхъ народовъ себи то право присвоили єсу, у оскудности онаковыхъ рѣченій, коя бы мнѣніе ихъ совершено исказала, нова *ковати*. Я самь отъ оваго права — но колико самь могао менше — употребленіе творіо. Зато я увѣренъ єсмь, да ни едно новое имя, чрезъ теченіе цѣле книге, найтисе нетьє, кое бы оному не-

вра-

(a)

— 35 —

не смеду ове посланике Фератагићеве пустити у свој логор, него ји уставе на другом месту, и изишавши им на састанак, кажу за Кара-Ђорђија, да је отишао по велике топове. Онда силиктар рече, да пишу Кара-Ђорђију, да се врати, да ове све Турке из Карановца изваде. Срби то једва дочекају, и одма пишу Кара-Ђорђију, те се врати, и по млогом цењкању и погађању уговоре, да Карановчани врате Кара-Ђорђијну некаку велику шешану, коју су Срби бежећи оставили, и да му даду једнога ата. И тако Карановчани, давши Кара-Ђорђију шешану и лепа кулатаста ата покривена црвеном чоом до копита, изиђу (на Петров дан) са свим из Карановца и отиду у Нови пазар, а Срби уђу у Карановац, и попале све, што је могло изгорети.

Кад се прота Ненадовић с Карановца врати с топом у нахију Ваљевску, онда Јаков позове Милана Обреновића с нахијом Рудничком, и Аџи-Мелентија, архимандрита Рачанског, с неколике стотине људи из нахије Сокоске, те пођу на Ужи-

(b)

Fig. 7. Database sample documents: (a) from the book entitled *Fisika* dated from 1802 written by Atanasije Stojković, (b) from the book entitled *Danica - magazine* dated from 1834 written by Vuk Stefanović Karadžić

with different kernel functions, i.e. linear, polynomial with order 3 and Gaussian radial basis with scaling factor 1. At the end, we use the linear kernel function because it obtains the best classification performances in this context.

Before any classification task, the values of each feature type have been normalized in the range [0,1]. In particular, let $\mathcal{X} = \{x_j^p, ..., x_j^q\}$ be the set of features of a given type, which is a subsequence of the feature vector x_j. Normalization of a given value $x_j^i \in \mathcal{X}$ is performed as follows:

$$\overline{x_j^i} = \frac{x_j^i}{\sum_{h=p}^{q} x_j^h}. \tag{6}$$

This value corresponds to the frequency of the i-th pattern inside the document represented by x_j.

We generate the confusion matrix for measuring the performances of the binary classification. It quantifies the number of correctly and wrongly classified documents between the ground truth division in the two classes (Serbian and Slavonic Serbian) and the division obtained by the classifier. From the confusion matrix, we compute three performance measures for each document class

(Serbian and Slavonic Serbian): (i) precision, (ii) recall, and (iii) f-measure [22]. Precision is the ratio between the number of correctly classified documents and all retrieved documents. Recall is the ratio between the number of correctly classified documents and all relevant documents. F-measure is the weighted harmonic mean of precision and recall.

Performance evaluation is realized by K-fold cross validation [14]. In particular, the database is randomly divided into K folds. Each of these folds is used as the test set, while the remaining $K - 1$ folds are merged to create the training set. Each time, the classifier uses the training set for learning and the test set for validation. Precision, recall and f-measure are computed from the classification of each test set and averaged over the K trials. We set K equal to 2, 5 and 10, which are typical adopted values in the literature. Also, we replicate the experiment 100 times for each K, by averaging the performance measures on these runs.

5 Results and Discussion

Tables 1 and 2 show the classification results obtained respectively by SVM and NB on the database of documents written in Serbian (Serb.) and Slavonic Serbian (Slav.) languages represented by ALBP1, and the combination of ALBP1 with

Table 1. Classification results obtained by SVM algorithm on the database. Cases when the extended features overcome ALBP1 are highlighted in bold. NBP_r with $r = 2, 3$ are named as ENBP2 and ENBP3. ANBP1 is the ANBP with $r = 1$. Standard deviation is given in brackets

		2-fold			5-fold			10-fold		
		prec.	rec.	f-m.	prec.	rec.	f-m.	prec.	rec.	f-m.
ALBP1	Serb.	0.88 (0.09)	0.83 (0.11)	0.85 (0.05)	0.91 (0.13)	0.83 (0.17)	0.85 (0.11)	0.90 (0.18)	0.83 (0.26)	0.84 (0.19)
	Slav.	0.73 (0.15)	0.75 (0.20)	0.70 (0.11)	0.71 (0.28)	0.78 (0.32)	0.71 (0.24)	0.64 (0.41)	0.79 (0.42)	0.69 (0.40)
ALBP1+ ENBP2	Serb.	**0.89** (0.08)	0.82 (0.11)	0.84 (0.06)	**0.93** (0.11)	**0.85** (0.19)	**0.87** (0.13)	**0.97** (0.08)	**0.86** (0.25)	**0.89** (0.19)
	Slav.	0.72 (0.15)	**0.76** (0.18)	0.70 (0.11)	**0.73** (0.32)	**0.84** (0.28)	**0.76** (0.28)	**0.85** (0.25)	**0.99** (0.04)	**0.89** (0.18)
ALBP1+ ENBP3+ ANBP1	Serb.	0.88 (0.08)	**0.85** (0.10)	**0.86** (0.06)	**0.97** (0.07)	**0.93** (0.12)	**0.94** (0.10)	**0.98** (0.06)	**0.97** (0.08)	**0.97** (0.08)
	Slav.	**0.74** (0.15)	0.75 (0.19)	**0.72** (0.13)	**0.88** (0.20)	**0.92** (0.16)	**0.89** (0.19)	**0.96** (0.11)	**0.98** (0.06)	**0.97** (0.09)
ALBP1+ ENBP2+ ENBP3	Serb.	**0.89** (0.08)	**0.84** (0.12)	0.85 (0.07)	**0.95** (0.08)	**0.87** (0.18)	**0.90** (0.13)	**0.97** (0.10)	**0.91** (0.22)	**0.93** (0.17)
	Slav.	0.73 (0.18)	**0.76** (0.19)	**0.72** (0.13)	**0.79** (0.28)	**0.88** (0.21)	**0.81** (0.24)	**0.90** (0.22)	**0.98** (0.06)	**0.93** (0.17)

Table 2. Classification results obtained by NB algorithm on the database. Cases when the extended features overcome ALBP1 are highlighted in bold. NBP_r with $r = 2$ is named as ENBP2. Standard deviation is given in brackets

		2-fold			5-fold			10-fold		
		prec.	rec.	f-m.	prec.	rec.	f-m.	prec.	rec.	f-m.
ALBP1	Serb.	0.85 (0.08)	0.85 (0.10)	0.84 (0.06)	0.92 (0.13)	0.85 (0.18)	0.87 (0.12)	0.95 (0.15)	0.85 (0.25)	0.87 (0.19)
	Slav.	0.70 (0.17)	0.65 (0.21)	0.64 (0.14)	0.74 (0.28)	0.82 (0.30)	0.75 (0.25)	0.76 (0.36)	0.90 (0.32)	0.81 (0.33)
ALBP1+ ENBP2	Serb.	0.85 (0.10)	**0.86** (0.09)	**0.85** (0.05)	**0.93** (0.12)	0.85 (0.17)	0.87 (0.11)	0.95 (0.14)	0.85 (0.25)	0.87 (0.19)
	Slav.	**0.72** (0.15)	**0.67** (0.24)	**0.66** (0.16)	**0.76** (0.25)	**0.83** (0.27)	**0.77** (0.21)	0.76 (0.36)	0.89 (0.32)	0.80 (0.33)
ALBP1+ ENBP2+ LBP1	Serb.	**0.86** (0.10)	0.84 (0.10)	0.84 (0.06)	**0.94** (0.11)	0.85 (0.18)	**0.88** (0.12)	0.95 (0.15)	0.85 (0.25)	0.87 (0.19)
	Slav.	0.69 (0.16)	**0.70** (0.25)	**0.66** (0.16)	**0.78** (0.25)	**0.87** (0.25)	**0.80** (0.21)	0.76 (0.35)	0.90 (0.32)	0.81 (0.32)

ENBP2, ENBP3 and ANBP1, and with LBP1 and ENBP2. For the different K values of the fold cross validation, the average values of precision (prec.), recall (rec.) and f-measure (f-m.) are reported together with the standard deviation (in brackets) for each document class.

In Table 1 we may observe that the combination of ALBP1 with ENBP2, ENBP3 and ANBP1 has better performances than ALBP1. In particular, the best results in performance measures are obtained by the combination of ALBP1 with ENBP3 and ANBP1, overcoming ALBP1 of 0.01–0.03 in 2-fold, of 0.06–0.19 in 5-fold, and up to 0.32 in 10-fold, which is a noticeable improvement. Also, the combination of ALBP1 with ENBP2 obtains an improvement up to 0.06 w.r.t. (with respect to) ALBP1 in 2 and 5-folds and a higher improvement up to 0.21 in 10-fold. Still, the combination of ALBP1 with ENBP2 and ENBP3 overcomes ALBP1 of 0.01–0.02 in 2-fold, up to 0.1 in 5-fold, and up to 0.26 in 10-fold. Finally, the standard deviation values of the extended features are small, and in some cases lower than the values of ALBP1. This demonstrates that our results are sufficiently stable.

The classification results obtained by NB in Table 2 are very encouraging, too. In particular, we may observe that the combination of ALBP1 with ENBP2 overcomes ALBP1 of 0.01–0.02 in 2 and 5-folds. Still, when ALBP1 is combined with LBP1 and ENBP2, the classification is improved up to 0.05 in 2 and 5-folds. In the case of 10-fold, the classification results of ALBP1 and the extended features are quite comparable. It is worth noting that the extended features improve the classification results especially for the Slavonic Serbian language. It is a noticeable aspect because the classification of this language is usually the most critical one. Finally, the standard deviation values are quite small and in most cases lower than the values obtained by ALBP1. Hence, also in this case, the classification results are quite stable.

Results in Tables 1 and 2 are graphically reported in Fig. 8 showing the f-measure values in the different cases.

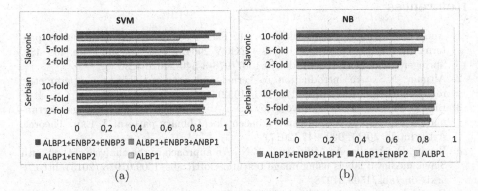

(a)   (b)

Fig. 8. F-measure values obtained by: (a) SVM, and (b) NB in the different cases

6 Conclusions

This paper presented a new method for the recognition of documents as given in evolving languages. Because in some cases the evolution of the language over time is associated with different historical periods, this method implicitly identifies the historical period of the document. In the first stage, the document is transformed into a sequence of four numerical codes, according to the position of the letters in the text-line based on their energy profile. The obtained sequence is considered as an image of four gray levels, on which LBP, NBP and their introduced derivations are applied for feature extraction. This determines the document feature vector, which is subjected to classification by SVM and NB algorithms for language recognition. An experiment performed on a database of documents in Slavonic Serbian and Serbian languages confirmed the discriminatory ability of the extended features in evolving language recognition. In particular, it demonstrated that the proposed feature representation is robust and accurate in the language identification which is not connected with a specific classifier. Hence, the good performances can also be found with different classifiers.

Future work will experiment the proposed feature representation with different languages, including the Italian dialects. Also, a set of different classifiers, including the convolutional neural networks, will be used on the feature representation for the language identification.

Acknowledgments. This work was supported by the Grant of the Ministry of Education, Science and Technological development of the Republic of Serbia within the project TR33037 and through Mathematical Institute of Serbian Academy of Sciences and Arts within the project III44006.

References

1. Ahonen, T., Hadid, A., Pietikäinen, M.: Face recognition with local binary patterns. In: Pajdla, T., Matas, J. (eds.) ECCV 2004. LNCS, vol. 3021, pp. 469–481. Springer, Heidelberg (2004). doi:10.1007/978-3-540-24670-1_36
2. Altman, N.S.: An introduction to kernel and nearest-neighbor nonparametric regression. Am. Stat. **46**(3), 175–185 (1992)
3. Brodić, D., Amelio, A., Milivojević, Z.N.: An approach to the language discrimination in different scripts using adjacent local binary pattern. J. Exp. Theoret. Artif. Intell. **29**(5), 929–947 (2017)
4. Brodić, D., Amelio, A., Milivojević, Z.N.: An approach to the analysis of the South Slavic medieval labels using image texture. CoRR abs/1509.01978 (2015). http://arxiv.org/abs/1509.01978
5. Brodić, D., Amelio, A., Milivojević, Z.N.: Characterization and distinction between closely related South Slavic Languages on the example of Serbian and Croatian. In: Azzopardi, G., Petkov, N. (eds.) CAIP 2015. LNCS, vol. 9256, pp. 654–666. Springer, Cham (2015). doi:10.1007/978-3-319-23192-1_55
6. Brodić, D., Amelio, A., Milivojević, Z.N.: Clustering documents in evolving languages by image texture analysis. Appl. Intell. **46**(4), 916–933 (2017)
7. Cortes, C., Vapnik, V.: Support-vector networks. Mach. Learn. **20**(3), 273–297 (1995)
8. Grangier, D., Bengio, S.: A discriminative kernel-based approach to rank images from text queries. IEEE Trans. Pattern Anal. Mach. Intell. **30**(8), 1371–1384 (2008)
9. Grothe, L., Luca, E.W.D., Nürnberger, A.: A comparative study on language identification methods. In: LREC. European Language Resources Association (2008)
10. Hamouchene, I., Aouat, S.: A new approach for texture segmentation based on NBP method. Multimedia Tools Appl. **76**(2), 1921–1940 (2017)
11. Heikkila, M., Pietikainen, M.: A texture-based method for modeling the background and detecting moving objects. IEEE Trans. Pattern Anal. Mach. Intell. **28**(4), 657–662 (2006)
12. Khan, A., Baharudin, B., Lee, L.H., Khan, K., Tronoh, U.T.P.: A review of machine learning algorithms for text-documents classification. J. Adv. Inf. Technol. **1**(1), 4–20 (2010)
13. Kim, J., Kim, B.S., Savarese, S.: Comparing image classification methods: K-nearest-neighbor and support-vector-machines. In: Proceedings of the 6th WSEAS International Conference on Computer Engineering and Applications, and Proceedings of the 2012 American Conference on Applied Mathematics, pp. 133–138. World Scientific and Engineering Academy and Society (WSEAS), Stevens Point, Wisconsin, USA (2012)
14. Lever, J., Krzywinski, M., Altman, N.: Points of significance: model selection and overfitting. Nat. Methods **13**(9), 703–704 (2016)
15. Mäenpää, T., Viertola, J., Pietikäinen, M.: Optimising colour and texture features for real-time visual inspection. Pattern Anal. Appl. **6**(3), 169–175 (2003)
16. Nosaka, R., Fukui, K.: Hep-2 cell classification using rotation invariant co-occurrence among local binary patterns. Pattern Recogn. **47**(7), 2428–2436 (2014)

17. Nosaka, R., Ohkawa, Y., Fukui, K.: Feature extraction based on co-occurrence of adjacent local binary patterns. In: Ho, Y.-S. (ed.) PSIVT 2011. LNCS, vol. 7088, pp. 82–91. Springer, Heidelberg (2011). doi:10.1007/978-3-642-25346-1_8
18. Ojala, T., Pietikainen, M., Maenpaa, T.: Multiresolution gray-scale and rotation invariant texture classification with local binary patterns. IEEE Trans. Pattern Anal. Mach. Intell. **24**(7), 971–987 (2002)
19. Ojala, T., Pietikinen, M., Harwood, D.: A comparative study of texture measures with classification based on featured distributions. Pattern Recogn. **29**(1), 51–59 (1996)
20. Roark, B., Saraclar, M., Collins, M.: Discriminative n-gram language modeling. Comput. Speech Lang. **21**(2), 373–392 (2007)
21. Sibun, P., Spitz, A.L.: Language determination: natural language processing from scanned document images. In: Proceedings of the Fourth Conference on Applied Natural Language Processing, ANLC 1994, pp. 15–21. Association for Computational Linguistics, Stroudsburg, PA, USA (1994)
22. Sokolova, M., Lapalme, G.: A systematic analysis of performance measures for classification tasks. Inf. Process. Manag. **45**(4), 427–437 (2009)
23. Zhang, H.: The optimality of Naive Bayes. In: Barr, V., Markov, Z. (eds.) Proceedings of the Seventeenth International Florida Artificial Intelligence Research Society Conference (FLAIRS 2004). AAAI Press (2004)

Usability Analysis of the Image and Interactive CAPTCHA via Prediction of the Response Time

Darko Brodić[1]([✉]), Alessia Amelio[2], Nadeem Ahmad[3],
and Syed Khuram Shahzad[3]

[1] Technical Faculty in Bor, University of Belgrade, V.J. 12, 19210 Bor, Serbia
dbrodic@tfbor.bg.ac.rs
[2] DIMES, University of Calabria, Via Pietro Bucci Cube 44, 87036 Rende, CS, Italy
aamelio@dimes.unical.it
[3] Department of CS and IT, University of Lahore,
1-KM Defence Road, Lahore, Pakistan
{nadeem.ahmad,khurram.shahzad}@cs.uol.edu.pk

Abstract. This paper introduces a new method for automatically predicting the response time of the Internet users to solve the CAPTCHA test by a regression tree strategy. The input to the model is a set of demographic features of the user: (i) age, (ii) education level, and (iii) Internet experience level. The experiment is performed on 114 Internet users who are invited to solve three image and interactive CAPTCHA tests: (i) FunCAPTCHA, (ii) home numbers, and (iii) picture of the CAPTCHA. Collected demographic features and response time for each user are processed by the regression tree approach in order to evaluate the prediction accuracy. Obtained results revealed the ability of the model in correctly predicting the response time of the specific CAPTCHA types. This represents an invaluable analysis in the state-of-the-art for designing new CAPTCHA types which are more accustomed to specific categories of Internet users.

Keywords: Prediction · Regression tree · Artificial intelligence · CAPTCHA

1 Introduction

CAPTCHA stands for "Completely Automated Public Turing test to tell Computers and Humans Apart". CAPTCHA is sometimes called reverse Turing test. It is valid, because it uses a reverse objective. Unlike the Turing test where the questioner is a human, who judges the answers from the human and the digital computers, here the questioner is a digital computer. In this sense, the digital computer questioner is used as a more neutral judge than human ones. However, the CAPTCHA is a challenge-response test used in computer science to determine whether or not the user is a human. In some way, we can think about it as a coded information which the human should recognize or decode unlike the digital computer programs commonly called computer robots or abbreviated as bots.

© Springer International Publishing AG 2017
S. Phon-Amnuaisuk et al. (Eds.): MIWAI 2017, LNAI 10607, pp. 252–265, 2017.
https://doi.org/10.1007/978-3-319-69456-6_21

Although the first CAPTCHA was invented in 1997 [20], the general concept has been later given. Firstly, CAPTCHA is a program that generates a test. Secondly, the CAPTCHA concept includes two premises about solving the given test: (i) most of the humans can pass the given test, and (ii) the computer programs (bots) cannot pass the test [2]. In that sense, such kind of program is able to differentiate humans from computers. The main paradox of the given concept is that the CAPTCHA as a program can generate and grade tests which cannot be passed by itself [3]. It can be used in many applications for practical security, such as: (i) Online pools, (ii) Free E-mail services, (iii) Search engine bots, (iv) Worms and spam, (v) Preventing dictionary attacks, etc.

The CAPTCHA types are usually categorized into the following groups: (i) Text-based CAPTCHA, (ii) Image-based CAPTCHA, (iii) Audio-based CAPT-CHA, (iv) Video-based CAPTCHA, and (v) Other types of CAPTCHA. Text-based CAPTCHAs were the first to be invented. They usually include letters or numbers displayed in a distorted form on a non-uniform background image. Still, the advanced Optical Character Recognition (OCR) program is able to decode and recognize the given set of letters and numbers. To advance the security level of the text-based CAPTCHA, new elements have been added such as noise and additional elevation. Obviously, it makes a challenge to the bots, but it decreases the success rate of solving the CAPTCHA by the human users. Image-based CAPTCHAs were proposed to overcome the problems of the text-based CAPTCHAs. Still, some of them lacks of flexibility and adaptability [19]. Audio-based CAPTCHA is suitable for the visually impaired humans. Basically, a text-based CAPTCHA is usually audio interpreted in a random interval. However, an advanced speech algorithm can easily recognize the audio signal, which leads to a low level of audio CAPTCHA security. Video-based CAPTCHA typically incorporates flowing text during the video projection. Usually this text is differently colored. Hence, it can be traced by advanced OCR programs and recognized as well.

In the research studies, the image-based CAPTCHA has shown many advantages especially in security and usability elements over the text-based [5,7] and audio-based CAPTCHAs [9]. Hence, we choose to explore the elements of the image-based CAPTCHA and their impact in terms of time for solving the CAPTCHA. It represents the CAPTCHA usability elements [4]. Also, we compare the usability elements of the image-based CAPTCHA with the elements of other types of CAPTCHA merging image characteristics and interactivity. For this reason, they are called game-based CAPTCHA.

In particular, we do not propose a new CAPTCHA test. On the contrary, we analyze the response time to solve known CAPTCHA tests and its dependence from demographic features of the users which solve the test. Demographic features are the elements proposed in the Turing test as input variables [23]: (i) The initial state of the mind, i.e. date of birth (age), (ii) The education to which the users are being subjected (education level), and (iii) Other experience, which was not previously described but to which the users have been subjected (Internet experience). Dependence of the response time from the demographic features of the users is explored as a regression problem, which is formalized by a regression tree. Its aim is the prediction of the response time to solve different CAPTCHA tests from the knowledge of the demographic features.

It will provide an invaluable starting point for designing new CAPTCHA types which may be more accustomed to specific types of users. In fact, the prediction of the response time of users with specific demographic characteristics (e.g. older age or low education level) for a given CAPTCHA type will reveal useful information for customizing a new CAPTCHA to that user's category. Furthermore, it will expand the process of creating new CAPTCHA categories which are currently unknown. The characteristics of the new CAPTCHA will be established by satisfying some elements, such as: (i) reduced solution time below the reference one (typically 30 s), (ii) solution time which is similar for different demographic groups, (iii) increased level of correctly solving the given CAPTCHA above the reference limit (at least 95% success rate), and (iv) extremely low level of correctly solving the CAPTCHA by bots (below 0.01% success rate).

Previously, only one thoughtful objective analysis was performed on different CAPTCHA types [14]. However, it was not reliable due to the small tested population and limited age groups used in the test. All other studies were based on the presumed conclusions that their new proposed CAPTCHAs had a clear advantage over some other types of CAPTCHA [13], which is far from our analysis. Recently, some works analyzed the usability of the image-based CAPTCHA in terms of dependence between response time and demographic features of the users [6,8]. Usually, the response time depends on many demographic factors. Typically, image CAPTCHAs with facial expression contents were solved in 2–3 s, while text-based CAPTCHA were solved in 20–25 s [8]. However, these analyses were performed by using statistical tools and association rule mining. Accordingly, a study about unsupervised correlation between demographic features and response time was only conducted. Hence, to the very best of our knowledge, we are the first to proposed a study about the prediction of the response time to successfully solve specific types of CAPTCHA. Consequently, a fair comparison with other state-of-the-art similar methods cannot be provided.

The paper is organized as follows. Section 2 introduces the image and game-based CAPTCHA. Section 3 presents the proposed model. Section 4 describes the experiment, including data gathering and dataset creation. Section 5 shows the results obtained by the experiment and makes a discussion. Finally, Sect. 6 draws the conclusions and outlines future work directions.

2   The CAPTCHA Types

Image and game-based CAPTCHAs are effortless and interesting for humans while controlled composite distortions make them difficult to decode for the AI programs [10]. Hence, these CAPTCHAs expose a challenging task. It is a win-win situation for both: (i) either the hardcore AI problem will be resolved, or (ii) the websites will be safe from attacks. Next, we will provide a few examples of image and game-based CAPTCHAs, as well as describe their characteristics.

2.1   Image-Based CAPTCHA

Microsoft Asirra is an image-based CAPTCHA in which the user has to recognize and select a specific animal from several images. As shown in Fig. 1, the user has to select all the images of cat from 12 distinct images.

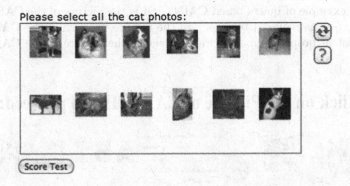

Fig. 1. Microsoft Asirra Project. The user selects all those images which depict the image of cat [11]

'What's Up' CAPTCHA is another image-based CAPTCHA in which the user is required to rotate the image. As shown in Fig. 2(a), an image of child or bird is shown upside down and the user has to rotate it to display in the correct orientation.

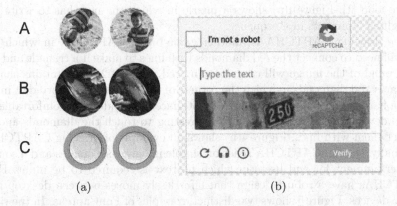

Fig. 2. 'What's Up' CAPTCHA: images with various orientation positions. The left side shows rotated images while the right side shows them in the upright direction (a), reCAPTCHA introduced by Google which includes home numbers acquired from the Google Street View application (b)

In 2013 Google has introduced the reCAPTCHA to protect the websites from the spam. reCAPTCHAs utilize human efforts in digitizing the text for preserving books and improve maps by encoding house numbers from google street view. Recognizing arbitrary multi-digit numbers from Street View images is a difficult problem. Figure 2(b) shows the reCAPTCHA in which street numbers are shown for human verification.

A last example of image-based CAPTCHA is the picture of the CAPTCHA, where the user is required to recognize the picture visualizing the CAPTCHA inside a list of proposed images. Figure 3 shows the picture of the CAPTCHA test.

Click on the Picture of CAPTCHA to proceed:

Fig. 3. The picture of the CAPTCHA test

2.2   Game-Based CAPTCHA

The animated CAPTCHA is a game-based CAPTCHA where the user needs to write alphabets with the presented sequence. The image will be in GIF type in which advertisement and alphabets will be appearing and disappearing in an infinite loop [1]. Figure 4(a) shows a puzzle in which the user has to write the highlighted alphabets in a sequence.

The drawing CAPTCHA is another game-based CAPTCHA in which the user will need to connect the red diamonds with lines to make it a triangle and the background of the image will contain many red dots [16, 21]. It contains shapes of squares and diamonds in which the corners of the shapes are distorted to make them a hard target for the attackers. Its interface is considerably comfortable on mobile devices and users find it very interesting to touch the diamonds and to connect them with lines. Figure 4(b) shows an example of drawing CAPTCHA.

Finally, the FunCAPTCHA relies on simple image-based games and a source of entertainment for end users in which no text is required to be input. FunCAPTCHAs have a robust design that effortlessly moves between desktop and mobile devices. Figure 5 shows two distinct examples of FunCaptcha. In the right side, the user has to move the image of woman at its proper place. In the left side, the user should rotate the image in its right upward orientation.

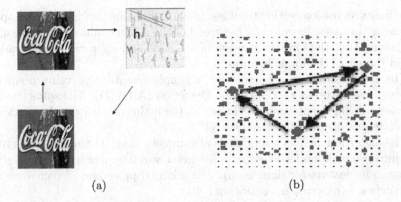

(a)   (b)

Fig. 4. Animated CAPTCHA: type highlighted characters in sequence [1,12] (a), Drawing CAPTCHA: the user will form the triangle by joining all three diamonds [16,21] (b) (Color figure online)

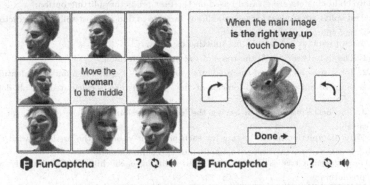

Fig. 5. Two different examples of FunCAPTCHA

3   The Proposed Model

The aim of the proposed model is predicting the solution time to the image and interactive CAPTCHA tests from known demographic features of the resolving users. In this sense, we analyze the predictability of the image processing and computer vision CAPTCHA tasks to be solved by the humans, such as image segmentation, object detection, scene understanding, object tracking and face recognition. Also, we analyze the role of the interactivity in the CAPTCHA usability by comparing the image and game-based CAPTCHAs. Finally, we study the influence of different devices, on which the CAPTCHA test is solved, on the predictability of solving the aforementioned tasks.

This is accomplished by using a regression tree strategy. It is one of the classical statistical methods used for numeric values predictive analysis [22]. Its quantitative analysis approach for continuous values of dependent variables distinguishes from other prediction tree techniques. Also, it overcomes the limitations of the linear regression getting troublesome with high dimensional data or rapidly increasing variables. In our case, the trend of the feature values cannot be a priori known. Also, the linear regression is not a general approach if we decide to extend the set of the input features.

The regression tree is based over a simple quantitative value prediction method named Automatic Interaction Detection (AID) [17]. AID splits the data stepwise starting from a single cluster and splitting it into two by retrieving candidate sets of predictor variables [17].

The algorithm creates a root node of complete data. The root node is being split into two child nodes based on a predictor variable, which refers to a single or composite feature (or dimension). The adopted procedure of regression tree construction is reported in Algorithm 1 [24].

Algorithm 1. Regression Tree construction.

Step 1. Create a root cluster of the complete dataset.

Step 2. Two child clusters are created based on the best predictor splitting option:

Step 2.1. Test splits are studied for each predictor variable to find the best splitting predictor before doing the actual split.

Step 2.2. Each predictor is analyzed for splitting as follows:

Step 2.2.1. The data is sorted all the cases of the predictor variable.

Step 2.2.2. For n possible cases of the predictor variable, $n - 1$ splitting points are identified.

Step 2.2.3. Sum of squares over the mean of the child clusters is calculated for all dependent variables.

Step 2.2.4. The best split is chosen having the least dispersion within the child cluster for each predictor variable.

Step 2.3. After completion of the testing for each predictor variable, the predictor with the least square value is selected for the first actual split into two child clusters.

Step 3. The regression tree is being constructed splitting each child cluster similarly with the remaining predictors.

The prediction using the regression tree is a simple decision over each split having predictor variable splitting criteria for each cluster.

4 Experiment

The experiment is conducted on 114 Internet users, who are invited to solve specific CAPTCHA tests. As an example, we selected the following image-based CAPTCHAs: (i) home numbers, and (ii) picture of the CAPTCHA, and the following game-based CAPTCHA: (iii) FunCAPTCHA.

In the first stage, some basic information is collected about the participants to the experiment, consisting in the following demographic features: (i) age, (ii) education level, and (iii) Internet experience (in number of years). In the second stage, the user is conducted in a separate room where a tablet computer of 7" screen size wide and a smartphone of 5" screen size wide are located. Then, the user is asked to solve the three CAPTCHA tests (FunCAPTCHA, home numbers CAPTCHA and picture of the CAPTCHA) on these devices. Hence, each user is associated with three CAPTCHA tests. The FunCAPTCHA is solved on the smartphone, while the image-based CAPTCHAs are solved on the tablet computer. The time (in seconds) needed for solving the three CAPTCHA tests, from the beginning until the completion of each task, is properly registered, and it is independent from the solving success.

Internet users are teachers, engineers, employees, officials and clerks of age between 18 and 70 years. All users are volunteer participants who were informed that their data would be used for study and research purposes. However, the type of registered data, such as the response time to solve the tests and the aim of the analysis were not known to the user for avoiding bias effects in the experiment.

Data collected during the interview are organized into three datasets, one for each CAPTCHA. Each dataset contains one instance for each user, for a total of 114 instances. Each instance is composed of the three demographic feature values for a given user: (i) age, (ii) education level, (iii) Internet experience, and of the response time value to solve a specific CAPTCHA test (FunCAPTCHA in the first dataset, home numbers in the second dataset, and picture of the CAPTCHA in the third dataset).

The age can take numerical integer values in the range $[18, +\infty)$. In the datasets, the maximum age is 70 years. The education level splits the Internet users in two categories: (i) higher (represented by the numerical value 1), and (ii) secondary (which means undergraduate, represented by the numerical value 2). The Internet experience (in number of years) can take numerical integer values in the range $[0, +\infty)$. However, in the datasets it ranges between 1 (one year of Internet experience) and 20 (twenty years of Internet experience). The response time to the CAPTCHAs (in seconds) can take real values in the range $(0.0, +\infty)$. It varies between 0.002 s and 10.23 s in the case of FunCAPTCHA, between 0.41 s and 9.83 s in the case of home numbers, and between 0.51 s and 14.01 s in the case of picture of the CAPTCHA.

Table 1 reports the feature values of the three datasets.

Table 1. Values of each feature of the three datasets

Feature	Domain	Dataset interval
Age	$[18, +\infty)$	$[18, 70]$
Education level	[higher, second.]	$[1,2]$
Internet experience (years)	$[0, +\infty)$	$[1, 20]$
Response time FunCAPTCHA (sec.)	$(0.0, +\infty)$	$[0.002, 10.23]$
Response time home numbers CAPTCHA (sec.)	$(0.0, +\infty)$	$[0.41, 9.83]$
Response time picture of the CAPTCHA (sec.)	$(0.0, +\infty)$	$[0.51, 14.01]$

Finally, each dataset is subjected to the regression tree strategy for predicting the response time to the specific CAPTCHA from the values of the input demographic features: (i) age, (ii) education level, and (iii) Internet experience.

5   Results and Discussion

The experiment has been performed in Matlab R2015b on a notebook with Quad-Core CPU at 2.2 GHz, 16 GB RAM and UNIX operating system.

We run the method on each dataset split into training and test sets: (i) FunCAPTCHA, (ii) home numbers, and (iii) picture of the CAPTCHA. In particular, we learn the regression tree from the training set. Then, we evaluate the prediction accuracy of the regression tree on the test set. Some examples of generated regression trees are shown in Figs. 6, 7 and 8.

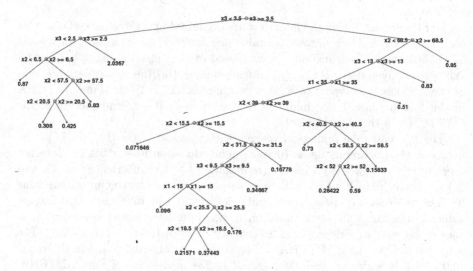

Fig. 6. Regression tree for FunCAPTCHA dataset. The legend is as follows: x1 - education level, x2 - age, x3 - Internet experience. Leaves have the response time, which is its average value over the cell represented by the leaf

For making the evaluation independent from the specific training and test sets, we employ the K-fold cross validation method [15]. In particular, the dataset is divided into K folds. Each fold in turn is used as the test set, while the remaining $K - 1$ folds are merged to be used as the training set. Each time, the performance measures are computed on the current training and test sets. At the end, the average measures over the different folds are computed for the final evaluation.

Two performance measure are used to quantify the prediction accuracy: (i) cross-validation loss, and (ii) resubstitution error.

The cross-validation loss (*cvloss*) is the mean squared error between the response time values in one fold and the response time values predicted for that fold by the regression tree trained by using the remaining $K - 1$ folds [18]. The resubstitution error (*resuberror*) is the mean squared error between the response time values of the training set and the response time values predicted

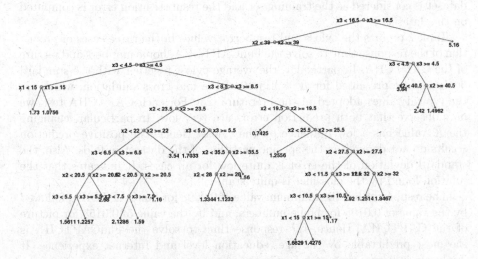

Fig. 7. Regression tree for home numbers CAPTCHA dataset. The legend is as follows: x1 - education level, x2 - age, x3 - Internet experience. Leaves have the response time, which is its average value over the cell represented by the leaf

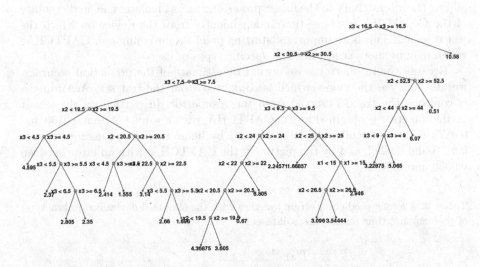

Fig. 8. Regression tree for picture of the CAPTCHA dataset. The legend is as follows: x1 - education level, x2 - age, x3 - Internet experience. Leaves have the response time, which is its average value over the cell represented by the leaf

by the regression tree based on the input training set [18]. In this case, the overall dataset is considered as the training set and the resubstitution error is computed on the dataset.

Table 2 reports the cvloss and resuberror values in the three cases of prediction of the response time to solve the FunCAPTCHA, home numbers and picture of the CAPTCHA. In particular, the average cvloss together with the standard deviation are presented for $K = 2, 5, 10$ of the fold cross validation, which are the typical values adopted in the literature [25]. For each CAPTCHA test, we may observe that both prediction errors are very low. In particular, changing the K value has a low influence on the cvloss. Hence, the positive prediction results do not depend on the specific partition of the dataset in folds. Also, the standard deviation of the error is quite low for all cases. It indicates that the solution found by the classifier is quite stable.

The resuberror has the minimum value of 0.0098 for FunCAPTCHA, followed by the value of 0.0105 for home numbers, and by the value of 0.0155 for picture of the CAPTCHA. Hence, the response time to solve the FunCAPTCHA is the most predictable by the age, education level and Internet experience. It implicitly indicates that such features are better connected to image processing and computer vision tasks which are "more interactive" in their core, e.g. object detection and motion tracking, which is the case of the FunCAPTCHA. Also, the good predictability of the response time to FunCAPTCHA is not influenced by the smartphone on which the test is solved. In fact, due to the touchscreen use on a very reduced surface, its response time should be highly variable. Consequently, it should be more difficult to obtain a correct prediction. This confirms that adding the interactivity to the image processing tasks increases the predictability of the CAPTCHA response time independently from the device on which the test is solved. This is an important starting point for designing new CAPTCHAs which may be more accustomed to specific types of users.

Because the resuberror is an optimistic estimate of the prediction accuracy, we also analyze the cvloss which is computed from the test set. Accordingly, it confirms the trend observed from the resuberror. In particular, the lowest prediction error is obtained by FunCAPTCHA, with a value between 0.0130 and 0.0175 in the different folds. It is followed by home numbers, ranging between 0.0178 and 0.0296, and by the picture of the CAPTCHA, with an error between 0.0380 and 0.0446.

Table 2. Average prediction errors together with the standard deviation (in brackets) of the response time for the three datasets

	resuberror	cvloss		
		$K = 2$	$K = 5$	$K = 10$
FunCAPTCHA	0.0098	0.0130 (0.0136)	0.0175 (0.0243)	0.0143 (0.0354)
Home numbers	0.0105	0.0178 (0.0097)	0.0280 (0.0214)	0.0296 (0.0385)
Picture CAPTCHA	0.0155	0.0446 (0.0158)	0.0380 (0.0165)	0.0421 (0.0308)

In order to extend the analysis, Fig. 9 shows the average cvloss together with the standard deviation (size of the vertical bars) at the different values of K between 2 and 10 for the three CAPTCHA tests. It confirms that the lowest prediction error and the most stable trend are obtained by FunCAPTCHA. On the contrary, the highest error and less stable trend are obtained by the picture of the CAPTCHA. Nonetheless, we can observe that the error never exceeds 0.05. In particular, it reaches a maximum of 0.045 for $K = 9$ in the case of the picture of the CAPTCHA, which is a satisfactory result.

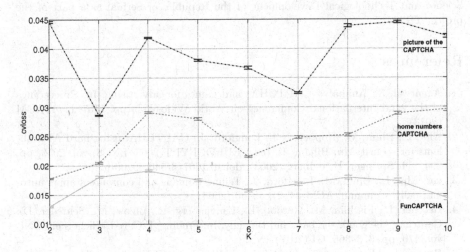

Fig. 9. Average cvloss together with the standard deviation (size of the vertical bars) obtained for $K = 2, ...10$ of the fold cross validation for the three CAPTCHA tests

6   Conclusions

This paper analyzed the predictability of the response time to image and game-based CAPTCHA tests from typical demographic features by using a regression tree strategy. This represents an invaluable analysis of the CAPTCHA usability, which revealed three important aspects: (i) the response time to the image-based CAPTCHA is highly predictable by using our model, (ii) the predictability increases when interactive tasks are added to the image-based CAPTCHA, in the example of the game-based CAPTCHA, (iii) the device on which the test is solved has a low influence on predicting the response time to the game-based CAPTCHA. This model represents a good starting point for creating new generation CAPTCHA tests which are more accustomed to specific types of users. Finally, an image and interactive CAPTCHA test requires multiple tasks of computer vision to be performed, i.e. face recognition, object detection, motion tracking, image transformations, etc. In that sense, the proposed analysis is of special interest in both AI and computer vision fields.

Future work will investigate the predictability of the response time to solve other CAPTCHA tests, which will extend the set of demographic features, and will provide larger datasets for the analysis. Also, the regression tree strategy will be compared with other regression methods, including the artificial neural network.

Acknowledgments. The authors are fully grateful to the anonymous participants for publicly providing their data.

This work was partially supported by the Grant of the Ministry of Education, Science and Technological Development of the Republic of Serbia, as a part of the project TR33037.

References

1. Aggarwal, S.: Animated CAPTCHAs and games for advertising. In: Proceedings of the 22nd International Conference on World Wide Web, pp. 1167–1174. ACM (2013)
2. Ahn, L., Blum, M., Hopper, N.J., Langford, J.: CAPTCHA: using hard AI problems for security. In: Biham, E. (ed.) EUROCRYPT 2003. LNCS, vol. 2656, pp. 294–311. Springer, Heidelberg (2003). doi:10.1007/3-540-39200-9_18
3. von Ahn, L., Blum, M., Langford, J.: Telling humans and computers apart automatically. Commun. ACM **47**(2), 56–60 (2004)
4. Baecher, P., Fischlin, M., Gordon, L., Langenberg, R., Ltzow, M., Schršder, D.: Captchas: the good, the bad, and the ugly. In: Freiling, F.C. (ed.) Sicherheit. LNI, vol. 170, pp. 353–365. GI (2010)
5. Brodić, D., Petrovska, S., Jevtić, M., Milivojević, Z.N.: The influence of the CAPTCHA types to its solving times. In: 2016 39th International Convention on Information and Communication Technology, Electronics and Microelectronics (MIPRO), pp. 1274–1277, May 2016
6. Brodić, D., Amelio, A.: Analysis of the human-computer interaction on the example of image-based CAPTCHA by association rule mining. In: Gamberini, L., Spagnolli, A., Jacucci, G., Blankertz, B., Freeman, J. (eds.) Symbiotic 2016. LNCS, vol. 9961, pp. 38–51. Springer, Cham (2017). doi:10.1007/978-3-319-57753-1_4
7. Brodić, D., Amelio, A., Draganov, I.R.: Response time analysis of text-based CAPTCHA by association rules. In: Dichev, C., Agre, G. (eds.) AIMSA 2016. LNCS, vol. 9883, pp. 78–88. Springer, Cham (2016). doi:10.1007/978-3-319-44748-3_8
8. Brodić, D., Amelio, A., Janković, R.: Exploring the influence of CAPTCHA types to the users response time by statistical analysis. Multimedia Tools Appl. 1–37 (2017). doi:10.1007/s11042-017-4883-7
9. Bursztein, E., Bethard, S., Fabry, C., Mitchell, J.C., Jurafsky, D.: How good are humans at solving CAPTCHAs? A large scale evaluation. In: Proceedings of the 2010 IEEE Symposium on Security and Privacy, SP 2010, pp. 399–413. IEEE Computer Society, Washington, DC (2010)
10. Datta, R., Li, J., Wang, J.Z.: Imagination: a robust image-based CAPTCHA generation system. In: Proceedings of the 13th Annual ACM International Conference on Multimedia, pp. 331–334. ACM (2005)

11. Elson, J., Douceur, J.R., Howell, J., Saul, J.: Asirra: a CAPTCHA that exploits interest-aligned manual image categorization. In: ACM Conference on Computer and Communications Security, vol. 7, pp. 366–374. Citeseer (2007)
12. Gossweiler, R., Kamvar, M., Baluja, S.: What's up CAPTCHA?: a CAPTCHA based on image orientation. In: Proceedings of the 18th International Conference on World Wide Web, pp. 841–850. ACM (2009)
13. Kim, J., Yang, J., Wohn, K.: Agecaptcha: an image-based captcha that annotates images of human faces with their age groups. TIIS **8**(3), 1071–1092 (2014)
14. Lee, Y.L., Hsu, C.H.: Usability study of text-based CAPTCHAs. Displays **32**(2), 81–86 (2011)
15. Lever, J., Krzywinski, M., Altman, N.: Points of significance: model selection and overfitting. Nat. Methods **13**(9), 703–704 (2016)
16. Lin, R., Huang, S.Y., Bell, G.B., Lee, Y.K.: A new CAPTCHA interface design for mobile devices. In: Proceedings of the Twelfth Australasian User Interface Conference vol. 117, pp. 3–8. Australian Computer Society, Inc. (2011)
17. Morgan, J.N., Sonquist, J.A.: Problems in the analysis of survey data, and a proposal. J. Am. Stat. Assoc. **58**(302), 415–434 (1963)
18. Nonparametric Supervised Learning: (2013). http://cda.psych.uiuc.edu/ multivariate_fall_2013/matlab_help/nonparametric_supervised_learning.pdf
19. Rao, K., Sri, K., Sai, G.: A novel video CAPTCHA technique to prevent BOT attacks. Procedia Comput. Sci. **85**, 236–240 (2016). International Conference on Computational Modelling and Security (CMS 2016)
20. Reshef, E., Raanan, G., Solan, E.: Method and system for discriminating a human action from a computerized action. Patent US20050114705, 1997, Pubblicated 26 May 2005 (2005)
21. Shirali-Shahreza, M., Shirali-Shahreza, S.: Drawing CAPTCHA. In: 2006 28th International Conference on Information Technology Interfaces, pp. 475–480. IEEE (2006)
22. Skrondal, A., Rabe-Hesketh, S.: Prediction in multilevel generalized linear models. J. Roy. Stat. Soc.: Ser. A (Stat. Soc.) **172**(3), 659–687 (2009)
23. Turing, A.M.: Computers & thought. In: Feigenbaum, E.A., Feldman, J. (eds.) Computing Machinery and Intelligence, pp. 11–35. MIT Press, Cambridge (1995)
24. Wilkinson, L.: Tree structured data analysis: AID, CHAID and CART. In: Sawtooth/SYSTAT Joint Software Conference, Sun Valley, ID (1992)
25. Yadav, S., Shukla, S.: Analysis of k-fold cross-validation over hold-out validation on colossal datasets for quality classification. In: 2016 IEEE 6th International Conference on Advanced Computing (IACC), pp. 78–83, February 2016

Generating Children's Stories from Character and Event Models

Bianca Trish Adolfo, Jerson Lao, Joanna Pauline Rivera,
John Zem Talens, and Ethel Chua Joy Ong[(⊠)]

De La Salle University, Manila, Philippines
{bianca_adolfo, ethel. ong}@dlsu. edu. ph

Abstract. Stories are inhabited by multiple characters who interact in the story world to achieve their goals. For computer systems to generate such stories, we propose the use of agents to model the needs and behavior, as well as formulate the individual plan of action of the different story characters. A central agent, the story planner, uses a simple turn-taking approach to maintain control over the asymmetric roles and goals of the character agents. It coordinates the various events that will be allowed to take place in the story by prioritizing candidate actions from the character agents based on their likelihood of increasing interaction, which may be verbal (conversations) or nonverbal (helping one another, playing together). The resulting stories are perceived by the human evaluators to have good character-to-character interaction, but acceptable level of coherence and cohesion of events in the story text.

Keywords: Story generation · Storytelling knowledge · Knowledge representation · Natural language processing

1 Introduction

Research works in automated story generation have devised different planning algorithms to enable computer systems to mimic the human's abilities to generate stories of various genre and domain in interactive environments. These include balancing between author-centric and character-centric approaches, as seen in MakeBelieve [1], Minstrel [2], Minstrel Remixed [3], and Picture Books [4–6]. Others utilize a combination of forward-chaining and backward-chaining as shown in Tale-Spin [7], case-based reasoning [8], corpus-based approaches [9, 10], and narrative prose generation in Author and Storybook [11].

In author-centric systems, the story planner focuses on the goal of the author to generate stories that follow a central theme, such as the acquisition of a desired positive behavior by the main character [4, 6]. Character-centric systems, on the other hand, focus on the individual goals of story characters. Planning revolves around helping the characters pursue these goals in a manner that is consistent with the character's traits and desires to generate stories with strong character believability [12].

Story planning should also consider the number of characters that are present in the story world. While single-character story generation systems can focus on planning the sequence of actions and events to help the character achieve his/her goal,

© Springer International Publishing AG 2017
S. Phon-Amnuaisuk et al. (Eds.): MIWAI 2017, LNAI 10607, pp. 266–280, 2017.
https://doi.org/10.1007/978-3-319-69456-6_22

multiple-character story generation systems must implement a turn-taking algorithm to give a slice of the story time to each character. In the author-centric approach, the planner should also consider how the actions that will take place in the story world will be distributed among the characters. A set of metrics to prioritize character goals and a termination criterion to determine when the story should end need to be defined.

Our work focuses on the genre of children's stories as these narratives contain events that may help children learn to make sense of their world [13]. Moreover, by targeting children's stories, our plots can revolve around story characters doing a misdeed, experiencing the consequences of such actions, and eventually learning to correct their mistakes to attain a lesson on proper behavior.

Character interaction is important in stories because this can teach children how to interact with others. Any form of communication between characters, be it verbal or non-verbal, can be considered character interaction. Verbal interactions range from simple greetings to long conversations, while non-verbal interactions pertain to any exchange that occurs between characters, such as giving an object to another character and helping another character perform a task.

In this paper, we present our approach in utilizing agents to model characters who can formulate their own plan of actions that can lead to the execution of actions with reasonably clear motives. Section 2 presents the knowledge representation to support story planning. Section 3 discusses the design of the planner with emphasis on selecting a set of events that prioritizes character interaction, while ensuring that characters receive equal opportunities (in terms of story time) to perform actions that will lead them closer to achieving their own goals. Results from evaluation by linguists are presented in Sect. 4.

2 Storytelling Knowledge

Story generation requires different forms of storytelling knowledge, namely, the story world model that represents dynamic character states, the static character model, a semantic ontology of commonsense knowledge, narratological concepts comprising of the plot structure and story themes, and a representation of story events.

2.1 Story World Model

The story world model maintains the current state of the characters (shown in Table 1), which includes a character's physical state and the interpersonal relationship scores that exist between two characters. The model is updated after the execution of action or occurrence of events in the story.

Table 2 shows the sample interpersonal relationship scores between two characters. These scores are used to guide the planner in deciding which actions a character could do based on his/her relationship with another character. Scores can range from 0 to 10, with 0 signifying a negative relationship and 10 signifying a positive one. 0–4 means enemies, with 0 being the worst enemy; 5 means acquaintances; and 6–10 means friends, with 10 being the closest friend. The score is a one-way point of view of the relationship, because character A might think of character B as a friend but character B

Table 1. Character state

Name	Rabbit	
Emotion	Neutral	
Location	Bedroom	
Item held	Ball	
Physical state	Hungry	False
	Thirsty	False
	Tired	False
	Asleep	False
Relationships	Pig	Friend = 6

Table 2. Interpersonal relationship scores

From	To	Relationship	Score
Tiger	Lion	Father	9
Lion	Tiger	Son	7
Rabbit	Pig	Friend	6
Rabbit	Tiger	Acquaintance	5

does not think of character A as one. The scores change as events take place in the story that may affect the relationship between two characters.

A world map is also maintained to track the story setting. It contains the place where the story takes place, the time of the day, and the objects present in the location.

2.2   Character Model

The character model is a representation of the static attributes of each story character, and includes the name, gender and a set of predefined traits. These traits affect the motivations, actions, and way of reasoning, planning and decision-making of the characters [14]. For example, a mean character would most likely sound bossy when speaking, while a shy character would sound meek. A shy character would prefer actions that do not involve interacting with other characters, while an outgoing person would choose to do things in a group.

2.3   Commonsense Knowledge

Commonsense knowledge refers to those that humans inherently possess to reason about everyday life [6]. It is used to provide the story planner with the concepts relevant to the supported themes. Concepts are abstract or general ideas that represent an entity, such as characters, places and objects; an abstract idea, such as emotion and state; or an event. Semantic relations are used to depict the relationship between two concepts. This representation has been adapted from ConceptNet [15]. Aside from the ConceptNet relations, relations such as *hasA*, *motivatedByGoal*, and *obstructedByGoal* were added to relate concepts that could later be used to encourage the selection of an interaction event.

Semantic relations are classified as either active or passive. Active semantic relations, such as *genderOf*, *traitOf*, *emotionOf*, *locationOf*, *isAsleep*, *isTired*, *isHungry*, *isThirsty* and *holds*, are used to model concepts depicting the emotional and physical states of a character that may change depending on the occurrence of a story event. This approach allows the story world model to be represented as assertions, which is consistent with passive semantic relations. In passive semantic relations, the concepts hold true within a story and across multiple stories. Some examples of assertions that use passive semantic relations are *usedFor(bed, sleep)*, *capableOfReceivingAction(ball, play)*, and *hasSubevent(investigate, see)*.

2.4 Narratological Concepts

Two important concepts of narrative serve as the framework in the generation of a story. These are the plot structure and the story themes. Our planner adopts the standard plot structure comprising of five elements or subplots - exposition, rising action, climax, falling action, and resolution. A plot is comprised of a causal network of events, an example of which is shown in Fig. 1.

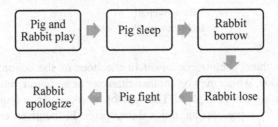

Fig. 1. Causal network of events

The generated stories center on themes that promote character interaction such as *learning to be friendly*, *generous* and *humble*. Each theme has an associated moral of the story, location, objects and character traits (shown in Table 3).

Table 3. Story themes

Theme	Location	Object	Trait
Friendliness	beach, playground	pail & shovel, ball	Shy
Generosity	bedroom	ball, puzzle	Selfish
Carefulness	beach	pail & shovel	Clumsy
Honesty	dining room, classroom	glass of water, magnifying glass	Dishonest
Neat	dining room	barbecue	Untidy

2.5 Event Model

An event is an action that a character performs in the story in order to achieve his/her goal or as a response to another character's actions. It is represented in an event model that contains the pre-conditions and post-conditions for its execution, interaction score (*IntScore*), interaction relationship score (*IRScore*), event type and dialogue type. Two definitions of the same event, *play*, are shown in Table 4.

Table 4. Event model

Concept	play(#agent, #patient, *location)		
Pre-conditions	isAsleep(#agent, false) ∧ isA(#patient, toy) ∧ capableOfReceivingAction(toy, play)		
Post-conditions	effectOf(play, happy) ∧ feels(#agent, happy)		
Interaction score	4	*IRScore*	+2
Event type	Agent support		
Dialogue type	Deliberation, Persuasion		
Concept	play(#agent, #patient, *location)		
Pre-conditions	isAsleep(#agent, false) ∧ capableOf(#patient, play)		
Post-conditions	isTired(#agent, true)		
Interaction score	7	*IRScore*	+3
Event type	Patient support		
Dialogue type	Deliberation, Persuasion		

An event has three parameters: *agent* or the doer of the action; *patient* or the recipient of an action, which may be another character or an object; and *location* or the place where the event can take place. The symbol '#' represents a required parameter, while the symbol '*' represents an optional parameter. In the given example, the first definition for *play* requires an object as the recipient of the action, e.g., *play with a ball*, as expressed in the assertion *isA(#patient, toy)*; whereas in the second model, the patient is another character, e.g., *play with a friend*.

Although the commonsense ontology can depict the causal chain of events using ConceptNet's semantic relations *EffectOf* and *FirstSubeventOf* [4], Ang and Ong [5] reported that this representation is "insufficient to support the planner in inferencing over the events chain". They propose augmenting an event's representation to support the definition of two sets of conditions or criteria for its occurrence. *Pre-conditions* are assertions that must be satisfied before an event occurs, while *post-conditions* assert the state of the story world after the occurrence of an event.

Consider event *play* in Table 4. The *pre-conditions* assert that *#patient* is *a toy* and *the toy is something that can be played with*. The execution of the event will trigger a change in *#agent*'s emotional state (stored in the story world model) to *happy*.

The interaction score specifies the extent of character interaction that may be promoted by performing an event. The higher the score, the greater the interaction. The *IRScore* pertains to the increase or decrease in the relationship between two characters after the event. Positive scores mean the characters would become closer to each other, while negative scores mean the event has caused a conflict between the characters. The event play, for example, may encourage interaction between characters and may even increase their relationship score by 3.

The *event type* dictates whether the supporting characters would be considered as agents or patients. A supporting character is considered as an agent if it is also performing the action along with the main character. A supporting character is considered a patient if it is the receiver of the action. Consider again the first definition of *play* with event type *agent support*. The planner will have to select a secondary character who will serve as the playmate of the main character and tagged them both as the *agents* of the event. This is discussed further in Sect. 3.3.

In some events, dialogues may be applied as a form of character-to-character interaction. The type of dialogue is defined in the *dialogue type* attribute, and can be emotion, deliberation, persuasion, negotiation, introduction and resolution [16]. Currently, we implemented template-based dialogue generation.

3 Planning the Story

The story world model is initialized based on the location, characters and objects that the user has specified through the system's Story Editor interface (shown in Fig. 2).

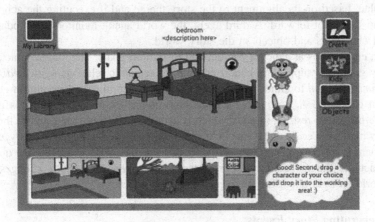

Fig. 2. Story editor

Story planning commences with the selection of a theme that aims to teach traits missing from the main character's attributes. The selected location and object/s are also considered. The next step is identifying the conflict and resolution. The conflict is an event which causes the main character to have an emotion opposite or conflicting with the theme of the story, while the resolution is an event that gives the main character the trait related to the theme of the story. These are identified by querying the commonsense ontology for events using relations *conflictOf* and *hasResolution*:

```
conflictOf(careful, lose)
hasResolution(lose, find)
```

A candidate conflict event would be *lose* (an object) if the theme is *learning to be careful*. If the only candidate conflict event for the trait *careful* is *lose*, then the resolution event would be *to find* (the object). If there are more candidate conflicts or resolutions, random selection would be applied.

3.1   Agents in Story Planning

Agents are used in story planning to enable story characters to formulate their own plan of actions that will lead them to achieve their assigned goals. This approach was adapted from [5]. Because children's stories should aim to teach lessons about proper behavior, for the main character agent, the goal is the acquisition of the missing trait or the moral of the selected theme. The goal of a secondary character is determined based on his/her relationship with the main character. That is, the goal of a "friend" will tend to be that of supporting the main character towards achieving the latter's goal. Alternatively, the secondary character may be assigned a goal that tends to obstruct or deter the main character towards achieving his/her goal.

A character agent submits its proposed action plan to the plot agent. The plot agent then makes a decision on whether to accept or reject a character agent's proposed action plan, based on its alignment to the story theme and if executing the action will move the story plot forward. A third agent, the world agent, monitors and updates the states of characters and objects in the story world.

Each character is assigned a conflict and resolution goals. The main character gets the story goal. The supporting characters use the semantic relations *motivatedByGoal* or *obstructedByGoal* to either motivate or obstruct the conflict and resolution goals of the main character. A story can be generated only if the main character is able to complete his or her resolution goal, which is acquiring the trait connected to the story theme, without exceeding the specified maximum allowed number of story events. While there is no explicit story text showing that the agents are observing the outcome of their actions, the next character's proposed action is dependent on the changes to the story world brought about by the agents' previous decisions.

3.2   Generating Story Events

Event selection occurs in a round-robin fashion to allow each character a slice of the story time. The main character gets the first turn from the exposition to the rising action subplots, and again from the conflict to resolution. At every turn, the character agent proposes a list of candidate events to the plot agent, taking into account the character's traits, interpersonal relationships and story world state. If the character agent's proposed event is rejected by the plot agent, the character skips that turn, and the next character gets to propose its plan of action.

Before the character proposes an event, it scores all candidate events it retrieved from the commonsense ontology using the semantic relation *capableOf*. However, it skips events that are already in the *action queue* and the *proposed queue*. The action queue records the character's past actions and has a maximum size of ten (10), excluding events that were proposed but rejected by the plot agent. The proposed queue, on the other hand, records the last five (5) proposed events. It does not differentiate between accepted and rejected events. The action queue prevents the character from proposing events that it had already performed. The proposed queue prevents the character from proposing events that just got rejected. The queues also remove the possibility of an infinite loop.

Once the list has been pruned, the score of each remaining event E is computed by finding the number of satisfied pre-conditions pertaining to the main character, denoted by semantic relation *semrelM(c1, c2)*, over the total number of pre-conditions for that event, as shown in (1). A threshold of 0.6 is then used to filter the candidate events. If the threshold is set too low, the set of candidate events can include illogical events that either satisfied the basic pre-conditions or they do not have a lot of pre-conditions in the first place. If the threshold is set too high, the number of candidate events would be greatly diminished, leading to incomplete stories. Events with scores passing the threshold would then be ranked according to their interaction score, and the highest scoring event will be submitted for approval to the plot agent.

$$Score(E) = \frac{\sum_{k=1}^{n} semrel_k M(c1, c2) \ == \ T}{n_E} \tag{1}$$

To prevent the generation of illogical stories, certain pre-conditions of an event may be marked as mandatory. A candidate event with an unsatisfied mandatory pre-condition is automatically given a score of zero. Consider an event *character takes exam* with three pre-conditions, one of which is *atLoation(#agent, classroom)*. If two of the three pre-conditions have been satisfied, and the third one, the location, say a *beach*, is not satisfied, there is still a chance that this event would pass the threshold in the latter phase of the filtering process and eventually be selected as the event. However, it seems illogical to *take an exam at the beach*. If the *location* is set to be a mandatory pre-condition, the planner would give this event a score of zero when it sees that the location of the story is not a *classroom*, thus preventing this event from passing the threshold.

Character traits are also used in scoring candidate events by specifying them as an assertion in an event's pre-condition. For example, an event *lose (an object)* may require the assertion *traitOf (#agent, clumsy)* as part of its mandatory pre-condition. However, the priority placed on achieving character-to-character interaction may lead to trait-based events to lose in the scoring scheme.

3.3 Selecting Supporting Characters and Objects

After the character agent proposes an event, the world agent, which manages the story world model, chooses the supporting characters and objects for that event. The number to be selected will depend on the *number of agents* and the *number of patients* attributes defined in the event model.

The type of event, which can be agent support and patient support, is then used to determine the role of the supporting characters and objects. If the event type is *agent support*, such as *investigate*, *search* and *play*, the world agent needs to find supporting characters who will perform the action with the main character. Otherwise, the world agent has to look for supporting characters or objects who will be the receiver of the action. Events that are tagged as *patient support* include *borrow*, *look* and *scold*.

Supporting characters are considered based on a scoring formula shown in (2) that is computed from the assertions pertaining to the supporting character, denoted by *semrelSC(c1, c2)*. A threshold of 0.5 is then applied to filter the list.

$$Score(SC) = \frac{\sum_{k=1}^{n} semrel_k SC(c1, c2) == T}{n_E} \tag{2}$$

If the number of remaining candidates is less than or equal to the number required by an event, then all candidates are selected. If there are more candidates than what is needed, the list is pruned based on user-specified priority, i.e., the sequence in which the user selected the characters at the Story Editor interface. If there are no candidates, this element is left blank if the pre-condition for a supporting character is not mandatory. Otherwise, the event is rejected.

The same scoring scheme is applied to choose objects for an event. However, if there are no objects present in the story world model, the world agent queries the commonsense ontology to find an object using the semantic relation *capableOf ReceivingAction(?patient, #event)*.

3.4 Realizing the Story Text

The output of the planner is a story plan consisting of a sequence of events and their details following the form Event("concept", "agents", "patients", "postconditions", event type, dialogue). A sample story plan is shown in Listing 1.

Listing 1: Excerpt of a Story Plan.

```
Event("exercise", "Jerry", null, "MainAgent:IsTired:true & MainAgent:IsThirsty:true &
MainAgent:IsHungry:true", "normal", null);
Event("play", "Jerry", "ball", "MainAgent:EmotionOf:happy & SupportAgent:IsTired:true &
SupportAgent:IsHungry:true", Event.TYPE_AGENTS_SUPPORT, Dialogue.DELIBERATION +","+
Dialogue.PERSUASION);
Event("break", "Jerry", "glass of water", "MainAgent:EmotionOf:nervous &
*MainAgent:IsHungry:false", Event.TYPE_PATIENTS_SUPPORT, null);
Event("ask", "Trisha", "Jerry", "MainAgent:EmotionOf:curious",
Event.TYPE_PATIENTS_SUPPORT, null);
Event("blame", "Jerry", "Trisha", "Patient:EmotionOf:innocent & Pa-
tient:EmotionOf:angry", Event.TYPE_PATIENTS_SUPPORT, Dialogue.EMOTION + "," + Dia-
logue.PLURAL);
```

This plan is transformed into surface text that proceeds in three main steps:

1. Lexicalization involves choosing a lexicon for each event concept in the story plan, i.e., the concept *'investigate'* is mapped to three lexical choices: *search*, *explore*, or *investigate*
2. Aggregation merges consecutive events with the same *patient* and *instrument*

3. Surface realisation generates either (i) the dialogue text for each event using a predefined template; or (ii) passing event details (*agents*, *action*, *patients*, and *post-conditions*) to SimpleNLG to generate a sentence.

A sample story for the plan in Listing 1 is shown in Listing 2. There are two characters, *Jerry* (main) and *Trisha* (secondary). The round robin approach for assigning a slice of the story time to each character is very evident in the second paragraph, when the two characters engage in a conversation-based interaction about what they are feeling. The story ends when *Jerry* achieves his goal, which is to learn about *honesty*.

Listing 2: Sample story - *Jerry learns to be honest.*

It was a cloudy afternoon. Jerry and Trisha were in the messy dining room. Trisha said, "Look, the dining room is so messy". Jerry said, "I agree, it is messy".

Jerry exercised. He said, "I am hungry". Jerry played the ball. He said, "I am happy". Jerry broke the glass of water. He said, "I am nervous". Trisha asked Jerry. Trisha said, "I am puzzled". Jerry blamed Trisha. Jerry said, "I am guilty". Trisha said, "I am angry". Trisha fought Jerry. Jerry said, "I am sorry". Jerry admitted Trisha. Jerry said, "I am honest".

Jerry said, "I learned a new lesson today. It is to be honest". Trisha said, "That is right Jerry". From then on, Jerry learned to be honest.

---

4   Test Results

Quantitative evaluation on the generated stories with character-to-character interaction was performed using metrics that focus on the story content. Qualitative comparison of stories with and without the character-to-character prioritization scheme was also performed to highlight significant differences in the selection of story events.

4.1   Story Content Evaluation

Ten (10) stories were generated from a knowledge base that currently contains 5 characters, 6 locations, 9 themes, 12 objects, 19 dialogue templates, 46 events, 115 concepts and 240 assertions. These were then given to four evaluators comprising of literature and English language professors. The evaluators rated the stories based on the following criteria: *coherence and cohesion*; *story elements* (*characters, objects, background*); and *content*. Each criterion has a set of questions that are scored as follows: 5 – strongly agree, 4 – agree, 3 – neutral, 2 – disagree, and 1 strongly disagree.

Table 5 shows the average evaluation scores of stories with character-to-character interaction (CC) and stories with a single character (SC). Because these stories were generated using different iterations of the planner, it should be noted that there were two sets of mutually exclusive evaluators.

CC stories did not fare well in all criteria compared to SC stories. For the *coherence* criterion, which is used to determine if the story text makes sense, the stories are easy to understand and are logically connected to each other, the low coherence score is attributed to the missing story text that highlights causal relationship between two events. Although our CC planner looks at pre-conditions to select events, surface realization did not use discourse markers to make the causal relation more explicit.

Table 5. Evaluator Scores for CC and SC Stories

Criteria	CC	SC
Coherence	3.63	4.25
Story elements	3.97	4.30
Content	3.38	4.20

Consider the story excerpt in Listing 3. Lines [1] to [3] wanted to portray that because *Jerry* and *Paula* played, they got tired. Since *Jerry* was tired, he decided to sleep. A person who is asleep should eventually wake up when he/she is no longer tired, and will resume his/her tasks. In the sample story, the events were not able to fully reflect this logic because the pre-condition of *being tired* was not explicitly stated as the cause for the event *sleep*.

Listing 3: Story excerpt with missing causal relations between events.

[1]   Jerry and Paula played.
[2]   Jerry slept.
[3]   Jerry woke up.
[4]   Jerry prepared a book.

The *story elements* criterion examines the characters, objects and background of the story. The insufficient description of the characters and their traits pulled down the evaluation score for CC stories. However, in the detailed breakdown of the items comprising the *story elements* criterion in Table 6, it can be seen that CC stories fared well in achieving interaction, receiving an average score of 4.38 in both cases.

Table 6. Evaluation scores for story elements

Question	Score
The characters were described	3.00
The objects were described	4.08
Character's actions are appropriate	3.70
Characters interact with the objects	4.38
Characters interact with characters	4.38
Character feels real to its environment	3.75

In the *content* criterion, CC stories got low scores in the proper resolution of the conflict and the sufficiency of story details. As seen in Listing 2, the story has insufficient details to describe how the characters arrived at the resolution, which is learning about *honesty*. This may be attributed to the event limit imposed by the story planner to prevent infinite loops when the same event is chosen again and again because there is no "termination" in the selection of events.

Increasing the event limit might address this issue, but the knowledge base currently does not contain enough events to significantly increase the length of the generated stories while trying to choose only those events that are relevant to the story theme. Another solution would be to consider including satisfied pre-conditions in the generated story plan to produce story text that flesh out character motivations and give meaning to character actions.

4.2   Comparison of Story Text

In this section, we show the effect of planning decisions on the resulting story text. Listings 4 and 5 depict the exposition subplot. Whereas line [1] from SC simply stated that the *camp was far*, lines [a–b] from CC use dialogue as a form of interaction for the characters to describe the location. Line [2] described the physical state and intent of Danny; whereas in lines [c–e] of CC, Trisha and Jerry deliberated on the action they would do together. In the Event Model in Table 4, the event *play* requires at least two characters, and the dialogue type may be either deliberation or persuasion.

Listing 4. Exposition for Single-Character (SC) Story
The evening was dark. Danny the dog was in the camp for an outing. He got a white marshmallow.
[1]   The camp was far. He felt tired.
[2]   Danny the dog felt hungry. He wanted to eat.
He brought a flashlight. Danny the dog felt sleepy because he ate the marshmallow. Danny the dog felt relaxed because he rested in tent.

Listing 5. Exposition for Character-to-Character (CC) Interaction Story
It was hot afternoon. Trisha and Jerry were in the messy camp.
[a]   Trisha said, "The camp is messy".
[b]   Jerry said, "You are right. It is messy".
[c]   Jerry said, "Do you want to play together?"
[d]   Trisha said, "Thank you. But I will have to decline".
[e]   Trisha said, "Okay then, let us play". Trisha and Jerry played. They said, "We are happy and hungry. Also, we are tired". Jerry and Trisha slept. They were asleep.

Listings 6 and 7 show the story text for the rising action, climax and falling action subplots. While Danny, all alone, did not know what to do when he saw a shadow in lines [3, 4], Trisha and Jerry shared their thoughts and feelings, and how they can possibly address their concerns (of finding out what the noise is all about). Eventually, Danny conducted a search for the source of the noise and arrived at his own realization in line [5]. On the other hand, Trisha and Jerry investigated together (line [f]).

Listing 6. Rising Action, Climax and Falling for SC Story

	He got the flashlight. He explored using the flashlight.
[3]	He saw a shadow. Danny felt scared.
[4]	He did not know what to do.
	He got the flashlight. He turned on the flashlight. Danny searched.
[5]	It was an owl.

Listing 7. Rising Action, Climax and Falling Action for CC Story

	Trisha and Jerry heard. They said, "We are scared".
	Jerry said, "I think I hear a snake". Trisha said, "No, I think it is an owl".
[f]	Trisha and Jerry investigated with the flashlight.
	They said, "We are brave". Trisha saw the owl.

Through this camping experience, Danny learned a lesson on bravery (Listing 8). In Listing 9, Jerry reminded Trisha about the importance of being brave.

Listing 8. Resolution for the Single-Character (SC) Story

From then on, Danny learned to be brave.

Listing 9. Resolution for Character-to-Character (CC) Interaction Story

Jerry said, "You should be brave from now on Trisha".
Trisha said, "Yes, I should be brave". From then on, Trisha learned to be brave.

5 Conclusion

We presented an agent-based approach to story generation that uses character agents to formulate a character's plan of action. A plot agent ensures the story structure is maintained by reviewing a character's proposed action against its ability to promote interaction and its alignment to the story theme. Currently, relationship scores are used to track the effect of interaction. These are discrete values that do not yet model the possibility of complex relationships that may exist between characters.

Human evaluators gave an average score of 4.38 in a scale of 1 to 5 in terms of character-to-character interaction, and 3.63, 3.97 and 3.38 in coherence and cohesion, story elements, and content, respectively. These scores may be attributed to the emphasis placed on giving each character a turn to contribute an action in the story timeline. This sometimes leads to the generation of story text that seems redundant, such as a secondary character echoing the main character's statement. Further work should explore alternative turn-taking schemes.

Including an event's pre-conditions in the story plan is currently being explored as an option to flesh out character motivations and help give meaning to character actions. These pre-conditions can also be used to give a vivid description of the world around the character and may include not only the location, but also the time, character mood or sensory expressions, circumstance and motivations. The pre-conditions should be weighted as over-usage may lead to lengthy and verbose text.

To enhance the story text, future work should look into NLG techniques for the production of dialogues as a form of interaction between characters. Moreover, discourse markers can be utilized to highlight the structure that exists between two or more spans of text and possibly lead to an increase in coherency of the text.

References

1. Liu, H., Singh, P.: Makebelieve: using commonsense knowledge to generate stories. In: Proceedings of the 18th National Conference on Artificial Intelligence, Edmonton, Alberta, Canada, pp. 957–958. Association for the Advancement of AI (2002)
2. Turner, S.: The Creative Process: A Computer Model of Storytelling. Lawrence Erlbaum Associates, Hillsdale (1994)
3. Tearse, B., Mateas, M., Wardrip-Fruin, N.: MINSTREL remixed: a rational reconstruction. In: Proceedings of the Intelligent Narrative Technologies III, Monterey, CA, pp. 1–7. ACM, New York (2010). https://doi.org/10.1145/1822309.1822321
4. Solis, C.J., Siy, J.T., Tabirao, E., Ong, E.: Planning author and character goals for story generation. In: Proceedings of the NAACL Human Language Technology 2009 Workshop on Computational Approaches to Linguistic Creativity, Boulder, CO, pp. 63–70. Association for Computational Linguistics (2009)
5. Ang, K., Ong, E.: Planning children's stories using agent models. In: Richards, D., Kang, B. H. (eds.) PKAW 2012. LNCS, vol. 7457, pp. 195–208. Springer, Heidelberg (2012). doi:10. 1007/978-3-642-32541-0_17
6. Yu, S., Ong, E.: Using common-sense knowledge in generating stories. In: Anthony, P., Ishizuka, M., Lukose, D. (eds.) PRICAI 2012. LNCS, vol. 7458, pp. 838–843. Springer, Heidelberg (2012). doi:10.1007/978-3-642-32695-0_82
7. Meehan, J.: Tale-spin: an interactive program that writes stories. In: Proceedings of the 5th International Joint Conference on Artificial Intelligence, pp. 91–98. Morgan Kaufmann Publishers Inc., Burlington (1977)
8. Gervas, P., Díaz-Agudo, B., Peinado, F., Hervás, R.: Story plot generation based on CBR. J. Knowl.-Based Syst. 18(4/5), 235–242 (2005). doi:10.1016/j.knosys.2004.10.011. Elsevier Science Publishers B.V., Amsterdam
9. McIntyre, N., Lapata, M.: Learning to tell tales: a data-driven approach to story generation. In: Proceedings of the Joint Conference of the 47th Annual Meeting of the ACL and the 4th International Joint Conference on Natural Language Processing of the AFNLP, Suntec, Singapore, pp. 217–225. Association for Computational Linguistics (2009)
10. Daza, A., Calvo, H., Figueroa-Nazuno, J.: Automatic text generation by learning from literary structures. In: Proceedings of the NAACL Human Language Technology 2016 5th Workshop on Computational Linguistics for Literature, San Diego, CA. Association for Computational Linguistics (2016)
11. Callaway, C., Lester, J.: Narrative prose generation. Artif. Intell. 139(2), 213–252 (2002). doi:10.1016/S0004-3702(02)00230-8. Elsevier Science Publishers Ltd, Essex
12. Riedl, M., Young, R.M.: Narrative planning: balancing plot and character. J. Artif. Intell. Res. 39(1), 217–268 (2010). AI Access Foundation
13. McKay, H., Dudley. B.: About Storytelling. Hale and Iremonger, Sydney (1996)
14. Carbonell, J.: Towards a process model of human personality traits. Artif. Intell. 15(1/2), 49–74 (1980). doi:10.1016/0004-3702(80)90022-3. ScienceDirect

15. Liu, H., Singh, P.: Commonsense reasoning in and over natural language. In: Negoita, M.G., Howlett, R.J., Jain, L.C. (eds.) KES 2004. LNCS, vol. 3215, pp. 293–306. Springer, Heidelberg (2004). doi:10.1007/978-3-540-30134-9_40
16. Walton, D., Macagno, F.: Types of dialogue, dialectical relevance and textual congruity. Anthropol. Philos. **8**(1/2), 101–120 (2007)

Text Dimensionality Reduction for Document Clustering Using Hybrid Memetic Feature Selection

Ibraheem Al-Jadir[1,2(✉)], Kok Wai Wong[1], Chun Che Fung[1], and Hong Xie[1]

[1] School of Engineering and Information Technology, Murdoch University, Perth, Australia
{I.Al-Jadir, K.Wong, L.Fung, H.Xie}@murdoch.edu.au
[2] College of Science, Baghdad University, Baghdad, Iraq

Abstract. In this paper, a document clustering method with a hybrid feature selection method is proposed. The proposed hybrid feature selection method integrates a Genetic-based wrapper method with ranking filter. The method is named Memetic Algorithm-Feature Selection (MA-FS). In this paper, MA-FS is combined with K-means and Spherical K-means (SK-means) clustering methods to perform document clustering. For the purpose of comparison, another unsupervised feature selection method, Feature Selection Genetic Text Clustering (FSGATC), is used. Two real-world criminal report document sets were used along with two popular benchmark datasets which are Reuters and 20newsgroup, were used in the comparisons. F-Micro, F-Macro and Average Distance of Document to Cluster (ADDC) measures were used for evaluation. The test results showed that the MA-FS method has outperformed the FSGATC method. It has also outperformed the results after using the entire feature space (ALL).

Keywords: Clustering · Feature · F-measure · Hybrid · Memetic · Selection

1 Introduction

The increasing number of digital documents has become a challenging issue that requires more sophisticated and efficient methods to handle the documents [1]. Feature selection is one of the steps used to reduce unwanted noisy text for efficient document clustering [2]. Feature selection is a complex step because of the large number of possible candidate solutions (solutions refer to the best combination of the selected feature subsets) due to the large number of documents. Presumably, for an n-dimensional problem (in this context, the dimensions refer to features), the possible number of candidate solutions might reach 2^n. The increasing number of n can potentially contribute to degrade the results from the applied machine learning methods used for document clustering [3].

Vector Space Model (VSM) is a standard representation for text in text mining. It is used to transform text into a vector format [4] and VSM represents each document as a vector. The vector components are the features selected to represent the documents.

© Springer International Publishing AG 2017
S. Phon-Amnuaisuk et al. (Eds.): MIWAI 2017, LNAI 10607, pp. 281–289, 2017.
https://doi.org/10.1007/978-3-319-69456-6_23

These features are often calculated using the term weighting schemes such as Term Frequency and Inverse Document Frequency (TF.IDF) [5].

In most cases, not all features are equally important. There are a lot of noises represented by the unimportant text features which are common, redundant, irrelevant or inconsistent [6]. In order to handle this problem, filter methods or ranker methods were first proposed. Filter methods calculate the significance of each feature statistically. Due to its simplicity, they are considered computationally efficient methods. Wrapper methods represent another feature selection category which is more complex than filter methods. They may be able to produce more accurate features due to their metaheuristic nature [7]. These methods iteratively update the existing feature sets by optimizing current feature subsets through generations. Evolutionary algorithms such as Genetic Algorithms are used for this purpose. In general, the use of filter methods and wrapper methods has some complementary advantages [8]. Thus, they can be combined to obtain an improved performance [8].

In optimization, Memetic Algorithms (MA) has been successfully used as hybrid evolutionary methods [9]. MA can enhance the performance of traditional GA to search in local areas of the search space (that the traditional GA is not capable to do the local search). Ideally, MA can be used to implement hybrid feature selection that integrates filter and wrapper methods [9].

The main objective of this paper is to utilize the advantages of both wrapper and filter methods by using MA. The proposed hybrid feature selection method uses Relief-F filter and GA-based wrapper feature selection methods. The aim is to fuse the robustness of the wrapper with the efficiency of the filter methods. K-means and Spherical K-means (SK-means) partitioning clustering methods are used after selecting the features using the proposed MA-FS method. For comparison purposes, the FSGATC [10] method and the entire feature space (ALL) were used to evaluate the performance of the proposed method. The comparison is performed by assessing internal and external clustering evaluation measures after and before feature selection.

The subsequent sections of this paper are arranged as follows: Sect. 2 is a review of related work and Sect. 3 provides a detailed explanation of the proposed method. A comparison test results is provided in Sect. 4 and lastly, a conclusion is presented in Sect. 5.

2 Hybrid Feature Selection Methods

From experience, it is known that performance of machine learning might be degraded if the entire feature space of a large dataset is used without processing of the features. Therefore, feature selection methods are used in an initial phase to process the data [1]. Feature selection can be classified into *filter* [2] and *wrapper* [3, 4] methods. Filters are straightforward in implementation, and they have a higher efficiency than wrapper methods. In most cases, filter methods rank features according to their significance in an ascending order [5]. Eventually, clustering or classification is applied to the filtered feature space [6]. Unlike filters, wrapper methods are implemented by using one of the machine learning methods and a classifier [7]. Despite its advantages over filter methods, wrappers may suffer from the issue of overfitting [6]. Therefore, hybrid scheme has been introduced that combines both wrapper and filter methods [8].

Hybrid methods can be performed in various ways. Some of the hybrid methods combine either two filters or two wrappers such as the method proposed in [9], that combines two wrappers which are the Artificial Bee Colony (ABC) and the Differential Evolution (DE). Still, the computational complexity will be high when two wrappers are used. The Filter-Filter methods are not common in literature unless more than one filter aggregated with some wrapper method. Therefore, Wrapper-Filter or Filter-Wrapper methods are more commonly proposed in the literature. Wrapper-Filter or Filter-Wrapper hybridizations can also be combined in different ways. For example, some of them are integrated using the Memetic Algorithm (MA). MA is hybrid population-based method that is proposed to enhance the exploitation capability of global search methods such as GA [10]. Furthermore, MA can also enhance the global search by integrating local search that manipulates the solutions iteratively [11]. In text feature selection, MA can be applied in two different ways. First it can be applied by using a filter inside a wrapper. For instance, in a previous work published by the authors in [7] it was shown that feature reduction can improve the performance of the traditional clustering methods using K-means and Spherical K-means in terms of the external and internal clustering evaluation measures.

Another MA hybrid feature selection has been used in the literature, the one that combines the wrapper with non-filter methods. Such hybrid methods use one of the local search methods like the derivative-based methods. For example, Hill climbing, Chaotic Search and Simulated Annealing (SA) methods [12]. Those methods are efficient in approximating the current solutions to its best nearest position. For example, the newly proposed population-based optimization named the Whale Optimization Algorithm (WOA) [13] is combined with SA in [14]. In that method, SA is used to enhance WOA wrapper to look for more accurate feature subsets. Moreover, MA is also used for a multi-classification data feature selection in [15].

3 The Proposed Feature Selection Method

3.1 Text Preparation

Text preparation is a pre-processing step that reconstructs text corpus into a structured format. The process starts by releasing the content of each document to generate a feature space referencing their original documents. Features are the keywords selected from documents; these features are calculated according to their frequency of occurrence within text corpus to produce weights. The weight must have a discriminatory power that can distinguish each document from another. However, the use of common features is impractical due to their incapability to identify the thematic topic of documents. Feature weights are varied from one document to another. It is noteworthy to mention that text preparation incorporates text tokenization, stop word removal and stemming steps before the weighting step [16]. Moreover, thresholding was applied to reduce the low-weighted features and all features with a low frequency of occurrence are discarded.

3.2   Feature Selection

After text pre-processing, the Memetic feature selection is applied as will be discussed in this section. First, randomly create the initial solutions that contain different combinations of features which are encoded as GA chromosomes (agents). Each agent is binary-encoded; with 0 bits refer to the absence of a particular feature while 1 bits refer to the existence of it. Second, each solution is evaluated using the K-nearest Neighbour *(knn)* fitness function where the classification accuracy is calculated, iteratively. Third, the local search modifier is used to refine the resulted solutions. The decision to keep or discard older individuals will be made according to the fitness function results after and before applying the local search. The Memetic feature selection in the proposed methods works on two modes or phases which are the wrapper and the filter modes. The wrapper mode is represented by the Global search while the local mode is represented by the filter method. The following steps explains in details these two modes:

Global Search Phase

The global search is represented by the GA-based search which involves the following steps:

- Initialize first population randomly; each solution in this population represents a random subset of features.
- Evaluate each one of these random solutions using the fitness function; the resulted fitness values represent the classification error ratio of that solution measuring its predictability.
- Apply the Metaheuristic operations *(Mutation and Crossover)* to produce new members to the population. The newly generated solutions will replace the older if their fitness exceeds their ancestors.

Local Search Phase

The local search is applied after the global search starts and initializes the first population. The LS operations are listed below:

- Select the *elite* individuals, whose fitness values are the best.
- Set the Local Search Length *(l)* and Local Search Interval values *(w)*. Where *l* is the maximum number of features *additions* and *deletions* operations are performed on the elite solutions while *w* is the maximum number of local search calls to each solution at a time.
- Apply the local search according to the *l* and the *w* parameters.
- Fine-tune the elite sub-population using local search.
- Calculate the fitness value of the new individuals resulted from local search.
- Compare the new fitness value with their corresponding older counterparts. The fitness function finds the accuracy of each solution. The classification performance is used to calculate the degree of discriminability of the solutions, where the *knn* classifier is used.
- Replace the preceding solutions with the new optimized solutions if their fitness values are less than the older one. Otherwise, discard the locally optimized solutions.

Finally, after performing one run, verify if the stopping criterion has been satisfied by comparing to the maximum number of generations which is set as 200 generations. After obtaining the reduced feature space two baseline clustering methods are used which are the K-means [17] and the Spherical K-means (SK-means) [18] are used to measure the quality of the resulted clusters using the evaluation measure that will be explained in the next section.

3.3 Performance Evaluation

In this paper, the F-macro and F-micro are used as external measures while the Average Document Distance to the Cluster Centroid (ADDC) is used as an internal measure in this paper. In contrast to the external F-macro and F-micro measures, internal measure using the ADDC does not need original class labels.

The reduced feature space of the feature selection step is entered to the partition clustering algorithms using K-means and SK-means. The produced clusters will be evaluated using those measures. Before calculating the F-macro and F-micro measures, the precision (P) and recall (R) measures should be calculated first. P and R calculated using Eqs. (1) and (2), while in Eq. (3) the F-micro is obtained after getting the results from (1) and (2).

$$p(x,y) = \frac{n(x,y)}{n(x)} \tag{1}$$

$$R(x,y) = \frac{n(x,y)}{n(y)} \tag{2}$$

here $n(x)$ is the number of documents in cluster x, $n(y)$ is the number of documents in class y and $n(x,y)$ are the number of the common documents in both cluster x and class y.

$$F(x,y) = \frac{2P(x,y)R(x,y)}{P(x,y)+R(x,y)} \tag{3}$$

After calculating the F-micro, it is used to calculate the F-macro as shown in Eq. (4).

$$F_{macro} = \frac{\sum_{i=1}^{k} F_i}{k} \tag{4}$$

where k is the entire number of clusters.

On the other hand, the ADDC is an internal evaluation measure and it is calculated in Eq. (5).

$$A = \left[\sum_{i=1}^{k} \frac{1}{n} \sum_{j=1}^{m_i} D(c_i, d_j) \right] / k \tag{5}$$

where k is the clusters number, m the number of documents in each cluster, D is the similarity measure, and d is a particular document (j) in a particular cluster (i).

4 Datasets and Experimental Results

The datasets used in this research are two criminal report datasets and two benchmark datasets. Table 1 shows the detailed information about the datasets. This paper presented the comparison of the clustering results using the proposed MA-FS method with FSGATC method, which is the state-of-the-art method. The proposed MA-FS method is also compared with the results from using the entire feature space (ALL). The different feature spaces resulted from these methods were then used for clustering. The two clustering methods used are the K-means and the SK-means. The resulted clusters were evaluated using the internal (ADDC) and the external (F-Macro and F-Marco) evaluation measures.

Table 1. Datasets

Dataset	D#	#Classes	Instances	Features
6 event crimes	D1	6	223	3864
10 types crime	D2	10	2422	15601
Reuters	D3	10	2277	13310
Pair 20news groups	D4	2	1071	9497
20 news groups (1–4)	D5	53	1489	6738

Tables 2 and 3 depicted the average clustering results after applying ALL, FSGATC and MA-FS methods. Table 2 shows the results of the K-means clustering while Table 3 lists the results of the SK-means clustering. In both tables the best results are highlighted in bold.

From the results shown in Tables 2 and 3, it can be concluded that by using the MA-FS method, the document clustering performance has generally improved. The internal evaluation measure which is represented by the ADDC shown lower values and that in turn indicated that the MA-FS method obtained more accurate results for the D2, D3, and D5 datasets while for the D1 and D4 the ADDC values of the MA-FS method have increased slightly. However, the corresponding F-macro and F-micro values for the D2 and D4 are much higher than the F-macro and F-micro obtained by the ALL and the FSGATC methods. The slight increase of the ADDC values for the D1 and D4 can be tolerated in favour of the higher leap achieved by the MA-FA method using the external measures. On the other hand, the external evaluation measures for the D2, D3 and D5 had shown higher values in both F-Macro and F-Micro after using the MA-FS method. At the same time, results for these datasets generated by using the MA-FS methods provided smaller ADDCs in comparison to those generated by using the FSGATC and the ALL methods as mentioned earlier.

Correspondingly, similar scenario in Table 2 can also be observed in Table 3. In Table 3, the results of the K-means clustering are shown. It is noted that in all datasets,

Table 2. The Average results of the 20 SK-means clustering runs

		ADDC	F-Macro	F-Micro
D1 6Events	All	0.57766	0.658635	0.698112
	MA-FS	0.245524	**0.788089**	**0.810925**
	FSGATC	**0.229833**	0.492082	0.529898
D2 Ten-types	All	0.677212	0.287809	0.313363
	MA-FS	**0.151185**	**0.322882**	**0.365718**
	FSGATC	0.172023	0.143143	0.178927
D3 20news (1 to 4)	All	0.543593	0.171355	0.202165
	MA-FS	**0.260621**	**0.238338**	**0.289229**
	FSGATC	0.338379	0.181858	0.240474
D4 pair of 20news	All	0.857462	0.936949	0.944229
	MA-FS	0.822826	**0.939442**	**0.947885**
	FSGATC	**0.637778**	0.804196	0.836257
D5 reuters (1 to 3)	All	0.653812	0.697164	0.740596
	MA-FS	**0.370575**	**0.697886**	**0.752983**
	FSGATC	0.516235	0.351788	0.473472

Table 3. The Average results of the 20K-means clustering runs

		ADDC	F-Macro	F-Micro
D1 6Events	All	0.56266	0.48357	0.520097
	MA-FS	**0.221446**	**0.674883**	**0.709189**
	FSGATC	0.248281	0.534229	0.566346
D2 Ten-Types	All	**0.20105**	0.143551	0.155976
	MA-FS	0.542752	**0.582856**	**0.669803**
	FSGATC	0.828157	0.1	0.1
D3 20news (1 to 4)	All	0.864935	0.2589	0.270064
	MA-FS	**0.475325**	**0.333333**	**0.333333**
	FSGATC	0.733333	**0.333333**	**0.333333**
D4 Pair of 20news	All	0.82733	0.800839	0.838016
	MA-FS	0.768131	**0.877231**	**0.89885**
	FSGATC	**0.637778**	0.804196	0.836257
D5 Reuters (1 to 3)	All	0.692387	0.915394	0.921158
	MA-FS	**0.485993**	**0.928727**	**0.935965**
	FSGATC	1	0.333333	0.333333

the K-means performance has been improved after using the MA-FS method by observing the F-macro and F-micro measures. A significant increase in performance achieved after using the MA-FS method for the K-means clustering. For the ADDC values, it can be noticed that the results for D2, D3, and D5, the MA-FS method obtained smaller values while it has higher F-macro and F-micro. On the other hand, for D1 and D4, despite that the FSGATC method obtained smaller ADDC than the

MA-FS method, the corresponding FSGATC external measure values are still less than those from MA-FS for both D1 and D4.

To summarize, the results shown in both Tables 2 and 3 can indicate the superiority of the proposed MA-FS methods in comparison to the ALL and the FSGATC methods. That was clear by using the ADDC measure that is an internal evaluation measure and the F-macro and F-micro measures that are two external evaluation measures. The relationship between these two measures can be stated in three cases, the first when the internal measure decreases and the external increases which is an ideal convergence state. This happened with the MA-FS method in Table 2 for the D2, D3, and D5 datasets while it is also clear in Table 3 for the D1, D3 and D5. The second case happens when the internal measure does not significantly decrease while the corresponding external measures are increases significantly which indicates to a notable improvement in the clustering accuracy, and that happened in Table 2 for the D1 and D4, and for the D2 and D4 in Table 3. Finally, the worst case that might happen when there is no improvement in the external measures, which is not visible from the results of the proposed MA-FS method with any of the datasets used. It can be clearly concluded that the MA-FS performed well with a more stable manner than using the ALL and the FSGATC methods for all datasets in this paper.

5   Conclusion

This paper presented a document clustering method that utilizes a hybrid feature selection. The proposed method integrates a GA-based wrapper with filter ranking methods and it is named Memetic-Algorithm-Feature-Selection (MA-FS). The MA-FS is combined with K-means and SK-means traditional clustering. The test results showed that using the proposed feature selection can enhance the performance of the traditional clustering. In the experimental comparison, the proposed MA-FS method outperformed the results obtained by the recently proposed method named FSGATC. The proposed MA-FS method also performed better when compared to the results generated using the ALL feature space.

Acknowledgment. Ibraheem wants to thank the Higher Committee for Education Development in Iraq (HCED) for the funning of his scholarship.

References

1. Luo, M., Nie, F., Chang, X., Yang, Y., Hauptmann, A., Zheng, Q.: Adaptive unsupervised feature selection with structure regularization. IEEE Trans. Neural Netw, Learn. Syst. **PP** (99), 1–13 (2017)
2. Nie, P.: A filter method for solving nonlinear complementarity problems. Appl. Math. Comput. **167**(1), 677–694 (2005)
3. Kohavi, R., John, G.H.: Wrappers for feature subset selection. Artif. Intell. **97**(1), 273–324 (1997)
4. Maldonado, S., Weber, R.: A wrapper method for feature selection using support vector machines. Inf. Sci. **179**(13), 2208–2217 (2009)

5. Souza, J., Japkowicz, N., Matwin, S.: Feature selection with a general hybrid algorithm. In: SIAM International Conference on Data Mining 2005, Newport Beach, CA, p. 45 (2005)
6. Saeys, Y., Inza, I., Larrañaga, P.: A review of feature selection techniques in bioinformatics. Bioinformatics **23**(19), 2507–2517 (2007)
7. Al-Jadir, I., Wong, K.W., Fung, C.C., Xie, H.: Text document clustering using memetic feature selection. In: Proceedings of the 9th International Conference on Machine Learning and Computing, pp. 415–420. ACM: Singapore (2017)
8. Vergara, J.R., Estévez, P.: A review of feature selection methods based on mutual information. Neural Comput. Appl. **24**(1), 175–186 (2014)
9. Zorarpacı, E., Özel, S.A.: A hybrid approach of differential evolution and artificial bee colony for feature selection. Expert Syst. Appl. **62**, 91–103 (2016)
10. Abualigah, L.M., Khader, A.T., Al-Betar, M.A.: Unsupervised feature selection technique based on genetic algorithm for improving the Text Clustering. In: 2016 7th International Conference on Computer Science and Information Technology (CSIT). IEEE (2016)
11. Ong, Y., Lim, M., Zhu, N., Wong, K.: Classification of adaptive memetic algorithms: a comparative study. IEEE Trans. Syst. Man Cybern. Part B: Cybern. **36**(1), 141–152 (2006)
12. Aarts, E., Laarhoven, P.V.: Simulated annealing: an introduction. Stat. Neerl. **43**(1), 31–52 (1989)
13. Mirjalili, S., Lewis, A.: The whale optimization algorithm. Adv. Eng. Softw. **95**, 51–67 (2016)
14. Mafarja, M.M., Mirjalili, S.: Hybrid whale optimization algorithm with simulated annealing for feature selection. Neurocomputing **260**, 302–312 (2017)
15. Lee, J., Kim, D.-W.: Memetic feature selection algorithm for multi-label classification. Inf. Sci. **293**, 80–96 (2015)
16. Uysal, A.K., Gunal, S.: The impact of preprocessing on text classification. Inf. Process. Manag. **50**(1), 104–112 (2014)
17. Hartigan, J.A., Wong, M.A.: Algorithm AS 136 a k-means clustering algorithm. Appl. Stat. **28**, 100–108 (1979)
18. Duwairi, R., Abu-Rahmeh, M.: A novel approach for initializing the spherical k-means clustering algorithm. Simul. Model. Pract. Theory **54**, 49–63 (2015)

Intelligent Information Systems

Location-Based Services for Surrounding Area with Myanmar Language on Mobile Devices

Myat Thiri Khine[(⊠)] and Myint Myint Sein

University of Computer Studies, Yangon, Myanmar
myatthirikhine@ucsy.edu.mm, myintucsy@gmail.com

Abstract. Location-based services provide the users who are not familiar with the region to find their desired location. There has been developed for many location-based services on the mobile devices but the location-based services with Myanmar native are still poor. The pronunciation error is still occurred in existing application and it is still necessary to develop the efficient and effective one. Spatial index can be used to quickly retrieve the geo-information efficiently and effectively. One of the problems in the mobile devices is spatial index because of the limited memory and low computation capacity. A new index structure is proposed to retrieve the desired location based information for user's surrounding area by using Myanmar language on the mobile devices. The proposed index structure is constructed by using Hilbert space filling curve and B-tree that combines the inverted file to reduce the searching time. Myanmar 3 is used as the Myanmar keyword in this paper to avoid the various sequence order of the character because the typing order of Myanmar language may be various form.

Keywords: Location-based service · Spatial query · Hilbert curve · B-tree · Index structure · Inverted file

1 Introduction

Although the effective Location-based services have been developed in the developed countries, it still lacks to develop the effective and efficient one in the developing countries as Myanmar. Location-based services application for Myanmar language has been developed but most of the applications mainly depend on the web services and still has the pronunciation error. So, it still needs to develop it on the mobile devices to easily search the location with Myanmar native language anywhere and anytime. Location-based Services that provide the surrounding area is developed based on the previous approaches [9, 10].

The geo-information is accessed from the existing spatial data which contain a location and is stored in Geographical Information System (GIS). Geospatial database is used for both storage of Spatial and Non-Spatial attributes and uses Geographic Information System (GIS) to locate and retrieve data effectively and efficiently [21, 25]. It can be used for indexing data structures to quickly retrieve the spatial queries. Spatial query can take the geographical features depend on location or spatial relationship. The more searching time will be taken as the database size increases.

Many index structures have been developed in recent years to quickly retrieve the geo-information. R-tree is mostly used to access the geo-information. R-tree with

© Springer International Publishing AG 2017
S. Phon-Amnuaisuk et al. (Eds.): MIWAI 2017, LNAI 10607, pp. 293–303, 2017.
https://doi.org/10.1007/978-3-319-69456-6_24

inverted file which named the families of IR-tree [1, 3, 4, 5, 11, 12, 24] is mainly used for both spatial and textual search. R-tree is utilized for indexing the spatial data and the inverted file is utilized for indexing the textual data. In R-tree, the unnecessary node might be visited and higher IO cost can be caused in the searching process as the data objects can be overlapping and covering each other [23].

Hybrid index structure that combines the K-d tree and the inverted file has been proposed for searching the spatial keyword query on the web services [13–15].

The nature of Myanmar language is complex. It has various types of characters such as consonants, medial, vowels, tones, etc. Myanmar word consists of one or more syllables that can contain one or more characters. Myanmar sentences do not have white space to specify words boundaries. Moreover, the sequence of the Myanmar characters is also important for matching the Myanmar word. The typing order of the Myanmar characters may be vary (pigeon, ခို→ ခ + ◌ ̊ + ◌ ̤ or ခ + ◌ ̤ + ◌ ̊). The sequence of characters must have the same order to match the word. In Myanmar 3 Unicode, the sequence of the character needs to be the correct order and the typing order of the character cannot be changed. For example, the sequences of လှေ(boat) syllable in Myanmar 3 Unicode is လ + ◌ှ + ေ (101C 103E 1031) [7]. Therefore, Myanmar 3 is used in this paper to avoid the various sequence order of the character in Myanmar language.

In this paper, a new index structure is presented to effectively and efficiently retrieve the location within the given range with Myanmar language on the mobile devices. This index structure is constructed by using Hilbert space filling curve and B-tree with the inverted file and it can reduce the searching time.

The rest of the paper is arranged as follows: the related works are presented in Sect. 2. Section 3 describes the Background theory. System overview and proposed index structure is discussed in Sect. 4. The experimental result is shown in Sect. 5. Section 6 concludes the paper with the directions for future work.

2 Related Works

There are many index structure has been developed to retrieve the geo-information. Among them, R-tree [1, 4, 11, 12, 24] is mostly utilized. Its variants are used for the spatial index and the inverted file is used to index the text. Both indices are constructed based on the combination schemes [18]. Felipe et al. [4] utilizes R*-tree to index the spatial data and inverted file is utilized for the text search. The IR tree [24] constructs R-tree whose nodes have a summary of the text content of the object. Cao et al. [19] proposed S2I index structure that is constructed depend on R-tree and the inverted file. The objects are stored differently depend on the document frequency and infrequency of the term.

Hariharan et al. [12] presented the KR*-tree that can process on both spatial and textual information and also proposed a framework for Geographical Information Retrieval systems. Wang et al. [17] proposed spatial keyword R-tree (SKR-Tree) which extended from the R-tree. The node of R-tree stores both spatial and keyword information. Cary et al. [1] proposed SKI which is constructed using R-tree with an inverted index to efficiently retrieve the nearest neighbour object that is processed on the Boolean constraints. Chen et al. [20] presents TUR-tree and TUA-tree to accelerate the query process. Query processing algorithms are designed for the three queries in social network, aiming to explore temporal dimension in users, relationships and social activities. Tao and Sheng [22] develop the spatial inverted index (SI-index) to answer nearest neighbor queries in real time. Chen et al. [6] developed COM-tree and also proposed the efficient algorithms for searching all-k-nearest-neighbour query in metric space. Cao et al. [18] proposed a system to efficiently access the spatial web objects using IR tree and the inverted file.

3 Background Theory

In this paper, Hilbert curve and B-tree with the inverted file is used in this proposed index structure. Hilbert curve is used to map the 2D coordinate point to 1D value. B-tree with the inverted file which is created according to the Hilbert value is used to quickly retrieve the location with Myanmar language.

3.1 Hilbert Curve

The Hilbert Curve is the space-filling curve which visits every point within a two dimensional space. The Hilbert curve is used for mapping an n-dimensional coordinate system to a 1-dimensional index. Figure 1 shows the Hilbert curve orders one, two and three.

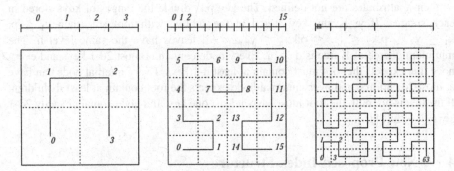

Fig. 1. Hilbert Curve Orders 1, 2, and 3 respectively.

The basic curve of the shape is an upside down "U". Firstly, a square is separated into 4 quadrants. In the first-order, the curve is drawn through their center points. The quadrants are ordered such that any two adjacent points in the ordering share a common edge. The top vertices are replaced by the previous order, and the bottom vertices suffer a rotation. The bottom left vertex is rotated 90 degrees clockwise, and the bottom right rotates 90 degrees counter clockwise. The curve starts on the lower left corner and ends on the lower right corner [2].

3.2   B-Tree

B-tree is balanced search tree and is similar to red-black trees but it is better at mini-mizing disk I/O operations. B-tree or variants of B-trees are used in many database systems to store information. B-trees keep values in every node in the tree, and the same structure may be used for all nodes. Unlike a binary-tree, each node of a b-tree may have a variable number of keys and children. The B-tree of order 2 can be seen in Fig. 2. In B-tree of order x, every node has at most x children and has at least x/2 children [8].

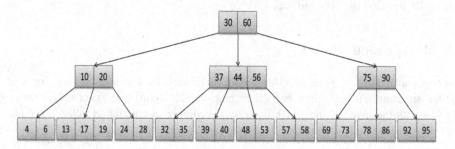

Fig. 2. B-tree of order 2

A B-tree R is a rooted tree whose root is R.root. In every node p, the number of keys p.n currently stored in node p. The p.n keys $(p.k_1, p.k_2, ..., p.k_{p.n})$ are stored in non-decreasing order so that $p.k_1 \leq p.k_2 \leq ... \leq p.k_{p.n}$. In p.leaf, the Boolean value is true if p is a leaf and false if p is an internal node. Each internal node p also contains p.n + 1 pointers $p.a_1, p.a_2, ..., p.a_{p.n+1}$ to its children. Leaf nodes have no children and so their a_i attributes are not defined. The key $p.k_i$ divide the ranges of keys stored in each subtree. If yi is any key stored in the subtree with root $x.a_i$, then $y_1 \leq p.k_1 \leq y_2 \leq p.k_2 \leq ... \leq p.k_{p.n} \leq y_{p.n+1}$. All leaves have the same level h. The minimum degree of B-tree is $d \geq 2$. Every node contain at most 2d-1 keys and every node that expects the root must contain at least d-1 keys. Every internal node can have at most 2d children and every internal node expects the root contain at least d children. If the tree is not null, the root must have at least one key. If a node contain exactly 2d-1 keys, it is full [16].

4   A New Proposed Index Structure

A new index structure is proposed to retrieve the surrounding area by using Myanmar Language efficiently and effectively. Overview of the system and proposed index structure is discussed in this section.

4.1   System Overview

This system is developed to provide the user to easily access the location with Myanmar languages on the mobile devices. The system architecture is shown in Fig. 3.

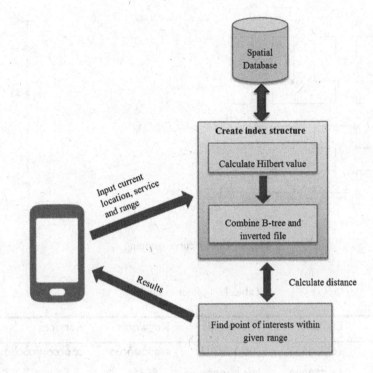

Fig. 3. System architecture

The data with their location (latitude, longitude) and services are stored in the spatial database. In this system, the user current location, services and desired range are taken as input. The desired point of interest is searched in the proposed index structure based on the user current location, given services and user desired range. The distance is calculated by using the Euclidean distance. Then, all the point which is within the given range is returned to the user and is displayed on the Map.

4.2 Proposed Index Structure

The proposed index structure is constructed by using Hilbert curve and B-tree with the inverted file. Before creating the B-tree, two dimensional coordinate points are converted to one dimensional value (h-value) by using the Hilbert curve. The mapping of the Hilbert curve can be seen in Fig. 4. Then, B-tree with the inverted file is constructed according to the h-value from Hilbert curve and services. The inverted file has keywords and location. The Example Dataset is shown in Table 1.

The calculation steps of the Hilbert value (h-value) have six steps. Firstly, (x,y) coordinate is taken as inputs. Then, the input coordinates is converted to binary representation in the first step. In the second step, bits of the two binary numbers are interleaved into one string. In the third step, the binary string is divided into 2-bit strings from left to right and then stores into the string S_i (i.e. i = 1, 2, ..., n). Then, each 2-bit strings is converted to the decimal value D_i according to the rules (Rules:

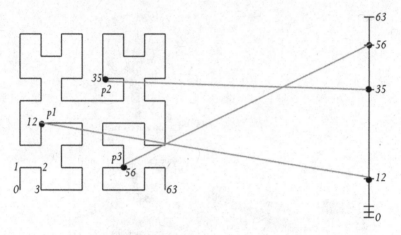

Fig. 4. Hilbert curve mapping

Table 1. Dataset example.

Id	Latitude	Longitude	Keywords	Services
Obj1	16.796433	96.176803	အောင်မင်္ဂလာ	ဘစ်ကား မှတ်တိုင်
Obj2	16.779908	96.140056	ဗဟိုစည်	ဘစ်ကား မှတ်တိုင်
Obj3	16.800442	96.162225	ဗိုလ်ချုပ်	ပန်းခြံ
Obj4	16.829281	96.155644	ဆီဒိုးနား	ဟိုတယ်
Obj5	16.816497	96.127464	ဖူဂျီ, ဂျပန်	စားသောက်ဆိုင်
Obj6	16.810881	96.176419	ရွှေဗဟို	ရုပ်ရှင်ရုံ

'00' to 0, '01' to 1, '10' to 3, '11' to 2) and stores into the array in the same order as the strings Si (i.e. i = 1,2, ..., n).

In the next step, the each value in the array is changed with the two conditions. The first one is 'if Di = 0 then every following occurrence of 1 in the array is changed to 3 and every following occurrence of 3 in the array is changed to 1' and the second one is 'if Di = 3 then every following occurrence of 0 in the array is changed to 2 and every following occurrence of 2 in the array is changed to 0'. Finally, each value in the array is converted to its two-bit binary strings and then all the string is concatenated from left to right. After that, the string is calculated as the decimal value [17].

The example of the calculation of the h-value is described in the following. Let X be latitude and Y be longitude. Let 'Sn' be a binary String and 'Dn' be a decimal value (i.e. n = 1,2,3,...).

$$X = 4 \qquad\qquad Y = 5$$

step 1:   X = <u>100</u>   Y = <u>101</u>

step 2:   <u>110001</u>

step 3:   S1=11   S2=00   S3=01

step 4:   S1=d1=2   S2=d2=0   S3=d3=1

step 5:   For d2,

          d1=2 d3=0 d3=3

          (This is the only switch in this step.)

step 6:   S1=10   S2=00   S3=11

          String=100011

          h-value=35

Then, B-tree with inverted file is constructed using h-value according to the services which is stored in the array. The proposed index structure is shown in Fig. 5.

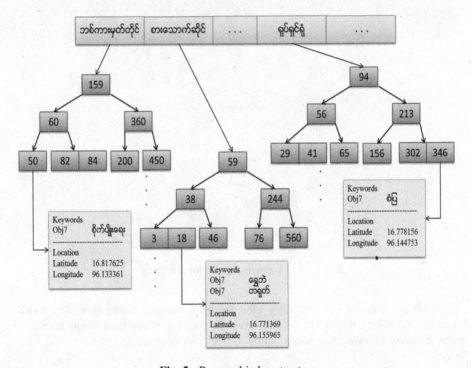

Fig. 5. Proposed index structure

5   Experimental Results

In this paper, the locations are searched based on the current location, given range and service. Current location is acquired by GPS and the desired service is chosen by the user. It takes these three inputs and search in the proposed index structure. This system is considered on the mobile devices and is tested on Yangon Region which has 46 townships. In this system, it is mainly focused on the 20 townships. It provides the user with 72 services and there are 3000 data in the database.

Figure 6 shows Input required query for searching. In this Figure, the desired service and range are required to choose to search the surrounding location. In Fig. 7, it shows the places which are searched by user based on the current location, services and given range.

Fig. 6. Input required query for searching

Figure 8 compares the searching time (second) between using proposed index structure and R-tree and K-d tree with inverted file. Searching time using proposed index structure is faster than R-tree and K-d tree with inverted file.

Fig. 7. Result after searching

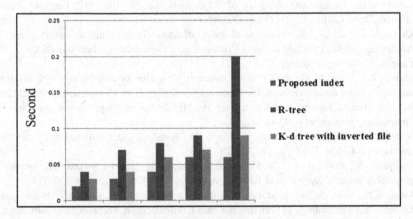

Fig. 8. Searching time comparison

6   Conclusion

This paper presents a new index structure that is constructed by using Hilbert space filling curve and B-tree with the inverted file to retrieve the locations by using Myanmar language within the given range. This system is intended to develop for the users who are difficult to use with English version. It is tested on Yangon region. This application is considered on the mobile devices. As a further extension, we will consider the system that will search the location with both English and Myanmar Language on the mobile devices and will work in an offline.

References

1. Cary, A., Wolfson, O., Rishe, N.: Efficient and scalable method for processing top-k spatial boolean queries. In: Gertz, M., Ludäscher, B. (eds.) SSDBM 2010. LNCS, vol. 6187, pp. 87–95. Springer, Heidelberg (2010). doi:10.1007/978-3-642-13818-8_8
2. Faloutsos, C., Roseman, S.: Fractals for secondary key retrieval. In: Proceedings of the Eighth ACM SIGACT-SIGMOD-SIGART Symposium on Principles of Database Systems, PODS 1989, pp. 247–252 (1989)
3. Cong, G., Jensen, C.S., Wu, D.: Efficient retrieval of the top-k most relevant spatial web objects. PVLDB 2(1), 337–348 (2009)
4. De Felipe, I., Hristidis, V., Rishe, N.: Keyword search on spatial databases. In: ICDE, pp. 656–665 (2008)
5. Rocha-Junior, J.B., Gkorgkas, O., Jonassen, S., Nørvåg, K.: Efficient processing of top-k spatial keyword queries. In: Pfoser, D., Tao, Y., Mouratidis, K., Nascimento, M.A., Mokbel, M., Shekhar, S., Huang, Y. (eds.) SSTD 2011. LNCS, vol. 6849, pp. 205–222. Springer, Heidelberg (2011). doi:10.1007/978-3-642-22922-0_13
6. Chen, L., Gao, Y., Chen, G., Zhang, H.: Metric all-k-nearest-neighbor search. IEEE Trans. Knowl. Data Eng. 28(1), 98–112 (2016)
7. Hosken, M.: Representing Myanmar in Unicode Detail and Example Version 4. SIL International and Payap University Linguistics Institute, Chiang Mai, Thailand
8. Kabat, M.R.: Design and Analysis of Algorithms, pp. 99–105. PHI Learning Private Limited, Delhi (2013). ISBN 978-81-203-4806-6
9. Khine, M.T., Sein, M.M.: Geo-spatial index structure for myanmar keyword query. In: Proceedings of the 15th International Conference on Computer Applications (ICCA 2017), Yangon, Myanmar, February 2017
10. Khine, M.T., Sein, M.M.: Poster: index structure for spatial keyword query with myanmar language on the mobile devices. In: Processing MobiSys 2016 Companion Proceedings of the 14th Annual International Conference on Mobile System, Application, and Services Companion, Singapore, p. 43 (2016)
11. Göbel, R., Henrich, A., Niemann, R., Blank, D.: A hybrid index structure for geo-textual searches. In: CIKM 2009, pp. 1625–1628 (2009)
12. Hariharan, R., Hore, B., Li, C., Mehrotra, S.: Processing spatial-keyword (SK) queries in geographic information retrieval (GIR) systems. In: SSDBM 2007, p. 16 (2007)
13. Aung, S.N., Sein, M.M.: K-nearest neighbours approximate keyword search for spatial database. In: Proceedings of 9th International Conference on Technological Advances in Electrical, Electronics and Computer Engineering (ICTAEECE), Bangkok, Thailand, pp. 65–68, 7 Feb 2015
14. Aung, S.N., Sein, M.M.: Hybrid geo-textual index structure for spatial range keyword search. Int. J. Comput. Sci. Eng. (CSEIJ) 4(5/6), 21 (2014)
15. Aung, S.N., Sein, M.M.: Index structure for nearest neighbors search with required keywords on spatial database. In: Zin, T.T., Lin, J.C.-W., Pan, J.-S., Tin, P., Yokota, M. (eds.) GEC 2015. AISC, vol. 388, pp. 457–467. Springer, Cham (2016). doi:10.1007/978-3-319-23207-2_47

16. Cormen, T.H., Leiserson, C.E., Rivest, R.L., Stein, C.: Introduction to Algorithm, 3rd edn., pp. 484–499. PHI Learning Private Limited, Delhi (2013). ISBN 978-81-203-4007-7
17. Wang, T., Li, G., Feng, J.: Efficient algorithms for top-k keyword queries on spatial databases. In: 12th IEEE International Conference on Mobile Data Management (2011)
18. Cao, X., Cong, G., Jensen, C.S., Ng, J.J., Ooi, B.C., Phan, N.T., Wu, D.: SWROS: A system for the efficient retrieval of relevant spatial web objects. http://www.ntu.edu.sg/home/gaocong/papers/vldb12swors.pdf
19. Cao, X., Chen, L., Cong, G., Jensen, C.S., Qu, Q., Skovsgaard, A., Wu, D., Yiu, M.L.: Spatial keyword querying. In: Atzeni, P., Cheung, D., Ram, S. (eds.) ER 2012. LNCS, vol. 7532, pp. 16–29. Springer, Heidelberg (2012). doi:10.1007/978-3-642-34002-4_2
20. Chen, X., Zhang, C., Ge, B., Xiao, W.: Temporal social network: storage, indexing and query processing. In: The Workshop Proceedings of the EDBT/ICDT 2016 Joint Conference, Bordeaux, France, 15 Mar 2016
21. Lifang, Y., Rui, L., Xianglin, H., Yueping, L.: Performance of R-tree with slim-down and reinsertion algorithm. In: Proceedings of International Conference on Signal Acquisition and Processing, pp. 291–294 (2010)
22. Tao, Y., Sheng, C.: Fast nearest neighbor search with keywords. IEEE Trans. Knowl. Data Eng. 26(4), 878–888 (2014)
23. Theodoridis, Y., Sellis, T.: Optimization issues in R-tree construction. Technical report, KDBSLAB-TR-93–08
24. Li, Z., Lee, K.C.K., Zheng, B., Lee, W.-C., Lee, D.L., Wang, X.: Ir-tree: An efficient index for geographic document search. IEEE TKDE 23(4), 585–599 (2011)
25. Wei, Z., Wanzhen, W., Xingguang, Y., Gang, X.: An optimized query index method based on R-tree. In: Proceedings of Fourth International Joint Conference on Computational Sciences and Optimization, pp. 1007–1010 (2011)

Processing and Monitoring Algorithm
for Solar-Powered Smart Home
in DC-Environment System Based
on RF-Radio Node

A.H. Sabry[1], W.Z.W. Hasan[2(✉)], MZA Ab. Kadir[2], M.A.M. Radzi[2],
and S. Shafie[2]

[1] Control and Automation, Faculty of Engineering, UPM, Serdang, Malaysia
ahs4771384@gmail.com
[2] Faculty of Engineering, UPM, Serdang, Malaysia
wanzuha@upm.edu.my

Abstract. The success of a design of an effective premises area network requires appropriate algorithm and communication strategy. The primary objective of this paper is to present an effective algorithm for low cost process and monitoring system integrated with energy management of a solar-powered home system. The proposed algorithm designed to serve a system of a low power consumption and recognized by a lower number of electronic components, the system includes only a pair of XBee RF modules to process signals of current, voltage and temperature sensors and to monitor the power consumption data rate variations. The proposed control algorithm able to manage the Xbee on-board micro-controller with the associated sensors to act as a remote integrated wireless sensor node. The processed information sent to base node attached to PC for monitoring the attained data and displaying over an appropriate GUI. The approach suits the XBee RF environment, but, based on a direct sensor link concept, can open horizon to other wireless sensor networking applications such as WiFi. The results have been validated by a real case study conducted in solar powered home appliances in the DC - environment system. A (11–123) Hz sampling frequency has been achieved to capture the possible surge power. This work serves as an essential stepping stone towards more efficient wireless circuit design for the smart home energy system.

Keywords: Premises area network · Home Energy Management System · Control algorithm · IEEE 802.15.4

1 Introduction

Recently, the challenges in Automatic Home Systems (AHS) have become on the processing and communication strategies that concentrate on the methods to process, control, monitor, and optimize the data flow for the use of energy by keeping maintain both low power consumption and cost. The solar-powered home electric energy management system equipped with communication, and sensor nodes to collect and process data, then to send that data for monitoring or analysis according to some

© Springer International Publishing AG 2017
S. Phon-Amnuaisuk et al. (Eds.): MIWAI 2017, LNAI 10607, pp. 304–314, 2017.
https://doi.org/10.1007/978-3-319-69456-6_25

activities and prospects of the occupants. Home control algorithm offers a distributed or centralized control of appliances, therefore, adding smart technologies to the solar powered home system would be possible to gain a greater level of comfort and energy savings. In general, the energy management of smart home refers to the application of data acquisition and administrative control for managing the energy, which includes the generation, transmission, and power distributions to form a concept of the smart grid, which has been usually interested in order to recommend future development trends of electricity grids.

After the above introduction, Sect. 2 discusses the previous related work focusing on the related algorithms with wireless or low cost energy management in the residential application. Then, highlighting the main contributions and the differences of this algorithm with respect to related work. Section 3 describes the Materials and methods, in which divides the proposed method into subsections for main system elements. An evaluation of the attained measurements has been discussed in Sect. 4. Finally, a last section highlights the significant conclusions.

2 Related Work

There are several approaches have been addressed to refer on in this study such as, smart home appliances [2], strategies of smart sensors [3], home energy storage system (HESS) with their algorithms [4], and home area network [5]. Home Energy Management System (HEMS) became necessary in the residential sector and deals with the real-time monitoring and managing the consumption of different appliances, through a Graphical User Interfaces (GUI) and intelligent ambient system in smart houses, and also, with electricity cost reduction target and efficiency improvements to energy management performance [6]. The importance of smart energy managements with the fast development in renewable energy technologies and advanced power electronics could be incorporated towards best utilization of stored energy sources in residential buildings that lead the expansion of energy home efficiency and conversion process [7]. The advanced communication strategies enable a reliable 2-way communications between the energy source and the consumer and, it has become possible for the utility company to offer the end-users with the time-dependent cost of electricity [8–12] so that, the consumer will then adjust his load schedule according to the price.

Algorithms have been proposed to serve for processing and monitoring the power rate with a renewable energy systems within a smart house environment [13], a distributed framework for the demand response algorithm for appliance scheduling in HEMS [14], where the demand side management promotes the user in a smart home to modify his electricity consumption according to prices variation of electricity [15]. A presented framework for the development of a complete HEMS for individual residential homes and several communities of household users, with consideration of both the power systems and the final users' perspectives [16].

This paper focuses on the algorithm of an integrated wireless management system applied on a solar-powered house with a DC environment and based on voltage matching concepts between the source and load. Some of the important features that recognize the proposed prototype framework are as follows:

- A circuit implementation of a new control algorithm for solar-battery charging process, which is based on utilizing the off-state energy at a high level of battery state of charge (SOC) period to be switched into another current path as an auxiliary load; surplus power could be a secondary battery or ventilation fan for cooling the solar panels, which improves its performance. The control algorithm adopts the variation range of both temperature and irradiance at the geographical site, which is used to set the operational voltage of the charging circuit. The detailed algorithm presented in our previous work [17], which seems to be inversely designed, starts from the appropriate value of the DC voltage for load to be assigned as a fully charged battery voltage.
- An energy-monitoring circuit for a DC-bus PV microgrid home system based on a single voltage (source-battery) matching concept to dispense the AC inverter, which is described in detail in a previous work [18].
- Low-power-consumption WSN for energy monitoring of both the charging process and the management of a DC-bus microgrid system. The proposed system is based on only one pair of XBee S1 Pro capabilities to access the data and RF communication.
- The proposed approach is quite efficient in terms of user cost level contribution by adopting the concept of the Source-Load voltage matching, which adopts the

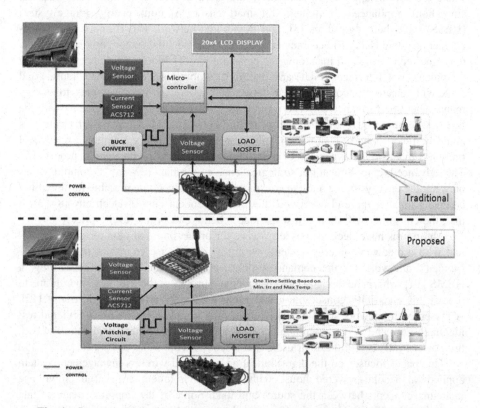

Fig. 1. Comparison diagram between the managed system by the control algorithm.

suitability of system component selection, leading to the dispensing of additional microcontrollers and allows achieving a solid economic cost reduction.

The difference between the proposed system algorithm and the common related management algorithm in terms of the system type that managed, can be described in Fig. 1. It is obviously in this figure that in the proposed control algorithm manges the monitoring and control system with less components in terms of the microcontroller, furthermore, the control and monitoring system in the traditional includes a micro-controller and wireless access card, while in the proposed work, the algorithm able to use only the wireless RF module as a signal processor and a wireless communication node.

3 Methodology

The proposed framework consists of two parts: the hardware prototype module and the PC-based software. The prototype consists of a wireless energy management module and a solar-battery controller module, while the software can be divided into a graphical user interface (GUI) for hardware driving and data monitoring and the initial configuration software. The proposed integrated prototype, which suits the function-alities required for the proposed scheme and the interconnection of system components, can be seen in Fig. 2.

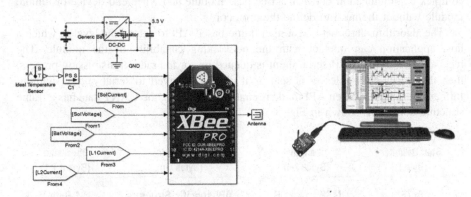

Fig. 2. Wireless energy measurement and management modules.

3.1 Base Station

The base station has the function as a coordinator between the XBee Pro module communication and it is connected to the monitoring computer, through a USB cable. Figure 2, shows the proposed base station, which is traditionally one to acquire the energy information from the remote node. A FT232 chip has used to provide a USB to UART interface. A MATLAB software driver, at the base station, allows the designed software to communicate with the remote Xbee module.

The wireless energy measurement and management module network consists of 6 analogue channel measurement node which acts as a remote end device and a coordinator node which acts as a central server attached to a PC or any operating system device such as any smart mobile phone.

The six analogue channels of the remote measurement node are classified as:-

1. Two channels to measure the voltage and current of the solar panels through their associated sensors.
2. One channel is used with appropriate sensor to measure the ambient temperature.
3. The load voltage and its two current branches were measured by three channels and their concern sensors.

All sensors are synthesized and connected to RF IEEE 802.15.4 module directly based on the capabilities of the RF wireless module itself, which is operated under its API mode, as shown in the above schematic diagram.

3.2 Communication Protocol

The communications technique through the serial bus to access the data can be defined as the serial interface protocol. XBees configuration is in transparent mode by default. But this work utilized Application Programming Interface API, one of the two XBee modes. The API mode provides a structured interface where data is communicated throughout the serial interface in structured packets. This will help to enable to create complex communication between XBee base module and Xbee end device or remote module without the need to define the protocol.

The algorithm starts with creating a frame-based API to extend the level to which a host application can interact with the networking capability of the module. The received data by the USB serial input is queued up for the radio transmission process, then data received wirelessly is sent as it exactly received to serial output, without further information. When API mode is enabled, (AP = 1), the UART data has a frame structure defined as shown in Fig. 3.

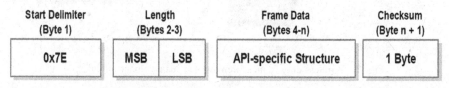

Start Delimiter (Byte 1)	Length (Bytes 2-3)		Frame Data (Bytes 4-n)	Checksum (Byte n + 1)
0x7E	MSB	LSB	API-specific Structure	1 Byte

MSB = Most Significant Byte, LSB = Least Significant Byte

Fig. 3. Shows frame structure when the API mode is enabled, (AP = 1).

This work also involves the command mode of XBee operation. Command mode is a state in which the firmware interprets incoming characters as commands. Command mode provides the project to adjust the device's firmware by changing the parameters that can be set using AT commands, also called Transparent Mode.

Since the XBee Module support ADC (Analog/digital conversion) as well as the digital I/O line passing. The proposed work used the maximum available 6 analogue channels for the temperature, currents and voltages while using the digital I/O lines to control appliances status.

3.3 XBees Initial Configuration

At the beginning, the Xbees (base and remote) configured with the proper parameters, so that they will communicate each other. In both XBee radios, XCTU is utilized to load the initial parameters as listed in Table 1.

Table 1. Parameter configurations of the remote and base modules.

Parameter	Remote configuration	Base configuration
CH channel	C	C
ID PAN ID	3332	3332
DL (destination address low)	DL = 0x1111	DL = 0x2222
MY (source address)	MY = 0x2222	MY = 0x1111
BD interface data rate	115200 [7]	
API operation	API disabled[0]	API disabled [1]
Analog-to-Digital Converter, DIO = Digital Input/Output	D0 = D1 = D2 = D3 = D4 = D5 = ADC [2];	N/A
IR (sample rate)	IR = 0x14	N/A
CE coordinator enable	N/A	Coordinator [1]
IU (enable I/O output)	Enabled [1]	Enabled [1]
IA (I/O input address)	N/A	0xFFFF
End device association		0100b [4]

The settings of the XBees configure the remote RF module to set AD0, AD1, AD2, AD3, AD4 and AD5 as analogue input and sampled once each every 20 ms. Then sending to the base RF module. The base must accordingly receive a 24-Byte transmission (12 Bytes of data and 12 Bytes framing) every 20 ms.

The hardware of the XBee base module includes only the connection between the base module and the monitoring PC via the transceiver chip ST232E, as shown in Fig. 4.

3.4 Flowchart and GUI Decoding

The flow chart of MATLAB GUI Decoding can be described in Fig. 5.

The XBee module software platform utilized in proposed kit prototype is initially adopted the XCTU for XBee IEEE 802.15.4 module parameters configuration, then, the MATLAB AT command functions have been used to control the access of the data transfer, which provides an API (Application Programming Interface) for

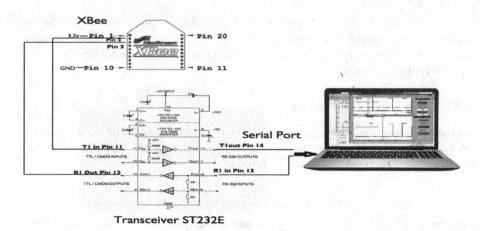

Fig. 4. The 2 pin connection of the base Xbee and PC through transceiver.

synchronization and communication between the remote and the base station. The designed MATLAB software provides an API to access the data peripherals which are available in the remote evaluation and energy management board.

The designed GUI display contains the Static Text for labeling and titles, the Edit Text is for data input or real-time editing, Check boxes to select between two options and two X-Y Axis display to monitor the appliances power consumption and status. The display of the proposed GUI always shows the online date and time while frozen at the starting time of energy system parameters recording. There are a 4 min data logging assigned by defaults while an optional change in the end logging time also allowed. Solar and Load energies were displayed through accumulating the power rate that recorded in the upper X-Y plotter as described in Fig. 6.

4   Measurements Evaluation

Practical measurements have been conducted on one of the most consumer appliances in domestic application to evaluate the performance of the proposed algorithm. Air-conditioner has been selected as a load in this experiment. Since the system serves processing and monitoring of DC-powered appliances, a Digital Inverter Technology (DIT) air-conditioner was used. Several measurements have been conducted to verify the best performance with lower consumption, according to algorithm compatibility to cover the surge power with an appropriate rate of processing and transmitting data in such system. One hour experimental power consumption and temperature measurements for the DC based system as a power source applied on 1 HP Air-conditioner. The result is shown in Fig. 7.

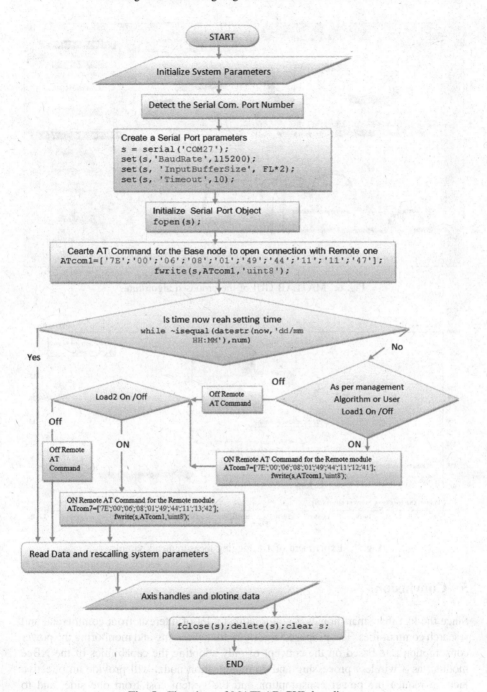

Fig. 5. Flowchart of MATLAB GUI decoding.

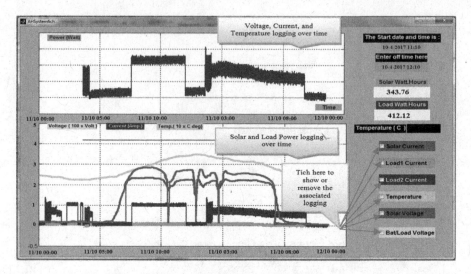

Fig. 6. MATLAB GUI of the proposed algorithm.

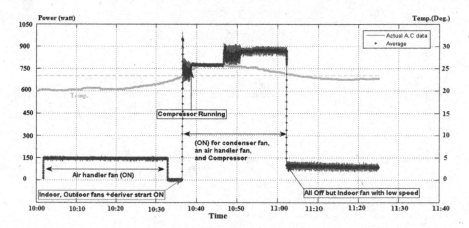

Fig. 7. Experiment of 1 h logging measurements sample.

5   Conclusion

Since the fact that smart homes go on to attract a lot of interests from commercial and research communities. The proposed algorithm for processing and monitoring the power consumption rate based on the concept of only adopting the capabilities of the XBee module, as a wireless processing and communication node, will provide an effective facts to reduce the power consumption and the system cost from one side, and to increase the energy management efficiency with less complexity to solve the problem of suboptimal control strategies. Therefore, simultaneously dropping the running costs of not only the solar-powered homes but also in traditional buildings. Ultimately, the idea has been validated by executing the algorithm with actual smart solar-powered system in DC-environment appliances, PV and battery system. A (11–123) Hz sampling frequency has been achieved to capture the possible surge power. This work serves as an essential stepping stone towards more efficient wireless circuit design for the smart home energy system.

References

1. Sabry, A.H., Wan Hasan Mohd Zainal, .W.Z., Amran, M., Shafie, S.B.: High efficiency integrated solar home automation system based on DC load matching technique. ARPN J. Eng. Appl. Sci. **10**(15), 6424–6434 (2015)
2. Bradac, Z., Kaczmarczyk, V., Fiedler, P.: Optimal scheduling of domestic appliances via MILP. Energies **8**(1), 217–232 (2015)
3. Ahmed, M.A., Kang, Y.C., Kim, Y.: Communication network architectures for smart-house with renewable energy resources. Energies **8**, 8716–8735 (2015)
4. Pascual, J., Sanchis, P., Marroyo, L.: Implementation and control of a residential electrothermal microgrid based on renewable energies, a hybrid storage system and demand side management. Energies **7**(1), 210–237 (2014)
5. Collotta, M., Pau, G.: A novel energy management approach for smart homes using bluetooth low energy. IEEE J. Sel. Areas Commun. **33**(12), 2988–2996 (2015)
6. Han, D.-M., Lim, J.-H.: Design and implementation of smart home energy management systems based on zigbee. IEEE Trans. Consum. Electron. **56**(3), 1417–1425 (2010)
7. Subbiah, R., Pal, A., Nordberg, E.K., Marathe, A., Marathe, M.V.: Energy demand model for residential sector: a first principles approach. IEEE Trans. Sustain. Energy **8**(3), 1–19 (2017)
8. Samadi, P., Mohsenian-Rad, A.-H., Schober, R., Wong, V.W.S., Jatskevich, J.: Optimal real-time pricing algorithm based on utility maximization for smart grid. In: 2010 First IEEE International Conference on Smart Grid Communications, pp. 415–420 (2010)
9. Chen, C., Kishore, S., Snyder, L.V.: An innovative RTP-based residential power scheduling scheme for smart grids. In: ICASSP, IEEE International Conference on Acoustics, Speech and Signal Processing - Proceedings, pp. 5956–5959 (2011)
10. Kaufmann, S., Künzel, K., Loock, M.: Customer value of smart metering: explorative evidence from a choice-based conjoint study in Switzerland. Energy Policy **53**, 229–239 (2013)
11. Celebi, E., Fuller, J.D.: A model for efficient consumer pricing schemes in electricity markets. IEEE Trans. Power Syst. **22**(1), 60–67 (2007)
12. Yang, P., Tang, G., Nehorai, A.: Optimal time-of-use electricity pricing using game theory. In: ICASSP, IEEE International Conference on Acoustics, Speech and Signal Processing - Proceedings, pp. 3081–3084 (2012)
13. Saha, A., Kuzlu, M., Khamphanchai, W., Pipattanasomporn, M., Rahman, S., Elma, O., Selamogullari, U.S., Uzunoglu, M., Yagcitekin, B.: A home energy management algorithm in a smart house integrated with renewable energy. In: IEEE PES Innovative Smart Grid Technologies Conference Europe. vol. 2015, no. January (2015)
14. Chavali, P., Yang, P., Nehorai, A.: A distributed algorithm of appliance scheduling for home energy management system. IEEE Trans. Smart Grid **5**(1), 282–290 (2014)
15. Pipattanasomporn, M., Kuzlu, M., Rahman, S.: An algorithm for intelligent home energy management and demand response analysis. IEEE Trans. Smart Grid **3**(4), 2166–2173 (2012)

16. Barbato, A., Capone, A., Carello, G., Delfanti, M., Falabretti, D., Merlo, M.: A framework for home energy management and its experimental validation. Energy Effic. 7(6), 1013–1052 (2014)
17. Sabry, A.H., Wan Hasan, W.Z., Zainal, M., Amran, M., Shafie, S.B.: Alternative solar-battery charge controller to improve system efficiency. Appl. Mech. Mater. 785 (February 2016), 156–161 (2015)
18. Sabry, A.H., Wan Hasan, W.Z., Zainal, M., Amran, M., Shafie, S.B.: DC loads matching technique as an alternative to ac inverter in residential solar system application evaluation and comparison. Appl. Mech. Mater. 785, 225–230 (2015)

GuARD: A Real-Time System for Detecting Aggressive Human Behavior in Cage Environment

Phooi Yee Lau[1(✉)], Hock Woon Hon[2], Zulaikha Kadim[2], and Kim Meng Liang[2]

[1] Centre for Computing and Intelligent Systems (CCIS), Universiti Tunku Abdul Rahman, Kampar, Malaysia
laupy@utar.edu.my
[2] MIMOS Berhad, Technology Park Malaysia, Kuala Lumpur, Malaysia

Abstract. The relative closeness in a cage environment, such as lock-up or elevator, will become a place that is conducive to conduct criminal activities such as fighting. Monitoring the activities, in the cage environment, therefore, became a necessity. However, placing security guards could be inefficient and ineffective, as it is impossible to monitor the scene 24 by 7. A vision-based system, employing video analysis technology, to detect abnormalities such as aggressive behavior, becomes a challenging and emerging problem. In order to monitor suspicious activities in a cage environment, the system should be able track individuals from the scene, to identify their action, and to keep a record of how often these aggressive behaviors happen. On top of the previous consideration, the system should be implemented in real-time, whereby, the following conditions were taken into consideration, being: (1) wide angle (fish-eye) (2) resolution (low) (3) number of people (4) lighting (low). This paper proposes to develop a vision-based system that is able to monitor aggressive activities of individuals in a cage environment. This work focuses on analyzing the temporal feature of aggressive movement, taking consideration of the acquisition limitations discusses previously. Experimental results show that the proposed system is easily realized and achieved real-time performance, even in low performance computer.

Keywords: Surveillance system · Behavior monitoring · Perspective correction · Background subtraction · Real-time video processing

1 Introduction

Recent work in vision-based surveillance system aims to learn about the presence and the behavior of a person in a given environment [1–4]. These works often focus on monitoring activities such as violent behavior, preferably in a fully automatic manner, and usually for surveillance purposes. Also, these systems often come with a well-designed alarm to be triggered depending on the situations defined, to connect to remote security control centers. In most of these video surveillance systems, some are devoted to using low cost off-the-shelf cameras [1].

© Springer International Publishing AG 2017
S. Phon-Amnuaisuk et al. (Eds.): MIWAI 2017, LNAI 10607, pp. 315–322, 2017.
https://doi.org/10.1007/978-3-319-69456-6_26

In the past, CCTV is often used as a surveillance tool, but humans are poor at remaining alert for long period of time and therefore, such limitations, prohibit human to participate in the detection chain especially in 7 by 24 h systems. As such, vast majority of installed CCTV cameras remain unwatched and therefore, it will be unlikely that incidents can be detected. Likely, when serious crime has happened, those videos will only be used to check what has happened, reducing it to a trace-driven tool, for verification or support.

In 2008, Chen reported that video surveillance has become a self-reporting tool with the ability to detect and to monitor potential aggressive behavior [2]. His work describes a framework to recognize aggressive behavior using a local binary motion descriptors. However, aggressive human behavior in this work focuses on the involvement of an object, e.g. chair, as it was difficult to notice, due to occlusion, an aggressive action by itself. In 2012, Quanane propose to recognize a boxing action as aggressive behavior. His proposed work are based on the geometrical approach associated with shape representation to recognize an aggressive human gesture. However, the work cannot resolve the occlusion when more than one person are present in the scene [3]. In 2014, Lyu proposed a violence detection algorithm based on the local spatio-temporal points and optical flow method [4]. His proposed work is able to detect aggressive action regardless of the context and the number of involved person. However, no real-time system implementation was discussed.

In this paper, we propose a new framework to extract *candidate* event(s) from a scene, and to classify them as potential aggressive behavior, named GuARD. GuARD is a surveillance system for detecting potential violent behavior in a scene, named *aggressive-behavior-like* region(s), in a cage environment. The usefulness of this proposed work is multiple; (1) analyses input scene in real-time, and raises an alarm when *aggressive-behavior-like* region(s) is detected, and (2) record the decision triggered in (1). The remainder of this paper includes: Sect. 2 that outlines the GuARD Framework; Sect. 3 that shows implementation with analysis; and Sect. 4 concludes the paper with future works.

2 GuARD Framework

The **AggR**essive behavior **D**etection system, named as GuARD, is developed using OpenCV libraries that is widely used in the real-time computer vision application. GuARD system flow is illustrated in Fig. 1. In *Step 1*, the video acquisition set-up is discussed. In *Step 2*, we obtained a foreground region(s), being a *candidate* region(s), using a background subtraction technique which extract the moving regions in a scene. In *Step 3*, the resultant image from *Step 2* will be thresholded using T_x, a value which represents the speed of motion detected, obtained by rigorous testing. In *Step 4*, we compensates the non-uniform perspective in the images, obtained using fish-eye camera, by rotating the image until the perspective could be represented vertically, i.e. part further away from the camera will be smaller and area closer to the camera be larger. *Step 5* compensates the region size in input scene, being further or nearer from the camera due to *Step 4*, for *candidate* region(s). *Step 6* classify all the *candidate* region(s) into *aggressive-behavior-like* region(s) or *non-aggressive-behavior-like*

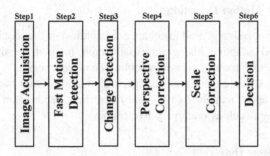

Fig. 1. GuARD framework.

region(s), and provide an alarm, as the output, to the system administrator. In this step also, *aggressive-behavior-like* region(s) will be stored in the system.

2.1 Step 1: Image Acquisition

The acquisition set-up for the experimental set-up is shown in Fig. 2 (a). A corner mount camera with the average vertical and horizontal field-of-view (FoV) set to 80° to 91° and 100° to 120°, respectively, is used in the acquisition. This large FoV would enable a room being monitored using single camera with minimum blind spot. The camera is installed at the most top of a corner, as indicated in Fig. 2 (a). To prevent the scene with the high resolution in which can greatly slow down the performance of the system, the input image is resized to 320 × 240 pixels, with RGB color format.

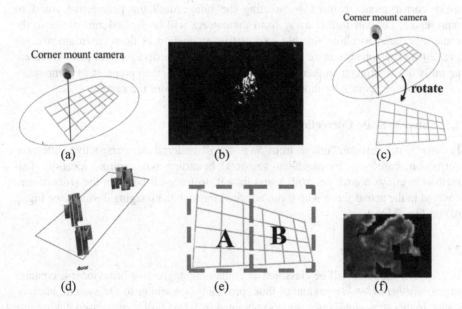

Fig. 2. System output: (a) Set-up and criteria of monitoring, (b) *Step 3* Change Detection, (c) *Step 4* Perspective Correction, (d) *Step 5* Correction Concept, (e) *Step 5* Scale Correction, (f) *Step 6* Individual region analysis

2.2   Step 2: Fast Motion Detection

Here, at first, pre-processing is used to enhance the contrast of the acquired image using the contrast-limited adaptive histogram equalization method. In this step also, a background subtraction method is used to obtain *candidate* region(s) for input scene, being $I_t(x,y)$. $I_{t1}(x,y)$, being the current image, are subtracted with background frame, being three-*frame* apart, namely $I_{t2}(x,y)$. The *frame* here depends on the selection of frame for processing, such as one every five frames.

2.3   Step 3: Change Detection

A threshold parameter is applied to obtained the binary motions between consecutive frames, being a *candidate* region(s) from *Step 2*. Taking into account that $I_{t1}(x,y)$ and $I_{t2}(x,y)$ are from the same source, a change detection analysis can be performed to calculate the desired change information by applying Eq. (1). To obtain the *Step 3 candidate* region(s), T_x is applied to investigate the change from non-aggressive behavior to aggressive behavior. After rigorous testing, herewith T_x is set to 40 – see Fig. 2 (b).

$$CD(I_{t1}, I_{t2}) = |I_{t1}(x,y) - I_{t2}(x,y)| \qquad (1)$$

2.4   Step 4: Perspective Correction

In *Step 4*, we compensates the non-uniform perspective in the images [5], obtained using corner mount camera, by rotating the image until the perspective could be represented, i.e. part further away from the camera will be far and area closer to the camera be near, to allow suitable quantitative evaluation of floor environments, see Fig. 2 (c). The rotation angle used should take into consideration that pixel representation is much stronger further from the camera, and this step prepares to compensate the pixel value, especially those pixel(s) further away from the camera.

2.5   Step 5: Scale Correction

In *Step 5*, the resultant image from *Step 4* will undergo the perspective difference correction, based on the *candidate* region(s) bounding box centroid location. This method overlays a grid, i.e. grid A and grid B, to trade-off between the sizes of area covered in the actual scene with those acquired through the imaging device – see Fig. 2 (d) ad Fig. 2 (e).

2.6   Step 6: Decision

In *Step 6*, a frame(s) will be classified as containing aggressive behavior if it contains *aggressive-behavior-like* region(s), thus, providing a warning to the system administrator. In this step, *candidate* region(s) obtained in *Step 5* will be processed, taking into account the features such as their area and bounding box positions.

Area. Herewith, aggressive behavior is being associated with large *candidate* region (s). Therefore, a threshold value, T_y, for the grid A and the grid B in *Step 5*, namely [A, B], after rigorous experimental results, are set to [60, 90].

The condition above allow, for instance, discarding foreground candidate regions that correspond to noise leaving only the *aggressive-behavior-like* candidate regions. All candidate regions, is further analyzed, using T_z, a threshold value, set to 50 after rigorous experiments, in subsequent region-based background subtraction, being a more refined process – see Fig. 2 (f). Later, the *H value* is collected, due to its relatedness to skin color and cloth color, to allow us to focus on the human actions analysis.

3 Experimental Results

A system was developed to evaluate the performance of the GuARD framework discussed in Sect. 2. The processes are tested on an Intel i5 Core 1.80 GHz with 4 GB of RAM. The evaluation includes analyzing the (1) success rate in detecting aggressive behavior in cage environment, and (2) performance in terms of processing time and latency. A totaled of five different videos based on the following conditions were evaluated:

- Different frame selection (processing) analysis
- Different scenario analysis
- Different scene resolution and performance analysis

3.1 Different Frame Selection (Processing) Analysis

In this experiment, we investigated different scene with different frame selection. As shown in Table 1, we have investigated with different frame selection options. A four minutes sequence were selected in this experiments, with 320×240 resolutions (15 fps): (1) video 1: processing every frame (2) video 2: processing every frames being 5 frames apart, and (3) video 3: processing every frames being 10 frames apart. As shown in Table 1, in order to have real-time system, the acquired image should be, at least, processed every 5 frames.

Table 1. Performance of different frame selection options and processing time

Input video	Frame selection	Performance (ave)
1	Every frame	832 s
2	Every 5 frames	177 s
3	Every 10 frames	89 s

3.2 Different Scenario Analysis

In this experiment, we investigated different scenes with different number of aggressive behavior involving different number of person(s). As shown in Table 2, all scene(s) with different fighting characteristic(s) are able to be detected.

Table 2. System performance: detection results for different aggressive behavior and number of person involved

Scenario	Detection Result
Scene 1 – 3 person fighting	
Scene 2 – 2 person fighting 3 group	
Scene 3 – 6 person fighting 1 group	
Scene 4 – 6 person fighting 2 group	

3.3   Different Scene Resolution and Performance Analysis

In this experiment, we investigated different scenes with different resolutions. As shown in Table 3, we have selected to investigate scenes with different video resolutions and length for aggressive behavior. All videos selected contain different type of aggressive behaviors. Four videos were selected: (1) video 1: four minutes of video with 320 × 240 resolutions (15 fps), (2) video 2: six minutes of video with 320 × 240 resolutions (15 fps), (3) video 3: two minutes of video 640 × 480 resolutions (14 fps), and (4) video 4: four minutes of video with 640 × 480 resolutions (14 fps). As shown in Table 3, experimental results shown that, for a real-time system, the resolution of processed image should be, at most, 320 × 240 resolutions.

Table 3. Performance of different input resolution and duration

Input video	Processing duration	Average performance
1	182 s	Ave. 180 s (3 min) to process 4 min video
	180 s	
	180 s	
	182 s	
	177 s	
	181 s	
	179 s	
2	270 s	Ave. 273 s (4 min 33 s) to process 6 min video
	293 s	
	270 s	
	276 s	
	264 s	
	270 s	
	271 s	
3	286 s	Ave. 268 s (4 min 28 s) to process 2 min video
	262 s	
	267 s	
	266 s	
	272 s	
	263 s	
	266 s	
4	572 s	Ave 535 s (8 min 55 s) to process 4 min video
	531 s	
	534 s	
	529 s	
	518 s	
	528 s	
	538 s	

4 Discussion and Conclusion

In this section we run a 13.14 min video with 320 × 240 resolutions. This video's has been annotated, i.e. the aggressive behavior appeared in the video has been detected, and listed in Table 4. Referring to the aggressive behavior detection from 2:56 – 3:15, the aggressive activity happens in the "front part of the camera" or Grid A, marked in green, see Fig. 3. However, for the aggressive behavior detection from 6:45 – 7:04, the aggressive behavior activity happens at the "far part of the camera" or Grid B, marked in blue, see Fig. 3. The detection accuracy is high for this video.

In general, it is now possible to study the aggressive behavior in cage environment by employing intelligent video analysis technology. The experimental results indicate that the aggressive behavior can be effectively detected.

Table 4. Ground Truth for Aggressive Behavior Analysis

Input video	Duration
Video length: 13 m 14 s	2:56–3:15
	3:33–3:52
	4:37–5:00
	5:25–5:43
	6:44–7:00
	7:09–7:30
	8:21–8:40
	8:54–9:17

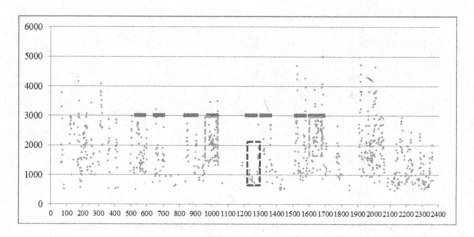

Fig. 3. System performance frame by frame (Color figure online)

References

1. Haritaoglu, I., Harwood, D., Davis, L.S.: W4: real-time surveillance of people and their activities. IEEE Trans. Pattern Anal. Mach. Intell. **22**(8), 809–830 (2000)
2. Chen, D., Wactlar, H., Chen, M.Y., Gao, C., Bharucha, A., Hauptmann, A.: Recognition of aggressive human behavior using binary local motion descriptors. In: 2008 30th Annual International Conference of the IEEE Engineering in Medicine and Biology Society, Vancouver, BC, pp. 5238–5241 (2008)
3. Ouanane, A., Serir, A., Kerouh, F.: New geometric descriptor for the recognition of aggressive human behavior. In: 2012 5th International Congress on Image and Signal Processing, Chongqing, pp. 148–153 (2012)
4. Lyu, Y., Yang, Y.: Violence detection algorithm based on local spatio-temporal features and optical flow. In: 2015 International Conference on Industrial Informatics - Computing Technology, Intelligent Technology, Industrial Information Integration, Wuhan, pp. 307–311 (2015)
5. Wakefield, W.W., Genin, A.: The use of a Canadian (perspective) grid in deep-sea photography. Deep Sea Res. Part A. Oceanogr. Res. Pap. **34**(3), 469–478 (1987)

DREAD-R: Severity Assessment
of ONOS SDN Controller

Muhammad Shakil, Alaelddin Fuad Yousif Mohammed[✉], Hyeontaek Oh,
and Jun Kyun Choi

Korea Advanced Institute of Science and Technology (KAIST), Daejeon, Korea
{shakilphd,alaelddin,hyeontaek}@kaist.ac.kr, jkchoi59@kaist.edu

Abstract. In few past years, popularity of Software Defined Networking
(SDN) among academia and industry is rapidly increased, and users are
conferenced about choosing suited and secured SDN controller. Recently,
Open Network Operating System (ONOS), which provides the control
plane for SDN, appears as best choice for service provider in term of high
availability, scalability, and security. There are some existing models for
security assessment of SDN. However, there is still a room for more assess-
ments. This paper address the severity assessment of ONOS using proposed DREAD-R model which considers traditional DREAD (Damage
potential, Reproducibility, Exploitability, Affected users and Discoverability) model with additional "Reputation" parameter. This paper found
that control plane vulnerabilities are critical in nature and disrupt entire
network functions and need immediate attention for solutions.

Keywords: SDN · ONOS · Severity assessment · DREAD-R

1 Introduction

Software Defined Networking (SDN) is a novel network approach that separates
control plane from forwarding plane. SDN provides several advantages over the
legacy network such as centralized network visualizing, the agility of control
plane programing, and central security implementation [1–3]. We can notice
from academia and industry that SDN is a promising and disruptive network
technology to solve legacy network challenges.

In the legacy network, control plane and data plane are packaged together.
However, in SDN, data plane is separated from control plane [4]. The separation
of control plane from data plane provides a global view of the network. Network
performance can be viewed and managed centrally from SDN controller (i.e. it
is the mainstay of SDN innovation).

SDN architecture can be viewed as a combination of three layers as shown
in Fig. 1. On the top is the application layer which, contains network functions.
Therefore, all kinds of applications remain in this layer (e.g. firewalls, load balancing, traffic monitoring). The SDN applications communicate to a controller
through northbound interface [4]. Many of the northbound Application program

S. Phon-Amnuaisuk et al. (Eds.): MIWAI 2017, LNAI 10607, pp. 323–330, 2017.
https://doi.org/10.1007/978-3-319-69456-6_27

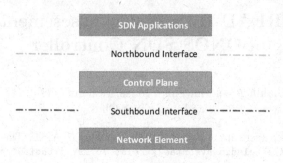

Fig. 1. SDN architecture.

interfaces (APIs) that exist are based on their applications. The commonly used APIs and protocols that communicate between application and controller are Representational State Transfer (REST) Application Program Interface (API). On the other hand, network element communicates using southbound interface with the controller. Southbound protocols are also open to adopt any protocol according to their needs (e.g. Network Configuration Protocol (NETCONF), Open vSwitch Database (OVSDB), and OpenFlow). However, OpenFlow, which is widely used, has become a de facto standard for SDN.

In SDN, the SDN controller is the brain of the network and the owner of virtual resources [4]. Control plane is also responsible for coordinate between network and virtual resources. Usually, a controller provides a concrete interface to the network, and the controller can have different types of access levels to users, devices, and applications [5]. The controller is the center-of-gravity in SDN concept, and it should be resilient against known and unknown attacks [2,6–9]. The controller has multiple north, south, and east/west bound interfaces which interact with applications, network elements as well as with other SDN controllers, respectively. The vulnerabilities of interfaces can be used to compromise the controller [4].

Open Network Operating System (ONOS) is one of the candidates for distributed SDN Controller which has been widely adopted in academia and industry [10]. Security of ONOS has been assessed in some recent studies (e.g. [5,7,11]). Authors in [5] assessed the security of ONOS using Microsoft developed threat modeling technique STRIDE (Spoofing, Tampering, Repudiation, Information Disclosure, Denial of Service (DoS), and Elevation of Privilege [12]) using Data Flow Diagramming (DFD). On the other hand, authors in [7] developed a security framework for SDN vulnerability assessment (named DELTA) using fuzzing techniques. Microsoft developed DREAD (Damage potential, Reproducibility, Exploitability, Affected users and Discoverability) risk assessment model to measure the severity of threats/attacks to find out severity [11]. Those previous studies concentrated on analyzing general ONOS security analysis.

In this paper, we assess the severity of threats/attacks utilizing the existing DREAD model with additional proposed parameter "Reputation" to test the trust of ONOS community. Furthermore, threats/attacks are categorized using the proposed DREAD-R model to find out the severity of SDN controller particularly, ONOS. We rate threats found by DELTA. It has to note here that DELTA is the first ever SDN security analysis framework (also known as SDN pentesting framework) [7] and STRIDE based assessment [5]. In this paper, we are interested in analyzing the security vulnerabilities/threats found using DELTA and STRIDE and rating them using proposed DREAD-R model. The goal of this paper is to check the validity of the following hypotheses:

- H1. Control plane vulnerabilities are more severe than northbound and southbound protocols;
- H2. Proposed DREAD-R model increase/decrease severity rating based on reputation.

The rest of this paper is organized as follows, Sect. 2 describes general ONOS architecture and literature review of STRIDE, DELTA and DREAD security assessment frameworks. Section 3 introduces proposed DREAR-R and the analysis of the severity assessment of ONOS. Section 4 presents our conclusion and future work.

2   Related Work

2.1   ONOS

ONOS is an open source distributed network operating system for service providers. ONOS core built on carrier grade features that provide high availability, scale out, and performance. It also provides abstractions to Northbound and Southbound interfaces [10] as shown in Fig. 2. ONOS is a JAVA based controller and uses Open Service Gateway Initiatives (OSGI) to develop different subsystems and provide web style agility to SDN control plane.

Commonly, ONOS releases do not provide any built-in security mechanism. However, a separate implementation released with the name of Security-Mode ONOS. In this study, we analyze ONOS Security-Mode that is referred as a conservative mode. The conservative mode has two features; (1) Application Authentication and (2) Role based/Permission based Access Control (least privilege applications) [5].

2.2   Security Assessment Frameworks for ONOS

STRIDE: STRIDE stands for Spoofing, Tampering, Repudiation, Information Disclosure, Denial of Service (DoS), and Elevation of Privilege [12]. Spoofing means misleading victim and attract them to make improper security decision [13]. Tampering includes alteration of data. Repudiation involves denying of action or lack of the ability of tracing the forbidden actions. Information disclosure involves revelation of data to unauthorized individuals. If a valid user cannot access any service then it is DoS attack. In Elevation of threats, an ordinary user

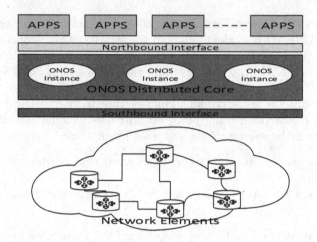

Fig. 2. ONOS architecture

can have super or privileged user access that supposed not to have [12]. STRIDE is a model-based technique for threat modeling and required Data Flow Diagram (DFD) [13]. DFD is visual diagram to describe logical model that defines data transformation in system without operation sequence. DFD defines scope of the security analysis and produce a model of underneath system. Authors in [5] used STRIDE model for ONOS controller analysis where. In our paper, we utilize threats that explored in [5] to rank risks. Furthermore, several threat modeling are available for implementation such as Trike [14], Secure UML [15], Flexible Modeling Framework (FMF) [16], and PASTA [17].

DELTA: SDN security evaluation framework DELTA developed by authors in [7] is the only available open source penetration testing tool to assess SDN security using fuzzing techniques and found known attacks as well as unknown attacks. Known attacks of DELTA targets SDN control flow based on the well-known protocol OpenFlow, dividing them into three categories such as symmetric flows, asymmetric control flows, and intra-controller control flows [7]. Numbers of SDN security hypothetical analysis work has been done in previous work (e.g. [18–20]). DELTA is the only empirical penetration framework based on SDN controller that includes ONOS for evaluation along with other SDN controllers [7]. Therefore, this is motivate us to use DELTA in our study. Additionally, DELTA also exposed unknown attacks that are not part of this study. In this study, we used only known attacks found authors in [7] and rate them according to proposed DREAD-R model.

DREAD: DREAD is a popular model to rank/priorities risks to related threats/attacks in numeric values. DREAD is acronym of Damage potential (How much is the damage if the vulnerability is exploited?), Reproducibility

(How easy is it to reproduce the attack?), Exploitability (How difficult is to exploit vulnerability?), Affected users (As a rough percentage, how many users are affected?), and Discoverability (How easy is it to find the vulnerability?) [11]. Also, Common Vulnerability Scoring System (CVSS) can be an alternative to DREAD for measuring the severity of threats [21].

3 Proposed DREAD-R Severity Assessment Modeling and Analysis

3.1 Proposed Model

This paper adds "Reputation" criterion (How much reputation of ONOS project/community is damage?) to DREAD model for measuring trust effects on ONOS community. If ONOS core is affected, that is categorized as high risk in damage potential, however, if an attacker can leak trivial information from third party application or ONOS subsystem, this can be categorized as low risk. An attacker can reproduce ONOS attack without any time window (whenever attacker want), this is categorized as high risk. On the other hand, an attacker may have knowledge of security loop hole and ONOS architecture, but it is still difficult to mount a similar attack, this is categorized as low in

Table 1. Proposed DREAD-R criteria for severity assessment

	Rating	High (3)	Medium (2)	Low (1)
D	Damage potential	Attacker can gain ONOS core access as privileged user, can change core code as well as exploit Apps and install malicious apps	Attacker can leak apps as well as ONOS core information and can disconnect underlying network elements or cause disruption of apps to controller	Attacker can have trivial information of others applications
R	Reproducibility	ONOS user can trivially exploit vulnerability without any time windows	Required few steps to exploit in particular case or in particular time	The attack cannot reproduce even with knowledge of the security hole
E	Exploitability	Attacker having knowledge little knowledge of SDN protocol or app can exploit	A skilled programmer having knowledge of ONOS could make the attack, and then repeat the steps	The attack requires an extremely skilled person and in-depth knowledge of ONOS as well as protocol, every time to exploit
A	Affected users/ Apps/modules	All apps/modules of ONOS/users, default configuration may be affected, key customers	Specific apps/modules of ONOS/users affected or underlying network element	Some of apps/users affected
D	Discoverability	Attack available publically and can easily found using search engines and is part of ONOS core features	The vulnerability is not part of ONOS core and only affect some protocol/North/South bound interface	Can be found by monitoring ONOSE core and apps
R	Reputation	Having Impact on repute of ONOS project and loss of user's and community trust	Having Impact on users trust but not all community	Having no impact on trust of user or ONOS community

term of "Reproducibility". Reputation is widely used among research community [22,23]. However, "Reputation" parameter used in our work is classified as the impact on ONOS user and community trust, which could damage ONOS reputation. Details of all DREAD-R threats categorization correspondence to ONOS summarized in Table 1.

3.2   Result Analysis

A simple scheme of threat rating as high (3), medium (2), and low (1) used as shown in Table 2. Threat ranked on a scale of 1 to 3 where higher number shows higher threat level. After obtaining ratings of individual threat, a sum of DREAD-R presented at the end. Over all rank determined by dividing threats into three categories. Rating of 0–6 as trivial (can be fixed in next release or later), 7–12 as near critical (n-critical) (need to be fixed in next release or earlier) and 13–18 as critical (need to be fixed as early as possible) as shown in Table 2.

Table 2. Severity ranking based on the DREAD-R

Threat studies	Threat detail		D	R	E	A	D	R	Total	Severity
Ramachandra/ STRIDE [5]	Component	Threats								
	South bound interface	Denial of service	2	2	2	2	2	2	12	n-critical
	Process controller core	Denial of service	3	2	2	3	3	3	16	critical
	Switches and north bound applications	Spoofing	1	2	1	1	1	0	6	trivial
DELTA [7]	Flow type	Attacks								
	Symmetric flows	Control message manipulation	3	3	1	3	2	2	14	critical
	Asymmetric	Control message drop	3	2	1	2	2	2	12	n-critical
	Flows	Control message infinite loop	3	2	1	3	2	2	13	critical
	Intra-controller control flows	PACKET IN flooding	1	2	2	1	2	1	9	n-critical
		Flow rule flooding	2	2	1	1	2	1	9	n-critical
		Flow rule modification	2	2	1	2	2	1	10	n-critical
		Switch firmware misuse	2	2	1	2	2	1	10	n-critical
		Flow table clearance	2	2	1	2	2	1	10	n-critical
		Eavesdrop	1	2	1	1	1	0	6	trivial
		Man-in-the-middle	3	2	1	3	2	2	13	critical
		Internal storage misuse	3	3	1	3	3	3	16	critical
		Application eviction	2	2	1	2	3	2	12	n-critical
	Non flow operations	System command execution	3	3	2	3	3	3	17	critical
		Memory exhaustion	2	2	1	3	2	2	12	n-critical
		CPU exhaustion	2	2	1	3	2	2	12	n-critical

Denial of Service (DoS) attack through ONOS southbound or data plane rated as critical. DoS attack can disrupt network element communication to ONOS core. ONOS core can be accessed by any of interface, this needs to be fixed in the next release or as early as possible. Spoofing attack on switches or application to leak information from them categorized as trivial and need to be fixed in the next release or later. Details of threats and attacks categorized are summarized in Table 2.

For severity assessment, 6 threats and attacks are critical and 5 out of 6 are using control plane vulnerabilities to exploit. Attacks affecting northbound and southbound interfaces/applications are trivial or near critical. By examining Table 2, the results confirm the hypothesis H1 that control plane vulnerabilities are more severe than others. However, adding "Reputation" to DREAD model for ONOS does not yield different result. Therefore, hypothesis H2 does not validated. Adding reputation to other systems/apps may have different result.

4 Conclusion and Future Work

This paper assess the vulnerabilities severity of ONOS. We have used DREAD model to rate attacks found by DELTA Security framework and previous study using STRIDE threat model. We have assessed vulnerabilities and found that control plane vulnerabilities are severe and need to be patched on priority. Moreover, we have enhanced DREAD model by using an extra parameter "Reputation" named as DREAD-R. We realized that adding the "Reputation" to DREAD model does not yield different result using on ONOS. We will continue the assessment of SDN controllers such as ONOS. This can help the developers and user of ONOS to understand the threats and attacks. Mitigation techniques for vulnerabilities are recommended as future work.

Acknowledgment. This work was partly supported by Institute for Information & Communications Technology Promotion (IITP) grant funded by the Korea government (MIST) [2015-0-00533, Development of TII (Trusted Information Infrastructure) S/W Framework for Realizing Trustworthy IoT Eco-system], and partly supported by BK 21 plus program.

References

1. Nunes, B.A.A., Mendonca, M., Nguyen, X.N., Obraczka, K., Turletti, T.: A survey of software-defined networking: past, present, and future of programmable networks. IEEE Commun. Surv. Tutor. **16**(3), 1617–1634 (2014)
2. Kreutz, D., Ramos, F.M., Verissimo, P.E., Rothenberg, C.E., Azodolmolky, S., Uhlig, S.: Software-defined networking: a comprehensive survey. Proc. IEEE **103**(1), 14–76 (2015)
3. Shin, M.-K., Nam, K.-H., Kim, H.-J.: Software-defined networking (SDN): a reference architecture and open APIs. In: 2012 International Conference on ICT Convergence (ICTC), pp. 360–361. IEEE (2012)
4. SDN Architecture. Technical report, Open Networking Foundation (2014)
5. Arbettu, R.K., Khondoker, R., Bayarou, K., Weber, F.: Security analysis of Open-Daylight, ONOS, Rosemary and Ryu SDN controllers. In: 2016 17th International Telecommunications Network Strategy and Planning Symposium (Networks), pp. 37–44. IEEE (2016)

6. Yan, Q., Yu, F.R., Gong, Q., Li, J.: Software-defined networking (SDN) and distributed denial of service (DDoS) attacks in cloud computing environments: a survey, some research issues, and challenges. IEEE Commun. Surv. Tutor. **18**(1), 602–622 (2016)

7. Lee, S., Yoon, C., Lee, C., Shin, S., Yegneswaran, V., Porras, P.: Delta: a security assessment framework for software-defined networks. In: Proceedings of NDSS, vol. 17 (2017)

8. Hong, S., Xu, L., Wang, H., Gu, G.: Poisoning network visibility in software-defined networks: new attacks and countermeasures. In: NDSS (2015)

9. Benton, K., Camp, L.J., Small, C.: Openflow vulnerability assessment. In: Proceedings of the Second ACM SIGCOMM Workshop on Hot Topics in Software Defined Networking, pp. 151–152. ACM (2013)

10. Berde, P., Gerola, M., Hart, J., Higuchi, Y., Kobayashi, M., Koide, T., Lantz, B., O'Connor, B., Radoslavov, P., Snow, W., et al.: ONOS: towards an open, distributed SDN OS. In: Proceedings of the Third Workshop on Hot Topics in Software Defined Networking, pp. 1–6. ACM (2014)

11. Meier, J.D., Mackman, A., Dunner, M., Vasireddy, S., Escamilla, R., Murukan, A.: Improving Web Application Security: Threats and Countermeasures. Microsoft Corporation (2003)

12. Adam Shostack: Threat Modeling: Designing for Security. Wiley (2014)

13. Thompson, D.R., Di, J., Sunkara, H., Thompson, C.: Categorizing RFID privacy threats with stride. In: Proceedings ACMs Symposium on Usable Privacy and Security held at CMU (2006)

14. Saitta, P., Larcom, B., Eddington, M.: Trike v. 1 methodology document [draft] (2005). http://dymaxion.org/trike/Trike_v1_Methodology_Documentdraft.pdf

15. Jürjens, J.: UMLsec: extending UML for secure systems development. In: Jézéquel, J.-M., Hussmann, H., Cook, S. (eds.) UML 2002. LNCS, vol. 2460, pp. 412–425. Springer, Heidelberg (2002). doi:10.1007/3-540-45800-X_32

16. Gilliam, D.P., Powell, J.D.: Integrating a flexible modeling framework (FMF) with the network security assessment instrument to reduce software security risk. In: Proceedings of Eleventh IEEE International Workshops on Enabling Technologies: Infrastructure for Collaborative Enterprises, WET ICE 2002, pp. 153–158. IEEE (2002)

17. UcedaVelez, T., Morana, M.M.: Risk Centric Threat Modeling: Process for Attack Simulation and Threat Analysis. Wiley, Hoboken (2015)

18. Schehlmann, L., Abt, S., Baier, H.: Blessing or curse? Revisiting security aspects of software-defined networking. In: 2014 10th International Conference on Network and Service Management (CNSM), pp. 382–387. IEEE (2014)

19. Chen, M., Qian, Y., Mao, S., Tang, W., Yang, X.: Software-defined mobile networks security. Mob. Netw. Appl. **21**(5), 729–743 (2016)

20. Shin, S., Yegneswaran, V., Porras, P., Gu, G.: Avant-guard: scalable and vigilant switch flow management in software-defined networks. In: Proceedings of the 2013 ACM SIGSAC Conference on Computer & Communications Security, pp. 413–424. ACM (2013)

21. FIRST. Common Vulnerability Scoring System v3.0: Specification Document

22. Selcuk, A.A., Uzun, E., Pariente, M.R.: A reputation-based trust management system for P2P networks. In: IEEE International Symposium on Cluster Computing and the Grid, CCGrid 2004, pp. 251–258. IEEE (2004)

23. Anantvalee, T., Wu, J.: Reputation-based system for encouraging the cooperation of nodes in mobile ad hoc networks. In: IEEE International Conference on Communications, ICC 2007, pp. 3383–3388. IEEE (2007)

Formal Specifications and Analysis of an Agent-Based Model for Cognitive Aspects of Fear of Crime

Azizi Ab Aziz[(✉)], Ahmad Hanis Mohd Shabli,
and Hayder M.A. Ghanimi

Human-Centred Computing Research Lab School of Computing,
Cognitive Artefacts Group, Universiti Utara Malaysia,
06010 Sintok, Kedah, Malaysia
{aziziaziz,ahmadhanis}@uum.edu.my, hayder.
alghanami@gmail.com

Abstract. This paper presents a cognitive agent model of fear of crime. The proposed model takes personality, environment, and perception of several events as input and calculates internal factors related to cognitive fear of crime, such as the belief about safety, community trust and likelihood of crime activities, and how they affect individual fear of crime. Simulation results suggest that community level of fear of crime and trust may emerge as the outcome of individuals' reaction towards perception of crime activities related to their exogenous properties. In addition, a formal approach is put forward to evaluate the behaviours of the proposed model by means of formal techniques namely; mathematical analysis, parameter evaluation, and automated logical verification. The first and second approaches analyse the equilibria conditions and follow by automatically checking a number of expected properties as depicted in the literature. One of the major contributions of this model is the possibility that an analytical engine could be further developed to support community wellbeing.

Keywords: Agent-based modeling · Cognitive analysis of fear of crime · Crime analytics · Decision support systems

1 Introduction

The incidence and risk of domestic crime has become linked with numerous perceived problems of social order of a neighbourhood. This will invoke unintentional fear of crime among residents and thus will harm their wellbeing and daily activities. The level or extent of the fear of crime depends on various factors like past experiences, belief about the environment, and many more [1, 2]. Often, individuals who are afraid of domestic crime expect the authorities to help them, but sometimes the authorities might not always be in a position to stop or prevent crime at that particular time due to lack of staff or mobile assets [1, 3]. As it common to acknowledge that to some extent, the fear of crime is normal and even essential for safety and well-being. However, when it becomes extreme, things become difficult for the communities. For example, one might

© Springer International Publishing AG 2017
S. Phon-Amnuaisuk et al. (Eds.): MIWAI 2017, LNAI 10607, pp. 331–345, 2017.
https://doi.org/10.1007/978-3-319-69456-6_28

becoming social phobic such as refuse to step out of their home after dark or have to frequently recheck their safety measurements and devices in their home [4].

Thus, it leads to constant fatigue as it causes them to believe that they need to be vigilant all the time [2, 5]. This paper explores the implementation of an agent-based modeling to simulate cognitive fear of individuals (local properties) and community (global emergence) during intense crime activities within the neighbourhood. By using this approach, the individual-level behaviours can be viewed as a collection of virtual agents and placed in a simulated environment that allows them to "travel" through space and time, behaving as they would do in the real world [6, 7]. This paper is organized as follows. Section 2 discusses a summary from the underlying concepts of cognitive fear of crime. In Sect. 3 the agent-based model is presented, and Sect. 4 discusses the results of the generated simulation trace. Section 5 presents a number of mathematical analysis using equilibria analysis approach. Later, Sects. 6 and 7 discusses some parameter analysis and temporal logic evaluation between a set of generated traces and literature. Finally, Sect. 8 is a concluding discussion about the approach.

2 Underlying Concepts

Cognitive aspects of fear of crime is related to the perceptions of the risk of personal victimization. For example, the cognitive side of fear of crime often includes public perceptions of the likelihood of becoming victims, public senses of control over the crime, or even estimations of the seriousness of the consequences of crime [2, 4]. People who feel vulnerable to crime activities (*crime displacements*) are likely to feel that they are likely to be targeted by criminals and are unable to control the possibility and that the consequences would be especially severe [4, 5]. Additionally, these different components of risk perception may interact; the impact of perceived likelihood on subsequent emotional response (feeling un safety) is likely to be especially strong among those who feel that consequences are high and self-efficacy is low [1, 8, 9]. In addition, people with a high *belief about safety*, aware about the *proactive policing* and low in neuroticism tend to have better *thought control* processes, less sensitive towards fear, and *trust the authority* more than those who were not [10]. For example, individuals with a high neuroticism level has difficulty accepting the prospect of the uncertain outcome (due to low trust in authority, thought control, and highly sensitive towards perception about crime) [1, 9]. In some cases, they exhibit a general intolerance of uncertainty and prefer structured and *proactive policing* even with a low risk area of crime [11].

Moreover, the *sensitivity to crime risk* can be used to anticipate the influence of likelihood on fear and it is moderated by perceptions of seriousness of the given perceived type of crime [12, 13]. Also, when people judged crime to be serious in its effect, it will stimulate high levels of personal *fear of crime*. Thus, coupled with the low *perceptions in civilities* within the neighbourhood (that later influences *perceived social cohesion*), it will reduce individual belief or trust in authorities and community trust [11, 14]. In the future, it will invoke the high sensitivity to a given level of *perceive likelihood of crime*. This is consistent with the risk sensitivity model suggests that once individuals associate a risk with high personal consequences and low personal thought control, only a relatively small level of perceived likelihood of crime is needed to evoke strong emotional response towards cognitive fear of crime [2, 5, 8, 11]. Similarly, perceived likelihood of crime may amplify the link between precursors of susceptibility (personality, belief about safety) and expressed perception (feeling of unsafety, likelihood of crime, and fear of crime) [11, 12].

3   Cognitive Agent-Based Modeling

In this section, a cognitive inspired agent-based model is presented that simulates the dynamics of fear of crime is discussed. In agent-based modelling, the fear of crime concept is modelled as a collection of autonomous computational entities called agents. Each agent individually evaluates its situation and makes decisions on the basis of a set of basic formal representations. At the *primitive level*, an agent-based model consists of a set of agents and the relationships between them. For example, the decisions of individuals and the underlying and cognitive aspects are addressed. From this level, a simple agent-based model can create complex behaviour patterns about the dynamics of the real-world condition that it emulates. At the level of the multi-agent system (*global*), the impact of such decisions on the community/society as a whole are addressed. Therefore, at this stage, these computational cognitive agents may be capable of evolving, allowing unanticipated behaviours to emerge. In our work, these cognitive agents adopt selected elements from previously developed conceptual models, particularly in [1, 12, 14]. For a graphical overview of the model, see Fig. 1 and for its abbreviations, see Table 1. The graphical overview incorporates several states (circles) and their dynamics as processes (arrows).

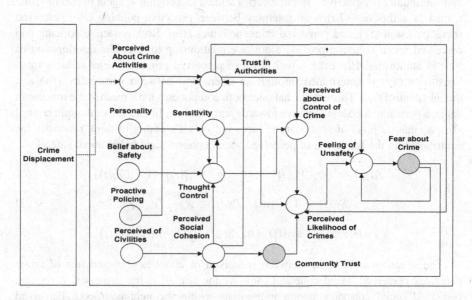

Fig. 1. Graphical representation of a cognitive agent model of fear of crime.

Table 1 provides an overview of the formalized concepts and its meaning (as depicted in Fig. 1).

Table 1. Nomenclatures of related concepts

Concept	Formalization
Perceived about crime activities	Ca
Personality	Py
Belief about safety	Bs
Proactive policing	Pl
Perceived of civilities	Pc
Trust in authorities	Ta
Sensitivity	Sy
Thought control	Tc
Perceived social cohesion	Sc
Perceived on control of crime	Cm
Feeling of unsafety	Us
Perceived likelihood of crime	Lc
Community trust	Cr
Fear about crime	Fc
Perceived about crime activities	Ca

This section explains the details of the model. The implemented relations between different concepts are based on earlier findings in literature on cognitive fear of crime and community perspectives. In the theories related to a cognitive agent of fear of crime i, trust in authorities (Ta) is an interplay between proactive policing (Pl), perceived social cohesion (Sc), and perceived crime activities (Ca). Both proactive policing and perceived social cohesion provide a positive relationship towards the development of trust in authorities. However, a high-level of perceived crime activities reduces trust. Sensitivity (Sy) is determined through an interaction between personality (Py) and thought control (Tc). This entails that once both components have reached the maximum value, a person will be less sensitive towards fear of crime. In the case of thought control (Tc), an intense level of sensitivity reduces individual's ability to think rationally (as contributed by the formation of perceived social cohesion and belief about safety).

$$Ta_i(t) = (\varphi_a . Pl_i, (t) + (1 - \varphi_a) . Sc_i(t)) . (1 - Ca_i(t)) \tag{1}$$

$$Sy_i(t) = 1 - (w_{sy1} . Py_i(t) + w_{sy2} . Tc_i(t)) \tag{2}$$

$$Tc_i(t) = (1 - Sy_i(t)) . (\eta_c . Sc_i(t) + (1 - \eta_c) . Bs_i(t)) \tag{3}$$

The negative relationship between perceived of civilities (Pc) and fear of crime generates perceived social cohesion (Sc). As the fear of crime increases, it reduces perceived social cohesion among individuals within the neighbourhood. Perceived about control of crime (Cm) is computed through a proportional contribution between trust in authorities and thought control. Interactions between sensitivity, trust in authorities, perceived on control of crime, and community trust (Cr) are important to control individual's perceived likelihood of crimes (Lc). Later, the feeling of unsafety (Us) is determined by the intensity of trust in authorities, perceived likelihood of crime and fear of crime. In this equation, total trust in authorities minimizes any possibilities of being sceptical about individual's thought of neighbourhood safety.

$$Sc_i(t) = Pc_i(t) \cdot (1 - Fc_i(t)) \tag{4}$$

$$Cm_i(t) = \psi_c \cdot Ta_i(t) + (1 - \psi_c) \cdot Tc_i(t) \tag{5}$$

$$Lc_i(t) = Sy_i(t) \cdot (1 - (w_{lc1} \cdot Ta_i(t) + w_{lc2} \cdot Cm_i(t) + w_{lc3} \cdot Cr_i(t))) \tag{6}$$

$$Us_i(t) = (1 - Ta_i(t)) \cdot (\phi_u \cdot Lc_i(t) + (1 - \phi_u) \cdot Fc_i(t)) \tag{7}$$

Those aforementioned equations use φ_a η_c, ψ_c, ϕ_u as proportional contributions, and w_{sy1}, w_{sy2}, w_{sy3}, w_{lc1}, w_{lc2}, w_{lc3} as weightage factors. Next, community trust (Cr) is primarily contributed the accumulation perception about social cohesion while the accumulated feeling about unsafety produces fear of crime (Fc).

$$Cr_i(t + \delta t) = Cr_i(t) + \beta_C \cdot [Sc_i(t) - Cr_i(t)] \cdot (1 - Cr_i(t)) \cdot Cr_i(t) \cdot \delta t \tag{8}$$

$$Fc_i(t + \delta t) = Fc_i(t) + \tau_C \cdot [(Us_i(t) - Fc_i(t)) - \lambda_{dc}] \cdot (1 - Fc_i(t)) \cdot Fc_i(t) \cdot \delta t \tag{9}$$

Note that the change process is measured in a time interval between $t + \delta t$ and In addition to all this, the rate of change for all temporal specifications are determined by flexibility rates β_C, and τ_C, while λ_{dc} represents a decay rate throughout time. Using all defined formulas, a simulator was developed for experimentation purposes; specifically to explore interesting patterns and traces that explain the behaviour of the cognitive agent model related to cognitive fear of crime. A collection of agents within an individual layer will interact to produce a global effect at the community layer (as in Fig. 2).

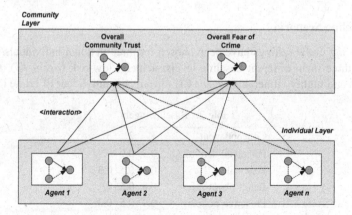

Fig. 2. Interaction between individual and community layers.

The community layer represents an overall perspective towards community trust (Ar) and community fear of crime (Ac). These two concepts are computed using an averaging approach.

$$Ar(t) = \frac{\sum_{i=1}^{n} Cr_i}{n} \tag{10}$$

$$Ac(t) = \frac{\sum_{i=1}^{n} Fc_i}{n} \tag{11}$$

where n represents the total number of agents and $n > 0$.

4 Analysis by Simulation Results

In this section some simulation results of cognitive fear of crime are discussed, first for the baseline cognitive agent settings, and next for the multiple agents setting that generates more variants of emergence behaviours (for larger agents/individuals). These agents are deterministic in itself (every time a simulation with specific settings is run, the outcome will be the same). The simulation runs are based on partially-defined stochastic settings, as intended to observe related agents' output. It is worth noting that the agent perceptions (exogenous factors) about crime activities are static in the simulations. However, the rest of the concepts for each agent and that of the group are dynamic.

For every time-step, the temporal values are updated with the current perceptions of that related time-point. Indirectly, the past is presented in every point in time, due to the updating mechanism happens dynamically. For example, the community trust value of the previous time-step is partially taken into account into the next point in time. This process repeats every time-step (duration of the scenario is 500 time points), making the past perception of the agent indirectly present in the current percept. In addition, these simulation processes used the following parameters settings; $t_{max} = 500$, $roman\delta t = 0.3$, temporal parameters $(\beta_c, \tau_c) = 0.3$, proportional contributions $(\varphi_a, \eta_c, \psi_c, \phi_u) = 0.5$, and weightage factors $(w_{sy1}, w_{sy2}, w_{sy3}, w_{lc1}, w_{lc2}, w_{lc3}) \approx 0.33$, and a decay rate $(\lambda_{dc}) = 0.0001$.

4.1 Baseline Scenario

The following initial settings have been chosen for three fictional individuals/agents to represent three main different baseline levels, namely; low-risk (*agent #1*), moderate (*agent #2*) and highly vulnerable (*agent #3*) towards cognitive fear of crime (Table 2).

Table 2. Baseline agent

Concept\agent	1	2	3
Perceived activities	0.9	0.9	0.9
Personality	0.9	0.5	0.3
Belief about safety	0.8	0.5	0.1
Proactive policing	0.9	0.5	0.2
Perceived of civilities	0.9	0.4	0.2

As can be seen in Fig. 3, the initial settings mentioned earlier lead to the following characteristics in the various baseline conditions related to the individual fear (fear of crime), trust towards community, perceived social cohesion, and perceived likelihood of crime.

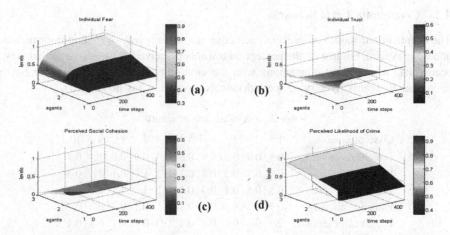

Fig. 3. Simulation results (for $n = 3$) (a) fear of crime, (b) trust, (c) social cohesion, and (d) likelihood of crime

As shown in Fig. 3(a) (individual layer), from the beginning of the simulation, both agents (#2 and #3) show the sharp increment of fear of crime levels. The same patterns also could be observed in perceived likelihood of crime. However, the agent #1 shows the opposite pattern, as it increases just a little bit due to the intense perceived crime events. An agent #1 also scores high results in trust and perceived social cohesion (as shown in Fig. 3(b) and (c)). The overall results show that agents with a less emotional personality and positive perception towards their community are unlikely to develop a high level of fear of crime. It is consistent with the findings in [10, 12].

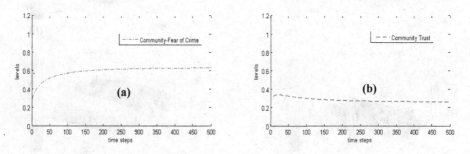

Fig. 4. Simulation results for $n = 3$ agents as a baseline level (a) fear of crime and (b) trust

In addition, from Fig. 3(d), although not directly visible in the graph, high individual fear, low trust and social cohesion causes an increase in of perceived likelihood of crime. As a result, at the community layer (as depicted in Fig. 4(a) and (b)), this close community experiences a quite high fear of crime and low community trust [9, 12]. Eventually, all generated patterns stabilise as expected after the mathematical analysis of the model.

4.2 Community Level Scenario

The agents in our model differ from each other not in their way of getting information about the system, but just on the perception towards perceived crime activities that they accumulate during their interactions with the environment. In this section, we have simulated 10 agents by varying the individuals' properties (as in Table 3).

Table 3. Extended size of agents

Concept\agent	1	2	3	4	5	6	7	8	9	10
Perceived activities	0.9	0.9	0.9	0.9	0.8	0.9	0.9	0.8	1	0.7
Personality	0.9	0.5	0.3	0.8	0.2	0.2	1	0.1	1	0.4
Belief about safety	0.8	0.5	0.1	0.9	0.1	0.1	1	0.1	0.8	0.3
Proactive policing	0.9	0.5	0.2	0.1	0.1	0.1	0.1	0.1	0	0
Perceived of civilities	0.9	0.4	0.2	0.8	0.1	0	0.1	0.1	0.1	0.4

Using the formulas to determine the individual cognitive fear of crime, some interesting patterns on human perception (bigger population) towards likelihood of crime and community level of trust and fear have been explored. The results of the simulations are shown in Figs. 5 and 6. Figure 5 displays the variations of simulation results with respect to the fear of crime, trust, social cohesion, and perceived likelihood of crime. Figure 6 displays the overall community level of fear of crime and trust.

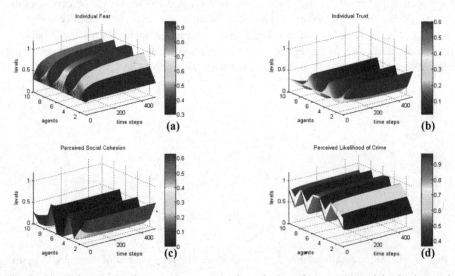

Fig. 5. Simulation results (for $n = 10$ agents) (a) fear of crime, (b) trust, (c) social cohesion, and (d) likelihood of crime

In addition, although not directly visible in the graph, the combination of high proactive policing, belief about safety, positive personal and perceived civilities among individuals within the neighbourhood causes an increase in of the individual stress skills that later reduces perceived likelihood of crime [9–11].

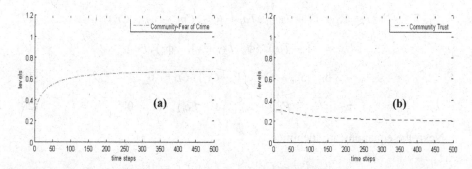

Fig. 6. Simulation results for $n = 10$ agents for the community-level (a) fear of crime and (b) trust

What stands out in this graph (Fig. 6) is the general opposite pattern of community level fear of crime and trust. These results suggest that fear of crime among community during is at the peak when all individuals within that neighbourhood are started to have negative feelings about safety, social cohesion, authority, and policing activities at their neighbourhood. Moreover, these findings are in line with those of previous studies as in [1, 8, 12]. As can be seen in all figures, perceived crime activities (through reports or social media channels) causes less perception of fear of crime if an individual perceives positive aspects in law enforcement, commitment from the community and precaution measurements [3, 11].

5 Mathematical Evaluation

In this section, the possible equilibria points are analyzed. A significant milestone in agent-based modelling is the successful representation of the behaviour of the "real" dynamical system by a model. Thus the temporal behaviour of variables is determined by the parameters of the models such as the equations describing the local properties and the parameters of those equations. One important assumption should be made; all exogenous variables are having a constant value. Assuming all parameters are non-zero, this leads to the following equations where an equilibrium state is characterized by:

$$Ta_i = (\varphi_a \cdot Pl_i + (1 - \varphi_a) \cdot Sc_i \cdot (1 - Ca_i) \tag{12}$$

$$Sy_i = 1 - (w_{sy1} \cdot Py_i + w_{sy2} \cdot Tc_i) \tag{13}$$

$$Tc_i = (1 - Sy_i) . \eta_c . Sc_i + (1 - \eta_c) . Bs_i) \tag{14}$$

$$Sc_i = Pc_i . (1 - Fc_i) \tag{15}$$

$$Cm_i = \psi_c . Ta_i + (1 - \psi_c) . Tc_i \tag{16}$$

$$Lc_i = Sy_i . (1 - (w_{lc1} . Ta_i + w_{lc2} . Cm_i + w_{lc3} . Cr_i)) \tag{17}$$

$$Us_i = (1 - Ta_i) . (\phi_u . Lc_i + (1 - \phi_u) . Fc_i) \tag{18}$$

$$\beta_C . [Sc_i - Cr_i] . (1 - Cr_i) . Cr_i = 0 \tag{19}$$

$$\tau_C . [(Us_i - Fc_i) - \lambda_{dc}] . (1 - Fc_i) . Fc_i = 0 \tag{20}$$

Next, the equations are identified,

$$\beta_C . [Sc_i - Cr_i] . (1 - Cr_i) . Cr_i = 0$$

$$\tau_C . [(Us_i - Fc_i) - \lambda_{dc}] . (1 - Fc_i) . Fc_i = 0$$

Assuming adaptation rates are equal to 1 and a decay rate λ_{dc} is zero, therefore, these are equivalent to,

$$(Sc_i = Cr_i) \vee (Cr_i = 1) \vee (Cr_i = 0) \vee (Us_i = Fc_i) \vee (Fc_i = 1) \vee (Fc_i = 0)$$

Hence, a first conclusion can be obtained where the stability points can only occur when $Sc_i = Cr_i$, or $Cr_i = 1$, or $Cr_i = 0$ (as in Eq. (19)). Thus, if these three conditions were combined, then a new set of relationship as in (A ∨ B ∨ C) ∧ (D ∨ E ∨ F) expression can be formed:

$$(Sc_i = Cr_i \vee Cr_i = 1 \vee Cr_i = 0) \wedge (Us_i = Fc_i \vee Fc_i = 1 \vee Fc_i = 0)$$

This expression can be elaborated using *Law of Distributivity* as (A ∧ D) ∨ (A ∧ E) ∨ (A ∧ F) ∨, …, ∨ (C ∧ F) and this will result:

$$(Sc_i = Cr_i \wedge Us_i = Fc_i) \vee (Sc_i = Cr_i \wedge Fc_i = 1) \vee$$
$$(Sc_i = Cr_i \wedge Fc_i = 0) \vee \dots (Cr_i = 0 \wedge Fc_i = 0) \tag{21}$$

Equation (21) later provides nine possible combinations of equilibria points to be further analyzed. In this paper, only three equilibria cases are discussed.

Case #1: $Sc_i = Cr_i \wedge Fc_i = 1$
In this case, from Eq. (12), this case is equivalent to:

$$Ta_i = (\varphi_a . Pl_i + (1 - \varphi_a) . Cr_i . (1 - Ca_i)$$

If $\varphi_a = 0.5$, therefore, $Ca_i = [Pc_i/Cr_i - Ta_i/(0.5Cr_i)] + 1$
Similarly, from Eq. (14), it follows.

$$Tc_i = (1 - Sy_i) . \eta_c . Cr_i + (1 - \eta_c) . Bs_i)$$

Equation (15) provides a set of equilibrium points through, $Sc_i = 0$.

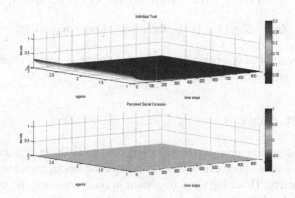

Fig. 7. The visual representation of an individual trust when $Sc_i \to 0$

This condition also reduces the overall individual perception about community trust throughout time as $Sc_i \to 0$, at later time points, $Cr_i \to 0$ (as shown in Fig. 7). In addition, from Eq. (18), the equilibria can be found,

$$Us_i = (1 - Ta_i) . (\phi_u . Lc_i + (1 - \phi_u))$$

Assuming $\phi_u = 1$ then $Ta_i = 1 + (Us_i/Lc_i)$ and Lc_i is nonzero.

Case #2: $Cr_i = 1 \wedge Fc_i = 0$
Consider Eq. (17), therefore this is equivalent to:

$$Lc_i = Sy_i . (1 - (w_{lc1} . (\varphi_a . Pl_i + (1 - \varphi_a) . Sc_i . (1 - Ca_i) + w_{lc2} . \psi_c . Ta_i$$
$$+ (1 - \psi_c) . Tc_i + w_{lc3}))$$

Taking into consideration of Eq. (15) provides,
$$Sc_i = Pc_i$$
From Eq. (18), it follows that this is equivalent to:
$$Us_i = (1 - Ta_i) . \phi_u . Lc_i \text{ and assuming } \phi_u \text{ is nonzero,}$$

$$Us_i = (1 - (\varphi_a . Pl_i + (1 - \varphi_a) . Sc_i . (1 - Ca_i)) . Sy_i . (1 - (w_{lc1} . Ta_i$$
$$+ w_{lc2} . Cm_i + w_{lc3} . Cr_i))$$

Case #3: $Sc_i = Cr_i \wedge Us_i = Fc_i$

In this case, Eqs. (12), (14), (15), and (17) will provide:

$$Ta_i = (\varphi_a . Pl_i + (1 - \varphi_a) . Cr_i . (1 - Ca_i)$$

$$Tc_i = \left(1 - \left(1 - \left(w_{sy1} . Bs_i + w_{sy2} . Tc_i\right)\right)\right) . \eta_c . Cr_i + (1 - \eta_c) . Bs_i)$$

$$Sc_i = Pc_i . (1 - ((1 - Ta_i) . (\phi_u . Lc_i + (1 - \phi_u) . Fc_i)))$$

$$Lc_i = Sy_i . (1 - (w_{lc1} . Ta_i + w_{lc2} . Cm_i + w_{lc3} . Sc_i))$$

The following part of this paper moves on to describe in greater detail of parameter and automated verification analysis.

6   Parameter Analysis

In our paper, the parameter analysis was conducted to evaluate possible variation of parameter/input-output space exploration to explain the model response to changes in the input parameters. This analysis is important in order to assess the extent to which results depend on specific parameter values. Accordingly, we have executed the model changing one parameter each time, while keeping all the others stable. Due to the excessive number of possible combinations, this paper only present a selection of the most significant findings.

Analysis #1: The Effect of Temporal Parameter, τ_C

For this analysis, we increased the contribution temporal parameter τ_C from 0.2 to 0.8 with time-steps of 1000 (at $\delta t = 0.3$) for all agents. Clearly, the experiments have a very similar outcome, with the only difference being gradual changes (increasing/decreasing).

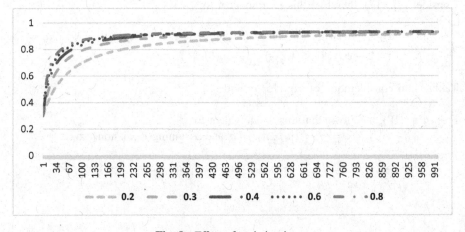

Fig. 8. Effect of variation in γ_C

The results are very interesting in light of our analysis. It shows the temporal parameter can be fine tune to represent variation within different individuals. This pattern can be visualized in Fig. 8.

Analysis #2: The Effect of Proportional Parameter ψ_c

The proportional parameter ψ_c is the parameter of the *perceived on control of crime*, related to *trust on authorities* and *thought control*. We increased from 0.1 to 0.5 by intervals of 100 (at $\delta t = 0.3$). By increasing ψ_c, the perceived on control of crime decreases gradually (see Fig. 9).

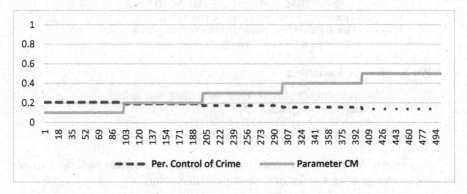

Fig. 9. Effect of different ψ_c values

However, as $\psi_c \rightarrow 1$, there is no significant difference of the simulated values (as the change factor is getting smaller than the previous value).

7 Automated Logical Verification

In order to verify whether the model is capable to generate traces that adherence to related cognitive fear of crime literatures, a set of dynamic properties have been identified from related literatures. For the model of the cognitive fear of crime, a number of such dynamic properties have been formalized in the Temporal Trace Language (TTL) [15]. TTL is built on atoms referring to time stamps t, states of the world *state*, and simulation traces γ. This relationship can be formalized as a *state* $(\gamma, t, output(R))| = p$. This representation means that state property p is true at the output of role R in the state of trace γ at time point t.

VP1: Low Perceived Social Cohesion Increases Perception of Likelihood of Crime

VP1 ≡ ∀γ. TRACE, ∀t1, t2:TIME, ∀R1,R2,D1,D2:REAL
[state(γ,t1)|= has_value(social_cohesion, R1) &
state(γ,t2) |= has_value(social_cohesion, R2) &
state(γ,t1)|= has_value(likelihood_crime, D1) &
state(γ,t2)|= has_value(likelihood_crime, D2) &
t1 < t2 & R2 ≤ R1] ⇒ D2 ≥ D1

VP2: High Fear of Crime Reduces Community Trust

VP2≡ ∀γ.TRACE, ∀t1, t2:TIME ∀M1, M2, D:REAL
[state(γ, t1)|= has_value(fear_crime, M1) &
state(γ, t2)|= has_value(community_trust, M2) &
M1 ≥ 0.8 & t2= t1+D] ⇒ M2 ≤ 0.3

VP3: Stability of Variable _x_

VP3≡ ∀γ. TRACE, ∀t1, t2: TIME, tb, te :TIME, ∀J1,J2:REAL
[state(γ,t1)|= has_value(x, J1) &
state(γ,t2) |= has_value(x, J2) &
tb < t1 < te & tb < t2 < te] ⇒ J1 − α ≤ J2 ≤ J1 + α

This property can be used to verify in which situations a certain variable does not fluctuate or change after a series of time-steps (stable point).

VP4: Monotonic Decrease of Variable x

VP4≡ ∀γ. TRACE, ∀t1, t2: TIME, tb, te:TIME, ∀J1,J2:REAL
[state(γ,t1)|= has_value(x, J1) &
state(γ,t2) |= has_value(x, J2) &
tb ≤ t1 ≤ te & tb ≤ t2 ≤ te & t1 < t2 ⇒ J1 ≥ J2

Property VP4 can be used to evaluate whether a variable decreases monotonically over a certain interval.

8   Conclusion

In this paper we present a cognitive agent-based model of fear of crime based on related theories, to analyse the potentially interaction between individuals and community during the event of crime. Using numerical analysis programing tool, a large number of simulation experiments under different parameter settings have been performed. The resulting simulation traces have been formally analysed by means of the verification of formal properties and were shown to behave as expected. Moreover, by a mathematical analysis the equilibria of the model have been determined, and a number of expected properties of the model have been verified to guarantee internal validity. For the next step, we aim to develop a community-aware analytics software agent that is able to monitor the overall cognitive fear of crime among residents within the neighbourhood in a timely and knowledgeable manner. Using this, it would be possible to give more detailed advices and prevention measurement based on the predicted effect of the cognitive of fear of crime.

Acknowledgements. This research was supported by the UUM-Internal Research Grant [S/O 13615].

References

1. Ferraro, K.F., Grange, R.L.: The measurement of fear of crime. Sociol. Inq. **57**, 70–97 (1987)
2. Bursik Jr., R.J., Grasmick, H.G.: Neighborhoods and Crime: The Dimensions of Effective Community Control. Lexington Books, Lexington (1993)
3. McGrath, S.A., Chananie-Hill, S.: Individual-level predictors of perceived safety: data from an international sample. Sociol. Focus **44**(3), 231–254 (2011)
4. LaGrange, R.L., Ferraro, K.F., Supancic, M.: Perceived risk and fear of crime: role of social and physical incivilities. J. Res. Crime Delinq. **29**(3), 311–334 (1992)
5. Zhao, J.S., Lawton, B., Longmire, D.: An examination of the micro-level crime-fear of crime link. Crime Delinq. **61**, 19–44 (2015)
6. Jackson, J.C.: Agent-Based Modeling: A Guide for Social Psychologists. Soc. Psychol. Pers. Sci. (2016)
7. Chatterjee, R.K., Sharma, M., Sarkar, A.: Modeling of multi agent system from analysis to design. Int. J. Softw. Eng. Appl. **10**(12), 149–168 (2016)
8. Braga, A.A.: Hot spots policing: theoretical perspectives, scientific evidence, and proper implementation. In: Teasdale, B., Bradley, M.S. (eds.) Preventing Crime and Violence. APS, pp. 269–279. Springer, Cham (2017). doi:10.1007/978-3-319-44124-5_23
9. Chadee, D., Ali, S., Burke, A., Young, J.: Fear of crime and community concerns: mediating effect of risk and pragmatic fear. J. Community Appl. Soc. Psychol. (2017)
10. Pearson, A.L., Breetzke, G., Ivory, V.: The effect of neighbourhood recorded crime on fear: does neighbourhood social context matter? Am. J. Community Psychol. **56**(1–2), 170–179 (2015)
11. Johnson, R.R.: Reducing Fear of Crime and Increasing Citizen Support for Police (2016)
12. Melde, C., Berg, M.T., Esbensen, F.A.: Fear, social interactions, and violence mitigation. Justice Q. **33**(3), 481–509 (2016)
13. Salem, G.W., Dan, A.L.: Fear of Crime: Incivility and the Production of a Social Problem. Transaction Publishers, Piscataway (2016)
14. Valera, S., Guàrdia, J.: Perceived insecurity and fear of crime in a city with low-crime rates. J. Environ. Psychol. **30**(38), 195–205 (2014)
15. Sharpanskykh, A., Treur, J.: A temporal trace language for formal modelling and analysis of agent systems. In: Dastani, M., Hindriks, K., Meyer, J.J. (eds.) Specification and Verification of Multi-agent Systems, pp. 317–352. Springer, Boston (2010)

An Anytime Algorithm for Scheduling Tasks for Multiagent Systems

Chattrakul Sombattheera[✉]

Faculty of Informatics, Mahasarakham University Khamreang,
Kantarawichai 44150, Mahasarakham, Thailand
chattrakul.s@msu.ac.th

Abstract. This research proposes an any time algorithm for a task scheduling problem among agents. The tasks are composed of atomic tasks and are to be distributed to coalitions of agents as subtasks for parallel execution. We model the problem and propose an algorithm for it. The algorithm calls other low level algorithms to recursively generate plans for agents. The results show satisfactory results that the convergent times are reasonably short and are close to termination time in many settings. We also found that the distribution of input values affect the performance of the algorithm similar to the optimal coalition structure problem.

Keywords: Multiagent systems · Task scheduling · Task allocation

1 Introduction

Multiagent systems (MAS) is an important area of research in artificial intelligence. Among many interesting topics in multiagent systems, optimal coalition structure (OCS) problem is at the heart of MAS research because it suggests how cooperation among agents should be done in order to leverage the maximal efficiency for the system. The objective of OCS problem is to find the maximal sum of coalition values of a coalition structure within the system. The problem is known to be NP-hard because the size of the search space grows exponentially and becomes large even for small inputs.

Much progress in OCS has been made during the past decade – several variation of the problem has been addressed. However, the original form of OCS, i.e. OCS with characteristic function, remains an interesting problem because other variations can be derived from it. Nevertheless, previous research suggests that the characteristics of the problem or the input data can guide us how the algorithm for solving the problem should be designed. It is shown that the distribution of input data can affect the performance of the algorithm significantly.

Unlike OCS where coalition values must be accumulated, we are interested in a different characteristic of MAS, where agents form coalitions but execute there tasks in parallel. The task cannot be split and be executed independently by individual agents. There are needs for agents to cooperatively work, i.e. forming

© Springer International Publishing AG 2017
S. Phon-Amnuaisuk et al. (Eds.): MIWAI 2017, LNAI 10607, pp. 346–359, 2017.
https://doi.org/10.1007/978-3-319-69456-6_29

coalitions, together. A simple reason for this is that agents might face unexpected problems. Executing the tasks as planned will result in poor performance of the whole system. Thus other agents can carry on these tasks, while the unfortunate agents may be able to execute others.

This kind of environment can be found in agent-based grid systems, where agents possess resources and are allocated tasks for execution. Forming coalitions means agents can support other agents in the same coalitions. The efficiency of the system is not the accumulated execution time of coalitions but it is the minimal accumulated execution time of agents in coalitions. Important questions yet to be addressed are the efficiency of such systems and how an algorithm for this system should be designed. We consider this as a task scheduling among agents.

The contributions of this research are two folds. (i) We show that the problem can be modeled and solved. (ii) We developed an anytime algorithm which can still yield satisfactory results in tight time constraint. The structure of the paper is as the following. We review related work both in coalition formation and grid scheduling. We then formulate the problem and address the optimal plan for agents. The algorithm for solving the problem is presented. The experiments and results are then discussed, followed by the conclusion.

2 Review

Multiagent systems (MAS) [2] are an efficient technique which can be used to solve complex problems. The solution concept for maximizing efficiency is optimal coalition structure (OCS), in which agents form coalitions such that the sum of their efficiency (value) is optimal. [1] proposes an anytime algorithm for this problem but is not suitable for our domain because the algorithm does not follow any fixed structure. [4], on the other hand, proposes a more suitable to our problem here and we follow this path. In general, it involves two underpinning algorithms to generate a certain structure [3] and recursively generate a subset [3]. MAS can also be used to schedule tasks among agents [12,13] However, our problem here is more complex and different. Therefore, we develop a new algorithm which in turn uses these algorithms for generating the solution.

Minimizing cost is also an important issue in Grid scheduling. Max-min and Min-min algorithms [10] are also used to select one of these two algorithms, dependent on the standard deviation of the expected completion times of the tasks on each of the resources. [9] proposed a QoS Sufferage algorithm, which considers network bandwidth and schedules tasks based on their bandwidth requirement as the QoS guided Min-min algorithm does. Compared with the Max-min, Min-min, QoS guided Min-min and QoS priority grouping algorithms, QoS Sufferage obtains smaller makespans. [11] minimizes the cost of the execution of workflows while ensuring that their associated QoS constraints are satisfied. [7] use advanced reservation and resource selection. The algorithm minimizes the total execution time of the individual tasks without considering the total execution time of all of the submitted tasks. [8] presented a multiple resources scheduling (MRS) algorithm, which takes into account both the site capabilities and the resource requirements of tasks.

3   Problem Formulation

Agents are to form coalitions to execute given tasks. The number of coalitions is, of course, equal to the number of tasks. Tasks are to be partitioned into sub-tasks. The number of sub-tasks of a task to be given to a coalition must be equal to the number of agents in that coalition. In other words, each agent is to execute a sub-task of a task given to the coalition to which the agent belongs.

3.1   Coalition and Coalition Structure of Agents

Given a set $\mathbb{A} = \{a_i | 1 \leq i \leq \mathbf{I}\}$ of $\mathbf{I}$ agents, a *coalition* $S \subseteq \mathbb{A}$, $S \neq \emptyset$, is a non-empty subset of $\mathbb{A}$. The set $\mathbb{A}$ itself is called the *grand coalition* while a coalition of one agent is called a *singleton coalition*. As in set theory, the *cardinality* of S, denoted by $|S|$, is the size of (the number of agents in) S. Let $\mathbb{S}$ be the set of all coalitions. The size, number of all coalitions, of $\mathbb{S}$ is $2^{\mathbf{I}} - 1$. For example, let $\mathbb{A} = \{a_1, a_2, a_3, a_4\}$, there are $2^4 - 1 = 15$ coalitions. Members of $\mathbb{S}$) include $\{a_1, a_2\}, \{a_1, a_3\}, \{a_1, a_4\}, \{a_2, a_3\}, \{a_2, a_4\}$. In our system, we assume coalitions are presented in lexicographical order, e.g. $\{a_2, a_1\}$ must always be presented as $\{a_1, a_2\}$

Forming coalitions is merely partitioning agents into mutually exclusive and exhaustive subsets. We define a *coalition structure*, denoted by CS, as a partition of $\mathbb{A}$. The size of CS, denoted by $|CS|$, is the number of coalitions within CS. As in set theory, The set of all CSs is denoted by $\mathbb{CS}$. the number of all CSs is known as *Bell number* [3]. Bell number grows exponentially. For example, Bell number of $2, 3, 4, 5, 6, 7, 8, 9, 10$ are $2, 5, 15, 52, 203, 877, 4140, 21147, 115975$, respectively. Partitioning agents can be done based on integer partition. Given the above set of agents, some CSs in $\mathbb{CS}$ include $[\{a_1, a_2\}, \{a_3, a_4\}]$, $[\{a_1, a_3\}, \{a_2, a_4\}]$ and $[\{a_2, a_3\}, \{a_1, a_4\}]$. These coalition structures are depicted in Fig. 1(a), where coalitions are agents attached together and coalitions of a CS are bounded by a dashed lines.

A CS of M coalitions, $|CS| = M$, can also be denoted by $CS = \{S_1, S_2, \ldots, S_M\}$, where $M \leq \mathbf{I}$. This implies that the number of coalitions must not exceed the number of agents. We shall refer to CS in this form later in Sect. 4.2.

3.2   Task, Task Structure and Task Configuration

Let $\mathbb{T} = \{T_n | 1 \leq n \leq \mathbf{N}\}$ be a set of $\mathbf{N}$ tasks. A task T_n can be divided into $\mathbf{K}_n$ atomic tasks, $T_n = \{t_{k,n} | 1 \leq k \leq \mathbf{K}_n\}$. Note that the number of atomic tasks in each task can be different from the rest, depending on the characteristics of each task. Given T_n, a *subtask*, $\tau_n \subseteq T_n$, $\tau_n \neq \emptyset$, is a non-empty subset of T_n. The size (or cardinality) of τ_n, denoted by $|\tau_n|$, is the number of atomic tasks in τ_n. Let

$\mathbb{T}_n$ be the set of all subtasks of T_n. The size, number of all subtasks, denoted by $|\mathbb{T}_n|$, of $\mathbb{T}_n$ is $2^{\mathbf{K}_n} - 1$. For example, let $\mathbb{T} = \{T_1, T_2\}$, $T_1 = \{t_{1,1}, t_{2,1}, t_{3,1}, t_{4,1}\}$ and $T_2 = \{t_{1,2}, t_{2,2}, t_{3,2}, t_{4,2}, t_{5,2}\}$. There are $2^4 - 1 = 15$ subtasks for T_1 and $2^5 - 1 = 31$ subtasks for T_2. Some subtasks of T_1 and T_2 are $\{t_{1,1}, t_{2,1}\}$, $\{t_{3,1}, t_{4,1}\}]$, $\{t_{1,1}, t_{3,1}\}$, $\{t_{2,1}, t_{4,1}\}]$ and $\{t_{1,2}, t_{2,2}\}$, $\{t_{3,2}, t_{4,2}, t_{5,2}\}$, $\{t_{3,2}, t_{4,2}\}$, $\{t_{1,2}, t_{2,2}, t_{5,2}\}$, $\{t_{2,2}, t_{4,2}\}$, $\{t_{1,2}, t_{3,2}, t_{5,2}\}$, respectively. As in coalitions, we assume subtasks and related elements are presented in lexicographical order, e.g. $\{t_{2,1}, t_{1,1}\}$ must always be presented as $\{t_{1,1}, t_{1,2}\}$.

Similar to agents, tasks can also be partitioned. We shall refer to each partition of a task T_n as *task structure*, denoted by TS_n. The size of TS_n, denoted by $|TS_n|$, is the number of subtasks within TS_n. The set of all TS_ns is denoted by $\mathbb{TS}_n$. Since TS_n is merely a set, the number of all TS_ns can also be identified by *bell number* [3]. Partition tasks can also follow integer partition. Given above $\mathbb{T}$, some TS_1s in $\mathbb{TS}_1$ include $[\{t_{1,1}, t_{2,1}\}, \{t_{3,1}, t_{4,1}\}]$, $[\{t_{1,1}, t_{3,1}\}, \{t_{2,1}, t_{4,1}\}]$ and some TS_2s in $\mathbb{TS}_2$ include $[\{t_{1,2}, t_{2,2}\}, \{t_{3,2}, t_{4,2}, t_{5,2}\}]$, $[\{t_{3,2}, t_{4,2}\}, \{t_{1,2}, t_{2,2}, t_{5,2}\}]$ and $[\{t_{2,2}, t_{4,2}\}, \{t_{1,2}, t_{3,2}, t_{5,2}\}]$.

To be able to designate a particular task structure or a particular subtask of that task structure, a TS_n of $\mathbf{J}_n$ subtasks, $|TS_n| = |\mathbf{J}_n|$ can be described by $TS_{j,n} = [\tau_{1,n}, \tau_{2,n}, \ldots, \tau_{\mathbf{J}_n,n}]$, where $\mathbf{J}_n \leq \mathbf{K}_n$. This implies that the number of subtasks of a task structure of a task must not exceed the number of atomic tasks. We shall refer to this form of task structure later in Sect. 4.2. Tasks, atomic tasks, subtasks and task structures are depicted in Fig. 1(b).

Given a set of $\mathbf{N}$ tasks, a *task configuration*, $\mathbb{TC} = \langle TS_1; TS_2; \ldots; TS_{\mathbf{N}} \rangle$, is an $\mathbf{N}$ tuple of a task structure of each task. For example, given above $\mathbb{T}$, task configurations include

$TC_1 = \langle [\{t_{1,1}, t_{2,1}\}, \{t_{3,1}, t_{4,1}\}]; [\{t_{1,2}, t_{2,2}\}, \{t_{3,2}, t_{4,2}, t_{5,2}\}] \rangle$,
$TC_2 = \langle [\{t_{1,1}, t_{3,1}\}, \{t_{2,1}, t_{4,1}\}]; [\{t_{2,2}, t_{4,2}\}, \{t_{1,2}, t_{3,2}, t_{5,2}\}] \rangle$,
$TC_3 = \langle [\{t_{1,1}, t_{3,1}\}, \{t_{2,1}, t_{4,1}\}]; [\{t_{3,2}, t_{4,2}\}, \{t_{1,2}, t_{2,2}, t_{5,2}\}] \rangle$.

Task configurations are shown in Fig. 1(c).

3.3   Plan

Given that we are to find out how agents should cooperatively and coordinatively execute the tasks, agents need to specify explicitly what each agent must do. A *plan* is an ordered pair

$$P = (CS : TC) = (\{S_1, S_2, \ldots, S_M\} : \langle TS_1; TS_2; \ldots; TS_{\mathbf{N}} \rangle)$$

where

(1) CS is a coalition structure defined previously,
(2) TC is a task configuration defined previously,
(3) $|CS| = |TC|$,
(4) $|S_m| = |TS_n|$, where $1 \leq m \leq M$, $1 \leq n \leq N$ and $M = \mathbf{N}$

The above conditions imply the followings. Firstly, $|CS|$ must be the same as $|\mathbb{T}|$, i.e. each S is to execute the corresponding TS. Moreover, it is important

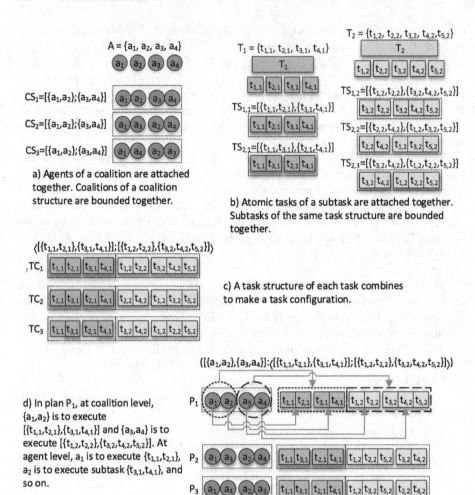

a) Agents of a coalition are attached together. Coalitions of a coalition structure are bounded together.

b) Atomic tasks of a subtask are attached together. Subtasks of the same task structure are bounded together.

c) A task structure of each task combines to make a task configuration.

d) In plan P_1, at coalition level, $\{a_1,a_2\}$ is to execute $[\{t_{1,1},t_{2,1}\},\{t_{3,1},t_{4,1}\}]$ and $\{a_3,a_4\}$ is to execute $[\{t_{1,2},t_{2,2}\},\{t_{3,2},t_{4,2},t_{5,2}\}]$. At agent level, a_1 is to execute $\{t_{1,1},t_{2,1}\}$, a_2 is to execute subtask $\{t_{3,1},t_{4,1}\}$, and so on.

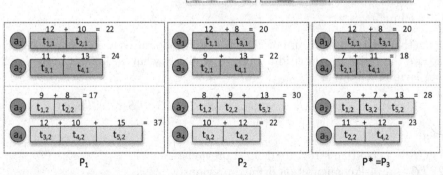

e) Graphical representation of the calculations for P^*. The width of each box representing an atomic task reflects its execution cost of the corresponding agent.

Fig. 1. Forming Optimal Plan. Graphical illustration of building blocks in calculation for an optimal plan.

that the number of agents in each coalition must also be equal to the number of subtasks in the corresponding TS_K, i.e. $|S_1| = |TS_1|, |S_2| = |TS_2|, \ldots, |S_M| = |TS_N|$. This implies that agent a_i, which is o-th member of S_m, is to execute all atomic tasks in the corresponding o-th subtask in TS_n.

For example, the ordered pairs

$$P_1 = ([\{a_1, a_2\}, \{a_3, a_4\}] : \langle [\{t_{1,1}, t_{2,1}\}, \{t_{3,1}, t_{4,1}\}]; [\{t_{1,2}, t_{2,2}\}, \{t_{3,2}, t_{4,2}, t_{5,2}\}]\rangle),$$

$$P_2 = ([\{a_1, a_3\}, \{a_2, a_4\}] : \langle [\{t_{1,1}, t_{3,1}\}, \{t_{2,1}, t_{4,1}\}]; [\{t_{1,2}, t_{2,2}, t_{5,2}\}, \{t_{3,2}, t_{4,2}\}]\rangle)$$

$$P_3 = ([\{a_1, a_4\}, \{a_2, a_3\}] : \langle [\{t_{1,1}, t_{3,1}\}, \{t_{2,1}, t_{4,1}\}]; [\{t_{1,2}, t_{3,2}, t_{5,2}\}, \{t_{2,2}, t_{4,2}\}]; \rangle)$$

are plans. In P_1, at coalition level, $\{a_1, a_2\}$ is to execute $[\{t_{1,1}, t_{2,1}\}, \{t_{3,1}, t_{4,1}\}]$ and $[\{a_3, a_4\}$ is to execute $[\{t_{1,2}, t_{2,2}\}, \{t_{3,2}, t_{4,2}, t_{5,2}\}]$. At agent level, a_1 is to execute $\{t_{1,1}, t_{2,1}\}$, a_2 is to execute subtask $\{t_{3,1}, t_{4,1}\}$, and so on. Note that in P_1 and P_2, CSs and TSs are different. However, the same principle for assigning tasks and subtasks to coalitions and agents applies. Figure 1(d) graphically explains the structure of a plan.

4   Task Scheduling

The ultimate goal of this research is to plan or schedule for the minimal completion time for an agent-based grid system. Tasks are to be distributed among agents as subtasks, each of which is a set of atomic tasks. Each agent, at the same time, executes the allocated atomic tasks one by one. The execution time for each agent is the time it takes to finish all subtasks. The completion time of the system is the point where the latest subtask is completed.

4.1   Execution Cost

In order to determine the completion time, there are many important factors involved with scheduling tasks in grid systems. The first one is *Communication Time* ($\mathcal{CT}$), which is the time for communicating, transferring information, etc. among agents. In general, computing $\mathcal{CT}$ involves geographical proximity, size of data, bandwidth and speed of communication channel. Another factor is the *Execution Time* ($\mathcal{ET}$) of the given (sub)tasks for an agent. Computing $\mathcal{ET}$ normally takes, in addition to the subtask itself, CPU, RAM and hard disks required for the task. There could be more factors involved but we limit the list by just two inputs. Additional inputs may be added without loss of generality.

For both $\mathcal{ET}$ and $\mathcal{CT}$, the algorithms used for calculating both factors can be linear programming or more complex techniques. The results vary depending on characteristics of the inputs, their values, etc. In this research, we shall leave the these low level calculations. We assume these values are calculated by the most appropriate algorithms. All of these factors are accumulated to the *Execution Cost* ($\mathcal{EC}$).

Execution Cost. Let there be an *Execution Cost Matrix*,

$$
\mathcal{ECM} =
\begin{bmatrix}
\alpha^1_{1,1} & \alpha^1_{1,2} & \cdots & \alpha^1_{1,I} \\
\alpha^1_{2,1} & \alpha^1_{2,2} & \cdots & \alpha^1_{2,I} \\
\vdots & \vdots & \ddots & \vdots \\
\alpha^1_{K_1,1} & \alpha^1_{K_1,2} & \cdots & \alpha^1_{K_1,I}
\end{bmatrix}
\begin{bmatrix}
\alpha^2_{1,1} & \alpha^2_{1,2} & \cdots & \alpha^2_{1,I} \\
\alpha^2_{2,1} & \alpha^2_{2,2} & \cdots & \alpha^2_{2,I} \\
\vdots & \vdots & \ddots & \vdots \\
\alpha^2_{K_2,1} & \alpha^2_{K_2,2} & \cdots & \alpha^2_{K_2,I}
\end{bmatrix}
\cdots
\begin{bmatrix}
\alpha^N_{1,1} & \alpha^N_{1,2} & \cdots & \alpha^N_{1,I} \\
\alpha^N_{2,1} & \alpha^N_{2,2} & \cdots & \alpha^N_{2,I} \\
\vdots & \vdots & \ddots & \vdots \\
\alpha^N_{K_N,1} & \alpha^N_{K_N,2} & \cdots & \alpha^N_{K_N,I}
\end{bmatrix},
$$

each element is of the form $\alpha^n_{t_{k,n},i}$, which specifies $\mathcal{EC}$ of agent a_i for executing atomic task $t_{k,n}$ of task i. Since we are interested in how quickly each agent can complete a given subtask, which is composed of atomic tasks, the building blocks of this is then the execution cost of each agent on an atomic task of each task.

Given the above $\mathbb{A}$, $\mathbb{T}$, CSs and TSs, an example of execution cost matrix can be

$$
\mathcal{ECM} =
\begin{bmatrix}
12 & 15 & 12 & 10 \\
10 & 14 & 9 & 7 \\
8 & 11 & 12 & 13 \\
13 & 13 & 13 & 11
\end{bmatrix}
\begin{bmatrix}
10 & 8 & 9 & 9 \\
13 & 9 & 8 & 11 \\
14 & 7 & 11 & 10 \\
11 & 11 & 14 & 12 \\
12 & 13 & 13 & 15
\end{bmatrix},
$$

which states that it takes agent a_1 12 units of time to complete $t_{1,1}$, 10 units of time to execute $t_{2,1}$, 8 units of time to execute $t_{3,1}$, ... 10 units of time to execute $t_{1,2}$ 13 units of time to execute $t_{2,2}$, and so on. Similarly, it takes agent a_2 15 units of time to execute $t_{1,1}$, 14 units of time to execute $t_{2,1}$, 11 units of time to execute $t_{3,1}$, ... 8 units of time to execute $t_{1,2}$ and 9 units of time to execute $t_{2,2}$, and so on. Note that there are 4 rows in the first matrix and 5 rows in the second one because there 4 and 5 atomic tasks in T_1 and T_2, respectively.

4.2 Optimal Plan

Given a plan P, let us consider a corresponding pair $S_m : T_n$. Let $a_i \in S_m$ is the at o-th position S_m and its corresponding subtask at the same oth position is $\tau_{j,n} \in TS_n$. the *Execution Cost of Agent* a_i on subtask $\tau_{j,n}$ is

$$
ExCoAg(a_i, \tau_{j,n}) = \sum_{t_{k,n} \in \tau_{j,n}} \alpha^n_{t_{k,n},i}.
$$

Since agents execute their given subtasks in parallel, we do not sum up the agents' execution cost for that of the coalition. The time needed for completing the given task of a coalition is merely the longest completion time of agents in the coalition. Therefore, the *Execution Cost of Coalition* S_m on corresponding task TS_n is

$$
ExCoCo(S_m, TS_n) = max(ExCoAg(a_i, \tau_{j,n}))
$$

where $a_i \in S_m$ and $\tau_{j,n} \in TS_n$.

Similarly, the coalitions execute tasks in parallel. Therefore, the time needed for completing all the tasks is the longest time needed by a coalition in the coalition structure. The *Execution Cost for Plan P* is

$$ExCoPl(P) = max(ExCoCo(S_m, TS_n))$$

where $S_m \in CS$ and $TS_n \in TC$.

Among the massive number of of possible plans, we are interested in the one that requires the shortest time to finish. The optimal plan is

$$\mathbf{P}^* = arg_{min}ExCoPl(P).$$

Note that it is possible that there might be multiple $\mathbf{P}^*$s in a given problem. However, finding the first one is good enough because it has already solve the problem.

4.3 Example of Optimal Plan

Based on above examples, we continue with an example to find out P^*. For P_1, we can see that $\tau_{1,1} = \{t_{1,1}, t_{2,1}\}$, $\tau_{2,1} = \{t_{3,1}, t_{4,1}\}$, and so on. Then, $ExCoAg(a_1, \tau_{1,1}) = 12 + 10 = 22$. Similarly, $ExCoAg(a_2, \tau_{2,1} = 11 + 13 = 24)$, $ExCoAg(a_3, \tau_{1,2} = 9+8 = 17)$ and $ExCoAg(a_4, \tau_{2,2} = 12+10+15 = 37)$. It can be seen that P_1's both $ExCoCo(S)$s are 24 and 37. Therefore, $ExCoPl(P_1) = 37$.

For P_2, all Ss in CS and TSs in TCs are different from P_1. Following the same principle, we can see that $\tau_{1,1} = \{t_{1,1}, t_{3,1}\}$, $\tau_{2,1} = \{t_{2,1}, t_{4,1}\}$, and so on. Then $ExCoAg(a_1, \tau_{1,1}) = 12 + 8 = 20$. Similarly, $ExCoAg(a_3, \tau_{2,1} = 9 + 13 = 22)$, $ExCoAg(a_2, \tau_{1,2} = 8+9+13 = 30)$ and $ExCoAg(a_4, \tau_{2,2} = 10+12 = 22)$. It can be seen that P_1's both $ExCoCo(S)$s are 20 and 30. Therefore, $ExCoPl(P_2) = 30$.

For P_3, almost all Ss in CS and TSs in TCs are different from P_2. We can see that $\tau_{1,1}$ and $\tau_{1,2}$ remain unchanged but $\tau_{1,2} = \{t_{1,2}, t_{3,2}, t_{5,2}\}$ and $\tau_{2,2} = \{t_{2,2}, t_{4,2}\}$. Then $ExCoAg(a_1, \tau_{1,1}) = 12 + 8 = 20$, $ExCoAg(a_4, \tau_{2,1} = 7 + 11 = 18)$, $ExCoAg(a_2, \tau_{1,2} = 8 + 7 + 13 = 28)$ and $ExCoAg(a_3, \tau_{2,2} = 11 + 12 = 23)$. It can be seen that P_3's both $ExCoCo(S)$s are 20 and 28. Therefore, $ExCoPl(P_3) = 28$. We can now conclude that $P^* = P_3$. Figure 1(e) depicts the whole process for determining P^*.

5   Algorithms

5.1   Generating CS and TC

Both CS and TC are main components of a plan. The complexity of generating both CS and TS (as parts of TC) are NP-Hard, it is better to use an algorithm which is looking for the (near) optimal solution and then diverge to the optimal one. In generating an (near) optimal plan, there are two main steps: (i) generating CSs as per $|\mathbb{T}|$, and (ii) for each $S^m \in CS$, generating TS as per $a^i \in S^m$.

Both generating CS and TS are generally the same problem that needs to follow a certain integer partition. For each part in the partition, we need to repeatedly generate a subset out of the remaining set of agents or atomic tasks. Once we reach the last part, we just have to step back to the previous part and generate its next subset out of the remaining set. The process of repeatedly generating subset continues until there is no further subset to be generated at the first part.

According to this idea, there are three basic algorithms involved, (i) integer partition (IP-alg), (ii) generating subset (GS-alg), and (iii) generating CS or TS (CS-alg). There are algorithms that can be modified for these three tasks, i.e. [kreher] for the first two algorithms and [4] for the last one. Both (i) and (ii) are well known algorithms. However, (iii) is unique and is a complex one. Complete explanation can be found in the papers.

Due to limited space, we will focus on the higher level algorithm, which is the main algorithm that calls the other three.

5.2   An Anytime Algorithm to Generate P^*

This algorithm acts as the main one. Basically, it requires $\mathbb{T}$ and $\mathbb{A}$. The first thing is to initialize both P^*, the (near) optimal plan, and VP^*, its value, to *null* and 0, respectively. The next thing is to initialize CS as an array of integer. While CS is not null, it enters the loop in which TS will be repeatedly generate to construct a plan. Plan P is initialized with its $P.CS$ is set to be CS.

The algorithm examines the cost of execution for each S^m within a loop. The execution cost of the plan, $ExCoPl$, is set to 0. TS is then initialized. Inside the loop, TS is included into TC of the plan. The maximal coalition's execution cost, $MaxExCoCo$, is set to 0.

The next thing is to find the execution cost of each agent in the present coalition. The maximal agent's execution cost, $MaxExCoAg$ is set to 0. The execution cost on each atomic task in the agent's subtask is accumulated into $ExCoAg$. $MaxExCoCo$ is set to $ExCoAg$ if it is greater.

Once all agents in the present coalition are finished with the execution costs, $MaxExCoCo$, the execution cost of the present P is updated with $ExCoAg$ if it is greater. After all TSs are finished with the execution costs, $ExCoPl$ will be updated by $MaxExCoCo$ it is greater. At this point, we know the execution cost of the present plan. After all TSs of the present TC are generated, Lastly, $VP*$ and P^* will be updated if $ExCoPl$ is less. This process is repeated until CS cannot be generated anymore. The pseudocode of this algorithm is presented in Algorithm 1. Due to limited space, we assume the implementation of $GenNextCS$ and $GenNextTS$ both generate only valid CS and TS.

5.3   Implementation and Improvement

The real implementation of this algorithm varies depending on the language and the operating system. Both CS and TS can be represented as two dimension

Algorithm 1. Main Algorithm to generate plans and determines (near) optimal plan P^*

Require: $\mathbb{T}$ and $\mathbb{A}$

1:   $P^* \leftarrow null$
2:   $VP^* \leftarrow 0$
3:   declare CS int array of size $tsize$
4:   initialize CS
5:   **while** $CS \neq null$ **do**
6:     initialize P
7:     $P.CS \leftarrow CS$
8:     **for each** $S_m \in CS$ **do**
9:       $ExCoPl \leftarrow 0$
10:      declare TS int array of size $|S_m|$
11:      initialize TS
12:      **while** $TS \neq$ **do**
13:       $P.TC \leftarrow P.TC \cup TS$
14:       $MaxExCoCo \leftarrow 0$
15:       **for each** $\tau \in TS$ **do**
16:         $MaxExCoAg \leftarrow 0$
17:         **for each** $t \in \tau$ **do**
18:           $ExCoAg \leftarrow ExCoAg + \alpha_{t_{k,n},i}^n$
19:         **end for**
20:         **if** $ExCoAg > MaxExCoCo$ **then**
21:           $MaxExCoCo \leftarrow ExCoAg$
22:         **end if**
23:       **end for**
24:       **if** $MaxExCoCo > ExCoPl$ **then**
25:         $ExCoPl \leftarrow MaxExCoCo$
26:       **end if**
27:       $TS \leftarrow GenNextTS(TS)$
28:      **end while**
29:     **end for**
30:     **if** $ExCoPl < VP^*$ **then**
31:      $VP^* \leftarrow ExCoPl$
32:      $P^* \leftarrow P$
33:     **end if**
34:     $CS \leftarrow GenNextCS(CS)$
35: **end while**

---

array in Java, which is the case in this research, where the first dimension refers to $S^m \in CS$ and the second dimension refers to $a^i \in S^m$. In this case, $|CS|$ and S^m can be determined by checking the size of array in each dimension, i.e. passing only the array itself is enough. We refer to an algorithm for generating CS and TS as $GenNextCS()$ and $GenNextTS()$, respectively. A good reference of such an algorithm can be [4] and modify it as needed. Here, the algorithm takes an argument, the present CS and TS, in order to find the structure of both CS and/or TS. The algorithm itself calls İP-alg and GS-alg repeatedly.

To make the algorithm more efficient, the branch and bound technique can be used to efficiently skip a lot of unnecessary search space and can yield good results at any time. This branch and bound technique can be applied when the algorithm examines for the next atomic task. If the present cost of the agent is more than VP^*, then it can ignore the remaining ts, τs and Ts. This is a simple if statement to be inserted in the most inner loop.

Another possible improvement is to arrange the cost of each agents on subtasks by ascending or descending order then accessing them by their costs. This approach follows the idea presented by [1] However, this may require a lot of effort to access the next valid subtask. The performance of this approach depends on the distribution patterns of the cost.

The other approach is to generate both CS and TS differently from lexicographic order as implement in [4]. This approach may be expensive in terms of time and effort in order to improve the performance of the algorithm because it requires at least three additional components: (i) more complex data structure to keep track of CS and TS being generated because there will be a lot of back tracking, (ii) the major modification in CS-alg implementation because the order of structures generated varies, and (iii) the major improvement in the main algorithm, including the pop and push actions. We have implemented the first improvement while generating TS.

6   Experiments and Results

The is research is not about executing tasks in grid computing but is about planning for executing task. By involving coalition of agents, the problem is similar to coalition formation problem because it is a combinatorial problem where the efficiency of the system depends on how coalitions of agents are formed. Therefore, we experiments the algorithm based on agent coalition practice.

6.1   Settings

As implemented in [1] where coalition values are related to cardinality of coalitions, we take into account the distribution of completion costs as per sizes of coalition. We consider 4 types of distributions as following: (i) IND: The average completion time increases when cardinality increases. (ii) DCD: The average completion time decreases when cardinality decreases. (iii) CCD: The average completion time is of the $\bigcup$ shape. (iv) CVD: The average completion time is of the $\bigcap$ shape.

The experiments were conducted on an i5 machine with 3.5 GHz and 8 GBs of RAM. The algorithms were implemented in Java. The experiments involved 10 to 16 agents. There are 100 runs for 10, 11 up to 16 agents for each distribution type. In each run, the completion times were generated by the Random class using $currentTimeMillis$ function.

6.2 Results

The data presented here is the time spent in scheduling, not the completion time of real execution. The results are the termination and convergence time of running scheduling algorithm. The algorithm terminates when (i) it cannot improve the results or (ii) the time is expired. The numbers are scaled down to the logarithmic value of execution time (Fig. 2).

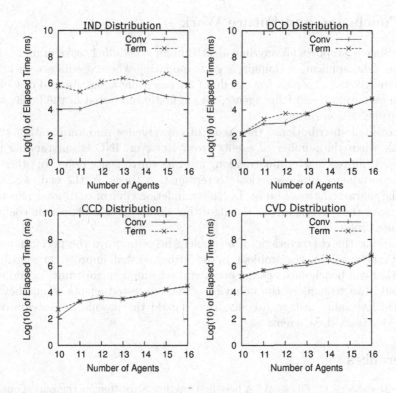

Fig. 2. Trends of Scheduling Times. The graphs show average convergence and termination times of generating (near) optimal plans for grid scheduling

In INC, the trend of both convergence and termination times is slightly increasing when the number of agent grows. This can be implied that when the number of agents grow, it brings more complexity to the problem and takes more time to yield results.

In DEC, the trend of both convergence and termination times are consistently increasing when the number of agent grows. This is opposite the behavior in INC. The algorithm can terminate soon after it converges.

In CCD, the trend of both convergence and termination times are similar to that of DEC. However, the average time is much less. This is similar to what happens in DEC but opposite to INC.

In CVD, the trend of both convergence and termination times increase when the number of agents grow. However, the average time is less, similar to INC but opposite to DEC.

Among all distributions, INC is outstanding that the algorithm reaches termination long after its convergence point. In other settings, convergence times are close to termination times. In all cases, the algorithm takes more time to reach convergence and termination when the number of agents grow.

7   Conclusion and Future Work

This research proposes an anytime algorithm for scheduling tasks in multiagent systems. The application domain is grid computing where agents act on behalf of resource owner and plan (or schedule) for executing tasks. Instead of looking for the execution time of the agents, we are firstly interested in the behavior of the scheduling algorithm.

Across all distributions, the trend of convergence and termination times increase when the number of agents grow. However, INC is outstanding that the algorithm reaches termination long after its convergence point. In other settings, convergence times are close to termination times. In the end, we found that the characteristics of input, i.e. the completion time of coalitions, affect the behavior or the performance of the algorithm similar to that of optimal coalition structure problem.

Knowing the characteristic of a problem helps improve the performance of algorithms for solving the problem. In the future, we shall improve the scheduling algorithm and benchmark against other grid scheduling algorithms. In addition, we would like to explore the behavior of self-interested agents when they are assigned low value task to execute. How should the payoffs be distributed in order to attract these agents.

References

1. Sombattheera, C., Ghose, A.: A best-first anytime algorithm for computing optimal coalition structures. In: Proceedings of the 7th International Joint Conference on Autonomous Agents and Multiagent Systems, pp. 1425–1428. ACM Press (2008)
2. Sycara, K.: Multiagent systems. AI Mag. **19**(2) (1998). Intelligent Agents Summer
3. Kreher, D., Stinson, D.: Combinatorial Algorithms Generation Enumeration and Search. CRC Press, Boca Raton (1999)
4. Rahwan, T., Ramchurn, S., Dang, V., Jennings, N.: Near-optimal anytime coalition structure generation. In: Proceedings of the 20th International Joint Conference on Artificial Intelligence (IJCAI 2007), pp. 2365–2371. Kaufman Morgan, January 2007
5. Mohammad Khanli, L., Analoui, M.: Resource scheduling in desktop grid by Grid-JQA. In: The 3rd International Conference on Grid and Pervasive Computing. IEEE (2008)
6. Mohammad Khanli, L., Analoui, M.: A QoS guided scheduling algorithm for grid computing. In: The Sixth International Symposium on Parallel and Distributed Computing (ISPDC 7). IEEE (2007)

7. Elmroth, E., Tordsson, J.: Grid resource brokering algorithms enabling advance reservations and resource selection based on performance predictions. J. Future Gener. Comput. Syst. **24**, 585–593 (2008)
8. Benjamin Khoo, B.T.B., Veeravalli, T.H., Simon See, C.W.: A multi-dimensional scheduling scheme in a grid computing environment. J. Parallel Distrib. Comput. **67**, 659–673 (2007)
9. Ullah Munir, E., Li, J., Shi, S.: QoS sufferage heuristic for independent task scheduling in grid. Inf. Technol. J. **6**(8), 1166–1170 (2007)
10. Etminani, K., Naghibzadeh, M.: A minmin max-min selective algorithm for grid task scheduling. In: The Third IEEE/IFIP International Conference on Internet, Uzbekistan (2007)
11. Afzal, A., Stephen McGough, A., Darlington, J.: Capacity planning and scheduling in Grid computing environment. J. Future Gener. Comput. Syst. **24**, 404–414 (2008)
12. Shehory, O., Kraus, S.: Formation of overlapping coalitions for precedence-ordered task-execution among autonomous agents. In: Proceedings of the 2nd International Conference on Multiagent Systems (ICMAS 96), Kyoto, Japan, pp. 330–337. AAAI Press, December 1996
13. Shehory, O., Kraus, S.: Methods for task allocation via agent coalition formation. Artif. Intell. **101**(1–2), 165–200 (1998)

Hybrid Model with Margin-Based Real-Time Face Detection and Tracking

Bacha Rehman[✉], Ong Wee Hong, and Abby Tan Chee Hong

Faculty of Science, Universiti Brunei Darussalam,
Bandar Seri Begawan, Brunei Darussalam
bachapk@gmail.com, {weehong.ong,abby.tan}@ubd.edu.bn

Abstract. Face detection and tracking algorithms mainly suffer from low accuracy, slow processing speed, and poor robustness when meet with real-time setup. The problem becomes crucial in real-time situations such as in human robot interactions (HRI) or video analysis. A margin-based region of interest (ROI) hybrid approach that combines Haar cascade and template matching for face detection and tracking is proposed in this paper to improve the detection accuracy and processing speed. To speed up the processing time, region of interests (ROIs) with fixed and dynamic margin concepts are used. A dataset comprising of ten RGB video streams of fifteen seconds have been created from real-life videos containing a person in lecture delivering environment. In each video, there exists person's movement, face turning and camera movements. An accuracy of 97.96% with processing time of 10.76 ms per frame has been achieved. The proposed algorithm can detect and track faces in sideway orientation apart from frontal face. The proposed approach can process the video streams at the speed above 90 frames per second (FPS). The proposed approach reduces processing time by ten times and with a boost to accuracy in comparison to the conventional full frame scanning techniques.

Keywords: Face detection · Face tracking · Haar cascade · Template matching · Dynamic margin · ROI

1 Introduction

Face detection within an image is an important field of research in human computer interaction and computer vision [1, 2]. It is also a necessary step in face recognition. Several researches on automatic face detection have been carried out. The inspiring work of Viola and Jones [3] has recognized the two basic principles in face detection for applied solutions as simple features and boosted cascade structure. Majority of the academia and industrial real-time face detector applications are based on the said two principles. Such face detection applications work quite good for nearly frontal faces under usual conditions. However, they lack the effectiveness for faces with non-frontal orientation in addition to challenges under rough real world situations, such as expression, lighting, and occlusion. The reason behind this ineffectiveness is because the simple Haar-based features are not sufficient to detect large variations in the face orientation and other facial and ambient properties. This technique also involves huge

© Springer International Publishing AG 2017
S. Phon-Amnuaisuk et al. (Eds.): MIWAI 2017, LNAI 10607, pp. 360–369, 2017.
https://doi.org/10.1007/978-3-319-69456-6_30

computational processing which leads to high computational time, not suitable for real-time system involving face detection [4].

In this paper, a combined face detector and tracker with margin-based ROI to improve both the speed and accuracy is presented. It combines both Haar cascade and template matching principles to improve accuracy. Haar cascade [3] algorithm requires some fine tuning to perform really fast and to deal with non-frontal face orientation. To overcome these deficiencies, template matching method [5] is used that finds the resemblance between the input images and the template images.

Template matching method can use the relationship between the input images and stored standard pattern of face features, to detect the existence of a face in an image. The benefit of this method is that any template image can be used regardless whether it is frontal or otherwise. Moreover, based on the correlation values i.e. corresponding to the template and input image common pattern, it is very easy to apply the algorithm. Further it can easily determine the face location as well as eyes, nose, mouth and other features of a face. The method can also be applied on various variations of the images.

In addition, the concepts of fixed and dynamic margin are used to improve the processing speed. Face tracking is used to provide the necessary information for the margin based algorithms to process subsequent frames. If face is found in the first place, the face position is stored for the computation of region of interest (ROI) in the next frame. In the ROI calculations, two variations are presented, i.e. fixed margin and dynamic margin. In fixed margin, fixed percentage extra pixels is added around the face area of the detection face in the initial frame. In the dynamic margin calculation, the margin corresponds to the change in the face position in the previous frames. This procedure significantly speeds up the detection process. As the algorithm is developed keeping in mind if Haar cascades fail, the template matching algorithm calculates the most prospective face position based on the face detected in previous frames. This variation of the detection algorithm makes it robust and reliable.

Six algorithms are implemented and compared in this paper. The detector and tracker presented takes around 10 ms on average which is 10 times faster than the conventional algorithm [3]. It also achieves high detection accuracy on the dataset [6] of 10 videos of 15 s. The videos contain a person who is moving around and occasionally turning his/her head in a normal lecture delivering environment. The main contributions of this paper are:

1. Proposed the face detection and tracking approach incorporating margin-based and template matching with Haar cascade detector to achieve high accuracy and fast speed face detection in real-time.
2. Implemented six variations of the proposed hybrid approach and evaluated their performance on real-life videos.

2   Related Work

Different face detection algorithms [1] have been developed and applied from time to time. One of the most popular algorithm regarding face detection is presented in [3, 7], which has become a benchmark in many software packages e.g. OpenCV [8]. However these conventional algorithms have some serious issues with speed and confronting non-frontal face images [4]. To address these issues, the work done in [4] presented variation of the conventional Haar cascade algorithm [3, 7]. This effort [4] significantly improves the processing time and reduce it to 28 m-sec per frame for a 40×40 frame size, and also improved the detection of non-frontal faces to some extent. However there is still a need to improve the detection technique and also the processing time to enable it to be used for real time system e.g. HRI. Nevertheless, algorithm presented in [4] can be considered as a good alternative of the conventional Haar cascade algorithm [3] for future reference. Having said that, there are other works going on currently to improve the conventional Haar cascade method and to be used for various purposes e.g. a cascade based Deep Neural Networks (DNNs) is proposed [9] to obtain pose estimation results with high precision. Similarly [10–12] adapted multi-task cascaded convolutional networks for face detecting using DNNs.

Template matching algorithm for face localization has been presented in [13], while few variations of template matching techniques are presented in [14]. As template matching algorithm is fast by its nature [5], therefore, it is worth a try to combine it with the conventional cascade algorithm in an intelligent way for effective face detection and tracking task.

Centered correlation filters based tracking systems have been discussed in [15]. Haar wavelet and edge orientation based feature are used to ROI grouping and classification for the purpose of pedestrian detection were discussed in [16]. Re-registration and dynamic template based approach has been developed for head motion recovery in [17]. Template matching based approach addressed issues regarding shape, color and motion was discussed in [18]. The works mentioned above helped understanding various concepts to develop the hybrid system with improved accuracy and processing time.

3   Proposed Margin-Based Hybrid Approach

The algorithm developed as a result of this work is a hybrid approach using Haar cascades and template matching. The main face detector is the Haar cascade, however, in case the Haar cascade fails, the system switches to the template matching detector under certain stopping scenario including time and edge detections. In addition, fixed or dynamic margin-based region of interest (ROI) is used to achieve fast face tracking.

Once a face is detected, its position, face region and template are stored and the ROI is calculated around it. In fixed margin, extra pixels around the face area are taken at fixed percentage i.e. 25% on each side. In the dynamic margin calculation, fixed margin is taken as initial margin with additional pixels corresponding to the change in the face position in previous frames. The detector, either Haar cascade or template matching is applied with this margin-based ROI (MROI) to achieve reliable tracking. Figure 1 describes the general algorithm of the margin-based ROI approach for face detection and tracking. The downscaling of frame size is taken as half. In this work the frame size is downsized to 320×240 from the original size of 640×480.

MROI Algorithm
FOR each frame in the video stream DO
1.   Get the next frame f from the video stream source
2.   Downscale frame size keeping the aspect ratio
3.   Obtain the ROI based on previous frame information
4.   Apply algorithm (Select from equation (5) to (10))
5.   IF face found
5.1. Update the face position
5.2. Update the ROI with the given margin m
5.3. Update the face template
5.4. Update the face area
END FOR

Fig. 1. Margin-based region of interest (MROI) algorithm.

Mathematically, the Haar cascade and template matching detector are expressed in Eqs. (1) and (2) respectively.

$$F(n)_z = \sum_{(0,0)}^{(x,y)} \sum_{\frac{m}{10}}^{\frac{m}{2}} (Multiscale_{HC_m})_z \tag{1}$$

$F(n)$ represents the conventional Haar cascade [3] where, z is the frame number and m is pixels scale window. The minimum size of the window is $\frac{m}{10}$ while the maximum is half of the image frame, i.e. $\frac{m}{2}$. The points represented by $(0,0)$ till (x,y) denote the whole frame scanning.

$$TM(x,y)_z = \left(\frac{\sum_{x'y'} \left(T(x',y') - I(x+x',y+y') \right)^2}{\sqrt{\sum_{x'y'} T(x',y')^2 . \sum_{x'y'} I(x+x',y+y')^2}} \right)_z \tag{2}$$

$TM(x,y)$ represents the equation for the template matching algorithm. I denotes the input image, T is the template, and TM is the result.

The proposed fixed and dynamic margin-based detectors are expressed mathematically in Eqs. (3) and (4) respectively.

$$F(fm)_z = \sum_{(x1,y1)}^{(x2,y2)} \sum_{r*\frac{1}{3}}^{r*\frac{6}{5}} (Multiscale_{HC_r})_z \tag{3}$$

$F(fm)$ represents face detection method in fixed margin-based ROI approach. In Eq. (3), r represents the region of interest area which is from the points $(x1,y1)$ to $(x2,y2)$. In fixed margin, extra pixels around the face area are taken at fixed percentage i.e. 25% on each side. The scale of the windows are taken as related to the ROI with the minimum size as one third of the ROI area and the maximum size is 20% extra from the ROI.

$$F(dm)_z = \sum_{(x1,y1)-Dy_r}^{(x2,y2)+Dy_r} \sum_{r*\frac{1}{3}}^{r*\frac{6}{3}} (Multiscale_{HC_r})_z \tag{4}$$

$F(dm)$ represents the equation for dynamic margin approach. It is quite similar to $F(fm)$ with an addition of Dyr, which represents the dynamic extra pixels taken which is proportional to the face movement in previous two frames.

Based on the algorithms in Eqs. (1) to (4), six further algorithms have been implemented and they are expressed mathematically in Eqs. (5) to (10). The six algorithms are labeled as below:

1. Normal Face Tracking (NT)
2. Fixed Margin Face Tracking (FMT)
3. Dynamic Margin Face Tracking (DMT)
4. Normal Template Matching Face Tracking (NTMT) without margin-based ROI
5. Fixed Margin with Template Matching Face Tracking (FMTMT)
6. Dynamic Margin with Template Matching Face Tracking (DMTMT)

$$F(NT)_z = F(n)_z \tag{5}$$

$$(FMT)_z = \begin{cases} F(n)_z & F(n)_{z-1} = 0 \parallel F(fm)_{z-1} = 0 \parallel z = 1 \\ F(fm)_z & otherwise \end{cases} \tag{6}$$

$$F(DMT)_z = \begin{cases} F(n)_z & F(n)_{z-1} = 0 \parallel F(dm)_{z-1} = 0 \parallel z = 1 \\ F(dm)_z & otherwise \end{cases} \tag{7}$$

$$F(NTMT)_z = \begin{cases} F(n)_z & n \geq 10 \parallel z = 1 \\ \sum_{n=1}^{10} TM(x,y)_z & F(n)_{z-1} = 0 \end{cases} \tag{8}$$

$$F(FMTMT)_z = \begin{cases} F(n)_z & F(n)_{z-1} = 0 \parallel z = 1 \\ \sum_{n=1}^{10} TM(x,y)_z & F(fm)_{z-1} = 0 \\ F(fm)_z & n \geq 10 \end{cases} \tag{9}$$

$$F(DMTMT)_z = \begin{cases} F(n)_z & F(n)_{z-1} = 0 \parallel z = 1 \\ \sum_{n=1}^{10} TM(x,y)_z & F(dm)_{z-1} = 0 \\ F(dm)_z & n \geq 10 \end{cases} \tag{10}$$

For algorithms involving template matching, $n = 1\ to\ 10$ means that whenever the routine is switched to the template matching, then it will process the next *10* frames before switching back to the Haar detector. In addition to the variables specified in the above equations, a distance variable is used to record the difference between the previous frame face position and the current frame face position. If the distance exceeds a certain threshold then it is considered as a wrong detections and the face tracking switches from Haar detector to template matching for continuation of face detection and tracking. Haar cascade detector sometimes has false detection. Therefore, by introducing the distance filter such situations are minimized.

4 Experimental Setup

4.1 Dataset

A database of 10 videos have been created in this work and are made available at [6]. The videos are extracted from open domain sources in YouTube. The videos in the database have the following properties:

1. All videos contain one face and there are changes in the face orientation.
2. The length of each video is about 15 s each, roughly 450 frames with resolution 640 × 480.
3. The videos contain some popular personalities in a lecture delivering environment.
4. Both the camera and the person in the video are moving.
5. 7 videos of male and 3 videos of female (Fig. 2).

Fig. 2. Screen shots of some of the videos in the database.

4.2 Experiment

Six algorithms have been developed and compared for face detecting and tracking. They have been described in Sect. 3. The conventional algorithm (NT) gives the base idea about accuracy and speed of the algorithm.

All these algorithms are tested on the dataset [6] to reach the conclusions in terms of accuracy (correct, incorrect, and not detected), average time taken per frame, and ability to process the number of frames per second.

Each algorithm is executed ten times on each video file. The accuracy, processing time and FPS performance are calculated as the average of the ten test results (Table 1).

4.3 Development Environment

Table 1. Hardware and software used in the development

Hardware	CPU	Intel® Core™ i5 CPU 650 @ 3.20 GHz
	RAM	8 GB
Software	OS	Widows 8.1 pro 64 bits
	Language	Microsoft Visual C++ community 2015
	Tool	OPENCV 3.1

5 Results

The accuracy threshold is taken as 10 pixels. If the distance between the face position detected and ground truth position is less than the threshold value, then it is considered as correct detection. If the above distance is greater than the threshold then it is incorrect detection. If face is not detected then it will be considered as Not Detected.

Figure 3 shows the average face tracking accuracy for each of the algorithms. It can be seen that the incorporation of template matching has significantly improved the accuracy of the Haar-based tracking from 66.63% (NT) to 99.25% (NTMT). The introduction of margin-based approach did not help in improving the accuracy as can be seen from the results for FMT, DMT, FMTMT and DMTMT. There appears to be slight decline in the accuracy when the margin-based approach is used. However, the

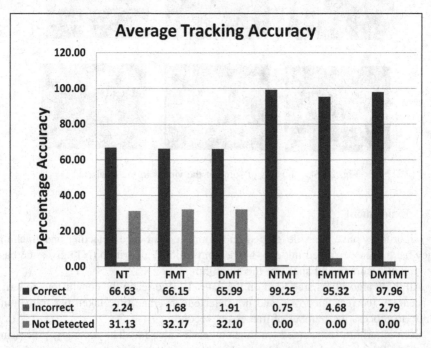

Fig. 3. Average face tracking accuracy.

decline is within 2% and DMTMT has achieved an accuracy of 97.96%. The result shows that the dynamic margin is more robust than the fixed margin in detecting faces.

Turning to the results shown in Fig. 4 will shade light on the merits of the proposed margin-based approach. Figure 4 shows the average time to process or detect a face in each frame. The lower the value the faster is the algorithm. From the result, it can be seen that the margin-based approach significantly improves the speed of the algorithm. For the Haar cascade detector, the fixed margin (FMT) has reduced the time per frame from 104.29 ms to 47.78 ms and the dynamic margin (DMT) has achieved a time per frame of 47.10 ms bringing the processing time down to 45% of the non-margin based algorithm.

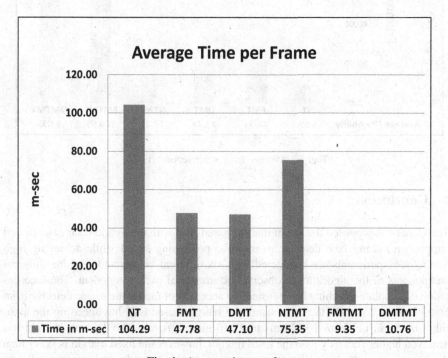

Fig. 4. Average time per frame.

Likewise, the time per frame for the hybrid Haar cascade and template matching approach (NTMT) was significantly improved from 75.35 ms to 9.35 ms with fixed margin (MFTMT) and 10.76 ms with dynamic margin (DMTMT). The longer time in the dynamic margin is due to the extra pixels taken proportional to the changes in the face position.

Figure 5 shows the average ability of each algorithm in processing the frames per second. It can be seen that FMTMT is the fastest approach and DMTMT the second. Both margin-based approaches can easily handle a frame rate of more than 60 fps.

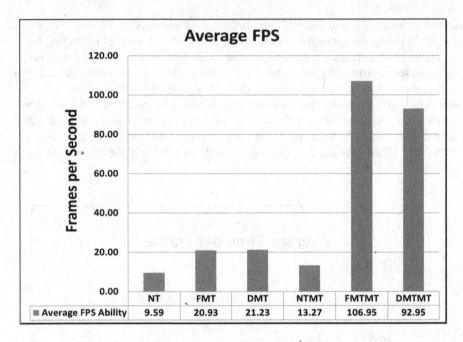

Fig. 5. Average frames per second (FPS).

6 Conclusion

This paper has proposed the use of margin-based ROI with the hybrid Haar cascade and template matching face detector to improve processing speed while achieving high accuracy. Experiments are conducted with six different combinations of the different components of the algorithm to observe the impact of each component. The incorporation of template matching has boosted the accuracy of the Haar cascade detector from 66.63% to 99.25%. On the other hand, the margin-based ROI has speed up the algorithm by 55%, i.e. from 104.29 ms to 47.10 ms per frame. The dynamic margin has achieved higher accuracy than the fixed margin, however the fixed margin is faster than the dynamic margin. If significant movement is involved, the dynamic margin will be a good choice. Further study can be made by evaluating these algorithms on videos that involve fast movement.

References

1. Yang, M.-H., Kriegman, D.J., Ahuja, N.: Detecting faces in image: a survey. IEEE Trans. Pattern Anal. Mach. Intell. **24**, 34–58 (2002)
2. Zhang, C., Zhang, Z.: A Survey of Recent Advances in Face Detection. Microsoft Research (2010)
3. Viola, P., Jones, M.: Rapid object detection using a boosted cascade of simple features. Comput. Vis. Pattern Recognit. **1**, I–511–I–518 (2001)

4. Chen, D., Ren, S., Wei, Y., Cao, X., Sun, J.: Joint cascade face detection and alignment. In: Fleet, D., Pajdla, T., Schiele, B., Tuytelaars, T. (eds.) ECCV 2014. LNCS, vol. 8694, pp. 109–122. Springer, Cham (2014). doi:10.1007/978-3-319-10599-4_8

5. Wei, L.-Y., Levoy, M.: Fast texture synthesis using tree-structured vector quantization. In: Proceedings of the 27th Annual Conference on Computer Graphics and Interactive Techniques - SIGGRAPH 2000, pp. 479–488 (2000)

6. http://ailab.space/projects/multimodal-human-intention-perception/

7. Viola, P., Jones, M.: Robust real-time face detection. Int. J. Comput. Vis. **57**, 137–154 (2004)

8. Bradski, G.: The OpenCV library. Dr. Dobb's J. Softw. Tools Prof. Program. **25**, 120–123 (2000)

9. Toshev, A., Szegedy, C.: DeepPose: human pose estimation via deep neural networks. In: The IEEE Conference on Computer Vision and Pattern Recognition (CVPR), pp. 1653–1660 (2014)

10. Zhang, K., Zhang, Z., Li, Z., Member, S., Qiao, Y., Member, S.: Joint face detection and alignment using multi - task cascaded convolutional networks. IEEE Sig. Process. Lett. **23**, 1499–1503 (2016)

11. Ranjan, R., Sankaranarayanan, S., Castillo, C.D., Chellappa, R.: An all-in-one convolutional neural network for face analysis. In: 12th IEEE International Conference on Automatic Face & Gesture Recognition (FG 2017), pp. 17–24 (2017)

12. Jiang, H., Learned-Miller, E.: Face detection with the faster R-CNN. In: 12th IEEE International Conference on Automatic Face & Gesture Recognition (FG 2017), pp. 650–657 (2017)

13. Dawoud, N.N., Samir, B.B., Janier, J.: Fast template matching method based optimized sum of absolute difference algorithm for face localization. Int. J. Comput. Appl. **18**, 975–8887 (2011)

14. Tan, T.K.T.T.K., Boon, C.S.B.C.S., Suzuki, Y.S.Y.: Intra prediction by template matching. In: 2006 International Conference on Image Processing, pp. 1–4 (2006)

15. Henriques, J.F., Caseiro, R., Martins, P., Batista, J.: High-speed tracking with kernelized correlation filters. IEEE Trans. Pattern Anal. Mach. Intell. **37**, 583–596 (2015)

16. Gerónimo, D., Sappa, A.D., Ponsa, D., López, A.M.: 2D-3D-based on-board pedestrian detection system. Comput. Vis. Image Underst. **114**, 583–595 (2010)

17. Xiao, J., Kanade, T., Cohn, J.F.: Robust full-motion recovery of head by dynamic templates and re-registration techniques. In: Proceedings of 5th IEEE International Conference on Automatic Face Gesture Recognition, FGR 2002, pp. 163–169 (2002)

18. Held, D., Levinson, J., Thrun, S., Savarese, S.: Robust real-time tracking combining 3D shape, color, and motion. Int. J. Rob. Res. **35**, 1–28 (2015)

Smart LED Street Light Systems: A Bruneian Case Study

Dk Nur Siti Khadhijah Pg Ali Kumar, Thien Wan Au[✉],
and Wida Susanty Suhaili

Universiti Teknologi Brunei, Jalan Tungku Link,
Mukim Gadong BE1410, Brunei Darussalam
Dnsk_909@hotmail.com,
{twan.au, wida.suhaili}@utb.edu.bn

Abstract. Smart LED Street Light System (SLSLS) could offer a more systematic and efficient approach that would be beneficial to the government, road users and community. This could reduce energy consumption by intelligently switching on and off and dimming of lights according to real-time data from sensors and control request from end-users. SLSLS could also minimise human intervention by incorporating dynamic faulty light detection through wireless communication. This paper presents the design of a low cost SLSLS using off-the-shelf Arduino based controller using wireless and sensor networks. This requires wireless data transmission between street light and storing data in the system database. The system includes an interactive interface that monitors and provides data visualisation of vital and up-to-date information to end-users. The SLSLS prototype units are developed to test the feasibility of these goals: to demonstrate the smart functionality of the wireless data transmission; a back-end database server to provide storage unit; and the monitoring control and display interface (MCDI).

Keywords: Smart street light · LED · Energy-saving · Fault detection · Wireless sensors

1 Introduction

Street light has been around for centuries, playing an important role in assisting road users, including drivers and pedestrians, to navigate their way mainly during night time. Not only that, street lights extend the hours in which light is available to further increase daily productivity. A well-lit area discourages criminal acts, thus giving the feel of safety to the community especially in residential areas.

However, the cost and energy spent to provide road lighting across Brunei all year round, 12 h a day, take a toll not only on the depleting natural gas used to generate electricity but also on the government's subsidized budget on electricity. In recent years, street lights become affected by the economy crisis faced by the country in that more and more lights are being switched off, particularly in residential area in order to save cost. The main causes to the high energy consumption come down to two factors: high high-pressure sodium (HPS) lights wattage and unnecessary lighting in the absence of road users.

© Springer International Publishing AG 2017
S. Phon-Amnuaisuk et al. (Eds.): MIWAI 2017, LNAI 10607, pp. 370–379, 2017.
https://doi.org/10.1007/978-3-319-69456-6_31

There is also an issue on how faulty lights are not attended either due to no or improper complaint from the public or due to lack of night-time patrolling in certain areas. Lights that fail to switch off during daytime waste electricity and lights that fail to switch on during night time create an unsafe environment.

Other countries were/are also facing the same problems. Many are turning to modern technologies for solution; and intelligent street light is their answer. They combine LED's power-saving feature with smart features acquired from integrating sensors with microcontroller to achieve efficient lighting. Some further incorporate the ideology of Internet of Things (IoT) into their system, connecting street lights to the Internet so that they can be monitored and managed remotely. According to [1], the global LED street light trial in 12 major cities from 2009 to 2012 achieved its 50–70% power-saving goal; and went beyond that figure when smart control were integrated. The result proven that smart street light is ready to be deployed on a wide scale.

Hence, this paper proposed a Smart LED Street Light System (SLSLS) using sensors and wireless network as an alternative solution to conserve energy and provide a more systematic way to manage street lights in Brunei.

With SLSLS, energy consumption would be greatly reduced mainly due to the utilization of LED lamp. Light dimming and the ability to detect faulty lights that fail to turn off preventing unnecessary wastage of energy further cut down electricity usage. Faulty light detection would be instant; human involvement is no longer needed. Because wireless media is used for data transmission, the SLSLS is scalable; new street lights can easily be added into the system without heavy cabling. Web based Monitor Control and Display Interface (MCDI) provides a single-platform for end-user to monitor, control, and access data, thus managing street light becomes more efficient. Maintenance cost is also reduced due to the longevity of LED lamp (five times longer than conventional HPS).

The next section will discuss the background and current development of smart street lights followed by the proposed system architecture. This will then followed by the implementation of the proposed prototype, tests, results and a conclusion.

2 Background and Current Development

Many countries are now switching to automatic control system for street lighting, and some are going for more advanced techniques; implementing the concept of IoT to make a smart or intelligent control system. Different systems have different objectives; majority are aiming for power efficiency and reduction in carbon dioxide emission by coupling the system with LED lights, others want autonomous operation and ease in street light management and maintenance.

Common approaches to smart street lighting systems use Microcontroller as the system's brain that control data input and output and in charge of data exchange between control center and street light via wired and/or wireless medium. Appropriate sensors are used as measuring instruments to aid the system or user in deciding whether to switch on or off or dim the lights. At the control center, end-user is provided with a GUI for easier remote system management and monitoring. Most systems integrate wired and wireless communication to provide seamless connection; wired connection between microcontroller and street light and wireless connection between microcontroller and server.

2.1 Street Light System in Brunei

Street lights in Brunei are using two types of lamps: high-pressure sodium (HPS) and light-emitting diodes (LED) lamps. According to Department of Electrical Services (DES) of Brunei, it is estimated that 42,063 street lights are installed in the Sultanate. here are 41, 244 HPS street lights installed across the country. Wattage used varies, ranging from 70 W, 150 W, 250 W, and 400 W, depending on the locations.

LED street lighting was first introduced in Brunei in 2011. As of 2016, there are a total of 819 LED street lights installed and the energy consumed was only 378 MWH according to Table 1. That translates into 0.49 MWH per LED lamp compared to 1.19 MWH for HPS lamp, more than 40% in energy saving. Accordingly 70% savings could be achieved if dimming is involved. This opens up opportunities to explore further into LED lights and how a smart LED street light system could start the Internet of Things and Smart City concept in Brunei.

Table 1. Statistics of energy consumption of street lights from 2013–2016 (DES Brunei)

Year	HPS (MWH)	LED (MWH)
2013	48.088	50
2014	48.088	64
2015	49.158	168
2016	50.099	378

2.2 Trends of Smart Street Light

In [3] a smart street light system has been developed based on generic infrastructure to reduce electricity and maintenance cost, and improves lights' availability. The system has two modes of operation: manual and automatic mode. For manual mode, data collected over a period of time is stored in the database and end-user can define each street light with the desired light intensity and other measures. For automatic mode, lights were switched on depends on cases and circumstances in which significant amount of electricity were saved. The downside of this system is that it does not take into account the presence of vehicles and pedestrians.

In [4], a digitally-controlled LED street lights and Ethernet-based communication with control center that aimed to reduce energy consumption was proposed. With digital controller, dimming is possible. Their experiment resulted in power efficiency of more than 90% and lighting efficiency higher than 85%. This paper highlighted the directionality feature of an LED light that ensure all lights are directed towards the roads and not wasted into the atmosphere (causing light pollution), hence achieved better luminance.

Sumathi et al. [5] designed stand-alone solar-powered LED street lights which depend heavily on sensors. Light dependent resistor (LDR) was used to measure light intensity, switching on lights when it is dark and switching them off when it is bright. Passive infrared (PIR) sensor detects presence of people and vehicles; if detected will switch on lights, otherwise switch them off. With their system, using LED lights cut yearly energy consumption from approximately BND\$41.80 to BND\$10.45 per light, and the operating hours reduced from 300 h per month to 108 h, saving about 67–71% of energy. Fault detection method is restricted to night time only; natural light during daytime would make readings unreliable.

In [6], Velaga and Kumar also proposed the same system as [5] and include cost comparison between the proposed and existing system and the result was overwhelming. The installation cost for proposed system per street light is six times more expensive than the usual street light. This is not a feasible solution for many developing countries due to the high cost.

In [7] the researchers integrated IEEE 802.15.4 standard into the existing HPS system. 6LoWPAN was selected to implement network layer and application layer as it allows mesh topology and Internet connection without any difficulties. The main drawback is that node-by-node hopping reduce battery lifetime as nodes receive and forward information from other nodes.

3 System Architecture

The 'smart' in SLSLS refers to how street light knows when to switch on, off or dim light based on readings from sensors and set threshold. It knows if street light is in normal or faulty state and notify end-user on the system website on the fly. Data send wirelessly from street light to the system server is in real-time, ensuring information displayed on the MCDI is up-to-date. End-users are also given the authority to control street light remotely from the website.

Figure 1 shows the proposed architecture of the SLSLS. The clock module, light sensor, motion sensor, and voltage sensor are connected to the brain of the system that is the microcontroller. This is where the intelligence or "smart" feature takes place; programs that determine the functionality of the whole system reside in the component. The microcontroller is powered using battery, therefore it is crucial to keep track of the battery life. This is to make sure street light are up at all times and able to receive and

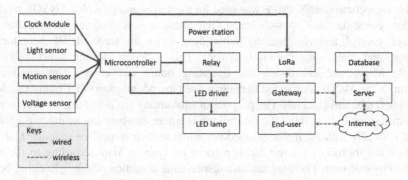

Fig. 1. Proposed smart LED street light system.

transmit data at any time, periodically or as requested. Voltage sensor is used to measure the current battery voltage.

The connection between the microcontroller and LED driver is bi-directional. Signal to dim light is transmitted from microcontroller to LED driver. Meanwhile, the amount of voltage flow to the lamp is transmitted from LED driver to microcontroller for light status and failure detection (fail to on and fail to off).

The network infrastructure for this system is based on LoRaWAN technology. LoRaWAN is long range, low power wide area network (LPWAN), implementing IEEE 802.15.4 g standard and is targeted for M2 M and Internet of Things. The two main features of LoRaWAN that makes it feasible as the network protocol for this system are its wider coverage range and longer battery lifetime compare to existing IEEE 802.15.4 standards. LoRa reviewed in [8] as a protocol that is able to establish communication between millions of nodes at a distance of up to 20 km through chirp spread spectrum modulation. It uses star-of-stars topology instead of the usual LPWAN mesh topology which eliminates synchronization overheads and node-by-node hopping. A centralized database server collects and stores data from all microcontrollers. These data in turn is accessible by all authorized end-users wirelessly via the Internet. A centralized system ensures no data duplication and fully utilized resources.

Communication between the microcontroller and server are also bi-directional. Microcontroller sends LED status (on or off), LED intensity (none, dim, or full), faulty status (fail to on, fail to off, or none), operating hours, and battery level (0–100%) to the server. Control light requests (switch on or off LED) are sent from the end-user of the server to the microcontroller.

4 System Design and Implementation

A small-scale prototype was developed to test the concept of the proposed architecture. Cytron ESP8266 Wi-Fi shield is used to provide wireless communication for the server to replace LoRa at this stage, stacked on top of the microcontroller without any soldering or wiring.

Figure 2 shows the overall components' connectivity of the SLSLS hardware prototype. All the LEDs, sensors, RTC, and other basic components are connected to the microcontroller, Arduino UNO. Arduino Sketch was used to develop the program for the microcontroller. XAMPP was used for the server and provided MySQL module for the system database. A web based GUI interface was designed for end-users to monitor, control, and visualize the lights' data, hence the name MCDI (Monitoring, Control, and Data visualization Interface). This includes locating street lights on Google Maps, and calculating the operating hours and energy consumption in real-time. The MCDI is expected to contain five tabs: Monitoring tab, Control tab, Map tab, Graph tab, and Data tab. The purpose of Monitoring tab is to have an overview of the entire street light system, the Control tab is where end-user can switch the light on or off manually with the lights grouped according to their respective area, the Map tab displays the location for street lights marked on Google Map according to the area selected by end-user. The Map tab also displays the condition of the light either being faulty or normal using different markers. The Graph tab is used to monitor and

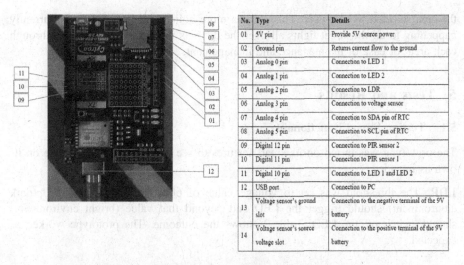

No.	Type	Details
01	5V pin	Provide 5V source power
02	Ground pin	Returns current flow to the ground
03	Analog 0 pin	Connection to LED 1
04	Analog 1 pin	Connection to LED 2
05	Analog 2 pin	Connection to LDR
06	Analog 3 pin	Connection to voltage sensor
07	Analog 4 pin	Connection to SDA pin of RTC
08	Analog 5 pin	Connection to SCL pin of RTC
09	Digital 12 pin	Connection to PIR sensor 2
10	Digital 11 pin	Connection to PIR sensor 1
11	Digital 10 pin	Connection to LED 1 and LED 2
12	USB port	Connection to PC
13	Voltage sensor's ground slot	Connection to the negative terminal of the 9V battery
14	Voltage sensor's source voltage slot	Connection to the positive terminal of the 9V battery

Fig. 2. Close up Arduino Microcontroller and components connectivity.

visualize the energy consumed by street lights daily, monthly, or yearly. Finally the Data tab is where end-users can access and view appropriate tables from the database.

Figure 3 shows a screenshot of the monitoring tab for the prototype. In the prototype only two LEDs were installed in area 1. The figure shows that one of the LEDs was detected faulty. Street lights are normally connected in parallel and therefore when one fails, the others are still on. Faulty light normally creates an open circuit and this is the concept that the prototype adopted where a zero current triggers a faulty alert.

Fig. 3. MCDI showing the Monitoring tab.

As SLSLS is run for every district in Brunei, the content of the Monitor tab is therefore simplified by grouping the necessary statistics from all nodes according to their respective area i.e. Area 1, 2 etc. instead of displaying a long list of street lights for the area selected by end-user. This gives a more holistic picture of what is currently happening to all the street lights all over the districts instead of having to go through each area for ease of maintenance and management.

5   Tests and Results

5.1   Testing Smart Functionality

The prototype was tested on its smart features to see whether it could operate on its own as intended.

LDR. The threshold was set to voltage value of 600. Readings below 600 (dark environment) should trigger the LED and beyond that value (bright environment) should switch off the LED. Table 2 shows the outcome. The prototype worked as expected.

Table 2. Result of LDR testing.

Environment	Light intensity voltage	Threshold voltage	LED expected	Status actual
Bright	990	600	Off	Off
Dark	540	600	On	On

PIR Sensors. Two tests were carried out: 1. the ability to detect vehicle and people; 2. determine the detection range. Table 3 summarizes the test result. Both normal-sized car and people could be detected as far as 7 m.

Table 3. Result of PIR sensor testing.

object	LED brightness	Distance from PIR sensor (m)						
		1	2	3	4	5	6	7
Car	Maximum	✓	✓	✓	✓	✓	-	-
	Dim	X	X	X	X	X	-	-
People	Maximum	✓	✓	✓	✓	✓	✓	✓
	Dim	X	X	X	X	X	X	X

Dual PIR Sensor Mechanism. Two consecutives street lights should switch at maximum intensity once presence is detected. The existence of non-detection area (NDA) due to 100-m light spacing could cause light to dim while vehicle or people is actually present. Therefore, both PIR sensors were programmed to work together to eliminate the NDA. If PIR1 detects presence, both LEDs light up and remain at their maximum intensity until PIR2 detects presence and wait until no more presence is detected. Table 4 summarizes the result. The mechanism managed to keep LED at

Table 4. Result of dual PIR sensor mechanism testing.

Object location	Object detection		LED intensity	
	PIR 1	PIR2	Dim	Maximmum
None	X	X	✓	X
PIR detection range	✓	X	X	✓
Non detection range	X	X	X	✓
PIR 2 detection range	X	✓	X	✓

maximum intensity when object was in non-detection area and while waiting for object to move out of the detection range.

Fault Detection. Two experiments were done: 1. Both LED1 and LED2 were working normally; 2. LED1 worked normally and LED2 was faulty. This was to see whether voltage readings changed for normal and broken lights. Table 5 shows the outcome. As expected, normal LED pulled in the required amount of voltage to emit light whilst broken LED had zero voltage reading.

Table 5. Result of fault detection testing.

No	LED		LED condition		Voltage readings	
	LED1	LED2	Normal	Unserviceable	Expected	Actual
1	✓	-	✓	-	>0	323
	-	✓	✓	-	>0	327
2	✓	-	✓	-	>0	404
	-	✓	-	✓	0	0

5.2   Testing Wireless Data Transmission

5.2.1   From Microcontroller to End-Users

Testing was based on fault detection. Two tests were carried out in order: 1. Using working LED; 2. Using faulty LED. Updates were monitored on MCDI. Periodic updates were received and displayed on the MCDI. Upon carrying out test 2, an alert appeared on the screen, indicating light failure was detected. This shows that data transmission was successful.

5.2.2   From End-Users to Microcontroller

Testing was based on remote light control. On the Control tab of the MCDI, ON and OFF request were issued to see if LED followed the control requests. Figures 3 and 4 show that the requests were received and successfully parsed by the microcontroller (Fig. 5).

```
closing connection... GET /light.json
result: {"light": "on"}
json: {"light": "on"}
LED ON
led1volt: 337
led2volt: 339
start time led1
start time led2
Duration led1: 0
statintfn: 991
count: 2
closing connection...
```

Fig. 4. The ON request from MCDI was received by the microcontroller and LED was switched on.

```
closing connection... GET /light.json
result: {"light": "off"}
json: {"light": "off"}
led off
statintfn: 111
count: 1
```

Fig. 5. The OFF request from MCDI was received by the microcontroller and LED was switched off.

6 Conclusion

This paper rightly demonstrated the proposed SLSLS to be beneficial in terms of saving energy and ease the maintenance of street lighting system. It also provides safe environment for road users both the car drivers and pedestrians.

More Intelligent or "smartness" can be added to reduce human intervention to save lighting consumption, maintaining a state of maximum visual comfort in the lighted areas, as there are many occasions where it is not necessary to maintain a maximum level of light intensity to provide optimal service to the area, which generally causes excessive consumption. The intelligent system included should have the ability to automatically ("smartly") or manually interact according to the lighting used. By using machine learning and datamining technique, some of the devices' life, such as the microcontroller, can be prolonged by allowing the microcontroller to sleep based on the prediction of weather pattern from the data gathered from the sensors.

References

1. Jessup, P., Finighan, R., Walker, J., Curley, P., Cai, H.: Lighting the clean revolution: the rise of LEDs and what it means for cities (2012). https://www.theclimategroup.org/sites/default/files/archive/files/LED_report_web1.pdf
2. Soni, N.B., Devendra, P.: The transition to LED illumination: a case study on energy conservation. J. Theoret. Appl. Inf. Technol. 4(11), 1083–1087 (2008)
3. Amin, C., Nerkar, A., Holani, P., Kaul, R.: GSM based autonomous street illumination system for efficient power management. Int. J. Eng. Trends Technol. 4(1), 54–60 (2013)
4. Chen, P.Y., Liu, Y.H., Yau, Y.T., Lee, H.C.: Development of an energy efficient street light driving system. In: Proceedings of the IEEE International Conference on Sustainable Energy Technologies, pp. 761–764. IEEE, Singapore (2008)
5. Sumathi, V., Sandeep, A.K., Kumar, B.T.: Arm based street lighting system with fault detection. Int. J. Eng. Technol. 5(5), 4141–4144 (2013)
6. Velaga, N.R., Kumar, A.: Techno-economic evaluation of the feasibility of a smart street light system: a case study of rural India. Procedia – Soc. Behav. Sci. 62(2012), 1220–1224 (2013)

7. Denardin, G.W., Barriqueello, C.H., Campos, A., do Prado, R.N.: An intelligent system for street light monitoring and control. In: Proceeding of the Brazilian Power Electronics Conference, pp. 274–278 (2009)
8. Anupriya, K., Yomas, J., Jubin, S.E.: A review on IoT protocols for long distance and low power. Int. J. Eng. Sci. Technol. 5(6), 344–347 (2015)

Optimal Route Assessment for Emergency Vehicles Travelling on Complex Road Network

K-zin Phyo[✉] and Myint Myint Sein

University of Computer Studies, Yangon, Myanmar
kzinphyo@ucsy.edu.mm, myintucsy@gmail.com

Abstract. Emergency cases happen fast, unintentionally and suddenly, and mostly will bring great harm to human lives and properties. According to the lack of the good structure road network and effective emergency route response system, there are many difficulties to get the rapid response and recovery actions immediately. It is essentially require the emergency vehicles to reach the accident location in time for saving lives and reducing the risks of emergency event. The effective response system is needed to provide a greater support in giving the exact location of the accident place, offering the close services to get quick response and solving route direction discovery problems. In spite of the motivation, the effective optimal route response system is developed by using proposed modified Dijkstra's algorithm for emergency medical service teams and ambulances in Yangon, Myanmar. The detailed database of the system consists of road network, accident locations, and emergency services locations. The developed system will help to know the exact location of accident case and the medical services which locate near with that place. And it also provides the optimal route for the ambulance to the accident place. It can also offer various kinds of emergency route respond system by changing and using appropriate databases.

Keywords: Emergency route response system · Modified Dijkstra's algorithm · Optimal route · Good structure road network

1 Introduction

Emergency cases can occur anywhere and anytime with several different ways and will make some risk. Emergency cases always require a rapid response in time. Nowadays, road accident cases are a serious problem in the world especially in developing countries. Routing on urban road networks for emergency vehicles is an essential application in daily life. However, the road network infrastructures are complex and weak in many developing countries. Calculating the optimal route to reach the accident location in time is one of the focuses in real world applications. The proper road network infrastructure is also essential to play in emergency responses and decisions. There are some difficulties in verification of incident location based on the received information, to notify the close emergency services and the optimal route to reach the accident location without any delay. If the optimal route is unknown, it is quite difficult to reach the location in time. To solve these problems, the optimal route assessment system is developed based on the previous approaches [1–4].

© Springer International Publishing AG 2017
S. Phon-Amnuaisuk et al. (Eds.): MIWAI 2017, LNAI 10607, pp. 380–390, 2017.
https://doi.org/10.1007/978-3-319-69456-6_32

According to Word Health Organization nearly 3,500 people die on the world's roads every day and tens of millions of people are injured or disabled every year [11]. Road traffic accidents have been an interesting issue as they have been one of the top causes of death among Myanmar people and caused substantially massive economic and social loss. The recent report from the World Health Organization said that Myanmar is the second-worst country in Southeast Asia for traffic deaths. Due to the rapid urbanization and increasing rate of vehicles, the emergency service teams face some problems to give rapid response to emergency event. In emergency situation, to know the exact location of accident site and the optimal route to go there in time is very important. It is possible to reduce the lives and damage when the emergency vehicles reach as fast as they can. If the exact location of incident place and the optimal route are unknown, it is quite difficult to give the effective response immediately. So, the development of well-organized emergency response system is vital to save the valuable lives.

In recent times, many research works were approved in the application of exiting studies for emergency route response system to solve the route choice problems. The GIS based transport system which support fastest, shortest and safest route to reach hospitals within Allahabad city is developed by Kumar et al. [5]. Even if it can determine the fastest and shortest route but it cannot work on a real road network in a city tends to hold different levels of crowding during different time periods of a day. To find the best route from the location of incident to any healthcare service providers had developed based on GIS by Gubara et al. [6]. The unit of the best route to the closest healthcare service providers in this system is calculated based on the distance. Route analysis for decision support system consists of geographic information systems technologies, GIS web services and how these interact with each other. Bhanumurthy et al. [7] to find shortest route between one facility to another at the time of disaster situation. Elsheikh et al. [8], proposed the system to produce digital route guided maps and to improve services in case of emergencies such as fire, accident, etc. Sivakumar and Chandrasekar [9] proposed Modified Dijkstra's Shortest Path Algorithm (MDSP). In this work, multiple features such as time, time factor and congestion factor are added to improve the original algorithm. Bagchi et al. [10] developed ambulance service using modified Dijkstra's algorithm which method provides a predefined set of data about the ambulance services available nearby and the shortest route to reach them.

The issue of identifying the optimal route on the complex road network is a main problem for emergency vehicles travelling on it. In the case of any incident, it is essential to give the rapid response to the damage people and to take them to the close medical service centers. To give the effective medical service and to save the lives of patient the ambulance drivers needed to know the suitable route to go there within short time. To provide these requirements, the effective emergency route response system is proposed. This system will guide the optimal route for the drivers much easier to reach the preferred location in time. It also reduces the delays caused by complex structure road network and also improves the response and evacuation processes by effectively and efficiently.

2 System Design

The system intended to provide close emergency services and can also provide the optimal route to reach the incident location for rescue teams during natural disaster or emergency event. The general processing steps of the system is shown in Fig. 1. By using ordinary phone call or message, users can report the address information of accident case to the recues teams. Once receive these information, the system gets the location and requested service for incident place. The system will match the address of incident place with coordinate information to determine the exact position. It will make the address query to find the accident location on the road map by using the residential address or street name. After identifying the location on the map, the system will provide the close emergency service for that. And then, the system calculates the optimal route among the emergency services and the accident location by using proposed Modified Dijkstra's Algorithm. It can provide the optimal route not only for one emergency service and incident site but also between multiple emergency services and incident site with related route direction information. Once knowing the optimal route to go the victim location, the emergency vehicles can reach there in short time and can reduce the damage and save the valuable lives.

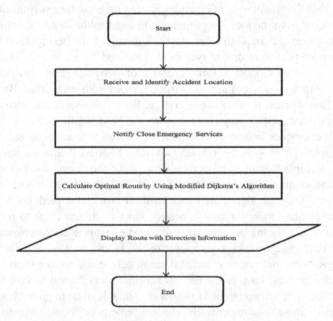

Fig. 1. System overview

2.1 Data Creation

The optimal route estimation for emergency vehicles has been developed for Yangon Region. This system prepares the database of road network, accident locations, and location of emergency services such as fire stations, hospitals and police stations. The emergency services locations of Yangon Region are collected from Myanmar Fire Service Department, Google Earth and GPS GARMIN etrex-10 device. In Yangon Region, there are 41 fire station, 47 police stations and 80 hospital services. In Table 1, the locations of some emergency services are described with related latitude and longitude. Table 2 shows the sample data to identify the incident location address. To calculate the optimal route, the road network table is created with relevant attribute as described in Table 3.

Table 1. Sample data for emergency services

No.	Name service	Latitude	Longitude
1	Hmawbi fire station	17.106246	96.060307
2	Tarmway fire station	16.803593	96.173997
3	Dawbon fire station	16.782553	96.187315
4	Thaketa fire station	16.793132	96.203339
5	Hlaing fire station	16.850763	96.124874
6	Mayangon fire station	16.864666	96.120911
7	Bayin Naung fire station	16.863489	96.107613
8	Mingalardon fire station	17.046965	96.140114
9	Acadamy hopital	16.790269	96.127969
10	Victoria hospital	16.877592	96.129881
11	Sakura hospital	16.796361	96.130711
12	OSC hospital	16.151433	96.155211
13	Thaketa hospital	16.805619	96.217417
14	Waibargi hospital	16.920511	96.156531
15	Shwe Baho hospital	16.809736	96.177211
16	Bahosi hospital	16.779447	96.139831
17	San Pya hospital	16.834058	96.190797
18	Tamwe police station	16.81338	96.169575
19	Bahan police station	16.813417	96.152593
20	Latha police station	16.779594	96.152512

Table 2. Sample data for location identification

Street name	Latitude	Longitude	Status
Myanandar 1st	16.84782046	96.11706937	0
Myanandar 5th	16.85299025	96.11654908	1
Myanandar 6th	16.85239008	96.11544029	1
Myanandar 7th	16.85216493	96.1168062	1
Myanandar 8th	16.85160707	96.11666655	0
Gantgaw 2nd	16.84203079	96.11908509	0
Gantgaw 3rd	16.84257339	96.11936848	0

(*continued*)

Table 2. (*continued*)

Street name	Latitude	Longitude	Status
Gantgaw 4th	16.84278308	96.11788918	0
Gantgaw 5th	16.84331773	96.11785638	0
Gantgaw 7th	16.84472742	96.11880049	0
Gonnisetyone	16.85113585	96.10967493	0
Hlaing Buter Yone	16.83711171	96.11861685	0
Hlaing Sabal	16.84931583	96.1249312	0
Hlaing Yandanar Mon	16.85385681	96.12812751	0
Htantapin	16.83396514	96.12609616	0
Kan	16.8380372	96.13336261	0
Kha Poung	16.83865384	96.1346037	1
KhaYae	16.84659139	96.11753962	0
KhaYae 3rd	16.84674745	96.11827388	0
Khine Shwe War	16.83276518	96.12310781	1

Table 3. Sample data for route calculation

From_Node	To_Node	Distance
1	5	59.58396639
1	3	63.56705376
1	9	95.44961733
2	4	54.58811319
2	6	62.34556288
5	3	119.1973968
5	3	119.1973968
6	4	116.8728413
6	5	133.7008945
7	18	44.69434051
7	10	45.89313512
7	24	85.98165463
8	2	96.68634637
8	9	130.7880717
8	5	137.9492925
9	5	35.89600655
9	6	135.6808953
9	1	95.44961733
10	7	45.89313512
10	18	90.58747563

3 Methodologies

Distance calculation between points or nodes is an important task of many research works which are associated with optimal route finding system. The efficient route finding methods are also essential to improve the working process on the large road network. The following sections discuss the methods which are applied in this work.

3.1 Point to Point Distance Calculation

There are many approaches to calculate between two points or locations. One of the main challenges to calculating distances is accounting for the curvature of the Earth. If only the Earth were flat, calculating the distance between two points would be as simple as for that of a straight line. The Haversine formula includes a constant r that represents the radius of the Earth. In order to calculate the distance, two geographic coordinates are needed. Both points must have their predefined geolocation coordinates. The point to point distance calculation formula is as follows:

$$d = 2r \arcsin\left(\sqrt{\sin\left(\frac{\phi_1 - \phi_2}{2}\right)^2 + \cos(\phi_1)\cos(\phi_2)\sin\left(\frac{\lambda_1 - \lambda_2}{2}\right)^2} \right) \qquad (1)$$

In above equation, where r is the radius of the earth which is 6378 km, d is the distance between two points with longitude λ_1, λ_2 and ϕ_1, ϕ_2 latitude, respectively.

3.2 Proposed Method

The shortest path algorithms are used to solve in the case of path finding problems. Most of road networks consist of millions of nodes and edges. Shortest path finding on large graphs might not be an easy task. When the size of graph is large the accuracy becomes more difficult to measure. Actually, the algorithms are needed to respond the result as fast as possible with high correctness. The original Dijkstra's algorithm finds the shortest path from one selected vertex (location) from all other remaining vertices (locations) in the graph (road network). Most of road networks consist of millions of nodes and edges. So, the processing time to find the optimal is long and the iteration steps are more complex. The main weakness of original Dijkstra's algorithm is that lots of memory usage and processing time when it applies on large road network. In order to reduce the search sequence and the processing time, the modified Dijkstra's Algorithm is proposed. In this modification, the variable *u_status* is used to determine and avoid the roads which are blocked, narrow, close or one-way. The statement $d[u] == \infty$ is used to eliminate the nodes which do not visit from source node. The pseudo code of the proposed modified Dijkstra's Algorithm is described as follow:

```
function ModifiedDijkstra(G, source, destination)
        int u_status;
        dist[source] := 0 ;
        Q := the set of all nodes in Graph ;
   while Q is not empty:
     u := vertex in Q with smallest distance in dist[] ;
           if  u_status= =1
             remove u from Q ;
                 else  if d[u] == ∞  || u_status == 0:
                 break ;
                 end if
           end if
           for each neighbor v of u
               temp_d := d[u] + d_between(u, v) ;
               if temp_d < d[v]:
                   d[v] := temp_d ;
                   previous[v] := u ;
                   decrease-key v in Q;
              end if
           end for
         end while
 return d[destination];
```

By applying the proposed method, the number of nodes which are not visited from the source node will eliminate and the result of optimal route will calculate based on road condition. As reducing the number of visited node, the number of iteration times will decrease and can reduce the processing time and can also improve the performance of the algorithm in optimal route finding.

4 System Implementation

The proposed system is tested in Yangon Region especially to support the emergency medical services. When the accident case happened, to save lives by giving care immediately is very important. To take the damage people from the accident location to the hospitals or medical service centers within short time is critical task for any accident. When the accident happened, the address information of emergency call could not determine the accident location accurately and it is difficult to determine the close hospital to give the needed facilities rapidly. To give the effective evacuation, the optimal route to go the accident location is also vital. In order to solve these problems, effective emergency response system is developed.

Figure 2 shows the locations of all emergency service points such as hospitals, fire stations and police stations in Yangon Region. It will accept the residential address or street name to identify the place of accident. After identifying the accident location as described in Fig. 3, the system displays the emergency services near the location as

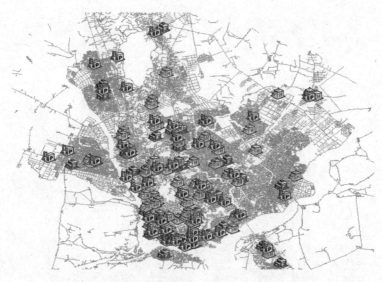

Fig. 2. Emergency services locations in Yangon division

Fig. 3. Incident location identification on road map

shown in Fig. 4. And then it calculates and shows the optimal route for the ambulance drivers with detail route direction information. The result of optimal route and detailed route direction information is shown in Fig. 5.

Fig. 4. Close emergency services for incident site

5 Experimental Result

The performance of the proposed system is recognized by computing the Yangon region road network with the number of edges 87038 and the number nodes 27852. In order to prove the effectiveness of proposed modified Dijkstra's algorithm, the

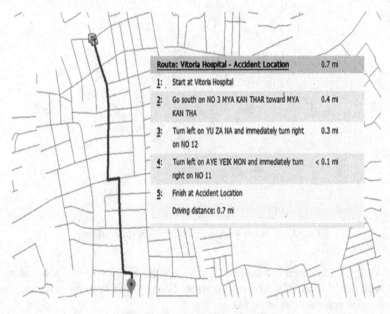

Fig. 5. Result of optimal route

traditional Dijkstra's algorithm is used to compare. The comparison result of the two algorithms is calculated by using number of visited nodes and processing time in route calculation. Table 4 describes the number of visited nodes by applying each methods and Fig. 6 shows tested results of processing time by comparing the original and proposed methods.

Table 4. Comparison of two algorithms in visited nodes

Modified Dijkstra's algorithm	Dijkstra's algorithm
8	20
14	40
28	60
36	80
40	100
64	200

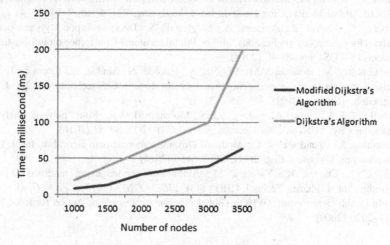

Fig. 6. Comparison in processing time

6 Conclusion

In this research work, we discussed and solved the problems faced by the emergency vehicles travelling on the complex structured large road network. The proposed system significantly solves the problem like confirming the accident location, providing the close medical service centers and the optimal route for the ambulances to go the accident site. The main advantages of this system is that it will make the work of the drivers much easier and make sure they get to the accident location within a short time to save the valuable lives and reduce the damage. Another advantage is that to know the importance well road network infrastructure. This system is also improved in evacuation actions effectively and efficiently. As future work, the proposed work is developed and advanced as mobile version to use in the world wide.

References

1. Phyo, K., Sein, M.M.: Effective emergency response system by using improved Dijkstra's algorithm. In: 14th International Conference on Computer Applications, ICCA 2017, Yangon, Myanmar (2017)
2. Zar, M.T., Sein, M.M.: Public transportation system for Yangon region. In: 12th International Conference on Computer Applications, ICCA 2015, Yangon, Myanmar (2015)
3. Zar, M.T., Sein, M.M.: Finding shortest path and transit nodes in public transportation system. In: The 9th International Conference on Genetic and Evolutionary Computing, ICGEC 2015, Yangon, Myanmar (2015)
4. Zar, M.T., Sein, M.M.: Using A* algorithm for public transportation system in yangon region. In: Proceedings of International Conference on Science, Technology, Engineering and Management, ICSTEM 2015, Singapore (2015)
5. Kumar, N., Kumar, M., Kumarsrivastva, S.: Geospatial path optimization for hospital: a case study of Allahabad city, Uttar Pradesh. Int. J. Mod. Eng. Res. 4(10), 9–14 (2014)
6. Gubara, A., Ahmed, Z., Amasha, A., El ghazali, S.: Decision support system network analysis for emergency applications. In: The 9th International Conference on Informatics and Systems (INFOS), pp. 40–46 (2014)
7. Bhanumurthy, V., Bothale, V.M., Brajesh, K., Urkude, N., Shukla, R.: Route analysis for decision support sytem in emergency management through GIS technologies. Int. J. Adv. Eng. Glob. Technol. 03(02), 345–350 (2015)
8. Elsheikh, R.F.A., Elhag, A., Sideeg, S.E.S., Mohammed, A.E.: Route network analysis in Khartoum City. SUST J. Eng. Comput. Sci. (JECS) 17(1), 50–57 (2016)
9. Sivakumar, S., Chandrasekar, C.: Modified Dijkstra's shortest path algorithm. Int. J. Innov. Res. Comput. Commun. Eng. 2(11), 6450–6456 (2014)
10. Bagchi, C., Chopra, K., Yamuna, M.: Ambulance service using modified Dijkstra's algorithm. Int. J. Pharm. Technol. (IJPT) 8(3), 17627–17633 (2016)
11. World Health Organization (WHO): Global Plan for the Decade of Action for Road Safety 2011–2020 (2009)

Pasang Emas: An AI Implementation of Brunei's Ancient Traditional Game

Pg. Hj. Asmali Pg. Badarudin[⊠]

School of Computing and Informatics, Universiti Teknologi Brunei,
Jalan Tungku Link, Gadong, Brunei Darussalam
salamdamit@gmail.com

Abstract. Pasang is a centuries-old traditional game of Brunei Darussalam. It is a strategy game that was popular among sections of Brunei society. This paper aims to discuss the game play and the game AI used in Pasang Emas, a computer implementation of the traditional board game. It outlines the use of search and evaluation algorithms and how the AI algorithm is played and implemented in Pasang and in comparison with recent development in AI board game implementation. A result of two experiments are presented here in the form of a contest between the game AI and an expert pasang player who was part of a national champion team and the second one from the experiment done by the creator to find out the complexity of the pasang game along with comparisons with other board games.

Keywords: Pasang gameplay · Pasang game complexity · Recent game AI development · Pasang emas AI vs human · Classic and non-classical board games

1 Background

Pasang is an ancient and traditional strategy board game from Brunei Darussalam. It is believed to have existed 600 years ago during Sultan Majid Hassan's reign. Legend has it that Sultan Bolkiah (Brunei's fifth Sultan and during whose reign, the old Brunei Empire was expanding in the region) brought pasang on board his royal barge as one of the two entertainment items for his many voyages — the other being the traditional gulingtangan musical set. The game is commonly played during celebrations of royal weddings and the annual birthday festivals of the Sultan of Brunei. The game is very fast to play with average game length of 56 plies or moves [1] but it has a lot of complex rules for beginners to learn.

A computer version of the game called Pasang Emas was first created around 2000 by Norjaidi Tuah, a local lecturer from Universiti Brunei Darussalam. Traditional pasang has an ancient royal background and in its physical form, can be played with two and up to four players. The Pasang Emas game, however, can only be played by two players. The computer game, nonetheless, can provide the platform for novices and experienced players alike to play and sharpen their skills.

Pasang is an abstract strategy game having complexity level between Chess and Checkers. It is defined as "…a board game with intricate rules. Played on an 11×11 grid

© Springer International Publishing AG 2017
S. Phon-Amnuaisuk et al. (Eds.): MIWAI 2017, LNAI 10607, pp. 391–405, 2017.
https://doi.org/10.1007/978-3-319-69456-6_33

with black and white tokens bears a superficial resemblance to Go, but with completely different game play. In fact, it's unrelated to any other board game, which makes it an appealing choice for anyone who's tired of the same old checkers and Parcheesi." [2].

The original traditional pasang game is played on a hand-made wooden board with clothing buttons used as tokens. It can be played by two, three and up to four players. The Fig. 1 below shows the starting positions of the game in its digital form, using the patterns of Kelabutan Berdarah Hitam which is one of the forty patterns available in the game. These patterns were derived from traditional patterns usually used as the design for the traditional kain songket, part of the country's national costume that have existed over the centuries. Pasang Emas has a custom pattern editor that makes it possible for players to create their own opening patterns.

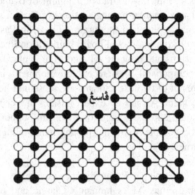

Fig. 1. One of the traditional patterns used by pasang emas game for starting positions.

2   Gameplay of Traditional Pasang

Aim of the Game: The object of the pasang player is to win the game by capturing as many as possible the 118 tokens available on the pasang board after each player turns one selected token as the capturing token or kas. The tokens initially comprise sixty white and sixty black tokens on the board as shown in Fig. 1 above. The white token is assigned two marks while the black one is assigned one.

Alternatively, a player can win by making the opponent unable to move the *kas*, the aforementioned special token used by both players to capture other tokens. This situation called *suntuk* or stuck and being unable to capture, is akin to a king being checkmated in a chess game. In pasang case, the kas cannot capture any token anymore. Since every move is a capture, being unable to capture means that the player loses and all the points are forfeited to the other player who automatically becomes the winner, regardless of the current score of both players.

2.1   The Opening

Agreeing on a Pattern: Before the game begins, both players must agree on the pattern to use for the game by choosing any one from the forty available patterns. New patterns can also be used if the players desire which can easily be created using a special editor in Pasang Emas. The Fig. 1 above is an example of a traditional pattern.

Creating a Passage: The first player starts the game by creating a passage which is done after a column of five tokens is captured on the first player's side of the board shown by the marked 11 × 5 grid lines in Fig. 2(a) below.

The second player will likewise choose a column and in the process captures another column of five tokens from an opposing side of 11 × 5 grid lines as well. However, unlike the first player that can choose any 11 of the columns, the second player is not allowed to choose a column that is of the same position but on the opposite side of the board (see Fig. 2(b) and (c) above.

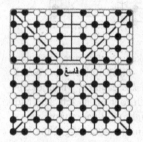 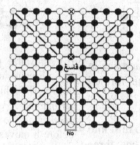 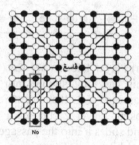

(a) Passage creation as the first player chooses one from eleven options of five tokens on her side as indicated by the box.

(b) The second player makes her move by choosing any column of five tokens on her side except on the indicated column above since player one chose the sixth column.

(c) Here, another illegal move on the indicated third column from the left. The move becomes invalid as the first player has chosen the third column from the right to create her passage.

Fig. 2. The opening by the first player and illegal opening moves by the second player.

Creating the Kas and Rules of Capturing: The first player moves a token to convert it into a kas by horizontally sliding it on the created passage. The kas can then be used to capture other tokens. The rules of capturing can be listed below;

- The *kas* moves in straight lines forward, backward, left or right along the grid
- Except on the first time when a chosen token on the two edges of the passage slides[1] into the passage to become a *kas*, the *kas* captures tokens that must be on its adjacent side and not on its direct line of sight. (See Fig. 3(a) below)
- The captured tokens must be of the same colours (See Fig. 3(b) below)
- The captured tokens must be in odd number of 1, 3, 5, 7 or 9 (See Fig. 3(b) below)

---

[1] Another variation of the creation of the *kas* is by selecting jumping over another token and into the passage rather than by sliding into it.

- The tokens being captured need not be continuous. (See Fig. 3(b) below)
- Captured tokens cannot be obstructed by an empty space called *gadong*[2] in the middle of the board or by the *kas* belonging to the other player (See Fig. 3(b) below)

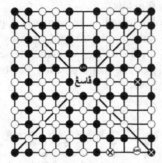 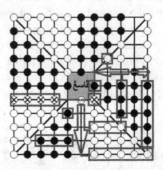

(a) Player 1 forms her *kas* (black *kas* in this case) by sliding into the formed passage and then captures a white token. Player 2 chooses a white token and slides it into the passage to turn into a white *kas*. The player 2 has three options (marked X) to choose from, the white and black tokens on the left and right and the black token at the front.

(b) Allowable tokens for capture is shown by all-white or -black tokens in boxes above. The white *kas* captures white tokens all marked X with four on its left side and another on the right of three empty spaces before it moves in for captureing. Note one captured token on the edge of a *gadong*, the middle shaded square. The *kas* is not allowed to cross the *gadong* or capture tokens obstructed by it.

Fig. 3. Kas formations and the rules of capturing: In (b) above, the black *kas* has four options to move either to the right to capture the five black tokens or to the left where there are three black, a white or a solitary black token. The white *kas* is also presented with four options: either to move and capture the odd groups of five white or three white or three black or a black token.

2.2 The End Game and the Battle for Odd-Numbered Tokens

The two players continue to move their respective kas,[3] in turns along the grid, looking for any odd (1, 3, 5, 7 or 9) tokens. The game continues until all the tokens are captured and total points are counted to determine the winner. In a suntuk situation, however, the game instantly ends and suntuk player's points are given to winning rival (Figs. 4 and 5).

---

[2] In the traditional board, the purpose of the *gadong* is for the first player to place the captured tokens as an honour for being the first to play. The second player has to place the captured tokens on other placeholder or simply on the area nearby outside the board.

[3] In traditional pasang, the token chosen as *kas* is changed with a coloured token, usually a button, to differentiate it from the rest of the tokens.

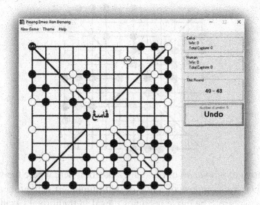

Fig. 4. The white *kas* penetrates the black *kas'* territory at midgame. Using *mamayongi* or shadowing strategy, it hopes to limit movement and eventually a *suntuk* situation for the rival.

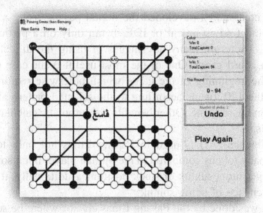

Fig. 5. The white *kas* succeeded in making the black *kas* into a *suntuk* situation

2.3 Unique Features of Traditional Pasang

There are some unique gameplay features in the traditional game that try to inculcate courteous behaviour and sportsmanship such as by not allowing a player to *mamacah* or literally breaking a position. In this situation, a player breaks an obvious capture by the opponent of a line or positions of odd number tokens (3, 5 and 7) by capturing one of the tokens in the line to make them even number (2, 4 and 6) thus rendering them invalid to be captured. Unless the player has no other choice, it is illegal to make the move and in a competition, the umpire will disallow the move (Fig. 6).

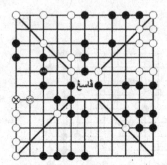

Fig. 6. The illegal move of *mamacah* or breaking a position here where the white *Kas* captures a white token which otherwise compose of a line of odd-numbered white tokens that the black *kas* has the opportunity to capture. The move becomes illegal in traditional pasang because the white *kas* has other options of capturing such as the three white tokens further up the board.

3   The Implementation in Pasang Emas

The Pasang Emas creator first developed the digital pasang using a commercial C++ integrated development environment or IDE. It ran only on a particular OS and was never released [2]. There are many advantages of using the digital pasang over the traditional wooden board game. One of the most useful is the ease of choosing what pattern to use at the beginning of the game which otherwise require both players to manually arrange the 120 tokens according to the selected pattern along the 11×11 grids on the wooden board game. Other benefits are automatic calculations and creating customised patterns.

Artificial intelligence (AI) is used in Pasang Emas not only to ensure that the computer gets as many tokens compared to the human player but also to ensure that the computer will not go into a suntuk or stuck position. Additionally, it seeks to increase the other player's chance of being suntuk.

An experiment was done by the Pasang Emas creator where he set the game demo mode to self-play where weak played against weak, weak played against strong, and strong played against strong in more than 3,000 games and more than 170,000 board positions [1]. It was observed that about 50% of the games ended up in suntuk [1]. One strategy often used by human players to increase the opponent chances of suntuk is the strategy of mamayongi or shadowing where the human player will try to break into the rival territory as early as possible and to always remain close to the rival kas in order to limit its movement and increase the chances of suntuk. This strategy is not visibly present and adopted by the AI player even though many cases are made where it is the human player's kas that becomes stuck while employing this strategy.

3.1   Branching Factors and the Game Tree Size

In the opening stage, exactly 11 possible moves are available for the first player who creates the passage but only 10 are available for the second one. This is because the rule dictates that the second player cannot create a passage at the exact opposite position to the one selected by the first player. Apart from the lesser options, this obviously gives the first player an early advantage by denying an early accumulation of points especially if the corresponding invalid position carries high points.

Statistics from the afore-mentioned experiment also shows that during the creation of the kas, there is an average of 31 possible moves which will be less if different moves are considered identical [1]. Theoretically, the maximum branching factor during this opening stage is 50 [1]. After the kas selection, a player has an average of 6 possible moves to choose from at each turn, less than the theoretical maximum of 40 according to Pasang Emas creator. The maximum seen during the experiment was only 26. Overall, the average branching factor is 7 [1].

The statistics from the experiment on Pasang Emas branching factors shows if the mean value 7 is used for the branching factor, the estimated tree size is 756, or approximately 2×1047. [1]. A comparison of pasang complexity against other popular board games is shown in the Table 1 below.

Table 1. Comparison of popular boards' game complexity to pasang

Game	Average branching factor	Game tree size (possible moves)	Average game length
Tac-Tic-Toe [3]	4	9!	9
Checkers [3]	2.8	10^{40}	70
Pasang [1]	7	2×10^{47}	56
Chess [4]	35	10^{123}	80
Go [4]	250	10^{360}	150

3.2   How the Game Complexity Is Addressed

The AI engine used in Pasang Emas is based on the minimax search algorithm with optimization techniques using Alpha-Beta pruning and depth-first iterative deepening. Negamax, which is an optimized version of minimax is used as to further improve the maximizing of the AI scores at the expense of the other player based on the zero-sum game theory. During a game, AI first obtains a rough result from shallow searches through minimax for the best move. Iterative deepening does the deeper searches, sorts the result of the heuristics evaluation from the highest to the lowest values of the scores. The game's AI prioritizes the best ones and in doing so is able to obtain a more efficient pruning.

These algorithms are mostly used effectively for other turn-taking, two-player games like chess and checkers. They also lend themselves to these algorithms for being deterministic, perfect information games. The branching factor of pasang though relatively lower than those found in games like Chess and Go as shown in Table 1 above, and the relatively big game tree size of 2×1047 require algorithms that are efficient and that do not need to go through all the nodes from the root to the end of the game tree. This will require large memory as well as extensive processing time to go through all the leaf nodes or possible moves which tend to increase exponentially after each depth or ply.

With average game length of 56 plies until the endgame and much shorter in suntuk situation, Pasang Emas is very quick to play from few minutes to 15 min at the most, thanks to the effective AI pruning algorithm as well as the optimization mechanism. Even at moderate strength, a computer can beat a very good pasang player quite easily. Pasang Emas however, in the Linux version, provides a tool to configure the machine's AI strength such that when playing against it, the machine can randomly miss the best move and can even choose a bad one. The purpose is to "humanise" the game so that the human player is motivated to continue playing in a more level playing field. This configuration includes setting up of the AI thinking time in seconds from the fastest of 1 s to slowest of 10 s, the number of moves to think ahead from the shallowest of 1 move to the deepest of 10 moves and lastly the ability to discern good positions from the fuzziest of 1 to the sharpest of 10.

The restriction of breaking of positions, or mamacah by a player on an obvious capture by an opponent is not implemented in Pasang Emas and the move is legal in the digital pasang. According to the creator, this restriction is very difficult to formalize due to the vagueness of the situation. In real physical games, the players are also expected to pick up the tokens in a very gentle way, something which the two dimensional version of the game like Pasang Emas may have difficulty to emulate due to the two dimensional look and feel of the game experience. However, Pasang Emas provides many themes of the board games and the tokens to choose from that can suit many players' individual preferences. Another exciting feature of Pasang Emas is its ability in self-playing mode which can enable human pasang player to learn new strategies. With further enhancement, example by storing the self-playing games' best moves in a data repository to enable machine learning, new game strategies may be uncovered and ma even can be eventually used for solving the pasang game.

4   Game Experiments and Results

In this paper, by pitting AI in in Pasang Emas against a human expert in pasang, the strength of the AI in Pasang Emas can be measured. How the searching for the best move is processsed and achieved by Pasang Emas AI can also be demonstrated. Being free software, Pasang Emas source codes are available and freely downloadable from sourceforge.net.

4.1   Testing the AI Strength Against Human

Five matches were arranged against a human expert player.[4] The latter was part of the winning team in Brunei's national pasang championships in the 1990s that won a number of titles in consecutive years. The tournament was unfortunately discontinued (Figs. 7, 8 and 9).

---

[4] Pg Hj Tarsat bin Pg Hj Abdul Rahman, a veteran expert pasang player, agreed to play five games on 30 May 2017 and the game moves and results were recorded.

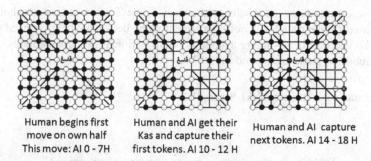

Human begins first
move on own half
This move: AI 0 - 7H

Human and AI get their
Kas and capture their
first tokens. AI 10 - 12 H

Human and AI capture
next tokens. AI 14 - 18 H

Fig. 7. The opening positions show the first six moves of the fourth game where in the first screenshot, the human expert player starts the first move with 7 points and ends up with 18 while AI 0 and ends up with 14

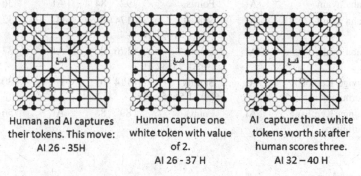

Human and AI captures
their tokens. This move:
AI 26 - 35H

Human capture one
white token with value
of 2.
AI 26 - 37 H

AI capture three white
tokens worth six after
human scores three.
AI 32 – 40 H

Fig. 8. The midgame positions show moves from the first six moves of the fourth game where in the first screenshot, the human expert player starts the first move with 7 points and ends up with 18 while AI 0 and ends up with 14

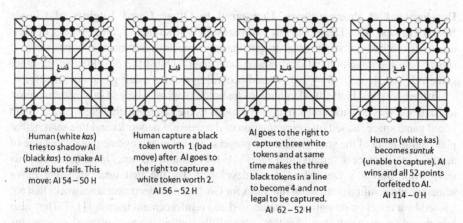

Human (white *kas*)
tries to shadow AI
(black *kas*) to make AI
suntuk but fails. This
move: AI 54 – 50 H

Human capture a black
token worth 1 (bad
move) after AI goes to
the right to capture a
white token worth 2.
AI 56 – 52 H

AI goes to the right to
capture three white
tokens and at same
time makes the three
black tokens in a line
to become 4 and not
legal to be captured.
AI 62 – 52 H

Human (white kas)
becomes *suntuk*
(unable to capture). AI
wins and all 52 points
forfeited to AI.
AI 114 – 0 H

Fig. 9. The endgame shows the last five moves of the fourth game where in the first screenshot, the human expert player tries to make AI *suntuk* but in the end the human player becomes *suntuk* himself.

This section presents the results as shown in Table 2 below and screenshots from Pasang Emas of one round of a non-tournament game between an experienced pasang player who was part of a winning team in previous national level competitions. A total of five rounds of game are played on 30 May 2017.

4.2   Human vs AI: Test of AI Strength

See Table 2

Table 2. Results of human pasang expert vs pasang emas AI.

Game	Pattern	Winner	Type of win	Points		First player	Total moves
				AI	Human		
Using Cincaluk (Pasang Emas Most Difficult Level)							
1	Paha ayam	AI	Points	92	84	AI	36
2	Paha ayam	AI	Suntuk (@AI 81–91 H)	174	0	H	32
3	Paha ayam	AI	Suntuk (@AI 93–82 H)	176	0	AI	37
4	Bunga Kembang Berhujan	AI	Suntuk (@AI 56–52 H)	114	0	H	30
5	Bunga Kembang Berhujan	AI	Points	89	88	AI	56

5   Discussions

5.1   Brief History and Recent Development in Game AI of Board Games

Development of Pasang Emas, Compared to Other Game Engines of Classic Board Games: The Table 3 below compares the milestones of development of various classic board games in order to put Pasang Emas development in perspective. It shows how the development of digital pasang fares against the development of other game AI. The games below are ordered according to increasing game complexity.

In the latest epic battle of AI vs human champion, AlphaGo beat a Go world champion in 2016 and was considered by many AI experts as the last great challenge for AI in the board game space. Based on a combination of deep neural networks and tree search, that plays at the level of the strongest human players, AlphaGo achievement achieved one of artificial intelligence's "grand challenges" [11]. For the match up, David Silver and his team from Google's DeepMind, have developed, for the first time, effective move selection and position evaluation functions for Go, based on deep neural networks that are trained by a novel combination of supervised and reinforcement learning [11]. They also introduced a new search algorithm that successfully combines neural network evaluations with Monte Carlo rollouts. Their program AlphaGo integrates these components together, at scale, in a high-performance tree search engine [11].

Table 3. Milestones of computer versions of popular classic board game

Game	Game engine	Milestones, algorithms and approach used	
Checkers	Chinook	Solved by Jonathan Schaeffer and team in 2007 where a perfect game strategy by both player and Chinook will always end in a draw. The first machine learning program that learnt to play checkers was written in 1952	'Best search' algorithm that allowed Schaeffer team to do a fraction of the calculations necessary to compute every single possible play in the game [5]. AI pioneer A.L. Samuel, used neural net that self plays and used alpha-beta pruning [6]
Pasang	Pasang Emas	Idea was mooted in 2000 and early versions were silently released on the Internet. Showcased by creator's students in a 2001 national competition [7] and was selected in APICTA[a] 2002 [2]. It also won Made-in-Brunei award in BICTA[b] under Cyberunai eServices, as part of a new foldable Pasang set and took part in APICTA 2010	Pasang Emas beat a former national pasang team champion in 2017, in an experimental set of game match ups. The Pasang Emas engine uses minimax with alpha-beta pruning. Minimax is optimized using the Negamax algorithm
Chess	Deep Blue	Deep Blue beat the reigning world Chess champions, Gary Kasparov in 1997. Powered by an IBM supercomputer, it searched deeply usually six moves or more [8]	An evaluation function was used at that depth then proceed similarly to the minimax algorithm. The move that led to the least bad worst-case scenario at this maximum depth was chosen [8]
Backgammon	Neurogammon, TD-Gammon (successor)	Neurogammon and TD-Gammon were both powered by neural nets but the former used supervised learning and the former used reinforcement learning [9]	The two AI games showed that machine learning was a viable alternative to the knowledge-based approach of hand-coding complex strategies [10]
Go	AlphaGo	AlphaGo beat a Go world champion in 2016' Le Sedol in a competitive tournament by 4 wins to one loss. Monte Carlo Tree Search (MCTS) to search game tree was used. By running many game simulations, selecting winning moves becomes accurate [8]	Convolutional neural networks reduce effective depth and breadth of the search tree: evaluating positions using a value network trained on 30 million game positions (deep reinforcement learning), and sampling actions using a policy network that self-plays [8]

[a]APICTA stands for Asia-Pacific ICT Award, an annual regional ICT competition.
[b]BICTA stands for Brunei ICT Award. Winners in BICTA represented the country in APICTA.

The approaches used by AlphaGo and by other AI programs as shown in Table 3 above can serve as alternative ways of designing a more powerful and feature-rich future game of pasang. In particular, pasang can become more challenging for future international tournaments since the experiments done to test its strength in this study were limited to a normal match albeit against a former national pasang champion team member.

The deep learning techniques and the self-learning features employed by many of the above AI engines can also be used to teach pasang gameplay without having to hardcode the gameplay. It may also dispense with or at least alleviate the use of brute-force that is mostly employed in perfect information and deterministic games like pasang which has relatively big game tree.

Checkers, an already solved game, for example, had been subjected to scientific enquiry since the early days of AI especially by AI and games pioneer A.L. Samuel. In 1952, in fact, he wrote the first computer learning program for the game of checkers, and the IBM computer that it played on improved at the game the more it played, studying which moves made up winning strategies and incorporating those moves into its program [12]. In 1959, he published the first academic account of machine learning entitled "Some Studies of Machine Learning Using the Game of Checkers", in which he presented the program's use of alpha-beta pruning [6].

Backgammon was another game, and an ancient board game, that attracted many scientists. Tesauro's neural network-based Neurogammon, was trained with a database of games played by expert human players, won the backgammon championship at the 1989 International Computer Olympiad. All top backgammon programs since Neurogammon have been based on neural networks. Search-based algorithms are not currently feasible for backgammon because the game has a branching factor of several hundred [13].

5.2   Recent Development of Game AI Approaches for a Non-classic Board Game in the Case of Tetris

This section briefly outlines a development of a non-classical and non-traditional board game, Tetris as comparisons to the afore-mentioned traditional classic games such as pasang. In [14], AI researcher, Phon-Amnuaisuak asserts the importance of the ability to automatically discover new knowledge whereby he proposes an evolutionary technique to search for good solutions and then employs a data mining technique to extract knowledge implicitly encoded in the evolved solutions. [14] uses Genetic Algorithm (GA) to evolve a solution for randomly generated tetromino sequences in the Tetris game.

Previously, an evolutionary strategy was employed to evolve weights (i.e., preferences) of predefined evaluation functions which were then used to determine players' actions, but in [14], the researcher directly evolves the gameplay actions. In the study, each chromosome represents a plausible gameplay strategy and its fitness is evaluated by simulating the actual gameplay using gameplay instructions from each chromosome [14]. In each simulation, 13 attributes relevant to the gameplay, i.e., contour patterns and actions of each tetromino, are recorded from the best evolved games. This produces 6583 instances which he then applies Apriori algorithm to extract association patterns from them [14]. In this respect, games like Pasang Emas may also use this new technique especially in preparation for playing in future international tournaments since the AI has not been tested to play against the best human player. The result from [14] studies illustrates that sensible gameplay strategies can be successfully extracted from evolved games even though the GA was not informed about these gameplay strategies. In pasang case, new game winning strategies may also be uncovered and this can increase the playability features such as in limiting the cases of suntuk experienced by some players. Furthermore, as mentioned earlier, Pasang Emas has that exciting feature of playing against itself.

5.3   Recommendation for the Future

The following are some points for discussions and recommendation arising from the study of the Pasang Emas software, which is an AI-based computer implementation of the traditional board game of Brunei Darussalam.

1. The Pasang Emas is an excellent software that is, in almost all areas, able to fulfil the needs of a pasang player.
2. The strength of the choice of searching algorithm, minimax/negamax with alpha-beta pruning are exceptionally utilized and optimized as shown by the difficulties of a former member of a national champion team to beat the game's AI.
3. It can be ascertained that pasang's complexity level is between chess and checkers.
4. There is currently no mechanism to address the *mamacah* or spoiling and breaking opponent potential points in a line of valid moves. The use of deep learning algorithm that enables supervised learning and self-play may enable computer pasang to learn the *mamacah* situation and considers it as an invalid move.
5. Can the pasang game be solved just like checkers was in 2007 by the Chinook team? Will the advent of deep learning be able to solve the game? Since Pasang Emas has been designed so well by its creator, and the software's source codes and algorithm is made available freely on the internet, opportunities for AI game researchers to take the challenge have now arisen using modern techniques.
6. The use of new techniques that employed reinforced deep learning approaches and genetic algorithms as well as data mining methods to uncover new winning strategies can also be useful to future pasang game design as well as enable new way of game development that will spawn many new interesting versions and variations of pasang game. The uniqueness of having many patterns in pasang starting positions can also be explored further in terms of their effects on strategies. In this respect, Pasang Emas impressive self-playing feature can be harnessed and thus be elevated to a whole new level in future game AI research and development.

6   Conclusion

The paper introduces pasang as a traditional game of Brunei Darussalam. It delves into pasang's unique gameplay and development. The AI mechanisms are well-designed and are successfully and efficiently implementated by Pasang Emas. The manner

Pasang Emas delivered comprehensive victories over a human pasang player can only conclude that it already plays at expert's level, even in its early days. Comparison between pasang's game AI developments may not be considered far behind the developments of other popular board games.

However, new development in game AI such as using new artificial neural network, genetic algorithm, deep learning and reinforced learning, and more advanced heuristic and evaluation functions can be explored in future pasang game versions. In most parts, the Pasang Emas software is an excellent piece of work that merit recognition and widespread use beyond board game hobbyists and AI researchers. The creator of Pasang Emas has already provided many wonderful and advanced game AI features that address most if not all, pasang player's needs such as by providing configurations to equalize the strength of the AI to that of normal human player.

Acknowledgements. The author gratefully acknowledges the kind assistance given by Pg Norjaidi bin Pg Tuah for explanations and guidance, in giving permission for use of parts of Pasang Emas for illustrations. The author is also grateful to Thein-Wan Au and Somnuk Phon-amnuaisuk for their kind guidance and advice.

The author gratefully acnowledges the kind cooperation of Pg Hj Tarsat bin Pg Hj Abdul Rahman for his willingness to play against the machine. The author also acknowledges and grateful for the valuable helpful comments and suggestions of the editors and reviewers, which have improved the content and presentation of this paper.

References

1. Tuah, N.: Pasang Emas: an exquisite rendition of a unique traditional board game of Brunei: game complexity (2010). http://pasang-emas.blogspot.com/2010/11/game-complexity.html
2. Sourceforge: Bored with your old board games? Try Pasang Emas (2009). https://sourceforge.net/blog/bored-with-your-old-board-games-try-pasang-emas/
3. Adamchik, V.: Game Trees. https://www.cs.cmu.edu/~adamchik/15-21/lectures/Game%20Trees/Game%20Trees.html
4. Koh, C.: How the Computer Beat the Go Master (2016). https://www.scientificamerican.com/article/how-the-computer-beat-the-go-master/
5. Madrigal, A.: How checkers was solved, the story of a duel between two men, one who dies, and the nature of the quest to build artificial intelligence (2017). https://www.theatlantic.com/technology/archive/2017/07/marion-tinsley-heckers/534111/
6. Samuel, A.L.: I Programmer, AI and Games Pioneer (2015). http://www.i-programmer.info/history/people/669-a-l-samuel-ai-and-games-pioneer.html?start=1
7. Tuah, N.: The birth of Pasang Emas (2010). http://pasang-emas.blogspot.com/2010/03/birth-of-pasang-emas.html
8. Google DeepMind's AlphaGo: How it works (2016). https://www.tastehit.com/blog/google-deepmind-alphago-how-it-works/
9. Tesauro, G.: Temporal difference learning and TD-Gammon. Commun. ACM **38**(3), 58–68 (1995)
10. Kurenkov, A.: A Brief History of Game AI up to AlphaGo. http://www.andreykurenkov.com/writing/a-brief-history-of-game-ai/
11. Silver, D. et al.: Mastering the game of go with deep neural networks and tree search. https://storage.googleapis.com/deepmind-media/alphago/AlphaGoNaturePaper.pdf

12. A Short History of Machine Learning Every Manager Should Read (2016). https://www.forbes.com/sites/bernardmarr/2016/02/19/a-short-history-of-machine-learning-every-manager-should-read/#785e199915e7
13. Cirasella, J., Kopec, D.: The history of computer games. CUNY Academic Works (2006). http://academicworks.cuny.edu/gc_pubs/174
14. Phon-Amnuaisuak, S.: Evolving and discovering tetris gameplay strategies. Procedia Comput. Sci. **60**(2015), 458–467 (2015)

Swarm Intelligence

Swap-Based Discrete Firefly Algorithm for Traveling Salesman Problem

How Siang Chuah[✉], Li-Pei Wong, and Fadratul Hafinaz Hassan

School of Computer Sciences, Universiti Sains Malaysia, Pulau Pinang, Malaysia
chs15_com085@student.usm.my, {lpwong,fadratul}@usm.my

Abstract. Firefly algorithm (FA) is an emerging nature-inspired algorithm which has been used to solve discrete optimization problems such as traveling salesman problem (TSP). However, during the discretization of firefly algorithm, one of the FA's characteristics, i.e. the movement of a dimmer firefly towards a brighter firefly is unapparent as the movement are random. Thus, in this paper, the usage of swap operation as the movement strategy is proposed. The proposed algorithm, Swap-based Discrete Firefly Algorithm (SDFA), is then integrated with Nearest-Neighborhood initialization, reset strategy and Fixed Radius Near Neighbor 2-opt operator (FRNN 2-opt). The proposed algorithm is tested on 45 TSP instances and is compared with several states-of-the-art algorithm. The findings of this research show that the proposed algorithm performs competitively compared to the Discrete Firefly Algorithm, the Discrete Cuckoo Search, the Discrete Bat Algorithm, the Hybrid Genetic Algorithm and the Discrete Bacterial Memetic Evolutionary Algorithm. On average, SDFA reports a percentage deviation of 0.02% from known optimum for TSP instances with dimension range from 14 to 318 cities.

Keywords: Discrete optimization · Combinatorial Optimization · Local search · Nature-inspired algorithm

1 Introduction

Traveling Salesman Problem (TSP) is a Combinatorial Optimization Problem (COP) which requires a finding of the optimum solution(s) in a discrete search space. Given a set of n cities and the corresponded distance matrix, TSP requires a salesman to start at a city, visit all cities once, and return to the starting city such that the generated tour is with minimum distance/cost [1]. TSP is widely studied by researchers due to its applicability to industrial usages such as data clustering, genome sequencing and logistics [2]. TSP is known to be an NP-Hard problem (i.e. hard to be solved in polynomial time). Generally, the approaches used to solve TSP can be categorized as exact approaches or approximation approaches. The exact approaches use mathematical model as their problem solving mechanism. Examples of exact approach include the Concorde TSP solver, Integer Linear Programming, and Branch and Bound [2].

© Springer International Publishing AG 2017
S. Phon-Amnuaisuk et al. (Eds.): MIWAI 2017, LNAI 10607, pp. 409–425, 2017.
https://doi.org/10.1007/978-3-319-69456-6_34

When large TSP instances are being solved, exact approaches are no longer feasible. In order to overcome the limitation of exact approaches, approximation approaches have been introduced to solve TSP. Approximation approaches utilizes heuristics and iterative improvement as their problem solving mechanism. Examples of approximation approach include improvement approaches (i.e. Lin-Kernighan (LK) algorithm [3] and Helsgauns LK algorithm [4]) and nature-inspired algorithms (i.e. firefly algorithm [5–10], genetic algorithm [11], particle swarm optimization [12], intelligent water drop algorithm [13], bee-inspired algorithms [14], and bacterial evolutionary algorithm [15,16]).

The firefly algorithm (FA) was initially proposed by Yang [5] to solve a set of continuous optimization problems. It was computationally realized as an algorithm by modeling the flashing characteristics of fireflies. The dynamics of this continuous FA are mainly affected by light intensity (i.e. brightness) and firefly attractiveness. In order to ensure that a less bright firefly moves towards a brighter firefly, a distance scheme and a movement scheme are proposed.

In recent years, the continuous FA proposed by Yang is modified to solve discrete optimization problems including TSP. In order to solve TSP, the continuous FA is discretized by having different distance and movement schemes which are discrete in nature as shown in [8–10]. Jati and Suyanto [8] proposed the Evolutionary Discrete Firefly Algorithm (EDFA) which utilizes arc distance and inversion mutation as its distance and movement schemes respectively. Kumbharana and Pundey [9] extends idea proposed in [8] by introducing swap distance and hamming distance as alternative distance scheme. They are denoted by EDFA and KPFA respectively in this paper. In these two papers, the characteristic of a less bright firefly moving towards a brighter firefly is not observed. To handle this issue, Jati et al. [10] proposed another discrete FA (DFA) which utilizes a new movement strategy (i.e. edge-based movement). This paper explores alternative movement scheme and a modified version of discrete FA, Swap-based Discrete Firefly Algorithm (SDFA) is proposed. SDFA utilizes swap distance and swap mutation as its discrete distance scheme and movement scheme respectively. SDFA also integrates other mechanisms such as the Nearest Neighborhood initialization, a reset strategy, and the Fixed Radius Near Neighbor 2-opt operator.

This paper is organized as follows. In the next section, related work are presented. In specific, the continuous FAs and the discrete FAs are described. Subsequently, Sect. 3 describes the proposed algorithm, i.e. the SDFA. Section 4 presents the results. Section 5 concludes this paper and provides some insight for future work.

2   Related Work

Fireflies are winged insects that can produce bio-luminescence (natural light) in order to attract mates and preys. This ability has inspired Yang [5] to develop FA. The FA proposed by Yang defines the artificial fireflies flashing characteristics as follows: (1) All fireflies are unisex. The fireflies will be attracted to one another regardless of their sex. (2) The attractiveness between fireflies are proportional to their brightness. A dimmer firefly will be attracted to a brighter firefly. If there is no brighter firefly than a particular firefly, it will randomly move. (3) The brightness of a firefly is determined by the objective function landscape of the problem being solved. FA is commonly used to solve both continuous and discrete optimization problems. The details of continuous FAs and discrete FAs are explained in Sects. 2.1 and 2.2 respectively.

2.1 Continuous FAs

The continuous FAs proposed by Yang [5–7] are used to solve mathematical optimization problems. Binary strings or real values representation are among the solution encoding for the continuous FAs. Binary representation encodes the solutions in 0s and 1s while the real values representation encodes the solutions in original value.

Two main issues are considered in these continuous FAs, i.e. the light intensity variation and the attractiveness formulation. According to the inverse square law $I(r) = I_s/r^2$ in physics, the light intensity, $I(r)$ decreases with distance, r from its sources, I_s. This formula serves as the basis for the light intensity formula. In addition, the light is absorbed when travel through medium. The continuous FA incorporates this concept in allowing the attractiveness to vary with the degree of light absorption. Thus, the overall formula of light intensity for the continuous FA is $I(r) = I_0 e^{-\gamma r^2}$ where the light intensity of a firefly, I, varies with the distance r in a medium with fixed light absorption coefficient γ. The light intensity or brightness of a firefly is often associated with an objective function of a problem being solved.

As the attractiveness of a firefly is assumed to be proportional to the light intensity when it is observed by other fireflies, the attractiveness, β_{ij}, between two fireflies (i.e. firefly i and firefly j) can be calculated using $\beta_{ij} = \beta_0 e^{-\gamma r_{ij}^2}$ where r_{ij} is the distance between two fireflies, β_0 is the attractiveness of firefly j when $r_{ij} = 0$, and γ is a fixed light absorption coefficient in the medium. The attractiveness of a firefly is relative. Each firefly will have different attractiveness values when it is viewed by another firefly as the distance between two fireflies varies. The longer the distance between two fireflies, the less attractive a firefly will be to a particular firefly. In the continuous FA, the distance in attractiveness is defined as Euclidean distance $(r_{ij} = \|x_i - x_j\| = \sqrt{\sum_{k=1}^{d}(x_{i,k} - x_{j,k})^2})$ between two fireflies.

In order to computationally realize the flashing characteristics of FA, i.e. a dimmer firefly will fly towards a brighter firefly, a movement scheme is formulated. The movement scheme used in continuous FA is determined the equation, $x_i = x_i + \beta_{ij}(x_j - x_i) + \alpha(rand - \frac{1}{2})$. The equation consists of three terms (i.e. original value of firefly, the effect of attraction on the differences between two fireflies and mutation value). The α is a randomized scaling number in the range of $[0, 1]$ and $rand$ is a random number that is set in uniform distribution of $[0, 1]$ [9]. Other than this movement scheme, uniform movement, Gaussian movement, Levy Flights and chaos distribution [17] can also be employed as the movement scheme of the continuous FAs proposed by Yang.

The light absorption coefficient, γ, is an important parameter to be carefully considered during experimentation. Theoretically, γ could be set in the range of $[0, \infty)$. When $\gamma \to 0$, the attractiveness will be a constant $\beta = \beta_0$ according to attractiveness function. When the attractiveness is constant, the light intensity of fireflies are not reduced when they are observed by another firefly. This implies that the environment is clear and an optima can be reached easily due to clear visibility of the best solution. On the contrary, when $\gamma \to \infty$, the attractiveness of a firefly will be close to zero when observed by another firefly. In this case, the environment is foggy and every firefly cannot see each other. Thus, all fireflies randomly move. By adjusting the value of γ within the range of two extreme cases, FA introduces a strategy to strike a balance in performing exploitation and exploration within the search space. Subsequently, this strategy enables FA to control its convergence speed. A suitable setting of value γ is vital to obtain optimum value for all problems. Yang [5] suggested that the value of γ could be set from 0.1 to 100 for most applications. Algorithm 1 shows the pseudocode of the continuous FAs.

Algorithm 1. Continuous FA

```
1: begin
2:     Generate an initial population of fireflies x_i(i = 1, 2, ..., pop)
3:     Objective function f(x), x = (x_1, ..., x_d)^T
4:     Light intensity I_i at x_i is determined by f(x_i)
5:     Define light absorption coefficient γ
6:     while t < maxGeneration do
7:         for i ← 1 : pop all pop fireflies do
8:             for j ← 1 : i all pop fireflies do
9:                 if I_j > I_i then
10:                    Move firefly i towards j in d-dimension via movement Scheme
11:                end if
12:                Attractiveness varies with distance r via e^{-γr^2}
13:                Evaluate new solutions and update light intensity
14:            end for j
15:        end for i
16:    end while
17:    Rank the fireflies and find the current best
18:    Postprocess results and visualization
19: end
```

2.2 Discrete FAs

Besides continuous optimization problems, FA is used to solve discrete optimization problems that involve the finding of optimum order for set of objects such as flow shop scheduling problem, traveling salesman problem (TSP) and job shop scheduling problem (JSSP) [17]. Discretization of continuous FA requires several changes such as the representation, attractiveness and movement schemes. Several discrete FAs which have been used to tackle TSP are described in this section.

TSP is a combinatorial optimization problem which the solutions can be encoded using the permutation without repetition encoding scheme. When a TSP is solved using a discrete FA, each firefly is encoded as a candidate TSP solution. The solution which is encoded using the permutation without repetition encoding scheme describes two properties, namely: the visiting order and the tour length. For example: [2 1 3 6 5 4] denotes the visiting order of a 6-city TSP solution. The tour starts at city 2, followed by cities 1, 3, 6, 5, 4, and eventually revisits the starting city to make a round-trip tour. When all the cities are visited, a tour length can be computed.

In discrete FA, the brightness of a firefly is proportional to the attractiveness of a firefly. When a discrete FA is used to address a TSP, tour length or visiting order of a TSP solution can be employed in the computation of the attractiveness for a firefly with regards to another firefly. If the tour length is employed, attractiveness between two fireflies are computed based on the phenotypic distance (i.e. the tour length difference is used to highlight the distance between the solutions encoded by the two fireflies). On the other hand, if the TSP solution visiting order is employed, attractiveness between two fireflies are computed based on genotypic distance. There are three different types of genotypic distances which are employed in discrete FAs: arc distance [8,10], Hamming distance [9], and swap distance [9] respectively. The details of these three distance schemes will be explained using two solutions encoded by two fireflies, i and j. Visiting orders of firefly i and firefly j are [1 3 4 2 5 6] and [2 5 3 6 1 4] respectively. Firefly j is referred to by firefly i as a reference solution such that the distance between these two solutions is established.

Arc distance between two solutions refers to the number of different edges. For example, the solution encoded by fireflies i and j are denoted by the following set of edges [1–3, 3–4, 4–2, 2–5, 5–6, 6–1], and [2–5, 5–3, 3–6, 6–1, 1–4, 4–2] respectively. The edges [1–3, 3–4, 5–6] in firefly i are not observed in firefly j. Thus, the arc distance of these two fireflies is 3. This distance is used in EDFA and DFA.

Hamming distance between two solutions is the number of positions at which the corresponding cities are different. For example, the Hamming distance between firefly i and firefly j is 6 (i.e. all the corresponding cities at each position are different).

Swap distance between two solutions refers to the number of required swaps (i.e. swapping of cities) performed on one solution such that it is similar to another solution. For example, in order to make the solution encoded by firefly i similar to firefly j, five swaps are required (i.e. swap distance is 5). These swap sequences are shown in Fig. 1.

In a discrete FA, a firefly will move towards a reference firefly, or, when a firefly fails to allocate a reference firefly, it will randomly move. The movement of a firefly towards a reference firefly is discussed first, followed by the discussion on random movement.

In order for a firefly to allocate a reference firefly and thus moving towards it, different strategies are observed in existing literature. In EDFA and DFA, each firefly attempts to find the most attractive firefly using the arc distance (i.e. genotypic distance). If the most attractive firefly cannot be found, then the firefly will randomly move. On the other hand, KPFA follows the procedure in continuous FA whereby a firefly will be compared with other fireflies. The firefly will move towards a reference firefly if the tour length (i.e. phenotypic distance) for the reference firefly is shorter.

When a firefly moves towards a reference firefly, it moves by permuting its encoded solution according to a specific movement scheme. The movement is expected to exhibit the characteristic of a dimmer firefly moves towards a brighter firefly as defined in the continuous FA [5]. When a firefly i (i.e. the dimmer firefly) moves towards a reference firefly j (i.e. the brighter firefly), the visiting order (i.e. genotypic distance) or the tour length (i.e. phenotypic distance) of firefly i should be similar to the reference firefly j.

In EDFA by Jati and Suyanto [8], inversion mutation is used as the movement scheme. In such inversion operation, a segment of TSP tour is reversed end to end. For example, if an inversion mutation is performed on a TSP tour [2 1 3 6 5 4] where the segment to be reversed is between cities 2 and 4, the resulting TSP tour after the inversion mutation is [2 5 6 3 1 4]. The inversion mutation movement scheme in EDFA requires arc distance as its parameter, which the working mechanism is as follows. Firstly, the distance between two fireflies, r_{ij}, is computated using a normalized arc distance with respect to number of cities, $r_{ij} = \frac{arc\ distance}{number\ of\ cities} \times 10$. Next, a value which represents a mutation length denoted by x, is randomly generated within a range of $[2, r_{ij}]$. The inversion mutation will then determine a segment of TSP tour with length of x for its operation. This inversion mutation is performed for multiple times for every firefly in a population. The changes made by one inversion mutation operation will persist before the next mutation operation. Similar to EDFA, KPFA employs an inversion mutation as its movement scheme which is based on Hamming distance and swap distance.

Since the inversion mutation movement scheme of EDFA and KPFA is performed on random segments, the resulting TSP tour is often random. This implies that after the movement scheme, the dimmer firefly might not show similarities in terms of visiting order when compared to the brighter firefly. In Fig. 2, firefly i performs an inversion mutation of length $x = 5$ to move towards firefly j. However, after the movement scheme, visiting order of firefly i' does not resemble firefly j and the correspond tour length does not improve. In other words, the resulting firefly does not show any indication of the dimmer firefly has moved towards the brighter firefly since it does not guarantee a decrement in either genotypic distance or phenotypic distance. Thus, this invokes an interest of whether a more appropriate movement scheme can be used.

Following this problem, the DFA which is based on the EDFA was proposed by Jati et al. [10]. The DFA employs an edge-based movement based on arc distance. The edge-based movement works around the concept of inversion mutation and the addition of an edge that exists in the brighter firefly j but does not exists in less bright firefly i. There are four possible combination of the edge-based movements and the DFA will randomly choose one of the combination and the selected edge-based movement will be executed once only. Besides, the edge-based movement also ensures that no similar edge existed previously are removed. Thus, this edge-based movement will guarantee a shorter arc distance.

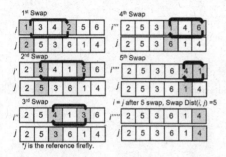

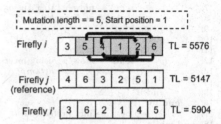

Fig. 1. The working mechanism of the swap distance identification.

Fig. 2. The movement of firefly i using inversion mutation

When a firefly fails to find a reference firefly, it will randomly move. For this random movement, the scheme used in EDFA and DFA is an inversion mutation which is executed for multiple times at different position in a TSP solution. However, random movement is not observed in KPFA.

3 Swap-Based Discrete Firefly Algorithm

In this section, the proposed Swap-based Discrete Firefly Algorithm (SDFA) which is used to tackle TSP is described. SDFA is a modified variation of EDFA [8] and DFA [10]. In the proposed SDFA, swap distance is used as the genotypic distance in the attractiveness computation and swap mutation is used as its movement scheme. They are introduced to computationally realize the movement of a dimmer firefly moving towards a brighter firefly. The termination condition used in the proposed SDFA is a fixed number of generations. Algorithm 2 shows the pseudocode of SDFA.

SDFA first computes the distance between two fireflies using swap distance scheme as described in Sect. 2. This swap distance is denoted by d_{swap}. Similar to EDFA, the distance between two firefly, r_{ij}, is computed using a normalized d_{swap}, $r_{ij} = \frac{d_{swap}}{number\ of\ cities - 1} \times 10$. In the proposed SDFA, d_{swap} is defined in a range of $[0, number\ of\ cities - 1]$. Therefore, the normalization is performed with respect to $number\ of\ cities - 1$. A fixed scaling parameter with a value of 10 is used in the computation of r_{ij}. Once the r_{ij} is established, the attractiveness, β_{ij}, between two fireflies (i.e. firefly i and firefly j) can be computed using $\beta_{ij} = \beta_0 e^{-\gamma r_{ij}^2}$. As the r_{ij} increases (i.e. approaching the fixed scaling parameter of 10), β_{ij} gradually reduces.

Algorithm 2. Swap-based Discrete Firefly Algorithm

Input: Population size of fireflies, pop, Light absorption coefficient, γ, Attractiveness coefficient, β_0, Number of moves, m, Accumulated Solution List, l
Output: A TSP solution with the shortest tour length
  1: Initialize a population of fireflies $x_i (i = 1, 2, ..., pop)$ using nearest neighborhood heuristic
  2: **while** termination condition are not met **do**
  3:   **for** $j \leftarrow 1 : pop$ all pop fireflies **do**
  4:     $x_j \leftarrow Find\_Reference\_Firefly(x_i)$
  5:     **if** $x_j \neq null$ **then**
  6:       **for** $k \leftarrow 1 : m$ **do**
  7:         $temp \leftarrow$ move x_i to x_j using swap mutation
  8:         $l \leftarrow Local\_Search(temp)$
  9:       **end for**
 10:     **else**
 11:       **for** $k \leftarrow 1 : m$ **do**
 12:         $temp \leftarrow$ move x_i using inversion mutation
 13:         $l \leftarrow Local\_Search(temp)$
 14:       **end for**
 15:     **end if**
 16:   **end for**
 17:   Select pop best distinct firefly from l
 18: **end while**

In the proposed SDFA, the movement of a dimmer firefly towards a brighter (i.e. reference) firefly is computationally realized. The working mechanism of allocating a reference firefly is as follows. Let's consider an example where a firefly i is trying to allocate a reference firefly from a set of four fireflies (refer to Fig. 3). The firefly i will first compare its tour length with other four fireflies. After the tour length comparison, a set of fireflies (i.e. fireflies 1, 2, and 4) which possess a shorter tour length compared to firefly i is selected. Based on this set of fireflies, the most attractive firefly (i.e. firefly 4 with highest β_{ij}) is selected as the reference firefly. The pseudocode of such reference fireflly allocation mechanism is shown in Algorithm 3.

Algorithm 3. Finding a Reference Firefly

Input: Firefly x_i
Output: Firefly x_j
  1: $bestAttractiveness \leftarrow -1$
  2: **for** $j \leftarrow 1 : pop$ all pop fireflies **do**
  3:   **if** $x_j.tourLength < x_i.tourLength$ **then**
  4:     **if** $\beta_{ij} > bestAttractiveness$ **then**
  5:       $bestAttractiveness \leftarrow \beta_{ij}$
  6:       $x_i \leftarrow x_j$
  7:     **end if**
  8:   **end if**
  9: **end for**

Once the reference firefly is successfully allocated, the dimmer firefly will move towards the reference firefly by performing the swap mutation for m times. Each time a swap mutation takes place, the swap operation is performed in the range of $[1, d_{swap} - 1]$. This range is to ensure that the dimmer firefly will at least has a minimal change in its encoded solution and at the same time preventing the dimmer firefly from having an identical encoded solution as what the reference firefly has. Let's consider an example as shown in Fig. 4 where a firefly i is moving towards a reference firefly j with d_{swap} between firefly i and firefly j is five. After a movement of 3-swap is performed, the dimmer firefly i will share similar visiting order with the reference firefly j. Note that the d_{swap} is now reduced to two. This movement scheme ensures the reduction of d_{swap} and it is able to reduce the genotypic distance between two fireflies. After each swap mutation, the encoded solution of the original firefly i is not changed. In other words, in the subsequent swap mutation, the swap operation will still be performed on the solution encoded by firefly i.

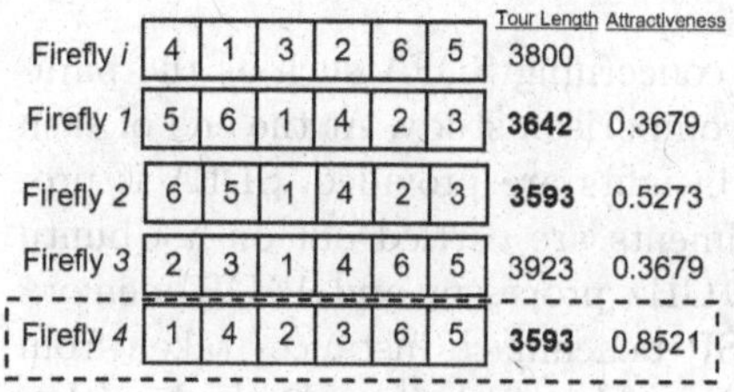

Fig. 3. Selection of the most attractive firefly.

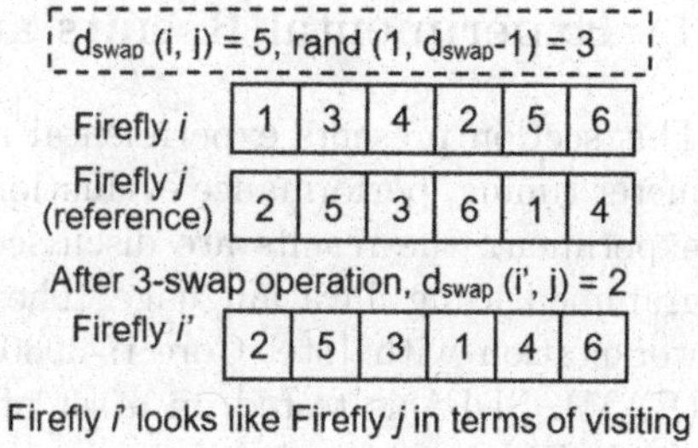

Fig. 4. The movement of firefly i using swap mutation.

When a firefly fails to find a reference firefly, then the firefly will randomly move using an inversion mutation with the length of [2, *number of cities*] for m times. This random movement scheme is adapted from EDFA.

In the proposed SDFA, a population of *pop* fireflies is maintained. The movement scheme (i.e. swap mutation or the inversion mutation) undergone by a specific firefly is executed for m times. When all the fireflies have undergone the movement scheme, it is considered as one complete generation. A total of $pop \times m$ solutions are accumulated in one generation. These accumulated solutions are stored in a list and *pop* best solutions are selected for the subsequent generation.

Besides computationally realizing the firefly flashing behaviour, the proposed SDFA is integrated with an initialization heuristic, i.e. the nearest neighborhood heuristic. The working mechanism of the nearest neighborhood heuristic is as follows. The heuristic starts with a random city and keeps on visiting the next nearest city until a round trip tour is generated. Random selection is performed when there is a tie in selecting the next nearest city. The main aim of this nearest neighborhood heuristic is to ensure that the SDFA has a population of non-randomly generated solutions to start with.

A reset strategy is also included to enable the FA to escape from local optimum. It is carried out when the best solution tour length remains the same for a fixed number of generations. The reset strategy works by reinitializing the firefly population using the nearest neighborhood heuristic. The best solution so far will be kept.

After a firefly has generated a complete TSP tour, the resulting TSP tour
will be undergoing a local optimization. The Fixed-radius Near Neighbor 2-opt
(FRNN 2-opt) is used in SDFA as it is a more computational efficient method
to implement 2-opt local optimization [18]. Traditionally, 2-opt local search is
an exhaustive method to find shorter tour by swapping two edges. FRNN 2-opt
reduces the computational search time by limiting the search to the area of a
circle with radius of the original edge length. The aim of integrating the FRNN
2-opt is to ensure that the solution encoded by each firefly is locally optimized
such that tour length can be reduced.

4   Experimental Results and Discussion

This section presents experimental results concerning SDFA such as the parameter tuning, performance evaluation and comparison study. At the end of each
experiment, the results are discussed and insights are provided. SDFA is programmed using Java language. The experiments are carried out on a Ubuntu
workstation with Intel Core i7-3930K 3.20 GHz processor and 16 GB memory
(RAM). SDFA is tested on a set of 45 TSP benchmark instances taken from
the TSPLIB[1] which the dimension ranges from 14 to 318 cities. Each algorithm
execution on a specific TSP benchmark instance is designated on a single specific
core.

The SDFA parameters are tuned using the Central Composite Design (CCD)
[19]. Five levels of parameters are defined as shown in Table 1. In this paper, 2^k
full factorial experiments with ten center points and ten axial points for five
factors, $k = 5$ is utilized. An α value of 2.37841 is used.

The parameter tuning experiments are designed using the Minitab software
version 17.3.1 according to TSP dimension. The 45 benchmark problems taken
from the TSPLIB are categorized into four categories as follows: [1–100], [101–
200], [201–300] and [301–400]. For each category, a TSP instance is chosen as
the representative problem instance (denoted as Rep. Problem) for the parameter tuning experiments. For example, the representative problem instance of
category [1–100] is eil51. A total of 52 experiments with different combination
of parameters as stated in Table 1 are generated. The optimal parameter setting
for each category is shown in Table 2.

The results of SDFA and SDFA with FRNN 2-opt (i.e. SDFA+FRNN_2-opt)
on a set of 45 TSPLIB benchmark problems are tabulated in Table 3. Both algorithms are integrated with a nearest neighborhood initialization heuristic and
a reset strategy. For each benchmark problem, a total of 30 replications (i.e.
runs) of algorithm execution are conducted. The stopping condition for both
algorithms is the maximum number of generation, $maxGen = 10000$. The experimental results in Table 3 are obtained using three key performance indicators,
namely: percentage deviation of average tour length from known optimum (δ_A),
percentage deviation of the best tour length from known optimum (δ_B), and
average computational time to obtain the best tour length for each replications

---

[1] http://www.iwr.uni-heidelberg.de/groups/comopt/software/TSPLIB95/.

Table 1. Values used for the parameter tuning experiments

Parameter	$-\alpha$	-1	0	$+1$	$+\alpha$
Number of times of movement, m	1	6	8	11	15
Attractiveness, β_0	1	4	6	8	10
Light absorption coefficient, γ	0.01	0.06	0.08	0.11	0.1
Number of firefly population, pop	10	15	18	21	25
Reset generation, rG	200	432	600	769	1000

Table 2. Optimal parameter settings

Dimension	Rep. problem	SDFA					SDFA+FRNN_2-opt				
		m	β_0	γ	pop	rG	m	β_0	γ	pop	rG
[1, 100]	eil51	11	4	0.11	21	769	8	6	0.08	10	600
[101, 200]	kroA150	6	8	0.11	21	432	8	6	0.08	10	600
[201, 300]	gr229	6	8	0.11	15	432	6	4	0.06	15	769
[301, 400]	lin318	15	6	0.08	18	600	6	4	0.06	15	769

in seconds (μ_T). A smaller deviation is favorable. The average of δ_A, denoted by μ_A is also computed. Based on 30 replications, the results also present the frequency of the algorithm obtained the optimum tour length (C_0), the percentage deviation $\leq 0.01\%$ from the known optimum (C_1), and the percentage deviation $\leq 0.05\%$ from the known optimum (C_5).

The results in Table 3 show that the SDFA+FRNN_2-opt outperforms SDFA. In terms of δ_A, SDFA+FRNN_2-opt outperforms SDFA in 42 TSP instances. For burma14, ulysses16, and ulysses22, both of the algorithm are able to solve the problems to optimum. In addition, the μ_A of SDFA+FRNN_2-opt is 3.9% better than SDFA. Besides, SDFA+FRNN_2-opt is also able to achieve optimality in 30 out of 45 TSP instances whereas SDFA is only capable of reaching optimality in 3 out of 45 TSP instances.

In order to benchmark the performance of SDFA, it is compared with the Discrete Firefly Algorithm (DFA) [10], the Discrete Cuckoo Search (DCS) [20], the Discrete Bat Algorithm (DBA) [21], the Hybrid Genetic Algorithm (HGA) [22] and the Discrete Bacterial Memetic Evolutionary Algorithm (DBMEA) [16]. DFA, as described in Sect. 2.2, utilizes edge-based movement as its movement scheme and it achieved better results when compared with EDFA. Thus, it is used as the main comparison with SDFA. The DCS is an improved version of original cuckoo search whereby it structures the cuckoos population in three different categories. In each category, the cuckoos will explore the search space using different strategies. The strategies are seeking solution nearby the best solution, finding new solutions far from the best solution and seeking solutions from the current position. With the defined strategies, the cuckoos move by permuting the visiting order using successive 2-opt moves and double bridge moves. On the other hand, the DBA is the discretized version of the bat algorithm to solve TSP. It uses 2-exchange crossover heuristic to update the bat positions and applies 2-opt local search procedure with probability. It is chosen as one of the comparison due to its similarities with FA that employs multiple movement schemes. The HGA is also included in the comparison study. It is integrated with two local optimization strategies. The first strategy focuses on four vertices and three lines inequality whereas the second strategy is the operation of inversion mutation on

Table 3. Comparison of SDFA and SDFA+FRNN_2-opt

Problem* instances	Known optimum	SDFA				SDFA+FRNN_2-opt			
		δ_B (%)	δ_A (%)	$C_0/C_1/C_5$	$\mu_T(s)$	δ_B (%)	δ_A (%)	$C_0/C_1/C_5$	$\mu_T(s)$
burma14	3323	0.00	0.00	30/30/30	0.20	0.00	0.00	30/30/30	0.08
ulysses16	6859	0.00	0.00	30/30/30	0.51	0.00	0.00	30/30/30	0.09
ulysses22	7013	0.00	0.00	30/30/30	0.52	0.00	0.00	30/30/30	0.12
att48	10628	0.19	0.87	0/0/0	12.48	0.00	0.00	30/30/30	0.43
eil51	426	0.23	1.25	0/0/0	23.41	0.00	0.00	30/30/30	45.09
berlin52	7542	0.00	2.24	18/18/18	16.26	0.00	0.00	30/30/30	0.29
st70	675	1.04	2.75	0/0/0	48.34	0.00	0.00	30/30/30	1.92
eil76	538	0.93	2.93	0/0/0	64.53	0.00	0.00	30/30/30	1.37
pr76	108159	0.00	2.62	1/1/1	64.45	0.00	0.00	30/30/30	1.32
gr96	55209	0.39	3.99	0/0/0	59.70	0.00	0.00	30/30/30	53.18
rat99	1211	1.07	3.82	0/0/0	98.00	0.00	0.00	30/30/30	1.47
kroA100	21282	0.00	2.20	3/3/5	90.04	0.00	0.00	30/30/30	0.86
kroB100	22141	0.17	2.20	0/0/0	97.40	0.00	0.00	30/30/30	2.30
kroC100	20749	0.00	3.13	1/1/1	82.63	0.00	0.00	30/30/30	1.11
kroD100	21294	0.86	3.28	0/0/0	94.89	0.00	0.00	30/30/30	5.88
kroE100	22068	0.31	1.98	0/0/0	58.12	0.00	0.09	17/17/17	130.82
rd100	7910	0.88	3.38	0/0/0	96.56	0.00	0.00	30/30/30	3.24
eil101	629	1.27	3.35	0/0/0	72.37	0.00	0.03	25/25/25	18.96
lin105	14379	0.77	2.89	0/0/0	66.20	0.00	0.00	30/30/30	0.84
pr107	44303	0.30	0.66	0/0/0	48.13	0.00	0.00	30/30/30	1.34
pr124	59030	0.37	2.33	0/0/0	47.53	0.00	0.00	30/30/30	1.79
bier127	118282	1.83	3.73	0/0/0	99.71	0.00	0.00	30/30/30	15.44
ch130	6110	1.08	5.31	0/0/0	111.38	0.00	0.02	28/28/28	12.13
pr136	96772	5.41	7.75	0/0/0	118.68	0.00	0.00	30/30/30	104.48
gr137	69853	3.35	7.57	0/0/0	103.06	0.00	0.00	30/30/30	4.84
pr144	58537	0.42	2.63	0/0/0	160.20	0.00	0.00	30/30/30	3.83
ch150	6528	1.09	2.01	0/0/0	105.91	0.00	0.00	30/30/30	142.47
kroA150	26524	3.86	6.37	0/0/0	137.31	0.00	0.00	29/30/30	123.17
kroB150	26130	2.51	4.30	0/0/0	139.16	0.00	0.00	26/30/30	3.79
pr152	73682	0.78	2.37	0/0/0	78.67	0.00	0.00	30/30/30	12.86
u159	42080	3.74	8.21	0/0/0	115.75	0.00	0.00	30/30/30	1.26
rat195	2323	3.06	5.23	0/0/0	144.85	0.00	0.19	5/5/5	33.44
d198	15780	1.11	2.98	0/0/0	191.88	0.00	0.02	16/25/25	164.86
kroA200	29368	1.06	3.96	0/0/0	201.16	0.00	0.00	30/30/30	15.80
kroB200	29437	3.71	7.60	0/0/0	196.10	0.00	0.00	30/30/30	31.25
gr202	40160	4.44	6.36	0/0/0	98.94	0.00	0.03	21/21/21	201.07
ts225	126643	0.63	3.99	0/0/0	119.75	0.00	0.00	30/30/30	8.25
tsp225	3916	3.32	6.49	0/0/0	133.63	0.00	0.10	26/26/26	162.08
pr226	80369	1.81	3.71	0/0/0	126.27	0.00	0.00	30/30/30	11.79
gr229	134602	2.45	4.08	0/0/0	122.76	0.00	0.00	28/28/30	267.82
gil262	2378	4.21	8.16	0/0/0	198.48	0.00	0.17	17/17/22	215.89
pr264	49135	4.12	7.77	0/0/0	160.32	0.00	0.00	30/30/30	125.48
a280	2579	2.75	5.41	0/0/0	194.50	0.00	0.00	30/30/30	13.54
pr299	48191	5.47	7.80	0/0/0	197.42	0.00	0.02	23/23/24	270.06
lin318	42029	3.75	6.70	0/0/0	394.44	0.00	0.12	17/17/17	748.56
μ_A			3.92				0.02		

*The numerical figure in the name of TSP instances denotes the problem dimension. For example, the dimension for lin318 is a TSP with 318 cities.

multiple vertices. DBMEA is an algorithm inspired by the microbial evolution (i.e. genetically driven changes that occur in microorganisms) [16]. It employs two operations, namely: bacterial mutation and gene transfer operation to evolve its population. The DBMEA is integrated with 2-opt and 3-opt local search to solve a set of TSP benchmark instances, i.e. very large scale integration (VLSI) dataset and TSPLIB dataset.

In conducting the comparison experiments (i.e. SDFA versus DFA, DCS, DBA, HGA, DBMEA), a total of 7, 14, 34, 32, and 6 TSPLIB benchmark instances as reported in the literature are used respectively (refer to Table 4). The performance evaluation of this comparison study is based on the same amount of solution constructions throughout an execution and same number of replications as indicated in Table 4.

Table 5 presents the comparison analysis of the proposed SDFA against DFA based on seven TSPLIB benchmark instances with the dimension ranges from 16 to 666 cities. Since the DFA is not integrated with a local search, the SDFA without local search is employed in such comparison. The reset strategy of the SDFA is also disabled. The SDFA is configured such that it has the similar parameter settings as DFA (i.e. $m = 1$, $\beta_0 = 1$, $\gamma = 0.001$) and it is executed for the same amount of the solution constructions depending on the problem dimension of TSP benchmark instances. In SDFA, the total number of solution constructions is converted into $maxGen$ by diving the total number of solution constructions by pop. For example, in ulysses16, SDFA uses $maxGen = 1149/5 = 230$ as its terminating condition. In addition, the benchmark indicator used here is accuracy(ϕ) with the formula of $\frac{X}{C} \times 100\%$ where X is average percentage deviation and C is the known optimum. The algorithm with a higher accuracy indicates a better performance. The table shows that SDFA is able to achieve better results in five out of seven TSP benchmark instances, i.e. gr202, tsp225, a280, pc442 and gr666. On average, the SDFA achieves 97.21% accuracy compared to DFA which achieves 95.13% accuracy. This indicates that SDFA is competitive with DFA.

Since the DCS, DBA, HGA, and DBMEA are integrated with a 2-opt local search, the SDFA+FRNN_2-opt is used in the comparison study. Table 6 presents the comparison analysis of the proposed SDFA+FRNN_2-opt against DCS, DBA, and HGA while Table 7 presents the comparison analysis of the proposed

Table 4. Algorithm execution settings used by other approaches and the proposed SDFA

Approach	Number of benchmark instances	Algorithm execution settings		Replication
		pop	maxGen	
DFA	7	5	PD*	50
DCS	14	20	500	30
DBA	34	15	200	30
HGA	32	PD*	PD*	10
DBMEA	6	100	PD*	10

*Depending on problem dimension

Table 5. Comparison of SDFA and DFA

Problem instance	Known optimum	Number of solution constructions	DFA	SDFA
			ϕ_A (%)	ϕ_A (%)
ulysses16	74.10	1149	100.09	97.37
ulysses22	75.67	8987	100.18	98.02
gr202	549.99	55690	100.17	102.91
tsp225	3859.00	445398	88.49	89.05
a280	2586.76	548930	88.38	89.21
pcb442	50783.55	1187428	88.53	93.15
gr666	3952.54	341519	100.08	110.74
μ_A			95.13	97.21

SDFA+FRNN_2-opt against DBMEA, based on a set of TSPLIB benchmark instances. The algorithm execution settings of the proposed SDFA+FRNN_2-opt is configured according to the benchmark algorithms. In DCS and DBA, the amount of solution constructions throughout an algorithm execution is 10000 (i.e. 20×500) and 3000 (i.e. 15×200) respectively. In HGA, the amount of solution constructions throughout an algorithm execution depends on the dimension of the TSP benchmark instances, i.e. the total number of solution constructions for problem dimensions [1, 100], [101, 200], [201, 300], [301, 400] is 2000, 20000, 20000 and 10000 respectively. In DBMEA, the algorithm is not stopped based on a fix amount of solution construction. It is stopped when the best-so-far solution

Table 6. Comparison of SDFA+FRNN_2-opt against other approaches

Problem instance	Known optimum (KO)	Known optimum (without rounding)	DCS		SDFA		IBA		SDFA		HGA*		SDFA*	
			δ_b (%)	δ_a (%)	δ_b (%)	δ_a (%)	δ_b (%)	δ_a (%)	δ_b (%)	δ_a (%)	δ_b (%)	δ_a (%)	δ_b (%)	δ_a (%)
eil51	426	429.98	0.00	0.00	0.00	0.16	0.00	0.00	0.00	0.20	0.00	0.00	0.00	0.00
berlin52	7542	7544.36	0.00	0.00	0.00	0.00	0.00	0.00	0.00	0.00	0.00	0.00	0.00	0.00
st70	675	678.59	0.00	0.00	0.00	0.00	0.00	0.00	0.00	0.00	0.00	0.00	0.00	0.00
eil76	538	545.38	0.00	0.01	0.00	0.00	0.00	0.74	0.00	0.00	0.00	0.12	0.00	0.00
pr76	108159	108159.43	0.00	0.00	0.00	0.00	0.00	0.00	0.00	0.00	0.00	0.09	0.00	0.00
rat99	-	1211.00	-	-	-	-	-	-	-	-	0.68	0.90	0.68	0.68
kroA100	21282	21285.43	0.00	0.00	0.00	0.00	0.00	0.00	0.00	0.00	0.00	0.13	0.00	0.00
kroB100	22141	-	0.00	0.00	0.00	0.00	0.00	0.00	0.00	0.01	-	-	-	-
kroC100	20749	20750.76	-	-	-	-	0.00	0.63	0.00	0.00	0.00	0.30	0.00	0.00
kroD100	21294	21294.28	-	-	-	-	0.00	0.38	0.00	0.00	0.00	0.24	0.00	0.01
kroE100	22068	-	-	-	-	-	0.00	0.33	0.00	0.14	-	-	-	-
rd100	-	7910.39	-	-	-	-	-	-	-	-	0.00	0.04	0.00	0.17
eil101	629	642.30	0.00	0.23	0.00	0.04	0.00	1.27	0.00	0.08	0.00	0.39	0.00	0.00
lin105	14379	14382.99	-	-	-	-	0.00	0.00	0.00	0.00	0.00	0.28	0.00	0.00
pr107	44303	44303.00	-	-	-	-	0.00	0.40	0.00	0.00	0.00	0.09	0.00	0.00
pr124	59030	59030.00	-	-	-	-	0.00	0.08	0.00	0.00	0.00	0.11	0.00	0.00
bier127	118282	-	0.00	0.07	0.00	0.00	0.00	0.35	0.00	0.01	-	-	-	-
ch130	6110	6110.86	0.00	0.42	0.00	0.04	0.00	0.74	0.00	0.02	0.00	0.32	0.00	0.08
pr136	96772	96772.00	-	-	-	-	0.00	0.72	0.00	0.02	0.01	0.26	0.01	0.04
pr144	58537	58537.00	-	-	-	-	0.00	0.00	0.00	0.00	0.00	0.00	0.00	0.00
ch150	6528	6532.28	0.00	0.34	0.00	0.18	0.00	0.86	0.00	0.28	0.00	0.39	0.00	0.27
kroA150	26524	26524.00	0.00	0.17	0.00	0.00	0.00	0.47	0.00	0.00	0.00	0.28	0.00	0.00
kroB150	26130	26130.00	-	-	-	-	0.00	0.52	0.00	0.00	0.00	0.79	0.00	0.00
pr152	73682	73682.00	-	-	-	-	0.00	0.18	0.00	0.00	0.00	0.11	0.00	0.02
rat195	2323	2323.00	-	-	-	-	0.04	1.59	0.00	0.27	1.04	1.42	0.61	0.66
d198	15780	15780.00	-	-	-	-	0.00	0.57	0.00	0.03	0.74	1.16	0.20	0.25
kroA200	29368	29368.00	0.05	0.27	0.00	0.00	0.00	1.27	0.00	0.00	0.00	0.31	0.00	0.00
kroB200	29437	29437.00	-	-	-	-	0.01	0.90	0.00	0.01	0.05	0.50	0.01	0.04
ts225	126643	3859.00	-	-	-	-	0.00	0.00	0.00	0.00	0.51	0.88	0.00	0.00
tsp225	3916	126643.00	-	-	-	-	0.00	1.89	0.00	0.15	1.18	1.30	0.00	0.00
pr226	80369	80369.00	-	-	-	-	0.00	0.50	0.00	0.00	0.08	0.21	0.00	0.00
gil262	2378	-	-	-	-	-	0.08	1.35	0.00	0.33	-	-	-	-
pr264	49135	49135.00	-	-	-	-	0.00	0.49	0.00	0.07	0.03	0.06	0.00	0.00
a280	2579	2586.76	-	-	-	-	0.00	1.24	0.00	0.02	2.82	3.46	0.00	0.03
pr299	48191	48191.00	-	-	-	-	0.00	0.75	0.00	0.07	2.64	3.25	0.01	0.07
lin318	42029	42029.00	0.23	0.97	0.00	0.21	0.30	1.63	0.00	0.24	1.42	2.02	0.03	0.17
μ_A				0.18		0.04		0.58		0.06		0.61		0.08

*The percentage deviations are computed with respect to the known optimal (without rounding).

Table 7. Comparison of SDFA and DBMEA

Problem instance	Optimum found by the modified Concorde algorithm	DBMEA	SDFA	
		δ_b (%)	δ_b (%)	δ_a (%)
berlin52	7544.37	**0.00**	**0.00**	0.00
lin105	14383.00	**0.00**	**0.00**	0.00
pr107	44301.68	**0.00**	**0.00**	0.00
ch130	6110.72	**0.00**	**0.00**	0.00
ch150	6530.90	**0.00**	**0.00**	0.16
lin318	42042.54	**0.00**	**0.00**	0.17
μ_A				0.06

does not change for 100 consecutive generations. For the SDFA+FRNN_2-opt specific parameters (i.e. γ, β_0 and rG), they are set according to Table 2.

The bolded numbers in Tables 6 and 7 indicate the superior or on-par percentage deviations. In terms of δ_a as shown in Table 6, the SDFA+FRNN_2-opt outperforms DCS, DBA, and HGA in 8 out of 14 instances, 25 out of 34 instances, and 27 out of 32 instances respectively. In terms of μ_A, the SDFA+FRNN_2-opt is found to be lower when compared with the μ_A of DCS, DBA, and HGA. The results in Table 7 show that SDFA+FRNN_2-opt is comparable to DBMEA in terms of δ_b. Based on the six problem instances, the SDFA+FRNN_2-opt achieves $\mu_A = 0.06\%$.

5   Conclusion

In order to computationally realize the movement of a dimmer firefly towards a brighter firefly, the proposed SDFA introduces an attractiveness computation scheme based on swap distance and a swap mutation movement scheme. The proposed approach is an alternative approach to the DFA proposed by Jati et al. [10]. Besides that, a strategy to determine a reference firefly such that other fireflies can move towards to is also devised. In order to improve the performance of SDFA, a fixed radius local search, an initialization mechanism and a reset strategy are employed. The proposed SDFA has shown comparable results and it is competitive with several state-of-the-art algorithms such as the Discrete Firefly Algorithm, the Discrete Cuckoo Search, the Discrete Bat Algorithm, the Hybrid Genetic Algorithm, and the Discrete Bacterial Memetic Evolutionary Algorithm. For future work, the mechanism to determine a reference firefly can be further explored. The proposed SDFA can be extended to solve TSP with high dimension (i.e. large number of cities) and address real world problems such as internet data packet routing, manufacturing scheduling, and multi-modal journey planning.

Acknowledgement. This work was supported by the Research University Grant (Grant No: 1001/PKOMP/814274) at Universiti Sains Malaysia (USM). Also, the first author acknowledges USM for the fellowship scheme to study Ph.D. degree at USM.

References

1. Wong, L.P., Low, M.Y.H., Chong, C.S.: Bee colony optimization with local search for traveling salesman problem. In: Proceedings of 6th IEEE International Conference on Industrial Informatics, INDIN 2008, pp. 1019–1025 (2008)
2. Applegate, D.L., Bixby, R.E., Chvátal, V., Cook, W.J.: The Traveling Salesman Problem. Princeton University Press, Princeton (2007)
3. Lin, S., Kernighan, B.W.: An effective heuristic algorithm for the traveling-salesman problem. Oper. Res. **21**(2), 498–516 (1973)
4. Helsgaun, K.: An effective implementation of the lin-kernighan traveling salesman heuristic. Eur. J. Oper. Res. **126**(1), 106–130 (2000)
5. Yang, X.S.: Firefly algorithms for multimodal optimization. In: Proceedings of 5th International Symposium on Stochastic Algorithms: Foundations and Applications, SAGA 2009, pp. 169–178 (2009)
6. Yang, X.S.: Nature-Inspired Optimization Algorithms. Luniver Press, Bristol (2010)
7. Yang, X.S.: Metaheuristic optimization: algorithm analysis and open problems. In: Proceedings of 10th International Symposium on Experimental Algorithms, SEA 2011, pp. 21–32 (2011)
8. Jati, G.K., Suyanto: Evolutionary discrete firefly algorithm for travelling salesman problem. In: Bouchachia, A. (ed.) ICAIS 2011. LNCS, vol. 6943, pp. 393–403. Springer, Heidelberg (2011). doi:10.1007/978-3-642-23857-4_38
9. Kumbharana, S.N., Pandey, G.M.: Solving travelling salesman problem using firefly algorithm. Int. J. Res. Sci. Adv. Technol. **2**(2), 53–57 (2013)
10. Jati, G.K., Manurung, R., Suyanto: Discrete firefly algorithm for traveling salesman problem: a new movement scheme. In: Yang, X.S., Cui, Z., Xiao, R., Gandomi, A.H., Karamanoglu, M. (eds.) Swarm Intelligence and Bio-Inspired Computation, pp. 295–312. Elsevier, Amsterdam (2013)
11. Osaba, E., Carballedo, R., Diaz, F., Onieva, E., Lopez, P., Perallos, A.: On the influence of using initialization functions on genetic algorithms solving combinatorial optimization problems: a first study on the TSP. In: Proceedings of IEEE Conference on Evolving and Adaptive Intelligent Systems, EAIS 2014, pp. 1–6 (2014)
12. Mahi, M., Baykan, Ö.K., Kodaz, H.: A new hybrid method based on particle swarm optimization, ant colony optimization and 3-opt algorithms for traveling salesman problem. Appl. Soft Comput. **30**, 484–490 (2015)
13. Alijla, B.O., Wong, L.P., Lim, C.P., Khader, A.T., Al-Betar, M.A.: An ensemble of intelligent water drop algorithms and its application to optimization problems. Inf. Sci. **325**, 175–189 (2015)
14. Wong, L.P., Low, M.Y.H., Chong, C.S.: Bee colony optimization with local search for traveling salesman problem. Int. J. Artif. Intell. Tools **19**(03), 305–334 (2010)
15. Tüű-Szabó, B., Földesi, P., Kóczy, L.T.: Improved discrete bacterial memetic evolutionary algorithm for the traveling salesman problem. In: Proceedings of Computational Intelligence in Information Systems Conference, CIIS 2016, pp. 27–38 (2017)

16. Kóczy, L.T., Földesi, P., Tüű-Szabó, B.: An effective discrete bacterial memetic evolutionary algorithm for the traveling salesman problem. Int. J. Intell. Syst. **32**(8), 862–876 (2017)
17. Fister, I., Fister, I., Yang, X.S., Brest, J.: A comprehensive review of firefly algorithms. Swarm Evol. Comput. **13**, 34–46 (2013)
18. Wong, L.P., Low, M.Y.H., Chong, C.S.: An efficient bee colony optimization algorithm for traveling salesman problem using frequency-based pruning. In: Proceedings of 7th IEEE International Conference on Industrial Informatics, INDIN 2009, pp. 775–782 (2009)
19. Eiben, A.E., Smit, S.K.: Evolutionary algorithm parameters and methods to tune them. In: Hamadi, Y., Monfroy, E., Saubion, F. (eds.) Autonomous Search, pp. 15–36. Springer, Berlin Heidelberg (2012). doi:10.1007/978-3-642-21434-9_2
20. Ouaarab, A., Ahiod, B., Yang, X.S.: Discrete cuckoo search algorithm for the travelling salesman problem. Neural Comput. Appl. **24**(7), 1659–1669 (2014)
21. Saji, Y., Riffi, M.E.: A novel discrete bat algorithm for solving the travelling salesman problem. Neural Comput. Appl. **27**(7), 1853–1866 (2016)
22. Wang, Y.: The hybrid genetic algorithm with two local optimization strategies for traveling salesman problem. Comput. Ind. Eng. **70**, 124–133 (2014)

An Efficient New Memetic Method for the Traveling Salesman Problem with Time Windows

Boldizsár Tüű-Szabó[1(✉)], Péter Földesi[2], and László T. Kóczy[1,3]

[1] Department of Information Technology,
Széchenyi István University, Győr, Hungary
tszboldi@gmail.com, tuu.szabo.boldizsar@sze.hu
[2] Department of Logistics, Széchenyi István University, Győr, Hungary
foldesi@sze.hu
[3] Department of Telecommunications and Media Informatics,
Budapest University of Technology and Economics, Budapest, Hungary
koczy@sze.hu

Abstract. In this paper we present a new memetic algorithm, which is called Discrete Bacterial Memetic Evolutionary Algorithm for solving the Traveling Salesman Problem with time windows (TSPTW). This method is the combination of bacterial evolutionary algorithm with 2-opt and 3-opt local searches. The algorithm was already tested on symmetric Traveling Salesman Problem (TSP) benchmark instances up to 5000 cities. It showed good properties in terms of tour lengths, runtimes and predictability of runtimes, so we decide to examine other variants of TSP with our algorithm. With some slight modifications our method was tested on TSP with time windows benchmark instances. Our test results were compared with the state-of-the art methods. In most cases our algorithm found the best-known solutions, and in terms of solution quality and runtime it is the second best method.

Keywords: TSP · Time windows · Memetic algorithm · Heuristic

1 Introduction

1.1 The Traveling Salesman Problem with Time Windows

The salesman has to visit all customers within a specific time window starting his journey from the depot and then he returns to the depot. Each customer has a service time and a time window defining its ready time and due time. If the salesman visits a customer after its due time, then this tour is called infeasible because not satisfy the constraints. If the salesman arrives to a customer before its ready time, he must wait because cannot be left before it. The task is to find the minimum cost tour which satisfy the time windows (a feasible tour with minimum cost).

The Traveling Salesman Problem with time windows (TSPTW) can be defined as a graph search problem with edge weights (1):

© Springer International Publishing AG 2017
S. Phon-Amnuaisuk et al. (Eds.): MIWAI 2017, LNAI 10607, pp. 426–436, 2017.
https://doi.org/10.1007/978-3-319-69456-6_35

$$G_{TSPTW} = (V_{costumer}, E_{conn})$$

$$V_{costumer} = v_0 \cup \{v_1, v_2, \ldots, v_n\}, E_{conn} \subseteq \{(v_i, v_j) | i \neq j\}$$

$$C : V_{customer} \times V_{customer} \rightarrow R, C = (cij)(n+1) \times (n+1) \qquad (1)$$

$$Ready\, time = \{a_1, a_2, \ldots, a_n\}$$

$$Due\, time == \{b_1, b_2, \ldots, b_n\}$$

$V_{costumer}$ is the set of customers

v_0 is the depot

C is called cost matrix, where cij is the sum of the service time of customer i and the cost of going from customer i to customer j

The goal is to find a feasible (which satisfying the time windows) permutation of vertices $(p_1, p_2, p_3, \ldots, p_n)$ that minimalizes the tour length (2).

$$Minimalize\, C(i) = c_{v_0, p_1} + \left(\sum_{i=1}^{n-1} c_{p_i, p_{i+1}} \right) + c_{p_n, v_0}$$

$$Subject\, to : D_{p_k} \leq b_{p_k}\, for\, all\, customers \qquad (2)$$

$$D_{p_k} = \max(A_{p_k}, a_{p_k})$$

$$A_{p_k} = D_{p_{k-1}} + c_{p_{k-1}, p_k}$$

D_{p_k} Departure time at customer p_k

A_{p_k} Arrival time at customer p_k

The TSPTW has also many application areas: logistics, transportation, postal and bank delivery.

The Traveling Salesman Problem with time windows is also NP-hard, even finding a feasible solution is NP-hard [1], so the exact algorithms can solve only small instances is reasonable time, heuristics are needed to handle this problem.

In the literature can be found some exact algorithms. Langevin et al. [2] introduced a two-commodity flow formulation for the traveling salesman and the makespan problems with time windows being able to solve instances up to 40 nodes. Dumas et al. [3] enhanced greatly the performance of the dynamic programming approach by new elimination tests that results the solving of instances up to 200 nodes with small time windows. Focacci et al. [4] combined in their methods the constraint programming with optimization techniques.

In contrast to the exact algorithms, the heuristic approaches can also produce optimal or near-optimal solutions for also bigger instances with bigger time windows in appropriate time. Carlton and Barnes [5] presented a tabu search approach for solving the TSPTW. Gendreau et al. [6] introduced an insertion heuristic with construction and post-optimization phases. This heuristic fails to results feasible solutions for some bigger instances with narrow time window. Calvo presented a new heuristic based on the solution of an auxiliary problem [7]. Calvo's heuristic don't find feasible solutions for some instances. Ohlmann and Thomas [8] combined the simulated annealing with a variable penalty method. Da Silva and Urrutia [9] proposed a general VNS heuristic with two stages, the constructive and optimization phases. The VNS heuristic improved some former best known results, and outperformed the other heuristic methods both in computational time and tour values.

1.2 Our Previous Work

In past few years we carried out extensive investigations to compare various population based algorithms (genetic algorithm [10], bacterial evolutionary algorithm [11], particle swarm algorithm [12] and their memetic versions [13, 14]) by testing them on several numerical optimization benchmark functions. The bacterial memetic evolutionary algorithm showed the best properties (accuracy, converge speed) [14].

In 2005 we introduced a version of the bacterial evolutionary algorithm extended with the Levenberg-Marquardt method for fuzzy rule extraction [13].

The first version of our Discrete Bacterial Memetic Evolutionary Algorithm (DBMEA) was presented in 2016 for the Traveling Salesman Problem [15, 16]. The algorithm showed good properties: it founded optimal and near-optimal solutions, and the runtime was more predictable than in the case of Concorde algorithm, but the runtimes were significant for instances above 1000 cities. In 2016 our algorithm was improved with bounded local search which led to significant improvement in runtime [17].

Considering the good properties for TSP we decided to examine our algorithm on other TSP variants.

2 The DBMEA Algorithm

The DBMEA combines the bacterial evolutionary algorithm with 2-opt, 3-opt local searches, so it is a memetic algorithm. The process of the DBMEA algorithm can be seen in Fig. 1.

Memetic algorithms extend the evolutionary based global search algorithms with local search methods. A local search heuristic is added to the searching process of the algorithm, applying it for the members of the population in each iteration [18]. Memetic algorithms can often handle efficiently NP-hard optimization problems improving both the accuracy of the solution and the convergence speed because they combine the advantages of both methods and eliminate the disadvantages. Local search techniques has fast convergence speed, but often get stuck in local optimums. The evolutionary based methods search in the global space, but they converge to the global optimum slowly.

The Bacterial Evolutionary Algorithm (BEA) [17] is based on the evolutionary development of bacteria. It uses two special operations for improving the properties of the individuals in the population, the bacterial mutation and the gene transfer operations.

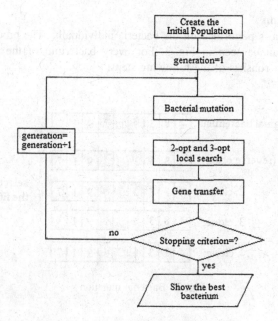

Fig. 1. The process of DBMEA algorithm

Creating the Initial Population

The Population is a group of individuals which mean solutions for the problem. In the DBMEA algorithm the individuals represent possible tours for the TSPTW.

In DBMEA the encoding is the following: The depot is indexed with 0, and each customer has an index $(1...n)$., so a sequence of indices represent an individual. Every tour in the graph starts from the depot, therefore the depot is not present in the code of the tours. Each index (excepting index 0) appears once, therefore the length of the string is $n-1$. An example of encoding can be seen in Fig. 2.

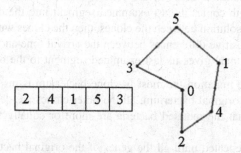

Fig. 2. The encoding of the tour

In the DBMEA for TSPTW the individuals in the initial Population are generated randomly.

Bacterial Mutation

Bacterial mutation is performed on the bacteria individually. The process of the bacterial mutation can be seen in Fig. 3. For every bacterium of the population, the bacterial mutation consists of the following steps:

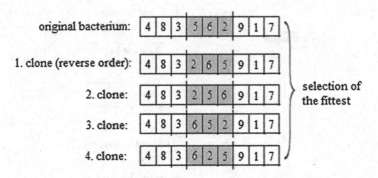

Fig. 3. Bacterial mutation

Initially N_{clones} clones are created from the original bacterium. The bacteria are divided into fixed length (I_{seg}) segments (genes) which are not necessary coherent. In our algorithm we use both loose and coherent segment mutations.

Next it chooses randomly one from the segments of the bacterium, and it randomly modifies the value of the selected segment in the clones but this gene in the original bacterium doesn't change. A deterministic clone with reverse ordering segment is generated, the others are created randomly.

Then the fitness value of each clone bacterium including the original are calculated. The gene of the best clone is copied back to the original bacterium and to all the clones.

In the case of TSPTW the evaluation of the clones is divided into two cases:

- if it is feasible solution between the clones, then the feasible solution with the shortest tour length copies its last examined segment into the others
- if it isn't feasible solution between the clones, then the clones with a smallest sum of delays (sum of positive differences between the arrival time and the due time of all customers in the tour) gives its last examined segment to the others

At the end of the mutation the most fit clone bacterium is inserted into the population instead of the original bacterium, all the other clones are deleted. The bacterial mutation provides that the mutated bacteria are more or equally fit than the original bacteria.

This process is repeated until all the genes of the original bacteria are mutated.

Coherent segment mutation: The coherent segments consist of adjacent elements of the code. The individual is cut into segments of equal lengths, so it can be executed easily (Fig. 4).

Loose segment mutation: The segments of the bacterium don't necessary consist of neighboring elements, it may come from different parts of the bacterium (Fig. 5).

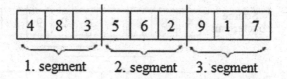

Fig. 4. Coherent segments

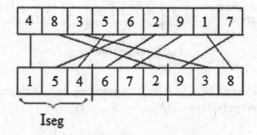

Fig. 5. Loose segments

The time complexity of the bacterial mutation is $O(N_{ind}N_{clones}n^2)$ in one generation, and the space requirement is $O(N_{ind}N_{clones}n)$ [19].

Gene Transfer

The gene transfer operation results in each iteration better and better bacteria in the population with transferring information from the bacteria with better properties to bacteria with worse properties.

In the gene transfer operation first the population is sorted in a descending order according to their fitness values and cut into two parts (an upper and a lower half). Next, the following is repeated N_{inf} times: it chooses randomly one bacterium (source bacterium) from the upper part and one bacterium (destination bacterium) from the lower part. Then a randomly selected part of the source bacterium with pre-defined length ($I_{transfer}$) is copied into the destination bacterium.

In the case of TSPTW first the population was sorted in ascending order according to their sum of delays (sum of positive differences between the arrival time and the due time of all customers in the tour), then the individuals with equal sum of delays are sorted again based on their tour lengths.

Gene Transfer in the DBMEA algorithm is the following: A source segment with pre-defined length is selected randomly from the source bacterium and this segment is transferred to the destination bacterium. The source and the destination offset are selected randomly, and it can be different.

In Fig. 6. the source segment is (6, 2, 9), and this segment is copied into the destination bacterium (after index 5). The double occurrence is eliminated with deleting the elements in the destination bacterium, which are same with the elements in the transferred segment to ensure the unchanged length of the code.

The total time complexity of the gene transfer operation is $C_{GT} = O(N_{ind}(n + logN_{ind}) + N_{inf}(n + N_{ind}))$, which consists of the fitness value calculation $O(N_{ind}n)$,

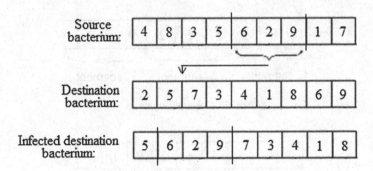

Source
bacterium:

| 4 | 8 | 3 | 5 | 6 | 2 | 9 | 1 | 7 |

Destination
bacterium:

| 2 | 5 | 7 | 3 | 4 | 1 | 8 | 6 | 9 |

Infected destination
bacterium:

| 5 | 6 | 2 | 9 | 7 | 3 | 4 | 1 | 8 |

Fig. 6. Gene transfer

sorting of the population $O(N_{ind}logN_{ind})$, reinserting the modified destination bacterium into the sorted population $O(N_{inf}(n + N_{ind}))$ [19].

Local Search

Local search techniques are crucial parts of every memetic algorithm because they can strongly influence the efficiency of the searching process.

A local search algorithm iteratively searches in the neighborhood of the current solution. In many optimization problems the combination of a local search technique with an evolutionary based metaheuristic results an efficient method (genetic algorithms, bacterial evolutionary algorithms etc.), which provides optimal or near-optimal solutions [20].

In the DBMEA for solving the TSPTW the local searches are the 2-opt and 3-opt techniques. First 2-opt, then if no further improvement is possible with 2-opt, 3-opt local search is applied on the tours. If the tour is infeasible, the local searches try to reduce the sum of the delays (sum of positive differences between the arrival time and the due time of all customers in the tour). If the tour is feasible (sum of delays is zero) the local searches try to reduce the length of the tour holding the feasibility of the tour with exchanging edges.

2-opt Local Search.

2-opt local search is a tour improvement heuristic, which aims to reduce the tour length with replacing edge pairs in the graph (Fig. 7).

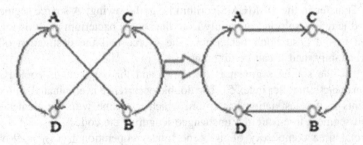

Fig. 7. 2-opt local steps

Edge pairs (AB, CD) are iteratively replaced with AC and BD edges and the following inequality is examined: $|AB| + |CD| > |AC| + |BD|$.

If the inequality holds then *AB* and *CD* edges are replaced with *AC* and *BD* edges (Fig. 7).

3-opt Local Search

The 3-opt local search improves the tour with replacing edge triples. There are 8 possible ways to create a new tour, but 4 of them is only a 2-opt step (Fig. 8). The output of the 3-opt step is the shortest tour from the original and the four new tours.

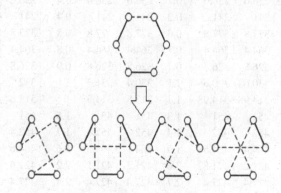

Fig. 8. 3-opt local steps

3   Computational Results

The DBMEA algorithm was tested on instances proposed by Gendreau *et al.* [6], which contains 140 instances grouped in 28 test cases between 20 and 100 customers with time window widths ranging from 80 to 200 time units.

The algorithm was tested with the following parameters:

- the number of bacteria in the population ($N_{ind} = 20$)
- the number of clones in the bacterial mutation ($N_{clones} = 20$)
- the number of infections in the gene transfer ($N_{inf} = 10$)
- the length of the chromosomes ($I_{seg} = 5$)
- the length of the transferred segment ($I_{trans} = n_{customer}/10$)
- Stopping criterion: maximum number of generations is 50

Our results are compared with the state-of-the-art methods, the general VNS Heuristic [9] and the compressed annealing [8]. Our algorithm was tested on an Intel Pentium Dual CPU T2390 1,86 GHz, 2 GB RAM workstation. The general VNS heuristic was run on a Pentium 4 2.40 GHz processor with 1 GB of RAM and the compressed annealing on a Pentium 4 2.66 GHz processor with 1 GB of RAM. Our results were calculated by averaging 10 test runs.

As it can be seen in Table 1, our algorithm produced the best known or near-best known solutions for all test cases. In 24 out of 28 test cases the DBMEA algorithm found the best-known results, in 4 cases the general VNS heuristic found a bit lower

Table 1. Comparison of results for TSP with time windows (*n*: number of customers, *w*: time windows width)

Instance		Best known	DBMEA			General VNS heuristic			Compressed annealing		
n	w		Best value	Avg. value	Avg. sec	Best value	Avg. value	Avg. sec	Best value	Avg. value	Avg. sec
20	120	265.6	265.6	265.6	0.2	265.6	265.6	0.3	265.6	265.6	3.1
	140	232.8	232.8	232.8	0.2	232.8	232.8	0.3	232.8	232.8	3.9
	160	218.2	218.2	218.2	0.2	218.2	218.2	0.3	218.2	218.2	4
	180	236.6	236.6	236.6	0.2	236.6	236.6	0.4	236.6	236.6	4
	200	241	241	241	0.2	241	241	0.4	241	241	4.1
40	120	377.8	377.8	377.8	0.6	377.8	377.8	0.8	377.8	378.1	6
	140	364.4	364.4	364.4	0.7	364.4	364.4	0.8	364.4	364.7	6
	160	326.8	326.8	326.8	0.7	326.8	326.8	0.9	326.8	327.1	6
	180	330.4	330.68	330.68	1.1	330.4	331.3	1	332	333.9	6.2
	200	313.8	314.98	314.98	1.7	313.8	314.3	1	313.8	315	6.3
60	120	451	451	451	1.3	451	451	1.5	451	452.9	8.3
	140	452	452	452	1.4	452	452.1	1.7	452.4	454	8.6
	160	464	464.4	464.58	1.9	464	464.5	1.6	464.6	465.4	8.4
	180	421.2	421.2	421.82	3.6	421.2	421.2	2.2	421.6	425.2	8.6
	200	427.4	427.4	427.4	2.7	427.4	427.4	2.4	427.4	430.8	8.4
80	100	578.6	578.6	578.6	1.4	578.6	578.7	2.3	579.2	581.6	11.5
	120	541.4	541.4	542.24	6.9	541.4	541.4	2.7	541.4	544	11.5
	140	506	506	506.88	6.4	506	506.3	3.2	509.8	513.6	11.3
	160	504.8	505.2	506.14	6.7	504.8	505.5	3.3	505.4	511.7	11.2
	180	500.6	502	502.8	7.4	500.6	501.2	3.7	502	505.9	11.4
	200	481.4	481.8	482.86	7.5	481.4	481.8	4.2	481.8	486.4	11.1
100	80	666.4	666.4	667.1	7.4	666.4	666.6	3.1	666.4	668.1	15.9
	100	642	642	642.86	10.4	642	642.1	3.7	642.2	645	14.6
	120	597.2	598.2	600.1	15.1	597.2	597.5	4.1	601.2	603.7	15
	140	548.4	548.4	548.66	8.8	548.4	548.4	4.4	579.2	582.5	14.9
	160	555	555	556.22	12.8	555	555	5.1	584	588.8	15
	180	561.6	562	562.7	14.1	561.6	561.6	6.3	561.6	566.9	14.9
	200	550.2	551.2	552.84	15	550.2	551	6.8	555.4	562.3	14.9

values than our algorithm. The average runtime of the DBMEA algorithm was smaller by 48,54% in comparison with the compressed annealing tested on the benchmark problems. The general VNS heuristic was faster by 49,78% than our method. The comparison of runtimes in Fig. 9 can be seen averaging the runtimes of the equal sized instances.

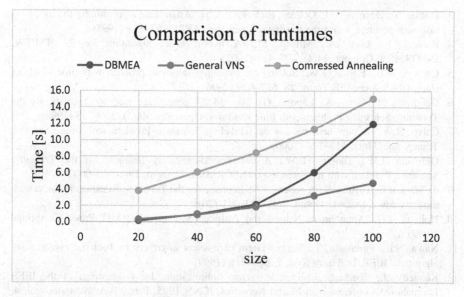

Fig. 9. Comparison of runtimes for the TSPTW

4 Conclusion

In this paper our DBMEA algorithm was tested on TSP with time windows benchmarks. The algorithm is efficient for solving TSP with time windows because in most cases found the best-known values, and it outperforms the Compressed Annealing in terms of runtime, however the general VNS heuristic is a bit faster.

In our further work we plan to test DBMEA algorithm on other TSP variants (time dependant TSP, Minimum Latency Problem etc.).

Acknowledgement. This research was supported by the National Research, Development and Innovation Office (NKFIH) K108405 and by the EFOP-3.6.2-16-2017-00015 "HU- MATHS - IN - Intensification of the activity of the Hungarian Industrial Innovation Service Network" grant.

 Supported by the ÚNKP-16-3 New National Excellence Program of the Ministry of Human Capacities.

References

1. Savelsbergh, M.W.P.: Local search in routing problems with time windows. Ann. Oper. Res. **4**(1), 285–305 (1985)
2. Langevin, A., Desrochers, M., Desrosiers, J., Gélinas, S., Soumis, F.: A two-commodity flow formulation for the traveling salesman and the makespan problems with time windows. Networks **23**(7), 631–640 (1993)

3. Dumas, Y., Desrosiers, J., Gelinas, E., Solomon, M.: An optimal algorithm for the travelling salesman problem with time windows. Oper. Res. **43**(2), 367–371 (1995)
4. Focacci, F., Lodi, A., Milano, M.: A hybrid exact algorithm for the TSPTW. INFORMS J. Comput. **14**(4), 403–417 (2002)
5. Carlton, W.B., Barnes, J.W.: Solving the travelling salesman problem with time windows using tabu search. IEE Trans. **28**, 617–629 (1996)
6. Gendreau, M., Hertz, A., Laporte, G., Stan, M.: A generalized insertion heuristic for the Traveling Salesman Problem with time windows. Oper. Res. **46**(3), 330–335 (1998)
7. Calvo, R.W.: A new heuristic for the Traveling Salesman Problem with time windows. Transp. Sci. **34**(1), 113–124 (2000)
8. Ohlmann, J.W., Thomas, B.W.: A compressed-annealing heuristic for the Traveling Salesman Problem with time windows. INFORMS J. Comput. **19**(1), 80–90 (2007)
9. da Silva, R.F., Urrutia, S.: A general VNS heuristic for the Traveling Salesman Problem with time windows. Discrete Optim. **7**(4), 203–211 (2010)
10. Holland, J.H.: Adaption in Natural and Artificial Systems. The MIT Press, Cambridge (1992)
11. Nawa, N.E., Furuhashi, T.: Fuzzy system parameters discovery by bacterial evolutionary algorithm. IEEE Tr. Fuzzy Syst. **7**, 608–616 (1999)
12. Kennedy, J., Eberhart, R.: Particle swarm optimization. In: Proceedings of the IEEE International Conference on Neural Networks, ICNN 1995, Perth, WA, Australia, vol. 4, pp. 1942–1948 (1995)
13. Botzheim, J., Cabrita, C., Kóczy, L.T., Ruano, A.E.: Fuzzy rule extraction by bacterial memetic algorithms. In: Proceedings of the 11th World Congress of International Fuzzy Systems Association, IFSA 2005, Beijing, China, pp. 1563–1568 (2005)
14. Balázs, K., Botzheim, J., Kóczy, T.L.: Comparison of various evolutionary and memetic algorithms. In: Huynh, V.N., Nakamori, Y., Lawry, J., Inuiguchi, M. (eds.) Integreted Uncertainty Management and Applications. AISC, vol. 68, pp. 431–442. Springer, Heidelberg (2010). doi:10.1007/978-3-642-11960-6_40
15. Kóczy, L.T., Földesi, P., Tüű-Szabó, B.: An effective discrete bacterial memetic evolutionary algorithm for the Traveling Salesman Problem. Int. J. Intell. Syst. **32**(8), 862–876 (2017)
16. Kóczy, L.T., Földesi, P., Tüű-Szabó, B.: A discrete bacterial memetic evolutionary algorithm for the Traveling Salesman Problem. In: IEEE World Congress on Computational Intelligence (WCCI 2016), Vancouver, Canada, pp. 3261–3267 (2016)
17. Tüű-Szabó, B., Földesi, P., Kóczy, L.T.: Improved discrete bacterial memetic evolutionary algorithm for the Traveling Salesman Problem. In: Phon-Amnuaisuk, S., Au, T.-W., Omar, S. (eds.) CIIS 2016. AISC, vol. 532, pp. 27–38. Springer, Cham (2017). doi:10.1007/978-3-319-48517-1_3
18. Moscato, P.: On evolution, search, optimization, genetic algorithms and martial arts - towards memetic algorithms. Technical report, Caltech Concurrent Computation Program, Report. 826, California Institute of Technology, Pasadena, USA (1989)
19. Földesi, P., Botzheim, J.: Modeling of loss aversion in solving fuzzy road transport Traveling Salesman Problem using eugenic bacterial memetic algorithm. Memetic Comput. **2**(4), 259–271 (2010)
20. Hoos, H.H., Stutzle, T.: Stochastic Local Search: Foundations and Applications. Morgan Kaufmann, San Francisco (2005)

A Novel Approach of Set-Based Particle Swarm Optimization with Memory State

Michiharu Maeda[1(✉)] and Takahiro Hino[2]

[1] Fukuoka Institute of Technology, Fukuoka 811-0295, Japan
maeda@fit.ac.jp
[2] JFE Systems, Handa 475-8611, Japan

Abstract. This paper presents a novel approach of set-based particle swarm optimization with memory state for solving traveling salesman problem. Particle swarm optimization achieves the social model of bird flocking and fish schooling and solves continuous optimization problem. Set-based particle swarm optimization functions in discrete space by using a set and solves combinatorial optimization problem with successfully applying to the large-scale problem. Our approach selects the best position among different positions from the current generation for creating a solution according to a velocity. In order to show the effectiveness of our approach, numerical experiments are presented for traveling salesman problem compared to existing algorithms.

Keywords: Set-based particle swarm optimization · Discrete space · Combinatorial optimization problem · Traveling salesman problem

1 Introduction

Particle swarm optimization (PSO) is an evolutionary computation algorithm [1]. When a particle finds the best solution, PSO moves each particle in the swarm to the best solution. Particles have a position and velocity. The position is a solution and the velocity is a vector of the difference between the current position and the next position. The application of PSO involves, for example, fuzzy-neural network for voice controlled robot system [2] and reactive power and voltage control considering voltage security assessment [3]. The traditional PSO algorithm is designed to work only in the continuous space. Discrete particle swarm optimization (DPSO) operates in binary space by using sigmoid function [4]. Memory binary particle swarm optimization (MBPSO) is developed based on DPSO [5]. MBPSO decides a position according to the previous position, in which mechanism is simple and effective. MBPSO memorizes the position which is updated according to a new defined velocity and shows superior results for discrete optimization problem. Set-based particle swarm optimization (SPSO) operates in discrete space [6]. All arithmetic updates in the position and velocity are redefined by the new operators and procedures. SPSO can approximately solve the traveling salesman problem (TSP) and is successful to apply to the

© Springer International Publishing AG 2017
S. Phon-Amnuaisuk et al. (Eds.): MIWAI 2017, LNAI 10607, pp. 437–449, 2017.
https://doi.org/10.1007/978-3-319-69456-6_36

large-scale problem comparatively. TSP is one of combinatorial optimization problems and searches for the shortest route that visits each city once and returns to the origin city. Max-min ant system (MMAS) is well-known for solving TSP in swarm intelligence [7]. For knapsack problem, we suggested set-based particle swarm optimization with memory state before this paper [8].

In this paper, we present a novel approach of set-based particle swarm optimization with memory state (SPSOMS) to decide the position based on the previous position for solving traveling salesman problem. Our approach selects the best position, except for the current position, among selectable sets which are generated by velocities. Experimental results are compared the proposed algorithm to MMAS and SPSO for six kinds of traveling salesman problems.

This paper is organized as follows. In the next section, traveling salesman problem and particle swarm optimization are described. Section 3 presents set-based particle swarm optimization with memory state. Section 4 describes numerical experiments and results. Finally, Sect. 5 summarizes conclusions.

2   Preliminary

2.1   Particle Swarm Optimization

Particle swarm optimization (PSO) is an optimization approach that achieves the social model of bird flocking and fish schooling [1]. Swarms move to a particle which finds out the best solution. Each particle has a position and velocity which are a candidate solution and a vector constructed the current position and the best position, respectively. Each particle stores the base position previously encountered by itself and the best position of all particles. The traditional PSO algorithm is operated by only continuance space. The update rules of velocity and position of i-th particle are defined as follows:

$$v_{ij}^{k+1} = wv_{ij}^k + c_1r_1(P_{ij} - x_{ij}^k) + c_2r_2(G_j - x_{ij}^k) \tag{1}$$

$$x_{ij}^{k+1} = x_{ij}^k + v_{ij}^{k+1} \quad (1 \leq i \leq n, 1 \leq j \leq d) \tag{2}$$

where n is the number of particles and d is the number of dimension in search space. v_{ij}^k is the i-th particle's velocity in j-th dimension for k-th generation and x_{ij}^k is the i-th particle's position in j-th dimension for k-th generation. P_{ij} in j-th dimension is the best position of i-th particle and G_j in j-th dimension is the best position of all particles. c_1, c_2, and w are the positive coefficients. r_1 and r_2 are random uniform values in $[0.0, 1.0]$. The procedure of PSO algorithm is described as follows:

Step 1. Initialize the positions and velocities.
Step 2. Evaluate the fitness of current position for each particle.
Step 3. Update the best position for each particle.
Step 4. Update the best position of all particles.
Step 5. Update the velocity according to Eq. (1).
Step 6. Update the position according to Eq. (2).

Step 7. If the current iteration is equal to the maximum number, then terminate, otherwise go to step 2.

We show the search concept of PSO in Fig. 1. x_i and v_i are the position and velocity of i-th particle, respectively. p_i is the best position previously encountered by particle i and g is the best position of all particles.

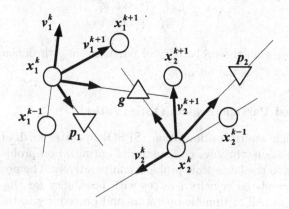

Fig. 1. Search concept of PSO

2.2   Discrete Particle Swarm Optimization

Discrete particle swarm optimization (DPSO) was proposed [4], in which the position is used as bit sequence for discrete problem. The velocity is the probability of real number for renewing the position. The position of i-th particle is updated as follows:

$$x_{ij}^{k+1} = \begin{cases} 1 & (r < s(v_{ij}^{k+1})) \\ 0 & (\text{otherwise}) \end{cases} \tag{3}$$

where r is a uniform random value in $[0.0, 1.0]$. s denotes a sigmoid function:

$$s(v_{ij}^{k+1}) = \frac{1}{1 + e^{-v_{ij}^{k+1}}} \tag{4}$$

2.3   Memory Binary Particle Swarm Optimization

Memory binary particle swarm optimization (MBPSO) shows a high quality for discrete optimization problem. MBPSO decides a position according to the previous position [5]. The velocity of i-th particle is updated as follows:

$$v_{ij}^{k+1} = wv_{ij}^k + c_1 r_1 \mathrm{E}(p_{ij}, x_{ij}^k) + c_2 r_2 \mathrm{E}(g_j, x_{ij}^k) \tag{5}$$

where $E(*, *)$ is defined as follows:

$$E(A, B) = \begin{cases} 1 & (A = B) \\ -1 & (\text{otherwise}) \end{cases} \tag{6}$$

The position of i-th particle is updated as follows:

$$x_{ij}^{k+1} = \begin{cases} x_{ij}^k & (r < s(v_{ij}^{k+1})) \\ \bar{x}_{ij}^k & (\text{otherwise}) \end{cases} \tag{7}$$

where v_{ij}^{k+1} represents the probability of particle i in j-th dimension to retain the current state. $\bar{x}_{ij}^k$ is the bit invert of x_{ij}^k.

2.4 Set-Based Particle Swarm Optimization

Set-based particle swarm optimization (SPSO) operates in discrete space [6]. SPSO can approximately solve combinatorial optimization problem and is successful to apply to the large-scale problem comparatively. The position is a candidate solution and the velocity is a set with possibility for the discrete optimization problem. All arithmetic operators and procedures in the position and velocity for the updating rule are redefined by new operators and procedures.

In SPSO for TSP, a universal set E is a collection of routes for all cities. E is illustrated as shown in Fig. 2 (a). The circles are the locations of cities and the lines are routes between two cities.

E^n is a subset of the universal set E for city n. By way of example, E^2 for city 2 is illustrated in Fig. 2 (b). Subset $E^2 = \{(1, 2), (2, 3), (2, 4), (2, 5), (2, 6)\}$ is described.

Position X is a feasible solution illustrated in Fig. 2 (c). Position $X = \{(1, 2), (1, 6), (2, 3), (3, 4), (4, 5), (5, 6)\}$ is shown.

In SPSO, the velocity is a set with possibility defined as follows:

$$V = \{e/p(e) \mid e \in E\} \tag{8}$$

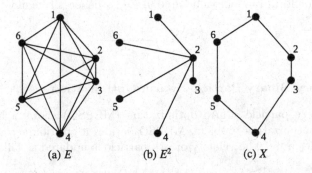

(a) E (b) E^2 (c) X

Fig. 2. Example of universal set E, subset E^2, and position X in TSP

where E is a universal set of elements and V has a possibility $p(e)$ in $[0.0, 1.0]$ of each element $e \in E$.

The set with possibility of i-th particle is defined as follows:

$$V_i = \{e/p(e) \mid e \in E\} \tag{9}$$

The set with possibility of i-th particle in j-th dimension is defined as follows:

$$V_i^j = \{e/p(e) \mid e \in E^j\} \tag{10}$$

where E^j is a universal set of j-th dimension.

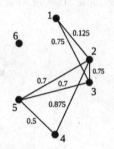

Fig. 3. Example of velocity

For explaining TSP, for example, we have velocity $V_i = \{(1,2)/0.125,$ $(1,3)/0.75$, $(2,3)/0.75$, $(2,4)/0.875$, $(2,5)/0.7$, $(3,5)/0.7$, $(4,5)/0.5\}$. The velocity V_i in j-th dimension is shown as: $V_i^1 = \{$ $(1,2)/0.125$, $(1,3)/0.75$ $\}$, $V_i^2 = \{(1,2)/0.125$, $(2,3)/0.75$, $(2,4)/0.875$, $(2,5)/0.7\}$, $V_i^3 = \{(1,3)/0.75$, $(2,3)/0.75$, $(3,5)/0.7\}$, $V_i^4 = \{(2,4)/0.875$, $(4,5)/0.5$ $\}$, $V_i^5 = \{(2,5)/0.7$, $(3,5)/0.7$, $(4,5)/0.5\}$, $V_i^6 = \phi$. V is illustrated in Fig. 3. The number near the line is a value of velocity.

At the beginning, we explain the velocity update. In SPSO, the update rule is defined as follows:

$$V_i^j = wV_i^j + c_1 r_1(P_{f_i(j)} - X_i^j) \tag{11}$$

where X_i^j is the position of i-th particle in j-th dimension. The position is given by a crisp set. $f_i(j)$ is adopted by the particle with high fitness for particle i when two particle are randomly selected [9].

We define K_i^j that keeps large possibility and converts a set with possibility to a crisp set. K_i^j of the i-th particle in j-th dimension is defined as follows:

$$K_i^j = \{e \mid e/p(e) \in V_i^j \text{ and } p(e) \geq \alpha_i\} \tag{12}$$

where α_i is a random value in $[0.0, 1.0]$ of i-th particle. For example, we suppose set K in Fig. 4. If a random value and a set are $\alpha = 0.5$ and $V = \{$ $(1,2)/0.1$, $(1,3)/0.6$, $(1,6)/0.8$, $(2,3)/0.6$, $(2,4)/0.7$, $(2,5)/0.8$, $(3,4)/0.8$,

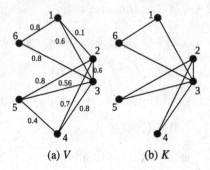

Fig. 4. Example of generation V to K

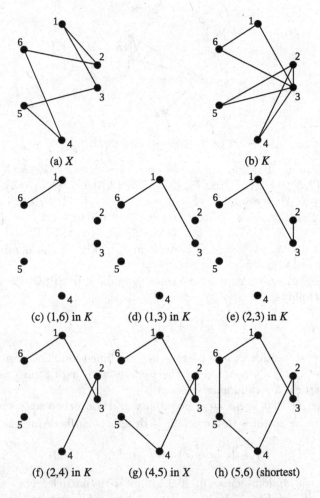

Fig. 5. Example of position update procedure in SPSO

$(3, 5)/0.56$, $(3, 6)/0.8$, $(4, 5)/0.4$ }, then we have $K = \{(1, 3), (1, 6), (2, 3), (2, 4),$ $(2, 5), (3, 4), (3, 5), (3, 6)\}$.

The position in SPSO is updated as follows:

$$X_i^{j,k+1} = \begin{cases} \{e \mid d(e \in K_i^j \text{ and } e \in \Omega^j)\} & ((K_i^j \in \Omega^j)) \\ \{e \mid d(e \in X_i^{j,k} \text{ and } e \in \Omega^j)\} & ((K_i^j \notin \Omega^j \text{ and } X_i^{j,k} \in \Omega^j)) \\ \{e \mid d(e \in \Omega^j)\} & (\text{otherwise}) \end{cases} \quad (13)$$

where $d(*)$ selects the shortest path in given sets. Ω^j is selectable sets of j-th dimension.

$X_i^{j,k}$ is the position of i-th particle in j-th dimension at k-th generation.

The update procedure in SPSO is described as follows:

Step 1. Select city j randomly.
Step 2. Generate selectable sets Ω^j.
Step 3. Update X_i^j in accordance with the update rule.
Step 4. If the closed path is completed, then terminate, otherwise select city j randomly and go to step 2.

We show the construction concept of route for SPSOMS in Fig. 5. We assume that $X = \{(1, 2), (1, 3), (2, 6), (3, 5), (4, 5), (4, 6)\}$ and $K = \{(1, 3), (1, 6), (2, 3), (2, 4), (2, 5), (3, 4), (3, 5), (3, 6)\}$ in (a) and (b), respectively. (c) selected element $(1, 6)$ in K, (d) selected element $(1, 3)$ in K, (e) selected element $(2, 3)$ in K, (f) selected element $(2, 4)$ in K, (g) selected element $(4, 5)$ in X, and (h) selected element $(5, 6)$ as the shortest path are illustrated.

3 Set-Based Particle Swarm Optimization with Memory State

Set-based particle swarm optimization with memory state (SPSOMS) decides the position based on the previous position.

The coefficient and set with possibility are multiplied as follows:

$$wV = \{e/p'(e) \mid e \in E\} \quad (14)$$

where

$$p'(e) = \begin{cases} 1 & (w \times p(e) > 1) \\ w \times p(e) & (\text{otherwise}) \end{cases}$$

For example, we show the multiplication operator of coefficient and set with possibility in Fig. 6. If the coefficient and set with possibility are $w = 0.8$ and $V_i = \{(1, 2)/0.125, (1, 3)/0.75, (2, 3)/0.75, (2, 4)/0.875, (2, 5)/0.7, (3, 5)/0.7, (4, 5)/0.5\}$, then $wV_i = \{(1, 2)/0.1, (1, 3)/0.6, (2, 3)/0.6, (2, 4)/0.7, (2, 5)/0.56, (3, 5)/0.56, (4, 5)/0.4\}$.

The minus operator is defined as follows:

$$P - X = \{e \mid e \in P \text{ and } e \notin X\} \quad (15)$$

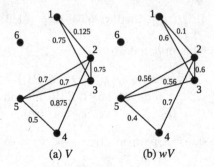

Fig. 6. Example of multiplication operator for coefficient w and set with possibility V.

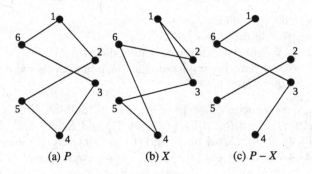

Fig. 7. Example of minus operator

For example, we show the minus operator in Fig. 7. If $P = \{(1,2), (1,6), (2,5), (3,4), (3,6), (4,5)\}$ and $X = \{(1,2), (1,3), (2,6), (3,5), (4,5), (4,6)\}$ are given, then we have $P - X = \{(1,6), (2,5), (3,4), (3,6)\}$.

The coefficient and set are multiplied as follows:

$$cE' = \{e/p''(e) \mid e \in E\} \tag{16}$$

$$p''(e) = \begin{cases} 1 & (e \in E' \text{ and } c > 1) \\ c & (e \in E' \text{ and } 0 \le c \le 1) \\ 0 & (e \notin E') \end{cases}$$

where E' is a subset of the universal set E and c is a coefficient. For example, we illustrate the multiplication operator of the coefficient and set in Fig. 8. If the coefficient and set are $c = 0.8$ and $(P - X) = \{(1, 6), (2, 5), (3, 4), (3, 6)\}$, then we have $c(P - X) = \{(1, 6)/0.8, (2, 5)/0.8, (3, 4)/0.8, (3, 6)/0.8\}$.

For the plus operator, two sets with possibilities are added as follows:

$$V_1 + V_2 = \{e/\max(p_1(e), p_2(e)) \mid e \in E\} \tag{17}$$

where $V_1 = \{e/p_1(e) \mid e \in E\}$ and $V_2 = \{e/p_2(e) \mid e \in E\}$ are defined on universal set E. For example, we illustrate the plus operator of two sets

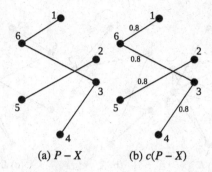

(a) $P - X$ (b) $c(P - X)$

Fig. 8. Example of multiplication operator for coefficient c and set $P - X$

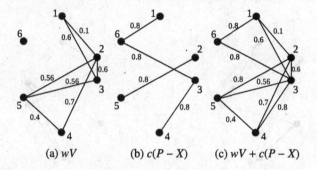

(a) wV (b) $c(P - X)$ (c) $wV + c(P - X)$

Fig. 9. Example of plus operator for two sets with possibilities wV and $c(P - X)$.

with possibilities in Fig. 9. If the sets with possibility are $wV = \{(1,2)/0.1,$ $(1,3)/0.6,\ (2,3)/0.6,\ (2,4)/0.7,\ (2,5)/0.56,\ (3,5)/0.56,\ (4,5)/0.4\}$ and $c(P - X) = \{(1,6)/0.8,\ (2,5)/0.8,\ (3,4)/0.8,\ (3,6)/0.8\}$, then we have $wV + c(P - X) = \{(1,2)/0.1,\ (1,3)/0.6,\ (1,6)/0.8,\ (2,3)/0.6,\ (2,4)/0.7,\ (2,5)/0.8,\ (3,4)/0.8,$ $(3,5)/0.56,\ (3,6)/0.8,\ (4,5)/0.4\}$.

The position in SPSOMS is updated as follows:

$$X_i^{j,k+1} = \begin{cases} \{e \mid d(e \in L_i^j \text{ and } e \in \Omega^j)\} & (L_i^j \in \Omega^j) \\ \{e \mid d(e \in X_i^{j,k} \text{ and } e \in \Omega^j)\} & (L_i^j \notin \Omega^j \text{ and } X_i^{j,k} \in \Omega^j) \\ \{e \mid d(e \in \Omega^j)\} & \text{(otherwise)} \end{cases} \qquad (18)$$

where $d(*)$ selects the shortest path and Ω^j is the selectable set of j-th dimension. L is defined as follows:

$$L = \{e \mid e \in K \text{ and } e \notin X\} \qquad (19)$$

where L is same as $K - X$. For example, we explain the minus operator of two sets in Fig. 10. If the sets are $K = \{(1,3),\ (1,6),\ (2,3),\ (2,4),\ (2,5),\ (3,4),\ (3,5),$ $(3,6)\}$ and $X = \{(1,2),\ (1,3),\ (2,6),\ (3,5),\ (4,5),\ (4,6)\}$, then we have $L = \{(1,6),\ (2,3),\ (2,4),\ (2,5),\ (3,4),\ (3,6)\}$.

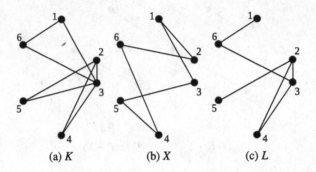

Fig. 10. Example of generation $L(K - X)$

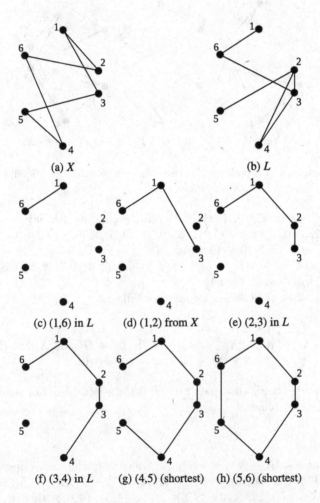

Fig. 11. Example of position update procedure in SPSOMS

We show the construction concept of SPSOMS in Fig. 11. We assume that sets $X = \{(1,2), (1,3), (2,6), (3,5), (4,5), (4,6)\}$ and $L = \{(1,6), (2,3), (2,4), (2,5), (3,4), (3,6)\}$ in (a) and (b), respectively. (c) selected element $(1,6)$ in L, (d) selected element $(1,2)$ in X, (e) selected element $(2,3)$ in L, (f) selected element $(3,4)$ in L, (g) selected element $(4,5)$ as the shortest path, and (h) selected element $(5,6)$ as the shortest path are illustrated.

Table 1. Results of TSP for each algorithm

Name	Optimal solution		MMAS	SPSO	SPSOMS
eil51	426.00	Best	426.00	426.00	426,00
		Worst	434.00	427.00	427.00
		Average	427.35	426.53	426.22
		SE	0.1266	0.0502	0.0416
		Opt	13	47	78
eil76	538.00	Best	538.00	538.00	538.00
		Worst	550.00	539.00	538.00
		Average	542.15	538.02	538.00
		SE	0.2375	0.1407	0.0000
		Opt	11	98	100
eil101	629.00	Best	629.00	629.00	629.00
		Worst	646.00	630.00	630.00
		Average	643.80	629.06	629.01
		SE	0.4467	0.0238	0.0100
		Opt	3	94	99
st70	675.00	Best	675.00	675.00	675.00
		Worst	690.00	676.00	676.00
		Average	680.46	675.36	675.14
		SE	0.3400	0.0482	0.0348
		Opt	11	64	86
berlin52	7542.00	Best	7542.00	7542.00	7542.00
		Worst	7902.00	7542.00	7542.00
		Average	7552.52	7542.00	7542.00
		SE	4.9056	0.0000	0.0000
		Opt	95	100	100
kroA150	26524.00	Best	26525.00	26535.00	26533.00
		Worst	27213.00	26781.00	26775.00
		Average	26813.17	26661.55	26651.16
		SE	14.8919	5.5401	5.1239
		Opt	29	100	100

4   Numerical Experiments

Experimental results are compared the proposed algorithm (SPSOMS) to max-min ant system (MMAS) and set-based particle swarm optimization (SPSO) for six kinds of traveling salesman problems. All TSP instances are taken from the TSPLIB benchmark library [10]. We used TSP instances of eil51, eil76, eil101, st70, berlin52, and kroA150. In experiments, $10000n$ solutions are generated and the population size is same as n, where n is the size of instance. The maximum iterations are 10000.

The best, the worst, the average, the standard error (SE), and the number of obtaining optimal solution (Opt) are shown in Table 1. Results are averages of 100 trials for each algorithm. SPSOMS shows superior outcomes to the existing algorithms in all instances.

5   Conclusion

In this paper, we have presented a novel algorithm of set-based particle swarm optimization with memory state (SPSOMS) to decide the position based on the previous position. It was possible to search effectively for solving traveling salesman problem. Experimental results were compared SPSOMS to SPSO and MMAS for traveling salesman problem and SPSOMS showed superior outcomes. For the future works, we will study more effective techniques of the proposed algorithm.

References

1. Kennedy, J., Eberhart, R.: Particle swarm optimization. In: Proceedings of IEEE International Conference on Neural Networks, pp. 1942–1948 (1995)
2. Chatterjee, A., Pulasinghe, K., Watanabe, K.: A particle-swarm-optimized fuzzy-neural network for voice-controlled robot systems. IEEE Trans. Ind. Electron. **52**, 1478–1489 (2005)
3. Yoshida, H., Kawata, K., Fukuyama, Y.: A particle swarm optimization for reactive power and voltage control considering voltage security assessment. IEEE Trans. Power Syst. **15**, 1232–1239 (2000)
4. Kennedy, J., Eberhart, R.: A discrete binary version of the particle swarm algorithm. In: Proceedings of IEEE International Conference on Systems, Man, and Cybernetics, pp. 4104–4109 (1997)
5. Ji, Z., Tian, T., He, S.: A memory binary particle swarm optimization. In: Proceedings of IEEE International Conference on Evolutionary Computation, pp. 1–5 (2012)
6. Chen, W., Zhang, J., Chung, H., Zhong, W., Wu, W., Shi, Y.: A novel set-based particle swarm optimization method for discrete optimization problems. IEEE Trans. Evol. Comput. **14**, 278–299 (2010)
7. Stützle, T., Hoos, H.: Max-min ant system. Gener. Comput. Syst. **16**, 889–914 (2000)
8. Hino, T., Ito, S., Liu, T., Maeda, M.: Set-based particle swarm optimization with status memory for knapsack problem. Artif. Life Robot. **21**, 98–105 (2016)

9. Liang, J., Qin, A., Suganthan, P.: Comprehensive learning particle swarm optimizer for global optimization of multimodal functions. IEEE Trans. Evol. Comput. **10**, 281–295 (2006)
10. Reinelt, G.: TSPLIB. http://comopt.ifi.uni-heidelberg.de/software/TSPLIB95/tsp/

A Spy Search Mechanism (SSM) for Memetic Algorithm (MA) in Dynamic Environments

Stephen M. Akandwanaho and Serestina Viriri$^{(\boxtimes)}$

School of Mathematics, Statistics and Computer Science,
University of KwaZulu-Natal, Durban, South Africa
viriris@ukzn.ac.za

Abstract. Searching within the sample space for optimal solutions is an important part in solving optimization problems. The motivation of this work is that today's problem environments have increasingly become dynamic with non-stationary optima and in order to improve optima search, memetic algorithm has become a preferred search method because it combines global and local search methods to obtain good solutions. The challenge is that existing search methods perform the search during the iterations without being guided by solid information about the nature of the search environment which affects the quality of a search outcome. In this paper, a spy search mechanism is proposed for memetic algorithm in dynamic environments. The method uses a spy individual to scope out the search environment and collect information for guiding the search. The method combines hyper-mutation, random immigrants, hill climbing local search, crowding and fitness, and steepest mutation with greedy crossover hill climbing to enhance the efficiency of the search. The proposed method is tested on dynamic problems and comparisons with other methods indicate a better performance by the proposed method.

Keywords: Memetic Algorithm · Local search · Spy search · Dynamic optimization · Hypermutation

1 Introduction

Memetic Algorithm (MA) is defined by the collaboration between cultural evolution and natural evolution to explore and exploit the search [1]. In order to prevent a search from falling into local optima, in addition to the global search, a local search technique is used to improve the neighborhood of solutions in the sample space. MAs follow a cultural process to evolve individuals. This concept was proposed by Dawkins [2] who expressed that memes or units of knowledge can move from one brain to another. When memes reach a brain they evolve into new memes based on the nature of the current brain in terms of dispositions, attitudes and others. From these concepts, Norman and Moscato [3] introduced a MA procedure which has been widely applied to solve combinatorial and other problems. The algorithm is known for its ability to diversify the population and

© Springer International Publishing AG 2017
S. Phon-Amnuaisuk et al. (Eds.): MIWAI 2017, LNAI 10607, pp. 450–461, 2017.
https://doi.org/10.1007/978-3-319-69456-6_37

intensify the search. Using MA, solutions are paired so that they can exchange their memes through interactions. This process results into memetic offspring from where an optimal solution can be obtained.

MAs have gone through four generations. In the first generation, a local search is added to the global search so as to incorporate aspects of cultural evolution. The second generation fuses the memetic material into the genotype of the evolutionary algorithm. In the third generation, the algorithms evolve to generate new methods based on the rules and patterns in the search space. In the fourth generation, learning evolves through a number of logical steps mimicking the cortex architecture in the human brain [4]. MAs have been applied to solve many problems. However, today's problems have increasingly become dynamic. As a result, MAs are being applied in dynamic optimization where the behaviors of elements in the search space keep changing [5]. This affects the fitness of individual chromosomes thereby causing a drift in the location of the optima [5,6]. In order to keep track of non-stationary optima and to optimally search the dynamic search environment, an intelligent search approach that is based on the search space information is required. There have been multiple strategies employed to enhance search quality such as, among others, intelligent search [7] and rule based search [8,9]. These mechanisms have been applied to various problems in optimization but they have not performed well when applied to hard and evolving dynamic problems [10].

In this paper, Spy Search Mechanism (SSM) is proposed to improve the memetic search in dynamic problem environments. This approach is made up of different components such as, hyper-mutation and random immigrants, fitness sharing and crowding and steepest mutation with greedy crossover hill climbing. The random immigrants and hypermutation are used to improve diversity which is important for changing environments. A spy individual is dispatched to collect valuable information from the environment. The method then draws on the collected information to perform the search. The approach is tested on four dynamic problems: oneMax, royalRoad, plateau and deceptive. The results indicate that an enhanced MA performs well in dynamic landscapes. The information collected before the search helps the method to direct more resources to more productive areas in terms of fitness and other features.

The remainder of this article is organized as follows. The related work is reviewed in Sect. 2. The proposed spy search method is presented in Sect. 3. In Sect. 4, the problems used for experiments are defined. The results and conclusion are presented in Sects. 5 and 6 respectively.

2   Related Work

Amen [11] presented a MA for dynamic problems which uses genetic algorithm (GA) with both mutation and crossover as operators for producing offspring in the generation. The hybrid method combines the genetic features of individual chromosomes in order to strengthen the outcome of reproduction. A similar principle was applied by Boudia and Prins [12] to solve an integrated production distribution problem which is divided into two phases namely, production and distribution. The landscape keeps changing and MA operators are used to evolve individuals and produce good offspring. However, there is no fast convergence since the search is explored without adequate prior search information.

Ferentinos and Tsiligiridis [13] proposed a MA for a dynamic optimization of a wireless sensor network design producing a sensor network that satisfies all the constraints of energy and communication which is similar to the aircraft problem that was solved by Bencheikh et al. [14] where various air-crafts are landed onto several airport runways. Every aircraft is assigned a distinct time, runway and other constraints. The dynamic memetic algorithm (DMA) used here combines the local heuristic search with an ant-colony algorithm to allow a dynamic scheduling of air-crafts. The variables in this problem keep changing all the time, like the in problem solved by Moser and Chiong [15] which is characterized by changing peaks. Weak performing individuals are replaced with high-fitness individuals. However, the methods take more time and generate high complexity when finding good outcomes in the sample.

Liu et al. [16] proposed a new split scheme strategy for a MA and applied it to a dynamic capacitated arc routing problem. The approach employs an operator known as path repair to deal with dynamic problem attributes. The technique that is baked into this mechanism is an extended-random-Ulusoy heuristic that helps to divide the individual chromosome in a way that produces a reduction in distance cost. This contrasts with the work of Tang et al. [17] that embeds a merge split component within its extended neighborhood search process to perform the search in big blocks to enhances the search efficacy. The merge split technique works by altering the different routes of the solution so as to refine them.

Isaacs et al. [18] proposed a MA for dynamic bi-objective problems. In this approach, a quadratic-programming based gradient evolve technique is applied to improve convergence. Similar concepts were proposed by Hamam and Almogren [19] where a coding-aware routing technique is based on the distributed DMA. The route optimization is implemented especially in wireless networks. Although this approach passes the meme phenotypes to nodes so as to easily find the optimal solution, it is not shown how diversity is improved in the search and how the fitness of weak individuals can be improved in order to apply to other problems.

Wang et al. [20] presented a MA that uses the local search for exploitation. Adaptive hill climbing is employed as a local search technique which is made up of both greedy crossover hill climbing and steepest mutation hill climbing. In order to prevent a convergence that is immature, adaptive dual mapping and triggered random immigrants are combined within a MA. This is similar to the work by Vaid and Verma [21] which hybridizes hill climbing with the replacement operator. The search by hill-climbing is applied to every individual. The approach shows that it preserves diversity and search exploitation. However, it doesn't show how moving optima can be tracked in a fluid problem environment.

Mavrovouniotis et al. [22] proposed a MA for dynamic environments. The algorithm used a combination of inherent capabilities for ant-colony optimization's adaptation and local search operators. The method was applied to a dynamic traveling salesman problem. In a similar vein, Duan and Yu [23] proposed a MA that used a hybrid ant colony optimization to tackle the traveling salesman problem. The approach used flexible parameters that are adjustable thus making the method responsive to dynamic environments. However, these methods do not do a rigorous assessment of the search space and its elements before conducting the search. As a result, the search is not guided well hence taking more and resources to complete the search. The neighborhood improvements also do not show how to keep track of the moving optima thus affecting the quality outcome of the improvements.

3 Spy Search Method (SSM)

The current search methods applied in optimization operate without first collecting information about the search space and its elements in order to direct and guide the search process. The proposed Spy Search Mechanism uses a spy individual to scope out the search space. The spy individual interacts with other individuals without revealing its identity to avoid being compromised and confused with other individuals in the sample. In addition, it does not keep individual profiles of solutions but collects all information which is then analyzed, filtered and ranked so that it is deployed wisely. The ranking is based on whether the information satisfies the parameters defined to guide information collection by the spy individual. The highest rank starts with fulfilling all the parameters, fulfilling some parameters, etc. The filtering is conducted to identify duplicated information and ensuring that only relevant information is captured.

The benefits of pre-reviewing the search include strategic resource utilization to direct more resources to areas that are likely to produce promising outcomes from the known data. The algorithm is made up of different components. These include, hybrid of hypermutation and random immigrants method, hill climbing local search, crowding and fitness and the steepest mutation with greedy crossover hill climbing.

3.1 The Structure of the Spy Search Method

Considering a population of individuals. The spy individual is initialized as part of the sample but with an aim of collecting information from the rest of the individuals.

In Fig. 1, the population of individuals in the search sample is initialized. The fitness is determined for individuals in the population and the spy individual is arbitrarily selected, but it must have a strong fitness. If the spy individual selected is not fit then another selection process is conducted until a strong individual is obtained.

The distance between individuals helps to know how far apart the solutions are placed between each other. This information determines the distance changes resulting from the changes in the environment. The initial individual fitness also changes with change in the environment. The positioning of the individual

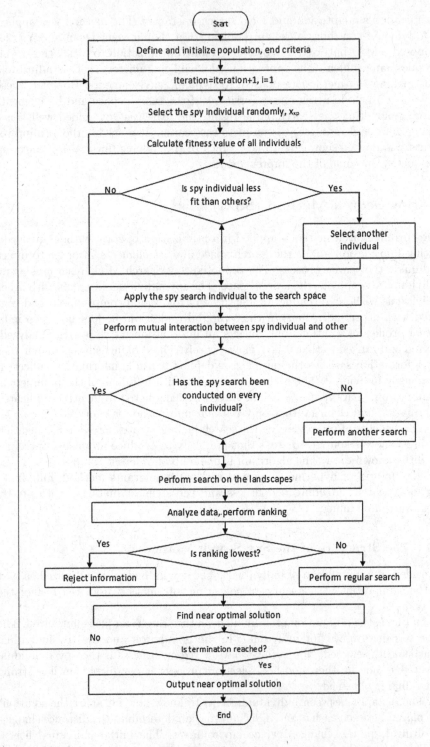

Fig. 1. SSM flowchart

Table 1. Notations used in this paper

Distance	Fitness	Positioning	Past direction change	Change severity
d_i	f_i	p_i	PC_i	ρ
Speed rate of change	Diversity	Speed calibration	Spy individual	Population
τ	μ	δ	x_{sp}	P
Information gathered	Exclusive operator	Offspring population	Binary template	Index for environment
g	$\oplus$	P'	T	k

solution is determined by its locus and environmental change patterns. The notation used in Eqs. 1, 2, 3 and 4 is defined in Table 1.

$$g_i = \sum_{i}^{n}(d_i + f_i + p_i + PC_i) \quad \forall i = 1, 2, \ldots n \tag{1}$$

The distance between individuals is calculated as a hamming distance defined in [20].

$$d(x_{sp}, x_{i,\ldots,n}) = \left\lceil \frac{\sum_{i}^{n}|x_{sp} - x_{i,\ldots,n}|}{n} \right\rceil \quad \forall i = 1, 2, \ldots n \tag{2}$$

Also, consider that x_{sp} achieves its aim within the search by gathering data about the search elements.

$$\forall n = i + 1 \tag{3}$$

$$\forall i = 1, \ldots, n, (x_{sp}, i \geq g_i) \tag{4}$$

Parameters control how the method reacts to changes in the problem environment. For example, when τ is increased, the technique is able to quickly find good individuals before the changes begin in the environment and the change severity is also balanced by parameter ρ while δ is for speed. In addition, operators ensure that the search is sufficiently exploited [24].

4   Dynamic Optimization Problems

Experiments in this paper are based on the test environments generated by a dynamic optimization problems generator [25]. These functions have been extensively used to test new dynamic algorithms [20,26–29].

The search environment is controlled by parameters τ and ρ which are defined as speed and severity respectively. When τ is at 0 the environment keeps intact but changes when τ is at 1. In the binary string, the dynamic oneMax keeps the number of ones to maximum within the binary string. The other functions contribute bits to the fitness of individuals as presented by [30].

The results in this work were compared with the known results for different methods that are presented in literature. These include, Memetic Algorithm with Adaptive Hill Climbing Operator (AHMA) [20], Deterministic Dominance Diploid Genetic Algorithm (DDDGA) [31], Memetic Algorithm greedy crossover hill climbing (CHMA) [20], Genetic Algorithm with Random Immigrants Scheme (RIGA) [20], Harmony Search Algorithm with Random Immigrant (HSA-I) [32], Cooperative particle swarm optimizer modified harmony search (CPSO-MHS) [33] Harmony Search Algorithm with Memory mechanism (HSA-M) [32], Multi Swarm Quantum Particle Swarm Optimization (mQSO) [34] and Harmony Search Algorithm with Random based immigrant mechanism (HSA-MI) [32]. The justification for using the above methods for comparisons is that most of them are dynamic and perform a memetic search in addition to combining different methods. They have also been widely used to solve dynamic optimization problems.

5   Results

5.1   Parameter Settings

There are different severities that are used to determine the rate of change in the environment so as to monitor the strength of each method under similar conditions, and the parameter for calibrating speed is δ which is set to 10, 20, 60 and 100 for oneMax, RoyalRoad, Deceptive and Plateau respectively and the severity change is respectively set at 0.1, 0.3, 0.5 and 0.7.

The experiments make performance comparisons between the proposed method with other known existing methods in the literature. All methods are configured with similar settings to determine their comparative performance. The population is set to 100, while 0.2 and 0.05 for crossover and mutation respectively. The evaluation rate is also set to 0.2. In SSM α, β, Δ and θ are set with 1.0, 1.2, 0.5 and 0.2 respectively to produce the results in Fig. 2. The execution of 24 individual runs was done with randomly similar seeds defined per generation with multiple landscape changes allowed. The best performance outputs are then recorded for each method as shown in Tables 2, 3, 4 and 5.

From the experiments, SSM performs better on all the dynamic optimization problems that were generated by the problem generator. The strength of SSM is increased by the components that have been incorporated to create a hybrid method so as to increase diversity and overcome the continuous changes of the search environment. In addition, an increase in performance is observed in Fig. 2 when the changes occur and intensify based on the variables set for the parameters. Moreover, SSM consistently shows bursts of strong performance at selective intervals of a dynamic search as demonstrated in Fig. 3.

5.2   Performance Evaluation

In the measurement of performance and in order to draw a direct contrast with existing methods, 24 runs are considered for the algorithms and the fitness over the runs is calculated as defined by Forrest and Mitchell [31]. The performance of SSM is generally better in relation with other existing methods owing to

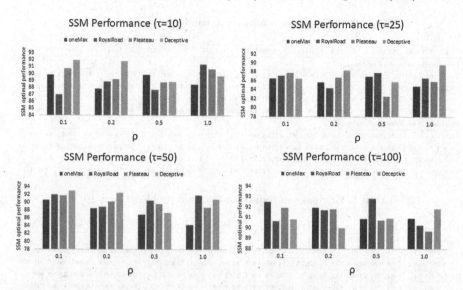

Fig. 2. SSM optimal performance when $\tau = 10, 25, 50$ and 100 for all the problems.

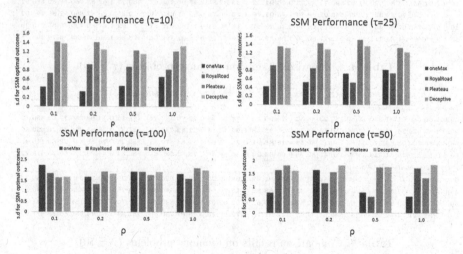

Fig. 3. SSM s.d for optimal performance for all the problems

diversity and search robustness created by the proposed method. The diversity of the population in each generation is defined based on the size of the population and the distance between individuals in the search [31]. The size of τ alternates between 10, 25, 50 and 100 so as to affect diversity accordingly as shown in Fig. 3. The generations are set to 100 for individual runs and it is noticeable that SSM is stronger although it struggles to compete in few multiple runs especially as observed in Tables 6 and 7 because of its rigorous search process that includes information collection and analysis.

Table 2. Comparison results on dynamic problems ($\tau = 10$)

τ	ρ	AHMA	DDDGA	CHMA	RIGA	SSM	HSA-I	CPSO-MHS	HSA-M	mQSO	HSA-MI
Performance on oneMax problem											
10	0.1	81.32 0.03	80.21 0.12	81.28 0.14	80.62 0.10	**89.8 0.43**	82.16 0.18	78.93 0.15	81.12 0.17	79.41 0.11	80.50 0.18
10	0.2	84.67 0.06	81.51 0.22	80.58 0.24	85.82 0.26	**87.82 0.33**	83.26 0.20	79.84 0.25	82.22 0.19	82.51 0.21	79.35 0.22
10	0.5	83.52 0.05	86.21 0.08	84.28 0.04	88.62 0.19	**89.82 0.45**	83.56 0.38	88.93 0.45	86.12 0.27	87.41 0.31	85.81 0.68
10	1.0	82.25 0.55	83.51 0.48	84.28 0.34	85.98 0.69	**88.42 0.65**	85.57 0.78	84.94 0.75	86.12 0.47	84.41 0.71	87.86 0.88
Performance on RoyalRoad problem											
10	0.1	83.43 0.83	78.58 0.62	85.11 0.45	85.68 0.81	**86.98 0.73**	79.73 0.38	78.93 0.95	82.13 0.77	74.91 0.78	83.52 0.18
10	0.2	84.43 0.67	85.47 0.68	83.22 0.59	78.64 0.92	**88.87 0.92**	76.70 0.28	76.32 0.14	82.43 0.74	84.19 0.68	85.75 0.39
10	0.5	88.47 0.57	82.71 1.37	63.48 1.45	68.82 0.87	**87.67 0.87**	79.98 1.13	86.75 0.56	87.78 0.68	86.21 0.82	84.26 1.23
10	1.0	90.21 1.78	86.84 0.67	86.52 0.92	83.24 1.83	**91.37 0.81**	89.27 0.89	88.69 0.94	90.45 1.58	87.57 0.71	86.91 1.78

Table 3. Comparison results on dynamic problems ($\tau = 10$)

τ	ρ	AHMA	DDDGA	CHMA	RIGA	SSM	HSA-I	CPSO-MHS	HSA-M	mQSO	HSA-MI
Performance on Plateau problem											
10	0.1	89.31 0.28	88.76 0.63	87.75 0.39	87.52 0.87	**90.72 1.42**	86.39 0.69	89.62 0.31	89.39 1.43	87.72 1.82	86.59 0.85
10	0.2	87.49 0.57	85.52 0.91	86.72 0.42	67.75 0.91	**89.18 1.41**	88.92 1.41	72.82 0.58	71.28 1.29	85.08 1.09	85.91 0.39
10	0.5	88.61 0.28	87.75 1.21	85.48 1.03	83.72 0.76	**88.79 1.23**	77.92 0.45	76.87 0.33	81.55 1.12	80.29 0.21	82.89 0.82
10	1.0	89.78 0.66	87.28 0.54	76.82 0.88	85.11 0.62	**90.68 1.21**	88.71 0.66	77.95 0.67	87.92 0.23	78.19 0.47	88.71 0.49
Performance on Deceptive problem											
10	0.1	91.85 1.54	89.92 0.81	82.59 0.71	89.35 0.76	**91.92 1.38**	82.87 0.47	90.74 0.82	89.27 1.62	83.76 0.18	82.57 0.91
10	0.2	90.64 0.76	89.39 0.98	88.54 0.92	89.73 1.46	**91.79 1.25**	90.72 0.82	71.38 0.19	72.85 0.66	87.88 0.52	86.28 0.62
10	0.5	87.78 0.65	88.43 1.06	87.72 0.76	86.39 0.46	**88.87 1.15**	86.81 0.71	82.62 0.81	87.92 1.87	86.72 0.76	85.91 0.29
10	1.0	88.63 0.71	84.71 1.23	86.94 1.17	85.26 1.08	**89.72 1.33**	87.29 0.88	83.79 0.54	79.88 1.59	84.48 0.69	79.39 0.75

Table 4. Comparison results on dynamic problems ($\tau = 50$)

τ	ρ	AHMA	DDDGA	CHMA	RIGA	SSM	HSA-I	CPSO-MHS	HSA-M	mQSO	HSA-MI
Performance on oneMax problem											
50	0.1	89.56 0.01	87.35 0.15	80.18 0.23	88.52 0.24	**90.56 0.77**	88.28 0.22	70.12 0.19	73.18 0.14	68.38 0.17	62.45 0.12
50	0.2	87.62 0.23	74.35 0.47	86.65 0.15	81.73 0.25	**88.48 1.64**	87.15 0.32	82.73 0.52	87.37 0.28	85.62 0.43	76.82 0.53
50	0.5	85.76 0.08	84.37 0.04	83.18 0.12	80.53 0.16	**86.91 0.78**	85.62 0.42	84.87 0.53	82.25 0.16	80.44 0.29	85.11 0.48
50	1.0	82.32 0.45	81.31 0.38	80.18 0.45	82.78 0.65	**84.24 0.63**	82.37 0.76	81.53 0.64	80.34 0.44	78.32 0.65	73.67 0.72
Performance on RoyalRoad problem											
50	0.1	89.76 0.76	75.63 0.52	83.23 0.56	76.54 0.78	**91.92 1.64**	90.35 1.43	87.92 0.76	85.26 0.82	71.84 0.85	75.78 0.24
50	0.2	87.54 0.75	86.12 0.64	88.14 0.64	73.47 0.18	**88.83 1.13**	70.65 0.32	71.56 0.28	80.75 0.83	70.43 0.54	82.63 0.32
50	0.5	88.42 0.25	87.58 1.32	64.67 0.48	62.78 0.82	**90.51 0.62**	82.61 1.22	78.84 0.32	81.76 0.67	79.18 1.82	82.54 1.45
50	1.0	91.34 1.74	82.82 0.72	82.34 0.65	81.53 1.74	**91.78 1.72**	90.76 0.78	87.73 0.86	82.84 1.64	74.65 0.83	85.97 1.92

Table 5. Comparison results on dynamic problems ($\tau = 50$)

τ	ρ	AHMA	DDDGA	CHMA	RIGA	SSM	HSA-I	CPSO-MHS	HSA-M	mQSO	HSA-MI
Performance on Plateau problem											
50	0.1	90.52 0.14	83.74 0.58	82.64 0.45	68.24 0.82	**91.68 1.82**	89.25 0.57	87.53 0.26	88.54 1.53	86.35 1.67	84.52 0.82
50	0.2	85.32 0.63	83.45 0.73	88.89 0.54	68.67 0.87	**90.27 1.56**	82.78 1.61	73.64 0.62	87.32 1.45	89.72 1.21	84.54 0.45
50	0.5	87.23 0.36	86.53 1.54	86.53 1.56	85.87 0.83	**89.64 1.75**	64.93 0.35	69.78 0.63	74.48 1.73	79.43 1.43	85.58 0.98
50	1.0	86.74 0.53	85.43 0.48	71.43 0.54	75.54 0.82	**88.76 1.34**	85.65 0.75	87.57 0.59	73.89 1.16	86.16 0.43	87.74 0.56
Performance on Deceptive problem											
50	0.1	92.81 1.76	85.95 0.93	85.63 0.76	84.73 0.78	**92.95 1.62**	89.75 0.42	87.67 0.75	88.32 1.58	87.72 0.54	91.65 1.54
50	0.2	91.52 0.56	90.54 0.87	90.87 0.87	90.67 1.56	**92.49 1.82**	79.65 0.42	81.45 0.23	87.49 0.58	75.68 0.73	91.27 1.42
50	0.5	86.93 0.47	84.76 1.73	83.86 1.95	82.56 1.58	**87.37 1.76**	86.73 0.67	85.75 0.93	84.78 1.79	82.78 0.84	83.87 0.35
50	1.0	90.68 1.68	87.82 1.94	88.85 1.82	82.76 1.28	**90.89 1.85**	88.32 0.94	87.75 0.45	73.76 1.75	87.38 0.48	89.35 1.73

Table 6. Comparison results on dynamic problems ($\tau = 100$)

τ	ρ	AHMA	DDDGA	CHMA	RIGA	SSM	HSA-I	CPSO-MHS	HSA-M	mQSO	HSA-MI
Performance on oneMax problem											
100	0.1	91.571.32	91.351.17	89.261.16	87.60 0.32	**92.48 2.24**	90.23 0.27	88.780.32	82.23 0.24	89.530.42	88.250.37
100	0.2	90.740.17	89.430.45	87.470.15	88.75 0.64	**91.95 1.68**	86.65 0.38	83.820.37	90.56 0.46	85.740.38	84.760.43
100	0.5	88.760.34	87.350.21	85.450.23	86.45 0.38	**90.85 1.94**	84.52 0.49	87.920.53	83.17 0.22	89.280.27	87.650.72
100	1.0	90.620.45	87.630.56	89.370.54	88.52 0.48	**90.93 1.84**	87.69 0.83	85.870.83	89.25 0.29	84.370.56	89.941.83
Performance on RoyalRoad problem											
100	0.1	89.750.14	87.370.85	88.230.59	89.72 0.92	**90.64 1.85**	79.85 0.54	85.740.86	83.27 0.85	82.710.62	81.760.56
100	0.2	90.590.87	87.450.82	85.540.63	82.85 0.65	**91.72 1.34**	85.85 0.46	84.560.32	84.73 0.72	86.280.76	89.870.41
100	0.5	91.670.45	89.571.42	86.651.49	89.86 0.75	**92.03 1.93**	91.45 1.45	90.260.39	88.59 0.51	92.121.85	81.161.18
100	1.0	88.441.67	85.730.87	89.480.71	84.38 1.43	**90.28 1.61**	89.61 0.78	85.740.83	85.78 1.62	85.680.53	87.851.64

Table 7. Comparison results on dynamic problems ($\tau = 100$)

τ	ρ	AHMA	DDDGA	CHMA	RIGA	SSM	HSA-I	CPSO-MHS	HSA-M	mQSO	HSA-MI
Performance on Plateau problem											
100	0.1	91.670.37	90.530.45	89.670.56	89.48 0.73	**91.94 1.65**	90.45 0.58	89.580.42	90.76 1.94	85.671.67	88.680.73
100	0.2	90.350.64	88.470.83	87.830.32	80.48 0.68	**91.81 1.94**	90.95 1.57	82.940.64	87.39 1.36	85.761.78	82.730.25
100	0.5	90.480.45	88.761.56	76.871.36	87.67 0.87	**90.73 1.78**	56.84 0.53	82.940.79	88.35 1.72	80.561.53	78.580.94
100	1.0	88.560.12	86.560.78	85.950.49	81.25 0.59	**89.72 2.12**	82.64 0.73	88.981.73	85.84 1.65	87.360.56	84.480.67
Performance on Deceptive problem											
100	0.1	89.931.76	86.430.75	88.610.53	76.72 0.83	**90.84 1.68**	83.48 0.39	89.670.74	88.52 1.54	81.821.87	79.890.75
100	0.2	87.720.87	86.520.87	86.940.73	88.71 1.68	**89.98 1.84**	82.84 0.45	83.450.63	88.94 0.78	83.710.63	82.570.87
100	0.5	88.890.87	84.781.86	86.581.69	85.45 1.57	**90.92 1.93**	89.75 0.92	85.570.95	85.84 1.74	89.630.84	89.760.34
100	1.0	90.780.86	88.831.94	89.731.65	79.73 1.53	**91.84 2.02**	90.16 0.74	87.370.76	82.88 1.58	82.270.51	80.540.94

It can be noticed that when τ is increased, there is an increase in the SSM output although a decrease is detected in some instances in the course of the run. The decrease is because of slow changes in the environment. The opposite is that when the changes are happening rapidly as calibrated by τ, there is quick convergence resulting from search exploitation by the local search. Figure 2 shows a high rate of performance due to a strong diversity created by a hybrid of immigrants method, hypermutation and crowding and fitness sharing. But when the environment begins to change, convergence slows down as seen in Fig. 3 when the $\tau = 25$. As the level of severity increases the diversity methods are invoked to counter the volatility of the changing search environment which in turn creates an increase in performance as noticed in Fig. 3 when τ changes from 50 to 100. OneMax performs relatively well when τ keeps increasing up to 100.

6   Conclusion and Future Work

In this paper, a new strategy for MA was introduced. The SSM guided the search in a dynamic search environment by collecting information on individuals and the sample space environment. A greedy crossover was combined with the steepest mutation to make individual refinements. In addition, diversity was preserved by a hybrid of triggered random immigrants, hypermutation and crowding and fitness sharing which improves convergence.

Experiments showed a better performance by SSM in relation to other existing methods. The more severity in the changes, the stronger performance showed by SSM. The adaptive hill climbing made neighborhood individual refinements. As part of future work multiple populations can be used and memory based approaches can be explored. Change pattern recognition of the search environment by the proposed method would also be an important area of research.

References

1. Burke, E.K., Hyde, M., Kendall, G., Ochoa, G., Ozcan, E.: A classification of hyper-heuristic approaches. In: Gendreau, M., Potvin, J. (eds.) Handbook of Meta-heuristics, International Series in Operations Research & Management Science. LNCS, vol. 146, pp. 449–468. Springer, Heidelberg (2010). doi:10.1007/978-1-4419-1665-5_15
2. Dawkins, R.: The Selfish Gene. Clarendon Press, Oxford (1976)
3. Norman, G.M., Moscato, P.: A competitive cooperative complex combinatorial search. In: Proceedings of Joint Conference on Informatics and Operations Research, pp. 15–29 (1991)
4. Meuth, R., Lim, M., Ong, Y., Wunsch, D.C.: A proposition on memes and meta-memes in computing for higher-order learning. Memetic Comput. 1, 86–99 (2009)
5. Fouladgar, N., Lotfi, S.: A brief review of solving dynamic optimization problems. Int. Acad. J. Sci. Eng. 2, 26–33 (2015)
6. Kell, D.B.: Scientific discovery as a combinatorial optimization problem: how best to navigate the landscape of possible experiments. BioEssays 34, 236–244 (2012)
7. Khan, M.B., Zhang, D., Jun, M., Li, Z.J.: An intelligent search technique to train scheduling problem based on genetic algorithm. In: International Conference on Emerging Technologies, pp. 593–598 (2006)
8. Ming, G., Li, H.: An improved algorithm based on max-min for cloud task scheduling. In: Recent Advances in Computer Science and Information Engineering, pp. 217–223 (2012)
9. Munir, E.U., Li, J., Shi, S.: QoS sufferage heuristic for independent task scheduling in grid. Inf. Technol. J. 6, 1166–1170 (2007)
10. Tsai, C., Huang, W., Chian, M.: A hyperheuristic scheduling algorithm for cloud. IEEE Trans. Cloud Comput. 2, 236–250 (2014)
11. Amen, A.: Memetic algorithm for dynamic optimization problems. Int. J. Comput. Appl. 136, 7–10 (2016)
12. Boudia, M., Prins, C.: A memetic algorithm with dynamic population management for an integrated production-distribution problem. Eur. J. Oper. Res. 195, 703–715 (2009)
13. Ferentinos, K.P., Tsiligiridis, T.A.: A memetic algorithm for optimal dynamic design of wireless sensor networks. Comput. Commun. 33, 250–258 (2009)
14. Bencheikh, G., Boukachour, J., Alaoui, A.E.H.: A memetic algorithm to solve the dynamic multiple runway aircraft landing problem. J. King Saud Univ. - Comput. Inf. Sci. 28, 98–109 (2016)
15. Moser, I., Chiong, R.: A Hooke-Jeeves based memetic algorithm for solving dynamic optimization problems. In: Hybrid Artificial Intelligence System, pp. 301–309 (2009)
16. Liu, M., Singh, H.K., Ray, T.: A memetic algorithm with a new split scheme for solving dynamic capacitated arc routing problems. In: IEEE Congress on Evolutionary Computation, pp. 595–613 (2014)

17. Tang, K., Mei, Y., Yao, X.: Memetic algorithm with extended neighborhood search for capacitated arc routing problems. IEEE Trans. Evol. Comput. **13**, 1151–1166 (2009)

18. Isaacs, A., Ray, T., Smith, W.: Memetic algorithm for dynamic bi-objective optimization problems. IEEE Trans. Evol. Comput. 31–47 (2009)

19. Hamam, S., Almogren, A.S.: Distributed dynamic memetic algorithm based coding aware routing for wireless mesh sensor networks. Int. J. Distrib. Sens. Netw. **2016**, 1–7 (2016)

20. Wang, H., Wang, D., Yang, S.: A memetic algorithm with adaptive hill climbing strategy for dynamic optimization problems. Soft. Comput. **13**, 763–780 (2009)

21. Vaid, M., Verma, A.: Memetic algorithm: hybridization of hill climbing with replacement operator. Int. J. Adv. Res. Comput. Sci. Softw. Eng. **4**, 738–743 (2014)

22. Mavrovouniotis, M., Muller, F.M., Yang, S.: An ant colony optimization based memetic algorithm for the dynamic traveling salesman problem. In: Proceedings of 2015 Annual Conference on Genetic and Evolutionary Computation, pp. 49–56 (2015)

23. Duan, H., Yu, X.: Hybrid ant colony optimization using memetic algorithm for traveling salesman problem. In: IEEE International Symposium on Approximate Dynamic Programming and Reinforcement Learning, pp. 92–95 (2007)

24. Lin, G., Lu, X., Kang, L.: Search direction made evolution strategies faster. In: Cai, Z., Li, Z., Kang, Z., Liu, Y. (eds.) ISICA 2009. CCIS, vol. 51, pp. 146–155. Springer, Heidelberg (2009). doi:10.1007/978-3-642-04962-0_17

25. Morrison, R.W., DeJong, K.A.: A test problem generator for non-stationary environments. In: Congress on Evolutionary Computation, vol. 3, pp. 2047–2053 (1999)

26. Yang, S.: Non-stationary problem optimization using the primal-dual genetic algorithm. In: Proceedings of 2003 Congress on Evolutionary Computation, vol. 3, pp. 2246–2253 (2003)

27. Yang, S., Yao, X.: Experimental study on population-based incremental learning algorithms for dynamic optimization problems. Soft Comput. **9**, 815–834 (2005)

28. Mitchell, M., Forrest, S., Holland, J.H.: The royal road for genetic algorithms: fitness landscapes and GA performance. In: Proceedings of 1st European Conference on Artificial Life, vol. 3, pp. 245–254 (1992)

29. Yang, S.: Memory-based immigrants for genetic algorithms in dynamic environments. In: Proceedings of 2005 Genetic and Evolutionary Computation Conference, vol. 2, pp. 1115–1122 (2005)

30. Forrest, S., Mitchell, M.: Relative building-block fitness and the building-block hyperthesis. In: Proceedings of Foundations of Genetic Algorithms, pp. 1–8 (1993)

31. Yang, S.: On the design of diploid genetic algorithms for problem optimization in dynamic environment. In: Proceedings of 2006 IEEE Congress on Evolutionary Computation, pp. 1362–1369 (2006)

32. Turky, A.M., Abdullah, S., Sabar, N.R.: Meta-heuristic algorithm for binary dynamic optimization problems and its relevancy to timetabling. In: Proceedings of 10th International Conference of the Practice and Theory of Automated Timetabling, pp. 26–29 (2014)

33. Zhang, G., Li, Y.: A memetic algorithm for global optimization of multimodal nonseparable problems. IEEE Trans. Cybern. **46**, 1375–1387 (2016)

34. Turky, A.M., Abdullah, S.: A multi-population harmony search algorithm with external archive for dynamic optimization problems. Inf. Sci. **172**, 84–95 (2014)

Hybrid Simulated Annealing for the Bi-objective Quadratic Assignment Problem

Mohamed Saifullah Hussin[1(✉)] and Thomas Stützle[2]

[1] SIAM, Universiti Malaysia Terengganu, Kuala Terengganu, Malaysia
saifullah@umt.edu.my
[2] IRIDIA, Université Libre de Bruxelles, Brussels, Belgium
stuetzle@ulb.ac.be

Abstract. Past research has shown that the performance of algorithms for solving the Quadratic Assignment Problem (QAP) depends on the structure and the size of the instances. In this paper, we study the bi-objective QAP, which is a multi-objective extension of the single-objective QAP to two objectives. The algorithm we propose extends a high-performing Simulated Annealing (SA) algorithm for large-sized, single-objective QAP instances to the bi-objective context. The resulting Hybrid Simulated Annealing (HSA) algorithm is shown to clearly outperform a basic, hybrid iterative improvement algorithm. Experimental results show that HSA clearly outperforms basic Hybrid Iterative Improvement. When compared to state-of-the-art algorithms for the bQAP, a Multi-objective Ant Colony Optimization algorithm and the Strength Pareto Evolutionary Algorithm 2, HSA shows very good performance, outperforms the former in most cases, and showing competitive performance to the latter.

1 Introduction

Finding the best assignment of facilities to locations is the basic idea of the Quadratic Assignment Problem (QAP), a classical NP-hard combinatorial optimization problem. The QAP has been used to represent many real world applications, such as the hospital layout [1] and keyboard layout [2], backboard wiring [3], and turbine balancing [4].

In general, the QAP can be explained as the problem of assigning n facilities to n locations, given the flows between the facilities and distances between the locations, with the objective being to minimize the function

$$f(\pi) = \sum_{i=1}^{n} \sum_{j=1}^{n} b_{ij} a_{\pi_i \pi_j}, \qquad (1)$$

where a facility can only be assigned to one location, and a location can only have one facility.

QAP formulations for solving problems with more than one objective have been proposed by Knowles and Corne [5], and by Hamacher et al. [6]. In this

© Springer International Publishing AG 2017
S. Phon-Amnuaisuk et al. (Eds.): MIWAI 2017, LNAI 10607, pp. 462–472, 2017.
https://doi.org/10.1007/978-3-319-69456-6_38

study, we adopt the former to derive the bi-objective QAP (bQAP). In particular, in the formulation by Knowles and Corne, the bQAP has two different flow matrices that are paired with one distance matrix.

The goal of a bQAP is to minimize $\boldsymbol{f}(\pi)$, where

$$\boldsymbol{f}(\pi) = (f^1(\pi), f^2(\pi)) \tag{2}$$

and

$$f^k(\pi) = \sum_{i=1}^{n}\sum_{j=1}^{n} b_{ij}a^k_{\pi_i\pi_j}, k = 2 \tag{3}$$

where a^k_{ij} refers to the k-th flow from item i to item j.

2   Algorithms

In this paper, we discuss several well performing metaheuristics that have been implemented for solving the bQAP. In particular, we discuss two algorithms on which our proposed algorithm is based. They are the two-phase local search (TPLS) and Pareto local search (PLS) methods. This particular idea has been discussed in [7,8]. Furthermore, we discuss in this section two well performing SLS algorithms for the bQAP, Multi-Objective Ant Colony Optimization (MOACO) and Strength Pareto Evolutionary Algorithm 2 (SPEA2) [9]. Next, we introduce the implementation of our new hybrid algorithm that combines a Simulated Annealing (SA) algorithm, an algorithm that performs well on large single objective instances, as the basic building block for TPLS, and hybridize this algorithm with PLS. The results obtained from the proposed improvements is then compared to MOACO and SPEA2.

Two-phase Local Search (TPLS) is a general concept that was proposed by Paquete and Stützle [7]. It consists of a scalarization-based multi-objective algorithm that can be divided into two phases. In TPLS, solutions returned by one scalarization will be used as the starting solution for the following scalarization. Solutions generated in the first phase serve as the first approximation of the Pareto global optimum set. Scalarization of objective functions can be done by providing a slight change in the weight vector. A solution returned in the second phase is stored in an archive if it is non-weakly dominated.

Pareto Local Search [10] (PLS) is an iterative improvement algorithm for multi-objective problems that can be seen as an extension of an iterative improvement algorithm for single objective problems. PLS uses an acceptance criterion that is based on Pareto dominance, instead of the acceptance criterion used for a single objective problem, and it keeps track of an archive of non-dominated solutions.

2.1   Multi-objective Ant Colony Optimization

The variant of MOACO considered in this study is the one of López-Ibáñez et al. [9], where $\mathcal{MAX} - \mathcal{MIN}$ Ant System [11] is used as the underlying ACO algorithm. Various ACO algorithms have been proposed for tackling the bQAP, and in MOACO, one pheromone matrix is assigned to each objective. When ants construct a solution, the pheromone information for the different objectives is aggregated using a weight vector. Heuristic information is not used as also in the state-of-the-art ACO algorithms for the single objective QAP, no heuristic information is used. Each pheromone matrix is updated by solutions with the best corresponding objective value [11]. The solution can either be taken from the set of nondominated solutions in the current iteration, ib or from the set of nondominated solutions since the beginning of the current trial, gb. The amount of pheromone deposited is set to a fixed value. We consider the use of multiple colonies, denoted as c. If more than one colony exists, ants construct solutions based on pheromone information of their own colony.

To determine the most suitable parameter settings of MOACO, we have ran extensive experiments using possible parameter settings. The first parameter is the local search strategy, where we will either use simply Iterative Improvement (II) or Robust Tabu Search (RoTS) [9] for a weighted sum scalarization. The length of RoTS run, $l = l' \cdot n$ iterations, where $l' \in \{1, 5, 10\}$. The total number of ants, m is equal to n, and for every colony, the number of ants is given by mc. For the number of colony, the values considered are $c \in \{1, 3, 5\}$. The pheromone evaporation factor, ρ is set to 0.9. The final parameter considered is the pheromone update strategy, u to be used, either ib or gb.

We found from our initial experiments that the best results are obtained when the MOACO are run using RoTS with $l' = 5$, $c = 5$, and $u = ib$.

2.2   Strength Pareto Evolutionary Algorithm 2

SPEA2 is an algorithm proposed by Zitzler et al. [12], which is an improvement over the original SPEA by [13]. SPEA2 adopted in this study is the variant that was implemented by López-Ibáñez et al. [9] for tackling the bQAP. SPEA2 starts with an initial population, generated either heuristically or randomly, together with an empty archive. The archive then is filled with non-dominated individuals based on their fitness evaluation. The maximum number of individuals allowed to be added into the archive is given by a parameter α. When the number of individuals inside the archive is larger than α, the individual with the smallest distance to another individual in the archive is discarded. If the archive is still not full, but all non-dominated individuals have already been added to the archive, the dominated individual with the smallest fitness value is then added into the archive. In the original implementation, [12] uses a single point crossover operator for recombination. In the implementation by [9], μ individuals are selected from the archive as parents to generate μ individuals using the CX recombination operator [14]. In addition, in SPEA2 by [9], iterative improvement or RoTS are applied to individuals from the initial population and individuals generated by recombination. The first parameter considered for SPEA2 is the local search strategy, whether iterative improvement or RoTS with length l. $l = l' \cdot n$ iterations, where $l' \in \{1, 5, 10\}$. The archive size considered, α is given by $\alpha' \cdot$

n, where $\alpha' \in \{1, 4, 5\}$. The final parameter, the number of new individuals generated in every iteration, μ is given by $\mu' \cdot n$, where $\mu' \in \{1, 5\}$.

The most suitable settings based on our initial experiments for the local search strategy are RoTS with $l' = 5$, $\alpha' = 4$, and $\mu' = 5$.

2.3   Hybrid TPLS-PLS Algorithms

Our SAR algorithm is essentially a standard SA algorithm that uses a temperature reheating during the run. The temperature reheating is intended to allow the algorithm to escape from particular local minima regions when the temperature reaches a very low value. An algorithmic outline of SAR is shown in Algorithm 1 [15]. Another restart-based simulated annealing was proposed earlier by Wang [16] for solving the QAP.

Algorithm 1. Outline of a Simulated Annealing algorithm

---

procedure *Simulated Annealing*
  $s := GenerateInitialSolution$
  $s_{best} := s$
  $T_0 := SetInitialT$
  while termination criterion not satisfied **do**
    $s' := GenerateRandomNeighbor(s)$
    $s'' := Accept(T, s, s')$
    if $f(s'') \leq f(s_{best})$ **then**
      $s_{best} := s''$
    end if
    $T := SetTemperature(T, Iterations, c)$
    $s := s''$
  end while
  return s_{best}
end *Simulated Annealing*

SAR starts by selecting an initial permutation uniformly at random. This permutation is set as the current best solution s_{best} and the current evaluation is set as $f(s_{best})$. The initial temperature is set to $T = 0.005 \cdot f(s_{best})$, which resulted in reasonable performance. In *GenerateRandomNeighbor(s)*, a neighbor s' of s is obtained by swapping the position of two items i and j. We apply the pair-swops sequentially for each solution s for all $k = \{1, \ldots, n\}$, following the suggestion of Connolly [17]. All moves that improve the current candidate solution are accepted, while moves that worsen it are accepted based on the Metropolis condition. This acceptance criterion is implemented by the function $Accept(T, s, s')$. For our cooling schedule, we retain the temperature level for $c \cdot n$ consecutive swaps, where c is a parameter. Some initial experiments showed that $c = 100$ results in satisfactory performance. We use geometric cooling, with the temperature at iteration $i + 1$ being set to $T_{i+1} = \alpha \cdot T_i$ with $\alpha = 0.9$. When the temperature drops below 1, we reset the temperature value to the initial value and restart the same cooling process. This temperature schedule is implemented in function $SetTemperature(T, Iterations, c)$. The SA algorithm continues until the maximum computation time limit.

We have developed two hybrid TPLS-PLS algorithms based on the work in [18]. The algorithm starts with a TPLS run that will provide a set of good initial solutions for PLS. During the TPLS stage, our algorithms use either SAR or II. SAR has been shown to obtain competitive performance when tackling single objective instances, especially when solving Euclidean Structured (ES) instances [15] (instances that show a flow distribution conceptually similar to one that is found in several real-world QAP instances and Euclidean distances for measuring the distance between locations), while II is the basic algorithmic component in most of the algorithms that we have studied. In II, *2-exchange-best* is used as the underlying local search procedure. The TPLS run will produce a set of non-dominated solutions. These solutions are then improved by using PLS. PLS is an iterative improvement procedure that exploits the 2-exchange neighborhood for the bQAP. Compared to the II in single objective problem, PLS adds a new solution into the archive only if the solution is not dominated by any solution in the archive. This results in two new hybrid algorithms that are named Hybrid Simulated Annealing (HSA) and Hybrid Iterative Improvement (HII). We have allocated in this experiment 5% of the total computation time for PLS part.

One of the decisions that need to be made is whether to use the classical TPLS or A-TPLS [18] in our HSA and HII implementations. A-TPLS is a TPLS variant that uses a different order of the weights for defining the scalarizations with the main objective of improving the anytime behavior of the TPLS algorithm. To ensure that HSA and HII are well-configured, we run preliminary tests to determine the most suitable TPLS variant to be used (either the classical TPLS or A-TPLS), the length of scalarization, and the parameter settings to be used.

To determine the most suitable TPLS variant, we have compared the performance of TPLS and A-TPLS on bQAP instances of size 100. Results on both instances show that A-TPLS has a clear advantage over the classical TPLS, whether on instances with no correlation between its flow matrices, or on instances with negative correlation between its flow matrices. Therefore, A-TPLS is adopted for HSA and HII implementation.

When a specific computation time is used to run the hybrid algorithm, we have to determine whether to give more priority to the number of scalarizations or the computation time for every scalarization. Having a larger number of scalarizations will allow a more diverse search to be performed, while allowing more time for every scalarization may result in higher quality solutions at each scalarization. Therefore, we have studied the effect of the number of scalarization, S and the cooling step for SA, cs. The considered values of S are $S \in \{20, 50, 100\}$, while $cs = cs' \cdot n$, where $cs' \in \{10, 50, 100\}$. Based on our preliminary experiments, the most suitable parameter settings for HSA is $S = 100$ and $cs' = 10$.

3 Benchmark Instances

In the study of SLS algorithms for solving the bQAP, we have generated our own set of instances. The idea of generating our own instance set is mainly to investigate whether the good performance of an algorithm on single objective instances can be extrapolated to bi-objective ones. We limit the study on bQAP instances to an instance set with an Euclidean distance matrix and two structured flow matrices (ESS). Note that this instance set is the extension of the instance set used in [15] and is different from the one of Knowles and Corne [5]. The correlation between the flow matrices however are based on the one used by Knowles and Corne. The flow matrix entries consist of many small values and few large values, and the entries can be represented by a lognormal distribution. The matrix is generated in the same way as the instances discussed in [19]. The distance matrix entries refer to the Euclidean distance between n points in the plane that are grouped into clusters of different sizes. While retaining the structure as in the single objective instances, we limit the entries to values between 0 and 100 to ensure that when calculated, the objective function values do not get too large. For the bQAP instances, we study also how the correlation between the two flow matrices affects the performance of an algorithm for solving an instance. We set the parameter that determines the correlation values between the two flow matrices, *corr*, as 0 and -0.75. In preliminary experiments, we found that instances with positive correlation do not pose a serious challenge to our algorithms, thus they were not included for comparison. We have also generated a set of instances of large size for bQAP, $n \in \{30, 50, 100, 200, 300\}$. A total of 60 instances were generated for every combination of instance size and correlation, so that the instances can be used for future experiments.

3.1 Performance Evaluation of SLS Algorithms for Solving Multi-objective Problems

In the study of the single objective SLS algorithms, the performance of algorithms can simply be compared based on their objective function value. However in the case of bi-objective and multi-objective algorithms, such a simple measure is not sufficient.

For tackling a bQAP for example, there are two objectives that are normally conflicting that need to be minimized. Minimizing one objective will cause the other objective to worsen, and vice versa. When comparing the performance of two algorithms for multi-objective problems, one may first check whether the output of one algorithm dominates the output of the other one. If this is the case, no further metrics are needed to decide that one algorithm is better than another one. If such a dominance relation does not hold, there are some solutions of each algorithms that are non-dominated w.r.t. the solutions of the other one. Additional performance indicators are useful to judge the quality of the approximations to the Pareto set. In the study of the bQAP and also other multi-objective problems, different measures have been proposed to evaluate the performance of SLS algorithms. It is in fact hard to define an appropriate quality measure for assessing the quality of approximation sets [20]. Therefore, until now there is no common agreement on what measure should be used.

In this research, we will focus on using the empirical attainment function (EAF) and the hypervolume indicator to evaluate the performance of the considered algorithms. The two indicators follow a different approach in interpreting the performance of algorithms. An attainment function is a measure that gives the probability that an arbitrary point in the objective space is obtained during a single run of the algorithm [21]. In general, it will describe the distribution of a set of random, non-dominated points in the objective space. The EAF can be seen as a quick graphical comparison method that can help us to understand the performance differences of algorithms at a glance. The EAF plots provided in this study were generated using the software introduced in [22]. The hypervolume indicator, on the other hand provides a numerical unary measure, and can be used to compare many algorithms at once. Hypervolume indicator is also known as the S-metric [23] or Lebesgue measure [24].

4   Experimental Results

In this section, we explain the setup of our experiments, followed by the experimental results. We have compared the performance of four algorithms. The first two are the HSA and HII explained before, while the rest are MOACO and SPEA2 [9] where they were reported to be state-of-the-art for solving bQAP. The experiments have been run using an AMD Opteron 6272, 2.1 GHz CPU with 16 MB cache running under Cluster Rocks Linux version 6/CentOS 6.3, 64 bits.

Figure 1 shows the results of comparisons between HSA and other algorithms on instances of size 300 with negative correlation. From the plots, HSA consistently shows an advantage over HII towards high quality solutions for both objectives in all cases. When compared to MOACO and SPEA2, HSA shows advantage over SPEA2 towards high quality solutions for both objective 1 and 2.

Comparisons on other instances show that HSA outperforms MOACO towards high quality solutions for both objectives, except on instances with $n = 30$ and 50. When compared to SPEA2 however, SPEA2 in most cases shows advantage over HSA except on negatively correlated instances.

The results of our experiment is also analyzed using the hypervolume indicator. The hypervolume for instances of size 30, 50, 100, 200, and 300 are shown in Table 1. Based on the hypervolume indicator, HSA has performed the best on instances of size 30, 100, and 300 (all having $corr = -0.75$) and the second best on five other instances. A good performance was also shown by SPEA2 where it performed the best on five instances, and the second best on three other instances. All instances where HSA shows the best results are the ones with negative correlation. MOACO shows the best performance on instance size 50 ($corr = 0$ and -0.75), which suggests that it has a potential to perform better if a suitable parameter setting is used for other instances.

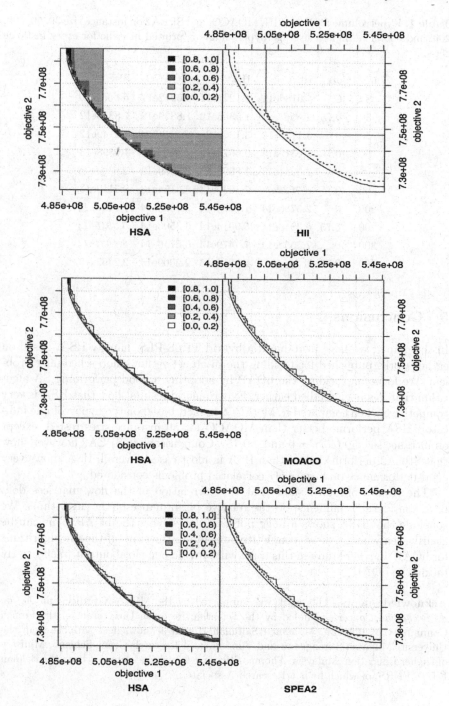

Fig. 1. Location of differences with respect to the comparison between EAFs for HSA and HII (top), HSA and MOACO (middle), and HSA and SPEA2 (bottom) on instances with $corr = -0.75$, $n = 300$.

Table 1. Hypervolume for HSA, HII, MOACO, and SPEA2 on instance size 30, 50, 100, 200, and 300. The highest average hypervolume is printed in italic for every instance class.

n	Corr	HSA	HII	MOACO	SPEA2
30	0	4.6186e11	4.1221e11	4.6042e11	*5.0667e11*
30	−0.75	*1.8385e12*	1.5356e12	1.8339e12	1.8316e12
50	0	3.1174e12	3.196e12	*3.2208e12*	3.2149e12
50	−0.75	1.0319e13	9.6670e12	*1.0611e13*	1.0598e13
100	0	2.5234e13	1.8693e13	2.5039e13	*2.5541e13*
100	−0.75	*8.7032e13*	7.5030e13	8.6154e13	8.5112e13
200	0	2.5786e14	1.7575e14	2.3363e14	*2.6398e14*
200	−0.75	6.3845e14	5.9014e14	6.3506e14	*6.3846e14*
300	0	7.5552e14	7.1479e14	6.5716e14	*8.1931e14*
300	−0.75	*2.3056e15*	2.0914e15	2.2009e15	2.2462e15

5   Conclusions

In this paper, we have introduced a hybrid TPLS-PLS, namely HSA, based on earlier works published for tackling the bi-objective flow-shop scheduling problem. We focus on tackling the bQAP by adopting a good performing SA algorithm that has been studied earlier. Experimental results show that HSA is very competitive when compared to MOACO. In fact, based on the hypervolume indicator, HSA performs better than MOACO for all instance sizes tested, except on instance size 50 ($corr = 0$ and -0.75). Comparisons to SPEA2 however show that SPEA2 performs better than HSA in most cases. Overall, HSA shows very good performance on negatively correlated problems considered.

The results obtained show that the correlation of the flow matrices does have considerable influence on the relative performance of the algorithms. We conclude that HSA shows a huge potential for solving the bQAP. This can be clearly seen when it shows competitive results to the state-of-the-art algorithms for bQAP. Further study in this topic will provide beneficial output to effectively tackle the bQAP.

Acknowledgments. This work was supported by the META-X project, an *Action de Recherche Concertée* funded by the Scientific Research Directorate of the French Community of Belgium. Mohamed Saifullah Hussin acknowledges support from the Universiti Malaysia Terengganu and Fundamental Research Grant Scheme, Ministry of Higher Education, Malaysia. Thomas Stützle acknowledges support from the Belgian F.R.S.-FNRS, of which he is a Research Associate.

References

1. Essafi, I., Mati, Y., Dauzère-Pèréz, S.: A genetic local search algorithm for minimizing total weighted tardiness in the job-shop scheduling problem. Comput. Oper. Res. **35**(8), 2599–2616 (2008)
2. Wagner, M.O., Yannou, B., Kehl, S., Feillet, D., Eggers, J.: Ergonomic modelling and optimization of the keyboard arrangement with an ant colony algorithm. J. Eng. Des. **14**(2), 187–208 (2003)
3. Steinberg, L.: The backboard wiring problem: a placement algorithm. SIAM Rev. **3**, 37–50 (1961)
4. Choi, W., Storer, R.H.: Heuristic algorithms for a turbine-blade-balancing problem. Comput. Oper. Res. **31**, 1245–1258 (2004)
5. Knowles, J., Corne, D.: Instance generators and test suites for the multiobjective quadratic assignment problem. In: Fonseca, C.M., Fleming, P.J., Zitzler, E., Thiele, L., Deb, K. (eds.) EMO 2003. LNCS, vol. 2632, pp. 295–310. Springer, Heidelberg (2003). doi:10.1007/3-540-36970-8_21
6. Hamacher, H., Nickel, S., Tenfelde-Podehl, D.: Facilities layout for social institutions. In: Chamoni, P., Leisten, R., Martin, A., Minnemann, J., Stadtler, H. (eds.) Operations Research Proceedings 2001, vol. 2001, pp. 229–236. Springer, Heidelberg (2001). doi:10.1007/978-3-642-50282-8_29
7. Paquete, L., Stützle, T.: A two-phase local search for the biobjective traveling salesman problem. In: Fonseca, C.M., Fleming, P.J., Zitzler, E., Thiele, L., Deb, K. (eds.) EMO 2003. LNCS, vol. 2632, pp. 479–493. Springer, Heidelberg (2003). doi:10.1007/3-540-36970-8_34
8. Lust, T., Teghem, J.: Two-phase Pareto local search for the biobjective traveling salesman problem. J. Heuristics **16**(3), 475–510 (2010)
9. López-Ibáñez, M., Paquete, L., Stützle, T.: Hybrid population-based algorithms for the bi-objective quadratic assignment problem. J. Math. Model. Algorithms **5**(1), 111–137 (2006)
10. Paquete, L., Chiarandini, M., Stützle, T.: Pareto local optimum sets in the biobjective traveling salesman problem: an experimental study. In: Gandibleux, X., Sevaux, M., Sörensen, K., T'kindt, V. (eds.) Metaheuristics for Multiobjective Optimisation. LNE, vol. 535, pp. 177–199. Springer, Heidelberg (2004). doi:10.1007/978-3-642-17144-4_7
11. Stützle, T., Hoos, H.H.: Improving the ant system: a detailed report on the $\mathcal{MAX}-\mathcal{MIN}$ ant system. Technical report AIDA-96-12, FG Intellektik, FB Informatik, TU Darmstadt, August 1996
12. Zitzler, E., Laumanns, M., Thiele, L.: SPEA2: Improving the strength Pareto evolutionary algorithm. Technical report, Swiss Federal Institute of Technology Zurich (2001)
13. Zitzler, E., Thiele, L.: Multiobjective evolutionary algorithms: a comparative case study and the strength Pareto approach. IEEE Trans. Evol. Comput. **3**(4), 257–271 (1999)
14. Merz, P., Freisleben, B.: Fitness landscape analysis and memetic algorithms for the quadratic assignment problem. IEEE Trans. Evol. Comput. **4**(4), 337–352 (2000)
15. Hussin, M.S., Stützle, T.: Tabu search vs. simulated annealing as a function of the size of quadratic assignment problem instances. Comput. Oper. Res. **43**, 286–291 (2014)

16. Wang, J.C.: Solving quadratic assignment problems by a Tabu based simulated annealing algorithm. In: Proceedings of 2007 International Conference on Intelligent and Advanced Systems, ICIAS 2007, Kuala Lumpur, Malaysia, pp. 75–80 (2007)

17. Connolly, D.T.: An improved annealing scheme for the QAP. Eur. J. Oper. Res. 46(1), 93–100 (1990)

18. Dubois-Lacoste, J., López-Ibáñez, M., Stützle, T.: A hybrid TP+PLS algorithm for bi-objective flow-shop scheduling problems. Comput. Oper. Res. 38(8), 1219–1236 (2011)

19. Hussin, M.S.: Stochastic local search algorithms for single objective and bi-objective quadratic assignment problems. Ph.D. thesis, Université Libre de Bruxelles, 190 p. (2015)

20. Okabe, T., Jin, Y., Sendhoff, B.: A critical survey of performance indices for multiobjective optimisation. In: 2003 Congress on Evolutionary Computation (CEC 2003), vol. 2, pp. 878–885 (2003)

21. da Grunert Fonseca, V., Fonseca, C.M., Hall, A.O.: Inferential performance assessment of stochastic optimisers and the attainment function. In: Zitzler, E., Thiele, L., Deb, K., Coello Coello, C.A., Corne, D. (eds.) EMO 2001. LNCS, vol. 1993, pp. 213–225. Springer, Heidelberg (2001). doi:10.1007/3-540-44719-9_15

22. López-Ibáñez, M., Paquete, L., Stützle, T.: Exploratory analysis of stochastic local search algorithms in biobjective optimization. In: Bartz-Beielstein, T., Chiarandini, M., Paquete, L., Preuss, M. (eds.) Experimental Methods for the Analysis of Optimization Algorithms, pp. 209–222. Springer, Berlin (2010). doi:10.1007/978-3-642-02538-9_9

23. Fleischer, M.: The measure of Pareto optima applications to multi-objective metaheuristics. In: Fonseca, C.M., Fleming, P.J., Zitzler, E., Thiele, L., Deb, K. (eds.) EMO 2003. LNCS, vol. 2632, pp. 519–533. Springer, Heidelberg (2003). doi:10.1007/3-540-36970-8_37

24. Goldberg, D.E.: Genetic Algorithms in Search, Optimization and Machine Learning, 1st edn. Addison-Wesley Longman Publishing Co., Inc., Boston (1989)

Solving the Manufacturing Cell Design Problem Using the Artificial Bee Colony Algorithm

Ricardo Soto, Broderick Crawford, Leandro Vásquez(✉), Roberto Zulantay(✉), Ana Jaime, Maykol Ramírez, and Boris Almonacid

Pontificia Universidad Católica de Valparaíso, Valparaíso, Chile
{ricardo.soto,broderick.crawford}@pucv.cl,
{leandro.vasquez.m,roberto.zulantay.a,ana.jaime.b,maykol.ramirez.g,
boris.almonacid.g}@mail.pucv.cl

Abstract. The manufacturing cell design problem (MCDP) proposes to divide an industrial production plant into a number of manufacturing cells. The main objective is to identify an organization of machines and parts in a set of manufacturing cells to allow the transport of parts to be minimized. In this research, the metaheuristic algorithm called Artificial Bee Colony (ABC) is implemented to solve the MCDP. The ABC algorithm is inspired by the ability of bees to get food, the way they look for it and exploit it. We performed two types of experiments using two and three cells, giving a total of 90 problems that have been used to solve the MCDP using ABC. In the results experiments, good results are obtained solving the 90 proposed problems and reaching the 90 global optimum values. Finally, the results are contrasted with two classical metaheuristics and two modern metaheuristics.

Keywords: Cell formation problem · Nature inspired algorithms · Artificial bee colony · Metaheuristic · Animal behavior

1 Introduction

In the manufacturing industry, there are many problems associated with the optimization of the resources such as time, costs and space to improve productivity. In this case, the Manufacturing Cell Design Problem (MCDP) appeared as a solution for this issue. Trying to find a mathematical interpretation of the problem to make it easier the organization of a factory or warehouse. For the resolution of MCDP, we apply a metaheuristic called Artificial Bee Colony (ABC). ABC is an optimization algorithm based on the intelligent foraging behavior of honey bee swarm.

The metaheuristic ABC that has been used to solve complex optimization problems such as Brain Tumor Segmentation [16], for human-machine interface layout of cabin driver's desk [14], for unsupervised classification of meteorological satellite images [7] and a for single machine scheduling problems [29], among others. In this paper, we perform tests to resolve MCDP using ABC and compared with the metaheuristics Simulated Annealing (SA) [5,27], Particle Swarm

S. Phon-Amnuaisuk et al. (Eds.): MIWAI 2017, LNAI 10607, pp. 473–484, 2017.
https://doi.org/10.1007/978-3-319-69456-6_39

Optimization (PSO) [9,10], Migrating Birds Optimization (MBO) [22,23] and the Shuffled Frog Leaping Algorithm (SFLA) [24] obtaining encouraging results.

The design of manufacturing cells is a topic that appeared a few decades ago, and that has emerged to improve and take advantage of the serial production. Two complementary lines of research have been used in resolving MCDP, the global optimization, and the approximate methods.

In the global optimization, one of the first investigations in trying to solve the MCDP was in 1963 with a production flow analysis [6]. Subsequent investigations were made in the formation of cells [13] and to group machines [20,21,26]. Other research proposed theoretical mathematical programming methods such as [1,4, 8,18,19] and solving the MCDP [5,25,28].

In the group of approximate methods used to solve the MCDP we can find: the Tabu Search (TS) [2,15,17]; the Simulated Annealing (SA) algorithm combined with Genetic Algorithms (GA) [11,27]; Particle Swarm Optimization (PSO) [10]; Shuffled frog leaping algorithm [24] and a Migrating Birds Optimization (MBO) [22,23].

The scope of the research is:

- Perform a strategy to integrate the ABC to solve the MCDP.
- Solve the MCDP with the ABC metaheuristic [12].
- Solve 90 instances of tests and compare results with other metaheuristics.

This study is divided into five main sections: Sect. 2 describes and models the MCDP. Section 3 gives an overview of ABC. Section 4 presents and discuss the experimental results. Finally, we conclude and provides guidelines for future work.

2   Manufacturing Cell Design Problem

The MCDP is a mathematical model focused on the optimization of the manufacture of products. The MCDP is that each manufacturing plant contains a set of machines and parts to use for processing. In which, the objective of the MCDP is to divide a manufacturing plant into cells so that each cell is independent of the other cells of production. This independence reduces the time spent in the manufacture of a product and the unnecessary movements of the pieces to be processed. It also increases productivity, the speed of production and efficiency of the factory.

The problem is modeled through 3 matrices. The first one represents the problem specification (see Fig. 1). Figure 2 shows a possible solution, where the left matrix represents the machines assigned to a cell, and the right matrix represents the parts assigned to a cell. Finally, using the incidence matrix $M \times P$, the solution matrix $M \times C$ and $P \times C$, we can determine the final solution of the problem (see Fig. 3).

	Part 1	Part 2	Part 3	Part 4	Part 5	Part 6	Part 7
Machine 1	1	0	1	0	0	0	1
Machine 2	0	1	0	1	0	1	0
Machine 3	0	1	0	0	0	1	0
Machine 4	1	0	0	0	1	0	1
Machine 5	1	0	1	0	1	0	1

Fig. 1. Initial incidence matrix $M \times P$

	Cell 1	Cell 2
Machine 1	0	1
Machine 2	1	0
Machine 3	1	0
Machine 4	0	1
Machine 5	0	1

	Cell 1	Cell 2
Part 1	0	1
Part 2	1	0
Part 3	0	1
Part 4	1	0
Part 5	0	1
Part 6	1	0
Part 7	0	1

Fig. 2. Matrix $M \times C$ and matrix $P \times C$

		Cell 1			Cell 2			
		Part 2	Part 4	Part 6	Part 1	Part 3	Part 5	Part 7
Cell 1	Machine 2	1	1	1	0	0	0	0
	Machine 3	1	0	1	0	0	0	0
Cell 2	Machine 1	0	0	0	1	1	0	1
	Machine 4	0	0	0	1	0	1	1
	Machine 5	0	0	0	1	1	1	1

Fig. 3. Rearranged incidence matrix $M \times P$

2.1   Representation of MCDP

The mathematical model of MCDP is represented by a set of parameters, variables, indexes, objective function and constraints.

Parameters:

- M : Number of machines.
- P : Number of parts.
- C : Number of cells.
- $Mmax$: Maximum number of machines per cells.
- $A = [a_{ij}]$: $M \times P$ matrix of incidence, where:

$$a_{ij} = \begin{cases} 1 & \text{if } j_{th} \text{visits the } i_{th} \text{ machine.} \\ 0 & \text{for all other cases.} \end{cases}$$

Variables:

- $Y = [y_{ik}]$: Variable solution with size $M \times C$, where:

$$y_{ik} = \begin{cases} 1 & \text{if the machine } i \text{ belongs to the cell } k. \\ 0 & \text{for all other cases.} \end{cases}$$

- $Z = [z_{jk}]$: Variable solution with size $P \times C$, where:

$$z_{jk} = \begin{cases} 1 & \text{if the part } j \text{ belongs to the cell } k. \\ 0 & \text{for all other cases.} \end{cases}$$

Indexes:

- i : Index of machines ($i = 1, \ldots, M$).
- j : Index of parts ($j = 1, \ldots, P$).
- k : Index of cells ($k = 1, \ldots, C$).

Objective function:

$$minimize \sum_{k=1}^{C} \sum_{i=1}^{M} \sum_{j=1}^{P} a_{ij} z_{jk} (1 - y_{ik}) \qquad (1)$$

Constraints:

$$\sum_{k=1}^{C} y_{ik} = 1 \quad \forall_i, \qquad (2)$$

$$\sum_{k=1}^{C} z_{jk} = 1 \quad \forall_j, \qquad (3)$$

$$\sum_{i=1}^{M} y_{ik} \leq M_{max} \quad \forall_k \qquad (4)$$

3   Artificial Bee Colony

Artificial Bee Colony (ABC) [12] is one algorithm inside the topic of swarm intelligence. It is inspired by the observations of the foraging behavior of honey bee swarms. ABC is a population-based metaheuristic algorithm. The solutions are called food sources, and they are modified by the bees which are the variation operators. The target of the bees is to find the food sources with better nectar. In the ABC algorithm, the bees move through the multidimensional search space, choosing the food sources according to the past experiences of them and the other bees from the hive. Some bees (scouts) fly and choose the food sources in a random way, and when they find a better one, they memorize its position and forget the previous one. This way, ABC combines global and local search methods, always trying to balance the exploring and exploiting search processes. The concepts associated with ABC are described in the Table 1.

Table 1. Elements of the ABC.

Element	Description
Food source generation	A food source is a solution for the problem. Is generated randomly and taking the constant values from a given problem
Working bees	Some working bees are the same as the food sources. Its job is to mutate the current solutions and check them to choose between the new solution and the old one
Onlooker bees	A number of onlooker bees. These bees choose a food source based on the information shared with the working bees through the dance. This dance is simulated by selecting the food source with the best-evaluated value from the objective function
Scout bees	These bees generate a new food source randomly to replace the food sources that could not be improved
Limits	Is the number of iterations that a food source can be without being improved. The limit is incremented every time that a solution is not modified by a bee

3.1 Pseudocode of Artificial Bee Colony

The pseudocode (see Algorithm 1) represents the algorithm of ABC and aims to show the steps followed to describe the behavior of bees which inspired this metaheuristic. The first step (see line 2) is to set an initial population that corresponds to the food sources that the bees are going to visit. Following the pseudocode, we get inside the main loop which contains the important steps to develop the metaheuristic. The first step (see line 4 and 5) is done by the working bees, which are going to analyze the initial solutions and through a local search, they are going to compare the new solutions with the ones taken from the initial population. If the fitness of the new solution is better, than the one taken from the initial population, they are gong to replace it. Otherwise, they are not going to make changes (see line 6). After that, the onlooker bees start with their job. They are going to generate a new solution by mutating one from the initial population and evaluate its fitness to see if it is better and replace it or not. If after a certain number of tries, the onlooker bees can't improve the fitness, the scout bees are going to start to generate new solutions to avoid the local optimums (see line 7, 8 and 9). Finally, the best solution is extracted (see line 11).

3.2 Integration of ABC with MCDP

The first step in solving the problem MCDP is a proper integration with the ABC metaheuristic. Therefore, we define the representation of the solution and integrates as metaheuristic. The Fig. 4 is a representation of the structure of

Algorithm 1. ABC Pseudocode

1: **Begin**
2: Init population.
3: **while** remain iterations **do**
4:    Select sites for the local search.
5:    Recruit bees for the selected sites and to evaluate fitness.
6:    Select the bee with the best fitness.
7:    Assign the remaining bees to looking for randomly.
8:    Evaluate the fitness of remaining bees.
9:    Update optimal solution.
10: **end while**
11: **return** Best Solution.
12: **End**

---

data that modeling the problem with the ABC algorithm. First, the circle FS_2 represents a solution. $M \times C$ represents a matrix, in which the rows represent the machines and the columns represent the cells in which a machine was assigned. $P \times C$ represents a matrix, in which the rows represent the parts and the columns represent the cells in which a part was assigned. Finally, Table 2 describes the concepts of the ABC algorithm, which are related to the integration of the MCDP.

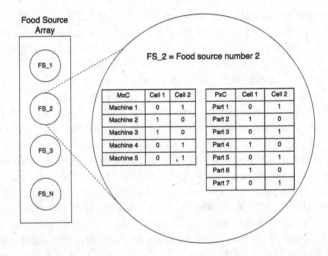

Fig. 4. Representation of the ABC applied to MCDP.

4   Experimental Results

The ABC algorithm for solving MCDP was coded in Java SE-1.8 (Java SE 8, 1.8.0_91) and was run on a computer with an Intel Core i3 Processor 2.53 GHz

Table 2. ABC concepts related to integration.

Element	Description
Food sources	This structure is formed by a bi-dimensional array which represents the amount of food sources that exists to be exploited. Generally it's length is half of the total number of bees from the hive. Our $M \times C$ arrays will be stored here, that's how we will have a matrix with dimension $M \times Food\_Sources$
Fitness array	The fitness of every food source are stored here. Its length is given by the amount of food sources available
Trial	Here are stored the number of tries from every food source. If this number is exceeded, the food source is changed
Probability	Is a probability array where a change percentage is associated with each one of the food sources. This corresponds to the probability of change from every food source. Inside this structure there are other elements that is not relevant to name

with 4 GB RAM 1600 MHz DDR3 running Windows 7. We have tested 90 problems (10 instances considering 5 values of $Mmax$ for $C = 2$ (Cells) and 10 instances considering 4 values of $Mmax$ for $C = 3$. The test data are available in [3]. The experiments for Artificial Bee Colony where done with 31 executions for each Boctor's problem [5], using the following parameters for ABC: Food Source $= 300$, Iteration $= 3000$ and Trial $= 100$.

In terms of results, Tables 3 and 4 describes the configuration of the 90 instances of tests. The description of each column of the table is shown below. Column 1 (Boctor Problem) corresponds to the identifier assigned to each Boctor's problem [5]. Column 2 (Mmax) describes the $Mmax$ value [5]. Column 3 (Optimum value) depicts the global optimum value for the given problem [23]. Column 4 (ABC) depicts the best value reached by using Artificial Bee Colony. Column 5 (ABC-Average) the average value of 31 executions is depicted. Column 6 (ABC-RPD%) represents the difference between the best known optimum value and the best optimum value reached by MBO in terms of percentage, which is computed as follows: $RDP\% = \frac{(Z-Z_{opt})}{Z_{opt}} \times 100$. Column 7 (SA) depicts the best value reached by using Simulated Annealing [5]. Column 8 (PSO) depicts the best value reached by using Particle Swarm Optimization [10]. Column 9 (MBO) depicts the best value reached by using Migrating Birds Optimization [23]. Column 10 (SLFA) depicts the best value reached by using Shuffled Frog Leaping Algorithm [24].

Concerning results, in the problems with $C = 2$ and $C = 3$, the results were that the average is equal to Boctor's global optimum and reaching it in every execution. Figure 5, we can be seen the convergence of the third problem of Boctor's with $C = 3$ and $M_{max} = 12$, the ABC reached the optimum in the iteration number 48 of 3000. We show that ABC has a fast convergence to solve Boctor's problems.

Table 3. Experiments using $C = 2$; Optimum values for ABC, SA, PSO, MBO and SFLA.

Boctor problem	Mmax	Optimum value	ABC	ABC average	ABC RPD%	SA	PSO	MBO	SFLA
1	8	11	11	11.00	0.00	11	11	11	11
1	9	11	11	11.00	0.00	11	11	11	11
1	10	11	11	11.00	0.00	11	11	11	11
1	11	11	11	11.00	0.00	11	11	11	11
1	12	11	11	11.00	0.00	11	11	11	11
2	8	7	7	7.00	0.00	7	7	7	7
2	9	6	6	6.00	0.00	6	6	6	6
2	10	4	4	4.00	0.00	10	5	4	4
2	11	3	3	3.00	0.00	4	4	3	3
2	12	3	3	3.00	0.00	3	4	3	3
3	8	4	4	4.00	0.00	5	5	4	4
3	9	4	4	4.00	0.00	4	4	4	4
3	10	4	4	4.00	0.00	4	5	4	4
3	11	3	3	3.00	0.00	4	4	3	3
3	12	1	1	1.00	0.00	4	3	1	1
4	8	14	14	14.00	0.00	14	15	14	14
4	9	13	13	13.00	0.00	13	13	13	13
4	10	13	13	13.00	0.00	13	13	13	13
4	11	13	13	13.00	0.00	13	13	13	13
4	12	13	13	13.00	0.00	13	13	13	13
5	8	9	9	9.00	0.00	9	10	9	9
5	9	6	6	6.00	0.00	6	8	6	6
5	10	6	6	6.00	0.00	6	6	6	6
5	11	5	5	5.00	0.00	7	5	5	5
5	12	4	4	4.00	0.00	4	5	4	4
6	8	5	5	5.00	0.00	5	5	5	5
6	9	3	3	3.00	0.00	3	3	3	3
6	10	3	3	3.00	0.00	5	3	3	3
6	12	2	2	2.00	0.00	3	4	2	2
6	11	3	3	3.00	0.00	3	4	3	3
7	8	7	7	7.00	0.00	7	7	7	7
7	9	4	4	4.00	0.00	4	5	4	4
7	10	4	4	4.00	0.00	4	5	4	4
7	11	4	4	4.00	0.00	4	5	4	4
7	12	4	4	4.00	0.00	4	5	4	4
8	8	13	13	13.00	0.00	13	14	13	13
8	9	10	10	10.00	0.00	20	11	10	10
8	10	8	8	8.00	0.00	15	10	8	8
8	11	5	5	5.00	0.00	11	6	5	5
8	12	5	5	5.00	0.00	7	6	5	5
9	8	8	8	8.00	0.00	13	9	8	8
9	9	8	8	8.00	0.00	8	8	8	8
9	10	8	8	8.00	0.00	8	8	8	8
9	11	5	5	5.00	0.00	8	5	5	5
9	12	5	5	5.00	0.00	8	8	5	5
10	8	8	8	8.00	0.00	8	9	8	8
10	9	5	5	5.00	0.00	5	8	5	5
10	10	5	5	5.00	0.00	5	7	5	5
10	11	5	5	5.00	0.00	5	7	5	5
10	12	5	5	5.00	0.00	5	6	5	5

Table 4. Experiments using $C = 3$; Optimum values for ABC, SA, PSO, MBO and SFLA.

Boctor problem	Mmax	Optimum value	ABC	ABC average	ABC RPD%	SA	PSO	MBO	SFLA
1	6	27	27	28.00	0.00	28	-	27	-
1	7	18	18	21.00	0.00	18	-	18	-
1	8	11	11	14.00	0.00	11	-	11	-
1	9	11	11	13.00	0.00	11	-	11	-
2	6	7	7	13.00	0.00	7	-	7	-
2	7	6	6	8.00	0.00	6	-	6	-
2	8	6	6	7.00	0.00	7	-	6	-
2	9	6	6	7.00	0.00	6	-	6	-
3	6	9	9	11.00	0.00	12	-	9	-
3	7	4	4	6.00	0.00	8	-	4	-
3	8	4	4	5.00	0.00	8	-	4	-
3	9	4	4	5.00	0.00	4	-	4	-
4	6	27	27	25.00	0.00	27	-	27	-
4	7	18	18	19.00	0.00	18	-	18	-
4	8	14	14	15.00	0.00	14	-	14	-
4	9	13	13	15.00	0.00	13	-	13	-
5	6	11	11	12.00	0.00	11	-	11	-
5	7	8	8	11.00	0.00	9	-	8	-
5	8	8	8	10.00	0.00	9	-	8	-
5	9	6	6	8.00	0.00	8	-	6	-
6	6	6	6	9.00	0.00	8	-	6	-
6	7	4	4	6.00	0.00	5	-	4	-
6	8	4	4	5.00	0.00	5	-	4	-
6	9	3	3	5.00	0.00	4	-	3	-
7	6	11	11	13.00	0.00	11	-	11	-
7	7	5	5	8.00	0.00	5	-	5	-
7	8	5	5	7.00	0.00	5	-	5	-
7	9	4	4	7.00	0.00	5	-	4	-
8	6	14	14	16.00	0.00	14	-	14	-
8	7	11	11	15.00	0.00	11	-	11	-
8	8	11	11	14.00	0.00	11	-	11	-
8	9	10	10	12.00	0.00	10	-	10	-
9	6	12	12	17.00	0.00	12	-	12	-
9	7	12	12	14.00	0.00	12	-	12	-
9	9	8	8	11.00	0.00	8	-	8	-
9	8	8	8	11.00	0.00	13	-	8	-
10	6	10	10	12.00	0.00	12	-	10	-
10	7	8	8	11.00	0.00	14	-	8	-
10	8	8	8	9.00	0.00	8	-	8	-
10	9	5	5	8.00	0.00	8	-	5	-

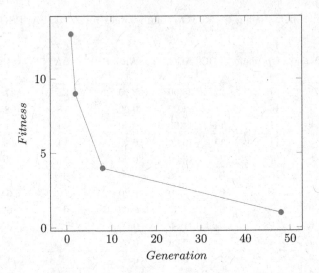

Fig. 5. Convergence graphic of the problem of Boctor's number 3 with $C = 2$ and $M_{max} = 12$.

5   Conclusions and Future Work

In this research, we have presented the resolution of the problem of the design of the manufacturing cell solved through the algorithm Artificial Bee Colony. The obtained results demonstrate that the algorithm is a good alternative for the resolution of the MCDP. Because the ABC in the tests performed (number of cell $C = 2$ and $C = 3$), it has been possible to reach all the optimum global values. In comparative terms, ABC has achieved good results compared to other metaheuristics in the literature.

As future work, it is expected to perform an ABC parameter adjustment, such as decreasing the number of iterations due to the rapid convergence of ABC. Also, decrease population numbers and trials. Finally, performing the MCDP resolution using the Constraint Programming in combination with the Autonomous Search can also be an interesting direction to follow.

Acknowledgements. Ricardo Soto is supported by Grant CONICYT/FOND-ECYT/REGULAR/1160455. Broderick Crawford is supported by Grant CONI-CYT/FONDECYT/REGULAR/1171243. Boris Almonacid is supported by Postgraduate Grant Pontificia Universidad Católica de Valparaíso, Chile (VRIEA 2016 and INF-PUCV 2015) and by Animal Behavior Society, USA (Developing Nations Research Awards 2016). Also, we thank the anonymous reviewers for their constructive comments.

References

1. Adil, G.K., Rajamani, D., Strong, D.: A mathematical model for cell formation considering investment and operational costs. Eur. J. Oper. Res. **69**(3), 330–341 (1993)
2. Aljaber, N., Baek, W., Chen, C.L.: A tabu search approach to the cell formation problem. Comput. Ind. Eng. **32**(1), 169–185 (1997)
3. Almonacid, B.: Dataset - Solving the Manufacturing Cell Design Problem using the Artificial Bee Colony, August 2017. https://figshare.com/articles/Dataset_-_Solving_the_Manufacturing_Cell_Design_Problem_using_the_Artificial_Bee_Colony_/5270983
4. Atmani, A., Lashkari, R., Caron, R.: A mathematical programming approach to joint cell formation and operation allocation in cellular manufacturing. Int. J. Prod. Res. **33**(1), 1–15 (1995)
5. Boctor, F.F.: A linear formulation of the machine-part cell formation problem. Int. J. Prod. Res. **29**(2), 343–356 (1991)
6. Burbidge, J.L.: Production flow analysis for planning group technology. J. Oper. Manag. **10**(1), 5–27 (1991)
7. Deriche, R., Fizazi, H.: The artificial bee colony algorithm for unsupervised classification of meteorological satellite images. Int. J. Comput. Appl. **112**(12) (2015)
8. Deutsch, S.J., Freeman, S.F., Helander, M.: Manufacturing cell formation using an improved p-median model. Comput. Ind. Eng. **34**(1), 135–146 (1998)
9. Duran, O., Rodriguez, N., Consalter, L.A.: Hybridization of PSO and a discrete position update scheme techniques for manufacturing cell design. In: Gelbukh, A., Morales, E.F. (eds.) MICAI 2008. LNCS, vol. 5317, pp. 503–512. Springer, Heidelberg (2008). doi:10.1007/978-3-540-88636-5_48
10. Durán, O., Rodriguez, N., Consalter, L.A.: Collaborative particle swarm optimization with a data mining technique for manufacturing cell design. Expert Syst. Appl. **37**(2), 1563–1567 (2010)
11. James, T.L., Brown, E.C., Keeling, K.B.: A hybrid grouping genetic algorithm for the cell formation problem. Comput. Oper. Res. **34**(7), 2059–2079 (2007)
12. Karaboga, D., Basturk, B.: Artificial bee colony (ABC) optimization algorithm for solving constrained optimization problems. In: Melin, P., Castillo, O., Aguilar, L.T., Kacprzyk, J., Pedrycz, W. (eds.) IFSA 2007. LNCS, vol. 4529, pp. 789–798. Springer, Heidelberg (2007). doi:10.1007/978-3-540-72950-1_77
13. Kusiak, A.: The part families problem in flexible manufacturing systems. Ann. Oper. Res. **3**(6), 277–300 (1985)
14. Li, B., Liu, F., Bai, X.: Artificial bee colony algorithm optimization for human-machine interface layout of cabin driver's desk. In: Proceedings of the Fourth International Conference on Information Science and Cloud Computing (ISCC 2015), Guangzhou, China, 18–19 December 2015 (2015)
15. Lozano, S., Adenso-Diaz, B., Eguia, I., Onieva, L., et al.: A one-step tabu search algorithm for manufacturing cell design. J. Oper. Res. Soc. **50**(5), 509–516 (1999)
16. Menon, N., Ramakrishnan, R.: Brain tumor segmentation in MRI images using unsupervised artificial bee colony algorithm and FCM clustering. In: 2015 International Conference on Communications and Signal Processing (ICCSP), pp. 0006–0009. IEEE (2015)
17. Nsakanda, A.L., Diaby, M., Price, W.L.: Hybrid genetic approach for solving large-scale capacitated cell formation problems with multiple routings. Eur. J. Oper. Res. **171**(3), 1051–1070 (2006)

18. Oliva-Lopez, E., Purcheck, G.: Load balancing for group technology planning and control. Int. J. Mach. Tool Des. Res. **19**(4), 259–274 (1979)
19. Purcheck, G.F.: A linear programming method for the combinatorial grouping of an incomplete power set (1975)
20. Seifoddini, H., Hsu, C.P.: Comparative study of similarity coefficients and clustering algorithms in cellular manufacturing. J. Manuf. Syst. **13**(2), 119–127 (1994)
21. Shargal, M., Shekhar, S., Irani, S.: Evaluation of search algorithms and clustering efficiency measures for machine-part matrix clustering. IIE Trans. **27**(1), 43–59 (1995)
22. Soto, R., Crawford, B., Almonacid, B., Paredes, F.: A migrating birds optimization algorithm for machine-part cell formation problems. In: Sidorov, G., Galicia-Haro, S.N. (eds.) MICAI 2015. LNCS, vol. 9413, pp. 270–281. Springer, Cham (2015). doi:10.1007/978-3-319-27060-9_22
23. Soto, R., Crawford, B., Almonacid, B., Paredes, F.: Efficient parallel sorting for migrating birds optimization when solving machine-part cell formation problems. Sci. Program. (2016)
24. Soto, R., Crawford, B., Vega, E., Johnson, F., Paredes, F.: Solving manufacturing cell design problems using a shuffled frog leaping algorithm. In: Gaber, T., Hassanien, A.E., El-Bendary, N., Dey, N. (eds.) The 1st International Conference on Advanced Intelligent System and Informatics (AISI2015), November 28-30, 2015, Beni Suef, Egypt. AISC, vol. 407, pp. 253–261. Springer, Cham (2016). doi:10.1007/978-3-319-26690-9_23
25. Soto, R., Kjellerstrand, H., Durán, O., Crawford, B., Monfroy, E., Paredes, F.: Cell formation in group technology using constraint programming and boolean satisfiability. Expert Syst. Appl. **39**(13), 11423–11427 (2012)
26. Srinivasan, G.: A clustering algorithm for machine cell formation in group technology using minimum spanning trees. Int. J. Prod. Res. **32**(9), 2149–2158 (1994)
27. Wu, T.H., Chang, C.C., Chung, S.H.: A simulated annealing algorithm for manufacturing cell formation problems. Expert Syst. Appl. **34**(3), 1609–1617 (2008)
28. Xambre, A.R., Vilarinho, P.M.: A simulated annealing approach for manufacturing cell formation with multiple identical machines. Eur. J. Oper. Res. **151**(2), 434–446 (2003)
29. Yurtkuran, A., Emel, E.: A discrete artificial bee colony algorithm for single machine scheduling problems. Int. J. Prod. Res. 1–19 (2016)

Evolving 3D Models Using Interactive Genetic Algorithms and L-Systems

Mariatul Kiptiah binti Ariffin$^{(\boxtimes)}$, Shiqah Hadi,
and Somnuk Phon-Amnuaisuk

Media Informatics Special Interest Group, Centre for Innovative Engineering,
Universiti Teknologi Brunei, Gadong, Brunei
mariatulit1990@gmail.com, shiqah@outlook.com,
span.amnuaisuk@gmail.com

Abstract. The modeling of 3D objects is popularly obtained using a shell/boundary approach. This involves manipulating vertices and planes in a three-dimensional space using computers. Manually creating a 3D model in this way allows a designer full control over the creative processes but at the expense of long working hours. In this work, we explore the hybrid framework between *the Interactive Genetic Algorithm (IGA)* and the *L-system*. The L-system generates a 3D model from its production rules and the IGA evolves the 3D model by evolving the L-system's production rules. In this study, we investigate whether the approach can successfully steer the 3D model design using subjective preference feedback from users. We analyze and discuss the creative processes in the proposed hybrid system and present the models generated by our approach.

Keywords: L-system · Interactive Genetic Algorithm · 3D modeling · Genetic · Algorithm

1 Introduction

Modeling a 3D object manually is a laborious task, especially, when modelling complex objects with intricate shapes and design patterns. Altering a portion of the 3D model often requires changes that results in either adding or removing vertices and edges. These local changes propagate through the overall structure; therefore the overall model must be modified to suit new changes. Hence, we are interested in automating this design process using computers. We explore nature-inspired algorithms to automatically generate many 3D models and let a user interactively guide the design process using IGA.

In brief, each member in the GA population is an L-system object. The L-system has a set of production rules where it is employed to generate a 3D shape. The production rules can be viewed as a recipe for creating 3D models. Each production rule is a chromosome, in a GA context, where each chromosome is a finite length of string composed of terminal and non-terminal symbols. A 3D model can be rendered from the L-system chromosome [1]. Hence the modeling process is the iterative process of the following three main activities: (i) the rendering of 3D models where the system

© Springer International Publishing AG 2017
S. Phon-Amnuaisuk et al. (Eds.): MIWAI 2017, LNAI 10607, pp. 485–493, 2017.
https://doi.org/10.1007/978-3-319-69456-6_40

interprets the chromosome strings and generates 3D models using the L-system, (ii) the evaluation of 3D models where the system accepts the user's interactive feedback, and (iii) the evolution of 3D models where GA evolves the L-system's production rules using its 2 reproduction schemes i.e., elitism, crossover and mutation. This process is repeated until the desired design is obtained. The paper is organized into five sections. The background of the genetic algorithm and the L-system is given in Sect. 2. Section 3 discusses the overall architecture and the key concepts of our method. Section 4 provides the illustration and discussion of the results. Lastly Sect. 5 provides the conclusions of the research and the future works.

2 Background

Applying genetic algorithm to a 3D modeling problem is challenging as the optimal solution is dependent on a user's subjective preferences. Translating a user's subjective preferences to computational constraints is difficult, if not impossible, as every human has his or her own preferences and it may not be explicitly quantified. This work resorts to the IGA framework which has been one of the popular approaches due to fitness functions' highly subjective nature, as those commonly observed in the creative domain such as music informatics [2, 3], user interface design [4], caricature generations [5] and product design [6–9].

Interactive Genetic Algorithm: In [6], the authors used IGA to evolve their preferred cola bottle shape design. According to the authors, IGA is chosen in this case because users have difficulty expressing their shape preferences as they are dependent on contextual and visual factors. The system allows users to flexibly and interactively express their preferences in a single evaluative quantity.

Depending on the domain, it may be natural to express the user's preferences using many criteria. In [10], the authors developed an IGA integrated generative design system using with multi-objective genetic algorithms. The IGA handles multiple objectives to optimize the qualitative and quantitative features in designing the artifact. The qualitative refers to the subjective human-based emotions which is a user-based fitness evaluation. The quantitative objectives refer to computable features such as the weight and size.

The L-System: Lindenmayer Systems (L-systems) describes a plant developmental structure using a set of production rules. These rules are expressed using strings of terminal and non-terminal symbols that can be interpreted as a 3D model. Hence, the modification of the L-systems' production rules allows for the exploration of the design search space. The authors in [11] describe a modeling system developed for the creation of three-dimensional animated models using the L-systems.

In [12], the L-systems are used to stimulate/for the stimulation of the evolution of artificial 2D plants. The genotype is represented by the mathematical formalism or the L-systems. The phenotypes are the branching structures resulted from the graphic interpretation of the genotypes. It provides IGA for a selection that allows users to control the simulated evolution through the phenotype. The overall results of the simulation have established that artificial evolution is a powerful tool for exploring a large and complex search space. But the experiment has only been tested on 2D graphics and employed the simplest type of L-systems (D0L-systems).

One of the old research methods [13], uses the 3Gmap L-system to model flowers. They combine the L-systems grammar writing with the interactive control of parameter settings. The models are created by operating the 3Gmap volumes. The flower model can also be modified interactively to allow users to create their intuitive model preferences. This modelling method also allows users to create the internal structure of the flower, giving more realistic results.

L-System also explores the 3D concept [14] for dynamic generation of agricultural crops. Here, the studies are more focused on generating crop heads using Fractal plant library. To manipulate the axiom and production of the 3D plant, it defines the type part and two angles; the minimum and maximum angle of the elements of parts. The parts consist of the element *stalk, leaf* and *bloom*, and provides individual information such as the radius, length and growth rate. The elements of stalk, leaf and bloom were created using polygon. E.g. the stalk can be represented using a green cylinder, leaves are represented using a green leaf-like rhombus and bloom is seven spheres that combines together to look like a flower.

3 Method

The proposed system is implemented in Blender. The L-systems and the GA components are developed in Python and are integrated in Blender as a software component interacting with the native Blender. Adopting dynamic language such as Python to L-systems [15] enhances the model by keeping the syntax simple, the code easy to execute and avoid compilation overhead. Models are also reusable and provide ways to build complex modular models. This enables easy access when running the simulation. The system has three main components as shown in Fig. 1: (i) the L-systems, (ii) the User-Evaluation, and (iii) the Genetic algorithm.

i. The L-systems component is a set of rewriting rules that translates a given string into a new string. It performs two main functions: (a) rewrite the string according to the rewrite rules, and (b) interpret the string as a 3D model and display the model. The L-system can be express as a tuple:

$$\text{L-system} = (V, S, P) \tag{1}$$

V is a set of symbols containing both non-terminal NT = {A, G, T, C} and terminal symbols T = {F, Q, > , ..., |}; S is a finite length start string S ⊆ V* and P is the production, here, only four production rules are defined for each model, P = {A → V*, G → V*, T → V*, C → V*}1. The table below summarizes some common terminal symbols and their semantics. A full detail of these terminal symbols and their corresponding semantics could be found in github (https://github.com/ento/blenderlsystem- addon) (Table 1).

The L-System program is implemented to Blender software as an addon. The parameters such as radius and positions are calculated using their own functions.

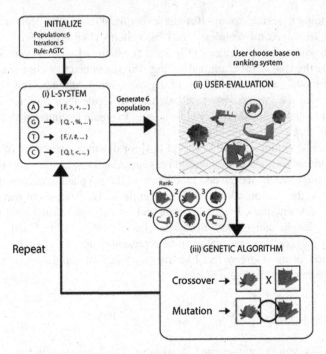

Fig. 1. The proposed framework, (i) L-system takes in the input and generate the models. (ii) User-evaluation lets user express their preferences based on models ranking approach. (iii) Genetic algorithm evolve the model using standard GA reproduction scheme: elitism, crossover and mutation operators.

Table 1. Summary of the terminal used in the system

Terminal symbols	Semantics
F	Create edge/branch segment
Q	Create quad or UV-mapped square/leaf
+, −	Rotate around the right axis (pitch)
/, \	Rotate around the up axis (yaw)
<, >	Rotate forward axis (roll)
[,]	Push or pop sack
&	Rotate random amount
!, @	Expand or shrink the size of a forward steps (branch segment or leaf)
#, %	Fatten or slink the mesh radius of a branch

The values are based on the user's input of the next component. With Blender's function, the 3D model is constructed using the instructions created by the L-System.

ii. The interactive user-evaluation component provides means for users to feedback their preferences back to the system. In each iteration, the L-system interprets and displays each chromosome as a 3D model. Users then exercise their preferences to select and rank these models. The selections are input manually via scripting console and these values will be calculated again through the L-System and GA.

iii. The GA takes the user's interactive preference feedback and uses it to guide its reproduction operations. Preferred models receive more opportunity for breeding. In our approach, GA performs standard elitism, crossover and mutation operations on the L-systems' rewrite rules. In other words, in each generation, the rewrite rules are evolved and the preferred models, i.e., preferred set of production rules are breeding.

4   Analysis and Discussion

We explore these concepts (finite generative rules and evolutionary strategy) to generate 3D models. Using Blender with L-system addons, we implement a hybrid IGA and L-system as a program component (IGAL) that communicates with the Lsystem. The IGAL performs all interactive GA functions (e.g., initialize population, evaluation, and reproduction) and communicates with the L-system (e.g., updating chromosome information). The IGAL starts with an initial population of L-system models. The number of models, the number of rewrite rule iterations, and other control parameters e.g., crossover rate, mutation rates, etc., can be determined by users.

The user then ranks their preferred models before repeating the generative processes until it creates a satisfied output. Figure 2 (top pane) shows representative examples of the generated 3D models. The models are randomly initialized in this case. The figure shows a gradual transformation towards the user's preferences. Comparing the first and its subsequent generation, the models appear to transform into new models using information from its parent's models (bottom pane).

Random evolution of 3D models may be preferred if one's design approach is in an organic style. Organic styles could produce interesting shapes and is a popular approach for evolving abstract shapes. The other alternative would be to start with a rough design and further evolve them. Our IGAL also allows users to define initial GA population with predefined 3D model.

Figure 3 shows representative examples of models evolved from different predefined shapes, here, a tree like structure. The models show different branching styles, balance and imbalance branching. As the generation progresses, we can observe that branching characteristics of different components are transferred from parents to their child model.

Though user's satisfaction is one of the main focus of the system, it does not completely adhere to user's idea of the model. Results are always mixed with one model being completely out of scope to their preference and the other might just be what user were looking for.

The idea that DNA is a recipe book for creating all organisms has been speculated in scientific communities long before we understand the structure of DNA. However, this topic is not well understood yet although we have learned a lot about the instructions to create proteins by DNA. This idea has also influenced many studies in computer generated models. Lindenmayer's L-system [16] and Wolfram's automata

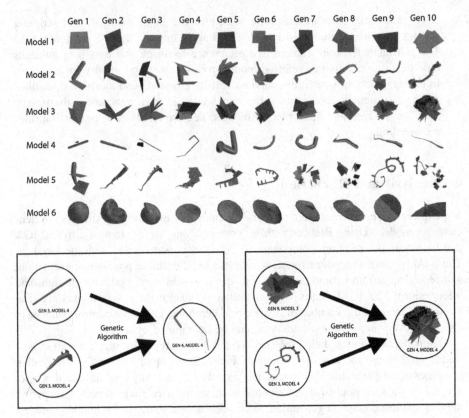

Fig. 2. Top pane – representative examples from random models initialization. Bottom pane - IGAL incorporates preferences of parents' 3D models to a new child model.

[17] explores the concepts that complex shapes can be generated from a simple set of rules. Dawkins further explores the concept of evolution. He implemented a program named *biomorph* which could create various forms which resemble trees, insects, birds (in a very abstracted shapes).

Challenges: It is observed that the proposed hybrid IGAL system could facilitate the 3D modelling process since the models are automatically evolved. However, there are many challenges in evolving the 3D models using IGAL. The following challenges are highlighted:

- Lacking specific/expressive feedback: In our implementation, preferences are expressed at a holistic level by ranking the models. The holistic approach is preferred since it is difficult to quantify different preferences. The lack of specific feedback makes it hard to control the direction of design. It may be important to allow hierarchical expression of preferences or multi-objective preferences.
- Lacking means to better steer the evolution: Lacking expressive feedback is one of the issue discussed earlier. Given a specific feedback, it will be fruitful if the information can be explicitly employed to influence the desired characteristics of

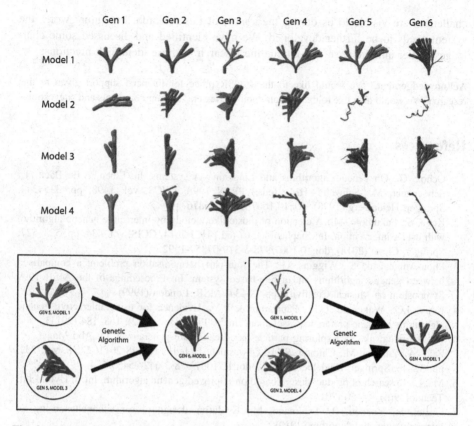

Fig. 3. Top pane – representative examples from predefined models initialization. Bottom pane - IGAL incorporates preferences of parents' 3D models to a new child model.

the model through specific knowledge intensive GA reproduction scheme. This requires some sort of control knowledge which may be expressed as a domain dependent knowledge source, or other machine learning tactics.

- Lacking semantic checking: During experiments, some of the generated models cannot be rendered by the L-system. We believe this is from non-well-formed combinations between the terminal and nonterminal symbols of the alphabets in the L-system. The current reproduction process (i.e., crossover and mutation) can only syntactically modify the production rules of the L-system. It does not perform semantic checking.

5   Conclusion and Future Work

This work explores ideas developed by Lindermayer, Wolfram and Dawkins. We have implemented a hybrid IGAL system that employs the interactive GA and the L-system to facilitate a 3D model design task. The approach has shown some potential and many challenges are visible to us during the course of this research. For future work, the system needs to be further developed. We have identified and discussed some challenges earlier and we wish to continue the research in those identified directions.

Acknowledgement. We would like to thank GSR office for financial support given to this research. We would also like to thank anonymous reviewers for their comments and suggestions.

References

1. Ochoa, G.: On genetic algorithms and Lindenmayer systems. In: Eiben, A.E., Bäck, T., Schoenauer, M., Schwefel, H.-P. (eds.) PPSN 1998. LNCS, vol. 1498, pp. 335–344. Springer, Heidelberg (1998). doi:10.1007/BFb0056876
2. Koga, S., Fukumoto, M.: A creation of music-like melody by interactive genetic algorithm with user's intervention. In: Stephanidis, C. (ed.) HCI 2014. CCIS, vol. 434, pp. 523–527. Springer, Cham (2014). doi:10.1007/978-3-319-07857-1_92
3. Phon-Amnuaisuk, S., Wiggins, G.: The four-part harmonisation problem: a comparison between genetic algorithms and a rule-based system. In: Proceedings of the AISB 1999 Symposium on Musical Creativity, pp. 28–34. AISB, London (1999)
4. Kelly, J.C., Wakefield, G.H., Papalambros, P.Y.: Evidence for using interactive genetic algorithms in shape preference assessment. Int. J. Prod. Dev. **13**(2), 168–184 (2011)
5. Phon-Amnuaisuk, S.: Exploring particle-based caricature generations. In: Abd Manaf, A., Zeki, A., Zamani, M., Chuprat, S., El-Qawasmeh, E. (eds.) ICIEIS 2011. CCIS, vol. 252, pp. 37–46. Springer, Heidelberg (2011). doi:10.1007/978-3-642-25453-6_4
6. Ma, L.: Research of product design based on improved genetic algorithm. Int. J. Hybrid Inf. Technol. **9**(6), 45–50 (2016)
7. Cluzel, F., Yannou, B., Dihlmann, M.: Evolutive design of car silhouettes using an interactive genetic algorithm (2010)
8. Dou, R., Zong, C., Li, M.: Application of an interactive genetic algorithm in the conceptual design of car console. Tianjin University (2014)
9. Kelly, J.C., Wakefield, G.H., Papalambros, P.Y.: Evidence for using interactive genetic algorithms in shape preference assessment. Int. J. Prod. Dev. **13**(2), 168–184 (2011)
10. Kielarova, S.W., Sansri, S.: Shape optimization in product design using interactive genetic algorithm integrated with multi-objective optimization. In: Sombattheera, C., Stolzenburg, F., Lin, F., Nayak, A. (eds.) MIWAI 2016. LNCS, vol. 10053, pp. 76–86. Springer, Cham (2016). doi:10.1007/978-3-319-49397-8_7
11. Viruchpintu, R., Khiripet, N.: Real-time 3D plant structure modeling by L-system with actual measurement parameters. National Electronics and Computer Technology Center, Bangkok (2005)
12. Boudon, F., Pradal, C., Cokelaer, T., Prusinkiewicz, P., Godin, C.: L-Py: an L-system simulation framework for modeling plant architecture development based on a dynamic language. Front. Plant Sci. **3**, 76 (2012)
13. Wyss, G.: Using L-systems for a dynamic generation of agricultural crops. BSc (Honours) thesis, University of Zurich (2013)
14. Petrenko, O., Terraz, O., Sbert, M., Ghazanfarpour, D.: Interactive flower modeling with 3Gmap L-systems. In: Proceedings of the 21st International Conference on Computer Graphics and Vision, pp. 20–24 (2011)

15. Boudon, F., Pradal, C., Cokelaer, T., Prusinkiewicz, P., Godin, C.: L-Py: an L-system simulation framework for modeling plant architecture development based on a dynamic language. Front. Plant Sci. **3** (2012)
16. McCormack, J.: Interactive evolution of L-system grammars for computer graphics modeling. In: Complex Systems: From Biology to Computation, pp. 118–130 (1993)
17. Wolfram, S.: Computation theory of cellular automata. Commun. Math. Phys. **96**(1), 15–57 (1984)

Author Index

Printed in the United States
By Bookmasters